Transition report 1998

Financial sector in transition

Contents

Part II: Financial sector in transition

Foreword

This *Transition Report*, with its special topic of the financial sector in transition, is the fifth in an annual series. Taken together, the Reports chart the progress of transition from the command to the market economy and identify and analyse the challenges of the coming years in central and eastern Europe, the Baltic states and the Commonwealth of Independent States.

The EBRD's mandate is to foster the transition to an open market-oriented economy and to promote private and entrepreneurial initiative in all 26 of its countries of operations. It is a participant investor with a private sector focus. It works with its partners on projects that are financially sound and advance the transition, and that would be unlikely to emerge or to function well without its participation. For the EBRD to implement its mandate effectively, it is of great importance to analyse and understand the complex process of transition and to share the Bank's analyses with its partners, other investors and policy makers in the region. The EBRD *Transition Reports* thus take an investment perspective on the transition. They focus both on the climate for investment and on the contribution that investment shaped by market forces can make to the transition and to overall economic performance.

The building of a market economy requires the creation of markets, of market-oriented enterprises, and of the wide range of institutions and business practices needed to support them. Some aspects of a market economy can and have been created quickly in transition economies, in particular through market liberalisation and privatisation. However, developing the institutions and business practices required for a well-functioning market economy takes much longer. There is thus an inherent imbalance in the transition process. The full implications of this imbalance are starting to reveal themselves.

There is a sense in which the creation of markets in transition economies has been a relatively simple task, requiring governments to reduce their activity by abandoning their control of prices, trade and access to foreign exchange. However, for markets to function well there must be robust entry into, and disciplined exit from, markets to ensure that the most efficient and innovative producers are those that operate in a market. This key aspect of competition does not yet operate well in transition economies, particularly those in the CIS where arbitrary government behaviour and corruption deter formation of new firms and soft-budget constraints sustain non-viable producers.

Strengthening markets and directing the focus of producers towards customers requires both economic freedom and the clear allocation and enforcement of property rights. Privatisation and private enterprise help to ensure that markets operate effectively by separating production decisions from government diktat and the imposition of hard-budget constraints on producers. Private ownership of firms also helps to focus the objective of firms and their managers on achieving a profit by serving their customers. In many transition economies, privatisation of state enterprises is well advanced. In some of these countries, however, dubious business practices and weak legal foundations for corporate governance seriously impair the ability of private owners to protect their investments and to secure a return on them.

In sectors where free markets and private enterprise cannot function effectively along simple competitive lines, as in some aspects of infrastructure and finance, they must be supported by government regulation. Effective regulation requires well-established objectives, rooted in a clear understanding of why markets do not work well in the circumstances at hand and how their functioning can be strengthened through government intervention. It also requires allocation of responsibility for regulatory enforcement to an authority that has the capacity and independence to meet its responsibilities and that is held accountable for its performance. In transition economies, developing the capacity of the state to regulate effectively, as well as to provide other institutional arrangements required in a market economy, demands a radical reorientation of government away from the direct control of economic activity to an effective supporting role. This reorientation inevitably takes time since it depends on the development of the necessary skills and practices. As the example of regulation shows, much remains to be done in transition economies in building this new role for the state.

The current crisis in Russia arose largely from a failure of the state – its inability to collect taxes, to enforce laws, to manage its employees and to pay them – and constitutes a significant setback in transition. From this experience, it is clear that the way in which markets are liberalised and state enterprises are privatised – that is, the nature of the early transition decisions – can have important implications for the capacity of governments to enforce the rule of law, to promote competition and to regulate effectively. Liberalisation that leaves large profits to be earned from flawed markets and favouritism in privatisation that places industry and finance in the hands of vested interests with powerful political connections can create serious obstacles to further advances in market-oriented reform.

In contrast to the crisis in Russia, however, stands the strong performance of many transition economies in central Europe. Having substantially liberalised markets and privatised state enterprises, they are now responding to the difficult challenges of the next phase of transition, building the necessary institutions and business practices. Countries such as Poland are now moving forward with restructuring difficult sectors, such as coal and steel, in preparation for greater private participation, with commercialising infrastructure and creating the necessary regulatory framework, and with completing the privatisation of commercial banks together with further enhancing prudential regulation. The benefits to a coherent and balanced approach to market-oriented reform are clear: high rates of economic growth, improved living standards and resilience to a difficult international environment. In addition to the considerable direct benefits, this reform process is further reinforced by the prospect of acceding to the European Union.

The stresses experienced by transition economies and the contrasts displayed within the region are prominent themes in this year's *Transition Report*. The turmoil in international capital markets has put the transition economies through a stress test that has revealed their strengths and weaknesses. Part I of the Report analyses progress in market-oriented reform, macroeconomic performance and cross-border private capital flows, focusing on the current crisis in Russia and highlighting the differing experiences among transition economies.

Each *Transition Report* has a particular theme. These themes are devoted primarily to a close analysis of the transition and the forces shaping its progress, together with an examination of policies to foster the development of those institutions and business practices that are required in a well-functioning market economy. It is thus important to see the Reports as a series in which each edition is complete in its own right, but is also inter-related and cross-referenced to previous editions. The analyses in the special topics for each year develop and complement the topics from earlier years. The special themes of the previous *Transition Reports* were:

- 1994 – Institutional reform and economic openness;
- 1995 – Investment and enterprise development;
- 1996 – Infrastructure and savings;
- 1997 – Enterprise performance and growth.

Part II of this year's Report examines the financial sector in transition. Financial institutions were essentially non-existent under the old regime. The analysis in the Report finds that, after nearly a decade of transition, the financial sectors in the region remain significantly underdeveloped in terms of delivering services to the real economy. The banking sectors appear stunted, in this sense, relative to those in developing countries at comparable income levels. Securities markets are still more severely underdeveloped. There has been significant progress in enacting the legal and regulatory framework for banking and securities activities, but their enforcement has lagged behind, particularly in CIS countries and in securities activities. The performance of the banking sector remains weak, with banks earning profits primarily from market power in deposit taking and from lending to governments rather than from lending to the real economy.

The evidence reveals a financial sector in transition, but one that is far from performing the role required in a well-functioning market economy. Challenges in the next phase of transition are to strengthen the legal and regulatory framework for financial activity, and within the financial sector itself to enhance the process of competition and to promote wider private ownership and effective corporate governance. The Report provides guidance on these key policy issues, with a particular focus on the banking sector.

The assessments and views expressed in this *Transition Report* are not necessarily those of the EBRD. The responsibility for them is taken by myself on behalf of the Office of the Chief Economist. While we have attempted to be as up to date as possible, the "cut-off" date for most of the information in the Report is September 1998.

Nicholas Stern
Chief Economist and Special Counsellor to the President

28 October 1998

Executive summary

1. Transition and volatility: a year of stresses and contrasts

The turbulent events of the past year have led to contrasting developments across the region. While some countries were severely affected by the crisis of confidence in emerging markets, others have shown more resilience and have been able to maintain growth, albeit at a slower rate. Although the crisis is not over, it is clear that countries – mainly in central and eastern Europe – that have pushed ahead with the more challenging structural and institutional reforms have survived the stress-test of the past year and have been able to maintain macroeconomic stability.

In a number of other countries, in particular Russia, the contagious effects of East Asia's crisis were readily propagated in an environment where reforms were unsound and incomplete. Problematic corporate governance, slow restructuring and weak financial systems imposed a serious handicap on the transition process, constraining growth prospects and exacerbating instability. In many cases, these defects in reform reflected weaknesses in the state itself. In Russia, the government failed to overcome strong and manipulative vested interests, both from the old structures and the new oligarchs, in its attempt to pursue reform. The recognition of these political bottlenecks led to a collapse in the confidence of financial investors and to crisis. The Russian experience further underscores that institutional reform is essential if the potential gains from privatisation and liberalisation are to be realised in terms of growth and stability.

Part I. Progress in transition and economic performance

2. Progress in market-oriented transition

This year, market-oriented reforms have generally been slow and inconsistent throughout the region, as reflected in the 1998 transition indicators. Policy reversals have become more common, partly in response to economic crisis. The imbalance has continued to widen between the earlier successes of privatisation and liberalisation and the more difficult structural and institutional challenges of the next phase of transition. These challenges include corporate governance and enterprise restructuring, financial sector reforms, infrastructure reform, and fiscal and social sector reforms. Despite the setbacks of the past year, some countries have begun to tackle these challenges, while others have made up lost ground with progress in liberalisation and privatisation. Recent developments and remaining challenges in each of the major dimensions of reform are analysed and linked to their role in promoting economic stability and growth.

The slow and uneven progress in tackling the challenges of the next phase reflects the policymaking environment in transition countries, shaped by the policies early in the transition and the broader legacies inherited in each country. These challenges require a substantial and constructive role of the state at a time when its capacity is still underdeveloped and subject to capture by powerful economic interests. Major breakthroughs in meeting these challenges have been made in several transition economies, often motivated by financial pressures. But whether crisis leads to renewed reforms or to backtracking depends in part on the functioning of democratic institutions and the constraints they place on interest groups and on policymakers.

3. Macroeconomic performance and prospects

The past year has been a turbulent one for Russia, the region's biggest economy, and for many other countries in central and eastern Europe (CEE) and the Commonwealth of Independent States (CIS). The fall-out from the crisis in Russia – where a large output decline and return to high inflation are projected – is affecting economic performance in the rest of the region, particularly in neighbouring CIS economies with weak macroeconomic fundamentals and strong trade links to Russia. Economies in CEE more advanced in the transition process are less affected by trade exposure to Russia and, with strong foundations for growth and stability, should be able to weather the turbulence on international markets. A slow-down in growth in western Europe would, however, significantly dampen economic prospects in CEE.

Reversals in macroeconomic stabilisation as the transition progresses point to the fragile foundations in many countries for sustained growth and stability. Large and persistent fiscal imbalances, particularly in the CIS, reflect underlying structural weaknesses, including soft budget constraints for loss-making enterprises, an opaque and distorted tax system, and inefficient tax administration. As a result the tax base is small (and shrinking), the burden on those enterprises still paying taxes is excessive, and tax avoidance and evasion is widespread. In some countries, fiscal imbalances are also contributing to current account deficits. In contrast, rapid export growth and buoyant investment activity in most of central Europe reflect the gains in competitiveness achieved through deep enterprise restructuring.

4. Cross-border capital flows

Significant integration into the international capital markets has come only recently to transition economies. After initial hesitancy, capital flows have increased sharply over the past three years, reaching levels comparable to those of other emerging market economies. Foreign direct investment (FDI), responsible for a third of private capital inflows in 1997, has advanced steadily over the past decade in line with the countries' progress in transition and macroeconomic stabilisation. However, other capital flows, in particular short-term portfolio investments, have surged in 1996 and 1997 and their geographical distribution has been less clearly related to underlying investment opportunities in the real economy.

Capital flows into the transition economies can make a significant contribution to realising the region's growth potential, helping to fill the savings-investment gap and to transfer business practices and technology. Against these benefits stand the risks of exposure to a volatile international environment. While capital flows are bound to contract in the wake of the Russian crisis, the main impact will be a more discriminating approach by the capital markets. Sound fundamentals, including a favourable investment climate, are now an even greater priority for the transition economies. But because implementation of the necessary structural and macroeconomic measures requires time to become effective, governments should explore market-based means of containing the volatility of short-term capital flows while significant vulnerabilities remain.

Part II. Financial sector in transition

5. Financial institutions and markets in transition economies

The financial systems of the transition economies remain underdeveloped, burdened by the legacies of central planning and the structural and macroeconomic upheavals early in the transition. When compared with those of market economies at comparable levels of development, the banking systems of transition economies appear relatively stunted, particularly in lending to the private sector. At the same time, their securities markets are even more severely underdeveloped. In other words, the financial sectors of transition economies are both small and heavily bank-based, a holdover from central planning's monobank system.

Looking ahead, it is important to consider how the financial systems are likely to evolve and how stable they will be. The ongoing advances in information technology and the reinforcing benefits from provision of both banking and securities services point to a more balanced future development of these financial sectors. But as they develop are these systems likely to become more stable? The experience of developing countries provides a salutary warning. The challenge will be to ensure that the legal framework keeps pace as the financial sectors grow in size and complexity. The failure of prudential regulation in Russia to contain the banks' exposure to foreign exchange risk further reinforces the point.

6. Legal foundations for sound finance

A survey of lawyers in the region, conducted by the EBRD's Office of the General Counsel, examines the extent to which transition economies have enacted and effectively implemented core principles of financial law. The survey shows that most transition countries have made considerable, but not uniform, progress in establishing the basic legal and regulatory framework for sound finance. It finds that transition economies have achieved greater progress in the extensiveness than in the effectiveness of financial laws. The effectiveness is greater in banking than in securities activities, reflecting in part the dominance of banking in the financial system of the region and the early priority that was placed on banking reform. Moreover, there is substantial variation within the region in both the extent and the effectiveness of financial laws, with countries in CEE typically more advanced than are those in the CIS.

The deficiencies in implementing and enforcing sound financial laws can exacerbate the region's vulnerability to financial crises. Moreover, lack of law enforcement undermines respect for the rule-of-law, which weakens the confidence of savers and investors in the financial markets and can slow the transition process. The EBRD is helping to improve the legal basis for sound finance in the region through legal assistance projects aimed at strengthening legal rules and institutions as well as adapting the legal culture.

7. Performance of financial institutions: lessons from transition banking

Given the challenge of expanding financial activity in transition economies, it is important to examine how well their financial systems are performing and to identify factors that can enhance this performance. Banking receives particular emphasis because of the region's bank-based financial systems. Evidence from 452 banks in 16 transition economies shows that macroeconomic instability is associated with low levels of banking activity, high interest margins and, in some instances, high rates of profitability. One response of banks to operating in a difficult environment has been to accumulate holdings of government securities. Banks in transition economies have not been able to generate significant profits from customer loans.

Further evidence suggests that the concentrated banking markets in many transition economies impede the performance of banks in mobilising savings. In fact, banks with a dominant share of their domestic market for customer deposits appear able to set deposit rates below those of smaller banks. Nevertheless, smaller banks are expanding their customer loans more rapidly than the dominant banks, as they seek to develop new banking opportunities, particularly among small and medium-sized enterprises. Newly established and privatised banks also tend to be more profitable than comparable state-owned banks. These findings point to the importance of strengthening competition and private participation in enhancing the performance of the banking sector.

8. Promoting the stable expansion of banking

Since fostering competition and promoting private ownership in banking are key to its expansion, particular consideration is given to these policy issues. A credible threat of exit is fundamental to competition in any sector, including banking. The "prompt corrective action" framework is one approach to responding to deterioration in a bank; however, this framework may have to be adapted to the conditions of transition economies, where regulators often have only limited information about the banks they supervise. Once there is the prospect of orderly exits from banking, it becomes possible to allow competitive entry. Effective entry requires a balance between the number and the quality of banks. One constraint on their desirable number is the regulatory authority's capacity to supervise them effectively.

Bank privatisation is essential because of the benefits it brings not only to the privatised bank but also to the process of competition. Privatisation can be expected to improve the management and productivity of the bank. Privatisation is also likely to lead to a hardening of the budget constraint on the bank by reducing the prospect of government bailouts. Achieving these benefits, however, requires sufficient concentration of ownership following privatisation so as to provide effective corporate governance, as well as types of owners that will not perpetuate connected lending and other practices so characteristic of the previous system.

Acknowledgements

The *Transition Report* was prepared primarily by the EBRD's Office of the Chief Economist with important contributions by the Office of the General Counsel – Annex 2.1 and Chapter 6 – and by the Environmental Appraisal Unit – Annex 2.3. The editorial team, under the general direction of Nicholas Stern, consisted of Steven Fries (lead editor), Joel Hellman and Martin Raiser. Joel Hellman and Christian Mumssen restructured and edited the country-by-country transition assessments.

Contents and authors

Contents	Authors
1. Transition and volatility: a year of stresses and contrasts	**Nicholas Stern and Vanessa Glasmacher**
Annex 1.1: The Russian crisis	Rory MacFarquhar
Part I: Progress in transition and economic performance	
2. Progress in market-oriented transition	**Joel Hellman and Christian Mumssen**
Annex 2.1: Legal transition indicators	David Bernstein, Anita Ramasastry and Stevfka Slavova
Annex 2.2: Infrastructure transition indicators	José Carbajo, David Kennedy, Magdalena Reynes and Maria Vagliasindi
Annex 2.3: Energy efficiency and greenhouse gas emissions	Nobuko Ichikawa and Tim Murphy
3. Macroeconomic performance and prospects	**Martin Raiser and Peter Sanfey**
Annex 3.1: From Asia to Russia – contagion and transition	Martin Raiser and Peter Sanfey
4. Cross-border capital flows	**Hans Peter Lankes, Martin Raiser and Marina Wes**
Part II: Financial sector in transition	
5. Financial institutions and markets in transition economies	**Barry Eichengreen and Christof Rühl**
6. Legal foundations for sound finance	**Douglas Arner, Anita Ramasastry and Gerard Sanders**
7. Performance of financial institutions: lessons from transition banking	**Steven Fries, Colin Rowat and Paul Seabright**
8. Promoting the stable expansion of banking	**Philippe Aghion, Patrick Bolton, Simon Commander and Laura Maria Valderrama**

Valuable research support was provided by: Stanislav Gelfer for Annex 1.1; Dmitry Gladkov, Libor Krkoska, Magdalena Reynes and Avyi Sarris for Chapter 2; Bartosz Mackowiak and Avyi Sarris for Chapter 3; Serhiy Filipov, Avyi Sarris and Garance Wattez for Chapter 4; Luba Habodaszova for Chapter 5; Stevfka Slavova for Chapter 6; and Andrij Halushka for Chapter 7.

The transition assessments and the selected economic indicators were prepared by the economists of the EBRD's Office of the Chief Economist, whose country responsibilities are as follows: Albania – Peter Sanfey; Armenia – Beatriz Merino; Azerbaijan – Martin Raiser; Belarus – Beatriz Merino; Bosnia and Herzegovina – Hans Peter Lankes; Bulgaria – Marina Wes; Croatia – Christian Mumssen; Czech Republic – Julian Exeter and Libor Krkoska; Estonia – Vanessa Glasmacher and Tanya Normak; FYR Macedonia – Peter Sanfey; Georgia – Magdalena Reynes; Hungary – Francesca Pissarides; Kazakhstan – Christof Rühl and Martin Raiser; Kyrgyzstan – Peter Sanfey; Latvia – Rika Ishii and Tanya Normak; Lithuania – Rika Ishii; Moldova – David Kennedy; Poland – Steven Fries and Marina Wes; Romania – Christof Rühl; Russia – Ivan Szegvari; Slovak Republic – Christian Mumssen; Slovenia – Francesca Pissarides; Tajikistan – Young-Man Hong; Turkmenistan – Martin Raiser; Ukraine – Julian Exeter; and Uzbekistan – Maria Vagliasindi.

Libor Krkoska, Magdalena Reynes, Avyi Sarris and Karina Sarukhanyan coordinated the preparation of, and data gathering for, the tables in the transition assessments. Avyi Sarris coordinated the preparation of the selected economic indicators. Maureen Brown, Stephanie Griffiths and Linda Mulcahy provided valuable secretarial support.

Sandy Donaldson and Anthony Martin of the EBRD's Publications Unit prepared the text for publication and managed the publication process. Steven Still, Nathalie Lava and Damon Bassett of the Design Unit designed the Report and saw it through production.

The Report benefited significantly from discussions with, and comments from, colleagues in the EBRD. Maria-Luisa Cicognani, Kurt Geiger, Rogers LeBaron, Victor Pastor and Dragica Pilipovic-Chaffey of the Financial Institutions Team provided important input for Part II of the Report. Nandita Parshad of the Power and Energy Team, David Cooper and Ken Lonnen of the Telecommunications Team and Paul Amos of the Transport Team provided valuable contributions to Annex 2.2. The Country Teams and Resident Offices made important contributions to the preparation of the transition assessments. Simon Commander, Mark Dutz, Ricardo Lago, Thomas Nowotny and especially Mark Schankerman of the Office of the Chief Economist commented extensively on the Report. Many helpful comments and suggestions were, in addition, received from members of the EBRD's Board of Directors and from members of its Executive Committee.

Staff of the European Commission, International Monetary Fund and World Bank generously provided extensive and valuable comments on the Report. In addition, background studies for this *Transition Report* were prepared under a technical cooperation project – Policy Studies for the Economic Analysis of Project Preparation and Appraisal in Transition Economies – funded by the European Union's Phare programme. This funding is gratefully acknowledged.

Transition report 1998

Financial sector in transition

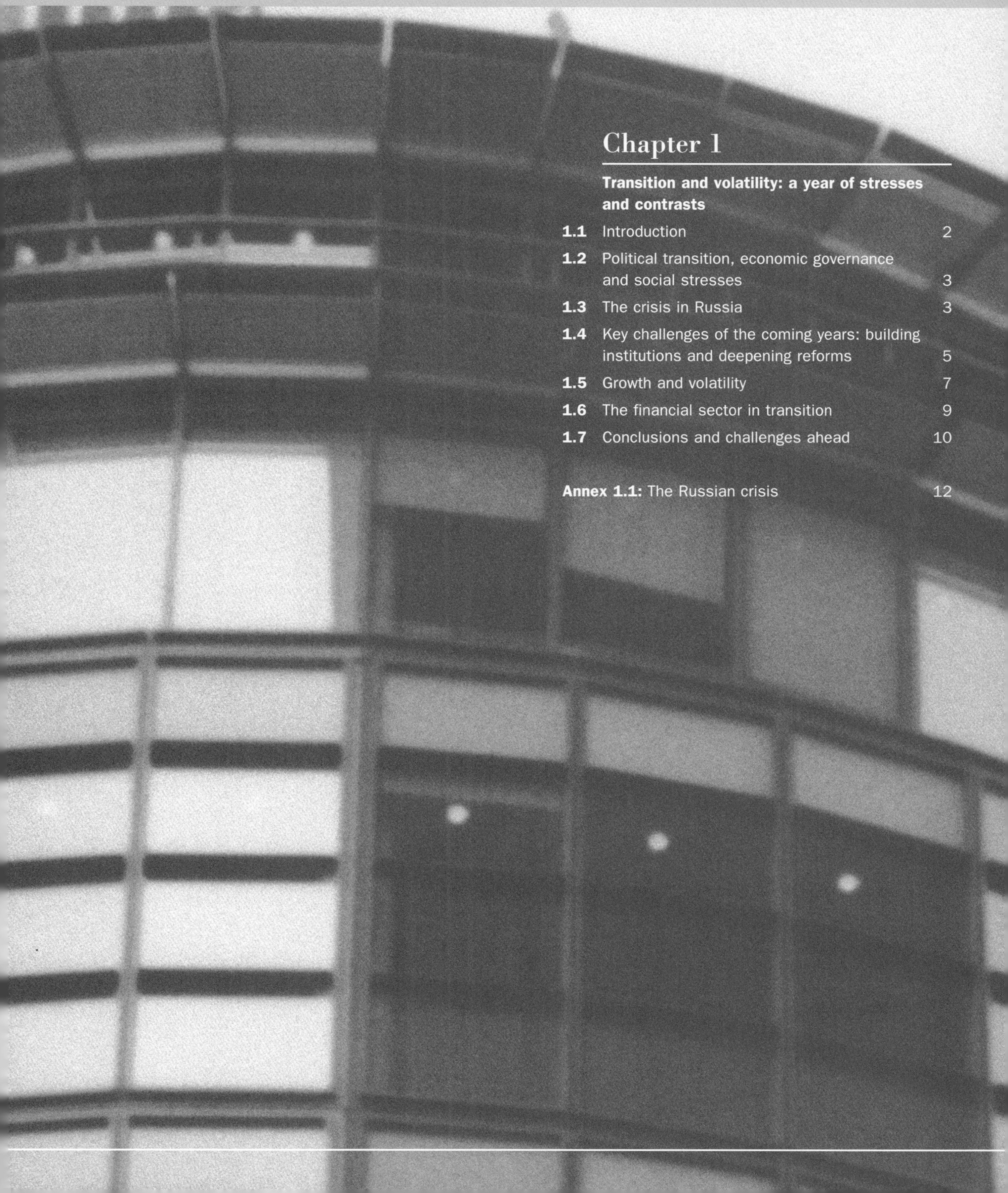

Chapter 1

Transition and volatility: a year of stresses and contrasts

Transition and volatility: a year of stresses and contrasts

1

1.1 Introduction

For the countries of central and eastern Europe, the Baltics and the CIS, 1998 has been a year of stresses and contrasts. The crisis of confidence in emerging markets sparked a collapse of the Russian financial system, forced Ukraine to renegotiate its domestic debt, unhinged the Slovak Republic's fixed exchange rate and required countries across the region to brace themselves against the dangers of contagion. The crisis is far from over and many of its effects are yet to be revealed. However, while the initial market reaction was severe across the region, a number of the transition economies have demonstrated an impressive resilience. Eurobond spreads, domestic money market rates and exchange rate shifts – key indicators of domestic and foreign investor confidence – already show a pattern of striking variation across the region as investors have begun to adopt greater selectivity in the wake of a broad reassessment of economic fundamentals and risk. The variation confirms the main message of this *Transition Report,* with its special focus on the financial sector, and of previous Reports: the hard-won achievements of liberalisation and privatisation must be balanced by progress in institutional reforms[1] in order to sustain macroeconomic stability and to build strong foundations for growth.[2]

This year has seen substantial variation in the progress of institutional reforms, as measured by the EBRD's transition indicators. Some countries of the region, such as Poland and Hungary, have shown further progress in tackling challenging institutional reforms in such areas as the financial sector and in corporate governance. But there has also been considerably more backtracking in reforms in 1998 than in previous years. Severe economic problems in a climate of uncertainty have prompted some countries, most notably Russia, to revert to direct state controls on economic activity. Other countries, such as Belarus, Turkmenistan and Uzbekistan, have continued to delay essential reforms and to reverse earlier achievements, suggesting a more general lack of commitment to market-oriented reforms. The reform paths of the transition economies are differing sharply.

There are several factors underlying these striking differences. As nearly all countries of the region begin to tackle the challenges of the next phase of transition – strengthening economic and corporate governance,[3] building effective regulatory frameworks, deepening financial intermediation and promoting enterprise restructuring – they face different obstacles shaped by their own historical experiences and by the results of the first phase of transition. Tackling these challenges goes beyond simple changes of government policy and requires broad efforts to transform expectations and deep-rooted patterns of behaviour, which are, in many respects, unique to each country. Like all major transformations, these tasks run the risk of intensifying political and social strains in societies that have already endured years of hardship and uncertainty. Indeed, a recognition of the implications of these strains is prominent throughout this Report. Governments in the region have already shown substantial differences in their willingness to take on such risks as well as in their capacity to develop and implement these challenging reforms. Explaining this variation calls for a recognition of different historical legacies and an understanding of the complex political economy of the transition process.

The first phase of transition has left many countries of the region with serious imbalances across different dimensions of market-oriented reforms. The rapid pace of liberalisation and privatisation has not been matched by concomitant progress in the development of institutions necessary to support a well-functioning market economy. These imbalances have caused serious market distortions in the transition economies, which can generate substantial gains to particular interest groups (often with close ties to the government) while imposing great costs on the rest of society. For example, liberalisation of the financial system without an effective regulatory framework has generated extremely high profits for banks in many transition economies, while the basic level of the financial intermediation that can support the real economy remains severely underdeveloped, as Part II of this Report demonstrates. In many countries of the region, rapid privatisation without effective corporate governance structures has resulted in big gains for enterprise managers without real improvements in enterprise performance. While the process of institution-building inevitably takes longer than the policy reforms and asset redistributions of the first phase of transition, some countries have made significant progress and have shown a strong commitment to these challenging reforms for the future. Where this commitment has been lacking, however, vested interests have emerged to sustain and to take further advantage of the market distortions rooted in reform imbalances, thereby preserving their extraordinary gains at a significant social cost. Recognising the problems associated with reform imbalances should not be taken to suggest that some countries should have pursued a slower course of liberalisation and privatisation, but rather emphasises the importance of the government's commitment to institutional reforms throughout the transition process.

1 The term "institutions" is used here to include: the functioning of the state and the behaviour of its officials, including the issues of corruption and of personal safety; the regulatory and legal framework and its effectiveness; the structure and functioning of enterprises – in particular their market-orientation; financial institutions; and political and social institutions, including the democratic process, the freedom of the press and a social safety net.

2 This was in large part also the central message of previous editions of the *Transition Report* and in particular the 1997 edition (which focused on growth).

3 Governance is defined as the "manner of governing".

The institutional challenges are manifested most strikingly in the financial sector, the special focus of this year's *Transition Report.* Financial institutions and markets in transition economies are relatively underdeveloped in their service to the real sector compared with countries at similar income levels. The legal framework for sound finance is also very weak. It is therefore imperative to foster an expansion of this sector, driven by the market, while ensuring that relevant laws and regulations, including the capacity for their enforcement, keep pace with this growth. Particular consideration is given to the role of sound banking in transition economies, as it is central to the stability of the financial sector and to promoting growth. The Report shows that competition and private ownership are crucial to enhance the performance of banks in mobilising savings and in allocating credit to the private sector. Yet competition must be managed effectively and careful consideration should be given to different approaches to bank privatisation, particularly from the perspective of their effects on post-privatisation corporate governance. The Report, therefore, provides guidance in these difficult policy areas.

1.2 Political transition, economic governance and social stresses

The political transition in the region has shown remarkable progress and has, in many cases, demonstrated its resilience. There remain, however, a number of authoritarian regimes, particularly in Belarus and in most of the countries of Central Asia, where effective multi-party democracy has not taken root. The experience of transition to date has shown that the reliance of these regimes on manipulation and control undermines sound economic decision-making and prevents an effective response to economic difficulties once they have arisen. Economic policy-making in a number of countries, notably Russia, is further distorted by powerful interconnections between industry, finance, the media and politics, which also weaken the functioning and stability of democracy. It is not by chance that the quality of economic governance is higher where the consolidation of multi-party democracy is stronger.

Weakness in democratic and economic governance is often associated with corruption which, in turn, inhibits both investment and further reform. As argued in last year's *Transition Report,* the CIS is widely perceived to be one of the most corrupt regions in the world. It is a serious issue, too, for central and eastern Europe and the Baltic states. Corruption not only causes severe stress in the everyday lives of the people of the region, but also stifles economic initiative. It destroys confidence in governmental and political processes and corrodes the political support that is vital if reforms are to be taken forward.

A reduction in bureaucratic controls and thus the advance of the transition itself is central to the fight against corruption. This fight also requires strong leadership from the top, which all too often is lacking. With a dismantling of controls and strong leadership, measures that can counter corruption have some chance of success. Without these essential ingredients, they will fail. International institutions can assist in combating corruption by setting standards of sound practice in their own and in their partners' activities in the transition countries. Fighting corruption requires cooperation and action from the government, business, the international community and groups within civil society. It must be high on the agenda in the next phase of transition.

Previous editions of the *Transition Report* have emphasised the social strains of the transition. In Chapter 2, attention is again drawn to the deep hardships in the region, particularly in the CIS. Although there has been a slight improvement in life expectancy across the region over the past years, only the countries in central Europe have now reached life expectancy levels that are higher than the levels in 1989. In the Baltic states and many of the members of the CIS, the levels are substantially worse than in 1989. Poverty has risen to disturbing levels, with particularly sharp increases during the periods of hyper-inflation in the early years of the transition. Dislocation is an inevitable part of the transition, but countries now need strong growth in new opportunities for those workers to be released from activities that are no longer viable; hence the importance of creating favourable conditions for entrepreneurship and particularly for small and medium-sized enterprises (SMEs). Discouraging new firms and propping up the old ones not only inhibits the structural change which is central to the transition, but also undermines the public finances which are crucial to the social safety net. The problem is compounded in many cases by the poor targeting of social benefits.

1.3 The crisis in Russia

In 1998, the eyes of the world focused on Russia, where the turbulence following the East Asian crisis exposed in a dramatic fashion the frailties of its economic governance and reforms. A detailed analysis of the development of the crisis is provided in Annex 1.1, which demonstrates how fundamental weaknesses in the enterprise sector and banking system set the stage for Russia's fiscal problems and vulnerability to changes in investor sentiment. From a broader perspective, however, the Russian crisis provides some vital lessons for our understanding of the economic, political and social dynamics of transition that go beyond more familiar stories of financial boom and bust in other countries. In Russia, we can see quite clearly the complex interaction between the inherited legacy of communism, the creation of new economic interests from the "first moves" of the transition process, and the development of new political pressures that together shape the political and social constraints on further progress in transition. Although the magnitude of Russia's problems appears to be unique, there are similar processes at work in a number of countries across the region, particularly but not exclusively in the CIS.

The legacy of communist industrialisation created a warped and profoundly inefficient structure for the Russian economy. Russia inherited a vast Rust Belt – a string of massive, largely obsolete, industrial firms, around which entire cities had been established, sometimes in very inhospitable, remote environments. At the start of the transition, these industrial behemoths employed the large majority of the workforce. During the years of partial liberalisation under Mikhail Gorbachev's policy of *perestroika,* managers took *de facto* control over most of these enterprises. In their search for rapid privatisation, reformers saw little alternative but to transform the *de facto* control of managers into *de jure* ownership rights. Having developed very close relationships with government authorities at all levels under the Soviet period, these managers-turned-owners used their influence to protect their enterprises from potential outside owners, from competition by new market entrants and from restructuring plans that would force substantial lay-offs. To keep these enterprises alive in their enfeebled condition required a massive drain on public resources and a reliance on wasteful practices, such as barter, to conceal the real state of affairs. The Russian experience is the most powerful example of the damaging consequences of insider ownership, which are particularly severe when insiders have inherited or developed strong ties to government.

The partial liberalisation of the Soviet economy under *perestroika* not only devolved *de facto* control over enterprises to managers, but also saw control over the financial system move away from the state towards new commercial banks. In stark contrast to banking reform in most of eastern Europe, enterprises were allowed to create their own banks. This began as early as 1989 and in the span of a few years of virtually unchecked growth, intensifying as the Soviet Union disintegrated, over a thousand commercial banks were created in the financial systems of the former Soviet Union. These systems were themselves still highly distorted by continuing state subsidies and poorly developed regulatory frameworks. In Russia, the banks grew at a particularly rapid pace, largely through arbitrage operations that took advantage of existing inefficiencies in the partially reformed and largely unregulated financial markets.[4] Soon many commercial banks outgrew their founders and, following the infamous "loans for shares" deals in 1996,[5] became themselves the owners of the "commanding heights" of the old system.

The rapid entrenchment of insider control and the rise of commercial bankers, and in a number of important cases their accumulation of vast resources, coincided with the collapse of the Soviet state. In Russia, the process of state-building was more contentious and complicated than in many other successor states of the former Soviet Union. Part of the explanation lies with the way in which the former Soviet Union disintegrated and the particular consequences for Russia. In addition, Russia was the only country to adopt a federal structure. Indeed, the distribution of economic authority and revenue between the federal and regional governments has still not been resolved nearly seven years after the birth of an independent Russia. With the state's authority and capacity thus ill-defined and inadequately developed, there were ample opportunities for managers and bankers to "capture" politicians and bureaucrats at every level of government. This was a fertile environment for the growth of corruption.

Not surprisingly, the managers and bankers who amassed great wealth from the distortions of a partially reformed economy sought to use their influence to attempt to preserve the special positions and monopolies that had allowed their enrichment. They were joined in their opposition to reform by those managers working in very weak enterprises, which were unlikely to survive in a genuinely competitive market system. Efforts by successive governments to reform the tax system, to protect shareholder rights, to implement a credible bankruptcy threat, and to eliminate direct and indirect enterprise subsidies were mostly opposed by these managers, who were hostile to both legislation and implementation.

A series of strong-willed reformers eventually managed to broker compromises that kept the reform process moving forward, if only in small steps. Under President Yeltsin's leadership, a precarious political equilibrium was maintained by a continual balancing of economic interests in successive governments. However, these various economic interests were not constrained and balanced in the context of a well-functioning system of democratic competition. Political parties were feeble and largely incapable of channelling popular interests into the political process. The power of the government to favour particular economic interests was virtually unchecked. The Duma was too weak to discipline the government but strong enough to hold up important policy initiatives. Civil society remained far too underdeveloped to assert effective checks on corruption and cronyism. In such an environment, investor confidence was largely determined by perceived shifts in the balance of reform forces within the Russian government, at times fuelling expectations that a breakthrough on structural reforms was imminent.

Yet such perceptions ignored several fundamental – and unpleasant – realities. Vested interests proved adept at blocking proposed reforms or configuring them in ways that were primarily to the benefit of relatively narrow groups in the population. Further, the Russian state's ability to provide even basic public goods – such as law and order and the defence of property rights – let alone pay its own employees and pensioners on a timely or complete basis, had become increasingly strained. A continuing, high incidence of poverty and a rapid growth in inequality also promoted a growing popular disillusion with "market reforms". These factors combined to promote a fundamental mistrust of, and a deep crisis of confidence in, government.

The fragile equilibrium that resulted began to falter as a result of persistent weaknesses in the enterprise sector and in the banking system. Although direct subsidies to enterprises had largely been phased out, a wide range of quasi-fiscal subsidies (in the form of tax arrears, payments-in-kind, utilities arrears, soft bank loans, etc.) increased claims on public resources over time. As Annex 1.1 demonstrates, the government's fiscal position steadily worsened and the level of borrowing, both domestically and internationally, rose sharply. Foreign investors saw very high returns on Russian

4 For example, the long delay in the execution of rouble payments and transfers, which for a prolonged period reached up to three to four weeks, allowed commercial banks to use the "float" to buy hard currency. They would then repurchase roubles at the time of payment at a sharply lower exchange rate (given the high inflation rate in the early years of transition).

5 Under this scheme, commercial banks offered to provide the government loans in exchange for managing the state's remaining shares in selected large enterprises, which, if the government did not repay, would be transferred to the banks. State stakes were offered in loan auctions, most of which had only one serious bidder. As a result, commercial banks with close ties to the government gained large stakes in major enterprises, often at a fraction of their value.

government securities and an apparent commitment to a fixed exchange rate. As a result, they herded into Russian financial markets.[6]

At the same time, banks provided little credit to the real economy and became dependent on high-yielding state securities for their survival. The government and the banking system thus became extremely vulnerable to the volatilities of international capital markets and to shifting investor sentiments. In the aftermath of the East Asian crisis and a series of strong external shocks (particularly the decline in energy prices), investors began to recognise the weaknesses of the underlying position and demanded ever higher interest rates. With these extraordinarily high rates, the fiscal burden of servicing obligations eventually became unsustainable.

Market sentiment improved briefly following the IMF-led "package" of late July 1998, but scepticism in the government's ability to deliver on its fiscal commitments and on other IMF conditionalities again grew rapidly in early August. On 17 August the government announced a moratorium on foreign debt servicing, a default on domestic debt and a rouble devaluation.[7] Shortly afterwards, the government of Prime Minister Kiriyenko was dismissed by President Yeltsin.

Russia has responded to the crisis with continued political stalemate, first over the appointment of a new government and then over the development of a coherent economic programme. The stalemate reflects the same problems that brought Russia to crisis in the first place: the continued influence of vested interests in the partially reformed economy and the government's reluctance to accept the social and political consequences associated with resolving problems of such great magnitude. As a result, macroeconomic stability has been undermined. Large parts of the banking system have collapsed and trust in the rouble has been severely eroded. Investment in the economy has dropped sharply following years of continued decreases. After appearing briefly in 1997, growth has once again stalled.

Of course, to understand the roots of the crisis is not to suggest that it was inevitable. The short-lived government of Sergei Kiriyenko had made some progress in a number of areas: pushing through elements of a new Tax Code, strengthening tax collection, protecting shareholder rights, improving inter-governmental fiscal relations and cutting the budget. However, these measures did not prove sufficient to create the investor confidence necessary to avoid a stampede for the exits. More effective efforts in these areas might have provided the breathing space for the reforms to have shown sufficient results to avoid the panic which precipitated the collapse.

However, it is also now clear that outside commentators and decision makers underestimated the obstacles to reform while at the same time feeling bound to support a government of committed reformers. The government lacked not only support from key vested interests and from parties in the Duma, but also, it seems, the support of the population at large. This undermined their ability to make the key advances that the situation demanded.

The climate for investment has been severely damaged. The task of rebuilding it will not be easy. But it is vital that it is not now undermined further through, for example, discriminatory tax collection, misguided direction of investment, heavy subsidies and avoidance of restructuring (or closure) of non-viable firms. Russia's actions are now crucial signals for investors concerning investment potential in the future. Notwithstanding the depth of its problems, Russia has seen the emergence of a vibrant and entrepreneurial private sector. This sector has suffered deeply in the crisis, but it is this private enterprise sector that remains the hope for Russia's economic future.

1.4 Key challenges of the coming years: building institutions and deepening reforms

While in the past year the pace of reform has been considerably slower than in previous years, many countries continue to push ahead in tackling the difficult institutional challenges of the next phase of transition. Other countries, where war and instability had long delayed basic reforms, continue to make up lost ground. Detailed assessments of the progress in institutional reforms are provided in Chapter 2.

In earlier editions of the *Transition Report*, we have argued strongly that progress in institutional development requires time. Such reforms involve learning and draw on the gradual accumulation of experience and the acquisition of skills. Governments have to learn how to provide sound economic governance. For its part, the private enterprise sector has to acquire the sound business practices that are the foundation for long-term success. Financial institutions suitable to an effective market economy are particularly dependent on experience and acquired skills.

Therefore, the institutional challenges lie in the public domain, in the private sector and in the private-public relationship; they are closely interconnected. The institutional challenges are summarised below (see also Box 1.1).

Governments

Governments across the region have to define a role for themselves in terms of providing a predictable, transparent and non-discriminating framework for sound market decisions and participation in economic activity. The key objectives should be to deliver macroeconomic stability, a transparent and effective legal framework (which defines property rights, contract, bankruptcy and liability law), a sound financial system, a social safety net, health, education, adequate infrastructure, and protection of the environment.[8] Central and east European states have been much

[6] Norman Stone wrote in his 1995 introduction to Charles Mackay's famous 1841 book on herd behaviour in financial bubbles and scandals (including the South Sea bubble and Tulipomania) that "elements may be seen in the former Communist bloc which is coming to terms with capitalism today". Stone was referring in 1995 to herding in relation to various dubious financial schemes, which had swindled sections of the population in Russia and elsewhere in the region. However, his remarks could also apply, mutatis mutandis, to the behaviour of international portfolio investors in Russia in the two or three years that followed.

[7] Formally, a change in the band for the exchange rate.

[8] See also Stern (1997) and Stern and Stiglitz (1997).

Box 1.1

The challenges of governance and institutions

Some of the challenges detailed below are also faced by countries outside the region, but they are intrinsic to the transition. Most of them arise in some shape or form in all countries of the region but, in many respects, they are deeper and more intractable in the CIS. They are interconnected and all of them relate to interactions between public and private sectors as well as to the functions of the individual sectors. They continue to create an investment climate that, notwithstanding the great opportunities in the region, can be discouraging and difficult.

State structures and behaviour that provide weak support for, or which are hostile to, the open competitive market economy include:

- bureaucratic interference and a civil service with limited understanding of the appropriate role of government in relation to the private sector;
- vexatious and ill-designed tax systems and weak tax administration;
- precarious fiscal positions arising from lack of adaptation of revenue and expenditure to the needs of a market economy (the result is excessive weight on monetary policy in achieving macroeconomic stability);
- difficult and ill-defined central-local government relations;
- weak regulatory and supervisory structures for banking/finance, infrastructure, environment, competition etc.;
- legal systems that provide inadequate foundations for contracts, investments and financial responsibility (including in relation to bankruptcy);
- crime, particularly organised crime; and
- corruption.

Systemic problems in markets include:

- weak financial systems that can be manipulated by insiders or governments;
- poorly developed capital markets;
- oligopolistic practices from special groups that acquired (or "grabbed") powerful positions in the first phase of transition;
- clogged payment systems and extensive use of barter;
- inflexible labour markets; and
- barriers to entry and expansion for SMEs, including harassment by organised crime and by government officials.

Systemic problems in enterprises and in infrastructure include:

- infrastructure that functions poorly (in terms of revenues, costs and delivery) and is inadequately oriented to the needs and principles of a market economy;
- ownership structures and practices that lead to weak corporate governance;
- unsound (often criminal) business practices in terms of relationships to customers, suppliers, workers, financiers and governments; and
- poor adaptation of older (particularly large) firms to the market – little restructuring.

Social issues include:

- the growth of poverty;
- extreme inequalities in income and wealth;
- deterioration in health care and public health;
- declining life expectancy in many CIS countries, particularly for males, with stress an important factor;
- problems in reallocating and restructuring pension responsibilities;
- serious problems of housing (functioning of market, stock, state of repair, responsibilities, etc.); and
- crime.

more successful than the CIS in providing these basic functions, but they too face major challenges in strengthening them further.

Legal systems still provide weak foundations for contracts, investments and financial responsibility. In central and eastern Europe, there has been substantial progress in adopting new laws. The effectiveness of their implementation is still weak, but those countries applying for membership of the EU are making significant headway. In the CIS, however, both the adoption and implementation of legislation has shown little progress. The complexity and uncertainty of the legal framework allows far too much discretion to public servants – a major factor contributing to the high level of corruption in the region.

Key to the fiscal stability of governments and the encouragement of entrepreneurial activity is the tax regime. The creation and effective operation of a market-oriented tax system is one of the central challenges of the transition (see *Transition Report* 1994). The challenge has met with very different responses across the region. In many countries, poorly designed tax systems and weak tax administration persist. The lack of adaptation of revenue and expenditure to the needs of a market economy have undermined fiscal stability. While revenue collection is much higher on average in the countries of central and eastern Europe than in the CIS, their fiscal positions have come under growing pressure as a result of high pension and health care commitments. For these countries, a major challenge will be to contain these expenditures and to target them more effectively in order to ensure long-term financial viability. In contrast, tax revenues as a share of GDP in the CIS are very low, resulting in large fiscal imbalances and a failure to deliver on some crucial basic tasks of the state (particularly health care, education and pensions).

Enterprise reform

The evidence on enterprise reform across the region suggests that in a number of countries restructuring has been extremely slow. This is particularly true in the CIS. A key determinant of performance has been the different conditions governing entry and exit of firms. Broadly speaking, in much of central and eastern Europe new firms have entered on a large scale. Increasingly they have joined the formal sector and have paid taxes. In Poland, for example, most of the substantial cumulative growth in the economy as a whole has come from new private firms. State and privatised firms have generally been forced to operate under hard budget constraints. There are, however, major challenges in restructuring heavy industries and in the enforcement of bankruptcy and exit where appropriate. In particular, enterprises in those countries applying for EU accession will be forced to restructure further to meet the accession requirements (see Box 1.2).

Box 1.2

Accession to the European Union

For the 10 applicant countries of central and eastern Europe and the Baltics, accession to the European Union will be a fundamental part of their transition and will require substantial institutional reforms in the areas identified in this section.[1] Indeed, the requirements for accession are very similar to the requirements for transition. There is a striking similarity between the Copenhagen criteria for accession, which were established at the European Council meeting in June 1993, and Article 1 of the Agreement Establishing the EBRD, which sets out the meaning of transition for the Bank. Both call for the creation of open, competitive market economies and democratic institutions.

Following the publication in July 1997 of the European Commission's 'Opinions' on progress with economic and political transition, the heads of government decided at the December 1997 Intergovernmental Council in Luxembourg to proceed initially with membership negotiations with five countries of the region (the Czech Republic, Estonia, Hungary, Poland and Slovenia). Accession negotiations with these countries began in March 1998. Accession partnerships have been agreed with all 10 applicant countries from the region, including Phare-funded investment programmes.

The task of meeting accession requirements, transforming enterprises, strengthening financial institutions and building infrastructure will take time and will make heavy demands on investment.[2] The challenges are particularly severe in manufacturing, services and infrastructure since these sectors will face increasing competitive pressure to accelerate modernisation and restructuring ahead of EU enlargement and in the light of past real appreciation of exchange rates. The accession requirements and adjustment pressures differ from country to country, but in general significant adjustment challenges are expected in heavy industries, mining, food and textiles.[3] In addition, the 10 EU accession countries will also face very specific requirements for investment in infrastructure to meet the EU *acquis* on the environment as well as to provide the necessary foundation for further progress in transition. These investments would be concentrated in the municipal infrastructure, power and heavy industry sectors. In addition to investments related to the environmental *acquis*, the programme for Trans-European Networks (TENs) should encourage a large increase in investments, mostly in transport infrastructure.

However, the timetable will be determined not only by these investment requirements and the progress in transition in the region itself, but also by developments within the existing 15-country EU. The EU will have to undergo a number of reforms, including reform of the Common Agricultural Policy and of the structural funds. These two processes of transition and reform within the EU and within the candidate countries can go on in parallel, but both will take time.

1 The applicants from central and eastern Europe and the Baltics are Bulgaria, the Czech Republic, Estonia, Hungary, Latvia, Lithuania, Poland, Romania, the Slovak Republic and Slovenia.

2 This will have important implications for the work of the EBRD and other international financial institutions over the coming years. In the last quarter of 1997, the European Commission launched an EC-IFI co-operation initiative in order to leverage Phare funds. A memorandum of understanding was signed in March 1998 between the EC, the World Bank and the EBRD with a view to developing co-financing opportunities, especially in the areas of infrastructure and the environment.

3 Results of a study of investment requirements in Poland by Mayhew and Orlowski (1998) that would, however, appear to have broader validity.

Further east, the story is far less encouraging. New firms have been deterred from entry by arbitrary public actions, pressure or threats from incumbent enterprises, pervasive corruption and punitive taxation. Notwithstanding these obstacles, there is a new private sector although much of it remains in the informal economy. In privatised firms in the CIS, there is weak corporate governance, partly as a result of insider control. In many cases, the state continues to intervene in enterprise decision-making or to support unprofitable enterprises. As a result, many firms that are effectively bankrupt have been able to survive. Their survival depends upon barter, payments in kind, and tax and utility arrears.

Financial system

The Russian crisis highlights the vulnerability of the economy to failures of the financial system. In many countries of the region, the financial sector remains underdeveloped. Evidence suggests that the health of the banking sectors in a number of central and east European countries has improved. This is largely the result of successful privatisation, restructuring, exit of unprofitable banks and increased competition. Still, in much of the CIS, the stability of the financial sector remains precarious due to weak prudential regulation and supervisory capacity, rapid entry of new undercapitalised banks, inadequate mechanisms for the bankruptcy of banks and the pervasiveness of connected lending. While prudential regulations are gradually being put in place across the region (with special efforts under way in those countries applying for EU accession), many key areas, such as central bank supervision, remain weak. Recent examples of important failures of bank regulation include the high volume of unhedged forward currency contracts in Russia and the large exposure of some banks of the region to Russian government securities.

1.5 Growth and volatility

The turbulent events of the past year have led to widening differences in macroeconomic outcomes across the region, as described in detail in Chapter 3. The broad crisis in emerging markets worldwide has weakened investor confidence in all the transition economies and has raised borrowing costs even for the countries with stronger economic fundamentals and lower risks.[9] Those countries that have pushed ahead with strong structural reforms should be able to withstand the pressures on their fiscal balances, external imbalances and exchange rates emanating from the crisis. While growth across the region has slowed, in those countries it is continuing. It must be remembered, however, that the crisis in world markets is far from over and many of its effects have yet to be revealed.

In those countries where structural reform has been slower and government and external deficits have been consistently high, the deterioration in the international environment poses

9 In October 1998, for example, Eurobond spreads for Russia increased to over 6,000 basis points over US treasuries and for Ukraine to over 10,000 basis points. Those for Poland increased to around 200 basis points.

still greater threats. This has been sharply illustrated by the Russian crisis, where, despite remaining uncertainty, all plausible macroeconomic outcomes entail a serious deterioration in macroeconomic performance in the short term.[10] The threat of contagion (see Annex 3.1) is particularly high in those countries where structural reforms have been weakest and trade and other links to Russia strongest.

Countries throughout the region will also be vulnerable to a slowdown in the world economy. They have opened their economies to world trade and are now crucially dependent on such trade to sustain development. Thus, it is vital that the richer countries, particularly the United States, Japan and the EU, take action to sustain demand and increase efforts to liberalise trade. It is particularly important to avoid any slackening in the process of accession to the EU.

Macroeconomic challenges

There are a number of macroeconomic challenges remaining in the region. They include: (i) fiscal imbalances arising from changing structures of government expenditures and revenues; (ii) rising investment demand, external imbalances and associated capital inflows, without a corresponding rise in the ability to service these flows; and (iii) the need for productivity improvements to sustain competitiveness as real exchange rates appreciate in fixed, or quasi-fixed, exchange rate systems.

Fiscal discipline

Generally fiscal discipline in the CIS has been poor, particularly in Russia and Ukraine. Tax revenues have been limited by a combination of factors. These include poor administration, erosion of the tax base, the development of barter and other forms of tax evasion, and the policy of keeping bankrupt firms alive. These problems require a strong policy response. The first is a clearly defined and market-oriented tax code. It has been quite possible, for example, to have zero or negative profits by normal OECD standards but large profits for tax purposes. The choice for firms is then between evasion and bankruptcy. Complicated structures also create possibilities for harassment and corruption by tax officers, which have a very damaging impact on entrepreneurial activity. Second, it is important to devote sufficient resources, of real quality, to tax administration, including training and effective supervision. Third, there must be strong commitment at the highest levels to tax collection. Without this, powerful vested interests will find ways of frustrating attempts at tax collection.

Increasing tax revenue in the CIS is important not simply to control deficits but also to provide revenues to meet obligations to pensioners and government workers, to maintain health and education expenditures, and to invest in rebuilding crumbling infrastructures. Without the revenues, the fabric of the state and of social expenditures cannot be sustained.

The fiscal challenges in many central and east European countries are also severe, although different in nature. Tax revenue is much higher than in the CIS, but expenditures are inflated by unusually high levels of pension and other social payments. The challenge is to change those commitments in a way that can avoid social hardships while relieving fiscal pressures. More careful targeting of benefits is crucial. While pension and social commitments must be manageable and credible, a "first pillar" of publicly provided pensions should be a central element of any pension system. There will, however, also be an important role in some countries for a "second pillar" of private and mandatory (defined contribution) pensions, in which people have clearly identified individual accounts. Such a move could facilitate the reform of underfunded public pension systems as well as contribute to the development of local capital markets and the institutions that support them. It would be dangerous, however, to underestimate the complexities and the costs of building the second pillar.[11] Recent events in financial markets and the problems of corporate governance in the region underline the necessity of creating an effective regulatory framework and appropriate conditions in financial markets. This represents a major challenge in a region where the relevant skills are scarce and political and corrupt pressures can be very strong.

Rising investment demand and associated external imbalances

The second of the macroeconomic challenges that must be faced in promoting growth while avoiding instability is rising investment demand and associated external imbalances.[12] While there have been differences across countries, investment in the region has tended to follow a pattern of rapid contraction in the early phase of transition, relative stability at low ratios to GDP during export-led recovery, and rapid expansion once economic growth has become established. Investment ratios are now rising fast in many of the advanced countries, probably exceeding 25 per cent (on average) of their GDP.[13] For sustainable growth, national savings rates should follow the upward trend of investment rates. However, on the available evidence, savings rates are not generally rising. In fact, in some cases they have been falling. This mirrors the deterioration in external balances (see Chapter 4 for a discussion on capital flows into transition economies).[14]

While recognising the advantages of foreign direct investment (FDI) and foreign saving during a period of reconstruction,[15] the ability to service debt-associated inflows must be created alongside the investment. As recent events in Russia and Ukraine have

[10] There will be a sharp increase in inflation, rouble depreciation and a strong decline in GDP for the rest of 1998. The macroeconomic prospects for 1999 look similar.

[11] The "third pillar" is that of non-mandatory private pensions.

[12] The risks of rising investment demand, external imbalances and associated capital inflows were discussed extensively in the *Transition Report* 1997.

[13] Note that these investment ratios are very rough estimates. Data on investment are particularly unreliable in the less advanced transition countries and in Russia, where the treatment of inventories and barter, among others, may account for ratios that appear unrealistically high.

[14] See also Lankes and Stern (1998).

[15] It should be understood that some capital inflow, or "foreign saving", during a period of reconstruction may well be a sensible economic policy. Investment for restructuring, combined with improved management and Western technology, offers opportunities for raising the yield of existing capital at relatively low cost. At the same time, domestic financial systems are able to offer only limited support to investors, and savings are lower than under the earlier regime. Foreign borrowing and associated current account deficits can therefore play a useful role in the region's development if channelled into quality investment.

illustrated, high debt levels and a short-term maturity structure can create great vulnerability to changing international sentiments. The problems of volatility in capital flows are, of course, most relevant for economies that have opened themselves to trade and capital markets. The experience of Russia shows the dangers of opening up rapidly to foreign portfolio investment before the financial and fiscal positions are robust. It is striking that Poland, with the strongest overall growth of any country in the region and a sound transition, has maintained some restrictions on short-term portfolio flows (such as those on capital and money market instruments, see Chapter 4).

In addition, there are many relatively poorer countries in the region, particularly the smaller economies of the CIS, which have been building international debt quite rapidly (mostly bilaterally from governments and from multilateral institutions).[16] Here, as we warned in Chapter 7 of last year's *Transition Report*, some of the countries will have to be very prudent about further sovereign debt if they are to avoid the problems of solvency and liquidity of the type that lead to the Highly Indebted Poor Country (HIPC) initiative of the World Bank and the IMF.

At the heart of the policy response to the challenge of sustaining growing investment and high capital inflows throughout the region must be sound fiscal policy (yielding public savings), measures to raise private savings, a favourable investment climate for equity investments, and strong financial institutions and corporate governance to provide productive use of investment. Public savings can be raised more quickly than private savings through fiscal measures. But raising private savings is crucial for the medium term. At the same time it is important to recognise the advantages of equity relative to loans in avoiding future debt service obligations.[17]

Rising real exchange rates

The third challenge is that of rising real exchange rates, which put strong pressure on productivity improvements. A rising real exchange rate is to be expected during the transition – markets produced low valuations on factors of production in the transition economies in the early years of transition, given the considerable uncertainty over their capacity to compete in world markets. As the transition progressed and trade and production began to be reoriented, real exchange rates have appreciated quite rapidly. However, this appreciation can lead to a lack of competitiveness if productivity does not increase to match it. The increase in productivity must come from further reforms and investments. Again, we see the close interrelation between macro-performance and structural reform.

1.6 The financial sector in transition

The special theme of this *Transition Report* is the financial sector in the process of transition. The performance of the financial sector has a major influence on the performance of the overall economy. By mobilising domestic and foreign savings and by allocating efficiently these funds to investment opportunities in the real economy, this sector can contribute directly to the processes of investment, restructuring and growth. A sound financial sector is also a source of stability, providing a mechanism for allocating risks and spreading financial losses that inevitably arise from economic activity. However, a poorly functioning and unsound financial sector imposes a serious handicap on any market economy, constraining growth prospects and exacerbating instability.

Recent developments in Russia underline these points. The vulnerability of the banking sector was exacerbated by the inadequate regulation of banks, in particular their open foreign exchange positions and off-balance-sheet activities. The breakdown of the banking system has had a devastating effect on much of normal economic life, with many of the basic trading and production activities disrupted or halted altogether. Thus, the crisis carries powerful lessons on the importance of building sound financial institutions.

Given that transition economies inherited few relevant financial institutions and markets from the era of central planning, it is not surprising that the banking systems of these economies remain underdeveloped compared with those of market economies at a comparable level of development (see Chapter 5, which analyses the progress in building financial systems). Their securities markets are even more underdeveloped. In other words, the relatively small financial sectors of transition economies are heavily bank-based. Looking ahead, it is important to consider what types of financial systems are likely to evolve in transition economies and how stable they will be.

The experience of developed and developing countries suggests that financial crises tend to occur when the financial sector develops too quickly and branches out into new activities, often following financial liberalisation. A fundamental challenge in the next phase of transition will be to ensure that the regulatory and supervisory framework keeps pace as the financial sector grows in size and complexity. This includes adequate rules of disclosure, auditing and accounting standards, rights for minority shareholders, deposit insurance and prudential regulation.

A survey of lawyers who work in the region, undertaken by the Office of the General Counsel of the EBRD, examines the extent to which international regulatory standards are met in the countries of the region (see Chapter 6). The survey reports strong progress in the adoption of core principles of financial law. However, the survey also shows that there has been less success in the implementation of financial laws, particularly those that apply to securities. There are several reasons for this. First, there are pervasive problems in securing the independence of regulatory bodies, resulting in failure to take corrective action. Second, there

[16] Four of the EBRD's 26 countries of operations have GDP of less than US$ 2 billion dollars. A loan of US$ 20 million represents 1% of GDP. This amount is the average size for the EBRD's contribution to a project, and the average size of the associated project would be about US$ 50 million. Thus, for a poor country with major infrastructural challenges, sovereign debt can build up very quickly relative to GDP.

[17] However, a balanced approach to foreign partnerships needs to be maintained in order to avoid the concern that assets are being sold to foreigners "on the cheap".

is a lack of experienced and trained personnel in the regulatory bodies. Third, there is insufficient transparency in both financial institutions and firms to achieve effective enforcement of financial laws. It is clear that the building of effective legal and regulatory institutions will be vital to the success of the transition. There is great potential for constructive outside assistance in this area.

The importance of expanding financial activity in transition economies lies in its potential for promoting the real economy. It is important, therefore, to examine how well financial institutions are performing as intermediaries, in particular by examining the activities (and profitability) of banks (see Chapter 7). The evidence suggests that macroeconomic instability is associated with low levels of activity, high interest margins and, in some instances, high rates of profitability. One response of banks operating in difficult environments has been to accumulate holdings of government securities. While these instruments often yield high returns, these reflect the risks associated with macroeconomic policy. Stabilisation and growth bring some expansion in bank lending, but the scale of banking in transition countries remains well below that in comparable market economies. Further evidence suggests that the concentrated oligopolistic banking markets of some transition economies often impede the performance of banks in mobilising savings. Smaller banks are expanding customer loans more rapidly than the dominant banks as they seek to develop new banking opportunities (particularly among SMEs).

There are a number of important and clear lessons arising from the evidence presented in Part II of the *Transition Report*. Progress in stabilisation and structural reforms are essential to increase the scale of banking activities. Second, the foundation for a stable expansion of banking activity requires a sound framework for effective prudential regulation and supervision of banks. Third, a reduction in market power, particularly in retail deposit taking, would serve to strengthen the banks' role in the mobilisation of savings and in strengthening their customer orientation. Fourth, greater private participation would serve to strengthen the performance of banks.

The evidence on bank performance in transition economies points to the importance of policies that foster effective competition and private ownership in the banking sector, including the resolution of failed banks, licensing requirements for new banks and bank privatisation (see Chapter 8). A credible threat of exit is fundamental to ensuring competition because the failure of one bank can sometimes spread contagiously through the banking system. Once there is the prospect of orderly exit from banking, it becomes possible to open the system to competitive entry. The process of competition promotes the selection by the market of banks on the basis of their ability to deliver the services that their depositors and borrowers require at the lowest cost.

Competition in banking, however, should not take the form of an unregulated free-for-all. The scope for fraud and other abuses is simply too great. Rather, effective competition in banking requires a balance between the number and the quality of banks. One clear constraint on the desirable number of banks is the capacity of the regulatory authority to supervise them effectively, a particularly important consideration in transition economies. Given the problems that have followed episodes of liberal entry of new banks in some economies, particularly in the CIS, the focus should now be on ensuring that new entrants into banking are of high quality. This requires the fair and transparent application of licensing requirements that help to ensure that new banks are both prudent and capable.

Bank privatisation in transition economies is important because of the benefits it brings not only to privatised banks but also to the process of competition. Privatisation can be expected to improve the capabilities and productivity of banks, particularly by imparting a strong focus on the customer and by introducing effective corporate governance. Privatisation is also likely to lead to a hardening of the budget constraint on banks by reducing prospects of a generous government bailout if performance deteriorates. This financial discipline serves to strengthen both the internal incentives within privatised banks and the process of competition in the banking system as a whole. The realisation of those gains, however, requires sufficient concentration of ownership following privatisation so as to provide appropriate corporate governance as well as types of owners that will not perpetuate connected lending and other practices so characteristic of the previous system. In these respects, the insider-led privatisation that has been widespread in the region has caused severe problems. The emphasis, wherever possible, should be on attracting strategic investors, both foreign and domestic.

1.7 Conclusions and challenges ahead

The theme that runs throughout this discussion is clear: growth and stability have been maintained in those countries where discipline in macroeconomic management and the depth of reform have been strongest. Structural reforms and effective macroeconomic management are closely intertwined. Weak reforms generate financial institutions and enterprises that are financially unsound and fail to meet obligations to customers, other enterprises and the government. In turn, financial institutions or firms can collapse, or where they do not, may fail to pay taxes. Fiscal positions deteriorate and macroeconomic difficulties arise. Heavy government borrowing requirements distort the development of financial institutions, which focus on the relatively easy task of lending to government rather than to private industry. In this way, financial intermediation is stunted, private investment is "crowded out" and long-term prospects are damaged. Investors have come to recognise this logic and the recognition of flawed reforms has led to crisis.

In order to avoid crisis and to sustain growth, countries must therefore push ahead with institutional reforms. The *Transition Report's* country-by-country analyses – the transition assessments – have been redesigned to present the key reform challenges facing each country along with a detailed description of the previous progress in reform, relying on both qualitative assessments and quantitative indicators across a number of areas. The main challenges still facing most countries include improving business practices and corporate governance, restructuring enterprises, strengthening financial institutions and reforming fiscal systems. Throughout the region, weaknesses in these areas are both a manifestation and a cause of the weaknesses of the state and its failure to adapt to its new role in a market economy.

This leads directly to the specific challenges faced by Russia. The priorities for the short-term should focus on fiscal adjustment and rebuilding the financial sector. A strong improvement in the fiscal position in the coming months, of about 5-6 per cent of GDP, is essential. In the absence of willing lenders or other outside funders in the near future, a fiscal balance is required and that is roughly the required adjustment, excluding the revenue required for meeting debt obligations. If this is not achieved, the likely reaction from the authorities would be to print money. This will not lead to the raising of significant resources (an inflation tax is unlikely to raise more than 1-2 per cent of GDP), but will lead to very high inflation, thereby effectively reducing real expenditures. The result would be great hardships of the type that occurred in Russia in 1993-94, with sharp increases in poverty and mortality rates. It must be emphasised, however, that the problem, at least in principle, is manageable. In the early part of 1998 there was a primary surplus, and tax revenues were starting to grow. It is essential that tax revenue performance is improved. Further reform of the tax code is a key ingredient.

It must be recognised that with the deterioration in the real economy in the last few months the revenue challenge is daunting. At the time of writing, the Russian authorities show little sign of a realistic response to this challenge in the future. Further, the above calculations of required revenue take no account of the roughly 5 per cent of GDP in sovereign debt service which is due in 1999. Pressures for rescheduling some of these payments will be strong.

The second urgent set of measures to restore the Russian economy concerns bank restructuring. Banks of strategic importance or those that are viable as going concerns will need rehabilitation. In many cases, the state will need to inject capital, acquire a controlling interest and replace management. Other non-viable banks should face liquidation. It is vital that those procedures move forward quickly and in an open, transparent and non-discriminatory manner. If the process reflects discrimination or cronyism, the old problems are likely to return.

It must also be emphasised that the root cause of the crisis lay in large part in the failure (for reasons described) to take on the problems of enterprise reform. Thus, a lasting solution to the current crisis also requires strong measures to increase the pace of restructuring and an improvement in the corporate governance of Russian enterprises. Experience in other transition economies strongly suggests that successful restructuring not only requires strategic investors but also limiting the scope for groups that might in the short run be adversely affected by restructuring from blocking those changes. What is required is a combination of policies aimed at increasing alternative employment prospects – including through growth in SMEs – and targeted income support.

In sum, the Russian crisis is not simply an economic crisis. It goes straight to the heart of the relationship between state and civil society. For reforms to proceed, a new and viable political consensus is required, just as much as a coherent programme. While assistance from outside can undoubtedly prove helpful at critical junctures, bringing forward the reform agenda will depend primarily on domestic decisions and leadership. At the present time, it is difficult to see a new political consensus for reform emerging rapidly. Yet the costs of prolonged delay are likely to be severe.

However, a response to the crisis should go beyond the reform efforts of the transition economies. The industrialised countries must also recognise that the current global market environment has powerful implications for the economies of the region. A special responsibility falls on the richer nations to take account of the effects of demand and of trade openness in industrialised countries on emerging markets. A loosening of monetary policy in industrialised countries would help to ease liquidity pressures and to dampen the re-balancing of global investment portfolios away from emerging markets. The United States, Japan and the European Union each has its own special structures and pressures and any policy measures they adopt will have to take them into account. However, the effects of their actions on emerging markets, and in particular for the process of transition in the region where the EBRD works, are profound and embody great responsibilities. It is vital that these responsibilities are reflected in the choices they make in response to the difficulties this global economy now faces.

References

H.P. Lankes and N. Stern, *Capital flows to eastern Europe and the former Soviet Union,* EBRD Working Paper, No. 27, February 1998.

C. Mackay, *Extraordinary Popular Delusions and the Madness of Crowds,* Wordsworth Edition Ltd., Ware, Hertfordshire, United Kingdom, 1995; original publication, Richard Bentley, London, 1841.

A. Mayhew and W.M. Orlowski, "The Impact of EU Accession on Enterprise Adaptation and Institutional Development in the EU-Associated Countries in Central and Eastern Europe", study prepared for EBRD, 1998.

N. Stern, *Macroeconomic policy and the role of the state in a changing world,* EBRD Working Paper, No. 19, April 1997. Published in *Development Strategy and Management of the Market Economy,* ed. E. Malinvaud et al. Clarendon Press, Oxford, 1997.

N. Stern and J. Stiglitz, *A framework for a development strategy in a market economy: objectives, scope, institutions and instruments,* EBRD Working Paper, No. 20, April 1997. Published in *Development Strategy and Management of the Market Economy,* ed. E. Malinvaud et al. Clarendon Press, Oxford, 1997.

Annex 1.1: The Russian crisis

On 17 August 1998 Russia simultaneously devalued its currency, defaulted on much of its domestic government debt and declared a moratorium on debt principal payments to foreigners by Russian companies and banks. The moves prompted a run on the banks, a sharp fall in the exchange rate well beyond the parameters of the announced devaluation and a substantial acceleration in monthly inflation to levels not seen since 1992. The severe strain on the banks led to a breakdown in the payments system, which along with the increased uncertainty caused a dramatic slowdown in economic activity. Within a week of the measures, the government of Sergei Kiriyenko had fallen after just four months in office. Following a three-week stalemate over the appointment of a new Prime Minister, the government of Yevgeny Primakov declared its intention to make substantial changes to the course of economic reform.

The origins of the crash of Russia's financial markets lay in the country's flawed stabilisation. Extremely high levels of inflation between 1992 and 1994 were fuelled by an enormous increase in the volume of credits from the Central Bank at highly negative real interest rates. These credits were provided to cover the federal government's persistently large budget deficits and to support enterprises that consistently resisted pressures to restructure. The government's stabilisation programme in 1995 managed to bring down inflation, but it did not address the underlying causes of macroeconomic imbalance. The government was not prepared to accept the consequences of enforcing hard budget constraints both in terms of the social and economic dislocation and the opposition of entrenched interest groups. Instead, it replaced monetary financing of the deficit with non-inflationary borrowing on a newly created Treasury bill market and on the international capital markets. It also used the exchange rate as an anchor to fight inflation. In principle, this approach bought the government time to make progress in deficit reduction and enterprise reform. However, channels of soft financing to enterprises remained significant.

As the exchange rate appreciated and as dollar wages outpaced productivity growth, the devaluation expectations of investors rose and with them the interest rates they required to hold the stock of increasingly short-term government debt. In addition, the onset of the East Asian financial crisis sharply raised the costs of borrowing throughout all emerging markets. The growing interest payments, in turn, aggravated the gap in the government's finances and thus compounded the already difficult problem of rolling over its short-term debt. This forced the Russian government to increase debt issues and further raise rouble interest rates to extraordinarily high levels. As the stock of debt grew without substantial progress in structural reforms, domestic and foreign holders of Russian debt increasingly believed that either the rouble would be devalued or the government would default on its domestic debt. Both results occurred, precipitating a profound financial crisis.

Chart 1.1.1

The Russian stock and bond market bubble

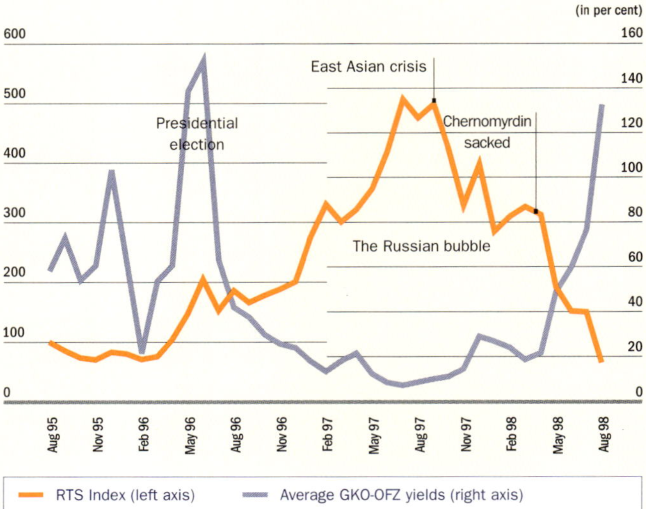

Sources: Russian Trading System and Central Bank of Russia.

This annex examines the asset bubble that preceded the crash, and then discusses the deficits and soft budget constraints that left the country so vulnerable to international contagion. The conclusion outlines policy options for the new government.

The Russian bubble

The re-election of President Yeltsin in July 1996 and the subsequent appointment of a team of high-profile economic reformers nine months later sparked a huge inflow of foreign portfolio investment into Russia's nascent equity and Treasury bill markets. This inflow was part of a worldwide boom in capital flows into emerging markets. The Yeltsin victory appeared to mark a turning point in Russia's reform process, holding out the promise that the country would belatedly follow the east European path of economic recovery after a cumulative 40 per cent decline in GDP since 1991. Backed by a new Extended Fund Facility from the IMF, the government committed itself to fiscal consolidation and a vigorous programme of structural reforms. With a framework of property rights apparently created by mass privatisation, investors were optimistic that substantial corporate restructuring would finally lead to sharp increases in asset prices. Meanwhile, growing international reserves would enable the Central Bank to maintain a predictable exchange rate policy within a sloping corridor. Although the opposition-dominated State Duma would continue to protest, a newly adopted constitution granted it minimal powers to block any reforms that had the President's strong backing. Agreements with the Paris and London Clubs of creditors on restructuring defaulted Soviet-era foreign debt cleared the way for a new wave of investment in Russia.

The capital inflows led to a spectacular asset price bubble, with the stock market rising 142 per cent in 1996 and a further 184 per cent in the first eight months of 1997 (see Chart 1.1.1). In the new

Chart 1.1.2

Stocks of GKO-OFZs and rouble deposits, 1995-98

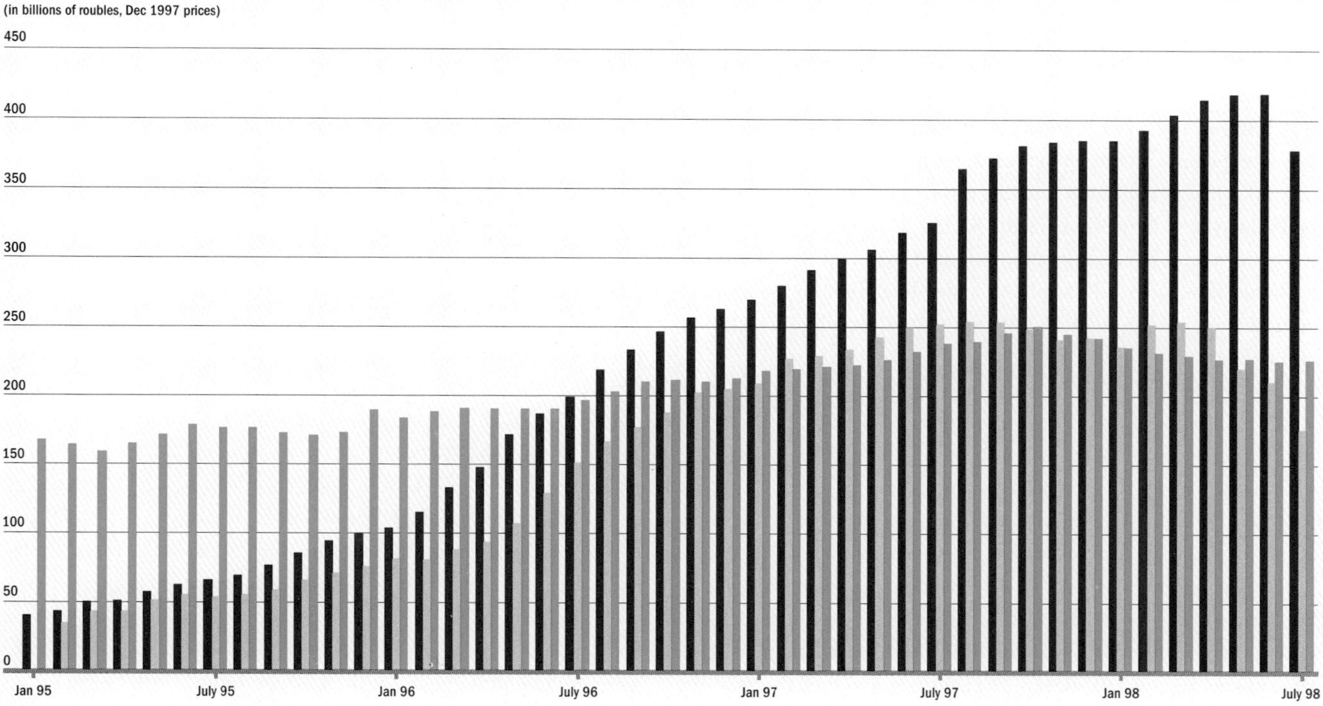

GKO-OFZs outstanding (face value) | GKO-OFZs outstanding (market value) | Rouble deposits

Source: Central Bank of Russia.

Chart 1.1.3

Federal deficit financing, 1995-98

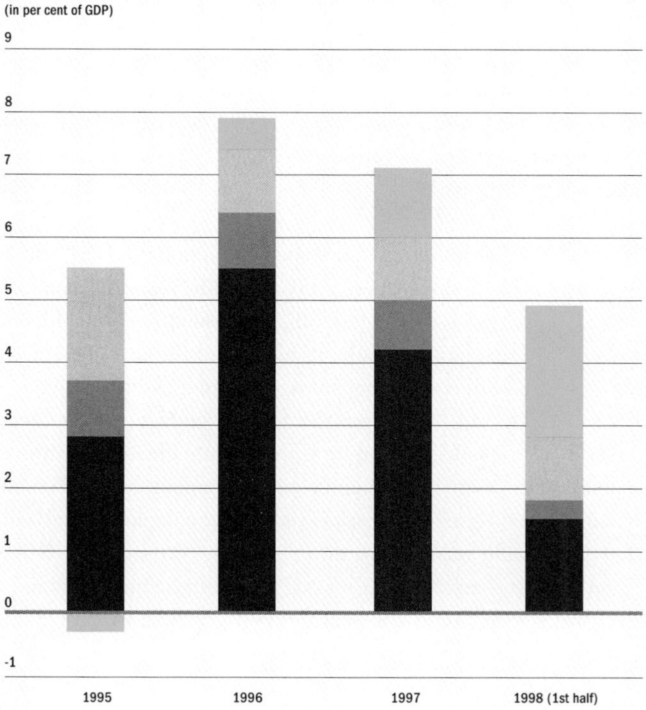

Other foreign | International financial institutions | Privatisation and gold | Domestic securities

Source: Ministry of Finance.

environment, commodity exporters and regional governments were able to borrow in dollars, avoiding high domestic interest rates. Commercial banks increasingly borrowed in dollars using the proceeds to buy high-yielding Treasury bills as well as corporate shares on sale at privatisation auctions and on the booming stock market. By summer 1997 investors appeared to be buying Russian securities indiscriminately.

The euphoria had a similar effect on the growing market for government debt. From 1995, the federal government financed much of its deficit by issuing short-maturity (less than one year) rouble-denominated Treasury bills (GKOs) and longer-dated coupon-bearing bonds (OFZs). As a result of a sharp increase in government spending and a broad tax amnesty leading up to the presidential elections, the market value of the stock of GKOs and OFZs grew by 170 per cent in real terms in the course of 1996, from 3.4 per cent to 8.2 per cent of GDP. By October 1996, the stock of GKOs and OFZs had exceeded the total stock of rouble deposits in the banking system (see Chart 1.1.2). Thereafter, the government relied increasingly on foreign financing (see Chart 1.1.3). In November 1996, the government issued its first US$ 1 billion Eurobond and, over the next two years, borrowed a further US$ 15 billion on international capital markets. At the same time, capital controls limiting foreign access to the GKO-OFZ market were gradually removed. Foreigners rushed into the high-yielding Russian debt market and, by the end of 1997, held an estimated 33 per cent of the total stock of GKOs and OFZs. Despite the rapid growth in the domestic debt stock, inflows of foreign capital caused yields to fall steadily from 170 per cent just before the 1996 presidential elections to 18 per cent in July 1997.

A consequence of the reliance on GKO-OFZ financing was that the fate of the rouble, the domestic debt stock and the banking system became intertwined. Foreign investors in the GKO market were at first obliged, and many later chose, to hedge themselves against the risk of devaluation by buying dollar forward contracts with Russian banks. These contracts apparently assured them a fixed rate of return in dollars by guaranteeing them a predetermined exchange rate at an agreed point in the future. At the same time, the hedge contracts increased the exposure of the Russian banking system to declines in the rouble. Conversely, fears about the government's fiscal position affected expectations about the exchange rate, since GKO-holders understood that the government might be tempted in the future to inflate (and devalue) its way out of the debt stock.

With the advent of the East Asian financial crisis in July 1997, investors began to reassess economic fundamentals and risk across all emerging markets, prompting a broader flight to "quality". In light of the newly increased awareness of the dangers of crony capitalism and weak banking systems following the crisis, Russia's economy, having still achieved only modest progress in key structural reforms and with looming fiscal problems, looked particularly vulnerable. Worse still, falling commodity prices hit Russia's main sources of export earnings, sending the current account into deficit and raising questions about the valuation of the rouble.

What began as a price correction turned into much deeper worries in March 1998 when President Yeltsin dismissed the political coalition under Prime Minister Viktor Chernomyrdin, which had been in government, with varying members, since late 1992. A prolonged nomination battle between the President and the Duma to appoint a successor threw into doubt the new government's ability to carry out its reform programme in the face of Duma opposition. Further doubts about the stability of the banking system arose following the Central Bank's decision to place Tokobank, which had been one of the most active in attracting foreign credits, under temporary administration. Foreign banks became increasingly unwilling to roll over maturing loans to Russian banks. With the value of their share and Treasury bill portfolios plunging, some large Russian banks were forced to make margin calls, which further depressed the stock and bond markets and put still more strain on the banks' balance sheets.

Throughout spring and summer of 1998 the government had increasing difficulty attracting buyers for the roughly US$ 1 billion of Treasury bills that needed to be rolled over each week. Budgetary wage and payment arrears rose sharply as the Ministry of Finance used tax revenues and Eurobond receipts to retire maturing GKOs. Meanwhile, the Central Bank's currency reserves dwindled as foreign portfolio investors retreated and capital flight accelerated. Months of extraordinarily high real interest rates began to hit enterprises, which cut back on production for lack of working capital. In July the IMF agreed to provide an emergency rescue package totalling US$ 17.1 billion in new loans with existing facilities bringing the total assistance package to US$ 22 billion. Within days of the arrival of the first IMF tranche, however, the capital outflow resumed. By early August, several banks were on the verge of default, and the Central Bank began pumping in liquidity to keep them afloat. Much of the 33 billion roubles in credits that the Central Bank issued in the first three weeks of August rapidly found its way onto the currency markets, further depleting reserves. By mid-month, the Russian authorities had spent the entire first tranche of IMF assistance (US$ 4.8 billion). Commercial banks had begun to default on their international obligations. On 17 August the government gave up its defence of the rouble.

Fiscal deficits

At the root of Russia's macroeconomic problems have been persistently high federal budget deficits, which came down dramatically in 1995 only to rise again in 1996 during the presidential election campaign (see Chart 1.1.4). Deficit reduction began in earnest again only towards the end of 1997, with the primary deficit (i.e. excluding interest payments) falling from its peak of 2.8 per cent of GDP in the first quarter of 1997 to 1.7 per cent in the fourth quarter, and moving into surplus in 1998. By that time, however, investor confidence had already begun a downward spiral.

The fundamental causes of the budget deficit were political: an inability to rein in government spending, weak tax discipline among politically influential firms and an excessive devolution of revenue to regional governments. Pressure to spend came both from the Duma, which repeatedly passed unrealistic federal budget laws, and from within the government, where line ministries resisted attempts by the Ministry of Finance to control their spending promises. As a result, the Finance Ministry's only lever of control was to sequester disbursements of cash from the Treasury to keep the deficit within the limits of available financing. This policy successfully averted a return to monetary financing, but caused a substantial build-up of wage and expenditure arrears. Federal government payment arrears reached 67 billion roubles (3 per cent of GDP) by 1 January 1997.

Poor control over spending commitments also worsened the deficit by contributing to the erosion of tax discipline. Non-payment for goods and services by the federal government and by budget-financed organisations made it easier for large companies, particularly utilities and companies with strong political connections, to withhold taxes from the federal budget. The federal government repeatedly tried to wipe the slate clean by clearing mutual debts between companies and the budget, but each time tax and spending arrears reappeared. Large companies realised that they could manipulate these schemes (known as KNOs, "money offsets" and "reverse offsets") to minimise their tax liabilities by "selling" their goods at inflated prices in exchange for clearing tax arrears. Soon, large companies became unwilling to pay their taxes in cash because of "powerful offset expectations", as one government analyst described it.[1] Non-cash tax payments to the federal budget amounted to 2.1 per cent of GDP in 1995, 4.0 per cent in 1996 and 3.6 per cent in 1997. After the most recent "reverse offset" scheme was announced in August 1997, federal tax revenues in cash fell by a third in a single month.

1 See Karpov (1997).

Chart 1.1.4

Federal deficits 1992-98

(in per cent of GDP)

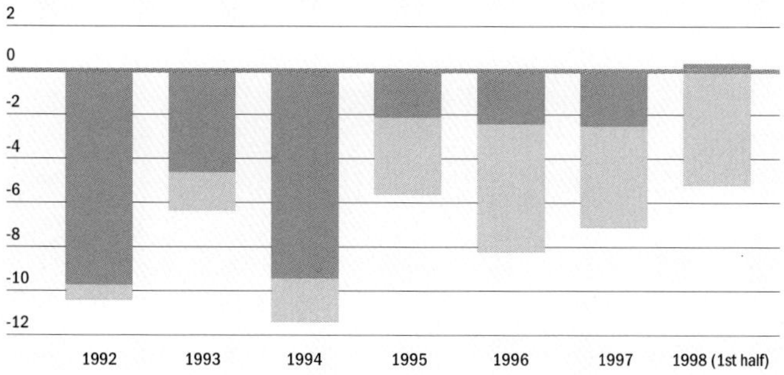

Sources: Ministry of Finance, Goskomstat and IMF.

Chart 1.1.5

General government revenues, 1993-97

(in per cent of GDP)

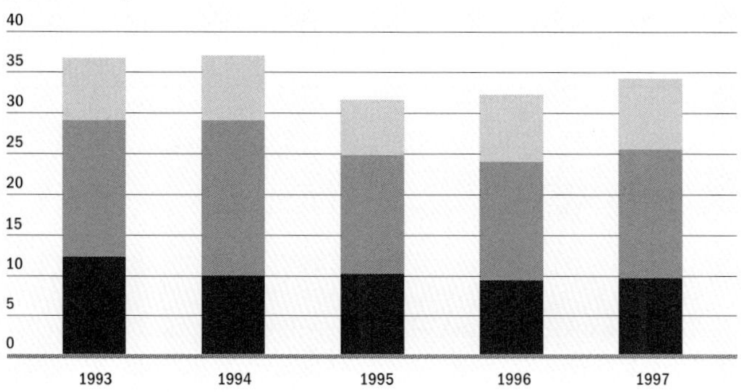

Sources: Ministry of Finance and Goskomstat.

Chart 1.1.6

Government spending in 1997

(in per cent of GDP)

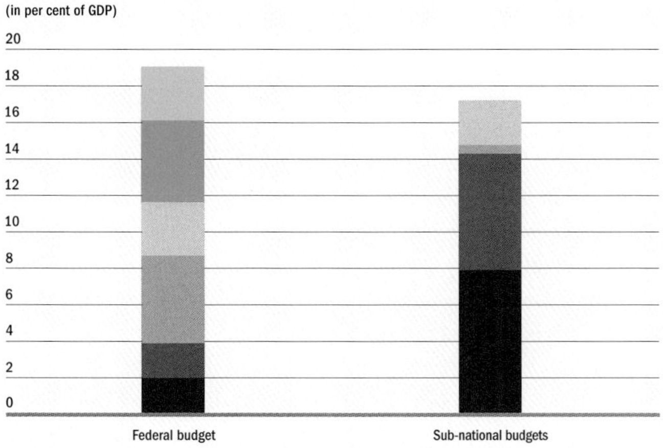

Sources: Ministry of Finance and Goskomstat.

In November 1997, the President signed a decree banning new clearing operations from 1 January 1998, but the parliament later overrode this decree in a clause of the 1998 Budget Law.

Federal revenues were also reduced by an outflow of revenue to sub-national governments. In the early years of reform, the federal government shifted expenditures to lower levels of government in an effort to alleviate pressures on the federal budget and to satisfy the separatist demands of its resource-rich ethnic republics.[2] To compensate for additional responsibilities, however, regional administrations gained a greater share of general government revenue by signing special bilateral deals with the centre and by creating non-transparent off-budget funds. Between 1992 and 1997, on-budget regional revenues (not including transfers) rose from 11.8 per cent of GDP to 13.5 per cent. Meanwhile, the federal budget bore the full brunt of the post-stabilisation revenue decline, with revenues falling from 15.6 per cent of GDP in 1992 to 12.0 per cent in 1997 (see Chart 1.1.5). Subsidies by regional and local governments continue to exceed 6 per cent of GDP (see Chart 1.1.6).

Finally, the system of intergovernmental transfers generated numerous possibilities for ad hoc bargaining and created incentives for regional governments to keep their spending high and their revenues low. A mathematical formula introduced in 1994 to calculate regional transfer needs created perverse incentives for regions to run wage arrears as a way of extracting transfers from the federal budget. In 1997, the President explicitly instructed the federal government to pay off wage arrears at both the federal and regional levels. General government wage arrears consequently fell from a peak of 11.3 billion roubles on 1 May 1997 to 4.2 billion roubles on 1 February 1998. However, as the President himself complained, many regions misappropriated the funds earmarked for this purpose and then proceeded to run up new wage arrears on the expectation of another bailout.

Enterprise restructuring and bankruptcy

Underlying Russia's fiscal problems has been a deeper set of difficulties afflicting the entire large corporate sector that has inhibited growth, encouraged capital flight, limited tax collection and reduced domestic savings. Politicians have been unwilling to draw sharp distinctions between public and private property or to impose hard budget constraints on large enterprises, both out of fear of the unemployment implications and to preserve rent-seeking opportunities for powerful vested interests. The rapid privatisation of state property between 1993 and 1995 moved over 125,000 enterprises into private hands, but it did not create effective corporate governance or place effective limits on state interference. The federal government gave up most attempts to intervene in company management, but regional governments have continued to exert a strong influence over the actions of key enterprises, whether or not they have been formally privatised. At the same time, small and medium-sized private companies are subject to harassment and expropriation by local officials and tax inspectors, leading them to hide as much of their operations as possible from the state. Thus, the large insolvent corporate sector inhabits

[2] See Treisman (1996).

Chart 1.1.7

Share of enterprises reporting losses

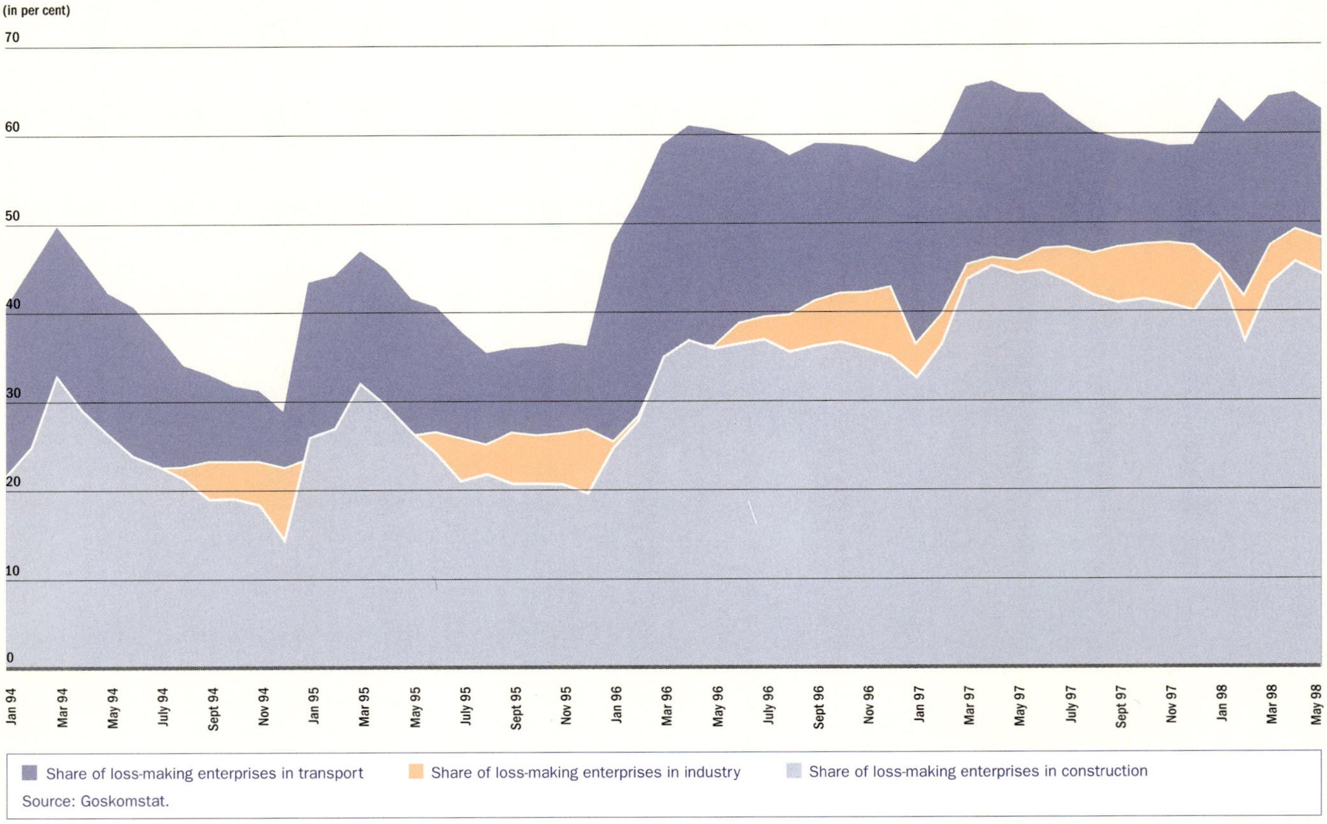

Source: Goskomstat.

what has been dubbed the "virtual" or "non-payments" economy, while smaller and new private firms conceal their activities and launder their profits in the shadow economy.[3] A third category of enterprise "particularly, profitable commodity exporters" have adopted a number of effective tax-avoidance strategies.

Much of the enterprise sector has faced undeniable economic hardship during the transition. As Chart 1.1.7 demonstrates, by the first half of 1997, a full 49 per cent of companies claimed to be operating at a loss. Yet neither the state nor private creditors took steps to liquidate these enterprises or even to replace the ineffective Soviet-era management. The courts considered only 4,300 bankruptcy cases in 1997, although over 65,000 medium-sized and large enterprises had overdue payables on their books. Instead, insolvent enterprises were kept alive, bartering whatever goods they did produce and running up ever-mounting debts to banks, suppliers, their putative employees and the budget. By June 1998, overdue payables on company balance sheets totalled 1,126 billion roubles, or over 40 per cent of GDP, and barter accounted for 50 per cent of industrial sales (see Chart 1.1.8). Meanwhile, tax arrears to the federal budget amounted to 129 billion roubles, not including accumulated penalties and fines; a third of the total was owed by just over 250 large debtors. In the absence of an adequate social safety net, the state sought to avoid the social and political consequences of unemployment from bankruptcies. Private creditors, for their part, were discouraged from taking legal action by the fear of losing customers and by an ineffective bankruptcy law, which gave them low priority in the list of claimants. They were also deterred by courts that were unwilling to enforce claims when local politicians objected, and by the political advantages of having overdue receivables.

Since the state has been unwilling to liquidate large insolvent enterprises, profitable companies, such as commodity exporters, have had a strong incentive to masquerade as bankrupt ones. Elaborate schemes involving "transfer pricing", shadowy intermediary companies, complex multilateral barter operations and offshore bank accounts have been used to hide profits and conceal income streams from the authorities and from outside shareholders. The State Tax Service has the authority to deduct funds from domestic rouble bank accounts, and did so with startling frequency (over 5 million times in 1997, according to its own figures), but it has had little success seizing property or accessing offshore accounts. In practice, draconian measures that stopped short of bankruptcy "such as heavy fines and frozen bank accounts" have made matters worse by driving debtor companies further into barter and the shadow economy.[4]

In contrast to the official indulgence shown towards large enterprises, fully private small companies and foreigners have experienced an extremely difficult business climate. Surveys of Russian shop-owners show a steady pattern of regulatory interference by local government officials and by criminal organisations.[5] Joint-ventures and foreign firms report having to obtain dozens of

3 On the "virtual economy", see Gaddy and Ickes (1998) and Karpov (1997), fn. 1. On the "shadow economy", see Kaufman and Kaliberda (1996) and Johnson, Kaufman and Shleifer (1997).

4 See Hendley, Ickes and Ryterman (1998).

5 See Frye and Shleifer (1997) and Frye and Zhuravskaya (1998).

licences, many requiring bribes to relevant bureaucrats, before they could start operations. The distorted and burdensome tax code, all but irrelevant for large enterprises, has been mercilessly applied to these private companies by tax inspectors. Some foreign companies operating in Russia have co-opted local authorities by giving them an equity stake in their business, further blurring the distinction between public and private responsibilities.

The pervasive soft budget constraints and weak property rights prevented Russia from experiencing an economic recovery and hence a revival in tax revenues, leaving the macroeconomic stabilisation extremely fragile. Ambiguous and unprotected property rights discouraged savings and investment, while giving companies and individuals a strong incentive to keep their capital offshore. The persistence of insolvent but politically influential enterprises blocked new private firms from entering the market. Given the courts' reluctance to take action against debtors, banks were understandably wary of lending to unaffiliated companies.

Together with fiscal deficits, these phenomena left the Russian financial system in a precarious position. Economic decline has, in turn, made political decisions to cut back budget entitlements and redistribute the tax burden much more painful and difficult. Yet unlike the fiscal situation, which was gradually improving in the first part of 1998, the enterprise sector has remained in an inefficient, unproductive equilibrium. The Russian crisis has demonstrated quite clearly that in the absence of necessary institutional reforms the economy is vulnerable to macroeconomic instability that, in turn, incurs a heavy cost on growth.

Policy challenges

In the aftermath of the crisis, Russia's immediate challenge is to move rapidly towards a sizeable fiscal adjustment while at the same time rebuilding a stable financial system. These will be no easy tasks. While default on domestic debt in the near term has reduced government expenditures, the fiscal deficit has nevertheless deteriorated as a result of the crisis and is projected to reach the equivalent of 6 per cent of GDP (annualised) in the new government's budget for the fourth quarter of 1998. This excludes the federal government's commitment to clear its wage and pension arrears, budgeted at about 1 per cent of GDP.

Default has also effectively eliminated any potential for domestic or foreign financing of the deficit, leaving money creation as the only financing option. Already by September 1998 monthly inflation had jumped to 38 per cent and, in the absence of a credible exchange rate anchor, upward pressures on the price level are undoubtedly strong. With a monetary base equivalent to 4 per cent of GDP, there is no inflation rate that could generate a sufficiently large inflation tax to close the budget gap, even assuming that the demand for base money remained constant as inflation took off. Any attempt to finance the existing deficit by money creation is thus doomed to fail and would simply lead to hyper-inflation. The costs to the real economy and to standards of living would be very damaging.

Yet predictions of high or hyper-inflation need not be self-fulfilling. Government debt prior to the crisis amounted to less than 60 per cent of GDP, of which roughly half was domestic debt. Even factoring in other commitments, overall indebtedness

Chart 1.1.8

Barter and arrears

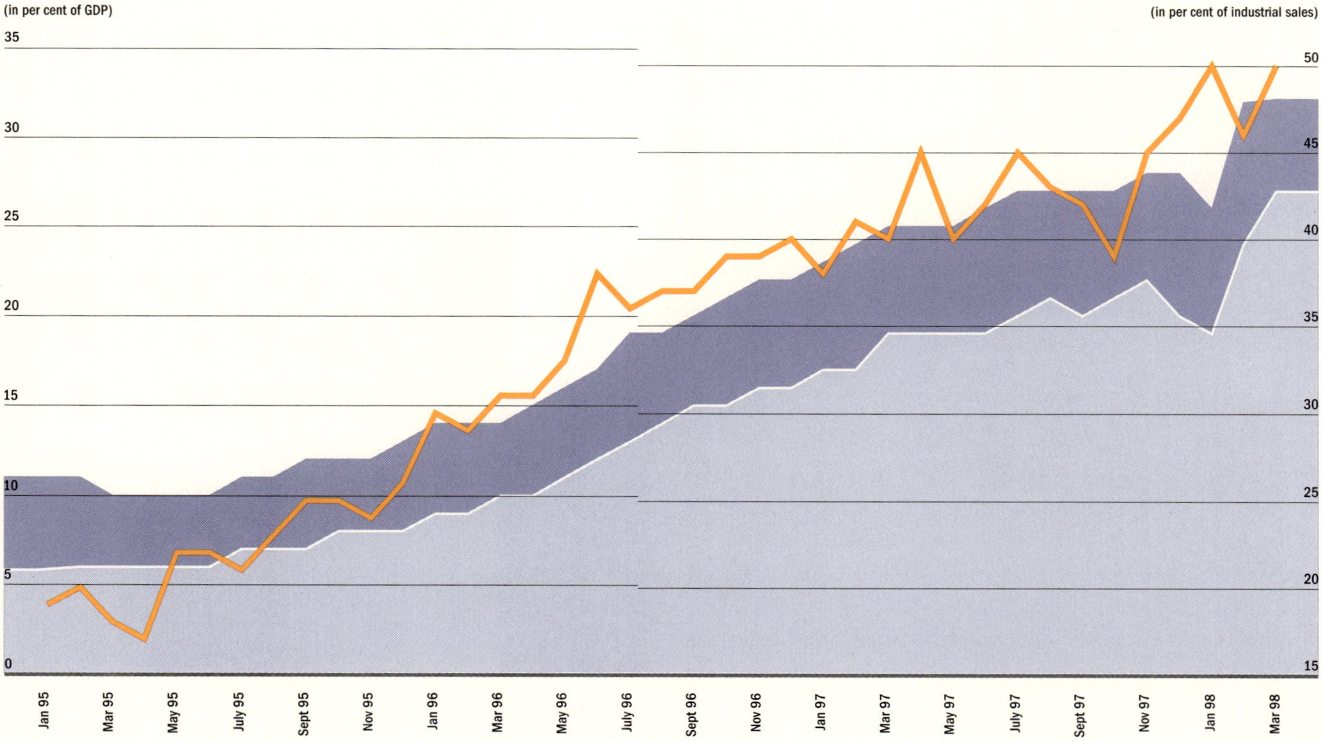

Overdue accounts receivable (left axis) Receivables over three months overdue (left axis) Share of barter in industrial sales (right axis)

Sources: Goskomstat, *Russian Economic Barometer* and *Russian Economic Trends.*

remains moderate. Further, there is considerable scope for raising federal government revenues, as well as restructuring and further reducing expenditures to increase efficiency. Soft support to enterprises needs to be drastically reduced. On the revenue side, the challenge is to take credible steps that will simplify the tax system, expand the tax net and develop a workable system of fiscal federalism. The use of tax offsets and non-monetary transactions should not be countenanced. The urgency of these revenue-enhancing measures is reinforced by the explicit sanction by government of tax offsets, which will only reduce federal revenues. Current government proposals for tax reform are scarcely credible in terms of the challenge of closing the deficit by 5-6 per cent of GDP. A further consolidation would be required to meet any interest payments on currently suspended debt.

Achieving fiscal and inflation objectives will require appropriate resolution of the banking sector's problems. Most insolvent and non-viable banks must be allowed to fail. Applying criteria of systemic importance, ongoing value and fairness, a well-targeted bank recapitalisation programme should not exceed a few per cent of GDP. Total household deposits in the Russian banking system amount to less than 5 per cent of GDP. The recapitalisation cost should be borne explicitly by the government rather than by the Central Bank. One way to implement a selective recapitalisation, without recourse to monetary financing, would be to issue government bonds in exchange for equity of the banks.

In short, a coherent programme for macroeconomic and financial stability cannot avoid some acceleration in inflation but it can avoid a prolonged bout of high inflation. This should involve robust measures to raise revenue at the federal level and to eliminate the still substantial areas of wasteful spending, including reducing the share of off-budgetary funds and implementing greater control and transparency over regional expenditures. Policies to achieve those objectives would have the additional advantage of attracting international support and allowing the amortisation of foreign debt due in 1998-99 to be financed. Around US$ 17 billion of sovereign debt service is due in 1999 (or 5 per cent of GDP). Pressures for rescheduling some of these payments are likely to be strong. Foreign creditors are likely to be more constructive if the Russians authorities show their willingness to continue reforms and confront the fiscal challenge. It must be recognised that, in relation to the severity of the challenge, current policies and practices seem inadequate to the task.

No enduring solution to the persistent fiscal crisis can be put in place without accelerating the pace of restructuring in Russian firms and clarifying the rules under which firms, old and new, are to be governed. To facilitate an efficient exit of loss-makers, the bankruptcy code should be implemented effectively and the continuing tolerance of arrears and payments-in-kind from branches of government, federal and sub-national, as well as from utilities should be drastically curtailed. The widespread use of mutual settlements and other non-monetary transactions should not be accepted.

The mitigation of the dislocation resulting from restructuring requires growth of new opportunities and some social protection. Thus the reduction of barriers to SMEs is of vital importance. Further, fiscal outlays on the unemployed and on social spending require radical restructuring to target groups in need and to provide an adequate level of benefits. The key is to reduce the role of firms as the sites of social protection and thereby raise the incentives for restructuring rather than minimal survival. Indeed, translating the existing implicit state subsidies to employment into explicit subsidies and/or a transparently financed scheme of unemployment benefits is likely to be fiscally advantageous in the current situation.

Better incentives for restructuring and closure of firms should be accompanied by changes in legislation and rules for new firms. Key here are improvements in tax administration and the simplification of tax structures for companies, not least to encourage new firms to cross over from the shadow to the taxed parts of the economy. To facilitate better corporate governance, rapid steps to make shareholder rights more transparent and enforceable will be crucial. Without such conditions, the level of investment both for restructuring and for new firms will remain low.

References

T. Frye and A. Shleifer (1997), "The invisible hand and the grabbing hand", *American Economic Review Papers and Proceedings*, Vol. 87, pp. 354-358.

T. Frye and Y. Zhuravskaya (1998), "Private protection and public goods: The role of regulation", Russian European Centre for Economic Policy, Moscow, mimeo.

C. Gaddy and B. Ickes (1998), "Beyond a bailout: Time to face reality about Russia's 'virtual economy'", *Foreign Affairs*, Vol. 77, pp. 53-67.

K. Hendley, B. Ickes and R. Ryterman (1998), "Remonetizing the Russian economy", http://econ.la.psu.edu/~bickes/barter.pdf.

S. Johnson, D. Kaufman and A. Shleifer (1997), "The unofficial economy in transition", *Brookings Papers on Economic Activity*, 2:1997:, pp. 159 -237.

P. Karpov (1997), "On the causes of low tax collection, general causes of the 'arrears crisis', and opportunities for restoring solvency", Interagency Balance Commission, Moscow.

D. Kaufman and A. Kaliberda (1996), "Integrating the unofficial economy into the dynamics of post-socialist economies," in B. Kaminski (ed.), *Economic Transition in Russia and the New States of Eurasia* (Armonk, New York: M.E. Sharpe).

D. Treisman (1996), "The politics of intergovernmental transfers in post-Soviet Russia", *British Journal of Political Science*, Vol. 26, pp. 299-335.

Part I

Progress in transition and economic performance

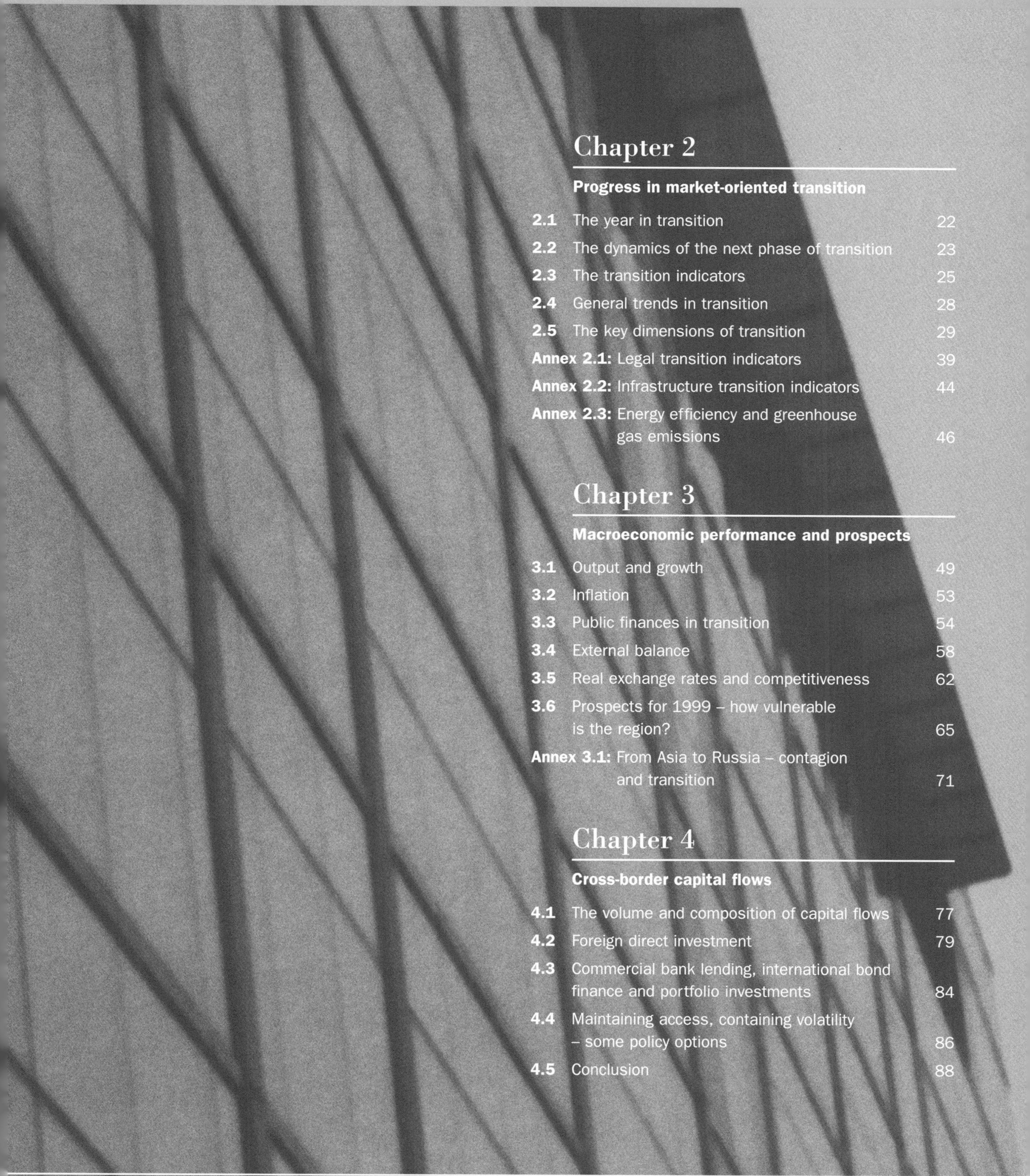

Chapter 2

Progress in market-oriented transition

Chapter 3

Macroeconomic performance and prospects

Chapter 4

Cross-border capital flows

Progress in market-oriented transition

2

2.1 The year in transition

The turmoil in emerging markets has put the quality of reforms in transition economies to the test. Although a wide range of factors has determined the vulnerability of these economies to crisis, the key to preserving macroeconomic stability and sustainable growth has been the strength of, and commitment to, market-supporting institutional reforms. The crisis has highlighted the critical importance of the capacity of the state to enforce laws and curb corruption, to collect taxes, to regulate banks and financial markets, to implement bankruptcies, to promote enterprise restructuring and effective corporate governance, and to build the social foundations for a well-functioning market economy. These are the key challenges of the next phase of transition and they remain at the top of the agenda for all countries of the region.

The transition economies face an increasingly similar set of challenges, but their responses, and hence their progress, have differed substantially. The crisis in emerging markets has highlighted ever more sharply the message of previous *Transition Reports:* the countries of the region have pursued strikingly different paths of macroeconomic stabilisation, structural reform and institutional development. The differences among them, both in terms of the nature of the reforms adopted and the pace of change in different dimensions of the reform process, have largely determined the vulnerability and the resilience of each country in the face of global market pressures.

While the gaps between countries may have grown, progress in tackling the difficult challenges of the next phase of transition has generally been slow throughout the region, especially in comparison with the rapid pace of the reforms of the first phase. For many countries, progress in transition, as reflected in the 1998 transition indicators presented below, has been slower and more erratic than in any year since the fall of the Berlin Wall. The contrast has become still more apparent between the achievements of the first phase – liberalisation and privatisation – and the modest progress in such areas as financial sector reform, governance and restructuring, competition policy and the development of market-oriented infrastructure. Policy reversals have become more common. A larger number of countries are resorting to administrative controls in response to crisis. The hard-won gains of the first phase of transition have been placed increasingly at risk.

The causes of the declining pace of progress and increased backtracking have been varied. In a small group of countries – Belarus, Turkmenistan and Uzbekistan – governments appear to be veering off the reform path, delaying basic reforms and reversing earlier achievements in pursuit of their own strategy of economic development. Each year they lag further behind the other transition economies. Other countries, such as Russia and Ukraine, have re-imposed a number of administrative controls over the economy in response to crisis. In most cases, backtracking and the postponement of necessary reforms can be traced to the opposition of strong vested interests in the political system, both inherited from the former command system and, more often, forged in the early stages of the transition itself. The politics of building the institutions necessary for economic stability and sustainable growth have proven to be extremely complex and fraught with risks to the entire reform process.

These risks were demonstrated all too dramatically with the unfolding of the crisis in Russia, where extreme fiscal pressures in the context of inadequate structural reforms and a highly uncertain political environment produced one of the sharpest setbacks of the reform process in the short history of the transition. In Russia, the gap between the rapid pace of liberalisation and privatisation and the stunted development of critical market-supporting institutions has been as stark as in any country in the region. Rapid privatisation was not combined with effective reforms to promote good corporate governance, competition through new market entry, and proper financial discipline. The explosive rise of commercial banks and complex financial instruments quickly outpaced the capacity of institutions to enforce effective prudential regulations. The state grew dependent on volatile foreign capital inflows without paying sufficient attention to the necessary improvements in the investment climate to secure sustained access to these inflows.

Russia became an emerging market of striking contrasts. Banks traded sophisticated financial derivatives, but were virtually unable to attract ordinary household deposits. Trading on the stock market reached volumes of over US$ 100 million per day, but stock owners were often unable to exercise their most basic shareholder rights. Vast financial-industrial groups (FIGs) were created to promote synergies between banks and large-scale enterprises, while an ever-increasing number of firms resorted to barter to stay afloat. The self-styled "oligarchs" in command of these FIGs amassed substantial fortunes, while leaving workers and the state with a mushrooming backlog of wage and tax arrears. Foreign portfolio investors moved aggressively into the Russian market, hedging their currency risks with Russian banks but taking inadequate account of the implications of an accumulating mountain of derivative contracts on the overall stability of the banking system. These imbalances, as suggested in Annex 1.1 of this Report, highlight the root causes of the ensuing turmoil in Russia.

However, the Russian crisis and reform reversals in other transition economies should not overshadow the progress that many transition economies have continued to make in 1998. Several countries in which reform was derailed by the pressures of war – Armenia, Azerbaijan, Bosnia and Herzegovina, Georgia and Tajikistan – have begun to make up lost ground, implementing long-delayed plans or adopting new reform programmes. The challenge ahead will be to maintain the commitment to implementing these reforms and to begin to tackle the difficult institutional reforms necessary for a well-functioning market economy.

Countries such as Hungary and Poland have begun to show real progress in tackling the challenges of the next phase of transition, particularly in the difficult areas of banking reform and enterprise restructuring. Indeed, the resilience that these economies demonstrated in the face of the crisis in emerging markets is a strong testament to the importance of these institutional reforms for maintaining stability and growth.[1]

2.2 The dynamics of the next phase of transition

Why has the pace of reforms slowed as countries face the challenges of the next phase of transition? Why do these challenges appear to entail even greater risks than the difficult tasks of the first phase? To answer these questions, we must recognise that the political and economic dynamics of the reform process have changed, both in response to the current challenges and to the new policy-making environment shaped by the early years of transition.

The tasks of the next phase of transition – promoting sound corporate governance and enterprise restructuring, deepening and effectively regulating financial markets, strengthening the fiscal system, building an adequate social safety net and fostering the rule of law – are of such magnitude and complexity that they cannot be completed overnight. Although rules, procedures and organisations can often be set in place rather quickly, the capacity of institutions to change expectations and shape behaviour – hence their effectiveness – can be developed only over the long term. Effective structural reforms require investments in the development of individual skills (human capital) and the slow accumulation of experience by learning and doing to alter entrenched patterns of behaviour and practices within society. As a result, the time needed for these reforms is substantially longer than the time required for the policy reforms and redistribution of state-owned assets associated with the first phase of transition.

Moreover, establishing market-supporting institutions while the market itself is functioning and developing at a rapid pace – likened by some to rebuilding a ship in the open sea[2] – is an extremely complex process with few historical parallels. While these institutions developed over many years, and even generations, in the advanced industrial countries, the transition countries are faced with the challenge of establishing them in a very short time span. Although the advanced industrial economies offer a rich variety of market-supporting institutions to choose from, the paths to attaining these institutions are much less clear. How can the state build the trust necessary to foster a law-governed society, especially in light of the difficult legacy of 70 years of communism in the former Soviet countries? How can effective enterprise restructuring be promoted before an adequate system of social protection is put in place, a task in itself complicated by the weak fiscal positions of most states in the region? How can efficient regulatory institutions be developed before the necessary long-term investments have been made in training and improving the civil service? There are no simple blueprints or models to provide answers to these questions, and success will inevitably depend on a lengthy process of experimentation and learning.

The state must play an important role in meeting these challenges and this role differs, in many respects, from the requirements of the first phase of transition. Liberalising reforms required the state to refrain from intervening in economic activity in order to allow market forces to determine outcomes. Privatisation required the state to redistribute its own assets to other groups in society, in many cases at a nominal cost to the recipients.[3] In contrast, the challenges of the next phase of transition require a much more constructive role for the state. These reforms entail fundamental changes in behaviour and expectations throughout society that are not necessarily generated by market incentives alone.[4] The state not only has to create market-supporting institutions but also to generate consent and compliance with the new rules across society. Consequently, in this new phase of transition the state requires more than just the administrative capacity necessary to design institutions but also the authority to ensure their effectiveness.

As regards the capacity of the state, there is substantial variation across the region but serious weaknesses persist in most transition countries. The absence of a well-functioning tax system, especially in the CIS, places severe fiscal constraints on the state at a time when its needs are most substantial. Salaries and benefits for civil servants have not kept pace with remuneration in the private sector, drawing the most talented individuals away from public service. Even more serious is the low level of state authority in many transition countries. Many states of the region face extremely low levels of public confidence and trust, thus undermining their authority to establish institutions that effectively alter the behaviours and practices of the population.

Corruption is both a fundamental cause for, and inevitable consequence of, weak state authority. It is a particularly severe problem in the CIS, where corruption, according to a number of different surveys, is perceived to be among the highest of any region in the world.[5] Corruption distorts state behaviour by allowing bureaucrats to intervene in areas where they should not, while undermining their capacity to act efficiently in those areas where they are urgently needed. Most importantly, corruption weakens the state's ability to gain consent for, and enforce compliance with, rules and institutions by undermining the public's trust that these

1 The contagion effects of the crisis in international capital markets on transition economies will be examined in Chapters 3 and 4.

2 See Elster, Offe, et al. (1998).

3 This is not to say that there were not existing stakeholders with *de facto* control of state property, whose interests did not have to be taken into account. For a discussion of the influence of existing stakeholders on the state's strategy of privatisation, see Boycko, Shleifer, et al. (1995).

4 For a broad discussion of market failures and the role of the state that can be applied to the process of transition, see Stiglitz (1989).

5 See the detailed discussion of corruption in Annex 2.1 of the *Transition Report* 1997, which presents several different measures of the perception of corruption across the regions of the world.

rules and institutions were designed to be fair and to be enforced without discretion or prejudice.

One further obstacle to progress in meeting the challenges of the next phase of transition is rooted in the power structures inherited from the early years of transition. Incomplete or imbalanced economic reforms at the very start of transition tended to generate flawed markets that often yielded extremely high benefits for small groups while imposing costs on the rest of society. For example, liberalising foreign trade without fully liberalising prices in the domestic economy allowed exporters to sell oil at world prices while enjoying the benefits of subsidised inputs and labour costs. Liberalising financial markets while retaining large flows of subsidised credits created enormous arbitrage opportunities for newly created banks, which frequently diverted credits from the intended recipients. To the extent that reforms in the next phase of transition reduce or eliminate these market flaws, they should be expected to provoke fierce opposition from those groups that initially gained from the rent-seeking opportunities.

Indeed, it is often the biggest "winners" of the first phase of reform that constitute the most difficult obstacles to the necessary reforms of the next phase. The greater the concentration of economic gains in the first years of transition – when the state itself is still in the process of transformation – the greater the ability of those winners to "capture" the political process and prevent further reforms in the next phase. Bankers who gained from speculative arbitrage operations and other off-balance-sheet activities have opposed strengthening prudential regulation and supervision. State managers who have become private owners – the big winners of privatisation in all too many countries – have prevented the establishment of effective corporate governance structures to ward off threats of outside control. Emerging financial-industrial groups have blocked efforts to promote competition and have called for barriers to new market entry. Criminalised business syndicates established early in the transition have undermined the formation of a viable legal system. Removing these obstacles to further reform has serious distributional implications and requires a state with the resolve and the capacity to break the power of vested interests.

The combination of a weak state and an extreme concentration of market power in many transition countries has created a policy-making environment characterised by the capture of the state by powerful economic interests, discretionary intervention by state bureaucrats into the market and high levels of corruption. In this environment, the state has been unable to finance itself in a sustainable way, to enforce a proper regulatory framework for the rapidly expanding financial markets or to respond credibly to economic shocks. Nor has it been able to enforce hard budget constraints on enterprises, to promote good corporate governance or to maintain investor and popular confidence in the market.

Despite these obstacles, many transition countries are making progress in building the institutional foundation for a well-functioning market economy. The factors that have brought about this progress, like the causes of delay described above, are varied. In most of the countries of central Europe and the Baltic states, steady progress has been made in tackling these challenges as governments of different political orientations have maintained a strong commitment to advancing market reforms. Such a commitment can derive from a number of inter-related sources, including cultural and historical receptiveness to the market economy, the attraction of accession to the European Union, broad social consensus in favour of continued reforms, and vigorous democratic political institutions that place constraints on the abuse of state power and the concentration of market power.

Major breakthroughs in tackling the challenges of the next phase of transition have also been the result of fiscal pressures, turmoil in the currency markets and banking crises.[6] Economic crisis, often accompanied by elections and a change of government, can serve to break the political deadlock of vested interests and unresponsive governments that hold back further reforms.

Fiscal pressures appear to have played a large role in encouraging states to move towards cash-based privatisations and international tenders of "strategic" enterprises to raise much-needed budgetary revenues. This has motivated many governments to increase private sector participation in infrastructure. Such measures have often been accompanied by greater efforts to improve transparency and corporate governance in large enterprises to increase their attractiveness to domestic and foreign investors. Similarly, fiscal considerations have led many governments to reduce state subsidies and to promote enterprise restructuring through liquidations as opposed to expensive bail-outs.

More dramatic breakthroughs have often been associated with banking and currency crises. In past years, serious turmoil in the banking sectors of Estonia and Lithuania has led to real improvements in the framework for prudential regulation. A currency crisis in the Czech Republic in 1997 pushed the government to pursue long-overdue bank privatisations and reforms in the securities markets, finally tackling the incestuous ties between banks, investment funds and large enterprises that have undermined real progress in corporate governance reform and enterprise restructuring. In Bulgaria, an extreme macroeconomic crisis in early 1997 prompted a new government to undertake long-delayed structural reforms that have already shown some success in securing stabilisation and promoting recovery.

However, as events in 1998 have shown quite dramatically, crisis can lead governments backwards as well as forwards. Belarus responded to a sharp decline in its currency in March 1998 by increasing state restrictions on prices and exchange rates as well as re-imposing state control over the Central Bank and banking activity more broadly. The immediate response to the crisis in Russia has tended to rely on administrative measures, reversing earlier achievements in price and trade liberalisation. Restrictions on currency convertibility have been implemented. Regional governments have resorted to price controls to combat inflation and have imposed restrictions on inter-regional trade.

6 For a discussion of the beneficial impact of crises on economic reform, see Drazen and Grilli (1993).

How governments respond to economic crisis appears to depend on the effectiveness of democratic institutions and on the commitment of political leaders. In most cases, elections brought on by crisis have produced governments that have renewed their commitments to market reforms, regardless of their ideological orientation. Strong political leadership has played a crucial role here. Governments less subject to the constraints of popular elections or parliamentary opposition have tended to rely on deepening administrative controls in response to economic crisis. These dynamics may account for the strong correlation between democratic political regimes and progress in transition.

2.3 The transition indicators

In an effort to analyse and compare the process of market-oriented transition in central and eastern Europe, the Baltic states and the CIS, the EBRD has presented annually a set of numerical transition indicators – across a number of dimensions – to summarise the progress of economic reforms since 1994. This year, for the first time, transition indicators are provided for Bosnia and Herzegovina, marking the onset of the reform process after the long and costly period of war.

The indicators, shown in Table 2.1, provide a snapshot of the cumulative progress in the movement from a centrally planned economy to a market economy. Although progress is measured against the standards of advanced industrial economies, it should be recognised that there is no perfectly functioning market economy, nor is there a unique end-point for the transition.[7] The numerical indicators in this table are intended to serve only as summaries of a detailed qualitative analysis of progress in each area of the transition. The evolving institutional reforms in each country are discussed in the transition assessments at the back of this Report. These assessments, presented in a new format this year, also describe past developments through a timeline and a new set of historical data and set out the key challenges ahead.

The categories covered by the transition indicators in Table 2.1 are selective and do not cover all the relevant aspects of the transition process. They continue to focus on three key elements of transition: enterprises, markets and trade, and financial institutions. On enterprises, the transition indicators are designed to measure the extent to which enterprises have been shifted into private ownership and have begun to alter their operations and governance structures in response to the market. On markets and trade, the transition indicators gauge how well these markets are functioning. In this regard they indicate the openness of markets, the extent of competitive practices and the degree to which prices reflect costs. On financial institutions, the indicators attempt to capture the extent to which the financial system provides financial discipline, effective intermediation between savers and investors and an efficient system of clearing and settlement.

Summaries of the progress in three additional areas of transition are also provided in separate annexes to this chapter. First, legal reform indicators are presented in Annex 2.1 to measure the extensiveness and effectiveness of commercial law, with a particular focus on laws critical for fostering market-based decision-making and investment, namely pledge law, company law and bankruptcy law. The annex also provides a summary of progress throughout the region in each of these areas.

Second, this year a new set of transition indicators is provided in Annex 2.2 to assess progress in the market-oriented development of infrastructure. The analysis focuses on three sectors: telecommunications, railways and electric power. The infrastructure indicators rate countries according to the overall progress achieved in the implementation of policies and the establishment of institutions typical of a market economy. As the infrastructure indicators are reported for the first time, no inferences can be made with respect to the incremental progress achieved since last year. Following the analysis in the *Transition Report* 1996, the infrastructure indicators are based on achievements in the areas of tariff reform, commercialisation (including private sector participation), and regulatory and institutional restructuring.

Third, Annex 2.3 looks at the environment from the perspective of energy efficiency and greenhouse gas emissions. Although total energy use has declined in most countries of the region due to the decline in economic growth, energy efficiency and air pollution remain two environmental priorities. The annex reviews energy use in transition countries, emphasising the challenges that lie ahead, and describes recent international agreements on the control of greenhouse gas emissions.

Although the discussion of legal reform, infrastructure and the environment are presented separately, progress in these areas should be recognised as an integral component of the overall process of transition whose importance is increasing over time.

The framework for a well-functioning market economy goes well beyond the areas covered by the transition indicators. It includes such vital features as the capacity of the state, the development of individual skills and entrepreneurship, and the provision of social services and an effective social safety net to alleviate poverty and limit its damaging consequences. The importance of these areas is becoming ever more clear as the transition enters the next phase. Yet these aspects of a market economy are difficult to measure succinctly and systematically in the form of simple numerical indicators. Their exclusion from the transition indicators does not reflect an assessment of their relative importance, but rather the difficulty in measuring the underlying concepts and the information available.

[7] The general advance of the transition indicators should not be misinterpreted to mean that countries are converging towards a standard model of the market economy; they in fact hide the considerable institutional diversity developing as the transition advances. At the more advanced stages, similar ratings in progress in transition should not be mistaken for similarities in the institutional forms that have emerged as a result of the transition.

Table 2.1

Progress in transition in central and eastern Europe, the Baltic states and the CIS [1]

Countries	Population (millions, 1997)	Private sector share of GDP in %, mid-1998 (EBRD estimate)[2]	Enterprises: Large-scale privatisation	Enterprises: Small-scale privatisation	Enterprises: Governance & enterprise restructuring	Markets and trade: Price liberalisation	Markets and trade: Trade & foreign exchange system	Markets and trade: Competition policy	Financial institutions: Banking reform & interest rate liberalisation	Financial institutions: Securities markets & non-bank financial institutions
Albania	3.2	75	2	4	2	3	4	2	2	2–
Armenia	3.7	60	3	3	2	3	4	2	2+	2
Azerbaijan	7.6	45	2	3	2	3	3	1	2	2–
Belarus	10.2	20	1	2	1	2	1	2	1	2
Bosnia and Herzegovina	4.1	35	2	2	2–	3	2	1	2	1
Bulgaria	8.3	50	3	3	2+	3	4	2	3–	2
Croatia	4.5	55	3	4+	3–	3	4	2	3–	2+
Czech Republic	10.3	75	4	4+	3	3	4+	3	3	3
Estonia	1.5	70	4	4+	3	3	4	3–	3+	3
FYR Macedonia	2.0	55	3	4	2	3	4	1	3	2–
Georgia	5.4	60	3+	4	2	3	4	2	2+	1
Hungary	10.1	80	4	4+	3+	3+	4+	3	4	3+
Kazakhstan	15.7	55	3	4	2	3	4	2	2+	2
Kyrgyzstan	4.6	60	3	4	2	3	4	2	3–	2
Latvia	2.5	60	3	4	3–	3	4	3–	3–	2+
Lithuania	3.7	70	3	4	3–	3	4	2+	3	2+
Moldova	4.3	45	3	3+	2	3	4	2	2+	2
Poland	38.7	65	3+	4+	3	3+	4+	3	3+	3+
Romania	22.5	60	3–	3+	2	3	4	2	2+	2
Russian Federation	147.2	70	3+	4	2	3–	2+	2+	2	2–
Slovak Republic	5.4	75	4	4+	3–	3	4+	3	3–	2+
Slovenia	2.0	55	3+	4+	3–	3	4+	2	3	3
Tajikistan	6.1	30	2	2+	2–	3	3–	1	1	1
Turkmenistan	4.7	25	2–	2	2–	2	1	1	1	1
Ukraine	50.9	55	2+	3+	2	3	3–	2	2	2
Uzbekistan	23.6	45	3–	3	2	2	2–	2	2–	2

1 The numerical indicators are intended to represent the cumulative progress in the movement from a centrally planned economy to a market economy in each dimension, rather than the rate of change in the course of the year. Legal transition indicators and infrastructure transition indicators are presented separately in Annexes 2.1 and 2.2, respectively.

2 The "private sector shares" of GDP represent rough EBRD estimates, based on available statistics from both official (government) sources and unofficial sources. The underlying concept of private sector value added includes income generated by the activity of private registered companies as well as by private entities engaged in informal activity in those cases where reliable information on informal activity is available.

Classification system for transition indicators [1]

Large-scale privatisation

1 Little private ownership.
2 Comprehensive scheme almost ready for implementation; some sales completed.
3 More than 25 per cent of large-scale enterprise assets in private hands or in the process of being privatised (with the process having reached a stage at which the state has effectively ceded its ownership rights), but possibly with major unresolved issues regarding corporate governance.
4 More than 50 per cent of state-owned enterprise and farm assets in private ownership and significant progress on corporate governance of these enterprises.
4+ Standards and performance typical of advanced industrial economies: more than 75 per cent of enterprise assets in private ownership with effective corporate governance.

Small-scale privatisation

1 Little progress.
2 Substantial share privatised.
3 Nearly comprehensive programme implemented.
4 Complete privatisation of small companies with tradable ownership rights.
4+ Standards and performance typical of advanced industrial economies: no state ownership of small enterprises; effective tradability of land.

Governance & enterprise restructuring

1 Soft budget constraints (lax credit and subsidy policies weakening financial discipline at the enterprise level); few other reforms to promote corporate governance.
2 Moderately tight credit and subsidy policy but weak enforcement of bankruptcy legislation and little action taken to strengthen competition and corporate governance.
3 Significant and sustained actions to harden budget constraints and to promote corporate governance effectively (e.g. through privatisation combined with tight credit and subsidy policies and/or enforcement of bankruptcy legislation).
4 Substantial improvement in corporate governance: for example, on account of an active corporate control market; significant new investment at the enterprise level.
4+ Standards and performance typical of advanced industrial economies: effective corporate control exercised through domestic financial institutions and markets, fostering market-driven restructuring.

Price liberalisation

1 Most prices formally controlled by the government.
2 Price controls for several important product categories, state procurement at non-market prices remains substantial.
3 Substantial progress on price liberalisation: state procurement at non-market prices largely phased out.
4 Comprehensive price liberalisation; utility pricing which approaches economic costs.
4+ Standards and performance typical of advanced industrial economies: comprehensive price liberalisation; efficiency-enhancing regulation of utility pricing.

Trade & foreign exchange system

1 Widespread import and/or export controls or very limited legitimate access to foreign exchange.
2 Some liberalisation of import and/or export controls; almost full current account convertibility in principle but with a foreign exchange regime that is not fully transparent (possibly with multiple exchange rates).
3 Removal of almost all quantitative and administrative import and export restrictions; almost full current account convertibility.
4 Removal of all quantitative and administrative import and export restrictions (apart from agriculture) and all significant export tariffs; insignificant direct involvement in exports and imports by ministries and state-owned trading companies; no major non-uniformity of customs duties for non-agricultural goods and services; full current account convertibility.
4+ Standards and performance norms of advanced industrial economies: removal of most tariff barriers; membership in WTO.

Competition policy

1 No competition legislation and institutions.
2 Competition policy legislation and institutions set up; some reduction of entry restrictions or enforcement action on dominant firms.
3 Some enforcement actions to reduce abuse of market power and to promote a competitive environment, including break-ups of dominant conglomerates; substantial reduction of entry restrictions.
4 Significant enforcement actions to reduce abuse of market power and to promote a competitive environment.
4+ Standards and performance typical of advanced industrial economies: effective enforcement of competition policy; unrestricted entry to most markets.

Banking reform & interest rate liberalisation

1 Little progress beyond establishment of a two-tier system.
2 Significant liberalisation of interest rates and credit allocation; limited use of directed credit or interest rate liberalisation ceilings.
3 Substantial progress in establishment of bank solvency and of a framework for prudential supervision and regulation; full interest rate liberalisation with little preferential access to cheap refinancing; significant lending to private enterprises and significant presence of private banks.
4 Significant movement of banking laws and regulations towards BIS standards; well-functioning banking competition and effective prudential supervision; significant term lending to private enterprises; substantial financial deepening.
4+ Standards and performance norms of advanced industrial economies: full convergence of banking laws and regulations with BIS standards; provision of full set of competitive banking services.

Securities markets & non-bank financial institutions

1 Little progress.
2 Formation of securities exchanges, market-makers and brokers; some trading in government paper and/or securities; rudimentary legal and regulatory framework for the issuance and trading of securities.
3 Substantial issuance of securities by private enterprises; establishment of independent share registries, secure clearance and settlement procedures, and some protection of minority shareholders; emergence of non-bank financial institutions (e.g. investment funds, private insurance and pension funds, leasing companies) and associated regulatory framework.
4 Securities laws and regulations approaching IOSCO standards; substantial market liquidity and capitalisation; well-functioning non-bank financial institutions and effective regulation.
4+ Standards and performance norms of advanced industrial economies: full convergence of securities laws and regulations with IOSCO standards; fully developed non-bank intermediation.

[1] The classification system is simplified and builds on the judgement of the EBRD's Office of the Chief Economist. More detailed descriptions of country-specific progress in transition are provided in the country-by-country transition assessments at the back of this Report. The classification system presented here builds on the *Transition Report* 1994. Pluses and minuses indicate countries on the borderline between two categories. The classification 4* which was used in previous years has been replaced with 4+, though the meaning of the score remains the same.

Chart 2.1

Average annual EBRD transition indicators and average variance, 1994-98

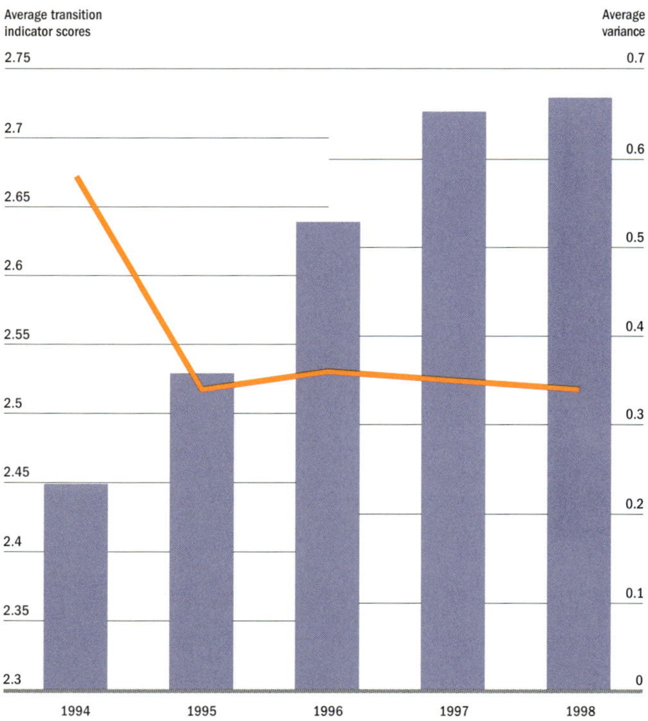

Average transition indicator scores across reform dimensions and countries

Variance of reform dimensions, average across countries

Note:
Bosnia and Herzegovina is not included as it has been rated with transition indicators for the first time this year.

2.4 General trends in transition

The EBRD's transition indicators now cover a five-year period. Some broad descriptions can be provided using the aggregates of scores from the transition indicators, both over all the dimensions of reform within each country and by progress across different dimensions of reform between countries.[8]

In 1998, the transition indicators show a significantly slower pace of overall progress than in previous years, as well as more frequent instances of backtracking on previously implemented reforms. Chart 2.1 shows the average of the transition indicators for the region as a whole over the past five years, which provides a broad measure of overall progress.[9] While the regional average shows progress in each year, the rate of change from 1997 to 1998 is significantly lower than in previous years. In 1998, 10 transition economies show net improvements in the transition indicators in comparison with 1997, six register a net decline, and 10 show no net change.

The progress over the year has been largely concentrated in countries that have been catching up on long-delayed reforms. These include Armenia, Azerbaijan and Tajikistan. The latter has recently adopted an IMF/World Bank recovery programme following the cessation of the civil war, which led to further progress in price and foreign trade liberalisation, small-scale privatisation and initial efforts to deal with enterprise arrears and to harden budget constraints. Azerbaijan continues to liberalise its trade and foreign exchange regimes as it approaches WTO standards. Armenia has accelerated its privatisation process by placing greater emphasis on cash auctions and international tenders.

Other countries have begun to show impressive progress in tackling the difficult challenges of the next phase of transition. Poland has made major strides in privatising its banking sector. Hungary has achieved real progress in governance and enterprise restructuring, owing to the important role that foreign investors have played in establishing effective corporate governance and the continued tightening of financial discipline.

Notwithstanding this progress, the 1998 transition indicators show more instances of backtracking on reforms than any previous year since the introduction of the indicators in 1994. Reform reversals were registered in ten instances across six countries. Russia stands out in this regard following the recent financial crisis. Indicators have been decreased in four areas: banking reform, securities markets, price liberalisation, and trade and foreign exchange liberalisation. This reflects the major retrenchment of the banking system and the virtual standstill of the financial markets following the rouble devaluation, forced restructuring of government debt, and the limited moratorium on commercial debt payments. Moreover, the indicators highlight the introduction of new price controls and currency convertibility restrictions that represent backtracking on earlier achievements. The crisis in Russia also had a limited effect on the indicators of other countries, most notably Latvia, where large bank holdings of Russian state securities revealed serious weaknesses in the effectiveness of the prudential regulation of Latvian banks.

Not all of the backtracking on reforms, however, can be attributed to the direct or indirect effects of the Russia crisis or broader pressures in emerging markets. One group of countries – Belarus, Turkmenistan and Uzbekistan – has demonstrated a consistent pattern in recent years of delaying or retreating from market-oriented reforms across a number of different dimensions. This pattern of backtracking does not appear to derive from economic constraints. Rather, governments in these countries have explicitly favoured alternative economic paths that have, over time, increasingly diverged from the reform patterns of other transition economies. In 1998 Belarus and Uzbekistan both introduced further price controls, leading to reductions in their transition indicators in this area. Turkmenistan continued to delay its modest programme for large-scale privatisation.

[8] While these aggregate scores provide a short-hand technique to illustrate some general trends, they must be treated with great circumspection. The aggregation of scores across dimensions by simple addition both allocates equal weight across dimensions and assumes that the distance separating the various thresholds of the 1-4 scale within each dimension is comparable. There are real difficulties in interpreting or justifying either assumption. We therefore confine ourselves to descriptions of general trends and patterns that are not particularly sensitive to how aggregate scores are calculated.

[9] The aggregated transition indicators for 1998 do not include the scores for Bosnia and Herzegovina, given that scores for this country were not included in previous years.

Chart 2.2

Regional patterns of reform

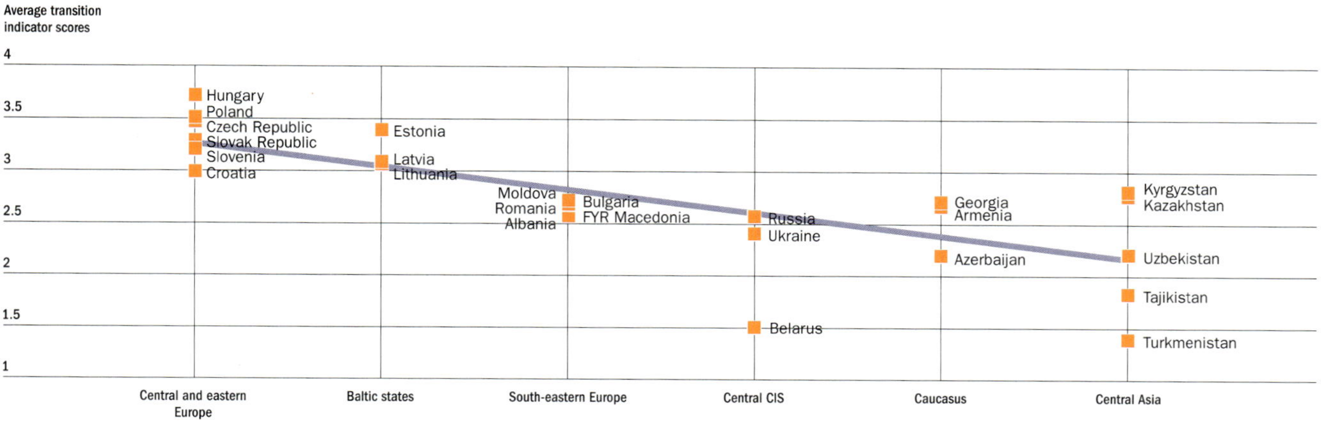

Over the years, there is some evidence of an increasing clustering of countries within each geographical region according to their average scores on the transition indicators, as well as increasing similarities in the patterns of reform across the regions. Chart 2.2 plots the average transition indicators for the countries grouped according to standard regional categories; the horizontal line represents the trend line marking the overall relationship between the different regional groupings and average transition indicator scores for individual countries. The chart shows that average transition indicator scores decrease as the focus moves from west to east, although it is important to recognise the outliers both above and below the trend line. Furthermore, the chart shows a tighter clustering of countries in eastern Europe than in the regions of the CIS. Over time, transition indicators have been converging in central Europe, south-eastern Europe and the Caucasus. The average indicators for the countries of the central CIS countries and Central Asia, however, have continued to diverge.

There are numerous possible explanations for this strong regional pattern of economic transition. These include historical and cultural links to the market economy, initial socio-economic conditions, opportunities for integration with international and regional institutions, regional demonstration effects, the structure of politics and political institutions, or differences among countries in the way in which the previous communist system collapsed. Disentangling these intricately related explanations would be extremely difficult. However, the maintenance of this regional pattern of variation in economic reform, even as the transition advances, suggests an interesting relationship between initial conditions, the early patterns of reform and later policy choices. Of course, this does not imply that progress in transition is shaped by some geographical determinism or trapped in an immutable path of reform. A comparison of the neighbouring states of Russia and Belarus or Kazakhstan and Turkmenistan, for example, clearly suggests that policy choices can lead countries to veer away from any regional pattern of reform.

To understand the challenges ahead, it is more important to look at the evolution of the average scores for each dimension of the transition for the region as a whole, as shown in Chart 2.3. The chart demonstrates the major imbalance between progress in those areas associated with the first phase of transition – small and large-scale privatisation, price liberalisation, and trade and foreign exchange liberalisation – and progress in the institutional reforms characteristic of the next phase of transition – governance and enterprise restructuring, competition policy, banking reform, and securities markets and non-bank financial institutions. As argued in the previous section, progress in institutional reforms has proceeded more slowly, in incremental steps rather than through "big bangs". However, there have been substantial differences in the extent of the governments' commitment to these institutional reforms across the region.

2.5 The key dimensions of transition

To provide a more in-depth comparison of the progress in market-oriented reforms across the region, the major trends within each of the reform dimensions are discussed below. This comparative analysis draws from, and complements, the individual transition assessments at the back of this Report and deepens the analysis of the reform process outlined above with more specific data and examples from trends over the previous year and over the entire transition.

Liberalisation

- Progress in liberalisation has exceeded all other dimensions of reform, with the recent advances spurred by efforts to join the World Trade Organisation (WTO) and the EU.
- To safeguard against macroeconomic instability, several countries have retained controls in such areas as public sector wages and short-term capital movements.
- The crisis in emerging markets has led to the re-imposition of state controls on prices and foreign exchange in some countries.

Most countries implemented comprehensive liberalisation of prices, trade and foreign exchange very early on in the transition, typically as the first steps in the reform process. Price liberalisation usually led the way and has shown continuous progress in recent years, as demonstrated by an EBRD survey of controls on 15 selected prices whose results are shown in Chart 2.4. In most countries, price controls remain only on utilities, rents and goods deemed to play a vital role in the economy.

Chart 2.3

Average annual EBRD transition indicators by dimension

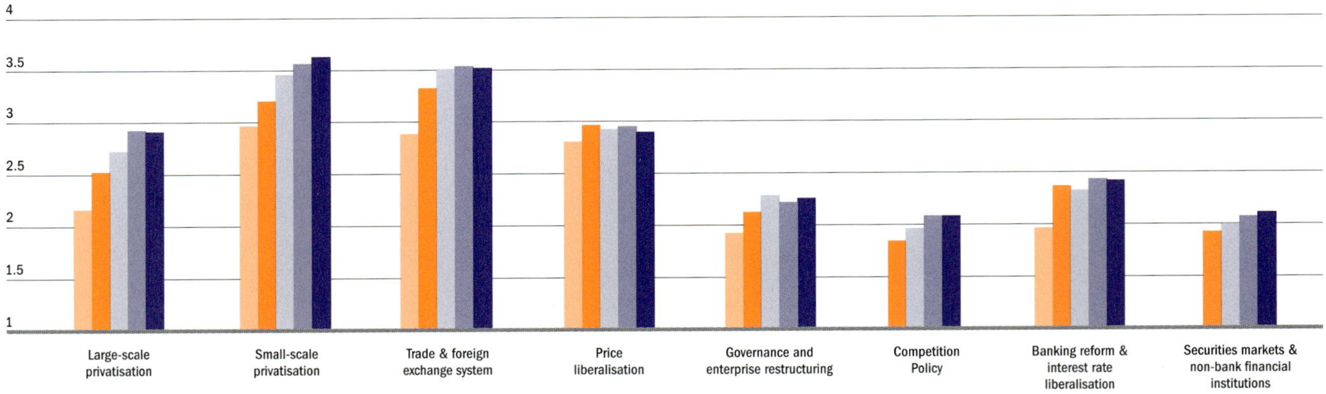

Note:
Bosnia and Herzegovina is not included in the averages as it has been rated with transition indicators for the first time this year.

Recent progress in liberalisation has been a result of efforts to join international organisations, such as the EU and the WTO. Ten transition economies have applied to the EU and 16 have applied to the WTO.[10] To support these bids, many governments have continued to liberalise their trade flows, capital accounts, commercial legislation, anti-dumping laws and tax laws.

However, adopting new laws has proven far easier than implementing them effectively. Land tradability has been particularly problematic. Most countries of the CIS have yet to establish a functioning market for land. Some still have restrictive laws inhibiting land trade; others have retained certain *de facto* barriers to land trade as well as restrictions on sales to foreigners. Incomplete land privatisation and inadequate land registration systems have remained serious barriers. Recently, a number of countries have made progress in these areas, including Albania, Estonia, Latvia and Moldova.

Competition policy is another area where effective implementation of legislation has proven difficult. Some countries, such as the Czech and Slovak Republics, the Baltic states, Hungary and Poland, have active competition offices with powers to impose fines for anti-competitive behaviour. However, none has reached the stage where significant enforcement has been implemented to reduce abuse of market power and to promote a competitive environment. In other countries, competition offices may exist, but these often have limited *de facto* powers over the main monopolistic enterprises.

In 1997 a number of countries adopted or re-imposed controls, in particular on public sector wages and short-term capital movements, to safeguard against macroeconomic instability. These controls came in response to high real wage growth, slowing exports and widening current account deficits. In the Slovak Republic, new wage ceilings were introduced on all enterprises at the end of 1997. Slovenia toughened its public sector wage regulation in mid-1997.

Some countries have temporarily increased controls on international trade and finance as a precautionary measure against destabilising macroeconomic developments. Croatia's central bank tightened capital controls in April 1998 in order to contain the rapid domestic credit growth that was partly financed by short-term capital inflows. In mid-1997, the Czech and Slovak Republics introduced temporary import barriers in response to growing current account deficits and downward pressure on their currencies.

The crisis in Russia has generated more serious reversals of earlier achievements in liberalisation. Following the currency crisis and debt moratorium in August 1998, Russia introduced new capital and exchange controls. Several regional governments re-introduced price controls on some goods and even placed restrictions on the movement of selected goods out of their regions. Earlier in the year, Belarus reacted similarly to a currency crisis by re-introducing wide-ranging controls, including on exchange rates, cross-border payments, external trade and prices.

Privatisation

- Privatisation has increasingly shifted from mass voucher programmes and management/employee buy-outs (MEBOs) to methods with greater revenue-raising potential, such as cash sales and international tenders of "strategic" enterprises.
- The privatisation of large loss-makers remains a major challenge.
- In response to economic crises, there have been calls for partial re-nationalisation of key enterprises and banks, although actual cases have been rare.

Progress in privatisation has differed significantly among transition economies. While small-scale privatisation is virtually complete in most countries, there has been significant variation in the privatisation of medium-sized and large companies. By mid-1998, the Czech Republic, Hungary and the Slovak Republic had

[10] Kyrgyzstan and Latvia have become the first countries of the former Soviet Union to join the WTO.

reached a degree of private ownership close to that of established market economies. In other central and east European countries, large-scale privatisation has been more sluggish, especially in Bulgaria, Croatia, FYR Macedonia and Romania, although these countries have recently intensified their privatisation efforts. In the CIS, Armenia and Georgia have initiated new momentum in large-scale privatisation during 1997-98 after lagging behind in previous years. By contrast, Belarus, Turkmenistan and Uzbekistan appear to have abandoned previous intentions to accelerate privatisation.

The dominant trend has been a shift away from MEBOs and mass voucher programmes towards cash sales to outsiders and international tenders, especially in Georgia, Kazakhstan, Lithuania, Poland, Romania and Ukraine. This trend has been accompanied by an increasing openness towards foreign participation in the privatisation process. Many governments have offered large state enterprises through international tenders, especially in financial services and infrastructure. Hungary has been at the forefront, with about half of its US$ 17 billion inflows of foreign direct investment (FDI) accounted for by privatisation. In 1997-98, strategic stakes in large companies were sold to foreign investors in Armenia (telecoms and cognac), Bulgaria (copper), Estonia (shipping), Kazakhstan (oil, mining and telecoms), Latvia (gas) and Lithuania (telecoms). In Georgia, management contracts with buy-out options have been awarded to foreign investors for two large industrial enterprises. Many other countries are at an advanced stage of preparing international tenders in key sectors.

While privatisation programmes in earlier years were driven mostly by social, political and distributional considerations, the recent trend has reflected greater attention to generating revenue for the state. However, revenue-oriented privatisation has not always been successful, slowing down the privatisation process in some cases. Many domestic cash auctions failed this year, partly due to the lack of domestic liquidity and partly due to unrealistic price expectations by the government. In Georgia, floor prices in cash auctions have been removed in order to accelerate the process. Other countries have recently rediscovered vouchers as a way to speed up privatisation. In Azerbaijan, Bulgaria and Croatia, new voucher schemes were introduced in 1997-98 to complement ongoing cash sales after initial delays in the large-scale privatisation process.

A major challenge for most transition economies remains the privatisation of their large loss-making enterprises. Creditor-led bankruptcy has been rare as these large firms are often deemed "too big to fail". More frequently, banks swap their claims for equity in the large loss-makers, which has contributed to the persistence of bad loan problems in many countries. Many large enterprises have been subject to financial and organisational restructuring efforts led by the state. Significant state-led restructuring programmes are currently being pursued in Albania, Bulgaria, Kyrgyzstan, Moldova and Slovenia, but their success has been uneven.

The recent crisis in international capital markets has disrupted the privatisation process in many of the transition economies. Financial risk premiums on exposure to transition economies have

Chart 2.4

Price regulation of 15 selected commodities, 1989-97

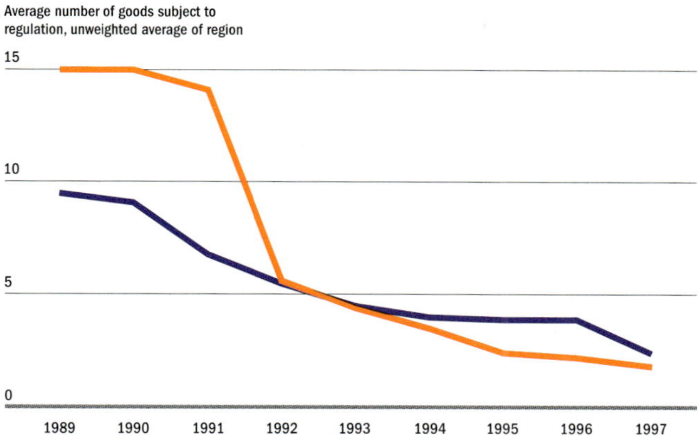

Central and eastern Europe — CIS and the Baltic states

Source: National authorities.

Note:

The 15 selected goods are: Flour/bread, meat, milk, gasoline or petrol, cotton textiles, shoes, paper, cars, television sets, cement, steel, coal, wood, rents and inter-city bus services.

increased substantially, weakening foreign interest in the privatisation process. Plans for international tenders in several countries have been put on hold until the markets stabilise. However, the long-term nature of foreign direct investment makes it less volatile than short-term capital flows.

More seriously, economic crisis has led to calls for a re-nationalisation of key companies in the enterprise and banking sectors in some countries. Yet efforts to move assets away from the "winners" of the first phase of the transition have already met with considerable political resistance, as demonstrated by the initial failure of Russia's attempts to re-nationalise some insolvent banks.

Enterprises

- Constrained by poor corporate governance and weak financial discipline, enterprise reform has continued to lag behind other dimensions of reform.
- While direct state intervention is being phased out, unprofitable enterprises continue to receive support through "soft budget constraints", including weak enforcement of bankruptcy and tolerance of tax arrears.
- The Russian crisis has underlined the importance of sound enterprise reform as a foundation for economic stability and sustainable growth.

Despite positive growth in labour productivity (see Box 2.1), the pace of enterprise restructuring remains slow and inconsistent in the transition economies. The most obvious indication of this is the persistence of unprofitable enterprises. In many countries, losses are concentrated among a few large enterprises. In Poland, state-owned companies in the chemicals, coal, steel and shipyard industries continue to record high losses. In the Czech Republic, two large conglomerates accounted for about a quarter of total losses in the industrial sector. In Russia, the majority of privatised large-scale enterprises in manufacturing were unprofitable even

Box 2.1

Industrial productivity

The transition process has brought about a radical structural change away from large-scale industrial and agricultural production and towards the new service sector. Industrial production dropped dramatically in the early years of transition, followed by the painful process of reducing industrial employment. Some industrial companies were closed, sometimes through state-led restructuring and liquidation programmes. However, the exit of unprofitable enterprises has been a very slow process.

Most countries in central and eastern Europe and the Baltics have gone a long way to complete this structural transformation. Today, a smaller more efficient industrial sector has emerged. The chart below shows that industrial productivity has recovered and surpassed the pre-transition level. Employment appears to have bottomed out, while output has been rising rapidly in recent years. In this process, most companies have drastically reduced their workforce and capacity, abandoning older and less efficient machinery and equipment. Many have successfully redirected their foreign trade away from old partners of the Council for Mutual Economic Assistance (CMEA) and towards western Europe (see *Transition Report* 1997, Chapter 4). The latter has required new investment and upgrading of quality standards. International capital markets have played an important role in providing this finance.

Industrial restructuring has been far less successful in Russia and some other countries of the CIS. The chart below shows that Russian industrial output fell even more dramatically during the transition process. However, this drop was never matched by equivalent reductions in employment. While hours worked may have fallen quite drastically, firms have not been willing or able to lay off employees. Labour productivity has grown moderately in recent years, driven by gradual reductions in employment. However, in stark contrast to central and eastern Europe and the Baltic states, industrial production has not yet started to grow and productivity has remained far below the pre-transition level.

Industrial production, employment and productivity

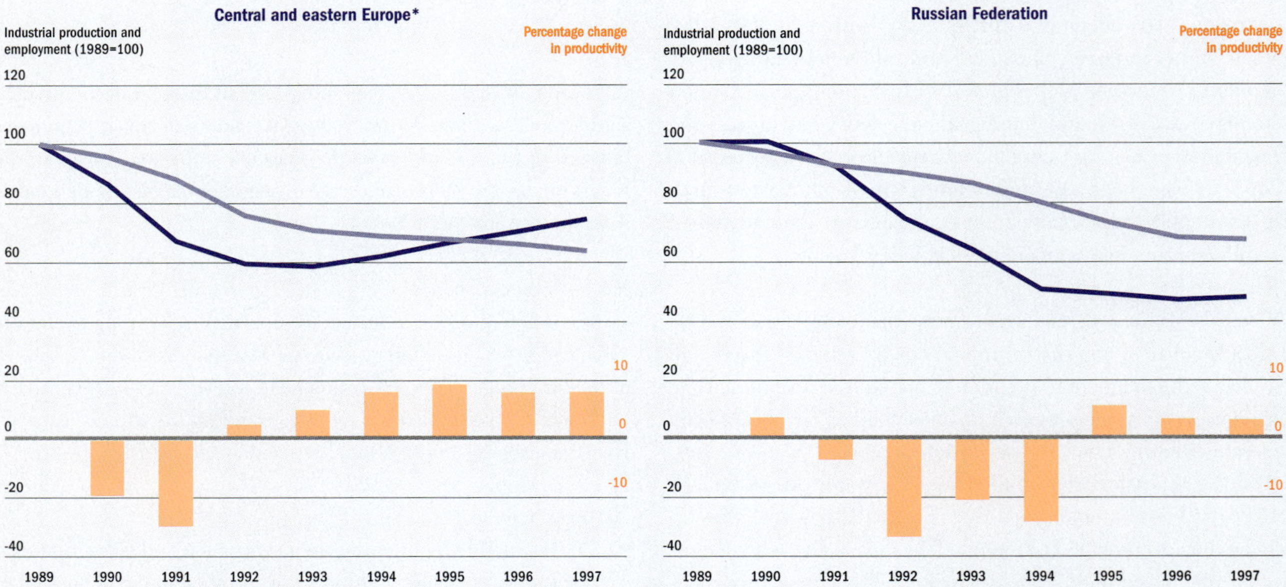

Productivity — Output — Employment

Sources: IMF, national authorities and EBRD staff estimates.
Note:
*Unweighted average of Bulgaria, Croatia, the Czech Republic, Hungary, Poland, Romania and the Slovak Republic. Data refer to manufacturing, except in Bulgaria and the Slovak Republic.

prior to the recent crisis. Restructuring the large loss-makers has proven to be a very difficult task, both in economic and political terms, especially in cases where these companies account for the livelihood of a whole city or even region, a particular problem in Russia.

Poor corporate governance remains a key obstacle to enterprise restructuring and sustainable growth. Privatisation through vouchers and MEBOs has produced insider-dominated governance structures in many countries. Corporate control is often exercised by management without effective checks by dispersed outside shareholders or by the state, which sometimes maintains residual stakes in privatised firms through its pension or privatisation funds. This mix of insider control, dispersed outside shareholders and residual state ownership has inhibited restructuring, especially reductions in the workforce. Yet there is little evidence that majority ownership by domestic outsiders has resulted in faster restructuring. Domestic banks and investment funds not only have little expertise in managing and restructuring firms, but often suffer from similar corporate governance problems themselves, most notably in the Czech Republic. There is evidence, however, that the profitability of new private enterprises and enterprises with a majority foreign owner exceeds that of state-owned and domestically privatised companies.[11]

[11] See *Transition Report* 1995, Chapter 8, for a discussion of the relationship between corporate governance, ownership and restructuring.

Perhaps the most damaging aspect of weak corporate governance has been the lack of transparency and accountability evident in enterprises across the region. Despite improvements in accounting standards, many firms do not strictly adhere to these standards as they trade on the unregulated segments of the stock exchange where reporting requirements are weak. Insider-dominated ownership has allowed them to remain non-transparent and unaccountable to minority outside shareholders and to creditors.

One consequence of the lack of transparency has been that access to finance has remained difficult for many privatised enterprises. Bank credit to enterprises is very low in all transition economies (see Chart 2.6). Enterprises have been forced to rely mostly on their internal cash flows and on inter-enterprise trade credits for working capital and to finance investment. Small and medium-sized enterprises (SMEs) are most severely affected by the lack of bank credit, which is typically their only source of outside finance. Most loans are extended to larger companies, in particular to those that are themselves shareholders in banks or which are partly owned by banks. Despite these problems, new private SMEs have been among the most dynamic enterprises in many transition economies.

Weak financial discipline has remained the Achilles heel of many transition economies and is among the most important challenges for the future. Despite efforts to harden budget constraints for enterprises, there has been surprisingly little market exit of loss-making firms. Creditor-led bankruptcy is almost non-existent in most transition economies, despite recent improvements in bankruptcy legislation in countries such as Azerbaijan, the Czech Republic, FYR Macedonia, Kyrgyzstan, Lithuania and the Slovak Republic. A common problem is the lack of institutional capacity on the part of the state to implement the legislation. Governments have often been unwilling to accept the employment implications of large-scale bankruptcies and to oppose existing vested interests that gained from the early stages of the privatisation process.

In their support for weak enterprises, governments have tended to move away from direct enterprise subsidies and towards greater use of indirect support through "soft budget constraints". These include low input prices and, increasingly, tolerance of tax arrears and arrears to the state-owned utilities. In Russia and Ukraine, there has also been a steep increase in barter and other non-monetary forms of payments. Payments in kind to tax authorities and utilities often overstate the true value of the goods. Subsidised bank credits and, more often, the continued extension of credits to firms with a poor debt service record are still common in many countries, especially when there is cross-ownership between loss-making enterprises and banks. The state has also taken a prominent role in pressuring large banks (including privatised ones) to continue extending credit to loss-making enterprises.

The Russian crisis has demonstrated how fundamental weaknesses in restructuring, corporate governance and financial discipline can expose transition countries to economic instability, as argued in Annex 1.1. By early 1998, Russia had liberalised trade, finance and prices, reduced inflation, stabilised the exchange rate, and privatised most of the enterprise and financial sectors. Yet Russian enterprises have generally made little progress in restructuring, especially in the large and inefficient industrial sector. Payments discipline was gradually deteriorating, with growing tax, wage and inter-enterprise arrears, as well as payments-in-kind, in the run-up to the crisis. The growing use of barter reduced transparency and helped to conceal the unfolding crisis of the industrial sector by overstating the value of barter sales (see *Transition Report* 1997, Box 2.2). These problems contributed to the weak fiscal position of the state, while increasingly obvious violations of minority shareholder rights further eroded investor confidence and made it vulnerable to sharp shifts.

Many other transition economies have made better progress in enterprise reform. In their quest to join the EU or WTO, many countries have opened up their economies to greater competition from abroad, increasing product market competition and generating incentives for restructuring. The need to raise capital, both at home and abroad, has compelled companies to restructure, become more transparent and improve minority shareholder rights. The fiscal constraints on the state have induced governments to cut subsidies and to limit expensive bail-outs of failed enterprises and banks. However, remaining fundamental weaknesses in restructuring, corporate governance and financial discipline not only constrain progress in fiscal and financial sector reform, but also expose transition economies to economic instability, putting the hard-won gains of the transition process at risk. Progress in enterprise reform is thus central both to the transition process as a whole and to a more stable environment for continued economic growth.

Infrastructure

- Progress has been made in upgrading the region's infrastructure, spurred by growing private sector involvement and foreign participation.
- Privatisation of infrastructure is under way in many countries, although regulatory mechanisms have not been fully developed.
- Tariff reform – an important pre-condition for further progress in infrastructure reform – continues to be undermined by weak payments discipline.

Improving infrastructure has become a central task of transition economies. The legacy of central planning included enormous inefficiencies in the production, distribution and consumption of many infrastructure services, especially energy, water and telecommunications.[12] A striking example is the inefficient use of energy discussed in Annex 2.3. Although the transition has brought some encouraging progress in infrastructure reform, improvements have varied substantially across countries and sectors.

The investment agenda and associated financing needs are monumental. With limited financial resources of their own, most countries have relied upon foreign capital to rebuild and improve their infrastructure. War-affected transition countries, such as Bosnia and Herzegovina, Georgia and Tajikistan, have drawn extensive official financing from other countries and multilateral

[12] See *Transition Report* 1996, Chapters 3, 4 and 5.

Box 2.2

Telecommunications privatisation

Stimulated by growing private sector involvement, considerable progress has been made with reforms in the telecommunications sector. Eleven of the 26 transition countries in the region have partially privatised the dominant fixed line service provider (see table). Most recently, Armenia and Lithuania sold majority stakes in their national telecommunications companies to foreign strategic investors. Privatisation plans are at an advanced stage in a number of other countries. Estonia is preparing for a second stage of privatisation, Bulgaria and Romania are planning to privatise through an international tender, while Croatia and Poland are planning to float shares on the stock markets. Albania, FYR Macedonia, Kyrgyzstan and Ukraine have also announced plans to privatise with a foreign strategic investor.

The extensive use of international tenders underlines the benefits of attracting foreign strategic investors and their sectoral expertise as well as the revenue-raising potential of telecommunications privatisation. Total privatisation revenues from selling stakes in the main fixed line service provider have amounted to over US$ 8 billion in transition economies. Two large transactions occurred in the mid-1990s: Hungary sold 67 per cent in two stages to strategic investors for over US$ 1.7 billion. The Czech Republic sold 27 per cent for over US$ 1.3 billion to a strategic investor and floated 19 per cent on the Prague Stock Exchange. In 1997, Russia sold a 25 per cent stake in Svyazinvest for US$ 1.9 billion to a consortium of financial investors.

The early privatisation of fixed line services has not been without its problems. Privatisation has sometimes proceeded ahead of the implementation of effective regulation, leaving pricing and licence requirements regarding investment and coverage subject to some degree of uncertainty. Most countries do not yet have a separate telecommunications regulator. If they do, they have not transferred all decision powers to the regulator. In most cases, regulators are responsible for granting licences and enforcing certain standards, while price regulation remains the responsibility of the government. Tariff policy is often partly determined by the terms and conditions of the privatisation contracts.

An important aspect of telecommunications privatisation is the extent of competition. In the 26 transition countries, as elsewhere, most fixed line services are currently provided by a single operator. When privatising the dominant operator, there is usually a trade-off between making the terms attractive to potential investors (and thus raising potential revenues) and encouraging longer-term efficiency by promoting competition. Most transition countries that have privatised telecommunications have granted a monopoly on fixed line services to the new private owners for a certain period. In recent sales, Armenia and Lithuania granted "exclusivity" on fixed line services of 15 and four years respectively.

However, the general trend has been towards allowing greater competition in both fixed line and mobile services. In Hungary, concessions for local telephone services have been awarded to local operators in 18 of the 54 regions of the network. In each region, the local operator has a monopoly until the end of 2001, when all telecommunications services will be liberalised. In Poland, TPSA's monopoly over local services has been abolished and a number of operators have started offering alternative services. Greater liberalisation of the sector is planned in many countries, motivated partly by the potential efficiency gains from increased competition and partly by the need to align their legislation with EU directives.

Telecommunications – Ownership, regulation and competition

	Fixed line services		Mobile operators	
Country	State share in dominant operator	Independent regulator [3]	Total	Private
Albania	100	Yes	1	0
Armenia	10	No	1	1
Azerbaijan	100 [1]	No	2	1
Belarus	100	No	2	0
Bosnia and Herzegovina	100	No	1	0
Bulgaria	100 [1]	Planned	2	2
Croatia	100 [1]	No	2	0
Czech Republic	51	Planned	2	0
Estonia	51 [1]	Planned	3	2
FYR Macedonia	100 [1]	No	1	0
Georgia	100	No	3	2
Hungary	6	Yes	2	2
Kazakhstan	45	No	2	1
Kyrgyzstan	90 [1]	Yes	1	1
Latvia	51	Yes	2	1
Lithuania	40	Yes	3	2
Moldova	100 [1]	No	2	2
Poland	100 [1]	Planned	3	2
Romania	100 [1]	Planned	3	2
Russia	75 [2]	No	>160	na
Slovak Republic	100	Planned	2	0
Slovenia	87	Planned	1	0
Tajikistan	95	No	1	0
Turkmenistan	100	No	1	1
Ukraine	100 [1]	No	4	3
Uzbekistan	100	No	4	3

Source: EBRD.

[1] Preparation of privatisation/intention to privatise announced.

[2] Svyazinvest.

[3] Independent body but the scope of power may vary across countries.

Chart 2.5

Average retail electricity tariffs, 1997

(in US¢ per kWh)

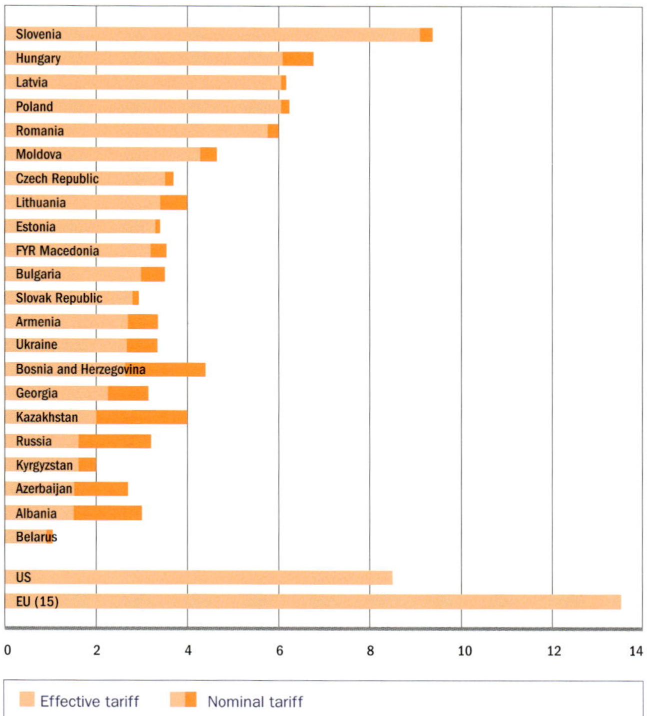

Sources: International energy agency and EBRD staff estimates.

Note:

Average tariffs on households and small businesses converted at current exchange rates. The effective tariff indicates actual collection of tariff revenues.

financial institutions. Private foreign financing of infrastructure-related investment has accounted for a large proportion of long-term capital flows in other transition economies. While the recent crisis in emerging markets has tightened access to international finance, infrastructure finance has proven more resilient than other types of capital flows. This is partly because this type of finance is often sovereign-guaranteed and partly because the cash-flow profile of projects is stretched over a relatively long term.

Apart from private provision of international finance, private sector involvement in infrastructure includes the growing use of service and management contracts, "build-operate-and-transfer" (BOT) schemes, concessions and the outright privatisation of infrastructure. These methods tend to promote economic efficiency in the provision of investment, operations and maintenance services, mainly by introducing competition for the market.

Infrastructure privatisation has accelerated rapidly in some sectors, such as telecommunications (see Box 2.2). Hungary, for example, now boasts a degree of private ownership in infrastructure similar to that of EU countries. Privatisation of infrastructure has increasingly involved foreign strategic investors that bring in new technical, organisational and strategic know-how and are often in a good position to realise many of the large efficiency savings that are possible. For the transition country, the political cost of giving up "strategic" assets to foreign owners is often outweighed by the benefit of high privatisation revenues and the future economic benefits resulting from efficiency improvements.

Effective price and quality regulation is vital for ensuring the socially efficient use of infrastructure, especially following privatisation. The process of developing the necessary regulatory rules and institutions has proved lengthy and difficult in transition economies, especially as there are no universally accepted rules on what constitutes "optimal" regulation. One complex and largely unresolved issue is to what extent competition should be fostered. A high degree of competition tends to boost operating efficiency and to lower market prices towards marginal costs, but may distort investment decisions. Governments have sometimes chosen to restrict competition for a predetermined time after privatisation in order to maximise privatisation revenues.

Further progress in infrastructure reform has been constrained by the poor financial condition of many utilities, which is partly due to distorted tariff structures. Household tariffs for electricity, heating, water and gas have remained below cost-recovery levels in most countries. Enterprises typically pay higher tariffs, cross-subsidising households. A large number of countries have recently tried to tackle the problem by raising household tariffs for these services; some have come close to cost-recovery levels.

Despite progress in tariff reform, many utilities in the CIS remain affected by low collection of tariff revenues among their customers (see Chart 2.5). The problem of late or non-payment has led to an increase in arrears to utilities in many countries. In Russia and Ukraine, the problem was exacerbated by an increase in barter payments. The combination of rising household tariffs and increasing tolerance of non-payment by enterprises has reduced the effective cross-subsidy from industry to households, but also introduced greater discretion in the tariff structure, based on the individual bargaining power of the user *vis-à-vis* the utility. In many countries, this mechanism has implied effective utility prices that are lower for large loss-making enterprises (privatised or state owned) than for profitable SMEs.

Increasing payments discipline will be vital not only to strengthen the financial health of utilities in the CIS, but also to enhance private sector involvement in infrastructure. Utilities that cannot collect their revenues are unattractive for investors, lowering their potential sales price. Still, this is not an easy task, not least because cutting off households or enterprises from infrastructure services can be socially and politically problematic. Greater use of direct and more targeted social benefits and the political will to phase out soft budget constraints for loss-making enterprises will therefore be essential for further progress in infrastructure reform.

Financial institutions

- The banking sector remains underdeveloped in most countries, characterised by a lack of financial intermediation, continuing bad loan problems and weak central bank supervision.
- However, the tightening of regulatory frameworks has contributed to an improvement of the overall health of banks, while bank privatisation and entry of foreign banks have led to greater competition in the sector.

- The contagion effects of the crisis in emerging markets have been most severe in transition countries with poorly developed banking systems and capital markets.

The banking sector in transition economies remains generally underdeveloped. With the exception of the Czech and Slovak Republics, the volume of credit to enterprises in central and eastern Europe is low by EU standards (where credit to enterprises is equivalent to more than half of GDP), as shown in Chart 2.6. In the CIS countries, lending to enterprises is even lower, although a modest improvement was recorded in 1997.

Bad loans remain a major problem (see Table 8.1) largely due to weak lending practices maintained during the transition. The persistence of bank lending to large loss-making enterprises has been particularly problematic in Albania, Romania and Turkmenistan, where the share of bad loans in total loans increased from 1996 to 1997. Imprudent lending practices have often resulted from connected lending or continued state influence.

Bank privatisation has advanced at very different speeds across the region. Progress has been made recently in Bulgaria, Croatia, the Czech Republic, Kazakhstan, Poland and Romania. In some transition economies – including Albania, Azerbaijan, Belarus, Bulgaria, Romania, Uzbekistan and Turkmenistan – extensive state control remains an impediment to the evolution of the banking sector. While directed credits have been largely phased out, many state-owned banks continue to provide loans at artificially low interest rates to "priority" sectors, especially to agriculture.

Prior to the Russian crisis and ensuing contagion effects, the financial health of the banking sector had been improving in most transition economies. These improvements have included higher profitability and capital adequacy as well as the exit of unprofitable banks (see Chapter 7). To some extent, this positive trend reflected increased competition in the banking sector. Privately owned profit-oriented banks (both domestic and foreign) have continued to displace state-controlled banks (see Chart 2.7). State banks have been restructured and privatised, some unprofitable banks have been closed, new private banks have expanded and foreign competition has grown. This has reduced the market share of the largest banks in most countries (see Chart 8.1).

Most transition economies have made progress in adopting and implementing tighter prudential regulation over the past year. Minimum capital requirements and capital adequacy standards have gradually been increased; international accounting standards and new regulations on connected lending and single-party exposure have been implemented. These measures have had an important impact on reducing the vulnerability of banking systems in the transition economies to the contagion effects of the recent financial crisis.

In many countries, however, central bank supervision remains very weak. In 1998 the most glaring weakness has been in Russia,

Chart 2.6

Average bank credit to enterprises

(in per cent of GDP)

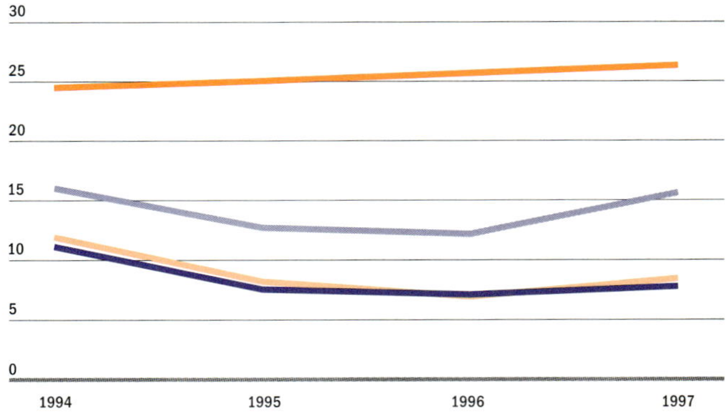

Sources: National authorities, IMF, World Bank and EBRD staff estimates.
Note:
Outstanding bank loans to domestic non-financial enterprises, all types of ownership, end of period. Data shown are unweighted averages of regions. Included in the CEE countries are Albania, Croatia, the Czech Republic, Estonia, FYR Macedonia, Hungary, Poland, the Slovak Republic and Slovenia; the Baltic states comprise Estonia, Latvia and Lithuania; while the CIS covers Armenia, Azerbaijan, Belarus, Georgia, Kyrgyzstan, Moldova, Tajikistan, Turkmenistan and Ukraine.

where the accumulation of a high volume of unhedged forward currency contracts by Russian banks facilitated and intensified the collapse of the sector in August 1998. The effects of the crisis spilled over into Latvia, where some banks proved to have excessive exposure to Russian state securities. Earlier in the year, Croatia's fifth-largest bank collapsed, following over-exposure to a single party with risky investment projects.

The non-bank financial sector remains as underdeveloped as the banking sector, despite gradual improvements in the regulatory and institutional framework. Market capitalisation on stock exchanges was relatively low in most transition economies in 1997 (see Chapter 5), and has decreased further in 1998 as a result of falling share prices. Many shares are illiquid and only a few are listed on the top tier of the market, where stricter reporting requirements apply. Initial public offerings (IPOs) and capital increases through the stock market remain very rare, except in the context of the privatisation process.

Contagion effects from recent crises in East Asia and Russia imply new risks for financial sectors in transition economies. Devaluation is a particular risk for banks with high levels of short-term foreign debt. Even if macroeconomic stability prevails at home, banks can suffer from the loss of business resulting from disruptions of regional trade flows. Another channel of risk is portfolio exposure to other countries, as demonstrated by losses world-wide following the default on Russian government debt. Finally, the strong reliance on foreign investors to provide liquidity to domestic stock markets implies vulnerability in times of global uncertainty. This has been reflected in the steep falls in stock markets across the region in 1998.

Chart 2.7

Bank ownership by assets, 1994-97

(in per cent)

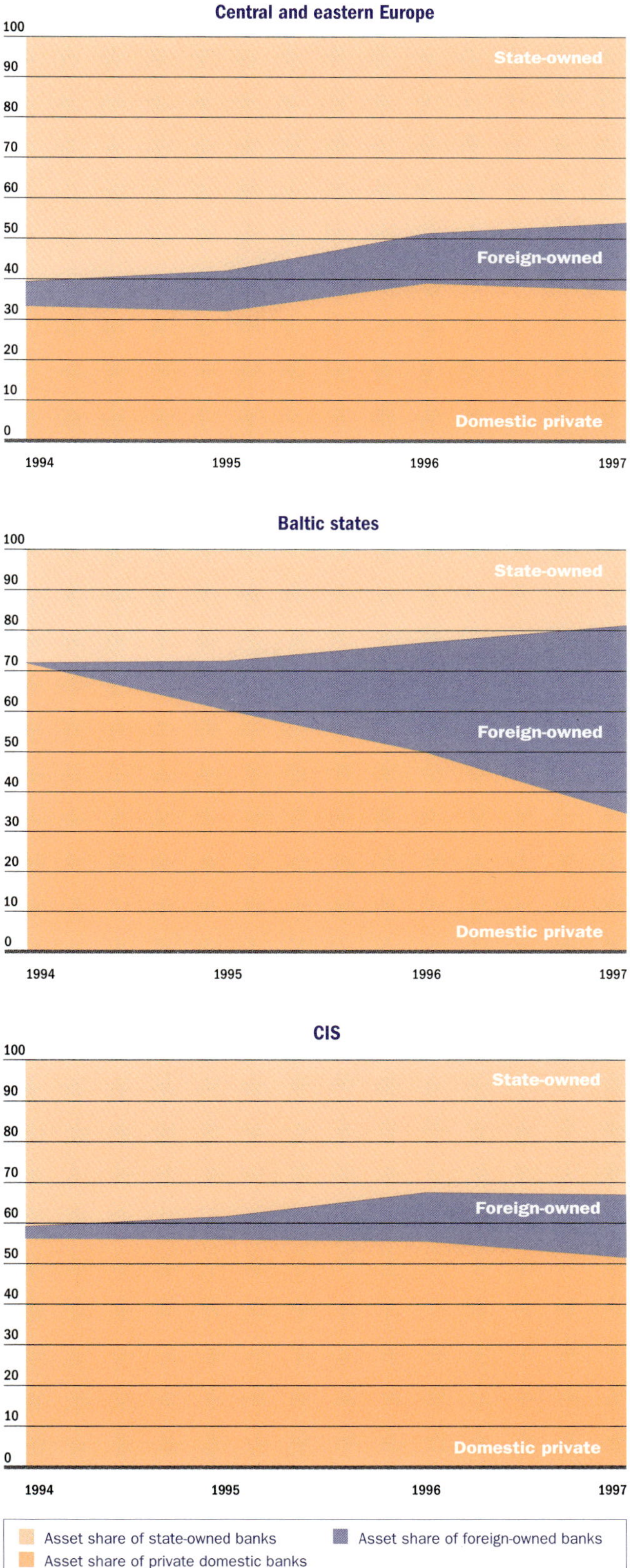

Source: National authorities.

Note:

Unweighted average of Albania, Croatia, the Czech Republic, Hungary, Romania, the Slovak Republic and Slovenia in central and eastern Europe; of Armenia Azerbaijan, Moldova, Kyrgyzstan and Uzbekistan in the CIS; and of Estonia, Latvia and Lithuania in the Baltic states.

Fiscal and social reform

- Meeting the challenges of the next phase of transition has been seriously hindered by persistent fiscal problems.
- In the CIS, the social problems are acute, but so are the weaknesses in tax collection. Little progress has been made on social reform.
- Many countries in central and eastern Europe and the Baltic states are preparing fundamental reforms of their pension systems in order to ensure the long-term viability of the state's finances.

Fiscal reform has moved to the top of the reform agenda in a number of transition economies. Slow structural reforms and inefficient tax policies have led to fiscal imbalances, making fiscal and social reforms increasingly urgent. Following some progress in this area, budget deficits have fallen gradually, to an average 4.4 per cent of GDP in the CIS in 1997 and 2.6 per cent in central and eastern Europe and the Baltic states.

The fiscal position of many CIS countries is undermined by low tax revenue collection, especially in Armenia, Azerbaijan, Georgia, Kazakhstan, Kyrgyzstan and Tajikistan. This has proven to be a serious destabilising factor in the economic, social and political structure of these countries. Vital investments in infrastructure, health and education have been severely constrained. A particularly pernicious aspect of low revenue collection has been the inability of the state to pay sufficient state benefits to pensioners and the poor. Chapter 3 discusses the causes of tax revenue problems.

Recent strategies to tackle the tax revenue problem have taken a number of forms. Some countries, such as Romania, Ukraine and Uzbekistan, have responded by raising indirect taxes. Armenia, Georgia and Moldova have streamlined and simplified their tax system by reducing the number of income tax rates while eliminating exemptions and concessions. An anti-corruption programme in Georgia is partly focused on ensuring that fewer tax payments are "lost" en route to the budget. In Ukraine, the tax system and registration procedures for small businesses have been simplified as an incentive for firms to operate in the formal economy. Some countries have also made efforts to strengthen their tax administration. Russia has given its tax police wide-ranging powers to clamp down on tax evasion, while Bulgaria has introduced a special tax office for the biggest taxpayers. Tajikistan has opened new regional offices of the national tax service.

Given the fiscal pressures, many transition economies have made efforts to economise on government spending. Some countries, such as Albania, have cut the number of civil servants. Others, such as Latvia and Poland, have reorganised and streamlined the civil service. Many other countries have implemented public sector wage limits.

However, social pressures on the budget have increased dramatically in many transition economies. In the CIS, the growth of poverty during the transition has reached alarming levels, due partly to the collapse of GDP and the onset of hyper-inflation in the early years of transition.[13] An increase in poverty has led to dramatically lower life expectancy in some CIS countries, as shown in Chart 2.8, although there have been modest improvements in recent years following partial economic stabilisation. The growth in poverty has also been accompanied by growing inequality. Chart 2.8 shows that earnings inequality has risen in all transition economies, increasing to a much greater extent in countries with weak structural reforms, such as Ukraine and Russia, where inequality is among the highest in the world.

The policy response to growing poverty has been inadequate in most CIS countries. Existing benefits are both insufficient and poorly targeted, thus doing little to alleviate poverty. There is some evidence that social policies in countries such as Russia may even be regressive.[14] Most CIS countries still rely heavily on indirect subsidies, such as low rents and utility tariffs and weak enforcement of payments, as ways to alleviate poverty. By contrast, social policies in the Czech and Slovak Republics (and to a lesser extent in Hungary and Poland) have tended to reduce inequality.

In central and eastern Europe and the Baltic states, the link between fiscal pressures and social reform is most visible in the areas of pensions and health care. The financial sustainability of pension systems has become increasingly uncertain. Like most other countries in the world, the transition economies rely on a "pay-as-you-go" pension system, by which payroll taxes directly finance the state's pension transfers. An important strain on this system is the often very low ratio of employees (contributing to the state pension funds) relative to pension recipients. In Bulgaria, Croatia and Latvia, there are already fewer than 1.5 contributors per pensioner. One reason for this unfavourable ratio is the generous use of early retirement policies, which were intended to cushion the impact of industrial restructuring and downsizing. Another reason is the ageing population. On average, the share of the population above 60 is expected to grow from 17.1 per cent in 1996 to 20.3 per cent by 2010.[15] In the CIS, the average ratio is expected to grow from 12.0 per cent to 12.9 per cent during the same period.

In light of these pressures, many countries have embarked on fundamental reforms of their pension systems.[16] In most countries, these reforms involve the introduction of a mix of voluntary and mandatory contributions to both public and private pension funds. Hungary, Kazakhstan and Poland have been the most advanced in this area. Fundamental reforms are also planned in Bulgaria, Croatia, the Czech Republic, FYR Macedonia, Slovenia and the Baltic states. As the transition from the pay-as-you-go system to a fully funded system implies a strain on the state's finances, many countries have taken steps to limit pension spending, and most are gradually raising the still relatively low retirement age.

Chart 2.8

Life expectancy and earnings inequality

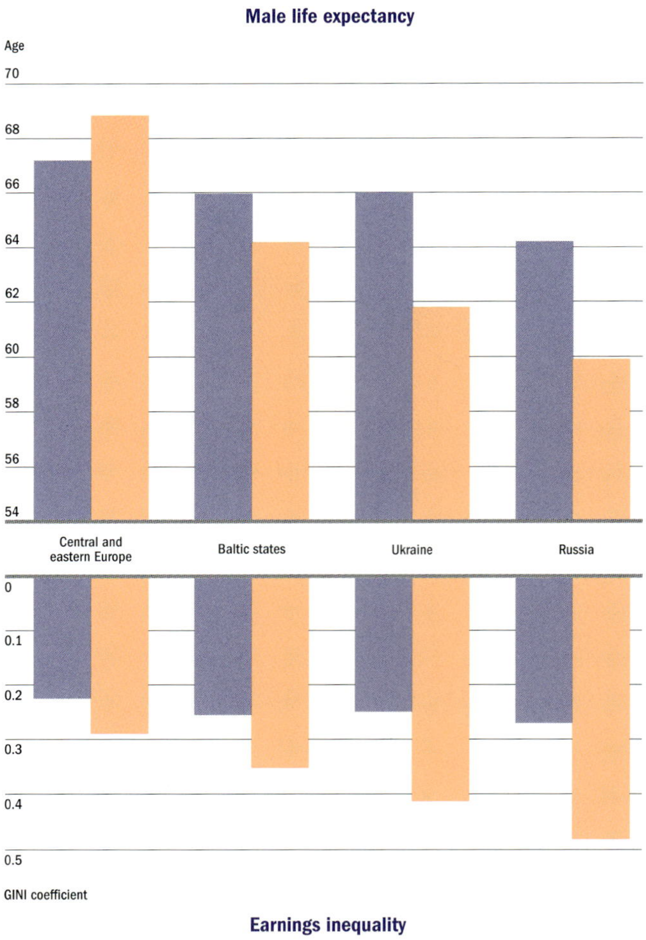

Source: TransMonee database Unicef, 1997.
Note:
For male life expectancy, the values for central and eastern Europe are unweighted averages of the Czech Republic, Hungary, Poland, the Slovak Republic and Slovenia. The values for the Baltic states are unweighted averages of Estonia, Latvia and Lithuania. In Ukraine the second bar refers to 1995.
For earnings inequality (GINI coefficient), central and eastern Europe are unweighted averages of the Czech Republic (1989/1995), Hungary (1989/1994), Poland (1989/1995), FYR Macedonia (1990/1996) and Slovenia. The values for the Baltic states are an unweighted average of Latvia and Lithuania.

References

M. Boycko, A. Shleifer, et al. (1995), *Privatising Russia,* The MIT Press, Cambridge, MA.

S. Commander (1997), "The impact of transition on inequality", *The Economics of Transition,* Vol. 5, No. 2, pp. 499-504.

A. Drazen and V. Grilli (1993), "The benefit of crises for economic reforms", *The American Economic Review,* Vol. 83, No. 3, pp. 598-607.

J. Elster, C. Offe, et al. (1998), *Institutional Design in Post-communist Societies: Rebuilding the Ship at Sea,* Cambridge University Press, Cambridge.

J. Stiglitz (1989), "On the Economic Role of the State", in A. Heertje, *The Economic Role of the State,* Bank Insinger de Beaufort NV.

13 For a discussion of poverty and inequality in transition economies, see *Transition Report* 1997, Annex 2.2.

14 See Commander (1997).

15 The ratios are calculated as an unweighted average of Albania, Bulgaria, Croatia, the Czech Republic, Estonia, FYR Macedonia, Hungary, Latvia, Lithuania, Poland, Romania, the Slovak Republic and Slovenia. Source: World Bank.

16 See *Transition Report* 1996, Chapter 7, for a discussion of pension systems in transition economies.

Annex 2.1: Legal transition indicators

1998 legal survey

Extensiveness and effectiveness of pledge, bankruptcy and company laws in the transition economies

For the second consecutive year, the EBRD conducted a survey in 1998 to assess the progress made to date in legal reforms in three major areas of commercial law: pledge, bankruptcy and company law. Table 2.1.1 contains both the 1997 and the 1998 survey results to show the changes that have taken place in the past year with respect to these areas of commercial law. The assessments were made on the basis of a survey distributed to private law firms, academics and other experts familiar with commercial laws in the transition economies. Private sector lawyers were selected on the basis of their expertise in advising on local law issues.

In 1995 and 1996, the EBRD surveyed the extensiveness and effectiveness of investment laws in general. These surveys examined how the legal environment in various jurisdictions facilitated foreign direct investment. The results demonstrated a significant correlation between the extensiveness and effectiveness of investment laws and other aspects of the transition process.

The 1997 and 1998 surveys mark a shift in emphasis from investment law to core areas of commercial law of particular importance to the private sector. Legislation in the areas of pledge, bankruptcy and company law must be both extensive and effective in order to facilitate commercial transactions. Commercial laws also have a direct impact on the pace of private sector investment activity. A section on general legal effectiveness has also been included in the survey. These questions attempt, as in past years, to evaluate those institutions that enforce and administer the three specific areas.

Table 2.1.1 provides a numerical assessment (as of August 1998) of pledge, bankruptcy and company laws on the basis of two criteria: (i) the extent to which commercial legal rules approach laws and rules of more developed countries in relation to their impact upon commercial transactions, such as secured lending, project finance, debt restructuring, and the formation and governance of joint-stock companies (referred to as extensiveness); and (ii) the extent to which such legal rules are clear and accessible and adequately supported administratively and judicially (referred to as effectiveness). The classification system is explained below.

The table is not based upon a comprehensive survey of all commercial laws and regulations. For example, it does not evaluate banking and taxation laws and regulations although they are pertinent to a well-functioning commercial legal regime. The EBRD conducted a separate survey in 1998 concerning the extensiveness and effectiveness of banking and capital markets laws and regulations. The results of this financial market survey are contained in Chapter 6.

Much of the material that forms the basis of Table 2.1.1 reflects the subjective assessment of survey respondents. Similarly, the information and views provided by respondents were not always consistent. The EBRD has been selective in using material provided by the survey. The final scores reflect an assessment of the effectiveness and extensiveness of the laws, based primarily on the survey results, but also reflecting the experience of EBRD bankers and lawyers who have worked on commercial transactions in the region. Accordingly, while the purpose of the survey and resulting analysis is to give an impression of how the laws in the region facilitate commercial transactions, care must be taken in reading and interpreting the results.

1998 results

The survey results indicate an overall improvement in the level of commercial law reform in the transition economies. Countries that have shown marked improvement include Armenia, Azerbaijan, Bulgaria, FYR Macedonia, Moldova and Romania. Most countries have established a fairly comprehensive commercial law system; the majority of countries received a rating of 3 or 4 for the extensiveness of their commercial laws. The area in need of the greatest improvement remains secured transactions legislation and its implementation. This field requires quite complex reform work due to its inter-connections with other areas of civil and commercial law. The introduction of registered non-possessory pledges over movable property, a model widely opted for in transition countries, requires expensive and technologically demanding centralised registration systems to be most effective.

In certain instances, countries received a lower effectiveness score in 1998, though they have a well-established legal framework. For example, while Croatia received a 4 for the extensiveness of its laws, its effectiveness has dropped from 4 to 3. Russia is another country where the effectiveness has decreased, from 3 to 2. This downward trend may be due to the impact of new and more sophisticated legal rules. New and comprehensive pledge or bankruptcy laws, for example, may have created problems of implementation and enforcement as courts and government bodies struggle with how to apply such reforms. Furthermore, the legal infrastructure (both institutions and personnel) in many transition countries may not be sufficiently equipped to cope quickly with major legal changes.

More generally, most respondents noted that the overall legal effectiveness in their countries had improved. Enforcement of commercial laws, however, remains less effective. Thus, many jurisdictions appear to have a more stable legal framework but still need further improvement in the implementation of bankruptcy, pledge and company laws.

Many countries have enacted new legislation. For example, in the past year a greater number of countries have moved towards a more centralised registration system for pledges. Several countries, including Kyrgyzstan and Russia, have also enacted new bankruptcy legislation. There were fewer changes in the area of company law. More generally, various jurisdictions seem to have amended their laws so as to streamline court proceedings, to strengthen enforcement of judgements, and to create clearer legal standards and criteria for various types of commercial transactions. Russia and Uzbekistan have enacted new laws aimed at making the court system more effective for enforcement of judgements and other legal proceedings. The effort to make commercial law more effective and efficient is discussed below as it relates to the three substantive areas of law.

Pledge law

The 1998 survey examined a number of key issues relating to the ability of a party to pledge movable property as a security for credit. In particular, the survey examined whether countries had reformed existing civil codes and/or adopted new laws to provide for non-possessory pledges of movable property. The survey also examined whether countries had provided for a cost-efficient mechanism for the registration and enforcement of pledges in movable property.

The 1997 survey confirmed that in most of the transition economies it was possible to obtain a non-possessory pledge in another party's movable property. However, the survey also revealed that only a few jurisdictions had established a functioning central registry for the registration of non-possessory pledges. The absence of such registries undermines the effectiveness of the non-possessory pledge. To be effective, pledges over movable property and the priority of competing pledges over the same property need to be established without undue delay or expense. The 1997 legal survey also demonstrated that fees relating to the notarisation or registration of a pledge were high.

During 1997, new pledge laws were enacted or came into force in Estonia, Kyrgyzstan, Lithuania and Moldova. This was followed in 1998 by Kyrgyzstan, Lithuania and Moldova moving ahead with plans to implement a centralised pledge registry to provide notice to third parties.

Moldova initially relied on a combination of pledge books and paper-based local and centralised registration, accompanied by a computer data base to allow easier retrieval of data. The country is now adopting a comprehensive central computerised registration system modelled on the one in use in Hungary. This system would also serve to keep registration costs at a minimum.

In 1997, a group of countries enacted changes to their secured transaction laws. Although they had yet to move to a streamlined system of registration and enforcement of pledges over movable property, they had legislation that permitted a creditor to obtain a non-possessory charge over a wide range of movable assets. They also had legislation that allowed parties to agree to enforce a pledge without the need to obtain a court order. In 1998, there has been less movement or change with respect to pledge law in this group of countries. This may be due to the fact that the drafting and implementation of such laws is a fairly detailed and lengthy process. A few changes have occurred, however.

Some countries have amended their pledge procedures in order to create a more cost-effective process for the registration and enforcement of pledges over movable property. Moldova recently set its pledge contract certification fee at 0.1 per cent of the pledged asset value. This is much lower than the original 2 per cent fee. Consequently, these countries appear to have taken notice of the problems caused by unduly high notary or registration fees.

A third category of countries still lacks pledge laws where non-possessory pledges may be obtained over a wide range of movable property. The Czech and Slovak Republics, Latvia and Romania, for example, have not yet amended their laws to permit non-possessory pledges over movable property. Romanian law, however, does allow agricultural products and inventory to be subject to a non-possessory pledge registered in a public register. Romania also recognises a *fond de comert* (a form of commercial pledge), which has arisen through practice but is not fully developed. Currently, Romania is considering a major reform of its secured transactions legislation.

Company law

The questions on company law in the 1997 and 1998 surveys focused on, among other things, the formation of joint-stock companies, the registration of shares and corporate governance – the duties and responsibilities of directors and the protection and rights afforded to shareholders.

By 1997, several countries had enacted modern company laws that included provisions for the protection of shareholder rights, such as the opportunity to be represented by proxy at shareholder meetings. The laws of many of these countries provided, in certain circumstances, that if a third party acquired more than a minimum percentage of the shares of a company, the third party must offer to purchase all of the remaining shares at the same price or, in some cases, at a price that is not less than the average purchase price of the shares in the six months preceding the acquisition.

Most countries have enacted legislation that gives shareholders pre-emptive rights in the event that a company issues new shares. Pre-emptive rights protect shareholders from having their stake in a company diluted.

In 1997, many jurisdictions did not require share registrants of companies to be maintained by an independent party. By 1998, however, several countries have established centralised share registries or depositories. For example, in September 1997, the Russian President issued a decree creating a national share depository, in which shareholders could register and hold shares in private and state companies. Azerbaijan has also created a national share registry and depository.

Company law is the area where improvement and refinement of existing legislation is still needed in almost every jurisdiction surveyed. Shareholder protections and procedures for ensuring proper corporate governance need to be enhanced. The survey revealed that the effectiveness of company law is quite weak in most countries. It is difficult for minority shareholders to enforce their legislative rights in many jurisdictions. Furthermore, it is often difficult to hold incumbent management or majority shareholders legally accountable for their actions. For example, in Russia, some minority shareholders have had to go to court to enforce their voting rights (e.g. with respect to nominating directors) against majority shareholders. Minority shareholders in some cases are foreign corporations. In response, the Russian government is considering a proposed change to the joint-stock company law to require that the majority of disinterested shareholders approve major transactions of a company.

Bankruptcy law

The bankruptcy and insolvency section of the survey included questions on reorganisation proceedings (whereby creditors and a debtor can reach a settlement rather than liquidate the company), liquidation and the role of the liquidator, trustee or manager. The survey also examined the efficacy of bankruptcy legislation, focusing on the time, frequency and manner of liquidation proceedings. During 1997, many countries enacted new bankruptcy legislation or amended existing legislation that was adopted in the early 1990s. Bankruptcy was the area in which the largest number of countries have made progress in adopting internationally accepted standards for corporate insolvency. Armenia, Azerbaijan, Croatia, the Czech Republic, Estonia, Latvia, Lithuania and Moldova, for example, all adopted new laws during 1997.

A new Russian law on insolvency came into force on 1 March 1998. Under the new law, a debtor is insolvent when it fails to meet its obligations for three months and when the aggregate amount owed to creditors reaches 67,000 roubles. Thus, the Russian law imposes both a time test and a monetary threshold. The head of a legal entity that is legally insolvent must file for liquidation within one month of that determination under the new law.

In autumn 1997, Kazakhstan adopted its third new bankruptcy law. The new law covers all legal persons, state institutions and the agricultural sector. Under the law, there is a high degree of court involvement. Secured and unsecured creditors are offered little freedom to execute upon collateral in a timely fashion. A liquidator has the authority, however, to declare certain contracts or transactions of the debtor void. These include, for example, certain property transfers that pre-date the liquidation by one year and credit obligations or property transfers that occur four months prior to the company's liquidation.

The Czech Republic amended its bankruptcy law in December 1997, the ninth amendment to the law since 1991. These new amendments grant courts additional powers that are designed to speed up the bankruptcy process and to assist creditors in the liquidation of the debtor's assets. Prior to these most recent amendments, the Czech Republic had an ambiguous standard for insolvency: a debtor was considered insolvent if it could not meet its financial obligations within 'a long period of time'. Under the 1997 amendments, a debtor is insolvent if it is unable to meet its obligations and there is a reasonable expectation that they will not be met in the future. A debtor is required to immediately file a petition for bankruptcy when it determines that it is bankrupt. The new amendments also provide for court-appointed bankruptcy administrators to submit their report on a company's finances within 18 months of appointment.

FYR Macedonia has also introduced new bankruptcy legislation, which came into force in early 1998.

In 1997, the EBRD noted that the rules for the distribution of liquidation proceeds varied across countries. In a number of countries, secured creditors did not receive the highest priorities in a liquidation proceeding. The costs of liquidation, unpaid employee compensation and certain taxes and other charges are examples of the types of claims that may have priority over the claims of secured creditors in liquidation. This is not, however, unique to central and eastern Europe or the CIS; many jurisdictions in other parts of Europe and elsewhere allow for the payment of liquidation costs and other amounts to be made prior to the payment of secured claims.

Kazakhstan's bankruptcy law ranks claims differently from the country's Civil Code, which gives priority to procedural and tort claims followed by secured, civil, tax and unsecured claims. In contrast, under Kyrgyzstan's bankruptcy law, secured claims have first priority and are not considered part of the debtor's estate for liquidation purposes.

This past year Romania introduced tough legislation on fraudulent bankruptcy. A debtor or a debtor's employees may receive a criminal sentence of up to 12 years for selling the assets of the company while it is technically bankrupt, for registering fictitious debts or for falsifying insolvency-related documents.

Effectiveness of laws

The scores for the effectiveness of the law are generally lower for some countries. This is explained in part by the recent enactment of new commercial laws in these countries.

The 1998 survey reveals continuing problems with the implementation and institutionalisation of new commercial laws. The main areas in which many countries need improvement include:

- modernising the procedures for the registration and enforcement of pledge agreements;
- removing the uncertainty regarding the recognition and enforcement of foreign judgements;
- improving the general mechanisms for the enforcement of civil judgements;
- shortening the time involved in court proceedings; and
- reducing the level of corruption and economic crime.

The recognition and enforcement of foreign judgements and arbitral awards remains a problem in a number of jurisdictions. In Ukraine, for example, the courts still do not recognise foreign arbitral awards. Russia has also received criticism with respect to the effectiveness of its laws for enforcing such judgements.

Table 2.1.1

Legal transition indicators, 1997-98

	1997			1998		
Country	Extensiveness	Effectiveness	Total	Extensiveness	Effectiveness	Total
Albania	2	2	2	2	2	2
Armenia	3	3	3	4	3	3
Azerbaijan	2+	1	1	3	2	2
Belarus	2	2	2	2	2	2
Bosnia and Herzegovina	2	1	1	2	1	1
Bulgaria	3	3	3	4	4	4
Croatia	4	4	4	4	3	3
Czech Republic	4	4	4	4	4	4
Estonia	4	4	4	3	4	3
FYR Macedonia	2	2	2	3	4	3
Georgia	3	2	2	3	3	3
Hungary	4	4	4	4	4	4
Kazakhstan	2	2	2	2+	2	2
Kyrgyzstan	3	2	2	3	2	2
Latvia	3+	3	3	3+	2	2+
Lithuania	4	3	3	4	3	3
Moldova	3	2	2	4	3	3
Poland	4	4+	4	4	4	4
Romania	3	3	3	4	4	4
Russian Federation	3+	3	3	4-	2	3
Slovak Republic	3	3	3	3	2	2
Slovenia	3	4	3	3	3	3
Tajikistan	na	na	na	2	3	2
Turkmenistan	na	na	na	na	na	na
Ukraine	2	2	2	2	2	2
Uzbekistan	2+	2	2	2+	2	2

To achieve effective implementation of new and amended commercial laws and regulations, countries in the region will need to devote substantial resources to the proper administration and enforcement of these laws. In many instances, countries have undertaken significant reforms of their commercial laws. These changes have not always been accompanied, however, by the development of effective institutions for their implementation. For example, large notary fees remain an impediment to secured lending in countries that have reformed their civil codes and pledge laws. In some jurisdictions there are significant disincentives to the commencement of reorganisation proceedings or bankruptcy proceedings, including high costs, extensive involvement of the courts in the proceedings, the lack of qualified insolvency practitioners, and the lack of certainty in the outcome of the proceedings. Similarly with secured transactions, many countries surveyed still required creditors seeking to enforce a pledge to sell the pledged asset through a court procedure or at public auction. Those countries that permitted private enforcement sales did so only in limited circumstances.

A number of countries have recently enacted legislation aimed at facilitating the enforcement of judgements (both foreign and domestic) and making the enforcement more certain. Uzbekistan also amended its Civil Procedure Code to provide for simplified court procedures for the service of summons. The Uzbek law also creates a new three-tier court system consisting of courts of first instance, appellate courts and a court of causation. Some respondents to the survey feared that this new system would prolong the time it took for cases to be resolved.

In October 1997, FYR Macedonia enacted new legislation to the execution of claims. The new law consolidates court procedures or commercial disputes and removes former prohibitions on a creditor's ability to seize assets considered "essential" to the economic functions of the debtor.

Classification system for the legal transition indicators

The extensiveness of commercial legal rules on pledge, bankruptcy, company formation and governance

1 Legal rules concerning pledge, bankruptcy and company law are very limited in scope. Laws impose substantial constraints on the creation, registration and enforcement of security over movable assets, and may impose significant notarisation fees on pledges. Company laws do not ensure adequate corporate governance or protect shareholders' rights. Bankruptcy laws do not provide for certainty or clarity with respect to the definition of an insolvent debtor, the scope of reorganisation proceedings or the priority of distribution to creditors following liquidation. Laws in these substantive areas often have not been amended to approximate those of more developed countries and the laws that have been amended contain ambiguities or inconsistencies.

2 Legal rules concerning pledge, bankruptcy and company law are limited in scope and are subject to conflicting interpretations. Legislation may have been amended but new laws do not necessarily approximate those of more developed countries. Specifically, the registration and enforcement of security over movable assets has not been adequately addressed, leading to uncertainty with respect to the registration and enforcement of pledges. Pledge laws may impose significant notarisation fees on pledges. Company laws do not ensure adequate corporate governance or protect shareholders' rights. Laws may contain inconsistencies or ambiguities concerning, among other things, the scope of reorganisation proceedings and/or the priority of secured creditors in bankruptcy.

3 New or amended legislation has recently been enacted in at least two of the three areas that were the focus of this survey – pledge, bankruptcy or company law – but could benefit from further refinement and clarification. Legal rules permit a non-possessory pledge over most types of movable assets. However, the mechanisms for registration of the security interest are still rudimentary and do not provide parties with adequate protection. There is scope for enforcement of pledges without court assistance. Company laws may contain limited provisions for corporate governance and the protection of shareholders' rights. Bankruptcy legislation contains provisions for both reorganisation and liquidation but may place claims of other creditors above those of secured creditors in liquidation.

4 Comprehensive legislation exists in at least two of the three areas of commercial law that were the focus of this survey – pledge, bankruptcy and company law. Pledge law allows parties to take non-possessory pledges in a wide variety of movable property and contains mechanisms for enforcement of pledges without court assistance. The legal infrastructure, however, is not fully developed to include a centralised or comprehensive mechanism for registering pledges. Company laws contain provisions for corporate governance and the protection of shareholders' rights. Director and officer duties are defined. Bankruptcy law includes detailed provisions for reorganisation and liquidation. Liquidators possess a wide variety of powers to deal with the property and affairs of a bankrupt.

4+ Comprehensive legislation exists in all three areas of commercial law that were the subject of this survey – pledge, bankruptcy and company law. Legal rules closely approach those of more developed countries. These legal systems have a uniform (i.e. centralised registration) system for the taking and enforcement of a security interest in movable assets and also provide for adequate corporate governance and protect shareholders' rights. In particular, the rights of minority shareholders are protected in the event of the acquisition by third parties of less than all of the shares of a widely held company. Bankruptcy law provides in a comprehensive manner for both reorganisation and liquidation. Liquidators possess a wide variety of powers and duties to deal with the property and affairs of a bankrupt, including wide powers of investigation of pre-bankruptcy transactions carried out by the debtor. There are specialised courts that handle bankruptcy proceedings. Liquidators must possess certain minimum qualifications.

The effectiveness of legal rules of investment on pledge, bankruptcy and company formation and governance

1 Commercial legal rules are usually very unclear and sometimes contradictory. The administration and judicial support for the law is rudimentary. The cost of transactions, such as creating a pledge over a movable asset, is prohibitive so as to render a potentially extensive law ineffective. There are no meaningful procedures in place in order to make commercial laws fully operational and enforceable. There are significant disincentives for creditors to seek the commencement of bankruptcy proceedings in respect of insolvent debtors.

2 Commercial legal rules are generally unclear and sometimes contradictory. There are few, if any, meaningful procedures in place in order to make commercial laws operational and enforceable.

3 While commercial legal rules are reasonably clear, administration or judicial support of the law is often inadequate or inconsistent so as to create a degree of uncertainty (e.g. substantial discretion in the administration of laws, few up-to-date registries for pledges).

4 Commercial laws are reasonably clear and administrative, and judicial support of the law is reasonably adequate. Specialised courts, administrative bodies or independent agencies may exist for the liquidation of insolvent companies, the registration of publicly traded shares or the registration of pledges.

4+ Commercial laws are clear and readily ascertainable. Commercial law is well supported administratively and judicially, particularly regarding the efficient functioning of courts, liquidation proceedings, the registration of shares and the orderly and timely registration of security interests.

Overall score

The overall score allocated in the third column of the table is the average of the scores given for the two indicators rounded down.

Annex 2.2: Infrastructure transition indicators

The restructuring of infrastructure is central to the process of transition in central and eastern Europe, the Baltic states and the CIS.[1] During the period of central planning, some infrastructure services, such as water and electricity, were abundantly supplied with limited regard to economic or environmental costs. Other services, such as telecommunications, were largely undersupplied. Overall, tariff structures were highly distorted. For example, power and water were provided to households free or at prices well below costs, supported by government funding and cross-subsidy from business users. Furthermore, economic inefficiencies caused by central planning affected the usage of infrastructure. For instance, railway systems could cover costs because production distortions meant that large volumes of bulk commodities were transported over long distances, while road haulage services were underdeveloped, car ownership levels were low and aviation infrastructure was poor.

After the collapse of communism, transition economies faced large infrastructure investment requirements coupled with severe constraints on government finance and decreasing demand levels for many services. Reforming infrastructure in a way that promoted efficient performance and financial viability thus became an urgent priority. The requirements for fostering the transition in infrastructure, as set out in the *Transition Report* 1996, include entry liberalisation, commercialisation, the introduction of competitive pressures and services that respond to demand, the move to cost-reflective prices, the establishment of effective regulatory institutions and the reduction of environmental costs.

This year, infrastructure transition indicators are presented for the first time as an initial attempt to assess current progress in the restructuring of infrastructure (see Table 2.2.1). Indicators are provided for three sectors – telecommunications, railways and electricity – in an effort to draw comparisons across countries. Three aspects of transition are emphasised: commercialisation, tariff reform and regulatory and institutional design. A rating (from 1 to 4+) is given, based on the progress in reform in these three areas since the beginning of the transition. Commercialisation encompasses the introduction of hard budget constraints and competitive pressures, including all types of private sector participation, from management service contracts to full private asset ownership and operations. Tariff reform includes setting cost-reflective tariffs, eliminating cross-subsidies and improving collection ratios. Finally, regulation and institutional design includes the establishment and implementation of legal and regulatory institutions that protect consumers by limiting monopoly power and protect investors by ensuring entry and fair competition in liberalised markets.

The indicators are sector-specific to reflect the different challenges faced in each sector. In telecommunications, for example, there has been more scope for competition due to the existence of large unmet demand and the possibility of low-cost new entry in certain segments of the market, such as mobile telephony. Electric power faces more complex organisational restructuring and tariff reforms. Railways are often subject to strong political pressures to maintain unprofitable passenger routes, for example, thus slowing down market-oriented reform. All infrastructure sectors, however, share the challenge of designing and implementing effective legal and regulatory systems.

The infrastructure transition indicators show considerable variation across countries and sectors. Overall, there is a positive correlation between the country average in the infrastructure transition indicators and its average in the general transition indicators as presented in Table 2.1. However, this correlation does not imply causality. It simply shows that progress in areas of economic policy covered by the traditional transition indicators tends to be accompanied by progress in infrastructure reforms.

Many of the factors influencing the current level of progress in infrastructure restructuring – initial conditions, speed and commitment of reforms, availability of finance, economic growth, etc. – are not addressed in the transition indicators. The next step will be to develop a more comprehensive assessment of the transition in infrastructure in all sectors, adding roads and municipal infrastructure (water supply and waste water) to the sectors discussed above. Such an assessment will examine the extent and speed of restructuring, taking into account the initial conditions, reform paths and transition outcomes, as measured by market performance.

Table 2.2.1

Infrastructure transition indicators, 1998

	Telecommunications	Railways	Electric power
Albania	1+	2	2
Armenia	2+	2	2
Azerbaijan	1+	2	2
Belarus	1+	1	1
Bosnia and Herzegovina	1+	2	2
Bulgaria	3	3	2
Croatia	2+	2+	2+
Czech Republic	4	2+	2
Estonia	4	4	2
FYR Macedonia	2	2+	2+
Georgia	2	3	2+
Hungary	4	3+	4
Kazakhstan	2	2	3+
Kyrgyzstan	2	1+	2+
Latvia	3	3+	2+
Lithuania	3+	2+	2+
Moldova	2+	2	2+
Poland	3+	3+	3
Romania	3	4	2+
Russian Federation	3	2+	2
Slovak Republic	2+	2	2
Slovenia	2+	3+	2+
Tajikistan	1+	1	1
Turkmenistan	1	1+	1
Ukraine	2+	1+	2+
Uzbekistan	2	2	1

[1] A market-oriented approach to infrastructure was the focus of the *Transition Report* 1996.

Classification system for the infrastructure transition indicators

Telecommunications

1 Little progress in commercialisation and regulation, i.e. minimal degree of private sector involvement, strong political interference in management, lack of cost-effective tariff-setting principles and extensive cross-subsidisation. Few other institutional reforms to encourage liberalisation envisaged, even for mobile phones and value-added services.

2 Modest progress in commercialisation, i.e. corporatisation of the dominant operator and some separation of operation from public sector governance, but tariffs still politically determined.

3 Substantial progress in commercialisation and regulation. Full separation of telecommunications from postal services, with reduction in the extent of cross subsidisation. Some liberalisation in the mobile segment and in value-added services.

4 Complete commercialisation (including the privatisation of the dominant operator) and comprehensive regulatory and institutional reforms. Extensive liberalisation of entry.

4+ Implementation of a coherent and effective institutional and regulatory framework (including the operation of an independent regulator) encompassing tariffs, interconnection rules, licensing, concession fees and spectrum allocation. Existence of a consumer ombudsman function.

Railways

1 Monolithic organisational structures. State railways still effectively operated as government departments. Few commercial freedoms to determine prices or investments. No private sector involvement. Cross-subsidisation of passenger service public service obligations with freight service revenues.

2 Laws distancing rail operations from the state, but weak commercial objectives. No budgetary funding of public service obligations in place. Organisational structures still overly based on geographic/functional areas. Separation of ancillary businesses but little divestment. Minimal encouragement of private sector involvement. Initial business planning, but targets general and tentative.

3 Laws passed to restructure the railways and introduce commercial orientation. Separation of freight and passenger marketing groups grafted onto traditional structures. Some divestment of ancillary businesses. Some budgetary compensation for passenger services. Design of business plans with clear investment and rehabilitation targets. Business plans designed, but funding unsecured. Some private sector involvement in rehabilitation and/or maintenance.

4 Laws passed to fully commercialise railways. Creation of separate internal profit centres for passenger and freight (actual or imminent). Extensive market freedoms to set tariffs and investments. Medium-term business plans under implementation. Ancillary industries divested. Policy development to promote commercial (including private) rail transport operations.

4+ Railway law exists allowing for separation of infrastructure from operations, and/or freight from passenger operations, and/or private train operations. Private sector participation in ancillary services and track maintenance. Establishment of rail regulator and/or implementation of access pricing and/or plans for a full divestment and transfer of asset ownership, including infrastructure and rolling stock.

Electric power

1 Power sector operated as a government department; political interference in running the industry. Few commercial freedoms or pressures. Average prices below costs, with external and implicit subsidy and cross-subsidy. Very little institutional reform with monolithic structure and no separation of different parts of the business.

2 Power company is distanced from government. For example, established as a joint-stock company, though there is still political interference. Some attempt to harden budget constraints, but management incentives for efficient performance are weak. Some degree of subsidy and cross-subsidy. Little institutional reform; monolithic structure with no separation of different parts of the business. Minimal private sector involvement.

3 Law passed which provides for full-scale restructuring of the industry, including vertical unbundling through accounting separation, setting up of regulator with some distance from the government, plans for tariff reform if effective tariffs are below cost, possibility of private ownership and industry liberalisation. Little or no private sector involvement.

4 Law for industry restructuring passed and implemented providing for: separation of the industry into generation, transmission and distribution; setting up of a regulator, with rules for setting cost-reflective tariffs formulated and implemented. Arrangements for network access (negotiated access, single buyer model) developed. Substantial private sector involvement in distribution and/or generation.

4+ Business separated vertically into generation, transmission and distribution. Existence of an independent regulator with full power to set cost-reflective tariffs. Large-scale private sector involvement. Institutional development covering arrangements for network access and full competition in generation.

Annex 2.3: Energy efficiency and greenhouse gas emissions

Energy production and consumption are directly related to the emissions of air pollution (including greenhouse gases) and to their associated impact on public health, welfare and the global environment. Overall energy use has declined in the region following the reduction in economic activity during the first phase of transition. However, transition economies are still characterised by high levels of energy intensity (energy used per unit of GDP) and, as a result, by relatively high levels of air pollution. Reducing energy intensity is a key challenge of the transition. Large energy intensities provide a wide scope for improvements in energy efficiency through energy-saving investments. Recent international developments in the reduction of greenhouse gas emissions, partly motivated by the efforts of some east European countries to meet EU environmental standards, will provide further impetus and financing to implement energy efficiency projects in the region.

Energy use

According to the International Energy Agency (IEA), commercial energy use in the region as a whole is estimated to have fallen by 23 per cent in the period 1990-95.[1] This fall corresponds to the drop in the level of economic activity estimated at 27 per cent of GDP for the entire region.[2] After seven years of output decline, the region experienced a resumption of economic growth in 1997, but at a rate of less than 1 per cent per annum. Correspondingly, IEA projections show a slow recovery in regional energy use, returning to the 1990 level by around 2010. These projections, however, will have to be revised downwards following the financial crises in East Asia and Russia and the associated slowdown in world economic growth (see Chart 2.3.1).

Chart 2.3.1

Energy consumption by region, 1990-2010

(in quadrillion British Thermal Units)

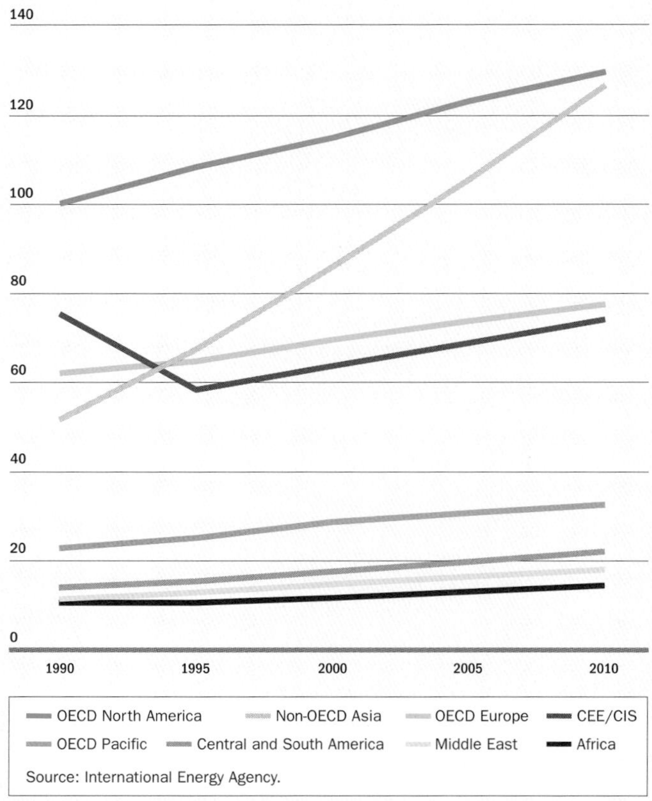

Source: International Energy Agency.

Total commercial energy use in the region declined from 22 per cent of world energy consumption in 1990 to approximately 16 per cent in 1995, while the United States accounted for 25 per cent and the EU for 14 per cent. The regional share is projected to decline further to 14 per cent by 2010.[3]

Energy use is also explained by the composition of output, energy prices and access to local energy sources. In this regard, countries in the region differ substantially in their fossil fuel endowments. Oil and natural gas are the main sources of energy for CIS countries, while coal is the principal energy source in central and east European (CEE) countries. Natural gas is expected to remain the major fuel source for electricity generation in the CIS. In central and eastern Europe, the share of natural gas is projected to more than double, from 8 per cent in 1995 to 18 per cent in 2015, as the countries in the region strive to diversify their fuel supplies with new pipeline construction to western Europe. By 2015, coal consumption in the entire region is expected to have declined slightly, while natural gas and oil use will increase by almost 70 per cent.[4]

Both energy intensity and air pollution can be reduced through energy-saving investments but also through a switch to cleaner fuels. This switch is being encouraged by an enhanced public awareness of environmental issues in transition economies. In the EU accession countries, for example, compliance with EU directives on air emissions, and with the Second Sulphur Protocol to the UNECE Convention on Long-Range Transboundary Air Pollution, will also trigger a switch from coal to oil and, particularly, to natural gas.[5] The substitution of natural gas for coal in the generation of electric power helps to reduce local air pollution problems.

Energy efficiency

The region remains the most energy intensive in the world. For example, energy intensities for individual transition countries vary between two to five times the average of the OECD countries. In

1 Commercial energy use refers to domestic primary energy use before transformation to other end-use fuels (such as electricity and refined petroleum products).

2 EBRD *Transition Report* 1997.

3 See World Bank (1998).

4 IEA, http://www.eia.doe.gov/oiaf/ieo97/world.html.

5 In order to further reduce acidification and low-level ozone pollution, the EC proposed in July 1998 new emission standards for future large combustion power plants that include more stringent standards for sulphur dioxide, nitrogen oxides and particulate matters.

Chart 2.3.2

Electricity consumption, 1989-96

(in kWh per US$ 1,000 of GDP at PPP)

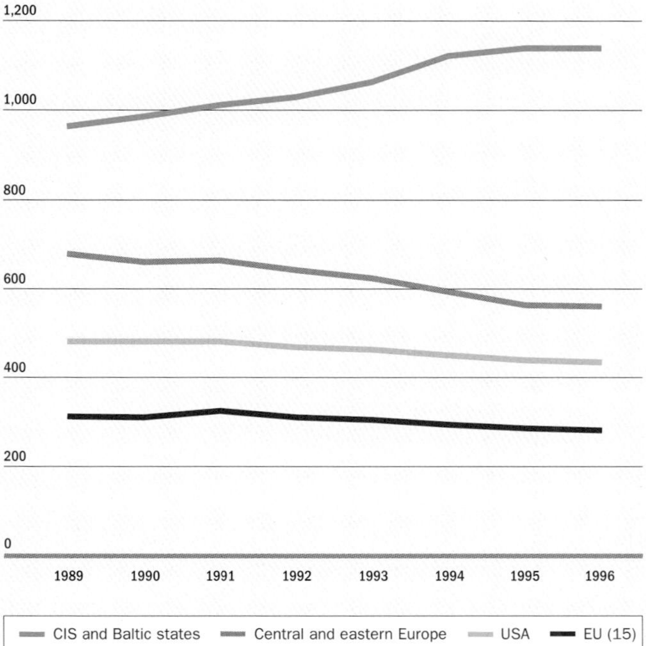

Sources: International Energy Agency and World Bank.
Note:
Unweighted averages.

centrally planned economies, heavy industry was a priority for economic development. Moreover, energy was considered a strategic commodity. To support such a policy stance, energy prices were kept artificially low, which promoted excessive consumption. Old and/or poorly maintained systems for production, transformation, transportation and consumption of energy resulted in substantial energy losses.

This legacy still shapes many energy systems of the region. Some countries, however, have been able to reverse the energy intensity. This is illustrated in Chart 2.3.2, which shows the evolution of electricity intensity as measured by electricity consumption per GDP (at purchasing power parity) over time. Since the start of transition, electricity consumption in CEE countries has become more efficient, while in the CIS countries electricity intensity has increased to levels almost twice as high as the CEE countries.

Energy intensity depends primarily on the structure of economic activity, particularly of processing and manufacturing industries, and on the degree of efficiency in the production, transformation, transportation and consumption of energy, especially by the final consumer. A recent IEA study, for example, has found both a significant decline in energy use in the manufacturing sector, but a simultaneous increase in the energy intensity of steel production for Bulgaria, FYR Macedonia, Hungary, Romania and Russia between 1990 and 1995.[6] This finding is likely to apply to a number of other energy-intensive industries and suggests a large potential for energy efficiency gains in the process and manufacturing sector in the region.

Indeed, improvements in energy efficiency are expected in the near future. According to the IEA, the region is predicted to have a greater decline in its energy intensity overall than any other region up to the year 2015. Transition economies are expected to reduce their inefficient energy use through the adoption of more efficient technology, the rationalisation of their energy systems and the introduction of prices that reflect adequately the production and distribution costs of fuel.

Very significant opportunities for energy efficiency improvements exist in the region through generation, distribution and consumption of heat and electricity by residential, public and commercial entities. Heat consumption (both space heating and water heating), in general, represents a substantial share of total energy consumption in the CIS countries. For example, in the Russian Federation, heat consumption in 1990 accounted for 30 to 35 per cent of the country's total primary energy consumption. Furthermore, district heating plays an important role in the energy systems of the CIS and many CEE countries. District heating provides about 75 per cent of the heat supply for residential, public and commercial entities in the Russian Federation, 65 per cent in Ukraine, 60 per cent in Estonia, and 50 per cent in Lithuania.[7] Energy efficiency improvements in district heating systems will have a significant impact on overall improvements in energy efficiency. Power plants that have considerably exceeded their service life, as well as poorly maintained power distribution systems, are another significant source of energy losses that prevent cost-effective energy production and distribution.

Climate change and greenhouse gas emissions

About 160 nations adopted the Kyoto Protocol at the Third Conference of Parties to the United Nations Framework Convention on Climate Change (COP3) in December 1997. Under the Protocol, overall greenhouse gas emissions will be reduced from their 1990 levels by an average of 5.2 per cent by 2008-12.[8] Among industrialised countries, it was agreed that the United States would reduce emissions by 7 per cent, the European Union by 8 per cent and Japan by 6 per cent.

The Protocol sets out three principal mechanisms for achieving the targets. The first is joint implementation (JI) among so called Annex 1 countries (the more advanced industrial countries). The Protocol allows any Annex 1 country to transfer to, or acquire from, any other Annex 1 country "emission reduction units" resulting from projects aimed at reducing emissions at source, or enhancing absorption of greenhouse gases by so-called carbon "sinks" (such as new forests). "Legal entities", such as private firms, may participate in transferring and acquiring emission reduction units with the authorisation of the relevant Annex 1

6 See IEA (1998).

7 See Martinot (1997).

8 Six types of gases were identified as greenhouse gases, namely carbon dioxide, methane, nitrous oxide, hydrofluorocarbons and sulphur hexafluoride.

Table 2.3.1

Total carbon emissions by region, 1990-2015

(million metric tons)

Region	1990	1995	2000	2005	2010	2015
Central and eastern Europe (CEE)	341	292	314	333	344	354
CIS	1,034	729	779	842	907	981
USA	1,377	1,413	1,490	1,584	1,659	1,733
Japan	310	333	375	401	417	435
EU	1,023	1,014	1,083	1,146	1,201	1,262

Sources: Energy Information Administration (EIA), *International Energy Annual* 1993, DOE/EIA, Washington DC May 1995; EIA, *Annual Energy Outlook* 1996, DOE/EIA-0219(93), Washington DC, January 1996, DOE/EIA-0383 (96), Table A 19, and World Energy Projection System, 1996.

governments. The second mechanism would be the yet-to-be-established Clean Development Mechanism (CDM). Under the CDM, "credits" would be allocated to developed countries that provide financial assistance to developing countries in their efforts to reduce greenhouse gas emissions. Details of JI and the CDM will need to be agreed at COP4 in Buenos Aires in November 1998, or at a later date. The third mechanism would be emissions trading.

Among the EBRD's 26 countries of operations, 13 agreed emission reduction targets as Annex 1 countries under the Kyoto Protocol. These countries are expected to reduce greenhouse gas emissions from their 1990 levels. Bulgaria, the Czech Republic, Estonia, Latvia, Lithuania, Romania, the Slovak Republic and Slovenia are required to reduce emissions by 8 per cent; Hungary and Poland by 6 per cent; Croatia by 5 per cent; while Russia and Ukraine will reduce emissions by zero per cent.

All of the above countries are entitled to participate in the transfer/acquisition of emission reduction units among Annex 1 countries. The whole region contributed 16 per cent of global emissions of carbon dioxide in 1995. During the period 1990-95, Russia is estimated to have reduced its carbon dioxide emissions by 26 per cent.[9] It is unlikely that Russia will increase its energy consumption to offset completely the 26 per cent reduction in carbon dioxide emissions during the period 2008-12 , assuming that improvements in energy efficiency take place. This means that Russia would have an "excess assigned amount" of greenhouse gases during the commitment period. In general, the region has experienced declining energy use due to economic contraction and this has resulted in a reduction in carbon emissions. Therefore, the region has available an "excess assigned amount" of greenhouse gases.

If the marginal costs of reducing greenhouse gas emissions are lower abroad, countries with relatively high reduction targets at home have an incentive to obtain carbon emission reduction units abroad. The United States and Japan have started discussions with Russia on how to cooperate to cut Russia's greenhouse gas emissions. The governments of Russia and Japan have agreed to begin feasibility studies on future JI projects to improve energy efficiency at Russian plants and reduce greenhouse gases. JI operations present opportunities for foreign firms to help cut emissions at Russian power plants or other facilities and, as a result, to offset at least in part the amount against their own emissions.

The outcome of the forthcoming discussions at COP4 in Buenos Aires is uncertain. Future agreements will need to overcome different national circumstances and expectations with respect to greenhouse gas reductions. Transparent and accountable systems will need to be in place to implement JI and CDM. Certification, verification and reporting of emission reduction units will be the key issues. It is, however, expected that a system for the trading of carbon emissions will be set up eventually. This may have important implications for the countries of the region, particularly in the power and energy, energy efficiency, oil and gas, and landfill sectors. In the meantime "emission reduction units" resulting from the EBRD's investments might be exchangeable through JI.

References

International Energy Agency (1998), *Energy Efficiency Initiative*, Paris.

E. Martinot (1997), *Investments to Improve the Energy Efficiency of Existing Residential Buildings in Countries of the Former Soviet Union*, World Bank, Washington DC.

S. Meyers, et al. (1997), *Global Climate Change Mitigation Assessment*, Washington DC.

World Bank (1998), *World Development Indicators*, Washington DC.

9 See Meyers et al. (1997).

Macroeconomic performance and prospects

3

The past year has been a turbulent one for Russia, with the largest economy in the region, and for many other countries in central and eastern Europe and the Baltics (CEE) and the Commonwealth of Independent States (CIS). While Russia's modest output recovery in 1997 was largely responsible for the first year of average growth in the region as a whole, its current crisis will cause a substantial downturn in its economy and at least a temporary return to high inflation (see Annex 1.1). The fall-out from the Russian crisis is affecting economic performance in the rest of the region, in particular in neighbouring CIS economies with weak macroeconomic fundamentals and strong trade links to Russia. Moreover, the outlook for a strong recovery in western Europe has been negatively affected by the spill-overs from East Asia and Russia to world financial markets. This will harm growth prospects in central Europe too, although its direct exposure to the Russian economy through trade and financial linkages is limited.

The overall picture from the 26 countries in the region, however, is positive in many respects. The severity of the current crisis in Russia and its potential consequences should not cloud the real strengths underlying robust economic performance in many transition economies in recent years, in particular in those countries that have achieved sound progress in the transition. Indeed, a number of countries have enjoyed annual real growth rates of 5 per cent or higher for more than two years, and data for the first half of 1998 show a consolidation of the recovery in a majority of cases. Several central European economies are now achieving official levels of output that are higher than before the transition, and considerably higher if the unrecorded economy were taken into account. Moreover, for most countries, the problem of high inflation appears to have been solved, although inflation persists at double-digit annual levels in a number of them. For many of the fast-growing countries, a continuing challenge remains the financing of large current account deficits. Prudent macroeconomic management will be required to prevent a further increase in external imbalances as conditions on international capital markets tighten.

On the other hand, economic performance has been disappointing in several other countries, most of them in the CIS, and all of them at an early or intermediate stage in the transition to a market economy. The crisis in Russia once again highlights the risk that progress in macroeconomic stabilisation can be quickly reversed when underlying structural weaknesses are not addressed. A primary concern in this regard, particularly in the CIS, is the problem of large fiscal deficits, combined in some countries with external imbalances financed by rapid increases in short-term foreign debt.

This chapter provides an overview of developments in growth and inflation in 1997, and discusses the macroeconomic outlook over the next two years against the background of the underlying strengths and weaknesses in the region's economies. The evidence reveals the close connection between lack of progress in structural reforms and the vulnerability to macroeconomic setbacks. An innovation in this year's *Transition Report* is the integration of the EBRD's survey of forecasters into the discussion of output and price developments in 1998. The chapter also analyses trends in government and external balances as well as real exchange rates and competitiveness. It concludes with a discussion of the outlook for growth and inflation in 1999. Annex 3.1 to this chapter provides a detailed evaluation of the potential implications of the Russian crisis for growth and macroeconomic stability across the region, examining both trade and financial linkages.

The chapter refers to international capital flows into the transition economies but does not discuss them in detail. Capital flows are both an indicator of success in transition and new investment opportunities as well as a crucial element of the region's vulnerability; they are discussed separately in Chapter 4. Another aspect of vulnerability to potential macroeconomic setbacks is the strength of the financial sectors; this is the topic of Part II of this Report.

3.1 Output and growth

Growth in 1997 – setback in 1998

The region as a whole experienced a landmark year in 1997, with positive growth recorded in both CEE and the CIS (see Table 3.1). GDP in Russia expanded in 1997 for the first time since 1989. In 1998 the reversal in Russia and its implications for economic performance across the region have been the main issues. Russia's GDP is likely to decline by 5 per cent or more, causing total GDP in the CIS to fall by over 3 per cent in 1998. A number of CIS economies are also directly affected by the Russian crisis and will record much lower growth than predicted earlier in the year. In CEE the momentum behind strong economic growth that was evident during the first half of 1998 will be moderated during the remainder of the year, and average growth will fall considerably below its 1997 level of 3.6 per cent.

An examination of official GDP data reveals considerable variation in cumulative growth performance across the region. Caution is warranted in comparing pre- and post-transition GDP figures, given the considerable conceptual and measurement difficulties highlighted in previous editions of the *Transition Report*. Bearing in mind these shortcomings, real GDP in the Slovak Republic and Slovenia in 1998 is projected to reach the 1989 level, joining Poland, where this was achieved in 1996. In contrast, official GDP levels in most CIS countries remain below 60 per cent of the 1989 level in spite of the return of growth to many former Soviet republics. Taking into account the substantial increases in the unofficial economy in this part of the region,[1] the differences in cumulative growth performance are less stark. However, per capita

[1] See Kaufmann (1997) for evidence. See also *Transition Reports* 1994 and 1997 (Chapter 4).

Table 3.1

Growth in real GDP in central and eastern Europe, the Baltic states and the CIS

	1992	1993	1994	(percentage change) 1995	1996	1997	1998	Estimated level of real GDP in 1997 (1989=100)	Projected level of real GDP in 1998 (1989=100)
Albania	-7.2	9.6	9.4	8.9	9.1	-7.0	9.0	80	87
Bulgaria	-7.3	-1.5	1.8	2.1	-10.9	-6.9	4.0	63	66
Croatia	-11.7	-8.0	5.9	6.8	6.0	6.5	4.2	76	79
Czech Republic	-3.3	0.6	3.2	6.4	3.9	1.0	-1.0	98	97
Estonia	-14.2	-9.0	-2.0	4.3	4.0	11.4	5.0	73	77
FYR Macedonia	-21.1	-9.1	-1.8	-1.2	0.8	1.5	5.0	56	59
Hungary	-3.1	-0.6	2.9	1.5	1.3	4.4	4.6	90	95
Latvia	-34.9	-14.9	0.6	-0.8	3.3	6.5	4.0	56	58
Lithuania	-21.3	-16.2	-9.8	3.3	4.7	5.7	3.0	61	63
Poland	2.6	3.8	5.2	7.0	6.1	6.9	5.2	112	118
Romania	-8.7	1.5	3.9	7.1	4.1	-6.6	-5.0	82	78
Slovak Republic	-6.5	-3.7	4.9	6.9	6.6	6.5	5.0	95	100
Slovenia	-5.5	2.8	5.3	4.1	3.1	3.8	4.0	99	103
Central and eastern Europe and the Baltic states [1]	*-3.8*	*0.4*	*3.9*	*5.5*	*4.0*	*3.6*	*3.0*	*96*	*99*
Armenia	-52.6	-14.8	5.4	6.9	5.8	3.1	6.0	38	40
Azerbaijan	-22.6	-23.1	-19.7	-11.8	1.3	5.8	6.7	40	42
Belarus	-9.6	-7.6	-12.6	-10.4	2.8	10.4	5.0	71	75
Georgia	-44.8	-25.4	-11.4	2.4	10.5	11.0	9.0	32	35
Kazakhstan	-2.9	-9.2	-12.6	-8.2	0.5	2.0	1.0	63	63
Kyrgyzstan	-19.0	-16.0	-20.0	-5.4	7.1	6.5	4.0	57	60
Moldova	-29.1	-1.2	-31.2	-3.0	-8.0	1.3	-2.0	35	35
Russia	-14.5	-8.7	-12.7	-4.1	-3.5	0.8	-5.0	58	55
Tajikistan	-29.0	-11.0	-18.9	-12.5	-4.4	1.7	3.0	40	41
Turkmenistan	-5.3	-10.0	-18.8	-8.2	-8.0	-26.0	5.0	42	44
Ukraine	-13.7	-14.2	-23.0	-12.2	-10.0	-3.2	0.0	37	37
Uzbekistan	-11.1	-2.3	-4.2	-0.9	1.6	2.4	2.0	87	88
Commonwealth of Independent States [2]	*-14.2*	*-9.3*	*-13.8*	*-5.1*	*-3.5*	*0.9*	*-3.6*	*57*	*55*
Central and eastern Europe, the Baltic states and the CIS	**-9.7**	**-5.1**	**-6.2**	**-0.6**	**-0.2**	**2.0**	**-1.0**	**73**	**72**

Notes:

Data for 1992-96 represent the most recent official estimates of outturns as reflected in publications from the national authorities, the IMF, the World Bank, the OECD, PlanEcon and the Institute of International Finance. Data for 1997 are preliminary actuals, mostly official government estimates. Data for 1998 represent EBRD projections. Estimates of growth for Bosnia and Herzegovina are only available since 1995 and therefore are not included in this summary table. Data for Bosnia and Herzegovina are provided in the selected economic indicators at the back of this Report.

1 Estimates for real GDP represent weighted averages for Albania, Bulgaria, Croatia, the Czech Republic, Estonia, FYR Macedonia, Hungary, Latvia, Lithuania, Poland, Romania, the Slovak Republic and Slovenia. The weights used were EBRD estimates of nominal dollar-GDP lagged by one year.

2 Here taken to include all countries of the former Soviet Union, except Estonia, Latvia and Lithuania. Estimates of real GDP represent weighted averages. The weights used were EBRD estimates of nominal dollar-GDP lagged by one year.

income levels remain significantly lower in the CIS, underlining the urgency of structural reforms that create a climate conducive to investment and growth.[2]

In CEE, output developments in 1997 and 1998 in three countries illustrate the benefits of decisive action to redress macroeconomic imbalances and to introduce financial discipline, as well as the considerable costs of delaying structural reforms. In 1997, Albania, Bulgaria and Romania experienced large falls in output, on the back of serious financial crises (Albania and Bulgaria) and the implementation of a macroeconomic austerity package (Romania). Negative growth rates in these three countries, and the considerable deceleration of growth in the Czech Republic following a currency crisis in spring 1997, were largely responsible for the fall in average growth in CEE to 3.6 per cent in 1997, down from 4 per cent in 1996.

Preliminary data for 1998 show a significant rebound of growth in Albania and Bulgaria, reflected in the positive growth projections for both countries shared by the majority of forecasters

2 Given the steep falls at the start of transition, more than a decade of growth at double-digit rates would be required in many CIS countries to reach official output levels recorded in 1989.

Table 3.2

GDP growth forecasts for 1998

(in per cent) [1]

Central and eastern Europe and the Baltic states	Average [2]	Range [3]	EBRD (Oct 98)	European Union (April 98)	OECD (June 98)	IMF (Sept 98)	United Nations ECE [5] (Sept 98)	Economist Intelligence Unit (Sept 98)	PlanEcon (Aug 98)	IWH [6] (Aug 98)	Kopint-Datorg [7] (July 98)	Vienna Institute (Aug 98)	CSFB [8] (July 98)	JP Morgan (July 98)	Dun & Bradstreet (Sept 98)
Albania	7.9	8.2	9.0	–	–	10.0	2.0	8.0	10.2	–	–	–	–	–	8.0
Bulgaria	3.1	4.5	4.0	2.3	3.0	5.5	3.6	1.0	3.6	2.0	3.0	2.0	–	4.0	3.0
Croatia	4.8	2.0	4.2	–	–	5.0	6.0	4.0	4.2	–	6.0	4.0	–	–	5.0
Czech Republic	0.9	2.9	-1.0	1.9	0.9	1.0	0.0	1.0	1.4	1.5	1.0	1.0	0.5	1.5	1.4
Estonia	6.7	3.0	5.0	6.8	–	6.0	6.5	6.0	6.4	8.0	–	8.0	–	–	7.5
FYR Macedonia	4.1	2.2	5.0	–	–	5.0	4.5	4.0	2.8	–	–	3.0	–	–	–
Hungary	5.0	1.2	4.6	4.5	4.3	5.2	5.1	5.0	5.4	5.0	5.0	5.0	5.5	5.4	5.0
Latvia	5.9	3.5	4.0	6.3	–	6.0	5.0	7.5	6.0	6.0	6.0	–	–	–	6.0
Lithuania	5.6	4.0	3.0	6.6	–	6.0	4.0	7.0	5.0	6.0	6.0	–	–	–	6.4
Poland	6.0	1.3	5.2	6.1	5.8	5.8	6.1	6.0	6.5	6.0	6.0	6.3	5.5	6.3	6.0
Romania	-2.8	5.0	-5.0	-1.6	0.0	-4.0	-3.7	-4.0	-2.1	-2.0	-2.0	-4.0	–	–	-2.0
Slovak Republic	4.6	1.6	5.0	4.4	4.0	4.0	5.6	4.0	4.1	5.0	5.5	5.0	–	–	4.5
Slovenia	3.9	1.7	4.0	3.6	3.5	4.4	3.2	3.8	4.9	4.0	3.5	4.0	–	–	3.8
Average	*4.3*	*1.5*	*3.6*	*4.1*	*3.1*	*4.6*	*3.7*	*4.1*	*4.5*	*4.2*	*4.0*	*3.4*	*3.8*	*4.3*	*4.6*
Weighted average [4]	3.9	–	3.0	–	–	3.9	3.8	3.8	4.3	–	–	–	–	–	–
Commonwealth of Independent States															
Armenia	5.3	2.2	6.0	–	–	5.5	5.0	6.0	3.8	–	–	–	–	–	–
Azerbaijan	6.8	1.1	6.7	–	–	7.0	7.0	7.0	7.1	–	–	–	–	–	6.0
Belarus	6.9	4.0	5.0	–	–	7.0	7.5	9.0	6.0	6.0	–	–	–	–	8.0
Georgia	9.8	1.2	9.0	–	–	10.0	10.0	10.0	10.2	–	–	–	–	–	–
Kazakhstan	2.3	3.4	1.0	–	–	1.5	3.5	1.0	4.4	–	–	–	–	–	2.5
Kyrgyzstan	6.3	4.0	4.0	–	–	6.0	7.0	6.0	6.5	–	–	–	–	–	8.0
Moldova	1.3	5.0	-2.0	–	–	3.0	3.0	1.5	1.2	–	–	–	–	–	–
Russia	-2.0	8.0	-5.0	–	2.0	-6.0	-3.7	-3.0	-2.5	-1.3	-1.5	-2.0	0.0	-3.0	1.5
Tajikistan	3.7	1.5	3.0	–	–	3.4	4.0	4.0	4.5	–	–	–	–	–	3.1
Turkmenistan	6.9	19.0	5.0	–	–	20.0	4.0	1.0	4.7	–	–	–	–	–	–
Ukraine	-0.1	2.1	0.0	–	–	-0.1	-1.6	0.0	0.0	0.5	-1.0	0.5	0.0	–	0.5
Uzbekistan	3.7	4.5	2.0	–	–	2.0	5.0	1.5	5.8	–	–	–	–	–	6.0
Average	*4.2*	*6.2*	*2.9*	–	–	*4.9*	*4.2*	*3.7*	*4.3*	*1.7*	*-1.3*	*-0.8*	*0.0*	–	*4.5*
Weighted average [4]	-1.1	–	-3.6	–	–	-4.2	-2.4	-1.9	-1.3	–	–	–	–	–	–

[1] All forecasts quoted here were published or reported to the EBRD between April and September 1998. The dates in brackets indicate the months in which the forecasts were reported or published by each institution. There may in some instances be substantial lags between preparation and publication of forecasts. The IMF, the Economist Intelligence Unit, United Nations (ECE) and Dun & Bradstreet reported revised forecasts in mid-September, taking into account developments since the Russian devaluation of 17 August. EBRD forecasts were revised in mid-October.

[2] The number at the bottom of this column refers to the mean of all the average forecasts shown in this table.

[3] This column shows the difference between the highest and the lowest of the forecasts.

[4] Weighted average based on EBRD estimates of nominal dollar GDP in each country in 1997. Several institutions calculate their own weighted average. The IMF estimates growth in eastern Europe, including Moldova at 3.7% in 1998 and 4.1% in 1999, Belarus and Ukraine at 3.4% in 1998 and 3.6% in 1999, and Transcaucasus and Central Asia at 4.1% in 1998 and 3.8% in 1999. The IMF also publishes a -6% growth forecast for Russia in 1999. The EU estimates the weighted average growth rate for 10 countries in eastern Europe and the Baltic states (this group excluding Albania, Croatia and FYR Macedonia) at 4.1% in 1998 and 4.5% in 1999. The IWH estimates a weighted average GDP growth for Bulgaria, the Czech Republic, Hungary, Poland, Romania, the Slovak Republic and Slovenia of 3.9% in 1998 and 4.4% in 1999. For Estonia, Latvia and Lithuania the IWH estimates a weighted average GDP growth rate of 6.5% in 1998 and 5.8% in 1999. For Ukraine, Russia and Belarus the estimates are -0.9% in 1998 and -1.1% in 1999.

[5] United Nations Commission for Europe.

[6] Institute for Economic Research, Halle, Germany.

[7] Kopint-Datorg is the Institute for Economic and Market Research, Hungary.

[8] Credit Suisse First Boston.

Table 3.3

End-year inflation in central and eastern Europe, the Baltic states and the CIS

(change in year-end retail/consumer price level, in per cent)

	1992	1993	1994	1995	1996	1997 (estimate)	1998 (projection)
Albania	236.6	30.9	15.8	6.0	17.4	42.1	10.0
Bulgaria	79.4	63.8	121.9	32.9	310.8	578.5	10.0
Croatia	938.2	1,149.0	-3.0	3.8	3.4	3.8	6.0
Czech Republic	12.7	18.2	9.7	7.9	8.6	10.0	9.0
Estonia	953.5	35.6	42.0	29.0	15.0	12.0	8.0
FYR Macedonia	1,925.2	229.6	55.4	9.0	-0.6	2.7	1.4
Hungary	21.6	21.1	21.2	28.3	19.8	18.4	13.5
Latvia	959.0	35.0	26.0	23.1	13.1	7.0	4.6
Lithuania	1,161.1	188.8	45.0	35.5	13.1	8.5	4.2
Poland	44.3	37.6	29.4	21.6	18.5	13.2	10.0
Romania	199.2	295.5	61.7	27.8	56.9	151.4	45.0
Slovak Republic	9.1	25.1	11.7	7.2	5.4	6.4	9.0
Slovenia	92.9	22.8	19.5	9.0	9.0	8.8	7.0
Central and eastern Europe and the Baltic states							
Median [1]	*199.2*	*35.6*	*26.0*	*21.6*	*13.1*	*10.0*	*9.0*
Mean [1]	*510.2*	*165.6*	*35.1*	*18.5*	*37.7*	*66.4*	*10.6*
Armenia	na	10,896.0	1,885.0	31.9	5.8	21.8	3.0
Azerbaijan	1,395.0	1,293.8	1,788.0	84.5	6.5	0.4	3.9
Belarus	1,159.0	1,996.0	1,960.0	244.0	39.0	63.0	60.0
Georgia	1,176.9	7,487.9	6,474.4	57.4	14.3	7.1	5.0
Kazakhstan	2,984.1	2,169.0	1,160.0	60.4	28.6	11.3	9.0
Kyrgyzstan	1,259.0	1,363.0	95.7	31.9	35.0	14.7	12.0
Moldova	2,198.0	837.0	116.0	23.8	15.1	11.2	30.0
Russia	2,506.1	840.0	204.4	128.6	21.8	10.9	150.0
Tajikistan	1,364.0	7,344.0	1.1	2,133.0	40.5	163.6	10.1
Turkmenistan	644.0	9,750.0	1,328.0	1,262.0	446.0	21.5	28.0
Ukraine	2,730.0	10,155.0	401.0	182.0	39.7	10.1	22.0
Uzbekistan	910.0	885.0	1,281.0	117.0	64.0	50.0	33.0
Commonwealth of Independent States							
Median [1]	*1,364.0*	*2,082.5*	*1,220.5*	*100.8*	*31.8*	*13.0*	*17.0*
Mean [1]	*1,666.0*	*4,584.7*	*1,391.2*	*363.0*	*63.0*	*32.1*	*30.5*

Notes:

Data for 1992-96 represent the most recent official estimates of outturns as reflected in publications from the national authorities, the IMF, the World Bank, the OECD, PlanEcon and the Institute of International Finance. Data for 1997 are preliminary actuals, mostly official government estimates. Data for 1998 represent EBRD projections. The figure for Albania for 1997 is based on information from parts of the country where data collection was possible. Estimates of inflation for Bosnia and Herzegovina (for the Federation and Republika Srpska separately) are provided in the selected economic indicators at the back of this Report.

1 The median is the middle value after all inflation rates have been arranged in order of size. In Table 3.3, the mean (unweighted average) tends to exceed the median, due to outliers caused by very high inflation rates in certain countries.

(see Table 3.2). Following changes in government, both countries rapidly adopted policy measures to stabilise their economies and to restore confidence in the domestic currency, and both have initiated the restructuring of their financial systems. In contrast, Romania is still in the midst of a macroeconomic crisis. EBRD projections of a decline in GDP in 1998 of 5 per cent reflect underlying macroeconomic weaknesses, such as large fiscal and current account deficits (see Section 3.3), exacerbated by political paralysis and delays in implementing necessary structural reforms. The Czech economy is also performing sluggishly. After growth of only 1 per cent in 1997, the majority of forecasters do not expect this performance to be improved upon in 1998.[3]

In the remainder of CEE, growth has been remarkably resilient over the 1997-98 period. Output grew in excess of 5 per cent in six out of 13 CEE countries in 1997, including the region's biggest economy, Poland. Growth in 1998 is likely to be lower in all of these countries, but to a significant degree only in Latvia and Lithuania due to close trade links with Russia. Growth has benefited from the revival of domestic demand in western Europe, particularly France and Germany, although it is not certain that this will continue. In general, however, the more advanced countries in central Europe have withstood well the stress test of their economies by the effects of the East Asian crisis, underlining their strong macroeconomic and structural foundations (see Annex 3.1 at the end of this chapter).[4]

3 The EBRD predicts a 1% decline, on the back of two subsequent quarter falls in GDP in the first half of the year.

4 See also Fries, Raiser and Stern (1998a, b).

While 1997 saw the return to positive growth in Russia and the CIS as a whole, 1998 will see renewed decline given expectations of a substantial output contraction in Russia. The causes of the Russian crisis are analysed in detail in Annex 1.1. At the heart of Russia's predicament lies a structural fiscal deficit associated with stalled tax reforms and slow progress in enterprise restructuring. After having turned to foreign investors to finance a large proportion of its fiscal deficit, the Russian government found it increasingly difficult to persuade them that it would be able to take the necessary remedial action to reduce future borrowing requirements. The financial panic surrounding the devaluation of the rouble on 17 August was exacerbated by regulatory failure in the banking sector and ill-conceived and badly executed policies in response to the crisis. Having suffered from real interest rates of 50 per cent or more during the first half of the year, Russia's real sector is now faced with a liquidity squeeze following the collapse of several major banks and the loss of confidence in the rouble. It is likely that this generalised loss of confidence will contribute to a drop in output of at least 5 per cent in 1998.

The extent of the downturn in Russia will have substantial implications for the remainder of the CIS. Given the close trade links with Russia, 1998 is likely to witness slow or no growth in a number of countries.[5] After a decline in GDP of 3.2 per cent, Ukraine's official level of production in 1997 fell below 40 per cent of its 1989 level. Ukraine shares many of the underlying structural weaknesses of Russia and has come under severe pressure following rouble devaluation. Economic recovery is therefore unlikely in 1998, although the IMF agreed a US$ 2.2 billion extended fund facility (EFF) programme in September.

The experience of 1997 and 1998 demonstrates that growth in many CIS countries is quite volatile. In some countries, such as Kyrgyzstan, Moldova and Uzbekistan, the agricultural sector is a key determinant; GDP growth is heavily dependent on the weather. The decline in oil and metal prices has significantly hurt Kazakhstan since the second half of 1997, and Turkmenistan's GDP has been dominated by gas and cotton exports, the latter's revival lying in part behind the recovery projected for this year. Tajikistan also remains very volatile, given the continuing political disturbances there, and the sustainability of the reported high growth rates in Belarus is highly questionable.[6]

3.2 Inflation

Strong disinflation in CEE – precarious stabilisation in CIS

Inflation has continued to decline in a majority of countries in 1997 and 1998. However, the past two years have been marked by reversals in macroeconomic stabilisation: Albania, Bulgaria, Romania and Tajikistan in 1997, and Belarus and Russia in 1998 (see Tables 3.3 and 3.4). Less pronounced increases in end-year inflation were also recorded in 1997 in Armenia and are likely this year in Moldova, Turkmenistan and Ukraine. The fragility of macroeconomic stabilisation, which has been a feature of the transition for some time, should not obscure the real achievements in stabilisation made in most countries, but points to the need to strengthen the foundations for stability.

In Russia the hard-won gains in the fight against inflation are in serious danger of being lost. Having reduced inflation to an end-year rate of 11 per cent in 1997, the collapse of the rouble and the crisis in the banking system means that end-year inflation in 1998 will almost certainly exceed 100 per cent (see Table 3.3). Macroeconomic stabilisation will now depend first and foremost on restoring confidence in the rouble through a comprehensive fiscal consolidation. It will then require deep structural reforms to ensure that an increase in the use of money in all economic transactions and a reduction in barter accompany the renewed build-up of liquidity in the country's financial system.

In CEE, achievements in the reduction of inflation in Albania and Bulgaria from high levels in 1997 are particularly notable. Both are forecast to achieve an end-year rate for 1998 of around 10-12 per cent. Improvements in Romania have been slower to materialise, largely because of stalled economic and political reforms and rising fiscal imbalances (see below). End-year inflation is projected to stay close to 50 per cent in 1998.

Elsewhere in CEE, inflation rates in 1997 continued to decline in the majority of countries, although small increases in end-year inflation were recorded in Croatia, the Czech and Slovak Republics and FYR Macedonia. Inflation rates have come down very rapidly in the Baltic states and to a lesser extent in Poland, while disinflation has been slower in Hungary. With the exception of Romania, inflation rates in all countries of CEE for 1998 are expected to be in single-digit or low double-digit figures. Two of the former Yugoslav republics, Croatia and FYR Macedonia, have had the lowest rates in the region in recent years, and come closest to the EU average of 2.1 per cent.

Turning to the CIS, the picture is one of average improvement but significant individual setbacks. The average end-year inflation rate was halved in 1997 to 32 per cent and, on the back of reductions to single-digit or low double-digit end-year levels in six of the 12 CIS countries, is projected to fall further in 1998. Lower inflation in many countries reflects the growing importance of securities markets, which have allowed persistent budgetary deficits to be financed in the short-term in non-inflationary ways. However, the reliance on monetary policy alone to bring down inflation carries very substantial risks, as demonstrated by the collapse of Russia's stabilisation efforts. Moldova's and Ukraine's inflation rates will also rise to over 20 per cent by year-end, as nominal exchange rate devaluations feed through to their domestic price levels. Stabilisation remains precarious in Turkmenistan – the major contributor to the decline in average inflation in 1997 – in light of continued directed credits to the agricultural sector.

[5] An exception is Turkmenistan, but this follows a drastic decline in real GDP in 1997. Wide output fluctuations in this country have been caused by volatile gas exports, although a greater part of these have not been paid and the decline in GDP hence tends to overstate the decline in real incomes of the population.

[6] While official figures suggest that Belarus is growing rapidly, increasing inflation, a burgeoning current account deficit and a collapse of the exchange rate on the black market point to the lack of sustainability of the country's present growth performance.

Table 3.4

Average inflation forecasts for 1998

(change in the average consumer price level, in per cent) [1]

Central and eastern Europe and the Baltic states	Average [2]	Range [3]	EBRD (Oct 98)	European Union [4] (April 98)	United Nations ECE [5] (Sept 98)	IMF (Sept 98)	Economist Intelligence Unit (Sept 98)	PlanEcon (Aug 98)	IWH [6] (Aug 98)	Kopint-Datorg [7] (July 98)	Vienna Institute (Aug 98)	CSFB [8] (July 98)	JP Morgan (July 98)	Dun & Bradstreet (Sept 98)
Albania	24.8	11.0	21.9	–	27.0	21.9	21.0	32.0	–	–	–	–	–	25.0
Bulgaria	27.3	28.0	25.0	31.0	25.0	26.9	24.6	28.0	28.0	12.0	35.0	–	40.0	25.0
Croatia	5.4	1.4	5.8	–	5.0	4.5	5.5	5.9	–	4.8	5.8	–	–	5.5
Czech Republic	11.3	2.5	11.0	9.5	11.4	11.0	12.0	11.9	11.0	11.5	11.0	12.0	11.8	12.0
Estonia	10.3	3.0	11.0	8.5	10.8	10.1	11.4	9.5	9.3	11.5	10.8	–	–	10.5
FYR Macedonia	4.2	6.7	1.3	–	8.0	2.5	2.0	5.1	–	–	6.0	–	–	–
Hungary	15.1	1.8	15.0	14.9	15.1	15.1	15.3	15.6	14.0	15.0	15.0	15.8	15.0	15.2
Latvia	6.2	2.8	5.3	6.6	7.8	5.0	6.0	5.9	5.2	6.5	–	–	–	7.3
Lithuania	6.7	2.8	5.5	6.8	8.3	7.2	6.0	6.3	6.2	6.2	–	–	–	7.5
Poland	12.1	2.4	11.0	13.4	12.8	11.9	12.3	12.2	11.2	11.0	12.0	12.5	12.3	12.2
Romania	56.1	21.0	60.0	60.0	40.0	61.0	58.0	57.2	45.0	60.0	60.0	–	–	60.0
Slovak Republic	7.2	1.8	7.5	7.0	7.5	7.0	7.5	7.3	6.0	7.5	7.0	–	–	7.8
Slovenia	8.7	2.4	8.5	8.8	8.0	7.6	8.4	8.9	10.0	9.5	9.0	–	–	8.5
Average	*15.0*	*6.7*	*14.5*	*16.7*	*14.4*	*14.7*	*14.6*	*15.8*	*14.6*	*14.1*	*17.2*	*13.4*	*19.8*	*16.4*
Commonwealth of Independent States														
Armenia	14.6	12.2	11.0	–	13.0	10.3	16.0	22.5	–	–	–	–	–	–
Azerbaijan	3.4	5.1	0.9	–	4.0	5.5	1.0	6.0	–	–	–	–	–	3.2
Belarus	66.1	55.0	50.0	–	69.0	53.3	50.0	95.3	45.0	–	–	–	–	100.0
Georgia	6.3	4.8	4.0	–	8.0	6.5	4.0	8.8	–	–	–	–	–	–
Kazakhstan	10.3	2.7	10.0	–	12.0	9.5	10.7	10.3	–	–	–	–	–	9.3
Kyrgyzstan	13.5	6.7	12.0	–	15.0	11.6	11.3	12.9	–	–	–	–	–	18.0
Moldova	10.0	6.0	13.0	–	10.0	8.0	7.0	11.8	–	–	–	–	–	–
Russia	21.7	40.4	40.0	–	22.0	48.4	12.5	26.9	9.0	12.0	15.0	8.3	8.0	37.0
Tajikistan	59.8	32.0	46.3	–	50.0	64.0	50.0	78.3	–	–	–	–	–	70.0
Turkmenistan	26.8	22.0	19.0	–	40.0	18.0	25.0	31.9	–	–	–	–	–	–
Ukraine	12.8	11.5	11.0	–	16.0	14.5	8.5	18.1	11.0	20.0	10.0	10.5	–	8.5
Uzbekistan	29.4	21.0	40.0	–	30.0	40.0	21.0	26.5	–	–	–	–	–	19.0
Average	*22.9*	*18.3*	*21.4*	–	*24.1*	*24.1*	*18.1*	*29.1*	*21.7*	*16.0*	*12.5*	*9.4*	–	*33.1*

1 All forecasts quoted here were published or reported to the EBRD between April and September 1998. The dates in brackets indicate the months in which the forecasts were reported or published by each institution. There may in some instances be substantial lags between preparation and publication of forecasts. The IMF, the Economist Intelligence Unit, United Nations (ECE) and Dun & Bradstreet reported revised forecasts in mid-September, taking into account developments since the Russian devaluation of 17 August. EBRD forecasts were revised in mid-October.

2 The number at the bottom of this column is calculated as the mean of all the average forecasts shown in this column.

3 This column shows the difference between the highest and the lowest of the forecasts.

4 Inflation is based on the private consumption deflator.

5 United Nations Economic Commission for Europe.

6 Institute for Economic Research, Halle, Germany.

7 Kopint-Datorg is the Institute for Economic and Market Research Information, Hungary.

8 Credit Suisse First Boston.

3.3 Public finances in transition

Persistent fiscal imbalances jeopardising macroeconomic stability and growth

A feature of the transition process, highlighted in previous Transition Reports, is the severe and continuing pressure on government budgets, and the resulting fiscal imbalances that have arisen in most countries in the region (see Table 3.5). The pattern has continued in 1997: with a few exceptions, governments are continuing to run budget deficits, which in many cases are large relative to the size of the economy. Revenue collection remains a pressing concern, especially in the CIS. EBRD estimates for 1998 indicate that the group of countries with fiscal deficits in excess of 5 per cent of GDP is likely to grow from six in 1997 to seven in 1998, five of which are in the CIS.

Managing the fiscal transition – overall trends

The substantial fiscal imbalances characteristic of most transition economies early in their reform process and still prevalent in many CIS countries are closely related to the process of structural reform in the public sector. On the revenue side, transition from a command to a market economy requires that governments collect revenues from individuals and private enterprises rather than directly retain resources from state-owned enterprises. Balancing the decline in profit and turnover taxes from the contracting state sector with increased revenues from other sources necessitates a major shift in the tax base, as well as a healthy and growing private sector.

Table 3.5

General government balances in central and eastern Europe, the Baltic states and the CIS

	1992	1993	1994	(in per cent of GDP) 1995	1996	1997 (estimate)	1998 (projection)	(in percentage points) Change 1996-97	Change 1997-98
Albania	-20.3	-14.4	-12.4	-10.3	-12.1	-12.7	-13.9	-0.6	-1.2
Bulgaria	-5.2	-10.9	-5.8	-5.6	-10.4	-2.1	-2.0	8.3	0.1
Croatia	-3.9	-0.8	1.6	-0.9	-0.4	-1.3	-0.5	-0.9	0.8
Czech Republic	-3.1	0.5	-1.2	-1.8	-1.2	-2.1	-2.4	-0.9	-0.3
Estonia	-0.3	-0.7	1.3	-1.3	-1.5	2.2	2.5	3.7	0.3
FYR Macedonia	-9.6	-13.8	-2.9	-1.2	-0.5	-0.4	-0.8	0.1	-0.4
Hungary	-6.8	-5.5	-8.4	-6.7	-3.1	-4.9	-4.9	-1.8	0.0
Latvia	-0.8	0.6	-4.1	-3.5	-1.4	1.4	1.0	2.8	-0.4
Lithuania	0.5	-3.3	-5.5	-4.5	-4.5	-1.8	-3.6	2.7	-1.8
Poland	-6.7	-3.1	-3.1	-2.8	-3.3	-3.1	-3.1	0.2	0.0
Romania	-4.6	-0.4	-1.9	-2.6	-4.0	-3.6	-5.5	0.4	-1.9
Slovak Republic	na	-7.0	-1.3	0.2	-1.9	-3.8	-4.0	-1.9	-0.2
Slovenia	0.2	0.3	-0.2	0.0	0.3	-1.1	-1.0	-1.4	0.1
Central and eastern Europe and the Baltic states [1]	*-5.1*	*-4.5*	*-3.4*	*-3.2*	*-3.4*	*-2.6*	*-2.9*	*0.8*	*-0.4*
Armenia	-13.9	-54.7	-10.5	-11.0	-9.3	-6.3	-5.8	3.0	0.5
Azerbaijan	na	-15.3	-12.1	-4.9	-2.8	-1.7	-3.6	1.1	-1.9
Belarus	0.0	-1.9	-2.5	-1.9	-1.6	-2.1	-3.0	-0.5	-0.9
Georgia	-25.4	-26.2	-7.4	-4.5	-4.4	-3.8	-2.5	0.6	1.3
Kazakhstan	-7.3	-1.4	-7.2	-2.5	-3.1	-3.7	-5.5	-0.6	-1.8
Kyrgyzstan	na	na	na	-17.0	-9.0	-9.4	-8.1	-0.4	1.3
Moldova	-26.2	-7.4	-8.7	-5.7	-6.7	-7.5	-8.0	-0.8	-0.5
Russia	-4.1	-4.2	-9.0	-5.7	-8.3	-7.4	-8.0	0.9	-0.6
Tajikistan	-28.4	-23.6	-10.2	-11.2	-5.8	-3.3	-3.3	2.5	0.0
Turkmenistan	13.2	-0.5	-1.4	-1.6	-0.2	0.0	-4.0	0.2	-4.0
Ukraine	-25.4	-16.2	-9.1	-7.1	-3.2	-5.6	-3.0	-2.4	2.6
Uzbekistan	-18.4	-10.4	-6.1	-4.1	-7.3	-2.3	-3.0	5.0	-0.7
Commonwealth of Independent States [1]	*-13.6*	*-14.7*	*-7.7*	*-6.4*	*-5.1*	*-4.4*	*-4.8*	*0.7*	*-0.4*

Notes:

Data for 1992-96 represent the most recent official estimates of outturns as reflected in publications from the national authorities, the IMF, the World Bank, the OECD, PlanEcon and the Institute of International Finance. Data for 1997 are preliminary actuals, mostly official government estimates. Data for 1998 represent EBRD projections. The figure for Albania for 1997 is based on information from parts of the country where data collection was possible. Estimates of government balances for Bosnia and Herzegovina (for the Federation and Republika Srpska separately) are provided in the selected economic indicators at the back of this Report.

[1] Unweighted average for the region.

On the expenditure side, the transition-related pressures have been equally severe, although the nature of these pressures in the more advanced transition economies of central Europe differs from those in the CIS. In central Europe, budgetary outlays on social security increased significantly in the early stages of transition and have led to the accumulation of large contingent liabilities in state pension systems. In the CIS and some east European countries, while price liberalisation allowed a reduction in most budgetary subsidies, various forms of "off-budget" support (directed credits, tax and energy payment arrears) have emerged that undermine the fiscal position of the consolidated government.

These observations suggest that government balances would follow a U-shaped pattern during the course of transition. Initially, large deficits would be expected as revenues declined sharply. With fiscal reforms progressing and growth returning to the region, these deficits should be reduced over time.

The presumption of a U-shaped development of government balances in the transition is borne out by the evidence for most countries, although deficits have re-emerged or remained persistently high in a number of cases. Charts 3.1 and 3.2 show that in both CEE and in the CIS, the gap between revenue and expenditure was at its widest about two to three years after the start of reforms. In CEE, there has been a very gradual narrowing of the gap from an average peak of -5.1 per cent of GDP in 1992 to -2.6 per cent in 1997, and a slow, steady decline in both revenue and expenditure as a percentage of GDP. However, both remain high relative to countries with similar levels of income, as general government expenditures in 1997 were still close to 40 per cent of GDP on average.

In the CIS, expenditures initially increased as a percentage of GDP following the break-up of the Soviet Union, leading to substantially wider initial imbalances. The subsequent rapid fall in expenditures and a mild recovery in revenues in the CIS, following the return of average positive growth after 1996, allowed the average fiscal deficit in this part of the region to fall from -14.7 per cent of GDP in 1993 to -4.4 per cent in 1997. In contrast to CEE, both revenues and expenditures are low in the CIS by international standards, reaching barely 10-15 per cent of GDP in countries such as Georgia and Tajikistan.[7] The decline in government outlays in absolute terms has been even more dramatic, as GDP has slumped, causing in many cases a disruption to the functioning of vital public institutions.

The seriousness of deficits also depends on the extent to which expenditure includes interest payments on government debt. For example, Russia's federal budget actually had a primary surplus (measured as the government balance when interest payments are ignored) of 0.4 per cent of GDP in the first half of 1998, but high interest rates and a large debt converted this to a 4.9 per cent deficit. The gap between the primary deficit (or surplus) and the overall deficit is an important indicator of a country's ability to repay its debts.

Macroeconomic consequences of fiscal imbalances

During the early transition period, fiscal deficits were associated with substantial inflation. More recently, the development of securities markets has allowed a number of countries to finance fiscal deficits in a non-inflationary way, at least in the short run. Public debt levels have increased rapidly in Russia and Ukraine, as they did earlier in Hungary. In Russia and Ukraine, foreign portfolio investors have accounted for a substantial share of new Treasury bill placements. However, relying on debt finance and in particular foreign portfolio investment is unsustainable if the underlying causes of government imbalances are not tackled. The inflow of capital into the government securities market will initially push up prices and allow interest rates to fall. Government debt can be cheaply refinanced, while the interest burden on current budgetary outlays is gradually reduced. Yet, if confidence in the government's ability to repay on time and over time is shaken, or if the attractiveness of government paper is reduced relative to other domestic or foreign assets, the cost of servicing the stock of accumulated government debt can increase very rapidly.

Fiscal deficits may also undermine long-run economic growth. Public borrowing requirements tend to crowd out private investment, particularly in the shallow capital markets of transition economies (see Part II of this Report). Moreover, in emerging markets, fiscal deficits are often seen as a sign of macroeconomic vulnerability causing higher borrowing costs in international markets. Under these conditions, the failure to maintain fiscal discipline can carry substantial costs, once adjustment becomes unavoidable because of a cut-off from external finance.

It should be noted, however, that high growth rates make deficit financing more sustainable in the short run. Several countries have managed to combine high deficits and high growth in the last couple of years, with Armenia, Georgia and Kyrgyzstan being the most notable examples. The rapid increase in output means that

Chart 3.1

GDP growth and share of general government and fiscal balance in GDP, central and eastern Europe and the Baltic states

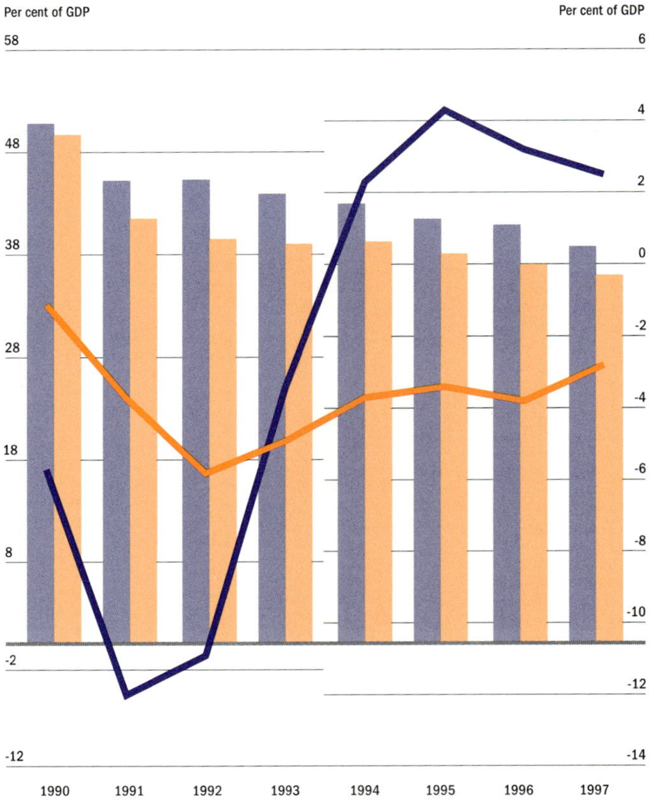

Spending (left axis) — Output growth (right axis)
Revenue (left axis) — Revenue expenditure (right axis)

Sources: Tables 3.1 and 3.5, national authorities and IMF.
Note:
The chart refers to unweighted averages for Albania, Bulgaria, Croatia, the Czech Republic, Estonia, FYR Macedonia, Hungary, Latvia, Lithuania, Poland, Romania, the Slovak Republic and Slovenia. GDP growth and the fiscal balance are on the right axis, revenue and expenditure are on the left axis.

government borrowing to fund the deficit does not necessarily raise the level of debt to GDP, and hence fiscal deficits of this magnitude may be sustainable in the short to medium term. However, given the observed fragility of recovery in a number of transition countries, it would be unwise for governments to expect to be able to run large deficits over long periods. In several transition economies, the level of external debt is such that the government has to be extremely cautious about borrowing abroad to fund current (or even capital) expenditure.

Challenges for fiscal policy

Raising revenues

Managing the fiscal transition will remain a crucial challenge for macroeconomic policy and structural reforms alike during the next stage of transition. This challenge has a number of features that are discussed briefly here. It is generally agreed that the structure of tax revenues and expenditure needs a major overhaul. The existing structure and recent changes are analysed in detail in

[7] It is important to note that Russia is one of the countries in the CIS with the highest share of general government revenues in GDP (total revenues were 31.8% of GDP in 1997). As shown in Annex 1.1, Russia's fiscal problems are related in equal measure to its inability to raise sufficient tax revenues and a wasteful and unaccountable use of public resources.

Box 3.1. This analysis shows that on average the former Soviet republics have been relatively unsuccessful in shifting the tax base from corporate profits to personal incomes and indirect consumption taxes, typically the largest revenue earners in developed market economies.

More generally, for a number of countries, particularly in the CIS, the problem of low revenue collection reflects a lack of tax discipline in three dimensions. First, tax evasion is widespread, especially in countries with a large informal economy. Many payments are by cash, and hence unrecorded (despite the ban on cash payments over a certain amount in many transition economies). Barter is also widespread in the CIS. Barter "prices" used for accounting are typically arbitrary and tax collection on such transactions is often impossible. In addition, evasion is facilitated by the ambiguous and complicated tax codes of many countries in the region, and by low remuneration for civil servants, which encourages corruption (for a description of Russia's complex tax system, see the *Transition Report* 1997, Box 7.1). Second, tax avoidance is also very common. Numerous tax concessions and tax breaks leave companies much room for manoeuvre.

Third, many governments remain lenient with enterprises that have large tax debts. This problem is particularly acute in Russia. Here, tax arrears have grown from 3.2 per cent of GDP at end-1994 to 12.2 per cent of GDP at end-1997. Also, in 1997 about 20 per cent of federal tax revenues were paid in barter or through offsets. These payments-in-kind tend to be valued at above cash market prices, thus exaggerating the true level of taxes paid. So far, however, the Russian federal government has failed to follow through on threats to declare the biggest debtors bankrupt.

Spending efficiently

The problems of revenue collection in the less advanced transition economies cannot be solved overnight. The overhaul of the tax system will take time, as will measures to strengthen tax administration. Given these constraints, governments will have to pay equal attention to an efficient use of public resources. A solution to the fiscal problems will have to tackle the waste of scarce resources through public sector over-employment, off-budget subsidies and corruption. Increasing efficiency in the use of public resources is all the more important as pressures on expenditure across the whole region will remain severe for the foreseeable future.

In many transition economies, pension reform is urgently required if spending in the future is not to rise uncontrollably. It is now clear that many previous commitments to pension spending are unsustainable in the long run. In addition to reducing these commitments, a number of countries are also exploring the possibility of moving away from purely state provision. Hungary, Kazakhstan and Poland have taken the first steps to introduce private and fully funded pension systems, which in the long run are expected to lead to increased private savings for retirement and a reduction of contingent pension liabilities for the budget. In the short run, however, the move to a funded system reduces the resources available in the existing state-managed pay-as-you-go systems, and may open up transitory deficits in public funds, which have to be taken into account in the formulation of fiscal targets.

Chart 3.2

GDP growth and share of general government and fiscal balance in GDP, Commonwealth of Independent States

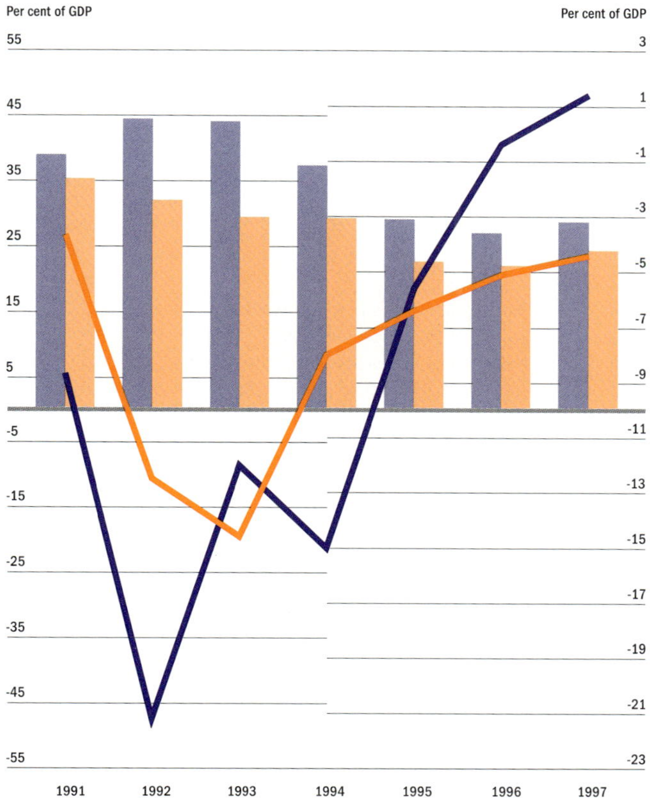

Spending (left axis) — Output growth (right axis)
Revenue (left axis) — Revenue expenditure (right axis)

Sources: Tables 3.1 and 3.5, national authorities and IMF.

Note:
The chart refers to unweighted averages for Armenia, Azerbaijan, Belarus, Georgia, Kazakhstan, Kyrgyzstan, Moldova, Russia, Tajikistan, Turkmenistan, Ukraine and Uzbekistan. GDP growth and the fiscal balance are on the right axis, revenue and expenditure are on the left axis.

Finally, most countries in CEE are beginning to address the issue of accession to the EU. Ten countries have formally applied for EU membership, with accession likely to take place in the first decade of the next century. Membership of the EU carries a number of responsibilities in terms of minimum environmental and regulatory standards and harmonisation of taxes, and therefore implies changes in revenue and expenditure, some of which are already taking place. The World Bank estimates that Poland, for example, will face direct investment costs over the period 1998-2000 of about US$ 6.6 billion in order to satisfy EU directives concerning regulatory and administrative structures on infrastructure and the environment.[8] This represents an annual cost of about 1.5 per cent of GDP. However, Poland (and other accession countries) will be eligible for substantial structural funds from the EU to help finance these expenditures, with the major inflow into the budgets of accession countries expected after 2000.

8 See World Bank (1997).

Box 3.1

The tax system in transition – accounting for the differences in revenue collection in CEE and the CIS

Both revenue collection and spending are much higher on average in CEE relative to the CIS. The difference in revenue reflects mainly better tax collection in the former region, rather than higher tax rates *per se*. In 1997, revenue exceeded 40 per cent of GDP in four countries of CEE, compared with only Belarus in the CIS. Indeed, revenue collection has virtually collapsed in a number of CIS countries, being only 10 per cent of GDP in Georgia for example.

This box looks at the structure of government revenues in particular to identify possible causes of the difference in revenue collection. It makes the point that the decline in revenues in the CIS is closely associated with the failure to shift the tax base away from corporate profit taxes. As corporate profits from the state sector have collapsed and excessive tax rates have driven the private sector to the informal economy, overall revenue has slumped. The box also examines the decline of expenditures, and emphasises that, despite the low level of expenditure in the CIS, much of this spending is quite wasteful and there is scope for efficiency gains.

Charts 1 and 2 reveal that the region as a whole has experienced a decline in tax revenues relative to GDP in almost every category, with the exception of social security taxes. The decline in revenues has been particularly accentuated in the area of enterprise profit taxes, and to a lesser extent in domestic taxes on goods and services (turnover and excise taxes, and/or value added tax (VAT)). As a share of GDP, tax revenues declined by 4.5 percentage points in CEE and 8.5 percentage points in the CIS since the start of the decade.

However, this general trend is qualified by substantial differences between regions. In CEE, the combined share of enterprise profit taxes and domestic taxes on goods and services declined from 62 per cent of tax revenue in 1989 to 41 per cent in 1997. In the CIS, the decline was only from 67 to 62 per cent. Moreover, in CEE (abstracting from the special case of Albania, by far the poorest country in this region) personal income taxes have not declined as a share of GDP and the decline in indirect domestic taxes has been marginal (1.7 per cent of GDP). Hence, almost the entire decline in tax revenues has been due to a fall in corporate profit taxation. By contrast, in the CIS, corporate profit tax revenues have fallen considerably less, while personal income tax revenues (except for Uzbekistan) have been halved and indirect domestic taxes have declined by close to 4 per cent of GDP. Countries that have lagged in reform, such as Belarus, Turkmenistan and Ukraine, still raised over 6 per cent of GDP in corporate income taxes in 1997, against an average of less than 3 per cent in the advanced transition countries.

This analysis suggests that major reform of the tax system in the CIS is essential. The transition assessments at the back of this Report highlight the efforts made recently by a number of countries to simplify the tax system and increase compliance. In addition, a shift in the tax base away from corporate profits towards personal income and expenditure taxes would relieve the corporate sector of an unduly high tax burden and would encourage new businesses back into the formal economy (see Johnson, Kaufmann and Shleifer (1997)). However, high VAT rates can also make life difficult, especially for small firms. It is therefore imperative that any reform is combined with tough measures against tax evasion and the reduction of tax arrears, so that tax rates can remain at reasonable levels.

A look at the structure of expenditures reveals that reductions across the region have been largest in the area of direct budgetary subsidies, falling from close to 10 per cent of GDP pre-transition to around 2 per cent in 1997. Investment outlays have also been reduced by half. However, social outlays have declined in the CIS, while they have increased on average in CEE. As argued in Annex 1.1, the lack of an adequate social safety net has been one reason behind slow enterprise restructuring in Russia. The reliance on a weak corporate sector as a primary source of revenue in the CIS is mirrored by the maintenance of excess employment in state firms, often propped up through lenient collection of taxes and utility charges.

While social outlays may not and should perhaps not be cut in response to lower revenues, there is considerable room to improve the efficiency of many government organisations. Although wages in the civil service are far from generous, outlays on the public wage bill and government administration have tended not to fall in most countries. An increasing gap between wages in the private and public sectors inevitably encourages low morale and corruption among workers in the latter sector. Reforms of public administration through efficiency gains and employment reductions should complement efforts to shift the tax base from profits to individual incomes and consumption. If such reforms are sustained, job losses in the state sector can be absorbed by a growing, dynamic private sector.

Conclusion

The key conclusions of the analysis of fiscal balances in transition are as follows:

- Fiscal deficits have been a feature of the transition in most countries. While the overall trend in recent years is towards lower deficits, the persistence of deficits in a number of countries is worrying.
- Deficits are a particular source of concern in countries with large government debt and high interest payments on this debt.
- On the positive side, the experience of a number of transition countries demonstrates that sustained efforts to reduce large fiscal deficits can enhance growth prospects.
- Fundamental changes in the tax base away from a reliance on corporate taxes are required in a number of CIS countries, but these changes must be combined with concerted efforts to reduce tax evasion and arrears and to improve the efficiency of public spending.

3.4 External balance

Persistent current account deficits

Current account deficits have been a feature of transition economies for several years, and 1997 was no exception. Table 3.6 shows that 17 out of 26 countries in CEE and the CIS had current account deficits in excess of 5 per cent of GDP, a level often seen as a "rule-of-thumb" danger signal, and in eight countries current account deficits exceeded 10 per cent of GDP. External balances in the transition economies in 1998 have been subjected to a combination of external shocks, including the impact of the East Asian crisis on world markets, and in particular on commodity prices, and more recently a dramatic swing in Russia's current account balance. After moving into deficit during the first half of the year, the devaluation of the rouble and the associated decline in demand for foreign goods is likely to lead to a positive end-year balance close to the result achieved in 1997. This swing in Russia's external balance is expected to have a deep impact on most countries in the CIS, and some countries in CEE, and will generally lead to wider current account deficits this year than were earlier anticipated.

Chart 1

General government revenue by category, central and eastern Europe and the Baltic states

(in per cent of GDP)

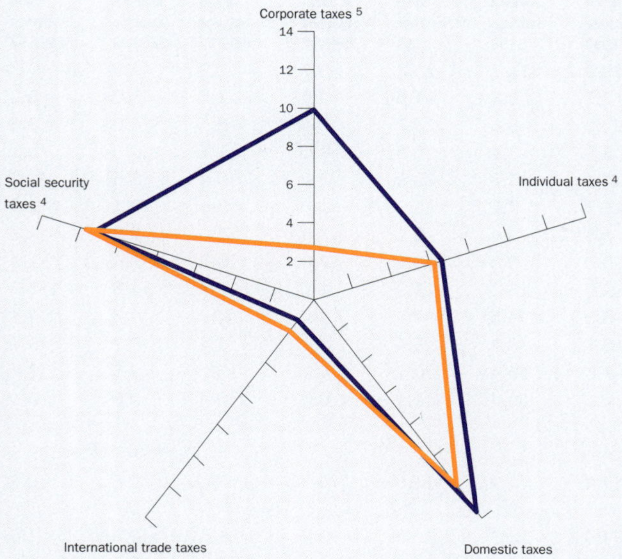

Source: See Table. Note: See Table.

Chart 2

General government revenue by category, Commonwealth of Independent States

(in per cent of GDP)

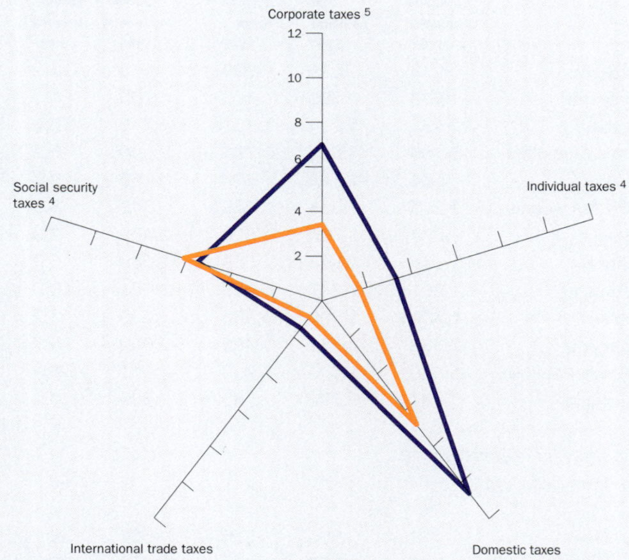

Source: See Table. Note: See Table.

General government revenue by category [1]

(In per cent of GDP)

Pre-transition [2]	Total revenue	Total tax revenue	Corporate taxes [3]	Individual taxes	Domestic taxes	International trade taxes	Social security taxes [4]
Central and eastern Europe and Baltic states [5]	49.5	39.0	9.9	6.6	13.6	1.3	11.3
Commonwealth of Independent States [5]	34.0	26.4	7.0	3.3	10.6	1.5	5.5
Today [2]							
Central and eastern Europe and Baltic states [5]	39.6	35.5	2.7	6.2	11.9	2.0	11.7
Commonwealth of Independent States [5]	21.8	17.9	3.4	1.7	6.8	0.9	6.1

Source: IMF, government financial statistics, recent economic developments reports, various issues, national authorities.

Notes:

1 General government includes local government and extrabudgetary funds.

2 Central and eastern Europe excludes Albania and Bosnia and Herzegovina because of substantially lower per capita incomes in the former and lack of comparable data in the latter. CIS excludes Belarus and Uzbekistan. Both have not experienced declining revenues – Belarus due to high corporate taxes and Uzbekistan due to increasing income taxes.

3 Pre-transition refers to 1989 for Bulgaria, Czech Republic, Kazakhstan, Kyrgyzstan, Lithuania, Poland, Romania, Russia, Slovak Republic, Tajikistan and Turkmenistan. It refers to 1990 for Hungary and to 1991 for Armenia, Azerbaijan, Estonia, FYR Macedonia, Georgia, Latvia, Moldova, Slovenia and Ukraine. Today is either 1996 or 1997 data. Data for 1989 refer to USSR in the case of Russia and former Czechoslovakia in the case of the Czech and Slovak Republics.

4 The distinction between individual and social security taxes is not always clear-cut. Some countries finance social security out of general government tax revenues, others from ear-marked payroll taxes. In most transition economies, the second system prevails.

5 In FYR Macedonia in 1997, profit taxes are included under individual taxation. In Hungary in 1990, individual taxes are included under corporate taxes.

Investment recovery in central Europe, "twin deficits" in less advanced transition economies

The size of external imbalances currently observed in several transition economies has raised concerns over their sustainability. In the majority of countries, current account deficits are driven by substantial increases in investment during the process of recovery, which in turn is contributing positively to export growth. However, in some countries, current account deficits have resulted at least in part from declines in domestic savings and increases in consumption, highlighting the need for corrective macroeconomic policies. Of still greater concern are current account deficits associated with large fiscal imbalances (hence the expression "twin deficits") in some less advanced transition economies, emphasising the need for fiscal adjustment discussed in the previous section.

There are two reasons why external deficits in the transition economies would tend to widen during the process of economic recovery. First, there are offsetting pressures on the aggregate savings rate as output recovers. Although enterprise profits tend to

Table 3.6

Current account and trade balances in central and eastern Europe, the Baltic states and the CIS

	(in millions of US dollars)				(in per cent of GDP)				(change in GDP-share, in percentage points)			
	Current account balance 1997	Merchandise trade balance 1997	Current account balance 1998	Merchandise trade balance 1998	Current account balance 1997	Merchandise trade balance 1997	Current account balance 1998	Merchandise trade balance 1998	Change in current account balance 1996-97	Change in merchandise trade balance 1996-97	Change in current account balance 1997-98	Change in merchandise trade balance 1997-98
Albania	-276	-519	-399	-675	-12.2	-22.9	-13.7	-23.3	-3.0	2.9	-1.6	-0.3
Bulgaria	433	381	-100	-200	4.2	3.7	-0.8	-1.6	3.0	1.5	-5.0	-5.3
Croatia	-2,435	-5,224	-1,737	-4,778	-12.6	-27.0	-8.6	-23.7	-8.1	-8.5	4.0	3.3
Czech Republic	-3,156	-4,600	-1,700	-3,000	-6.1	-8.8	-3.1	-5.5	1.5	1.7	2.9	3.3
Estonia	-564	-1,129	-576	-1,250	-12.0	-24.1	-10.6	-22.9	-2.9	-0.8	1.5	1.2
FYR Macedonia	-275	-388	-238	-349	-8.3	-11.7	-7.5	-11.0	-1.0	-3.6	0.7	0.6
Hungary	-987	-1,700	-1,600	-2,400	-2.2	-3.8	-3.4	-5.1	1.6	2.0	-1.2	-1.3
Latvia	-345	-848	-514	-1,000	-6.2	-15.3	-8.6	-16.8	-2.0	0.2	-2.4	-1.5
Lithuania	-981	-1,147	-1,563	-1,651	-10.3	-12.0	-15.1	-15.9	-1.1	-0.7	-4.8	-3.9
Poland	-4,300	-11,300	-6,500	-14,000	-3.2	-8.3	-4.5	-9.7	-2.2	-2.3	-1.3	-1.4
Romania	-2,338	-1,971	-3,400	-2,600	-5.7	-5.7	-6.4	-6.4	1.4	1.4	-0.7	-0.7
Slovak Republic	-1,340	-1,470	-1,950	-2,117	-6.9	-7.6	-9.4	-10.2	4.3	-19.7	-2.5	-2.7
Slovenia	37	-772	-80	-785	0.2	-4.2	-0.4	-1.1	0.0	0.4	-0.6	0.1
Central and eastern Europe and the Baltic states [1]	–	–	–	–	*-6.2*	*-11.4*	*-7.1*	*-12.0*	*-0.7*	*-2.0*	*-0.8*	*-0.6*
Armenia	-472	-560	-535	-500	-29.0	-34.4	-28.7	-26.8	-2.2	-5.0	0.3	7.6
Azerbaijan	-915	-567	-1,480	-850	-23.7	-14.7	-32.7	-18.8	1.8	-6.1	-9.0	-4.1
Belarus	-799	-1,335	-950	-1,350	-6.0	-10.0	-7.7	-11.0	-2.3	-1.7	-1.8	-1.0
Georgia	-347	-484	-500	-600	-6.6	-9.3	-9.0	-10.8	-0.5	-1.5	-2.3	-1.5
Kazakhstan	-953	-385	-1,800	-1,100	-4.2	-1.7	-7.5	-4.6	-0.6	-0.1	-3.3	-2.9
Kyrgyzstan	-139	-15	-165	-40	-8.3	-0.9	-9.5	-2.3	15.2	13.0	-1.2	-1.4
Moldova	-292	-319	-293	-330	-13.4	-14.7	-13.2	-14.9	-0.1	-1.4	0.2	-0.2
Russia	3,300	17,300	4,000	17,000	0.7	3.8	1.4	5.9	-2.1	-1.5	0.7	2.0
Tajikistan	-60	-64	-69	-70	-5.4	-5.7	-5.5	-5.5	2.0	-2.0	-0.1	0.2
Turkmenistan	-596	-245	-676	-431	-32.5	-13.3	-32.8	-20.3	-34.7	-21.6	-0.3	-7.0
Ukraine	-1,300	-4,200	-1,200	-3,000	-2.6	-8.4	-2.9	-7.3	0.1	1.2	-0.3	1.1
Uzbekistan	-584	-72	-492	-242	-4.1	-0.5	-3.8	-1.9	3.1	4.7	0.3	-1.3
Commonwealth of Independent States [1]	–	–	–	–	*-11.3*	*-9.2*	*-12.7*	*-9.9*	*-1.7*	*-1.8*	*-1.4*	*-0.7*

Notes:

Data for 1996-97 represent the most recent official estimates of outturns as reflected in publications from the national authorities, the IMF, the World Bank, the OECD, PlanEcon and the Institute of International Finance. Data for 1998 represent EBRD projections. Change in current account and merchandise trade balances in 1996-97 represents the difference between the ratios of current account and merchandise trade balances to GDP in respective years. Estimates of trade and current account balances for Bosnia and Herzegovina (for the Federation and Republika Srpska separately) are provided in the selected economic indicators at the back of this Report.

1 Unweighted average for the year.

improve with the resumption of growth, household savings rates are likely to fall as expectations of future incomes rise and uncertainty recedes.[9] Second, since much of the capital stock has been both rendered obsolete by the introduction of market prices and product market competition and depleted by years of neglect, the returns to fixed investment are high and demand tends to surge with growing output and increasing confidence (see *Transition Report* 1995, Chapter 4).

The case of Poland is a good example for the typical pattern of domestic private savings and investment that may be observed in a number of transition economies during the process of economic recovery (see Chart 3.3).[10] Poland's private savings rate and the difference between government savings and investment have remained roughly constant as a share of GDP since 1993. At the same time, the share of private investment in GDP has increased from 12.5 per cent in 1993 to 19 per cent in 1997 and this is chiefly responsible for an aggregate savings-investment imbalance of around 5 per cent of GDP by the latter year.[11] Poland's positive

9 The factors influencing the development of aggregate savings during the course of transition are more complex than the simple juxtaposition between profits and household savings made here. For a discussion, see Denizer and Wolf (1998a; b). It should be noted that the output decline experienced by all transition economies at the start of market-oriented reforms has been associated with a uniform decline in aggregate savings rates.

10 The picture looks very similar in the Czech and Slovak Republics, with private savings rates constant at around 23% of GDP and private investment rising rapidly from roughly 20% to 30% of GDP over the 1993-96 period, and a subsequent downward adjustment in 1997, following the Czech currency crisis.

11 These figures refer to national accounts data. They may differ from balance of payments measures of the current account deficit as shown in Table 3.6 because of under-reporting of economic activities in the national accounts, the existence of cross-border trade flows and other measurement discrepancies.

example is in contrast to developments in Latvia and Romania (see Chart 3.3), where a fall in private savings (an increase in consumption) and rising fiscal deficits respectively were the main factors behind the growth in the current account deficit in both countries to well over 5 per cent of GDP in 1997.[12]

Is investment growth in the advanced transition economies creating the basis for future export revenues? Chart 3.4 relates private investment rates for the sample of countries to the growth rate of exports. Over the period 1994-97, countries with larger private investment rates have recorded higher export growth. Although the short-term volatility of the supply of international funds could force corrective policy measures to reduce current account deficits across the region (see Chapter 4), the evidence reviewed here suggests that for the more advanced transition economies, and on the basis of macroeconomic fundamentals, external imbalances remain sustainable. That is, these countries should be able to service their current account obligations without drawing down reserves and without recourse to repeated devaluations of their currencies.

On the other hand, the examples of Romania in 1998 and Hungary during 1994-95 highlight the danger of running large government and external imbalances. In both countries substantial macroeconomic instability has been associated with the drying-up of capital inflows in view of weak fundamentals. Tough, corrective action has since greatly improved the situation in Hungary. Twin deficits are also characteristic of a number of CIS countries, including Armenia, Georgia, Kyrgyzstan, Moldova and (in 1998) Turkmenistan. With the exception of the latter two countries, the reliance on official sources to finance these deficits has so far attenuated the risk of serious balance of payments difficulties, but further efforts are needed if a costly external adjustment including a fall in private investment is to be avoided.

External shocks and prospects – moderate adjustment pressures in CEE, large current account swings in Russia and the CIS

External balances in the transition economies in 1998 have been affected by a combination of shocks, starting with the impact of the East Asian crisis on world trade and on commodity prices, and, from August 1998, the Russian devaluation. Trade linkages between the region and East Asia are minor and competition on third markets has been offset by the strength of the recovery in western Europe in 1998. The impact of falling commodity prices and reduced Russian import demand, however, is expected to lead to a substantial deterioration of external balances in natural resource exporting countries and Russia's main trading partners, most of them in the former Soviet Union. At the same time, the availability of external financing to cover current account deficits has declined (or at least such financing has become much more costly). As a result, a decline of both exports and imports is likely,

[12] Latvia's case is partially mirrored in the other Baltic countries, too. Estonia has had a very substantial decline in private savings between 1993 and 1994, followed by a fall in government savings, which against constant investment rates has contributed to very high external deficits. Lithuania has experienced a fall in government savings since 1993 against the background of recent increases in both private consumption and investment.

Chart 3.3

Savings and investment balances, government and non-government sectors

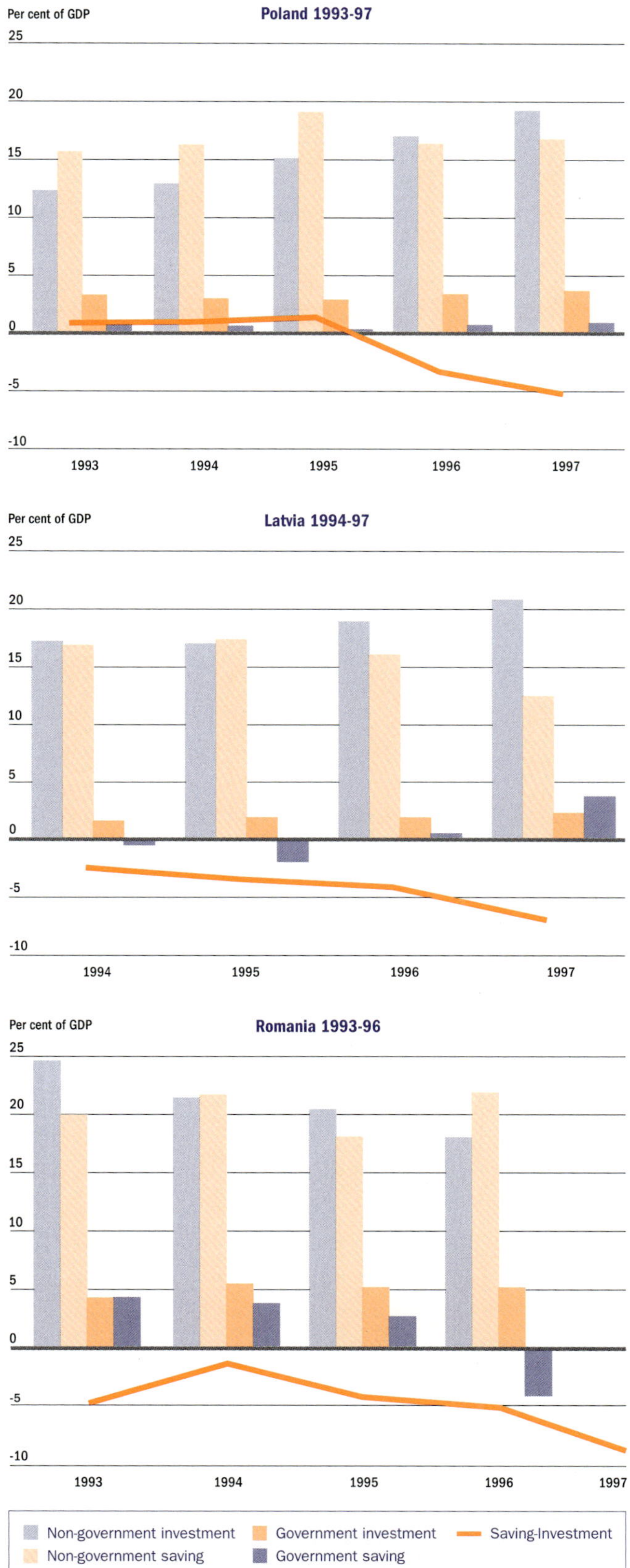

Sources: IMF, recent economic developments and national authorities.

Note:

Non-government investment is calculated as total investment minus general government capital expenditures. Government saving is equal to revenues minus current expenditures for general government. Non-government saving is calculated as total saving minus government saving. All data are in current prices. Changes from year to year do therefore partly reflect relative price changes.

Chart 3.4

Non-government investment and export growth in selected transition economies, 1994-97 average

(In per cent)

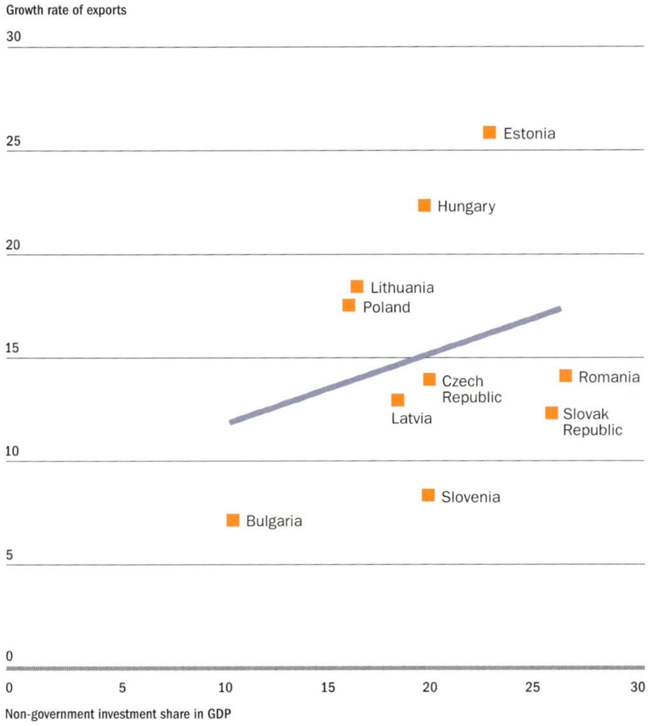

Sources: Table 3.8, national authorities and IMF.
Note:
The private investment rate is calculated as total investment minus general government capital expenditures over GDP at current prices.

particularly in countries that are unattractive for foreign direct investment (see also Chapter 4).

Since their peak in June 1997 and the beginning of the East Asian crisis, oil prices have declined by over 50 per cent. This has had an impact on external balances in Azerbaijan, Kazakhstan, Russia and Turkmenistan, each of which rely on oil for more than 20 per cent of export revenue. Data for the first half of 1998 indicate that export values in Azerbaijan, Kazakhstan and Russia were down by 10 per cent or more – no recent data is available for Turkmenistan. In all four countries, margins for oil producers were substantially reduced, and this negatively affected fiscal revenues, which are dependent to a large extent on their share of profits from natural resource extraction. In Azerbaijan and Kazakhstan expenditure policies have been tightened accordingly, but in Russia and Turkmenistan, falling oil and gas-related revenues contributed to government dissaving and to the twin deficits reported further above. Russia's devaluation can be understood in part as an attempt to restore profit margins to this important sector in the Russian economy.

In the remainder of the region, falling oil prices have had the opposite effect on external balances, as import growth was moderated in value terms. Indeed, for much of CEE low commodity prices provide a relief to external balances at the very moment when the momentum of rapid export growth that could be observed during the first half of the year may come under threat from the fall-out from Russia.

The impact of the Russian crisis on trade balances across the region will be highly differentiated. The CIS countries in particular conduct significant export trade with Russia (see Annex 3.1). The Baltic states and to a lesser extent Poland (on account of its substantial cross-border trade) also could be affected by the projected contraction in Russia's GDP and the resulting slump in demand for their exports. For most countries in CEE direct trade linkages and competition on third markets are far less important. However, the general outlook for exporters from the region has become less favourable and macroeconomic policy will have the challenge of preventing further increases in current account deficits against the background of tighter international capital markets.

Conclusion

The analysis of the sources of external imbalances in the transition economies in this section leads to the following conclusions:

- Current account deficits remain a feature of the transition. More than half the countries in the region had deficits in excess of 5 per cent of GDP.
- In some countries in CEE, these deficits reflect increased private investment, which can generate sustained export growth and long-term solvency.
- In other countries, especially in the CIS, current account imbalances are twinned with fiscal imbalances. Concessionary loans from external sources can finance current account deficits in the short run, but not indefinitely.
- The Russian economic crisis and currency devaluation may significantly worsen current account deficits in some CIS countries.

3.5 Real exchange rates and competitiveness

Real exchange rate appreciation moderates – diverging trends in competitiveness

A characteristic feature of macroeconomic developments in the transition so far has been the real appreciation of exchange rates. This trend has continued in 1997, as evidenced by Chart 3.5.[13] However, in 1997 and the first half of 1998, there has been a sharp moderation of pressures for real exchange rate appreciation, particularly in the CIS and the Baltic states as inflation rates have come down. In a number of countries, 1997 saw nominal devaluations, such as in the Czech Republic. In others, such as Bulgaria and Romania, the stabilisation of the nominal rate following an

[13] Developments since the Russian devaluation are not covered here. Russia's real exchange rate is likely to depreciate sharply during the remainder of the year. A more moderate real depreciation is also likely for Ukraine.

Chart 3.5

Real exchange rate index to the DM, CPI based, January 1994=100

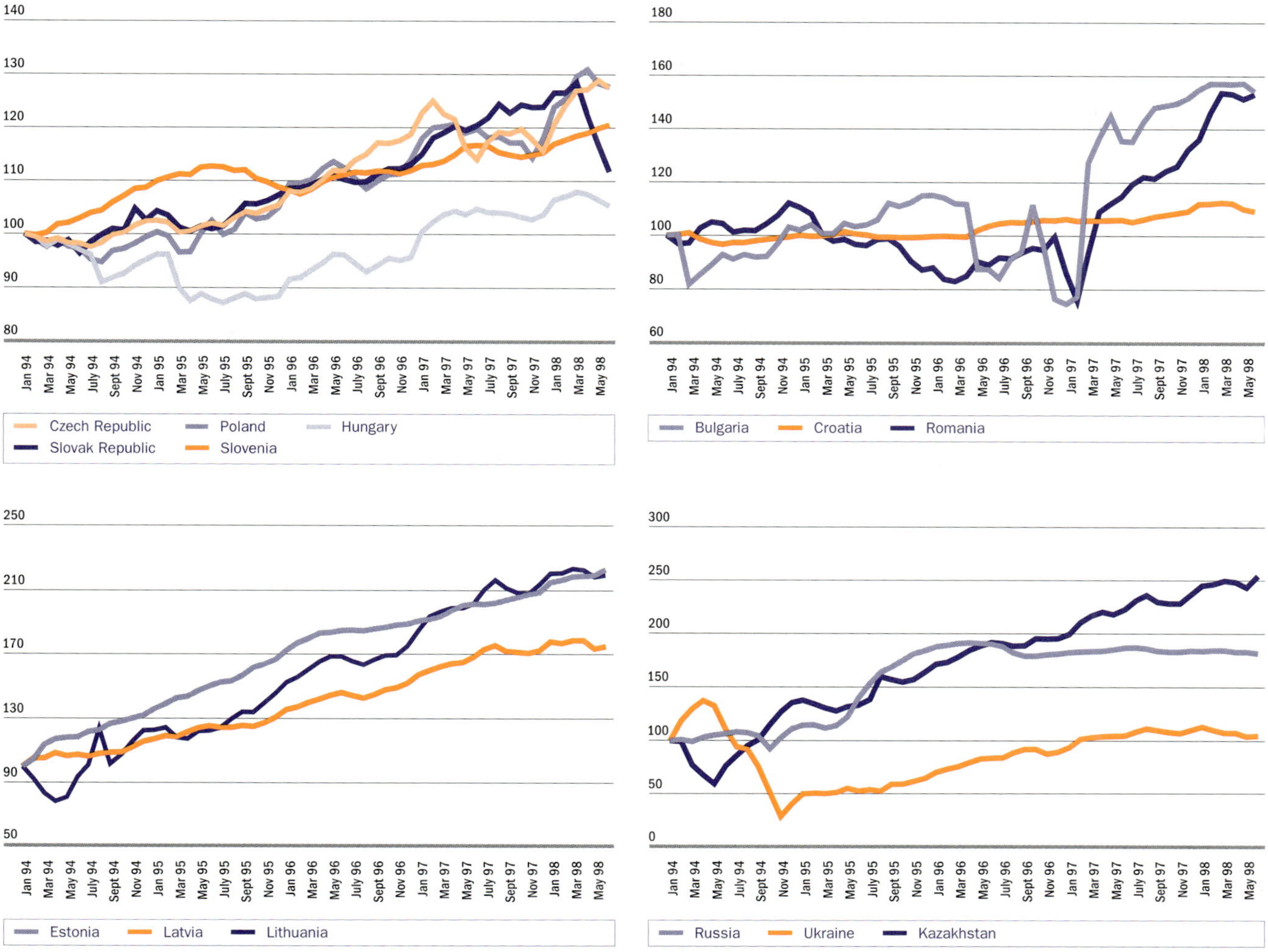

Source: National authorities.
Note:
The real exchange rate is calculated as the price of local currency in foreign currency terms, adjusted for the difference in consumer price inflation rates:
RER = FCU(1+CPI)/LCU(1+CPI*), where RER = real exchange rate FCU = foreign currency units LCU = local currency units CPI, CPI* = domestic, foreign consumer price inflation rate, in per cent. The rate to the DM is used, since most east European exports are factored in DM. For Russia, Ukraine and Kazakhstan the DM rate is also used for comparative purposes. US-dollar rates show a more moderate appreciation in 1995-97 due to the strength of the US currency during that period.

earlier currency crisis lay behind a large increase in the real exchange rate, as inflation was reduced more gradually.[14]

The real exchange rate is a key macroeconomic variable as it determines the relative profitability of selling goods abroad or in the domestic market. It is defined as the ratio of the domestic price level to the foreign price level, where the latter is converted to domestic units at the nominal exchange rate. Other things being equal, an increase in the real exchange rate (an appreciation) makes it harder for a country to sell its goods abroad, and in this sense makes a country less "competitive". On the other hand, real exchange rate appreciation may reflect productivity increases in the traded goods sector which enhance a country's competitiveness.[15]

Exchange rate policy in transition economies was initially targeted primarily at providing price stability. Hence, the majority of countries throughout the region have opted against a fully floating exchange rate, as attempts were made to stabilise inflationary expectations using a nominal exchange rate anchor. Given the substantial currency depreciation and low levels of the real exchange rate experienced at the start of transition, the subse-

[14] We focus on the real exchange rate against the DM in this section, taking into account the substantial share of trade conducted with western Europe, which is factored in DM. The DM's weakness against the US$ in 1997 tended to increase real appreciation in those countries operating a partial US$ peg, while any strengthening of the DM in 1998 would work in the opposite direction.

[15] An increase in productivity in the traded sector will tend to attract scarce resources to that sector, driving up their prices. This would in turn affect production costs in the economy as a whole, which implies a real appreciation of the exchange rate. However, in this case, the impact of real appreciation on the competitiveness of domestic goods is offset by productivity increases in the tradables sector.

Table 3.7

Indicators of competitiveness (change, in per cent)

	1994	1995	1996	1997	1998 Q1
Bulgaria [1]					
Industrial gross output	8.5	4.9	-1.0	-7.0	na
Productivity in industry	12.6	7.3	2.1	-3.8	na
Real wage in industry *(PPI-based)*	-12.1	3.3	-17.9	-15.9	na
Real D-Mark exchange rate *(CPI-based)*	-5.2	14.2	-12.2	40.9	na
D-Mark unit labour costs	-32.1	5.4	-23.7	5.3	na
Croatia [2]					
Industrial gross output	-2.7	0.3	3.1	3.9	6.9
Productivity in industry	1.6	5.8	11.4	12.0	14.2
Real wage in industry *(PPI-based)*	29.8	30.8	11.0	8.2	12.8
Real D-Mark exchange rate *(CPI-based)*	13.3	1.4	3.0	3.5	6.0
D-Mark unit labour costs	33.6	25.9	2.0	0.4	-0.9
Czech Republic [3]					
Manufacturing gross output	0.1	8.2	5.5	6.4	11.1
Productivity in manufacturing	4.9	11.1	9.6	11.1	15.0
Real wage in manufacturing *(PPI-based)*	11.2	9.5	12.0	8.3	6.0
Real D-Mark exchange rate *(CPI-based)*	6.7	2.6	10.1	5.3	0.4
D-Mark unit labour costs	11.3	1.5	10.0	1.0	-12.2
Estonia [4]					
Manufacturing gross output	-3.2	2.9	2.2	16.9	14.2
Productivity in manufacturing	6.7	0.4	3.7	17.8	na
Real wage in manufacturing *(PPI-based)*	26.9	14.1	7.8	11.0	11.7
Real D-Mark exchange rate *(CPI-based)*	44.0	26.6	21.4	9.2	12.8
D-Mark unit labour costs	61.7	35.2	19.3	1.1	na
Hungary [5]					
Manufacturing gross output	9.3	5.3	3.5	15.0	19.4
Productivity in manufacturing	7.3	11.2	9.1	14.5	16.3
Real wage in manufacturing *(PPI-based)*	9.2	-5.9	-0.2	1.4	4.3
Real D-Mark exchange rate *(CPI-based)*	-1.6	-6.9	5.5	9.6	4.9
D-Mark unit labour costs	-3.6	-19.3	-3.5	0.4	-6.3
Latvia [6]					
Manufacturing gross output	-12.0	-8.1	0.8	8.1	18.6
Productivity in manufacturing	9.5	-1.0	8.6	28.0	14.3
Real wage in manufacturing *(PPI-based)*	36.6	11.3	-0.1	17.3	7.6
Real D-Mark exchange rate *(CPI-based)*	57.3	14.8	16.3	16.4	10.9
D-Mark unit labour costs	73.0	17.9	5.2	4.2	3.0

	1994	1995	1996	1997	1998 Q1
Lithuania [7]					
Manufacturing gross output	-29.7	0.9	3.5	5.0	11.8
Productivity in manufacturing	-12.1	12.0	8.5	4.6	15.1
Real wage in manufacturing *(PPI-based)*	13.8	14.0	15.0	19.1	25.1
Real D-Mark exchange rate *(CPI-based)*	65.7	29.5	29.0	23.2	15.7
D-Mark unit labour costs	85.1	23.3	30.5	36.7	13.3
Poland [8]					
Manufacturing gross output	13.6	11.6	10.5	13.9	15.6
Productivity in manufacturing	13.9	7.0	9.9	13.9	15.1
Real wage in manufacturing *(PPI-based)*	5.1	5.4	18.3	8.8	11.0
Real D-Mark exchange rate *(CPI-based)*	1.4	4.4	11.6	7.1	6.1
D-Mark unit labour costs	-6.1	2.9	12.6	1.5	-1.8
Romania [9]					
Manufacturing gross output	3.8	12.1	12.5	-11.3	-23.7
Productivity in manufacturing	10.1	20.0	12.1	1.0	-22.0
Real wage in manufacturing *(PPI-based)*	0.7	16.6	3.6	-23.9	-1.3
Real D-Mark exchange rate *(CPI-based)*	43.9	-5.3	-5.1	23.2	70.5
D-Mark unit labour costs	2.2	-4.2	-3.8	-4.9	105.9
Russia [10]					
Manufacturing gross output	-20.9	-3.3	-4.0	1.9	-0.6
Productivity in manufacturing	-14.3	5.5	3.2	3.0	na
Real wage in manufacturing *(PPI-based)*	-17.5	-31.3	6.0	4.2	11.2
Real D-Mark exchange rate *(CPI-based)*	75.4	18.2	36.5	14.9	10.8
D-Mark unit labour costs	72.7	-5.5	45.2	18.6	na
Slovak Republic [11]					
Industrial gross output	4.7	8.3	2.5	2.7	4.7
Productivity in industry	6.8	4.0	2.5	4.8	6.5
Real wage in industry *(PPI-based)*	7.0	5.7	10.1	7.2	5.3
Real D-Mark exchange rate *(CPI-based)*	2.7	3.4	6.2	9.5	8.3
D-Mark unit labour costs	2.5	6.2	13.8	12.2	4.9
Slovenia [12]					
Industrial gross output	6.4	2.0	1.0	0.9	7.1
Productivity in industry	11.4	7.2	6.6	5.2	9.8
Real wage in industry *(PPI-based)*	8.1	3.9	7.0	5.3	4.7
Real D-Mark exchange rate *(CPI-based)*	1.5	7.0	-0.5	4.0	4.1
D-Mark unit labour costs	-1.6	4.9	-1.6	3.8	-1.0

Note:

Data for 1994-97 represent the percentage change of annual averages based on actual data. Figures for the first quarter of 1998 represent preliminary official estimates. Productivity is calculated as the ratio of manufacturing/industry production over manufacturing/industry employment. The real DM exchange rate is calculated as the domestic CPI divided by the product of the German CPI and the exchange rate. A positive sign represents a real appreciation. DM unit labour costs are calculated as wages divided by productivity. Data on the exchange rate to the DM, on CPI and PPI are based on national authorities, the IMF and EBRD estimates.

1 Industrial production, employment and wages are taken from the *Statistical Yearbook*, various issues, annual reports by the National Bank of Bulgaria, and the Bulgarian Statistical Office. Real wages are calculated as average gross monthly wages in industry, deflated by the PPI in industry.

2 Industrial production, employment and wages are taken from the 1996 *Statistical Yearbook* and various issues of *Monthly Statistical Report*, published by the Central Bureau of Statistics. Real wages are calculated as average monthly wages in industry, deflated by the PPI in industry. The 1994 growth rate refers to net wages, subsequent growth rates refer to gross wages.

3 Production, employment and wages are taken from annual and monthly publications of the Czech Statistical Office. Real wages are calculated as average monthly gross wages in manufacturing, deflated by the PPI in industry.

4 Production, employment and wages are taken from annual and monthly reports by the Estonian Statistical Office. Real wages are calculated as average gross monthly wages in manufacturing deflated by the PPI in manufacturing.

5 Production, employment and wages are taken from the *Monthly Bulletin of Statistics* of the Hungarian Statistical Office. Real wages are calculated as average monthly gross wages in manufacturing deflated by the PPI in industry.

6 Production, employment and wages are taken from the *OECD Short-term Economic Indicators*, various issues. Real wages are calculated as average monthly gross wages in industry deflated by the PPI in industry.

7 Employment and wages are taken from the *OECD Short-term Economic Indicators*, various issues. Output is taken from the *International Financial Statistics*, various issues. Real wages are calculated as average monthly gross wages in manufacturing deflated by the PPI in industry.

8 Production, employment and wages are taken from monthly and quarterly reports of the *Polish Statistical Office*. Real wages are calculated as average monthly gross wages in manufacturing deflated by the PPI in manufacturing.

9 Production, employment and wages are taken from the *OECD Short-term Economic Indicators*, various issues. Real wages are calculated as average net wages in manufacturing deflated by the PPI in industry.

10 Production, employment and wages are taken from the *OECD Short-term Economic Indicators*, various issues. Figures for 1997 refer to industry rather than manufacturing and wages are taken from *Russian Economic Trends*. Real wages are calculated as average gross monthly wages in manufacturing deflated by the PPI in industry.

11 Production, employment and wages are taken from the *OECD Short-term Economic Indicators*, various issues, and from annual and monthly publications by the Slovak Statistical Office. Real wages are calculated as average gross monthly wages in industry deflated by the PPI in industry.

12 Production, employment and wages are taken from the Slovenian Institute for Macroeconomic Analysis and Development. Real wages are calculated as average gross monthly wages in industry deflated by the PPI in industry.

quent real appreciation does not seem to have negatively affected the external balance in most transition economies (see *Transition Report* 1997).[16] However, as inflation rates have come down decisively since 1992 in central and eastern Europe and more recently in most of the former Soviet Union, the focus of exchange rate policy has shifted more towards sustaining external equilibrium.

Table 3.7 reveals that real exchange rate appreciation has been associated with rising unit labour costs in foreign currency terms. However, strong productivity growth and lower real wage growth in 1997 have moderated the impact of real exchange rate appreciation on the competitiveness of manufacturing across the region. Unit labour costs in DM on average increased by 6.7 per cent in 1997 in the 12 countries for which official data was available, compared with 8.8 per cent in 1996. Trends for the first quarter of 1998 indicate further strong productivity growth in most countries and little sign of an acceleration of real wages.

This general pattern is subject to a number of important qualifications, however. First, productivity growth has been highest in central Europe and in the Baltics, while it has stagnated or declined in Bulgaria, Romania and Russia. In the latter countries, the challenge will be to sustain earlier productivity improvements achieved primarily through labour shedding and to accelerate deep enterprise restructuring, which lies behind the better performance of countries at more advanced stages in transition. Second, real wage growth continues to be rather high in Estonia and Lithuania. Particularly in the latter, a slowdown in wage growth in 1998 will be required to prevent a further deterioration in competitiveness.

How much room is there for further real exchange rate appreciation before the competitiveness of exports from the region would be negatively affected? In a recent study, it has been found that in 1995 US$ wages across the region remained significantly below their equilibrium levels, as determined by various measures of productivity (see Box 3.2).[17] A recalculation for 1997 by the EBRD basically confirms this result, although wage gaps have been significantly reduced in a number of countries, including Croatia, Latvia, Lithuania, Kazakhstan, Moldova and Slovenia. Furthermore, if wage gaps were adjusted to account for differences in the directions of trade, the competitive position of several CIS countries would look much weaker – primarily because of their substantial trade dependence on Russia.

Conclusion

Real exchange-rate appreciation remains a characteristic of the macroeconomic environment in most transition economies, although the implications for competitiveness differ across countries:

- In central Europe and the Baltic states, productivity improvements have limited the increase in unit labour costs associated with appreciating real exchange rates. Further disinflation, and wage moderation in particular, will be required, however, if competitiveness is to be maintained.
- In eastern Europe (Bulgaria, Romania) and Russia, productivity has lagged. This has led to large increases in unit labour costs against the background of exchange-rate-based stabilisation programmes. Russia's dollar wages will fall significantly in 1998. However, to achieve international competitiveness, the policy challenge will be to raise productivity through deep structural change.

3.6 Prospects for 1999 – how vulnerable is the region?

Growth – moderate declines in CEE, extent of recovery in CIS largely dependent on Russia

Growth prospects for 1999 across the region are subject to a considerable amount of uncertainty. The direct impact of the Russian crisis on the region is likely to be quite different across various exposure groups, with the CIS most affected. For most countries in CEE, growth prospects largely depend on the performance of the west European economies. Declining share prices worldwide and their potential impact on investor confidence and consumer spending have led forecasters to revise downwards their growth projections for western Europe. The October *World Economic Outlook* of the IMF, for instance, predicts an average growth rate of 2.5 per cent in the EU, against 2.8 per cent in the May forecast.

This section reports the projections for growth and average inflation submitted to the EBRD during the course of May-September 1998. Forecasters were invited to re-evaluate their projections in the aftermath of the Russian crisis, but only a limited number of observers (Dun & Bradstreet, EIU, IMF and the EBRD) were able to adjust their projections at short notice. All the data in Tables 3.8 and 3.9 should therefore be interpreted both with a view to the timing when the forecasts were made and to the impact that unfolding events in Russia and the world economy might have. A more detailed analysis of the mechanisms linking economies to one another through trade and capital flows and the degree of exposure of individual countries to Russia in particular is provided in Annex 3.1 to this chapter. It provides a basis for the EBRD's forecasts as well as a bridge to the analysis of capital flows in Chapter 4.

Bearing in mind substantial forecasting uncertainty, growth forecasts for 1999 indicate a continuation of variations in output developments across the region, with the gap between countries in CEE and the CIS projected to widen. The regional difference is in part a reflection of the continued decline predicted for Russia by all post-crisis forecasts. This negatively affects the average growth projections for the CIS because of the weight of the Russian economy in aggregate CIS output and the close trade links between all countries of the former Soviet Union. However, the varying strengths in the foundations for growth and macro-

[16] For a less sanguine view, see Roubini and Wachtel (1997).

[17] See Kraijnak and Zettelmeyer (1997).

Box 3.2

Competitiveness and wage levels

Changes in real exchange rates and unit labour costs over time are useful only as indicators of competitiveness if they can be related to some benchmark level. However, standard approaches that derive an equilibrium real exchange rate from historical information on external balance or the long-run determinants of the real exchange rate are unavailable for the transition economies. Indeed, in the context of fundamental structural changes, shifts in relative productivity levels, substantial uncertainty and remaining imperfections in domestic goods markets, any comparison of real exchange rate levels with the pre-transition period would seem to be virtually meaningless.

Against these difficulties, two recent studies suggest looking at US dollar wages as a measure of the real exchange rate level, and derive a benchmark using cross-country information on the main determinants of dollar wages (Halpern and Wyplosz, 1996; Krajnyak and Zettelmeyer, 1997). The underlying idea is that wage levels across economies should be a function of their productivity. This is approximated using GDP per capita (at purchasing power parities), human capital endowments (secondary school enrolment), an indicator of the structure of the economy (the weight of agriculture in GDP) and a set of additional measures of the level of development.

The table in this box reports the results of Krajnyak and Zettelmeyer based on a panel of 75 middle income developing and industrialised countries over the 1990-95 period. This indicates that in 1995, all transition economies included in their sample had US dollar wages considerably below the equilibrium levels predicted by the cross-country regression results.

We have repeated the exercise for 1996 and 1997, using the co-efficients reported in Krajnyak and Zettelmeyer. Since the measures of human capital endowment and the share of agriculture in GDP tend not to change significantly from year to year, fitted wages for 1996 and 1997 were calculated based on changes in GDP only. This allowed us to use the original data on schooling and the structure of GDP for 1995, which we obtained from the authors and keep a consistent data source for these variables. The left panel reports the results using the IMF's 1995 GDP figures and updating to 1996 and 1997 with real GDP growth and the US inflation rate. In the right panel, we use the World Bank's data for GDP in purchasing power parities. In general, actual wages have remained below fitted wages for most countries, although wage gaps would seem to have diminished significantly in some depending on the sources used for GDP.

How should this evidence be interpreted and what are the implications for the region's competitiveness? Two factors arguably are of particular relevance in explaining the persistence of wage gaps in the transition economies. First, as many prices of non-tradables (for example, utilities) remain controlled, nominal wages may be lower than in countries with similar per capita incomes, without affecting purchasing power. As prices of public utilities and rents are adjusted, the real exchange rate would appreciate towards its market equilibrium – arguably not posing a major threat to competitiveness. Second, low US dollar wages may also be a reflection of low unit prices for manufactured exports on Western markets due to remaining quality differences relative to other exporters, for example from the newly industrialising countries (see Landesmann and Burgstaller (1997)). In this case, equilibrium wages may have been overestimated by not adjusting measures of relative productivity for such quality differences and the room for further real exchange rate appreciation would be correspondingly reduced.

Competitiveness and US dollar wages

	Ratio of actual to fitted equilibrium wages [1]						US dollar actual wages		
	IMF GDP per capita [2]			World Bank GDP per capita [2]					
Country	1995	1996	1997	1995	1996	1997	1995	1996	1997
Bulgaria [3]	0.34	0.28	0.24	0.39	0.31	0.28	126	93	82
Czech Republic	0.54	0.58	0.57	0.44	0.49	0.46	296	341	332
Hungary	0.71	0.69	0.67	0.69	0.67	0.62	309	309	308
Poland	0.64	0.67	0.66	0.68	0.75	0.70	271	319	320
Romania	0.41	0.40	0.36	0.36	0.35	0.27	102	105	87
Slovak Republic [3]	0.51	0.55	0.55	0.53	0.55	0.52	252	280	283
Belarus [3]	0.22	0.24	0.21	0.34	0.27	0.23	101	83	79
Kazakhstan	0.69	0.92	1.04	0.59	0.68	0.75	128	150	173
Kyrgyzstan [3]	0.40	0.37	0.35	0.36	0.35	0.31	51	52	49
Moldova	0.38	0.56	0.64	–	0.57	0.69	47	65	81
Russia	0.40	0.62	0.63	0.32	0.51	0.53	107	165	175
Ukraine [3]	0.28	0.53	0.50	0.34	0.49	0.50	60	82	82
Estonia	0.48	0.53	0.52	0.65	0.73	0.68	211	249	257
Latvia [3]	0.63	0.69	0.66	0.75	0.83	0.79	174	189	219
Lithuania	0.64	0.86	1.00	0.43	0.59	0.69	124	167	207
Average	**0.48**	**0.54**	**0.54**	**0.48**	**0.53**	**0.52**	–	–	–

Sources: Table 3.8 and national sources for actual wage and exchange rate data, IMF and World Bank for GDP data, and Kraijnak and Zettelmeyer (1997) for equilibrium wages.

1 Data are gross average monthly wages per employee in manufacturing. Equilibrium wages were calculated based on co-efficients of a cross-country regression of gross US-dollar wages against GDP per capita in purchasing power parities, the share of agriculture in GDP, and a measure for the stock of human capital. See Kraijnak and Zettelmeyer (1997) for details.

2 GDP data in purchasing power parities are from the IMF's *World Economic Outlook* database (1995 data) and the *World Bank Atlas* (1996 data). Data for 1996 and 1997 were calculated using real GDP growth and the US GDP deflator (IMF, *World Economic Outlook*).

3 Wages refer to industry.

economic stability are also reflected in the forecasts for individual countries, and among the CIS countries those most advanced in structural reforms seem to be most sheltered against adverse developments in the Russian economy.

Growth prospects for the countries of CEE are generally evaluated positively by most observers (see Table 3.8). The average of growth forecasts for every country in CEE is positive for 1999 and, according to EBRD projections, the weighted average growth rate will increase from 3.0 per cent in 1998 to 3.6 per cent in 1999. However, this is largely due to the return to (marginally) positive growth in Romania, the fourth-largest economy in the region. The unweighted average shows no change in CEE growth while the output expansion in Croatia, Hungary, Poland and the Slovak Republic is expected to slow from its previous high levels. In particular, the substantial reductions in growth forecast for the Slovak Republic and (less) for Croatia indicate observers' scepticism that the high growth rates of past years could be sustained without a more thorough commitment to structural reforms and given the need to reduce high external imbalances. The relatively high trade exposure of the Baltic states to Russia and the western parts of the CIS underlies their substantially lower post-crisis growth forecasts for 1999, with Estonia – as in 1998 – least affected.

A number of CEE countries may see improved output performance in 1999, mainly those where growth has been negative (Romania) or subdued (Bulgaria, Czech Republic and Slovenia) in recent years. Initiatives to improve the attractiveness of these economies to foreign direct investment will be key to sustaining the recovery against the background of a less accommodating international environment.

Average projections for the CIS are largely driven by projections for Russia. The majority of observers forecast a further decline in Russian GDP by around 4-7 per cent, reflecting the depth of crisis gripping the country. If a successful stabilisation programme can be implemented, the decline could be contained to the lower end of this range, but should stabilisation fail, an even larger decline would be possible, as demonetisation and the absence of effective governance lead to further disintegration of the official economy.

The variation in growth projected for the other CIS countries is illustrative of the gains from structural reforms for macroeconomic resilience. Armenia and Georgia are projected to continue growing at rates of 5 per cent or more, as is Azerbaijan. For the latter – as for Turkmenistan – this is primarily on the back of growing commodity exports. In contrast, Ukraine and Uzbekistan will see their recovery further hindered by the Russian crisis as foreign investment inflows dry up and the environment for domestic business formation remains clouded by government interference. Furthermore, Belarus and Moldova are likely to fall into recession due to close trading linkages with Russia and unsustainable macroeconomic foundations.

Inflation – further reversals possible unless underlying fiscal imbalances are addressed

No further reduction in average inflation is predicted for the CIS, as forecasters have factored in the acceleration of inflation in Russia and Ukraine, continuing high inflation in Belarus and Uzbekistan, as well as the possibility of stabilisation reversals in several other countries (including Turkmenistan and – to a lesser extent – Moldova and Tajikistan). In CEE, most forecasters, however, predict further reductions in inflation rates to an average rate of just above 10 per cent. As in 1998, 1999 will therefore see a growing gap in average inflation rates between CEE and the CIS. Part of the explanation lies in the higher fiscal deficits in the latter, which have become more costly to finance in non-inflationary ways following the fall-out from Russia.

Given rapid inflation during the closing months of 1998, average inflation in Russia in 1999 is projected to be above the 1998 average by all post-crisis forecasts, although observers differ dramatically in their assessment of the size of the inflationary shock (see Table 3.9). EBRD forecasts assume that the new Russian government will take corrective fiscal measures at the beginning of 1999, although inflation is expected to fall only gradually as some monetisation of fiscal deficits remains likely.

The devaluation of currencies in the CIS in the wake of the Russian crisis underlies projections for an increase in average inflation in Moldova and Ukraine and, much less, in Armenia. As in Russia in 1997, Ukraine has relied on portfolio investment inflows into its Treasury bill market to bring inflation down in the face of structural government imbalances, and there is considerable disagreement among forecasters concerning the ability of the authorities to reduce borrowing requirements and maintain investor confidence. Fiscal prudence will also be required in Armenia and Moldova if the increase in inflation is to be contained as projected. The use of central bank credits to finance quasi-fiscal deficits underlies a fragile macroeconomic situation in Belarus and Turkmenistan, both of which will also experience accelerating inflation. On the other hand, inflation is projected to stay roughly constant in Azerbaijan, Georgia, Kazakhstan and Kyrgyzstan, assuming the absence of any strong pressure on these countries' currencies.

The majority of countries in CEE are projected to have single-digit inflation rates in 1999, although only limited reductions relative to 1998 are predicted among this group. Poland and Hungary are slowly edging towards single-digit inflation levels. The major outlier in this part of the region continues to be Romania, which is not predicted to return to lower two-digit inflation rates soon by most observers, reflecting the general scepticism regarding the ability of the government to close its substantial fiscal deficit.

Table 3.8

GDP growth forecasts for 1999

(in per cent) [1]

Central and eastern Europe and the Baltic states	Average [2]	Range [3]	EBRD (Oct 98)	European Union (April 98)	OECD (June 98)	United Nations ECE (Sept 98)	Economist Intelligence Unit (Sept 98)	PlanEcon (Aug 98)	IWH [5] (Aug 98)	Kopint-Datorg [6] (July 98)	Vienna Institute (Aug 98)	CSFB [7] (July 98)	JP Morgan (July 98)	Dun & Bradstreet (Sept 98)
Albania	8.4	3.0	7.0	–	–	–	7.0	9.7	–	–	–	–	–	10.0
Bulgaria	4.0	4.0	3.0	3.8	6.0	4.4	2.0	5.4	4.0	4.0	3.0	–	5.0	3.8
Croatia	3.7	3.5	3.0	–	–	–	5.0	1.5	–	4.0	4.0	–	–	4.7
Czech Republic	2.5	2.5	1.0	2.6	1.2	1.6	3.0	3.3	3.0	2.5	3.0	3.5	3.0	2.6
Estonia	5.7	2.6	5.0	7.0	–	–	4.4	5.5	7.0	4.5	–	–	–	6.5
FYR Macedonia	3.8	0.6	4.0	–	–	–	4.0	3.4	–	–	–	–	–	–
Hungary	4.9	1.2	4.4	4.6	4.6	5.3	4.5	4.5	5.5	5.0	5.0	5.0	5.6	5.0
Latvia	5.2	4.2	2.6	6.6	–	–	5.0	3.9	6.0	6.8	–	–	–	5.5
Lithuania	5.1	4.0	3.0	6.7	–	–	3.0	5.0	5.0	7.0	–	–	–	6.2
Poland	5.6	1.5	5.0	6.0	5.6	5.9	5.6	5.9	5.5	6.0	6.0	4.5	5.6	5.2
Romania	1.7	4.2	1.0	1.4	3.0	4.2	1.0	3.3	1.0	0.0	0.0	–	–	2.0
Slovak Republic	3.3	5.1	3.0	3.5	4.0	5.1	0.0	2.6	4.0	4.5	3.0	–	–	3.0
Slovenia	4.5	4.6	4.5	3.9	3.5	7.9	3.3	5.1	4.5	4.0	4.0	–	–	4.0
Average	*4.5*	*1.4*	*3.6*	*4.6*	*4.0*	*4.9*	*3.7*	*4.5*	*4.6*	*4.4*	*3.5*	*4.3*	*4.8*	*4.9*
Weighted average[4]	4.3	–	3.6	–	–	–	4.0	4.6	–	–	–	–	–	–
Commonwealth of Independent States														
Armenia	5.5	1.6	5.0	–	–	–	5.0	6.6	–	–	–	–	–	–
Azerbaijan	7.1	3.0	6.5	–	–	–	6.0	9.0	–	–	–	–	–	7.0
Belarus	0.8	14.1	-4.0	–	–	–	5.0	-7.1	3.0	–	–	–	–	7.0
Georgia	8.0	4.1	6.0	–	–	–	8.0	10.1	–	–	–	–	–	–
Kazakhstan	1.3	6.3	0.5	–	–	–	-2.5	3.8	–	–	–	–	–	3.5
Kyrgyzstan	5.2	4.0	4.0	–	–	–	3.0	6.8	–	–	–	–	–	7.0
Moldova	1.2	10.6	-4.0	–	–	–	1.0	6.6	–	–	–	–	–	–
Russia	-1.3	11.0	-7.0	–	4.0	-2.9	-5.0	-4.0	-1.5	0.0	0.0	2.0	0.0	-0.2
Tajikistan	4.1	2.1	4.0	–	–	–	3.0	5.1	–	–	–	–	–	4.1
Turkmenistan	7.4	8.1	6.0	–	–	–	4.0	12.1	–	–	–	–	–	–
Ukraine	-0.1	6.0	0.0	–	–	-3.0	-2.0	-2.0	2.0	-1.0	1.5	3.0	–	1.0
Uzbekistan	3.7	5.5	1.5	–	–	–	2.0	4.3	–	–	–	–	–	7.0
Average	*3.6*	*5.1*	*1.5*	–	*4.0*	–	*2.3*	*4.3*	*1.2*	*-0.5*	*0.8*	*2.5*	–	*4.6*
Weighted average[4]	-0.7	–	-5.5	–	–	–	-3.9	-3.0	–	–	–	–	–	–

1 All forecasts quoted here were published or reported to the EBRD between April and September 1998. The dates in brackets indicate the months in which the forecasts were reported or published by each institution. There may in some instances be substantial lags between preparation and publication of forecasts. The Economist Intelligence Unit, United Nations (ECE) and Dun & Bradstreet reported revised forecasts in mid-September, taking into account developments since the Russian devaluation of 17 August. EBRD forecasts were revised in mid-October.

2 The number at the bottom of this column refers to the mean of all the average forecasts shown in this table.

3 This column shows the difference between the highest and the lowest of the forecasts.

4 Weighted average based on EBRD estimates of nominal dollar GDP in each country in 1997. Several institutions calculate their own weighted average. The IMF estimates growth in eastern Europe, including Moldova at 3.7% in 1998 and 4.1% In 1999, Belarus and Ukraine at 3.4% in 1998 and 3.6% in 1999, and Transcaucasus and Central Asia at 4.1% in 1998 and 3.8% in 1999. The IMF also publishes a -6% growth forecast for Russia in 1999. The EU estimates the weighted average growth rate for 10 countries in eastern Europe and the Baltic states (this group excluding Albania, Croatia and FYR Macedonia) at 4.1% in 1998 and 4.5% in 1999. The IWH estimates a weighted average GDP growth for Bulgaria, the Czech Republic, Hungary, Poland, Romania, the Slovak Republic and Slovenia of 3.9% for 1998 and 4.4% for 1999. For Estonia, Latvia and Lithuania the IWH estimates a weighted average GDP growth rate of 6.5% for 1998 and 5.8% for 1999. For Ukraine, Russia and Belarus the estimates are -0.9% for 1998 and -1.1% for 1999.

5 Institute for Economic Research, Halle, Germany.

6 Kopint-Datorg is the Institute for Economic and Market Research Information, Hungary.

7 Credit Suisse First Boston.

Table 3.9

Average inflation forecasts for 1999

(change in the average consumer price level, in per cent) [1]

Central and eastern Europe and the Baltic states	Average [2]	Range [3]	EBRD (Oct 98)	European Union [4] (April 98)	United Nations ECE (Sept 98)	Economist Intelligence Unit (Sept 98)	PlanEcon (Aug 98)	IWH [5] (Aug 98)	Kopint-Datorg [6] (July 98)	Vienna Institute (Aug 98)	CSFB [7] (July 98)	JP Morgan (July 98)	Dun & Bradstreet (Sept 98)
Albania	12.4	9.0	8.0	–	–	8.0	16.6	–	–	–	–	–	17.0
Bulgaria	12.7	12.0	14.0	13.0	12.0	8.5	16.0	13.0	8.0	20.0	–	10.0	12.0
Croatia	5.7	6.3	4.5	–	–	4.0	10.3	–	5.0	6.0	–	–	4.2
Czech Republic	9.0	3.0	8.5	8.4	9.8	9.4	9.8	8.0	10.0	7.0	10.0	8.4	9.8
Estonia	8.7	4.6	9.0	7.5	–	8.5	8.6	5.9	9.5	10.5	–	–	10.0
FYR Macedonia	4.7	2.0	4.0	–	–	4.5	4.1	–	–	6.0	–	–	–
Hungary	12.2	2.7	12.5	11.5	12.7	13.7	11.8	11.0	12.5	11.0	13.5	11.9	12.5
Latvia	6.2	6.4	4.0	5.7	–	6.0	10.4	4.1	6.0	–	–	–	7.0
Lithuania	6.0	3.8	4.2	6.2	–	8.0	5.6	5.3	5.8	–	–	–	7.0
Poland	9.9	3.3	10.0	12.3	10.1	9.0	9.1	9.2	9.7	10.0	10.5	9.4	9.5
Romania	31.8	25.0	35.0	30.0	–	25.0	25.7	26.0	25.0	50.0	–	–	38.0
Slovak Republic	8.3	4.5	8.0	7.0	6.5	11.0	10.7	7.5	8.0	9.0	–	–	7.0
Slovenia	9.0	5.3	7.5	7.9	–	6.7	7.3	10.0	10.0	12.0	–	–	10.2
Average	*10.5*	*6.8*	*9.9*	*11.0*	*10.2*	*9.4*	*11.2*	*10.0*	*10.0*	*14.2*	*11.3*	*9.9*	*12.0*
Commonwealth of Independent States													
Armenia	14.1	9.4	13.0	–	–	10.0	19.4	–	–	–	–	–	–
Azerbaijan	6.1	6.5	5.0	–	–	7.0	9.4	–	–	–	–	–	2.9
Belarus	75.0	60.0	70.0	–	–	75.0	59.9	55.0	–	–	–	–	115.0
Georgia	6.4	6.1	4.0	–	–	5.0	10.1	–	–	–	–	–	–
Kazakhstan	11.7	12.0	11.0	–	–	19.5	8.6	–	–	–	–	–	7.5
Kyrgyzstan	11.1	2.0	10.0	–	–	11.0	11.4	–	–	–	–	–	12.0
Moldova	16.6	14.3	25.0	–	–	14.0	10.7	–	–	–	–	–	–
Russia	47.6	214.0	220.0	–	20.0	45.0	90.9	12.0	14.0	40.0	6.8	6.0	21.0
Tajikistan	31.8	33.4	16.6	–	–	24.5	36.2	–	–	–	–	–	50.0
Turkmenistan	35.7	11.0	36.0	–	–	30.0	41.0	–	–	–	–	–	–
Ukraine	22.9	60.8	25.0	–	–	25.0	68.5	12.0	25.0	10.0	10.0	–	7.7
Uzbekistan	26.6	22.2	27.0	–	–	33.0	34.2	–	–	–	–	–	12.0
Average	*25.4*	*37.6*	*38.6*	–	–	*24.9*	*33.4*	*26.3*	*19.5*	*25.0*	*8.4*	–	*28.5*

1 All forecasts quoted here were published or reported to the EBRD between April and September 1998. The dates in brackets indicate the months in which the forecasts were reported or published by each institution. There may in some instances be substantial lags between preparation and publication of forecasts. The Economist Intelligence Unit, United Nations (ECE) and Dun & Bradstreet reported revised forecasts in mid-September, taking into account developments since the Russian devaluation on 17 August. The IMF provides average regional inflation forecasts for 1999: for central and eastern Europe, including Moldova but excluding Belarus and Ukraine -10.2%; including Belarus and Ukraine, -14.7% and for Transcaucasus and Central Asia, -11.7%. The IMF forecasts Russian average inflation at 73.2% in 1999. EBRD forecasts were revised in mid-October.

2 The number at the bottom of this column is calculated as the mean of all the average forecasts shown in this column.

3 This column shows the difference between the highest and the lowest of the forecasts.

4 Inflation is based on the private consumption deflator.

5 Institute for Economic Research, Halle, Germany.

6 Kopint-Datorg is the Institute for Economic and Market Research Information, Hungary.

7 Credit Suisse First Boston.

Conclusion

The international macroeconomic environment for the transition economies has become less favourable and this will affect economic performance across the region. However, those countries where the foundations for solid economic performance have been laid through persistent structural reforms should be able to withstand the pressures on their external balances, exchange rates and output growth emanating from the crisis in Russia and any general decline in investor confidence. For countries where government imbalances and external deficits remain high, the coming year will pose a crucial stress test of their governments' commitment to structural reform. A retrogression in transition is no solution to present circumstances and would almost certainly increase the costs of adjustment to a changing global economy.

References

C. Denizer and H. Wolf (1998a), "Aggregate Savings in the Transition: A cross-country study", World Bank, mimeo, April.

C. Denizer and H. Wolf (1998b), "Household Savings in Transition Economies", NBER Working Paper, No. 6457.

S. Fries, M. Raiser, N. Stern (1998a), *Macroeconomic and financial stability: transition and East Asian contagion.* EBRD Working Paper, No. 28.

S. Fries, M. Raiser, N. Stern (1998b), "Stress Test for the East", *The Banker,* July 1998, pp.18-21.

L. Halpern and C. Wyplosz (1996), "Equilibrium Exchange Rates in Transition Economies", Working Paper 96/125, IMF, Washington DC.

S. Johnson, D. Kaufmann and A. Shleifer (1997), "Politics and Entrepreneurship in Transition Economies", Working Paper Series No. 57, The William Davidson Institute, University of Michigan.

D. Kaufmann (1997), "The Missing Pillar of a Growth Strategy for Ukraine Institutional and Policy Reforms for Private Sector Development", Harvard Institute for International Development, mimeo.

K. Krajnyák and J. Zettelmeyer (1997), "Competitiveness in Transition Economies: What Scope for Real Appreciation?", Working Paper (Research Department), IMF, Washington DC.

M. Landesmann and I. Burgstaller (1997), "Vertical Product Differentiation in EU Markets: The relative position of East European producers", Research Report No. 234a, Vienna Institute for Comparative Economic Studies (WIIW).

N. Roubini and P. Wachtel (1997), "Current Account Sustainability in Transition Economies", mimeo, Stern School of Business, New York University, November.

Annex 3.1: From Asia to Russia – contagion and transition

Since mid-1997, the international environment has become less favourable for emerging markets around the world. The financial crisis unfolding in East Asia during the second half of 1997 led to a first round of capital outflows from emerging markets, accompanied by a significant shift in world trade flows and a general fall in commodity prices.[1] More recently, Russia's devaluation and effective default have reinforced these tendencies. Having been among the major beneficiaries of the substantial capital flows to emerging markets since 1995 (see Chapter 4), the transition economies are now facing higher borrowing costs on international markets and may see the demand for their products reduced as the Russian market contracts and world growth slows.

This annex examines recent developments in financial markets across the region and analyses the linkages that bind the transition economies to events in global markets, and in Russia in particular. The main conclusion is that – once the dust of the recent turmoil in financial markets worldwide settles – the impact on the region is likely to be highly differentiated. Four channels for contagion are analysed: direct trade linkages, banking sector exposure, financial linkages through the capital markets, and vulnerability to a global economic slowdown. In a number of transition economies underlying weaknesses in the foundations for macroeconomic stability have been brought to the fore by the shift in investor sentiment. In these countries, the stabilisation of market confidence will succeed only if governments underline their commitment to reform with strong action to reduce government and external imbalances and accelerate structural reforms.

This annex should be read in conjunction with Chapters 3 and 4 of this Report. The analysis draws on the weaknesses in macroeconomic fundamentals, particularly with respect to fiscal and external imbalances identified in Chapter 3. Cross-border capital flows form a major channel for contagion. The evolution and composition of capital flows in the transition and the particular importance of foreign direct investment are analysed in Chapter 4.

The market reaction – the immediate impact from Russia

The Russian crisis has had a deep impact on financial markets across the whole region. The immediate determinant of the market's reaction in many instances has been an adjustment to the worldwide shift in portfolio preferences. Hence, even in countries with strong underlying fundamentals, stock markets have slumped and exchange rates have come under pressure following Russia's devaluation on 17 August. However, as argued below, in the more advanced transition economies, the exit of international investors may turn out to be temporary. In others, the market's response to the crisis has been more muted so far despite underlying weaknesses, and a build-up of stronger pressures in the future cannot be excluded.

Table 3.1.1 reports for the month after the onset of the Russian crisis changes in equity markets, nominal exchange rates against the Deutschmark, money market rates and international reserves as an indication of the markets' immediate response.[2] Chart 3.1.1 complements this analysis by showing spreads of selected Eurobonds from the region over US and German treasury securities. Between 14 August and 14 September, stock markets fell substantially in Croatia, the Czech Republic, Hungary, Latvia, Lithuania, Poland, Romania and Ukraine, and less so in the Slovak Republic and Slovenia. The Tallinn stock index actually increased in the month after the Russian devaluation, mainly as a result of a rally in the share price of Hansapank following takeover rumours from a Swedish investor (but it has recently declined). Exchange rates in countries operating a floating exchange rate or a wide currency band also depreciated substantially in the immediate aftermath of Russia's devaluation. For instance, the Polish zloty and the Czech koruna both lost around 10 per cent of their value in the week following 17 August before recovering during early September. Currencies in many CIS countries were temporarily under severe pressure. For instance, the Georgian lari was trading at a 34 per cent discount during late August but has since recovered. The Moldovan leu had lost around 20 per cent of its value against the US dollar by mid-October. In Belarus the rouble has depreciated to a third of its official level on the parallel market, and in Turkmenistan and Uzbekistan the parallel market premium has increased significantly.

The fall in share prices and exchange rates across the region does not show a strong relationship with the underlying macroeconomic strengths and weaknesses analysed in the preceding chapter. However, developments in domestic money markets, in the secondary market for Eurobonds and in international reserve positions show a much clearer differentiation among countries, and one that conforms better with prior expectations of potential vulnerability. Estonia, Lithuania, Romania, the Slovak Republic and Ukraine have all experienced a significant tightening of domestic liquidity as their currencies have come under strong pressures – culminating in the shift in the exchange rate band in Ukraine on 4 September and the abandonment of the fixed exchange rate in the Slovak Republic on 1 October. The change in international reserves further reveals that the tightening of domestic liquidity was associated with a net resource outflow in Romania, Ukraine and, to a lesser extent, the Slovak Republic, while the Baltic states seem to have benefited from an inflow of foreign currency, as many Russians in particular shifted deposits across the border.

[1] On the impact of the East Asian crisis on world trade flows, see Zhang and Cline (1998). Their estimates suggest that the required adjustment to trade balances could shave around 0.8% off GDP growth in the USA and 0.6% in the European Union.

[2] For the first three variables the change is measured between 14 August and 14 September 1998. For international reserves the change is from end of July until the end of August. The simple one-month change masks significant volatility of stock indices and exchange rates between the two dates. This presentation is chosen to give a snapshot overview for as many countries as possible rather than tracking day-to-day movements for individual countries.

Table 3.1.1

The immediate impact of the Russian crisis – a one-month snapshot

Country	Stock Market index, change in per cent, 14.08-14.09.98[1]	Exchange rate against DM, change in per cent 14.08-14.09.98	Interbank offering rate (3 months) in per cent 14.08.98	Interbank offering rate (3 months) in per cent 14.09.98	International reserves – end July (US$ billion)	International reserves – end August (US$ billion)
Bulgaria [2]	na	0.00	5.26	5.08	2.534	2.428
Croatia [3]	-25.08	1.61	15.15	14.7	na	na
Czech Republic	-14.61	-1.61	14.42	13.09	11.43	11.367
Estonia [4]	25.30	0.00	10.5	15.91	0.731	0.823
Hungary	-36.29	5.19	16.53	16.6	9.8	9.35
Kazakhstan	na	8.49	17.21	17.7	2	1.8
Latvia	-33.90	-3.20	6.31	6.4	0.813	0.815
Lithuania [5]	-23.76	5.52	9.6	13.11	1.665	1.618
Poland	-17.16	8.26	19.07	18.07	25.811	na
Romania	-31.11	0.00	49.42	61.77	2.616	2.3
Russia	-44.45	40.96	61.5	na	13.4	7.7
Slovak Republic	-3.02	3.48	15.03	26.1	3.745	3.623
Slovenia [6]	-11.14	0.94	6.2	6.4	3.551	3.53
Ukraine	-26.30	22.37	78.7	200	1.5	0.8
Georgia	na	39.88	37.89	39.13	0.144	0.135

Sources: Bloomberg and national authorities.

1 Stock indices refer to: Crobex for Croatia, PX 50 for the Czech Republic, Talse for Estonia, DJRSE for Latvia, Litin for Lithuania, WIG 20 for Poland, BET for Romania, RTS for Russia, SAX for the Slovak Republic, PFTS for Ukraine.

2 Interest rates are for 3-month T-bills. The pre-crisis date is 11 August 1998.

3 The pre-crisis stock market index is for 15 August; the stock market was closed on 14 August.

4 The interbank rates are respectively for 12 August and 16 September.

5 Interest rates are for 3-month T-bills. The dates are 11 August and 18 September.

6 The interbank rates are overnight rates. No 3-month offering rates were quoted.

Developments in spreads on Eurobonds show that international capital markets are already differentiating strongly among borrowers. Kazakhstan, Romania, Russia and, to a lesser extent, the Slovak Republic have all recorded large increases in secondary market spreads – in contrast with moderate or small increases in Croatia, and Poland and Slovenia respectively (see Chart 3.1.1).[3] The result is a much larger divergence in spreads between the more and less advanced transition economies after the lending spree of early 1997 had led to a convergence in terms beyond what would seem to have been justified by macroeconomic fundamentals. The Kazakhstani case is particularly interesting in that the substantial increase in Eurobond spreads since mid-August has not been reflected by an increase in the domestic money market rates. Yields on Kazakhstani dollar-denominated securities as of mid-September were higher than on domestic Treasury bills, reflecting the government's attempt to calm financial markets by refusing to raise interest rates.[4]

Channels of contagion

In the medium term the impact of the Russian crisis on the region is likely to be more differentiated than the immediate market reaction suggests, although developments in money markets and in Eurobond spreads already point to some significant differences across countries. In evaluating the impact that current events in Russia and in the world economy are likely to have on the region, it is useful to distinguish between four channels of contagion: trade linkages, banking sector exposure, capital markets and a potential world economic slowdown. The extent of the repercussions resulting from recent events cannot at present be fully ascertained. EBRD growth forecasts presented in Chapter 3 give an approximate order of magnitude. According to these projections, growth in 1998 and 1999 in central and eastern Europe may be slowed moderately due to lower export demand from Russia and a slowdown in west European growth. The Baltic states and the CIS will be more strongly affected by trade linkages with Russia. In a number of countries, weak underlying fundamentals pose a significant risk of financial contagion. In these cases, growth could be slowed by a contraction in domestic demand following a rise in real interest rates and a reduction of current account imbalances forced by more limited access to international capital flows.

Trade linkages

The loss of exports due to demand contraction and/or real exchange rate depreciation in a major trading partner can directly squeeze incomes and weaken the balance of payments.[5] This may in turn force the government to adopt contractionary macroeconomic policies to restore external balance, thereby amplifying the impact on aggregate demand.

3 Lithuania also falls in the category of moderate increases in spreads, from around 100 basis points at launch to 500 basis points after the Russian devaluation.

4 This strategy may not be sustainable in the medium term unless public borrowing requirements are dramatically reduced. In a recent evaluation of the East Asian crisis, the IMF points to the need to raise interest rates early to fend off a build-up of pressure on the currency market (Adams et al., 1998).

5 Customs officials in Russia estimate that imports declined by 19% year-on-year in August 1998. EBRD growth forecasts in Chapter 3 assume a decline in Russian import demand for the year as a whole by about 20%.

Chart 3.1.1

Spreads on Eurobond issues by selected transition economies

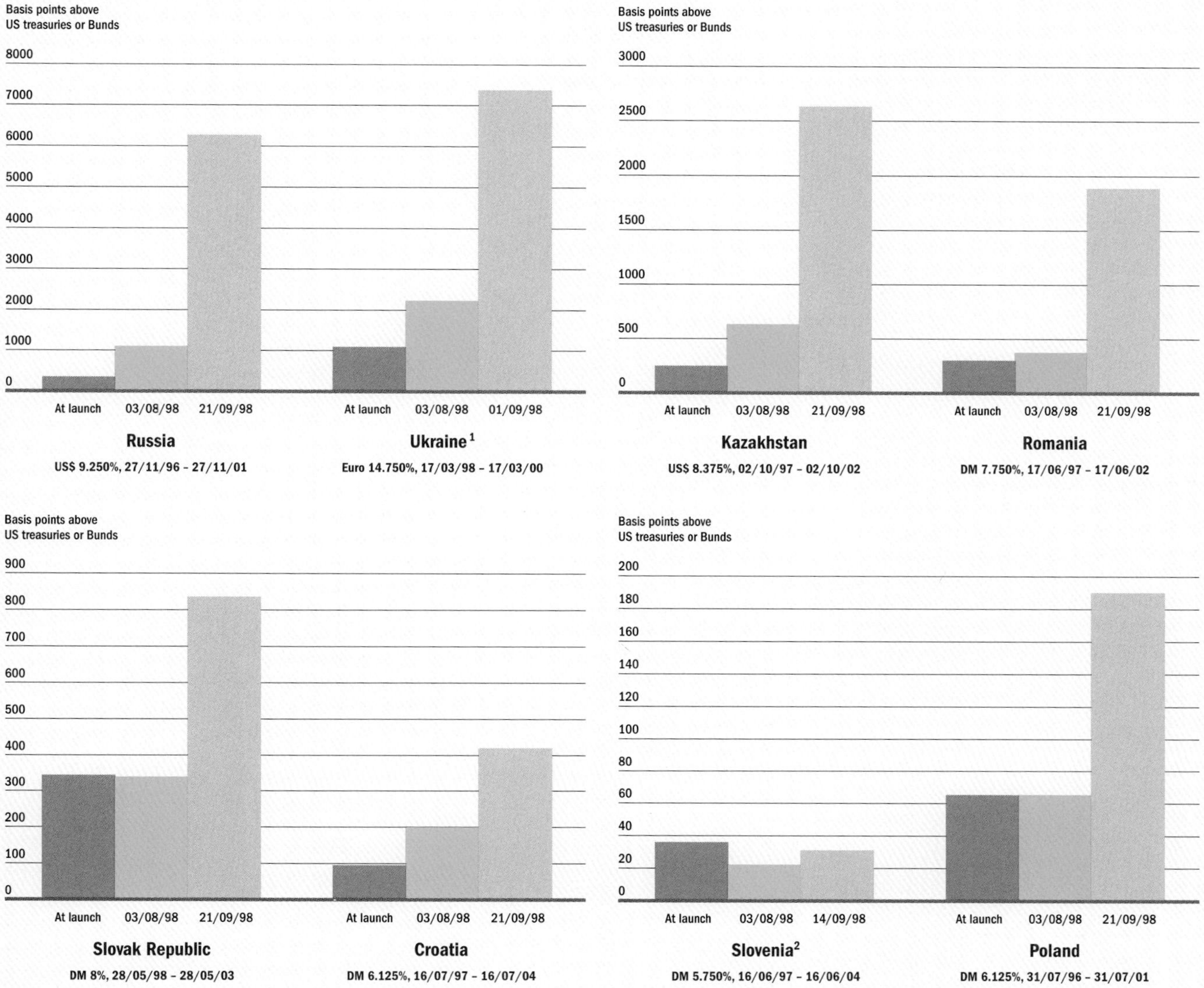

Source: Bloomberg.
Note:
Russia, Ukraine, Kazakhstan and Poland have issued several Eurobonds. Issues presented here were chosen according to maturity dates - taken to be as close as possible to each other.
1 For Ukraine no spread was available after 1 September.
2 For Slovenia the spread was only available on 14 September.

Trade exposure to Russia is most important for the CIS. All CIS countries with the exception of Tajikistan and Turkmenistan[6] conduct 20 per cent or more of their merchandise export trade with Russia, and this share is above 50 per cent in Belarus and Moldova and close to 40 per cent in Kazakhstan. If one further includes trade exposure to Ukraine and Belarus as countries likely to experience a sharp contraction in import demand over the next 18 months, Latvia and Lithuania are also strongly affected by trade linkages (see Table 3.1.2). Note that Table 3.1.2 reports only merchandise trade exposure as recorded by the IMF's Direction of Trade Statistics. Service trade, including above all transport of energy, is of considerable importance in the Baltic states[7] as well as in Belarus and Ukraine.

Trade linkages are far less important for central and eastern Europe. Most vulnerable are Bulgaria and Poland, each with 10 per cent combined trade exposure to Russia, Belarus and Ukraine. In Poland there is additional exposure through substantial cross-border trade not captured by trade statistics. In addition, indirect trade links exist through intermediary markets. For instance, in Hungary indirect trade exposure was recently estimated at 30 per cent of total exports, and anecdotal evidence

6 Turkmenistan's trade exposure is considerably higher than the figures in Table 2 suggest, since its export performance depends to a large extent on a resumption of gas transit through Russia. Turkmen officials have indicated that the present crisis may make an agreement with Gazprom less likely; hence Turkmenistan is also highly vulnerable to trade linkages.

7 National Bank data indicate Estonia's share of total exports to Russia was 13% during the first half of 1998. Similar figures for Latvia and Lithuania point to trade exposure in excess of 30%.

Table 3.1.2

Trade exposure to Russia

(in per cent)

Central and eastern Europe and the Baltic states[1]	Share of exports of goods to Russia[2]	Share of exports of goods to Ukraine[2]	Share of exports of goods to Belarus[2]	Total	Share of exports in GDP[2]	GDP exposure[3]
Bulgaria	7	3	0	**10**	47	5
Croatia	4	0	0	**4**	22	1
Czech Republic	2	1	–	**4**	43	2
Estonia	6	5	2	**13**	49	6
FYR Macedonia	2	8	1	**11**	36	4
Hungary	5	1	0	**7**	43	3
Latvia	21	4	3	**28**	32	9
Lithuania	7	9	12	**28**	44	12
Poland	4	5	1	**10**	20	2
Romania	3	1	0	**4**	28	1
Slovak Republic	3	3	–	**6**	45	3
Slovenia	4	1	–	**5**	47	2
Average	*6*	*4*	*2*	***11***	*38*	*4*
Commonwealth of Independent States						
Armenia	23	2	1	**26**	14	4
Azerbaijan	23	4	0	**28**	21	6
Belarus	59	15	–	**74**	55	41
Georgia	30	4	0	**34**	9	3
Kazakhstan	39	3	–	**42**	30	13
Kyrgyzstan	21	1	1	**23**	37	9
Moldova	63	5	2	**70**	38	26
Russia	–	9	6	**15**	20	3
Tajikistan	8	1	1	**10**	60	6
Turkmenistan	5	–	–	**5**	41	2
Ukraine	22	–	5	**27**	31	8
Uzbekistan	31	6	2	**39**	26	10
Average	*29*	*5*	*2*	***33***	*32*	*11*

Sources: IMF, *Direction of Trade Statistics Yearbook*, 1997; and EBRD staff calculations.

1 Data for Albania and Bosnia and Herzegovina were not available from the IMF. National sources for Albania indicate only minor trade exposure to Russia.

2 Exports of merchandise only. Figures from national authorities for total exports give considerably higher figures for all three Baltic countries.

3 Calculated as the total share of exports of goods to Russia, Belarus and Ukraine multiplied with the share of exports of goods in GDP.

suggests that a significant proportion of FYR Macedonia's exports through Yugoslavia may ultimately be destined for Russia. Some sectors of industry in central and eastern Europe are also particularly affected, such as food processing and pharmaceuticals.

Banking sector exposure

Heavy banking sector exposure to an economy in crisis and resulting capital losses from exchange rate movements and falls in asset prices may precipitate banking crises with potential knock-on effects on economic activity and macroeconomic stability. Direct banking sector exposure would seem to be a major risk only in the case of Latvia. Some Latvian banks are heavily exposed to the Russian GKO market; total exposure may equal 10 per cent of banking sector assets. Indirect exposure through the reduction of trade finance opportunities and economic difficulties of borrowers engaged in exports to the Russian market may nonetheless present a financial burden for many banks in the region.

More generally, financial systems in many transition economies remain weakened by low capitalisation of some banks, the lack of competition and inadequate regulation (see Part II of this Report). A weak banking system is an element of vulnerability that may interact with spill-overs in goods and capital markets to precipitate financial instability. While there has been no evidence so far of such indirect financial linkages through the banking sector, present circumstances highlight the need to strengthen prudential regulations and banking supervision (see Chapter 6).

Portfolio shifts in capital markets

Shifts in investor sentiment can increase the cost of borrowing and put (possibly acute) pressure on currencies. This can force countries into contractionary policies and lead to disruption in financial markets. Financial linkages may spawn contagious effects both directly, through the pressure on international investors to sell parts of their portfolio in order to meet liquidity needs, and indirectly, through a general "flight to quality" leading to an outflow of capital from all emerging markets.

Both direct and indirect financial linkages have been important in spreading financial turmoil to the transition economies. Russia was affected by the partial liquidation of Brazilian and South Korean GKO holdings in early December, estimated at around

US$ 4 billion. More recently, capital losses in the Russian GKO market have put several large investors under pressure to sell parts of their emerging market portfolio. The flight to quality by international investors was evidenced in the substantial decline in equity markets in all transition economies following the Hong Kong stock market slump in late October 1997, and more dramatically since the end of July 1998. However, a closer look at the effects of the East Asian crisis on the region reveals that once the dust of the initial turmoil settles, international investors differentiate strongly among countries according to their underlying strengths and weaknesses.[8] Indeed, one effect of the recent turmoil has been to fully expose the weaknesses in macroeconomic policies in several transition economies. Their problems as a result of the Russian crisis have at least as much to do with inadequate domestic policies as with financial contagion per se.

Evidence from episodes of currency or balance of payments crises in other emerging market economies suggests that vulnerability to financial contagion results from a combination of weak macroeconomic fundamentals and the accumulation of short-term domestic and/or foreign liabilities.[9] Among the macroeconomic fundamentals, the existence of "twin" fiscal and current account deficits in a number of transition economies are at present the biggest source of concern (see Chapter 3). On this count, Romania appears to be particularly vulnerable to a loss of investor confidence. Large current account deficits in the Baltic states, Croatia and the Slovak Republic also raise concerns about these countries' ability to mobilise sufficient financing, and some macroeconomic adjustment may be required. In most CIS countries, the weight of FDI and/or official financing in their capital accounts limits the degree of vulnerability to financial contagion, despite the existence of large fiscal and current account deficits in some cases.

The large financing requirements of some governments in eastern Europe and the CIS and their accumulation of short-term debts pose particular risks to the balance of payments and the exchange rate regime. Short-term debt can pose a significant risk to an exchange rate commitment if a substantial amount of debt is coming due and investor sentiment about the country deteriorates. Most short-term debt in the transition economies has been placed with the banking sector and in the domestic money markets.[10] In this context, the ability of monetary authorities to fend off a sudden decline in the demand for domestic assets depends to a considerable extent on the strength of its reserve position relative to the size of outstanding domestic liabilities. In Russia, for example, in early August 1998 domestic government debt maturing up to the end of the year was estimated at around US$ 16.5 billion, well in excess of the central bank's foreign exchange reserves at that time.[11] With a third of total domestic government liabilities of around US$ 60 billion held by foreigners, the government's precarious liquidity situation was one main factor precipitating the crisis of confidence in the run-up to the 17 August devaluation. On a smaller scale, a similar problem has emerged in Ukraine, where total Treasury bill holdings as of mid-September 1998 equalled 12.5 billion hryvnia (US$ 4.25 billion), or over five times the international reserves (foreign holdings alone were equal to around 65 per cent of reserves).

Chart 3.1.2 presents the ratio of liquid domestic assets (broad money plus outstanding Treasury bills and other money market instruments) to international reserves as an indicator of vulnerability to shifts in portfolio preferences for selected transition economies as of March 1998.[12] The same ratio is also given for five Asian countries for June 1997. This confirms the particular vulnerability of Ukraine in addition to Russia's unrivalled position. Belarus and the Slovak Republic also have a ratio of liquid domestic liabilities to international reserves comparable to the levels in East Asia prior to the latter's financial crises. In Belarus the loss of confidence in the currency has led to a collapse of the exchange rate on the parallel market since mid-August 1998. While convertibility restrictions may limit the immediate impact on the country's balance of payments, the external financing constraint is nonetheless likely to severely dent growth prospects. The Slovak koruna was devalued on 1 October in response to repeated speculative attacks.

World economic slow-down

Since the onset of the crisis in Russia, the financial turmoil that has spread from East Asia across emerging markets since mid-1997 has also reached out to the economies of western Europe and North America, and seems to have dented the optimism that bolstered asset prices and growth in recent years. For the economies of central and eastern Europe and the Baltic states, a slow-down in economic growth particularly in western Europe would have significant negative implications, more so than developments in Russia per se. Thus, in central Europe, where exports to the European Union account for between 20 and 40 per cent of GDP, a reduction in import demand from western Europe by only 2 per cent could shave around 0.5-1 per cent off growth in 1999. Among the CIS countries, the resource-rich economies of Central Asia would be particularly affected through depressed commodity prices as a result of a downturn in world economic activity. In the remainder of the CIS, the degree of trade integration with the rest of the world is much less significant, and the additional impact of a slowdown in world growth is likely to be small.

Containing contagion – policy implications

The Russian crisis has brought into sharp relief the underlying weaknesses in macroeconomic fundamentals and imbalanced structural reforms in a number of transition economies. Belarus and Ukraine have been particularly affected among the countries

8 This argument is developed in detail in Fries, Raiser and Stern (1998a;b).

9 See, for instance, Kaminski, Lizondo and Reinhardt (1996).

10 Short-term foreign liabilities are large by international comparison only in Russia and in the Baltic states. In the latter, however, the largest share of short-term liabilities is made up of Russian bank deposits, which have increased in the wake of the recent crisis and would not seem to present any immediate threat to the balance of payments.

11 This estimate was after the conversion of around US$ 6.5 billion GKOs into Eurobonds at the end of July 1998.

12 This indicator has been suggested among others by Calvo (1996) and successfully applied as a leading indicator of currency crises in emerging markets by Kaminski, Lizondo and Reinhardt (1997) and Sachs, Tornell and Velasco (1996).

Chart 3.1.2

Ratio of liquid domestic assets to international reserves

(March 1998 for transition economies, June 1997 for East Asian economies)

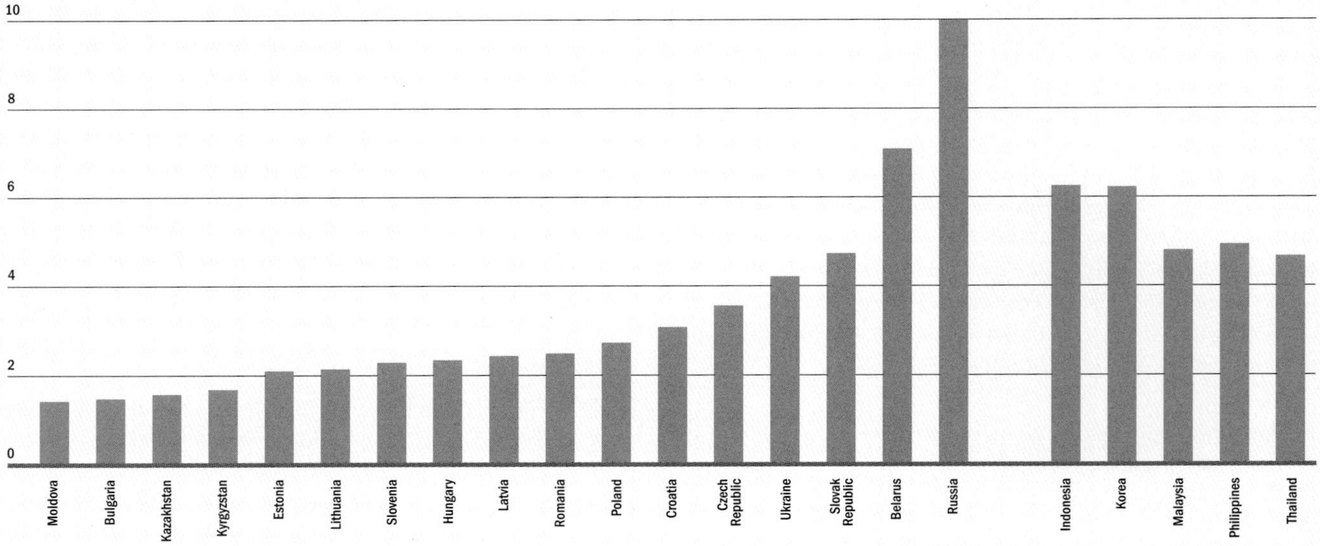

Sources: *International Financial Statistics* (IFS) and national authorities.
Note:
Liquid domestic assets are equal to the sum of money, quasi money and money market instruments. In the case of the transition economies, the latter is equal to the stock of Treasury bills, as reported by national authorities. Money market instruments for the Asian countries are from the IFS.

in this group by the combination of weak foundations for sustained growth and macroeconomic stability and close trade linkages with Russia. The Russian crisis is also highlighting the urgency of measures to reduce fiscal and/or external imbalances in a number of CIS countries, as well as in Romania, in the Slovak Republic and to a lesser extent in the Baltic states and Croatia. In other central and east European countries there is less need for corrective policy measures, but prudent macroeconomic management will be called for throughout the region. Several governments have already signalled their readiness to reduce expenditures and tighten monetary policy in response to the crisis.[13] Nonetheless, if experience to date with the impact of the Asian crisis at the turn of the year is anything to go by, the most advanced transition countries should be able to weather the present turmoil relatively well.

References

C. Adams, D. Mathieson, G. Schinasi, B. Chadha – lead authors (1998), *International Capital Markets. Developments, Prospects, and Key Policy Issues.* International Monetary Fund, World Economic and Financial Surveys, advance Internet version.

G. Calvo, (1996), *Why is the market so unforgiving? Reflections on the Tequilazo.* University of Maryland, mimeo, September.

S. Fries, M. Raiser, N. Stern (1998a), *Macroeconomic and financial stability: transition and East Asian contagion.* EBRD Working Paper, No. 28.

S. Fries, M. Raiser, N. Stern (1998b), "Stress test for the East", *The Banker,* July 1998, pp. 18-21.

G.L. Kaminski, S. Lizondo, and C.M. Reinhardt (1997), *Leading Indicators of Currency Crises.* Board of Governors of the Federal Reserve System, mimeo, June.

J. Sachs, A. Tornell, A. Velasco (1996), *Financial Crises in Emerging Markets: The Lessons from 1995.* Brookings Papers on Economic Activity (August), pp. 147-214.

[13] For instance, the Kazakhstani government will reduce expenditures by 25% in 1998, Hungary is drawing up a new budget taking under the assumption of only 3-4% growth in 1999, while Poland's finance ministry has also called for further fiscal restraint.

Cross-border capital flows

4

Capital flows into the transition economies can make a significant contribution to realising the region's growth potential. Foreign capital can benefit the transition process by helping to fill the savings-investment gap that has characterised the transition, by lowering financing costs, and by setting standards, tightening financial discipline and raising the intensity of competition. Against these benefits stand the risks of exposure to a volatile international environment. As argued in Annex 3.1, these risks are highest in countries that have integrated themselves into the international capital markets but have failed so far to establish the foundations for macroeconomic and financial stability.

Integration into the international capital markets is a very recent phenomenon for the transition economies (see Section 4.1). After some initial hesitancy, capital flows have increased sharply over the past three years, reaching levels that compare well with most other emerging market economies. The recent surge in net inflows means that, by the end of 1998 on current projections, three-quarters of all private capital will have entered the region during 1996-98. Foreign direct investment (FDI), responsible for a third of private capital inflows in 1997, has advanced gradually throughout the decade in line with the region's transition profile (see Section 4.2). Other flows of finance, especially short-term forms, have seemingly tried to catch up with the reform process and have grown exponentially during 1996 and 1997. However, their geographical distribution has been less clearly patterned on countries' progress in transition (see Section 4.3).

There are significant opportunities for foreign investors in the region. In most transition economies domestic savings are low (see Chapter 3) and financing costs high, due to underdeveloped financial systems. While the physical and human capital stock in the region is large by the standards of middle-income countries, it is inefficiently employed and partially obsolete. The potential productivity (and profitability) of new capital is therefore likely to be higher than in more settled market environments. Investment for restructuring, combined with improved management and advanced technology, offers opportunities for raising the yield of some of the existing capital at relatively low cost. Foreign capital can help to realise this potential, but governments must unlock it by creating a strong investment climate.

Access to the international capital market for all countries in the region will become more difficult in the wake of the Russian crisis. Capital flows to emerging markets are bound to contract, and all borrowers in the region will be burdened with additional risk premia for some time to come. However, the capital markets will also become much more discriminating among countries, reflecting differences in underlying macroeconomic fundamentals as well as the conditions for long-term investment. Long-term private flows have been of limited importance in countries at earlier stages of transition. Significant short-term flows, however, have in some of these countries been attracted by arbitrage opportunities that arose from inconsistencies in reforms. As cautioned in last year's *Transition Report*, the rapid growth of certain types of short-term capital flows has contributed to the volatility witnessed in 1998. In contrast, more advanced transition economies have attracted a much larger proportion of FDI, and consequently are likely to experience a less sharp contraction of capital inflows. Determined structural and institutional reform should be more than ever a priority for the transition economies.

It should be recognised that implementing the necessary structural and fiscal reforms that must underlie prudent macroeconomic management will take time. Shortcutting the transition by liberalising capital flows ahead of the establishment of an appropriate regulatory and institutional framework carries considerable risks. One lesson of the recent experience is that governments should explore market-based means of constraining the volatility of short-term capital flows as long as serious deficiencies remain in reform (see Section 4.4).

4.1 The volume and composition of capital flows

The socialist economies as borrowers – capital flows pre-transition

Irrespective of ideological misgivings, the central planners were no strangers to the international capital markets. Since the late 1970s, the Soviet Union, Poland, Yugoslavia and Hungary, and later Bulgaria, approached the syndicated loan market, generally through their foreign trade banks, and expanded the use of export credit and short-term trade finance.[1] East Germany relied more on its ability to extract bilateral credits from the Federal Republic of Germany. Equity finance was obviously foreign to socialism, and the decentralised nature of bond finance was not in favour with planners. The sovereign risk of these economies was well-regarded, as evidenced by their ability to rapidly raise their levels of indebtedness – although Poland underwent a series of debt restructurings from as early as 1981. At 1990 prices,[2] gross medium- and long-term capital flows into the region averaged US$ 7.7 billion per year in 1981-85 and US$ 20 billion in 1986-90, compared with US$ 2.7 billion in 1976-80. Except for Albania, Czechoslovakia and Romania, the countries of the region entered the transition process with heavy debt burdens on which – apart from Hungary – they eventually defaulted.[3]

1 Forfeiting developed into an art in COMECON trade finance, perhaps more so than in any other part of the world.

2 Deflated by the US GDP deflator.

3 The Soviet external debt was taken over by Russia after the break-up of the Soviet Union. The other CIS countries were thus essentially debt free at the start of transition. The problem of East German debt resolved itself through unification.

Table 4.1

Net capital flows to central and eastern Europe and Russia

(in millions of US dollars)

	(annual average) 1976-80	1981-85	1986-90	1989	1990	1991	1992	1993	1994	1995	1996	1997 (revised)
Total flows	**1,179**	**1,805**	**4,871**	**4,032**	**3,396**	**14,464**	**24,874**	**23,832**	**16,035**	**33,399**	**40,704**	**61,122**
Private flows	**862**	**973**	**3,935**	**2,866**	**-8,355**	**-6,409**	**6,213**	**14,272**	**12,214**	**28,427**	**33,079**	**51,033**
Equity investment	15	18	152	458	571	2,464	3,996	6,013	5,679	14,553	11,412	17,865
Direct equity investment	15	18	122	187	431	2,143	3,657	5,157	4,548	12,282	9,242	14,494
Portfolio equity investment	0	0	30	271	140	321	339	856	1,131	2,271	2,170	3,371
Commercial banks	694	680	76	908	-15,089	-8,226	996	1,412	1,976	8,412	11,102	7,800
Other private creditors	153	275	3,707	1,500	6,163	-647	1,221	6,847	4,559	5,148	10,565	25,368
Official flows	**317**	**831**	**936**	**1,166**	**11,751**	**20,873**	**18,661**	**9,560**	**3,821**	**4,972**	**7,625**	**10,089**
International financial institutions	204	625	-126	-1,143	1,112	5,729	3,607	3,124	3,001	3,459	3,756	4,257
Official bilateral creditors	113	206	1,062	2,309	10,639	15,144	15,054	6,435	820	1,514	3,869	5,832

Source: Institute for International Finance.

Note:
Data cover Bulgaria, the Czech Republic, Hungary, Poland, Romania, Russia and the Slovak Republic.

From official finance to private investments – capital flows in the transition

The transition process radically changed both the volume and composition of external capital flows. Capital flows from 1989 to 1993 were shaped by Western governments' determination to make the transition "stick", coupled with a wait-and-see approach by private sources of funds. In the early years of transition, central economic coordination was lost, with markets only gradually taking its place. Macroeconomic conditions were highly unsettled, relative prices adjusted sharply, and there was political uncertainty, especially in the former Soviet Union and former Yugoslavia. Correspondingly country and commercial risk was, and was perceived to be, extremely high. When economic performance improved and the transition progressed, private capital began to enter the market, first tentatively, then with great speed.

Reflecting these developments, capital flows into the region have followed a distinct sequence: official funding, FDI, non-guaranteed bank loans, dedicated equity funds, and lastly international bond issues and direct local stock and money-market investments. There are serious data problems with measures of capital flows in the transition economies. Commercial bank syndicated lending and bond issues, on a gross commitment basis, tend to be reasonably well covered by the Euromoney databases.[4] The recording of FDI flows is improving, but measures of portfolio investments can differ enormously.[5] The aggregate flows reported here use information on a subset of countries compiled by the Institute for International Finance (see Table 4.1).

Beginning in 1989-90, official funding increased sharply, while private sources of funds were largely absent from the region. A large share of the official capital flows were on account of German transfers to the former Soviet Union, as part of the German unification agreement (e.g. housing for repatriated Soviet soldiers). But substantial official support was also forthcoming from a range of bilateral and multilateral sources (e.g. the IFI contribution to the zloty stabilisation fund in 1991).[6] Net official flows peaked in 1991 at US$ 21 billion. After 1993, they declined both as a share of the total and in absolute terms.

Private flows began to exceed net official flows in 1993, and by 1997 accounted for 84 per cent of total net capital flows (excluding net resident lending abroad) into the seven recipient countries covered by Table 4.1.[7] This represented over 5 per cent of the region's GDP and 22 per cent of aggregate net private flows into the emerging markets.[8] The transition economies were among the few emerging market regions where inflows continued to increase during the second half of 1997, following the East Asian crisis (see Chart 4.1). However, this trend has been reversed following the Russian crisis, and inflows for the year as a whole will fall substantially below the 1997 level.

After a relatively minor presence in earlier years, private flows of all types have, since 1996 and especially in 1997, been increasingly destined towards Russia. Despite a slowdown after the onset of the East Asian crisis, Russia was still estimated to account for more than a third of all private flows into the region in the first six months of 1998. While foreigners have invested in Russia, however, Russians have increasingly transferred funds abroad or

4 Euromoney Bondware and Loanware.

5 Purchases by foreigners on domestic securities markets, in particular, are only collected sporadically. Below we report information on net portfolio flows for a limited number of countries drawn from the IMF's *International Financial Statistics*.

6 In addition, Paris Club reschedulings were granted to Poland (1991, concessional terms), Bulgaria (1991, '92, '94) and Russia (1993, '94, '95, '96).

7 Bulgaria, the Czech Republic, Hungary, Poland, Romania, Russia, and the Slovak Republic. Data from Institute for the International Finance.

8 Total flows as reported by the Institute for International Finance, May 1998.

Chart 4.1

Net private and official capital flows to central and eastern Europe and Russia, 1989-97

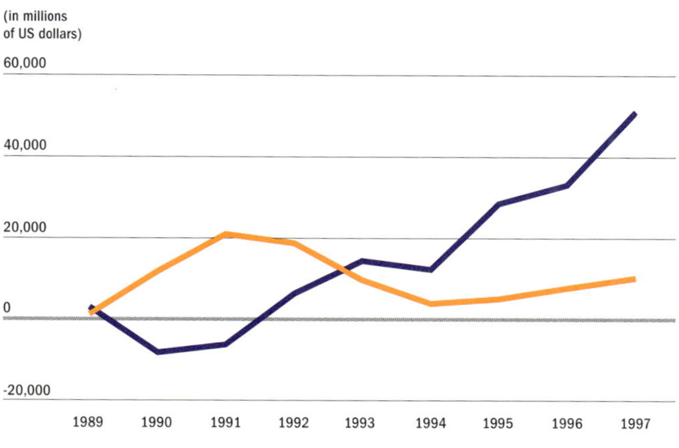

Source: Table 4.1.
Note:
Data cover Bulgaria, the Czech Republic, Hungary, Poland, Romania, Russia and the Slovak Republic.

engaged in capital flight. These transfers would appear to have been of similar magnitude to that of net foreign capital inflows into Russia during 1996 and 1997. The main channels have been the non-repatriation of export proceeds and currency purchases by the population.[9]

The impact of East Asia and Russia – recent developments and prospects

The East Asian and Russian crises are fundamentally altering conditions on international capital markets. The scale of losses made by international private investors in Russia as well as in Asia is likely to moderate sharply their appetite for risk. Large institutional investors, which provided an important contribution to the increase in capital flows to emerging markets since the early 1990s, may retreat from these markets for some time. Moreover, the scramble for liquidity since mid-August has led to "technical" sales by international investors to meet margin calls, driving down asset prices and leading to an outflow of short-term funds across emerging markets. Thus, to some extent, all borrowers from the region will be affected by the changing international environment, through rising risk premia and through a reduction of the supply of funds, as savings shift into less risky assets.

Nonetheless, the impact is likely to be highly differentiated both across countries and across types of capital flows. Markets discriminate between borrowers on the basis of their macroeconomic fundamentals.[10] Spreads on international bond issues by borrowers from the region are already reflecting a sharp differentiation (see Annex 3.1). After having been overly optimistic in the run-up to the present crisis, international investors are likely to display considerable caution towards the less advanced transition economies for some time. Government and external imbalances, in particular, will be watched very closely and corrective measures may be required.

With respect to the types of capital flows, in the short run, countries relying primarily on FDI are likely to be less affected by the present volatility in international capital markets than are countries where short-term portfolio investment played a major role in external financing. FDI in particular is motivated by the long-term economic opportunities in the region and comes together with significant changes in corporate governance in the recipient enterprises. Foreign direct investors therefore have both the ability and the incentives to maintain the value of their assets through "voice" or active involvement, rather than through "exit". Indeed, recent projections for FDI into seven major recipient countries in the region do not suggest a significantly negative impact of the Russian crisis, except for Russia itself (see Charts 4.2a and 4.2b).[11] A slow-down of FDI inflows into the region is nonetheless a possibility, and it would become far more likely if growth worldwide were to slow down sharply.

The impact on other types of capital flows is likely to be more pronounced than in the case of FDI. A number of transition economies including Moldova and Kazakhstan have postponed Eurobond issues planned for later in the year. Syndicated lending will also be cut back, as banks become more cautious lenders and take time to rebuild their capital – a process already in evidence during the first half of 1998. More immediately, a large number of countries, including the most advanced transition economies, have been affected by an outflow of short-term portfolio investments in the domestic money and equity markets. For instance, as of end-August 1998, it has been estimated that US$ 2 billion had been withdrawn from the fixed-income markets of Poland (US$ 1 billion), Hungary and the Czech Republic (US$ 0.5 billion each).[12] Capital outflows have also been registered from the Treasury bill markets of Romania, Bulgaria and several CIS countries.

The following two sections look at the determinants and impacts of FDI and other forms of capital flows in more detail. The analysis reveals that the structure of external financing to the transition economies is significantly related to the degree of progress achieved in transition to date. Maintaining access to the international capital markets and limiting vulnerability to volatile capital flows will require continued reform momentum.

4.2 Foreign direct investment

Continued rise and increasing diversification of FDI

FDI into the region in 1997 far surpassed previous levels at US$ 17 billion, accounting for roughly 14 per cent of FDI outside the developed market economies. The destination of FDI flows has

[9] Russian media estimates of dollar holdings by the Russian population range between US$ 30-40 billion.

[10] Fries, Raiser and Stern (1998) show that the impact of the East Asian crisis on the region was highly differentiated and initial falls in asset prices and pressures in money markets in central Europe turned out to be temporary in contrast to Russia and Ukraine.

[11] This is corroborated by the experience of the EBRD. Project sponsors in EBRD-financed FDI projects remain committed to their investment plans and new demand has remained healthy. The EBRD has been associated with around 10 per cent of FDI into the region.

[12] Merrill Lynch (1998).

Chart 4.2a

Net private flows to central and eastern Europe and Russia, 1996-99

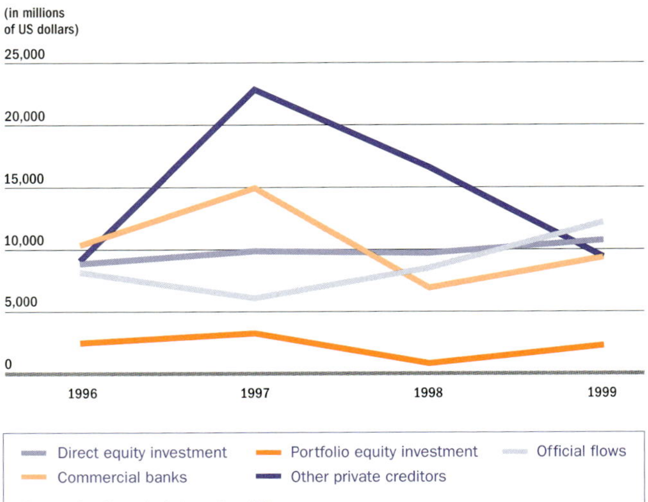

Source: Institute for International Finance.
Note:
Data cover Bulgaria, the Czech Republic, Hungary, Poland and Russia. Figures for 1998-99 are forecasts. Revised forecasts for Romania and the Slovak Republic were not available. The data are not comparable to figures in Table 4.1.

Chart 4.2b

Net capital flows to Russia, 1996-99

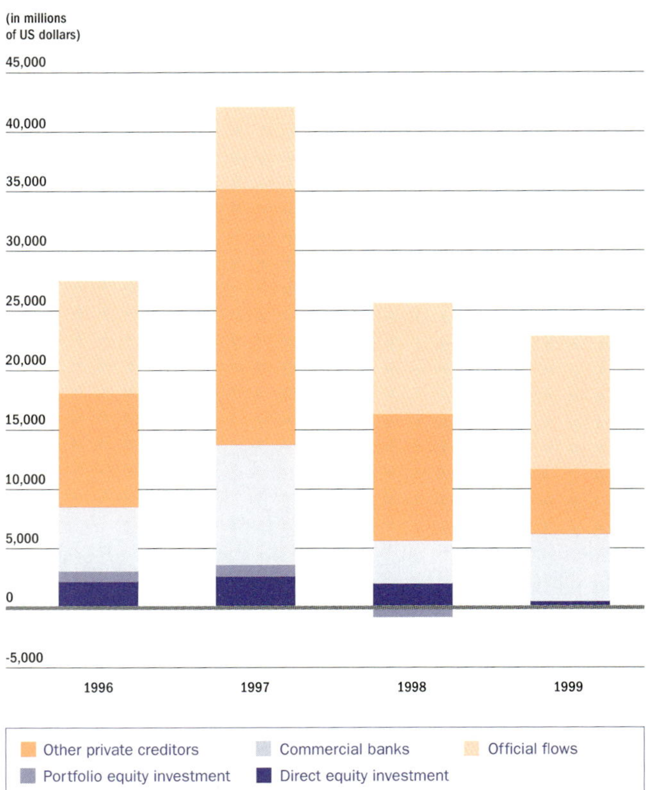

Source: Institute for International Finance.
Note:
Figures for 1998-99 are forecasts.

clearly been diversifying in recent years. Most FDI is still concentrated in a few countries, but whereas Hungary and the Czech Republic were lead destinations in earlier years, Russia and above all Poland dominate at present. Still, flows into Hungary have continued at a strong pace, and a number of countries (e.g. Azerbaijan, Bulgaria and Romania) have recorded significant increases. Net direct equity investments into the region are presented in Table 4.2. Because of the exclusion of intra-company loans and reinvested earnings, these are lower bound estimates (see Box 4.1).

Across the region, privatisation policies have been a significant determinant of trends and fluctuations in FDI flows. For instance, the early start of the Hungarian cash-based privatisation programme largely explains the FDI inflows shortly after the onset of the transition. In the period 1993-95, privatisation proceeds in Hungary accounted for 85 per cent of FDI inflows. In the latter year, FDI inflows into the Czech Republic also experienced a significant increase, driven by the privatisation of SPT Telecom and a large oil refinery (jointly accounting for 60 per cent of inflows in 1995). Despite the privatisation-related increase in FDI in Russia during 1997, foreign investment in the region's largest economy remains modest. For example, at the end of 1997 the total FDI stock in Russia was only half of the sum invested in Hungary between 1989 and 1997.

Data on the sectoral distribution of FDI reveal that manufacturing remains the single largest host sector, accounting for 40-60 per cent of the FDI stock. However, FDI into the service sectors is becoming increasingly important as a result of liberalisation and privatisation in telecommunications and electricity distribution. In some of the more advanced transition countries (the Czech Republic, Estonia, Hungary and Poland), substantial foreign investments are also taking place in financial services. These investments are contributing to increased competition and improved performance of financial systems across the region (see Chapter 7). In Russia and a few other CIS countries with vast natural resources, the primary sector accounts for the largest share of inward FDI.

The European Union continues to account for most FDI flows into the region. In central and eastern Europe and the Baltic states (CEE) it accounted for 64 per cent of all FDI inflows. The dominant position of the European Union (and especially Germany) is only challenged in Russia and some of the other CIS states, where the United States accounted for more than half of all FDI inflows in 1997. Japan accounts for only a very small percentage of the region's FDI stock.

While CEE and the CIS are primarily recipients for inward FDI, the region is also becoming a source of some outward direct investment flows. Although large discrepancies in data exist, one source suggests that annual outflows increased by more than five times in 1997, to an estimated US$ 3.4 billion. Outflows from Russia, which accounts for the bulk of these outward direct investments (US$ 2.0 billion), appear to be motivated partly by the desire of investors to diversify assets as a safeguard against domestic instability. However, in many other transition economies, outward FDI reflects local companies' growing ability to build and rebuild foreign trade and investment links, especially within the region. Transition economies that are registering significant outward FDI flows (Croatia, Estonia, Hungary, Russia and Slovenia) tend to

Table 4.2

Foreign direct investment

(net inflows of equity capital recorded in the balance of payments)

	(in millions of US dollars)							(in US dollars)		
	1993	1994	1995	1996	1997 (revised)	1998 (projection)	Cumulative FDI-inflows 1989-98	Cumulative FDI-inflows 1989-97 per capita	FDI-inflows per capita in 1997	FDI-inflows as % of GDP in 1997
Albania	45	65	89	97	42	95	473	148	13	1.9
Bulgaria	40	105	82	100	497	300	1,222	147	60	4.8
Croatia	77	95	83	509	196	450	1,422	297	41	1.0
Czech Republic	552	749	2,526	1,388	1,275	1,000	8,473	823	124	2.4
Estonia	157	215	199	111	128	200	1,010	695	88	2.7
Hungary	2339	1,097	4,453	1,986	2,100	1,500	16,903	1,667	207	4.6
Latvia	40	238	180	210	347	300	1,358	543	139	6.3
Lithuania	30	31	65	127	218	800	1,271	344	59	2.3
FYR Macedonia	na	24	13	12	30	45	124	59	14	0.9
Poland	580	542	1,134	2,741	3,044	4,000	12,442	321	79	2.2
Romania	97	341	417	263	1,224	900	3,370	149	54	3.5
Slovak Republic	107	236	194	199	51	220	1,223	227	9	0.3
Slovenia	111	128	176	186	321	200	1,274	639	161	1.8
Central and eastern Europe and the Baltic states	*4,175*	*3,866*	*9,610*	*7,928*	*9,473*	*10,010*	*50,566*	*439*	*82*	*2.4*
Armenia	na	3	19	22	51	170	265	72	14	3.1
Azerbaijan	20	22	282	661	1,093	1,155	3,233	425	144	28.4
Belarus	18	11	7	70	190	50	346	34	19	1.4
Georgia	na	8	6	54	189	255	512	95	35	3.6
Kazakhstan	473	635	964	1,137	1,320	1,200	5,729	365	84	5.9
Kyrgyzstan	10	45	96	46	83	29	309	67	18	4.9
Moldova	14	18	73	56	64	100	342	80	15	2.9
Russia	na	539	1,710	1,700	3,752	1,500	9,201	63	25	0.8
Tajikistan	9	12	17	20	11	18	87	15	2	1.0
Turkmenistan	79	103	233	129	108	110	762	162	23	5.9
Ukraine	200	100	400	526	600	700	2,696	53	12	1.2
Uzbekistan	48	73	-24	90	167	60	423	18	7	1.2
Commonwealth of Independent States	*871*	*1,569*	*3,783*	*4,511*	*7,628*	*5,347*	*23,905*	*84*	*27*	*1.3*
Total	**5,046**	**5,435**	**13,393**	**12,439**	**17,101**	**15,357**	**74,471**	**187**	**43**	**1.8**

Sources: IMF, central banks and EBRD estimates.

Note:
For most countries, figures cover only investment in equity capital and in some cases contributions-in-kind. For those countries where net investment into equity capital was not easily available (e.g. Estonia and the Slovak Republic), more recent data include reinvested earnings as well as inter-company debt transactions.

be those economies where inward FDI has been greatest. Rather than making investments via major cash privatisations or into greenfield manufacturing sites, intra-regional foreign investors have typically acquired existing manufacturing plants and have concentrated on building regional supply and distribution networks.

Progress in transition matters for foreign direct investment

FDI exploits long-term economic opportunities in the recipient countries. The economic potential of the region continues to be great, but countries have differed in their willingness and ability to unlock this potential through market-oriented reforms. This is reflected in the regional distribution of FDI. Leaving out the three oil and gas economies of Azerbaijan, Kazakhstan and Turkmenistan, the rank correlation coefficient for 22 countries between the EBRD's average transition indicator in 1997 and cumulative FDI per capita for 1989-97 is 0.89 (it is 0.87 for FDI per capita in 1997 alone). The association between FDI per capita and progress in transition for 25 countries is depicted in Chart 4.3.

This association supports the conclusion that it is the reform process which opens opportunities for profitable investment and which, through its mitigation of risk, motivates investors to take advantage of them. An investment climate conducive to FDI inflows goes beyond macroeconomic stability and the non-discriminatory treatment of foreign investors. FDI requires an ability to exercise corporate governance without arbitrary bureaucratic interference and a transparent and fair regulatory and legal

Box 4.1

Foreign direct investment data

Estimates of FDI flows and stocks into transition economies differ greatly depending on the source and it can be difficult to reconcile these statistics. This box analyses some of these discrepancies.

According to the IMF balance of payments definition, there are three main components to FDI: (i) equity capital – the purchase of shares of the investor in a foreign country; (ii) reinvested earnings; and (iii) capital loans – the borrowing and lending of funds between direct investors and affiliates.

Balance of payments data on FDI may or may not include reinvested earnings and capital loans. In general, most transition economies are recording only the equity capital component of FDI (Table 4.2 reports equity investments only). Sometimes these data are supplemented by estimates of contributions in kind, based on customs data.

Some countries in the region are now beginning to alter the way FDI data are collected. Estonia (since 1992) and Poland (since 1990) have been recording reinvested earnings and inter-company debt. Lithuania started in 1995, Latvia and the Slovak Republic in 1996. The Czech Republic will start recording reinvested earnings in 1999. The table in this box reports completed gross FDI statistics for Estonia and Poland. It shows clearly that equity contributions represent only a share (albeit the largest) of total FDI into these countries. Tax incentives can significantly influence the reporting of FDI as equity contributions or intra-company lending, and the results in the table cannot be extrapolated to the case of other countries. Nonetheless, they highlight the fact that FDI statistics based on equity contributions only, as reported in Table 4.2, are lower bound estimates.

Further distortions limiting the comparability of FDI data across countries are introduced by differences in the minimum equity stake necessary for an investment to qualify as direct investment (rather than portfolio investment). Although in general, direct investment transactions cover investments by an investor that holds 10 per cent or more of the ordinary shares or voting power, there are some exceptions to this rule. For instance, since the beginning of 1996, Estonia has changed this number to 20 per cent. In Slovenia, prior to 1997 all transactions in equity were recorded under direct investment. Beginning in 1997, an equity ownership threshold of at least 50 per cent and investments in shares to be held for more than seven years were introduced for recording direct investment transactions.

Other sources of discrepancies relate to methodology and currency translation adjustments. Whereas some countries use the balance of payments methodology, other countries base their FDI data largely on surveys. Some countries present data based on FDI intentions. Some countries use mid-year exchange rates whereas others use end-year rates; this can make a major difference when inflation rates are high and exchange rate fluctuations are significant. It can thus be difficult to reconcile cross-country statistics.

Gross foreign direct investment inflows

(in US$ millions)

Into Estonia	1993	1994	1995	1996	1997
FDI	163.1	216.9	201.1	151.2	265.8
Equity capital	93.5	145.5	101.4	18.0	97.9
Reinvested earnings	27.7	42.3	15.5	18.0	93.8
Other (loans)	41.9	29.0	84.8	115.2	73.8

Into Poland	1991	1992	1993	1994	1995	1996
FDI	291	678	1,715	1,875	3,659	4,498
Equity capital	216	433	1,109	2,105	1,096	3,159
of which contributions in kind	na	na	na	212	298	314
Reinvested earnings	50	154	199	382	888	244
Other (loans)	25	91	407	397	666	1,098

environment. Moreover, effective markets and sound financial institutions are important elements of a sound investment climate. The case of Bulgaria demonstrates how resolute action to overcome gaps in the reform process can elicit additional growth in investment. Following the financial crisis of 1996 and the subsequent stabilisation and structural reform efforts of the government, in 1997 more FDI was directed towards Bulgaria than in all previous years together.

Additional factors, which are hard to separate from the EBRD's measure of progress in transition, are likely to have played a role in location decisions. These include in particular the proximity (both physical and cultural) of investment locations to Western markets and the prospects for market (and political) integration with the EU. However, these factors are themselves closely associated with the achievements in market-oriented reform; partly because the prospect of accession to the EU has served to stimulate reform commitments, and partly because Association Agreements with the EU have brought early benefits of market access and generous technical assistance.

Foreign direct investment matters for enterprise restructuring

FDI contributes to the transition and economic performance across the region in three major ways. First, FDI may directly increase capital accumulation.[13] Second, it raises the productivity of the enterprise sector and benefits export performance. Third, it generates technological and organisational benefits for domestic suppliers and competitors. More generally, in the context of transition, FDI tends to have a "package" of attributes that can contribute to forming market-oriented institutions and behaviours. It does so through upstream and downstream linkages and demonstration effects. Thus, while a favourable investment climate and progress in transition may attract FDI, the causality also runs the other way.

In some countries, FDI has played an important role in addressing the capital shortage related to low domestic savings and limited financial intermediation. Table 4.2 shows that in 1997 the share of FDI in GDP exceeded 2 per cent in 15 countries. In Azerbaijan

[13] Even in the context of acquisition investments, capital accumulation tends to take place as part of modernisation and restructuring strategies.

and Kazakhstan, FDI into new oilfield developments contributed 90 per cent and 27 per cent respectively to gross fixed capital formation in 1997. Evidence for emerging markets in general indicates that FDI inflows complement rather than substitute for domestic investment – in other words, a dollar's worth of FDI may generate more than a dollar's worth of investment in the economy.[14]

The benefits from FDI are not only derived from its quantity, but also from its quality. One important area is enterprise restructuring and productivity. Foreign investors tend to restructure companies more quickly and, in the process, tend to cut employment more than state-owned or domestically privatised firms. Companies with foreign management also provide more intensive training.[15] Aggregate evidence for the Czech Republic, Hungary, Poland and the Slovak Republic shows that foreign-owned enterprises invest more, operate more capital intensively and have higher labour productivity than the domestic enterprise sector.[16] Foreign-owned enterprises also export more (see Chart 4.4). This benefit of FDI is particularly important in the present context, since it suggests that the significant current account deficits in several transition economies with high FDI inflows may be transitory (see Chapter 3).

Both the management of restructuring processes and training can "spill over" into the domestic enterprise sector and there are some indications that this is actually happening.[17] The presence of foreign investment enterprises affects local firms through greater competition, and through a variety of forward and backward linkages. Especially in monopolised markets (often remnants of the command economy) FDI may have the muscle needed to provide greater competition.[18] Direct backward linkages occur when local firms are employed as suppliers or subcontractors to firms with foreign participation. These relationships can, for instance, force modern standards of product quality and supply reliability upon local producers through their procurement management.[19] In turn such higher standards may spread to other suppliers through demonstration effects. The importance of these backward linkages will, of course, depend on the extent of local sourcing of foreign investment enterprises. One example of strong backward linkages from FDI is that of a foreign investor in the glass sector (with participation of the EBRD), which required the producer of its inputs to upgrade the quality of their products. In this particular case, the local upstream sand producer also serviced other suppliers, and quality improvements induced by the foreign investor thus fed back to other (local) downstream firms.

[14] In an empirical study covering 69 developing countries, Borenszstein, de Gregorio and Lee (1995) find that the inflow of foreign capital does not crowd out but may instead stimulate domestic investment.

[15] For an overview of case studies and enterprise-level data on restructuring in foreign-owned enterprises, see Szanyi (1997).

[16] See Hunya (1997).

[17] See Hunya, (1997) and Mayhew and Orlowski, (1998). For instance, the correlation between the stock of FDI and the growth in labour productivity since 1989 across all transition economies is 0.7, and highly significant.

[18] For instance, in some sectors in Hungary (including electronics) the composition of production has changed significantly following the entry of foreign investors. Market-seeking investments in telecommunications can have strong implications for local market structures.

[19] See Matouschek and Venables (1998).

Chart 4.3

Correlation between FDI inflows in 1997 and progress in transition

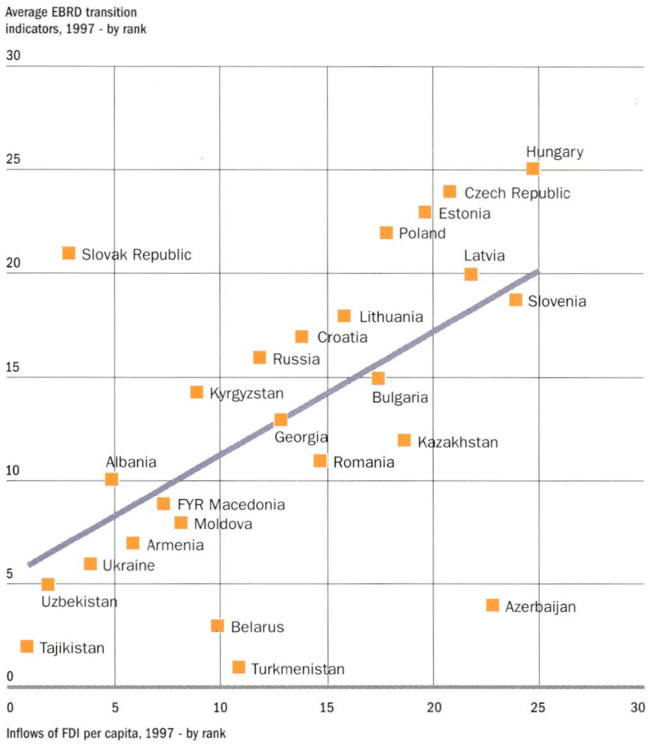

Sources: IMF, central banks and EBRD.

Chart 4.4

Productivity and export performance of foreign enterprises

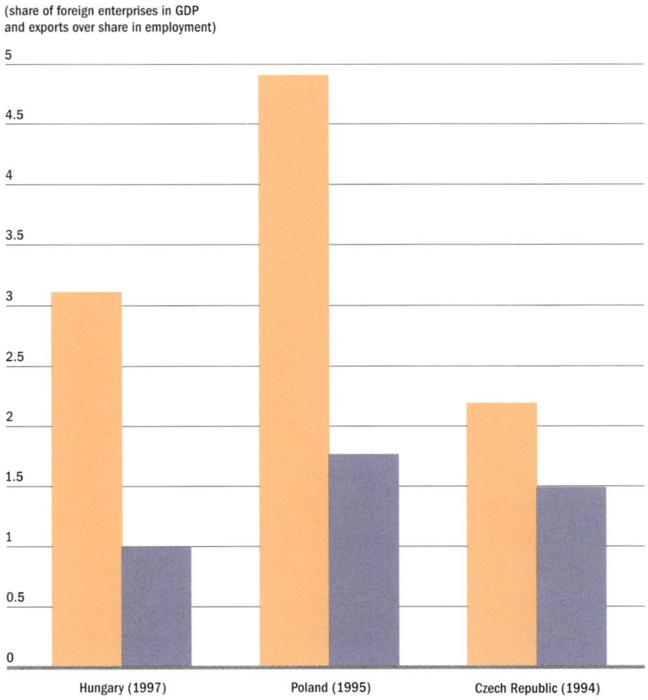

Share of foreign-owned companies in exports normalised by share in employment
Share of foreign-owned companies in GDP normalised by share in employment

Source: Hunya (1997).
Note:
Data for employment in Hungary refer to 1996.

4.3 Commercial bank lending, international bond finance and portfolio investments

Catching up with the transition – non-FDI private capital flows

In addition to foreign direct investment, other types of capital flows into the transition economies have expanded rapidly in recent years, after first emerging in 1993. These include commercial bank lending, international bond issues by governments and corporates from the region, and portfolio investments into the regional equity and money markets. The share of private sector counterparties in non-FDI transactions has continuously increased, and experienced a surge during 1997 and the first half of 1998 – as if to catch up with progress in transition. While private equity issues have remained restricted to the most advanced transition economies, portfolio flows into the government securities markets have characterised a number of countries at less advanced stages in transition.

Charts 4.5a and 4.5b provide a graphic representation of developments in commercial bank lending and international bond issues by sub-region.[20] In both cases, there was a gradual increase in flows over several years followed by a sharp acceleration in 1997. International equity issues picked up somewhat later and experienced a similar surge in 1997. Abstracting from the US$ 430 million issue of American Depository Receipts by Russia's Gazprom, private equity issues remain concentrated on central Europe. In the first half of 1998, transition economies had a strong presence in the bond markets but experienced a slowdown in syndicated loans and equity offers.

During the early transition period, loans to or guaranteed by governments and public bond issues dominated across the region, and the former Soviet Union took a major share in this. Since 1996, however, the number of syndicated loans to private counterparties has exceeded lending to public borrowers and, in the first half of 1998, surpassed public sector loans in volume, too (see Chart 4.6a). Borrowers from Russia were particularly active in this market during 1997. While banks have been very active as borrowers, the market has recently been dominated by the oil and gas sector and Russia's Gazprom in particular. Following a US$ 3 billion syndicated loan in November 1997, Gazprom accounts for more than a fifth of the cumulative total of loan commitments.

Sovereign and other public sector issuers have remained prominent on the international bond markets – with Lithuania, Moldova, Kazakhstan, Russia, the cities of Moscow and St Petersburg, and Ukraine making debut offerings since late 1996. More recently, significant issues have been made by "blue-chip" commercial firms and banks, especially in the advanced countries of central and eastern Europe. In 1997, the number of bond offerings by private issuers actually exceeded that of public issuers, even though the funding volume remained far lower (see Chart 4.6b).

[20] Note that Chart 4.2b excludes hard currency bonds issued by the Russian Federation in exchange for domestic Treasury bills in July 1998. The total value of these bonds was US$ 6.4 billion.

Chart 4.5a

Syndicated loan commitments by sub-region, 1991-98

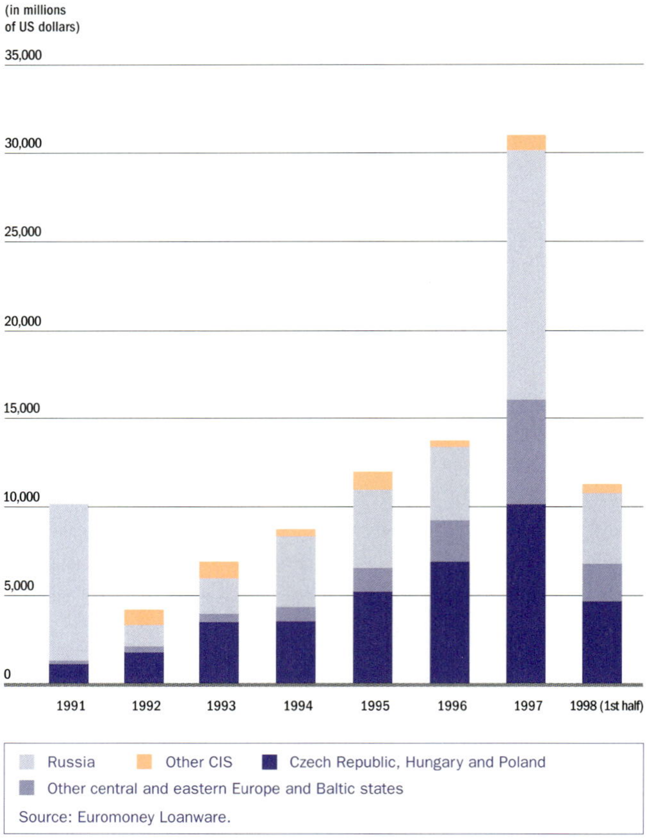

Source: Euromoney Loanware.

Chart 4.5b

International bond issues by sub-region, 1991-98

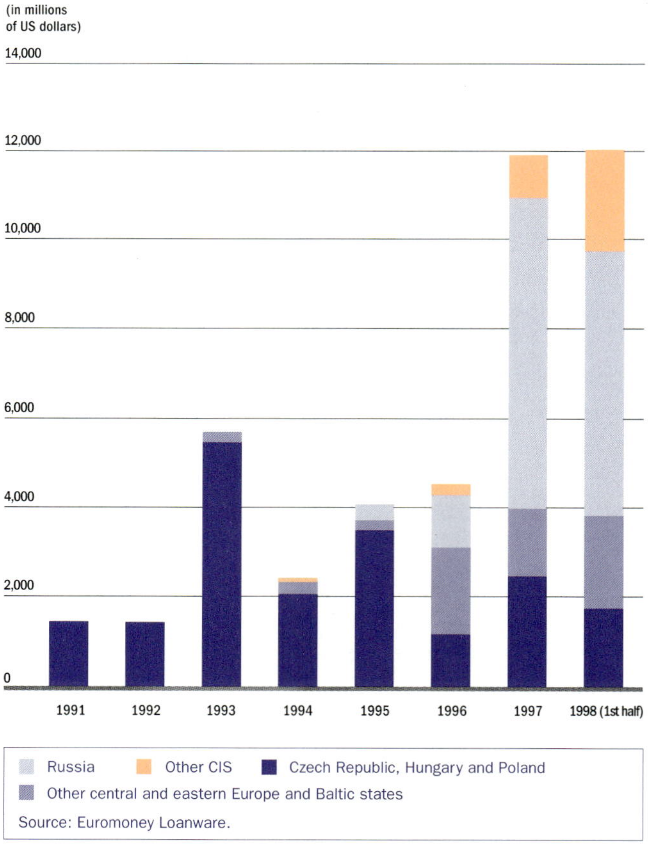

Source: Euromoney Loanware.

While the region as a whole has benefited from increasing capital inflows into its loan, bond and equity markets, the terms of external borrowing have nonetheless remained far more favourable for the more advanced transition economies. For instance, maturities of less than one year have been characteristic of loans to Russia during 1997 and 1998. In the advanced transition economies, in contrast, maturities of 5-10 years have accounted for almost half of the total number of loans in the past two to three years. Moreover, while the rapid fall in bond yields and loan spreads during the first half of 1997 led to a convergence of pricing beyond levels that might have been justified by underlying risk differentials,[21] the East Asian and Russian crises have led to a sharp differentiation in yields across the region.

Lastly, portfolio investments in the local stock and money markets experienced an equally rapid expansion starting around 1995. While portfolio flows were initially significant only in the Czech Republic (mainly in equities) and in Hungary (in government securities), in 1996 and 1997 the list of recipient countries broadened. For instance, Romania, Russia and Ukraine started to attract significant portfolio inflows into their government securities markets. While statistics on portfolio flows into local money markets are not systematically collected, estimates suggest that during 1996 and 1997 foreign investment in short-term domestic government securities may have represented more than a quarter of net private capital flows into the transition economies.[22] The bulk of these investments were made in Russia, where the stock of foreign-held Treasury bills has been estimated at US$ 17 billion (face value). More generally, it is the less advanced countries in transition that have recently relied particularly strongly on portfolio investment inflows (see Chart 4.7).

Chart 4.6a

Syndicated lending by type of borrower in 1991-98

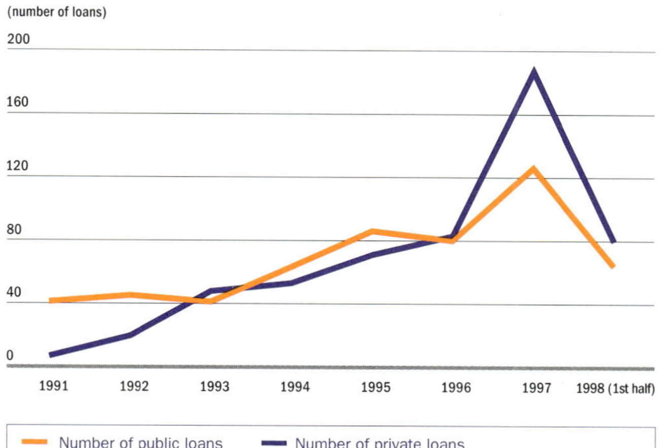

Source: Calculated on the basis of Euromoney Loanware.

Chart 4.6b

International bond issues by type of borrower in 1991-98

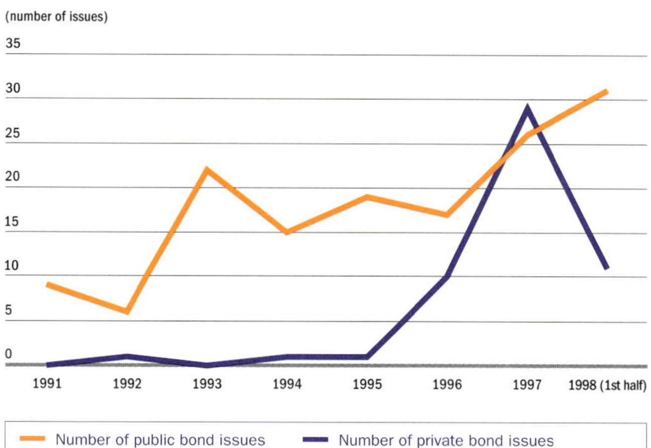

Source: Calculated on the basis of Euromoney Bondware.

Building long-term relationships or exploiting short-term gains – capital flows in the transition

Commercial bank lending can usefully complement FDI in providing access to trade and project finance, transferring financial technologies and exposing private counterparties to financial discipline. International bond issues from the region have presented a means of raising revenues for governments in the context of underdeveloped domestic securities markets, and often at more favourable terms. International equity issues have exposed corporate counterparties across the region to international disclosure and accounting standards and thereby have contributed to improving corporate governance. However, the recent dramatic shift in investor preferences against emerging markets has highlighted the vulnerability of less advanced transition economies, in particular to the volatility of capital flows.

Commercial banks were the main source of external funds for central and eastern Europe and the Soviet Union during the 1980s. During that period, close working relationships were built with foreign trade banks. These relationships survived the uncertainty and debt defaults of the early transition years, though the volume and nature of lending changed. Commercial banks participated in export finance insured by export credit agencies, and provided short-term trade finance collateralised with balances on correspondent accounts. By 1992-93, as trade flows between CEE and western Europe surged, terms on these transactions began to soften for CEE obligor banks. Collateral requirements were gradually replaced by uncovered forms of documentary credit and medium-term refinancing facilities. Project finance developed during that period in the context of FDI projects and syndications with international financial institutions, such as the EBRD. This was assisted by improvements in the legal basis for secured lending.

[21] See Barnes and Cline (1997).

[22] Aggregate net portfolio inflows reported by the *International Financial Statistics* into Bulgaria, the Czech Republic, Hungary, Poland, Romania, Russia and the Slovak Republic equalled US$ 21.1 billion in 1997. Subtracting the US$ 3.4 billion in aggregate portfolio equity flows to these seven countries in Table 4.1 yields an estimate for non-equity portfolio inflows of US$ 17.7 billion. Alternatively, the item "Other private creditors" (which captures residuals) in Table 4.1 may be adjusted by subtracting net flows on bonds, yielding estimates of portfolio investments into government debt markets plus trade credits (another residual) of US$ 9,453 million in 1996 and US$ 16,308 million in 1997.

Chart 4.7

Ratio of net portfolio investment to FDI flows in 1997

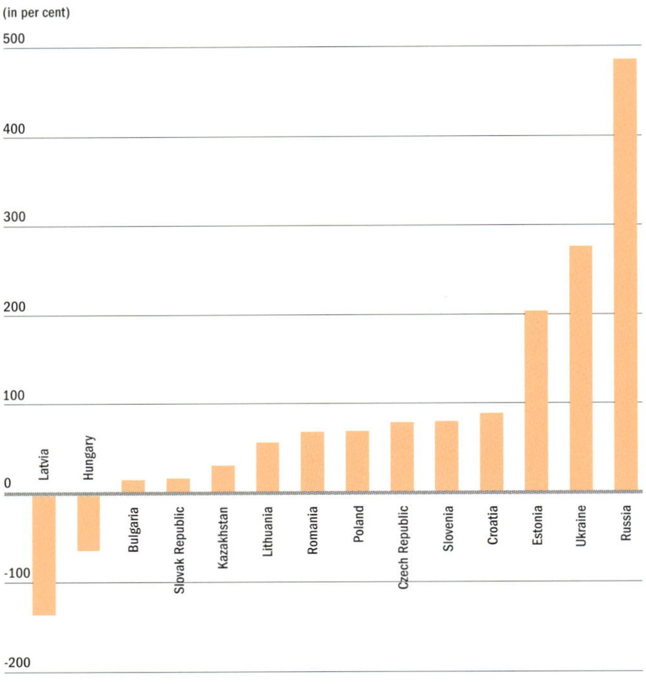

Source: IMF, *International Financial Statistics.*

When commercial bank lending expanded rapidly in 1995-97, it was mostly on the basis of these relationships.[23] In addition, privatisation in many countries moved into a new phase with infrastructure and large enterprises increasingly on offer. Together with FDI, this has vastly increased the opportunities for project finance. Infrastructure financing raised from foreign banks, for instance, grew from US$ 960 million in 1994 to US$ 3 billion in 1995. The sharp increase in competition from other sources of capital inflow during this period led to a very rapid fall in spreads, possibly beyond what was justified by underlying risk. Spreads on foreign borrowing have consequently been adjusted sharply upwards since the Russian crisis.

Apart perhaps from some of the equity funds that have long been operating in the region, the supply of portfolio flows and bond finance have, by their nature, relied far less on direct relationships built over time. As in other markets, they are motivated in part by the well-established benefits of portfolio diversification. However, their rapid growth during 1996-97 has been driven by a combination of macroeconomic tensions in the recipient countries, the "discovery" of the region by international investors, and a period of high liquidity on international capital markets.

Tensions within the macroeconomic policy mix of several countries have been a major source of attraction for short-term portfolio flows. Significant uncovered interest differentials emerged as the result of tight monetary policies and pegged exchange rates, combined with a loose fiscal stance. In Russia, for instance, returns on investments in government securities in mid-1997 averaged 50 per cent in foreign currency terms. Even higher returns were offered in some other CIS economies. As Chart 4.8 demonstrates, the combination of high real domestic interest rates and pegged exchange rates led to extraordinary returns in foreign currency terms on government securities, particularly in the CIS, reflecting significant underlying macroeconomic risks. As noted in Chapter 3, inconsistent macroeconomic policies have often resulted from severe structural imperfections. Thus, for at least part of these flows, it was the absence of transition combined with a reasonably liberal access for foreign investors that made investment attractive.

Macroeconomic tensions have been present in many transition economies for some time. The timing of the expansion in portfolio and bond finance during 1996 and 1997 has thus also to do with the liquid state of international capital markets during that period, as well as with leads and lags in the perception of underlying risk. The region does not have a history of credit ratings, and first formal ratings came for most countries at a time when reform had already progressed. This put these countries "on the map" over the last two years. In 1996-97, first credit assignments by Moody's and/or Standard & Poor's were given to Bulgaria, Croatia, Kazakhstan, Latvia, Lithuania, Moldova, Romania, Russia and the cities of Moscow, St Petersburg and Nizhny Novgorod (see Table 4.3). Partly as a result, international fund managers "discovered" the region, and it is interesting to note how the most aggressive funds moved from one security to the next successively in search of new arbitrage margins (such as from Russia to Ukraine and Bulgaria, or from Russian federal Treasury bills to regional ones). In the case of Russia in particular, moral hazard associated with the notion that Russia was simply too big to fail probably also played a role.

4.4 Maintaining access, containing volatility – some policy options

Maintaining access to the international capital markets will be crucial for the transition economies if they are to finance external imbalances associated with transition and to benefit from technological and organisational spill-overs associated with foreign investments. The most important lesson from the Russian crisis and from previous financial crises in emerging markets is that prudent macroeconomic management supported by vigorous structural reforms is the basis for a healthy integration into the international capital markets. The risks of volatility are highest in countries where the underlying fundamentals are weak. While all transition economies will be temporarily affected by the tightening of international liquidity, long-term rates of return to capital across the region remain undoubtedly high. Unlocking this potential requires the creation of an investment climate favourable to FDI and other long-term flows.

At the same time, capital inflows in the context of incomplete structural reforms carry considerable risks and may indeed magnify underlying macroeconomic and structural weaknesses. First, capital inflows may themselves be a cause of rising external imbalances. If these inflows are used to cover excessive public borrowing or a rapid increase in consumption, rather than laying

[23] For the CIS, bank-to-bank lending has been much slower to develop, in part because most existing relationships of Western banks were with Russia's Vneshekonombank.

Chart 4.8

Foreign currency returns and real domestic returns on money market investments, March 1997

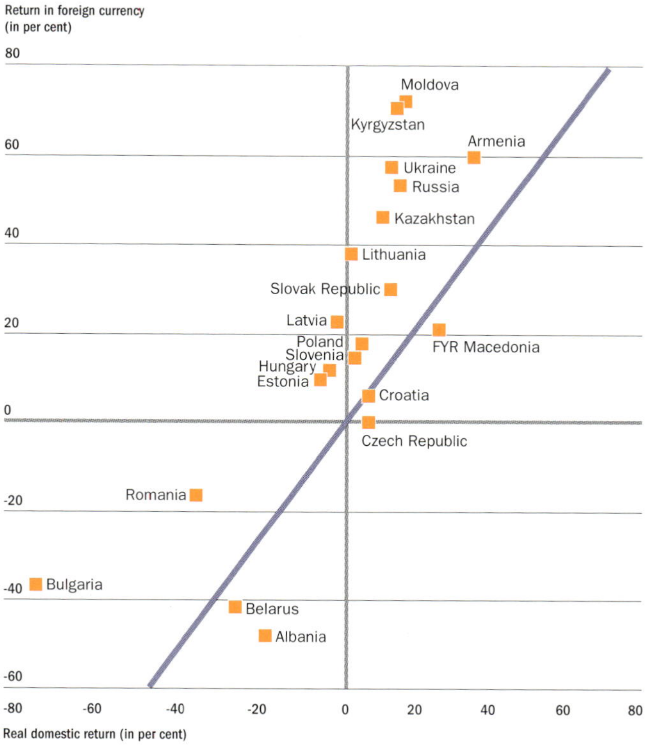

Sources: National central banks, statistical authorities and Bloomberg.
Note:
Foreign currency and real domestic returns were calculated based on Treasury bill yields in March 1997, deflated by the annualised average exchange rate depreciation and consumer price inflation during January-June 1997.

the basis for productivity improvements and future export earnings, they may exacerbate the underlying imbalances and eventually precipitate a loss of investor confidence (see Chapter 3). Second, the financial institutions and markets that intermediate part of these funds are still highly immature in many countries in transition. This heightens the risk of bank failures and associated dangers of volatility in capital flows.

A well-functioning banking system is thus essential to contain the risks of instability and a key factor of an investment climate that attracts long-term foreign investors (see Part II of this *Transition Report*). A related conclusion is the need to develop local sources of long-term finance. Pension reform, when combined with funded pillars and determined financial sector reform, could be an important source of such finance.

Prudent macroeconomic management

A sound macroeconomic policy framework is a central component of a strong investment climate. It includes responsible fiscal, monetary and exchange-rate management. Public sector solvency is a crucial factor in maintaining the confidence of investors, especially in countries where policy-credibility is not yet well-established.

The potential volatility of international capital flows points to the need for a consistent macroeconomic policy mix. Governments cannot hope to address several problems at the same time with the use of a single macroeconomic policy instrument. Monetary stabilisation combined with a nominal exchange rate anchor requires complementary fiscal adjustment to be credible. Simultaneously, banking sector supervision has to be strengthened to prevent domestic banks from running up large open foreign-exchange positions that link the stability of the financial sector to the survival of the nominal exchange-rate anchor. Macroeconomic policy consistency is also essential to mitigate the consequences of excessive capital inflows. In order to reduce the costs of sterilisation, the Polish and Estonian governments, for instance, both significantly tightened fiscal policy to cool down domestic demand and also tightened reserve requirements to rein in the rapid expansion of domestic credit.

In a number of transition economies, macroeconomic policy is complicated by the existence of large structural imbalances, as analysed in Chapters 2 and 3 of this Report. For instance, fiscal deficits are often associated with the implicit subsidisation of loss-making enterprises. Because many of the necessary structural reforms require time, these economies are particularly vulnerable to volatile short-term capital flows. While it will be vital for the region to maintain current account convertibility, a sequencing of capital account liberalisation may therefore need to be considered.

Capital controls[24]

A gradual approach to financial market integration could allow economies at earlier stages of transition to reap some of the benefits of exposure to international capital. The empirical evidence on capital controls suggests that, during the early stages of international financial integration, specific controls on short-term capital inflows have been able to affect temporarily the level and the composition of capital flows.[25] In practice, restrictions on capital flows have taken many forms and have varied greatly in effectiveness.

It is interesting to note that few transition economies have fully liberalised portfolio flows, whereas most lifted restrictions on FDI inflows early in the transition. Most countries have also guaranteed the free repatriation of both profits (current account convertibility) and FDI capital.[26] Treatment of trade credits has also been liberal and in most countries individuals are allowed to hold and operate foreign-exchange accounts at local banks, a privilege that most OECD countries accorded only at the latest stages

[24] The following draws in particular on Temprano-Aroyo and Feldman (1998).

[25] The efficacy of capital controls depends on a large number of factors, such as the size of misalignment motivating inflows and outflows, the types of cross-border flows targeted by the controls, the size of trade flows (determining the scope for under- and over-invoicing as well as for altering leads and lags on trade credit), the structure of the domestic financial system, the state of technology and the efficiency of the controlling bureaucracy (for more detail, see World Bank 1997). In general, domestic residents may be more prepared than foreign residents to evade restrictions, making controls on outflows less effective than controls on inflows.

[26] For detailed country-by-country information on current account convertibility, see the country assessments at the back of this Report.

Table 4.3

Sovereign long-term foreign currency credit ratings

(21 Sept. 1998)

Category	Country	Moody's	Standard & Poor's	Standard & Poor's Outlook	Fitch IBCA
A	Slovenia	A3	A	Stable	A-
A/BBB	Czech Republic	Baa1	A	Stable	BBB+
BBB	Estonia	Baa1	BBB+	na	BBB
	Latvia	Baa2	BBB	Stable	NR
	Hungary	Baa2	BBB-	Positive	BBB
	Poland	Baa3	BBB-	Positive	BBB
	Slovak Republic	Ba1	BB+	Negative	BBB-
	Croatia	Baa3	BBB-	Stable	BBB-
BBB/BB	Lithuania	Ba1	BBB-	Stable	BB+
BB	Kazakhstan	Ba3	BB-	Stable	BB
BB/B	Romania	Ba3	B+	Negative	BB-
	Russia	B3	CCC-	Negative	BB
	Bulgaria	B2	NR	na	NR
	Ukraine	B2	NR	na	NR

Sources: Moody's, Standard & Poor's and Fitch IBCA.

of capital account liberalisation. In general, non-FDI-related transactions remain restricted in many countries, there are tighter controls on outflows than on inflows, and more serious restrictions on short-term than on long-term transactions. Only the Baltic states (and in particular Estonia) opted for a very high degree of capital account openness at the onset of the transition process. Since 1995 there has been a gradual easing of restrictions on capital movements led by the Czech Republic, Hungary and Poland as part of their accession to the OECD.

Table 4.4 provides indices of liberalisation for selected categories of capital flows in CEE. They can take values between 0 and 100, with 100 representing the maximum degree of liberalisation. The evidence in Table 4.4 shows that, within CEE, capital flows have been most liberalised in countries at advanced stages of transition. This part of the region thus conforms to the recommendations of a gradual approach to liberalisation. In contrast, in Russia and Ukraine capital account liberalisation progressed rapidly from the beginning of 1997 against a background of weak fiscal and financial positions, and the results have been destabilising.

While this evidence supports those arguing for a cautious stance on capital account liberalisation, capital controls are not easy to enforce. In addition to the difficulties in recording and monitoring capital account transactions, relying on administrative controls also creates incentive problems, particularly in countries where government officials may have vested interests in maintaining access to budget financing from abroad. A lesson from the Russian crisis may thus be that tax-based mechanisms to stabilise capital flows should be further explored by the transition economies.

4.5 Conclusion

Cross-border capital flows support the transition in many ways. The region's economic opportunities and potential as a location for production and as a growing market remain large. This chapter shows that foreign investment, FDI as well as bank lending, bond finance and portfolio equity flows, is helping to develop these opportunities in many transition economies. However, investors will commit themselves in a lasting way only if they encounter a sound investment climate, including stable macroeconomic conditions, and reliable and non-distortionary government policies. Foreign investors are increasingly appreciating the region's growth potential, as evidenced by the acceleration of capital inflows over the past two years – however, it is up to governments to unlock this potential through their economic policies.

Foreign direct investment, after some temporary hesitancy, is likely to grow further, although political stability in Russia and the medium-term performance of world financial markets are clearly key to this forecast. The prospects for other capital flows are more difficult to judge. The rapid acceleration of the last two to three years is unlikely to be maintained, since it was in part due to a one-off adjustment in perceptions. After the Russian crisis, flows are likely to contract and become far more selective. Countries with sound fundamentals will continue to have access to the international financial markets, if at a higher price. Countries with a "reform deficit" may not be able to access the markets, even at high prices, for some time to come.

Subject to continued advance in the transition, and greater security of their assets through the legal and administrative system, investors will be looking particularly closely at fiscal policies. In much of the region, monetary policies have led the way in restoring macroeconomic stability resulting in, at times, extraordinarily high real rates of interest. If the macroeconomic position is to be secured, the fiscal position must be put on a sound long-term basis. As on most dimensions of the transition, improving policy on the fiscal front requires not only careful attention to building institutions, but also promoting and enforcing responsible behaviour both inside and outside government.

Given that the fiscal and structural reforms underpinning improvements in the investment climate may take time to become fully effective, in the short run some of the less advanced transition

Table 4.4

Indices of capital account liberalisation in central and eastern Europe and the Baltic states[1]

(position as of December 1997)

	Albania	Bosnia and Herzegovina	Bulgaria	Croatia	Czech Republic	Estonia	FYR Macedonia	Hungary	Latvia	Lithuania	Poland	Romania	Slovak Republic	Slovenia
Controls on direct investment[2]	66.7	33.3	66.7	83.3	100.0	100.0	66.7	100.0	100.0	83.3	100.0	83.3	83.3	83.3
Controls on real estate investment	75.0	0.0	50.0	0.0	50.0	75.0	0.0	75.0	75.0	50.0	50.0	0.0	50.0	50.0
Controls on credit operations[3]	0.0	50.0	37.5	83.3	62.5	100.0	37.5	75.0	100.0	62.5	75.0	0.0	50.0	37.5
Controls on portfolio flows	0.0	0.0	25.0	35.0	70.0	100.0	0.0	33.3	100.0	100.0	35.0	0.0	0.0	25.0
Overall index of liberalisation of the capital account	16.7	17.6	35.3	44.4	73.7	97.6	23.3	59.5	97.6	85.7	55.3	12.5	23.7	40.5

Source: Temprano-Arroyo and Feldman (1998).

1 The index can take values between 0 and 100, with 100 representing the maximum degree of liberalisation of capital flows under consideration. The index for a given country is constructed by adding up the values contained in each category of capital flows and dividing the total by the maximum possible score. Flows not subject to controls are assigned a value of 2; flows classified as being subject to partial controls are assigned a value of 1; flows subject to serious controls are given a value of 0. When information on a given capital transaction is not available, a value of 0 was assigned to both the numerator and the denominator.

2 With the exception of sectors normally considered sensitive or of strategic national interest.

3 Borrowed or extended by residents other than banks.

economies should consider carefully when to lift restrictions on capital flows. In particular, tax-based mechanisms to discourage excessive short-term capital flows may provide a useful policy tool to contain volatility. However, such measures are no substitute for structural reforms that encourage the mobilisation and more effective utilisation of domestic resources.

References

K. Barnes and W. Cline (1997), *Spreads and Risk in Emerging Markets Lending*, Institute of International Finance Research Papers, No. 97-1.

E. Borensztein, J. de Gregorio and J.-W. Lee (1995), *How does foreign direct investment affect economic growth?*, NBER Working Paper, 5057.

A.S. Bulatov (1998), "Russian direct investment abroad: main motivations in the post-Soviet period", *Transnational Corporations*, 7, 1.

A. Elteto, P. Gispir and M. Sass (1995), *Foreign direct investment in east central Europe in comparative analysis with Spain and Portugal*, IWE HAS Working Paper, No. 51.

S. Fries, M. Raiser and N. Stern (1998), *Macroeconomic and financial stability: transition and East Asian contagion*, EBRD Working Paper, No. 28.

G. Hunya (1997), "Large privatisation, restructuring and foreign direct investment", in Z. Salvatore (Ed.), *Lessons from the economic transition: central and eastern Europe in the 1990s*, Kluwer Academic Publishers, London.

N. Matouschek and A.J. Venables (1998a), *Evaluating investment projects in the presence of sectoral linkages: theory and application to transition economies*, unpublished manuscript.

N. Matouschek and A.J. Venables (1998b), *Evaluating investment projects in the presence of sectoral linkages: case studies*, unpublished manuscript.

A. Mayhew and W.M. Orlowski (1998), *The impact of EU accession on enterprise adaptation and institutional development in the EU-associated countries in central and eastern Europe*, study done for the EBRD.

Merrill Lynch (1998), *Convergence not Contagion*, monthly report.

M. Szanyi (1997), *The role of foreign direct investments in restructuring and modernisation of transition economies: an overview of literature on Hungary*, unpublished manuscript.

H. Temprano-Arroyo and R.A. Feldman (1998), *Selected Transition and Mediterranean Countries: An Institutional Primer on EMU and EU Relations*, IMF Working Paper, No. 82, June 1998.

UNCTAD (1998), *World Investment Report*.

World Bank (1997), *The Road to Financial Integration – Private Capital Flows to Developing Countries*, World Bank, Washington DC.

Financial sector in transition

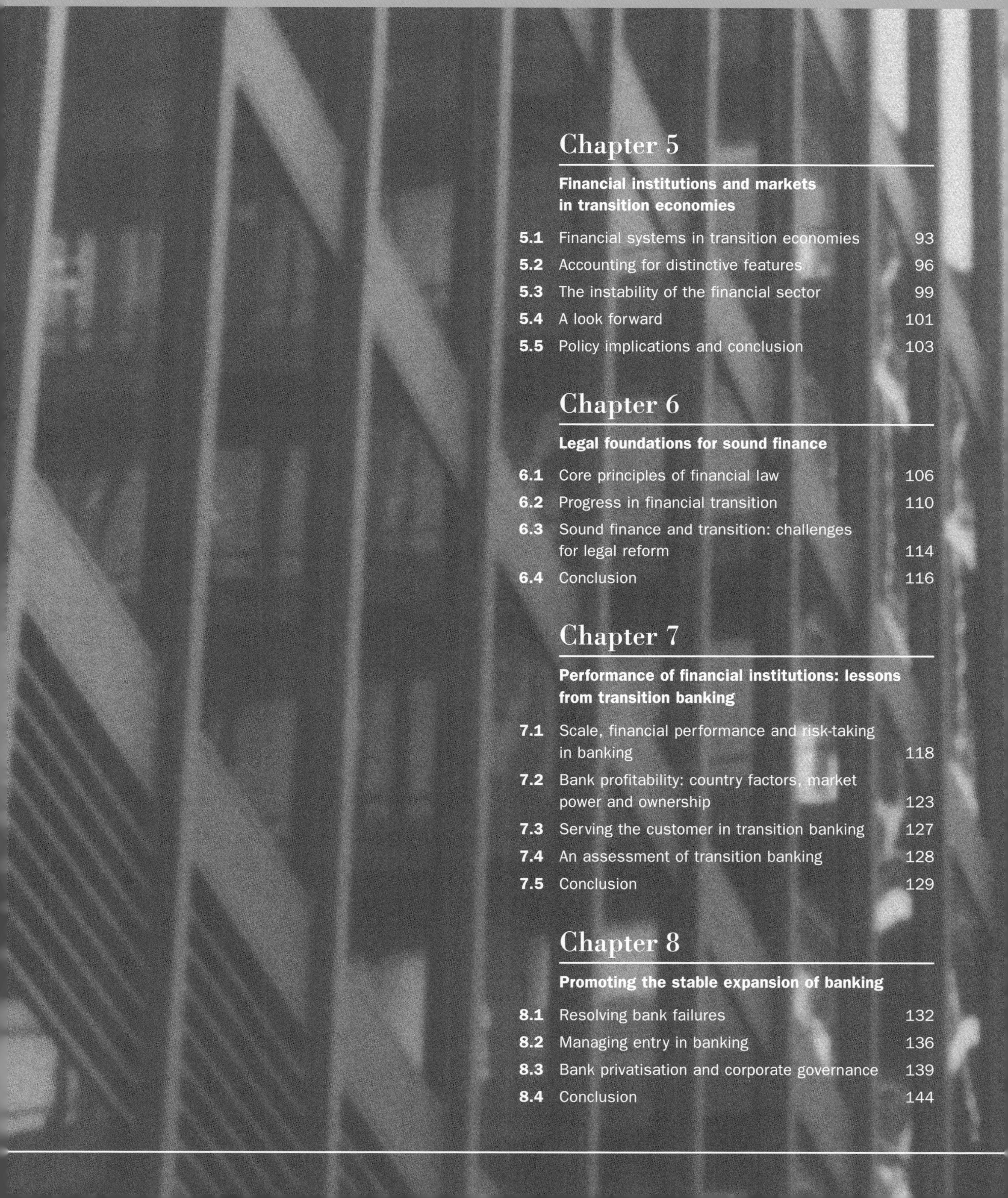

Chapter 5

Financial institutions and markets in transition economies

Chapter 6

Legal foundations for sound finance

Chapter 7

Performance of financial institutions: lessons from transition banking

Chapter 8

Promoting the stable expansion of banking

Financial institutions and markets in transition economies

5

Building a sound market-oriented financial system is fundamental to the transition from a command to a market economy. Financial institutions and markets play a central role in the allocation of resources in all market economies, intermediating between savers who seek safe and remunerative repositories for their funds and entrepreneurs seeking external finance for investment projects. They rank projects by risk and return, monitor the uses to which borrowed funds are put, and sanction managers who fail to maximise shareholder value. In so doing, they help to establish hard budget constraints on enterprises. Financial institutions, banks in particular, also provide ways of making monetary payments that substantially lower the cost of market transactions. The efficiency with which financial markets and institutions carry out these tasks is a crucial determinant of economic performance.

The transition economies inherited few of the relevant financial institutions and markets from the era of central planning, such as commercially oriented banks and insurance companies, pension and investment funds, and securities markets. Under planning, the financial system was little more than a bookkeeping mechanism for tabulating the authorities' decisions about the resources to be allocated to different enterprises and sectors. Securities markets were absent, since the authorities created no marketable financial instruments. So-called mono-banks simply created and distributed bookkeeping claims to finance, tracking whatever activities were mandated by the plan. Since there was no demand for banks to carry out the tasks of financial intermediaries, they developed little capacity to do so. And there was no need for the prudential regulation and supervision of financial activities beyond that inherent in the direct control of these accounting activities by government. The problem for the transition economies was thus to create a functioning financial system where none had existed before.

In doing so, they were encumbered by an inheritance of state banks that inevitably formed the foundation of the nascent financial system. The portfolios of these banks were dominated by non-performing loans, and their personnel possessed few of the capabilities expected of financiers in market economies. Building a functioning financial system around the vestige of the old institutions is an understandably difficult task. At the same time, the state inherited little capacity from central planning to regulate effectively a decentralised banking system.

Given the problems of restructuring the banking sector, it might have been tempting to seek to short-circuit the process of its restructuring by building a financial system centred on securities markets instead. But such thoughts would have been unrealistic. Banks were already in place. In addition, banks have played a dominant role among financial institutions in the early stages of development in virtually all market economies: the legal and institutional prerequisites for efficiently functioning securities markets are more demanding, and historically such markets have been relatively late to develop. In any case, the formerly planned economies lacked the preconditions for the development of active and efficient securities markets, such as prudential regulations and company and investor-protection laws. Lastly, there was the fact of proximity to Germany and the rest of western Europe, where financial systems are based largely on banks. In these universal banking systems, banks not only make commercial loans but also invest in equities and other securities. They consequently provide the bulk of finance to enterprises and dominate the financial sectors.

Developing vibrant financial sectors in transition economies was inevitably going to be a long and difficult up-hill climb, and, as the first decade of transition draws to a close, it is possible to see how much of the hill has been scaled. The evidence provided in this chapter reveals that not only is banking stunted relative to the situation in other emerging market economies at comparable stages of development but securities markets are even more severely underdeveloped. In part this reflects unfavourable conditions at the start of the transition and in part different policy choices along the way. For example, the degree of macroeconomic instability at the start of the transition continues to have a significant influence on the scale of banking, while advances in large-scale privatisation in some countries have provided a boost to securities activities.

To meet the challenge of building stable market-oriented financial systems in transition economies, it will be necessary to develop the skills and practices both in financial institutions and markets, which will take considerable time. In addition to this process of learning-by-doing, several factors are likely to shape the further expansion of finance. These include the legacies not just of central planning but also of the early decisions in transition, the ways that alternative forms of finance combine to enhance overall efficiency, and the ongoing changes in information technology that serve to increase the scope for securities activities. But to support the expansion of finance, government must put into place the kind of prudential regulations and supervision, disclosure and reporting requirements, auditing and accounting, and corporate governance practices that promote development of active and efficient banks and securities markets (see Chapter 6). Building robust financial systems will also require real competition among prudent and well-managed financial institutions, together with their private ownership and effective corporate governance. These issues are taken up in Chapters 7 and 8.

The remainder of this chapter is organised as follows. Section 5.1 compares the financial systems of transition economies with those of market economies at comparable stages of development. The second section accounts for the distinctive features of the financial sectors of transition economies by examining how both the legacies from central planning and early decisions in the transition

Chart 5.1

Ratio of domestic credit provided by banks to GDP by countries' level of per capita income, 1996

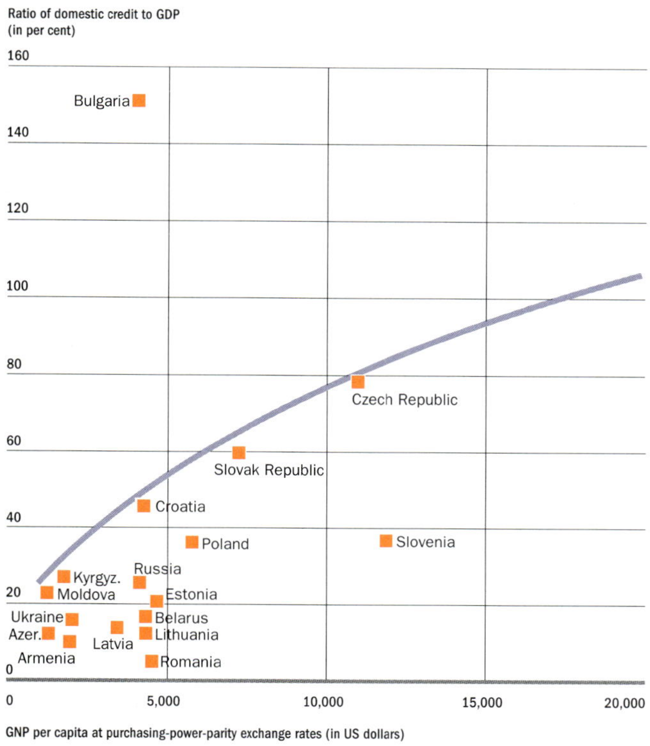

Sources: IMF, *International Financial Statistics*, and World Bank, *World Development Indicators*.

Note:

Domestic credit is credit provided by the banking system to the public sector and to the non-financial private sector.

have shaped the development of finance. Section 5.3 argues that the costs of financial instability will increase as the financial sectors expand and that prudential regulations must keep in step with market developments. The fourth section identifies three factors that are likely to shape the further expansion of finance in transition economies: history, technology, and interdependence of alternative forms of finance. Section 5.5 concludes the chapter by drawing out the implications for economic policy.

5.1 Financial systems in transition economies

The single most important fact about financial systems in transition economies is that they have less depth and breadth than those of market economies at comparable levels of development (where development is measured, for simplicity, by per capita GNP).[1] This section provides a comparative perspective on banking and securities activities in transition economies.

The banking sector

Chart 5.1 shows the ratio of domestic credit provided by banks to GDP for countries at different levels of development, where the solid line is the average relationship for 120 countries world-wide, excluding the transition economies with which this chapter is directly concerned.[2] Lending by banks is a measure of their activity that captures some of the vital services they provide to the real economy, particularly in the allocation of credit.[3] Virtually all the transition economies lie below the line which depicts the relationship between economic development and the expansion of banking in market economies. This shows that banking sectors in transition economies are unusually shallow.[4]

Charts 5.2a and 5.2b suggest that it is mainly the private sector that suffers from the underdevelopment of banking – it is credit to the private sector, not credit to the public sector, that is undersupplied. Governments have been able to use financial institutions as their quasi-fiscal agents, and intermediaries have invested disproportionately in government bonds in countries where property rights are poorly defined and corporate finance lacks transparency. The charts also point to significant differences within the region, with private sector credit less available in the CIS than in central and eastern Europe and the Baltic states.

Not only are the scale of bank lending and advances to the private sector at a lower level than those in comparable market economies, but spreads between deposit and lending rates are higher, often dramatically so (see Chart 5.3). In part this reflects macroeconomic instability and high inflation and in part inefficiencies and market power in transition banking. Notable exceptions are the Czech Republic, Estonia, Lithuania, Poland and the Slovak Republic, which are relatively stable economies at more advanced stages of transition and with some degree of access to foreign sources of finance. The high interest rate spreads, especially in CIS countries and Bulgaria, allow banks to maintain the real value of their capital in the midst of high inflations. However, the spreads also reflect the consequences of large government financing requirements crowding out private investment. Chapter 7 examines in greater detail the factors that influence interest rate spreads in transition economies.

Entry by foreign banks, together with the extent and maturity structure of foreign lending, provides an indicator of whether countries have succeeded in establishing safe, transparent and enforceable rules and regulations for financial markets. Foreign ownership and entry also presuppose the existence of private banks or considerable bank privatisation, since otherwise foreign institutions are unable to invest in local banks and are not enthusiastic about competing with domestic banks that enjoy public

1 Note that these differences would be even more pronounced if the measure for economic development were to include indices such as human capital (see *Transition Report* 1997, Chapter 6).

2 The relationship is calculated by regressing the domestic credit ratio on per capita income and per capita income squared. The database is all countries included in the World Bank's *World Development Indicators* database. All comparisons in this chapter use per capita GNP in international US dollars at purchasing power parity for 1996, as calculated by the World Bank. Additional regressors, such as average inflation for 1990-96 and an index of the effectiveness of the legal system, were also tried, but they were almost always insignificant and their inclusion had little impact on the co-efficients on per capita income.

3 The ratio of M2/GDP is an alternative measure of banking activity that captures the role of banks in mobilising savings. An analysis of this ratio for transition economies would confirm the conclusion drawn from Chart 5.1. By this measure as well, depth of banking is unusually shallow in all transition economies aside from Bulgaria, Croatia and the Czech Republic.

4 The one transition economy that has an unusually large banking sector is Bulgaria. However, this observation simply reflects the extreme monetary dis-equilibrium that prevailed in Bulgaria in 1996. Following the outburst of inflation in early 1997, the ratio of domestic credit to GDP fell to 30%.

Chart 5.2a

Ratio of bank credit to the private sector to GDP by countries' level of per capita income, 1996

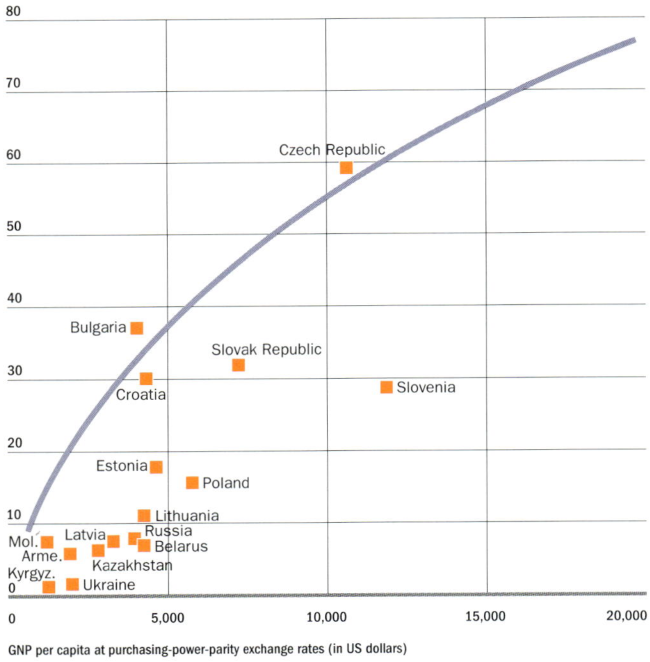

Fitted line for market economies ■ Transition economies

Sources: IMF, *International Financial Statistics*, and World Bank, *World Development Indicators*.

Chart 5.2b

Ratio of bank credit to the public sector to GDP by countries' level of per capita income, 1996

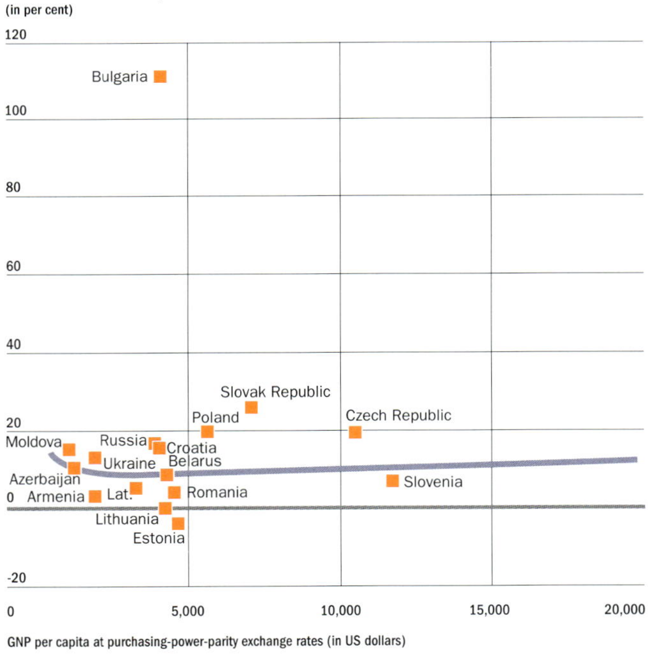

Fitted line for market economies ■ Transition economies

Sources: IMF, *International Financial Statistics*, and World Bank, *World Development Indicators*.

subsidies. Foreign participation as measured by the share of foreign-owned banks in the total assets of the banking system is unusually low in the transition economies (see Chart 5.4). Two countries where foreign participation has reached significant levels are Latvia and Hungary, which have made considerable progress in bank privatisation. In Latvia, both Nordic and Russian banks have gained a significant presence. Hungary, which has long had the most liberal policy towards foreign bank entry of any east European country, has attracted foreign banks from many advanced economies.[5]

Development of securities markets

Regarding securities markets, two measures for comparing the size and activity levels of equity markets across countries are market capitalisation and the value of market turnover. Market capitalisation provides a measure of the capacity of securities to provide finance to the real economy, while turnover is a measure of liquidity of the securities. To reflect the fact that securities markets are a relatively recent phenomenon not only in the transition economies but also in other emerging market economies, a group of emerging market economies serves as the reference group for the transition economies.[6]

Compared with this reference group, the stock market capitalisation in the transition economies remains low (see Chart 5.5).[7] Even the Czech Republic, with the most highly capitalised stock market in the region, has only about half the capitalisation typical for a market economy with its level of per capita income. The pattern of market capitalisation over time in transition economies is also considerably lower than in other emerging markets. Explanations for this include the short time during which these markets have been operating (and correspondingly low levels of public awareness and confidence), inadequacies in the legislative and regulatory framework for disclosure by enterprises issuing securities and the low level of privatisations of large-scale enterprises through public offerings in transition economies compared with other emerging market economies.

Even though stock-market capitalisation is uniformly low across the region, turnover has been high in the Czech Republic, Hungary, Poland and Slovenia (see Chart 5.6). Turnover has been relatively high in Poland since the creation of the securities exchange, reflecting the existence of a particularly strong regulatory framework. In the Czech Republic, in contrast, turnover has risen recently, stimulated by the amendment of the commercial code requiring the disclosure of substantial minority stakes and creating an independent securities and exchange commission. The pattern of stock-market turnover over time in transition economies reveals the importance of privatisation programmes and a subse-

5 Already in 1992, 21 joint-venture banks with some foreign participation were operating in Hungary. See Caprio and Levine (1994).

6 As in the analysis of banking, the solid lines in Charts 5.5 and 5.6 represent the relationship between measures of stock market performance and GNP per capita for 38 emerging market economies as calculated by simple non-linear regressions. This statistical relationship excludes the transition economies themselves, which are the focus of the analysis and are plotted individually.

7 The analysis of securities markets in transition economies focuses on stock markets. There are relatively few corporate bonds in transition economies, although some countries do have relatively well-developed markets for government securities.

Chart 5.3

Spread between bank loan and deposit rates by countries' level of per capita income, 1996

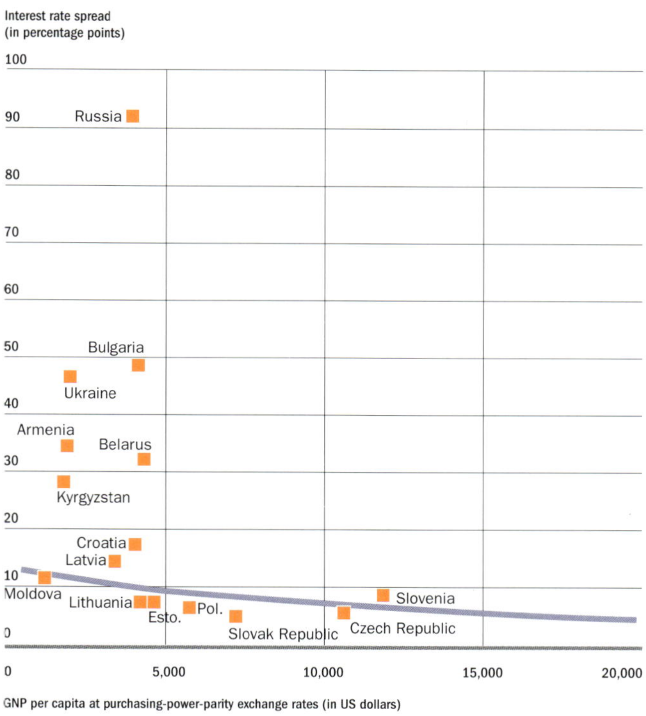

Fitted line for market economies ■ Transition economies

Sources: IMF, *International Financial Statistics*, and World Bank, *World Development Indicators*.

Chart 5.4

Share of foreign-owned banks in total bank assets by countries' level of per capita income, 1996

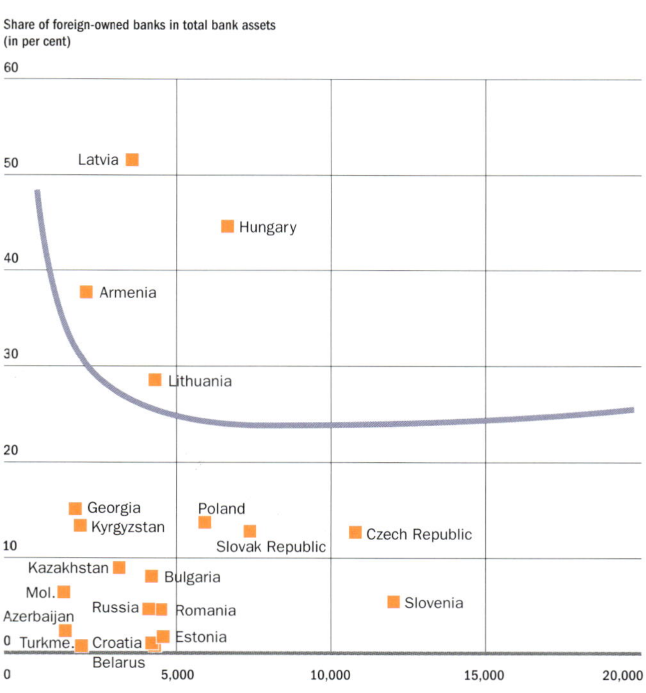

Fitted line for market economies ■ Transition economies

Sources: BankScope, central banks and World Bank, *World Development Indicators*.

quent phase of consolidation in the stock markets, as discussed in Section 5.2 below. In addition, there was sustained growth in stock-market activity in 1996-97 in a number of other countries, such as Estonia and Russia, accompanied by rapid run-ups in equity prices. The collapse of prices in the second half of 1997 and 1998 following the outbreak of the East Asian crisis has been associated with some fall in turnover, confirming that not all this progress was sustainable. The overall picture remains one of relatively low levels of activity in the region's equity markets.

Not only are stock markets relatively small by international standards, but most transition economies have virtually no corporate bond market.[8] And where bond markets exist, the value of short-term bonds relative to long-term issues is unusually high compared with other emerging markets.

Access to international capital markets

International capital flows are the main subject of Chapter 4. However, no discussion of financial intermediation in transition economies would be complete without considering briefly cross-border bank lending and foreign investment in domestic bond and equity markets.

For the Czech Republic and Hungary, where cross-border lending by foreign banks accounts for between 3 to 6 per cent of GDP, its contribution to the mobilisation of resources for capital formation is significant, equivalent to between 10 and 30 per cent of domestic credit provided by local banks.[9] Elsewhere in the region, where economic conditions have been less attractive to foreign banks, the quantitative importance of their lending is considerably less.

Loans by foreign commercial banks have been directed at the banking sector, the non-bank private sector and the public sector in proportions that differ markedly across recipient countries. To a large extent, the split among these recipients of foreign bank lending appears to depend on the state of macroeconomic stabilisation in the recipient country. In economies that were relatively early to stabilise, and where stabilisation has been accomplished without heavy reliance on bond financing of large budget deficits, foreign bank loans are increasingly directed towards the non-bank private sector, reaching fully half of the total in Hungary and Poland, and somewhat less in the Czech Republic.[10] These countries are also at the more advanced stages of transition, suggesting that foreign banks are more willing to lend directly to the local commercial sector where the transition is more advanced. In countries where enduring stabilisation has been slower in coming, and large budget deficits are still present after inflation has been brought down (Russia and Ukraine, for example), the government's financing needs have remained large, and the public sector is still the recipient of the vast majority of foreign bank lending. This same contrast is evident in the maturity structure of foreign bank lending; short-term loans are prevalent throughout the region, but they especially predominate in Romania, Russia and Ukraine.

8 For an analysis of domestic short-term and long-term bond markets in selected transition and developing economies, see World Bank (1998).

9 Claims of domestic financial intermediaries, excluding the monetary authorities, are typically in the range of 20% to 30% of GDP.

10 Based on data from the Bank for International Settlements.

Chart 5.5

Ratio of stock-market capitalisation to GDP by countries' level of per capita income, 1996

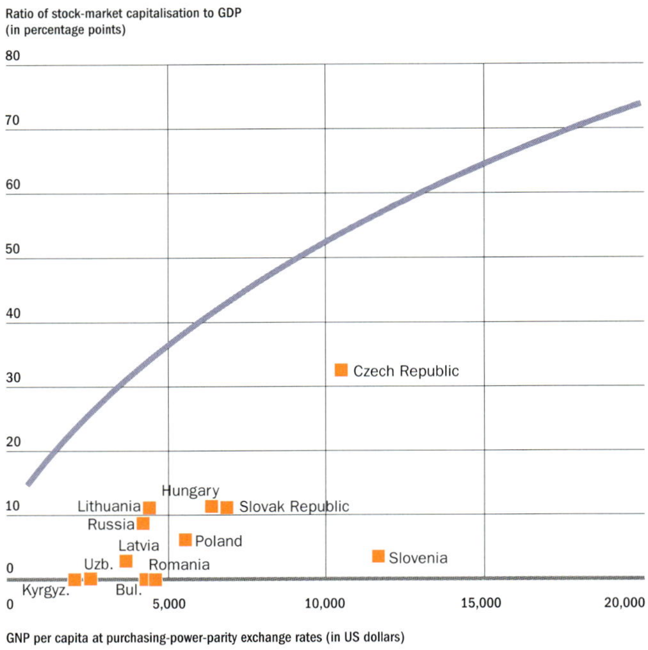

Sources: International Finance Corporation, *Emerging Stock Markets* Database, and World Bank, *World Development Indicators*.

Chart 5.6

Ratio of stock-market turnover to market capitalisation by countries' level of per capita income, 1996

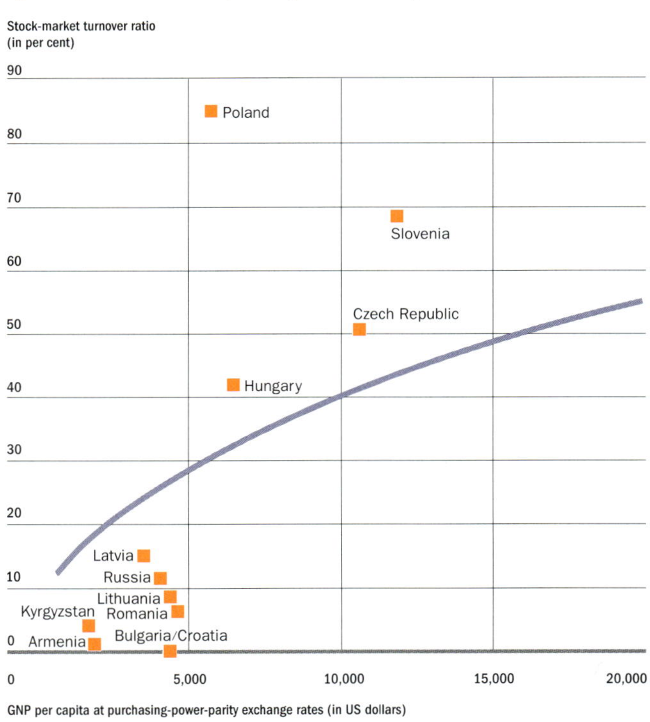

Sources: International Finance Corporation, *Emerging Stock Markets* Database, and World Bank, *World Development Indicators*.

Portfolio capital inflows into bond and equity markets have generally been smaller than foreign bank lending (and smaller than inward direct foreign investment).[11] However, some countries, such as Russia and Ukraine, have experienced large portfolio flows into government securities issued to finance intractable fiscal deficits. These speculative inflows have been attracted by very high yields associated with weak stabilisation efforts. Available evidence suggests that portfolio flows into equities has gained in relative importance over time, particularly once macroeconomic stabilisation appears to be sustainable.[12]

Summary

In summary, both bank and securities-based intermediation are relatively underdeveloped in the transition economies compared with market economies at comparable levels of per capita GNP. The data indicate that while bank credit is undersupplied, stock and bond markets are even more underdeveloped: the ratio of bank credit to securities market capitalisation is higher in the transition economies than in other emerging markets at comparable levels of per capita GNP. Thus, in cultivating active securities markets typical of countries at their stages of economic development, the transition economies have a long way to go – even further than in banking.

5.2 Accounting for distinctive features

Distinguishing features of the financial systems in transition economies are the legacies of central planning and the policies of the early transition. Of particular significance to the development of banking and securities activities as the transition advances are privatisation, macroeconomic stabilisation and the regulatory environment.

Pre-transition reform and its consequences

Historically, planned economies with their mono-bank systems drew no distinction between the central bank and a second tier of banks engaged in commercial activities. There was no two-tier banking system because there was no scope for independent commercial-bank activities. However, a few communist countries partially reformed their financial systems in the 1980s. The steps they took had important implications for subsequent developments.

In the Soviet Union, banking was one of the first economic activities to be liberalised and reformed under *perestroika*. Joint ventures and semi-private cooperative banks were allowed to be formed as early as 1987. The number of banks mushroomed in the final years of the Soviet empire. Thus, after the dissolution of the Soviet Union, virtually all of its successor states found themselves with an unusually large number of banks by the standards of market economies. This number continued to grow during the first years of transition (see Chapter 2), reflecting the tendency for non-financial enterprises to set up their own in-house banks and the

[11] Exceptions such as Bulgaria in 1997 are generally associated with extraordinary events, such as recent inflation stabilisation causing the reversal of capital flight. Note that bond portfolio investment here refers almost exclusively to investment into government securities, because the corporate bond market in transition economies is still largely absent (see Rühl 1998).

[12] An exception is the Czech Republic, where there was a spurt of foreign purchases of domestic equities starting in 1993, coincident with the country's voucher privatisation.

low capital requirements, which did little to deter entry. In Kazakhstan, for example, a country with 16 million inhabitants and a per capita income of US$ 1,300, the number of banks rose from 30 in 1990 to 204 in 1993 before consolidation set in. While the number of banks declined to 76 by the middle of 1998, this was still considerably above what one would expect in a comparably sized market economy. Across the region, most new banks were small, some were of dubious quality, and many were founded to support a single enterprise. Closely related to "strategic" enterprises and often in cross-ownership relations with them, some of these new banks ended up at the heart of the new financial-industrial groups that characterise parts of the industrial structure in the CIS today. Others were wiped out as soon as capital requirements were strengthened and effective regulations enforced.

In contrast to the former Soviet Union's entry-friendly, "bottom-up" approach to financial reform, central and east European countries reformed their financial systems "top down", limiting entry as state-owned commercial banks were spun-off from the mono-bank system, restructured and eventually prepared for privatisation. The length of this process varies from country to country. The mono-bank system had been abolished or significantly weakened prior to 1989 not just in the Soviet Union but also in the former Yugoslavia, Hungary and Poland. This early start allowed some of these countries to privatise at least some state banks relatively early in the transition and to allow relatively free foreign participation compared with other parts of eastern Europe. The former Czechoslovakia gave priority to macroeconomic stabilisation and enterprise privatisation rather than bank privatisation and regulation, which proceeded more slowly. In Bulgaria and Romania, significant attention was focused on banking reform only after instability was perceived as a systemic risk in the middle to late 1990s. Thus, different starting points largely dictated the pace of development of banking systems.

Central and east European countries that restructured their banks quickly as a result of the limited reforms of the 1980s also succeeded in strengthening prudential supervision and regulation. In addition, countries that are relatively advanced in terms of transition (as captured by the EBRD's transition indicators – see Chapter 2) tend also to have the edge with respect to measures of the quality of banking regulation and to display greater banking-sector growth.

Where the banking sector lags, however, there is no obvious tendency for securitised finance to substitute for it. From all appearances, the two segments of the financial system seem to grow in step with each other. Countries that have succeeded in developing well-regulated banking systems have also established relatively active security markets. Banking and securities activities may also serve to complement and reinforce, rather than substitute for, one another. Thus, the historical starting point and the policies adopted prior to comprehensive market reforms provide a significant explanation for the speed with which both viable commercial banking and securities activities were established.

The role of economic policy in transition

The growth of both components of the financial sector is also influenced by policy choices made during the transition itself. Important determinants of the development of financial institutions and markets are the scope of privatisation, the effectiveness of macroeconomic stabilisation and the implementation of a well-functioning regulatory framework.

Privatisation and equity markets

It would be reasonable to expect the development of stock markets to be driven by the extent and the method of privatisation, since this is the market for ownership claims to private companies. To this straightforward relationship, Chart 5.7 shows that stock-market turnover over time has been affected even more strongly than stock-market capitalisation by the timing and method of privatisation. Between 1992 and 1995, the period of most intense privatisation, turnover typically overshot the levels characteristic of other emerging markets. The explanation for this unsustainable surge of stock-market activity lies in the structure of privatisation in many transition economies. Most mass privatisation programmes were not carried out through initial public offerings on the stock market. Rather, they were accomplished by voucher privatisations like those in the former Czechoslovakia and in Russia. This method of privatisation implied low initial asset valuations, which translated into low market capitalisation. Shares were given to households at a fraction of their true costs.[13] This "give-away" stage of privatisation was then followed by the consolidation of new ownership structures, partly through the operation of newly established equity markets, generating unusually high rates of turnover relative to market capitalisation. Following the period of consolidation, the turnover on these stock markets declined. The approach taken to privatisation in the region thus helps to explain the rise and fall in stock-market turnover in the mid-1990s.

The strong link between privatisation and stock-market development is confirmed by Chart 5.8, which shows the relationship between stock-market capitalisation and the EBRD transition indicator for large-scale privatisation. The chart shows that market capitalisation tends to increase with the extent of privatisation; the turnover ratio is heavily influenced by the design of privatisation, with mass privatisation requiring more subsequent adjustment in ownership structures than sales to strategic investors, initial public offerings or other methods of case-by-case privatisations. Thus, the extent and method of privatisation strongly influence the size of securities markets across transition economies and their activity levels over time.

[13] This tendency was more pronounced in cases where "mass" privatisation took place with a large portion of assets distributed quickly, whether to insiders or not, and less so in cases where it took place at a slower pace with greater reliance on case-by-case sales, strategic investment and initial public offerings. The fact that market turnover is higher in Slovenia and Poland (69% and 85% of GDP respectively) than in the Czech Republic or Russia (50% and 11% respectively, all 1996), despite the latter's earlier implementation of comprehensive privatisation programmes, reflects this history. The low initial evaluation of, say, Russian industry at privatisation auctions is well known. Boycko, Shleifer and Vishny (1995), for example, calculated an aggregate value of Russian industry based on voucher auctions of under US$ 12 billion – less than that of most Fortune 500 companies in the United States.

Chart 5.7

Ratio of stock-market turnover to market capitalisation in emerging market economies and transition economies, 1991-96

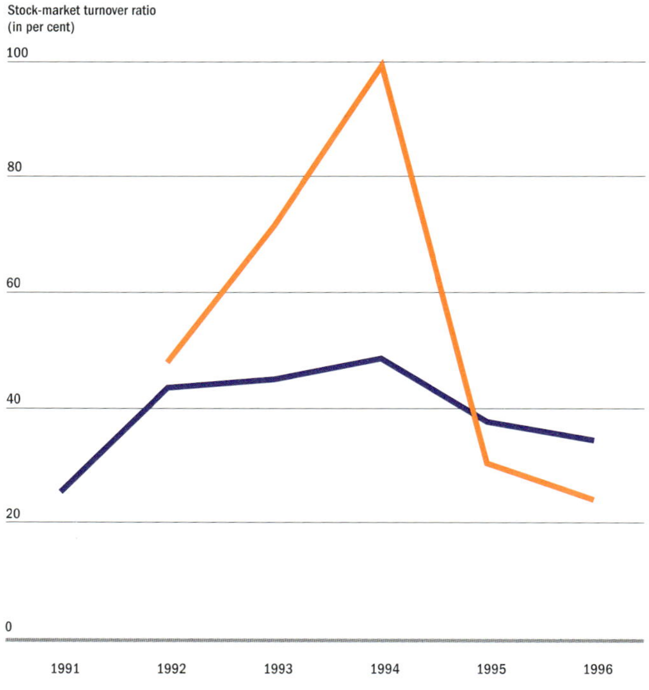

Source: International Finance Corporation, *Emerging Stock Markets* Database.

Chart 5.8

Ratio of stock-market capitalisation to GDP in transition economies by countries' progress in large-scale privatisation, 1996

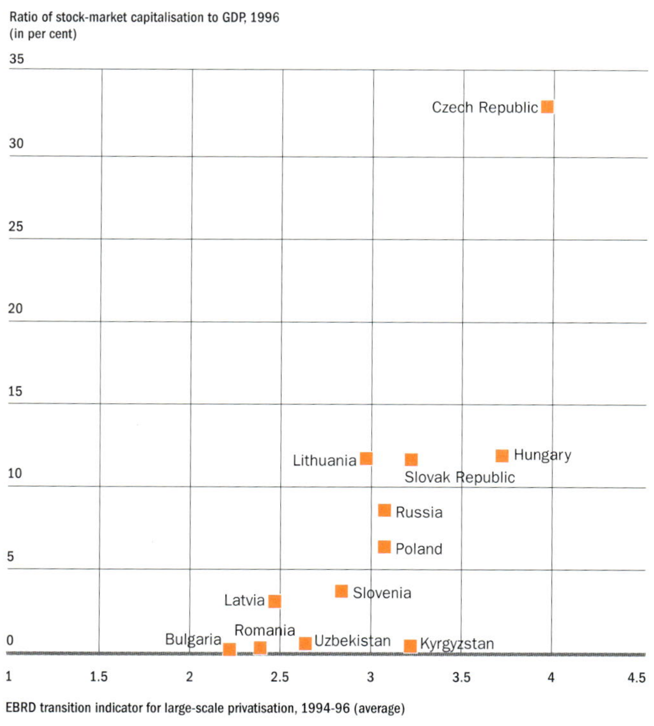

Sources: EBRD, *Transition Reports*, and International Finance Corporation, *Emerging Stock Markets* Database.

Macroeconomic stabilisation and the banking sector

Stabilisation policies have a significant effect on the environment in which banks perform their deposit taking and lending operations. High inflation distorts the ability of both borrowers and lenders to perform the financial calculations necessary to carry out long-term transactions. In particular, rapid inflation typically brings with it highly variable relative prices and increased uncertainty about the financial returns to economic activity. Reducing rapid inflation, moreover, often requires high real interest rates and is associated with output declines. For these reasons, an unstable macroeconomic environment is detrimental to the development of commercial banking.[14]

All transition economies went through a period of high inflation followed by a stabilisation in prices, at least on a temporary basis. In other respects, however, they differed. In most central and east European countries, the decline in output was arrested relatively early, inflation remained under control, and output grew briskly. Real interest rates, as a result, have settled to levels considered normal by international standards. Members of the second group, consisting mainly of CIS countries such as Russia and Ukraine, took longer to stabilise; although inflation remained low until recently, they have not succeeded in reversing the decline in output. Stabilisation was accompanied by persistent budget deficits, the associated high yields on government bonds and high real interest rates. Lastly, there is a third group, including Bulgaria and Romania, where output recovered but then collapsed again and where that collapse has been associated with a resurgence of inflation.

Among transition economies, those with higher average rates of inflation have had slower rates of growth of credit to the private sector (see Chart 5.9). This relationship suggests that inflation not only discourages the development of credit relations but also stunts the growth of the banks in charge of facilitating them. Moreover, inflation has had an adverse impact on the development of securities markets. In other words, while retarding the development of the banking sector, inflation did not induce the significant substitution from bank to non-bank intermediation.

The post-stabilisation environment was particularly difficult for enterprises in transition economies partly because of the very high level of real interest rates. Where stabilisation was not sustained, this reflected the failure to bring down government budget deficits. Banks responded by investing in government securities. The consequences are apparent in declining claims of deposit money banks on the private sector, crowding out the emerging private sector as finance at reasonable rates ceased to become available. Not surprisingly, this development is particularly pronounced in the CIS, where this post-stabilisation problem is most severe.

Monetary stabilisation with high fiscal deficits and real interest rates, moreover, did nothing to shelter the development of nascent equity markets. If anything, available data indicate that the oppo-

[14] Credit relationships are affected more than most, with uncertainty about future prices drastically shortening contractual agreements. Thus, for example, even during the modest US inflation in the 1970s, the market for 30-year mortgages and Treasury bonds all but disappeared. See Heymann and Leijonhufvud (1995).

site is true: where stabilisation resulted in a prolonged period of high interest rates and stagnant economic growth, the development of securities markets was stunted even more than bank-based intermediation. As governments turned from the inflation tax to wholesale issues of government paper and yields on the latter tended to rise, banks could protect their business by curtailing their lending to the private sector in order to invest in government bonds. Comparable yields were also unavailable on the equity markets, and levels of capitalisation as well as turnover suffered as a result.

Similar to high inflation, monetary stabilisation associated with sizeable fiscal deficits thus impedes private financial sector activities in two ways: by curtailing bank lending to the private sector, and by taking resources away from and preventing higher activity levels in the equity markets.

Role of prudential regulation

The development of deeper financial systems depends significantly on the effectiveness of regulatory and institutional reform. Chart 5.10 illustrates the close relationship by comparing the EBRD's transition indicators for banking reform with a measure of the extent of bank intermediation in transition economies. These relationships confirm the link between both segments of the financial sector and the scope and effectiveness of legal and regulatory reform. Thus, the growth of banking and security markets both seem to depend crucially on the effectiveness of institution building and legal reform. And over time, the expansion of financial activity will create yet further demand for more effective legal and regulatory frameworks.

Summary

No single factor explains the development of banking and securities activities in the transition economies. Clearly, the initial conditions at the start of transition were important, with the partial reforms in the last days of planning giving some countries a significant head start. But the policies that followed – for example, the approach taken to privatisation, and the timing and durability of stabilisation as well as the success of efforts to establish an effective legal and regulatory framework – were important as well. Understanding the development of financial systems thus means tracing the interaction of inherited circumstances with subsequent policies.

5.3 The instability of the financial sector

With time and the right policies, financial systems in transition economies will deepen, become more competitive and resemble more closely financial systems in other countries at comparable stages of economic development. This does not mean that they will become more stable. Financial instability and banking crises in particular have been endemic in developing and industrialised market economies, particularly over the past three decades with the widespread liberalisation of financial activity. Financial development is no guarantee against them.

Chart 5.9

Bank lending to the private sector in transition economies by countries' average inflation, 1996

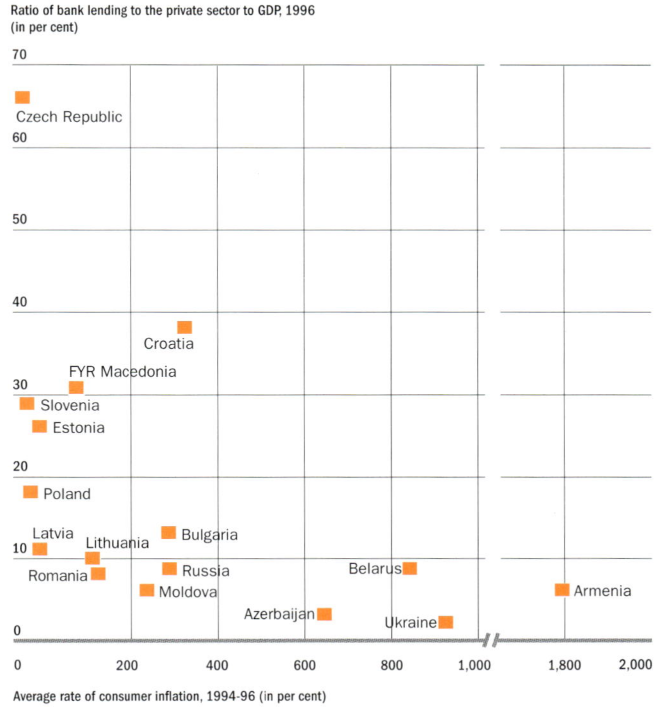

Sources: EBRD, *Transition Reports*, and IMF, *International Financial Statistics*.

Chart 5.10

Bank claims in the private sector in transition economies by countries' progress in banking reform, 1996

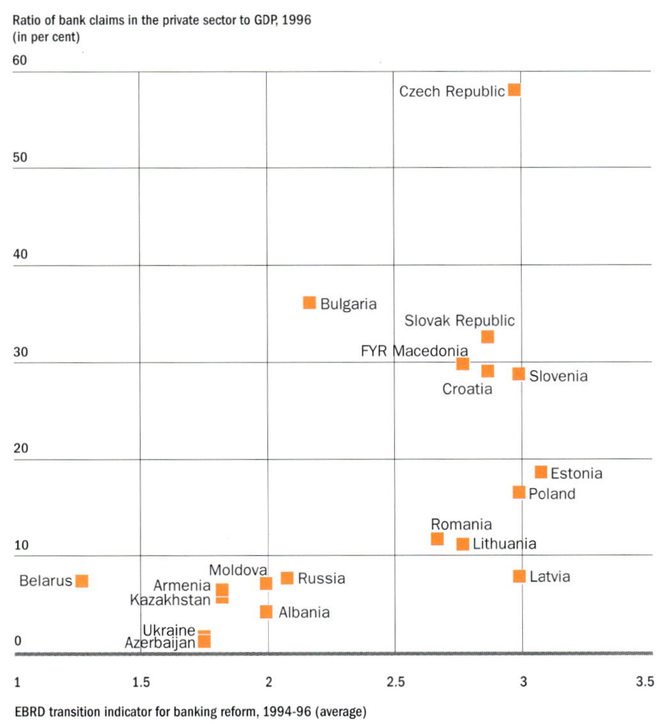

Sources: EBRD, *Transition Reports*, and IMF, *International Financial Statistics*.

Banking crises, in which a large number of banks or a number of large banks fail, have already occurred in the region. They have been prevalent in countries at relatively advanced stages of transition, where the financial environment has been liberalised but the regulatory framework has not been developed sufficiently to contain the additional risks. They have also occurred in countries where macroeconomic stabilisations have failed. A banking crisis was experienced by Estonia in 1992 and by Latvia and Lithuania in 1995. The Czech Republic saw the failure of several medium-sized and large local banks in 1996, and Bulgaria experienced a full-fledged banking crisis that same year. In Estonia, insolvent banks accounted for more than 40 per cent of the assets of the financial system. In Latvia, more than one-third of the total number of banks, accounting for 40 per cent of total bank assets, were suspended. These included Bank Baltija, which prior to its suspension was the repository of 30 per cent of bank deposits in the country. Following interventions in two smaller banks, the Lithuanian Central Bank suspended the operations of the country's two largest banks.[15] In Bulgaria's banking panic, more than a third of all banks were placed under administrative control or entered bankruptcy proceedings. The current crisis in Russia has engulfed much of the banking system.

Yet banking crises in the transition economies have not always produced the very severe real-side disruptions typical of other countries. Available research has shown that a banking crisis in an emerging market economy typically depresses growth by 1 percentage point in the year of the crisis and by 3 percentage points in the following year, before recovery sets in.[16] In contrast, the Czech Republic, Latvia and Lithuania continued growing at about the same pace as other transition economies during their banking crises in 1995-96. The Estonian economy contracted during the 1992-93 banking crisis, but output actually fell by less than in other transition economies. But the picture is very different in Bulgaria, where output contracted by 17 per cent in 1996-97, while growth was positive and accelerating in the other transition economies.[17]

The differences between transition economies and other emerging markets reflect in part the relative underdevelopment of financial intermediation in the former. As long as financial institutions and formal financial markets are underdeveloped, non-financial firms depend on financial intermediaries only to a limited extent. This leaves them less vulnerable to disruption by turbulence in financial markets. But as credit markets deepen and external finance grows in importance, the effects of banking crises are likely to become more severe. This contrast between transition economies and other emerging markets thus suggests that the impact of the unfolding banking crisis in Russia may have a less damaging impact on its real economy than have the recent crises in East Asia.

As financial development and deepening continue, it will become even more important for countries in transition to guard against banking crises. Historically, banking crises around the world have tended to occur when financial markets were recently liberalised but supervision and regulation were not upgraded to cope with new risks.[18] There is a propensity for banks with weak balance sheets to take on excessive risks because the shareholders and managers of the bank would not necessarily bear the full consequences of any losses. That risk is particularly great when the capital account is open and inter-bank borrowing is unrestrained, permitting risk-seeking banks to fund themselves externally and lever their bets. In addition, opening the capital account increases the sensitivity of revenues and funding costs to interest rates abroad. Not surprisingly, several recent studies have identified increases in foreign interest rates as a leading indicator of banking crises.[19]

These lessons indicate how important it is for transition economies to upgrade supervision and regulation as domestic financial markets develop and the capital account is opened. Prudential regulations need to be strongest where the financial safety net, in the form of explicit or implicit government guarantees and lender-of-last-resort facility, provides an incentive for banks to take on additional risk. Where guarantees are extended, regulators should consider raising capital requirements and tightening limits on open positions to offset the guarantee-related incentive for excessive bank-to-bank lending. Lastly, regulators should require adherence to internationally accepted auditing and accounting standards and mandate disclosure of banks' financial condition as ways of strengthening market discipline.

A related regulatory issue is whether supervisors should limit banks' involvement in securities markets to contain excessive risk taking. The argument for allowing banks to hold equity stakes in non-financial firms is that transition economies need concentrated shareholders to provide the corporate governance that would otherwise be unavailable as a result of the wide disbursal of securities holdings and that banks can play this important role. The argument against is that the banking system can be destabilised by sharp stock-price decline. In fact, looking across countries and over time, there is no strong association between universal banking and the stability of the financial system. When the macroeconomy is stable and financial markets are well regulated, allowing banks to branch into the securities business and to hold corporate securities as collateral poses no threat to financial stability. But when these conditions are not present, there is an argument for limiting banks' involvement in securities markets to prevent stock-market corrections and crashes from spilling over to the banking system and destabilising the real economy.[20]

[15] More extensive lists of bank failures and systemic banking crises have been enumerated. See, for example, Bank Austria (1998).

[16] These estimates are derived by comparing output growth in the year of (and the years following) the crisis with that in developing countries not experiencing crises. See Eichengreen and Rose (1998).

[17] This is not to imply that the cost of bank recapitalisation has been low. On the contrary, Bank Austria (1998) estimates that costs of recapitalisation have been as high as 10% of GNP in Hungary and 15% of GNP in Bulgaria.

[18] This summarises the findings of Demirgüç-Kunt and Detragiache (1997) and Eichengreen and Rose (1998).

[19] See Gavin and Hausmann (1995) and Eichengreen and Rose (1998).

[20] This idea that universal banking can pose problems when regulation is poorly structured or enforced is emphasised by Kaufman (1994).

Finally, careful consideration must be given to early liberalisation of the capital account. As Section 5.1 showed, cross-border bank lending significantly supplements domestic bank intermediation in some transition economies and foreign investors can make a significant contribution to activity on domestic stock and bond markets. Because of the large investment needs in the real economy and of the low rates of domestic savings, there is a strong argument for capital account liberalisation to permit capital to be imported from abroad.

At the same time, recent experience, not only in East Asia, has demonstrated the dangers of opening the capital account before the banking system has been well capitalised and supervision and regulation have been upgraded. Where banks are undercapitalised and poorly regulated, they will be prone to excessive risk taking. And where they receive government guarantees against failure, foreign investors will fund them freely in response to their offer of high interest rates. In these circumstances, opening the capital account will allow domestic banks to lever up their bets, amplifying pre-existing distortions in the pattern of lending. The implication is that the capital account should be fully opened only after recapitalisation has taken place and supervision and regulation have been strengthened. To the extent that implicit guarantees cannot be eliminated (because, among other things, banks are a key component of the payments system), particular caution should be exercised in opening the capital account to banks' borrowing from abroad.

The recent financial crisis in Russia further reinforces the point. Some Russian banks took large open foreign exchange positions, in part by writing forward foreign exchange contracts for foreign portfolio investors in the Russian Treasury bill market. Many of the contracts were inadequately hedged by Russian banks with counterparties of poor credit risk or unhedged altogether. These practices were largely unchecked by prudential regulation and supervision. The heavy reliance on these contracts by sophisticated foreign investors, such as international investment banks and hedge funds, suggests either that they failed to perform adequate credit-risk assessments of Russian banks or that they assumed that these banks benefited from implicit official support.

5.4 A look forward

This section asks whether finance in the transition economies is likely to remain as heavily bank-based in the future as it has been to date. There are at least three factors that are likely to shape the expansion of finance in transition economies: history, changing technology and interdependence among various forms of finance. Understanding how these influences will operate and interact, however, first requires a thorough understanding of the role of banks and securities markets in a mature financial system.

Banks versus markets

The experiences of industrialised market countries provide only limited guidance as to the kind of financial systems that transition economies can expect to develop. The ratio of stock-market capitalisation to the claims of banks on the private sector varies widely across OECD countries. It is relatively high in Canada, the United Kingdom and the United States and relatively low in Austria and Germany. There is no single representative pattern or financial system.

Economic analysis provides some guidance as to why. Markets tend to provide for an efficient allocation of resources when information about the goods or services being exchanged is widely available and reliable, when entry into the market by alternative providers is free, and when the exchange is not dependent upon an ongoing relationship between buyer and seller. Assuming that these pre-conditions are met, a securities market, like any other market, can deliver an efficient allocation of resources.

In reality, of course, these pre-conditions are difficult to satisfy. Perhaps most importantly in financial activities, reliable information about potential borrowers and issuers of securities can be difficult to obtain, creating the potential for them to mis-represent their financial conditions and prospects and to undermine the operation of markets.[21] This potential failure of markets creates the scope for financial institutions to take some of the financial activities "out of the market". Banks can be thought of in these terms – as providing an alternative to decentralised securities markets. These institutions gather information on behalf of their depositors, evaluating alternative investment opportunities and monitoring how funds are used once investments are made. They can surmount problems of imperfect information by investing in skills, practices and technologies that reduce these information barriers to sound finance. By developing long-term relationships with their customers, they can also mitigate the problem of reneging on financial obligations that would otherwise discourage the flow of finance.

These advantages do not come for free. Because they have proprietary knowledge and their balance sheets are less than transparent, creditors will find it difficult to distinguish good banks from bad banks, creating the possibility of contagious losses of confidence and depositor runs. In response to this problem, regulators not only provide a financial safety net, but also limit banks' activities to prevent their managers from taking on additional risk in response.

History

The structure of finance is heavily influenced by initial conditions.[22] In places where banks dominated financial markets in the past, evidence suggests that they will continue to do so in the future. Similarly, where securities markets have played the dominant role, they will continue to do so.

There are several reasons why a particular financial structure might become "locked in". One reason is that the cost of doing business in a certain way declines as others engage in the same business practices. If most borrowers and lenders transact through securities markets, for example, those markets will be deep, broad and liquid, encouraging others to use them as well and crowding

[21] See, for example, Jensen and Meckling (1976), Stiglitz and Weiss (1981) and Myers and Majluf (1984).

[22] See, for example, Soskice (1996) and Eichengreen (1996).

out bank intermediation. However, where banks do most of the business, lack of liquidity will hinder the development of securities markets. Where banks have previously captured the most reliable customers, the problem is that unreliable issuers will come to the securities market. Investors will find it difficult to distinguish between good and bad issuers, preventing a significant volume of securities activity from taking place.

Another reason why an initial financial structure can become locked in is the political power of the incumbents. Both banks and securities markets require a supportive regulatory environment, which needs to be provided by the political process.[23] Markets require an information environment supported by disclosure requirements for enterprises issuing publicly traded securities and by adherence to minimally acceptable auditing and accounting standards. They require investor protection laws to discourage insider trading and price manipulation. They require strong property rights for minority shareholders.[24] Banks, whose assets are illiquid and which are vulnerable to the contagious loss of confidence, require a financial safety net in the form of deposit guarantees and lender-of-last-resort facility. In return for their provision, they are subjected to prudential regulations designed to prevent them from taking on additional risk.

Whether these regulations promote or stifle bank- and market-based finance depends on how they are formulated and administered. Where banks are influential, they can be expected to use their political sway to lobby for a regulatory environment that sustains their initial advantage. The same goes for participants in securities exchanges.

The implication is that where banks dominate initially, they will continue to dominate, and similarly for securities markets.[25] It follows that only exceptional events that shift the system from one path to another can overcome the role of different starting points and the historical inertia they create. These include the issues discussed in Section 5.2, such as the extent and method of privatisation, the decisiveness of macroeconomic stabilisation or the effectiveness of the regulatory framework.

Changing technology

It is frequently suggested that the revolution in information and communications technologies is shifting the balance of advantages between these two forms of financial intermediation.[26] Computers, the Internet and satellite communications are making it easier for market participants to overcome information barriers to sound finance. Increased computing power facilitates the creation of complex financial derivative instruments that enable portfolio investors to assume some risks by avoiding others. More broadly, a host of technological advances is working to encourage securitisation at the expense of bank finance. There is also some evidence that higher incomes, which are themselves largely associated with technological advance, tend to be associated with a growing reliance on market- rather than bank-based finance. The implication is that the transition economies, like the rest of the world, should expect to see securities markets play a growing role relative to banks in the allocation of financial resources.

Interdependence of banking and securities activities

There are a number of reasons for thinking that banking and securities activities interact in ways that lower the overall cost of finance and that both can play an active role in a mature financial system.[27] It is frequently argued that bank debt is the cost-effective source of external finance for small enterprises with intangible assets and a limited track record, while securities markets provide a low-cost source of finance for large, established enterprises with a reputation and tangible, readily-valued assets. Bank finance will be more efficient for industries in which demand and technology are stable and in which there is a broad consensus on financial prospects, since it will then pay to exploit economies of scale in monitoring these industries. In contrast, where technology is evolving rapidly or the borrowing firm is large and its management must make complex decisions, no such consensus is likely to exist, and it will be preferable to use stock markets to pool diverse assessments and use the price mechanism to summarise this information.[28]

The efficiency of monitoring and corporate governance, moreover, is greatest in the presence of both banking and securities activities.[29] Bank finance provides an appropriate corrective against a firm's management taking on excessive risk. Since creditors do not share upside returns but incur significant losses when outcomes are poor (and debt is defaulted upon), they will attempt to discourage management from taking on additional risk. Since equity holders, on the other hand, benefit from upside risk but cannot lose more than their entire stake, they will encourage management to undertake high-risk, high-return projects. Thus, the efficiency of corporate governance is greatest and the cost of finance to the firm is lowest when both securities to provide equity finance and banks to provide debt finance exist in appropriate proportions.

23 These regulatory preconditions are discussed in Mendelson and Peake (1993).

24 See Modigliani, Perotti and Oijen (1998).

25 Thus, the prevalence of securitised finance in the "Anglo-Saxon" markets of Canada, the United Kingdom and the United States is thought to reflect the conditions prevailing a century and more ago conducive to the growth of securities markets and the lingering effect of those early conditions today (Allen (1993)). Similarly, the dominance of banks in Austria and Germany is thought to reflect reliance on bank finance to economise on scarce entrepreneurial resources in the nineteenth century and the influence of those earlier conditions even today (Gerschenkron (1964)).

26 For a powerful statement of this view, see Greenspan (1998).

27 See, for example, Boyd and Smith (1996) and Levine (1998).

28 It follows that securitised financial markets, which are better at providing finance to new enterprises employing novel technologies, tend to be associated with the development of venture capital firms. See Pardy (1992).

29 A nice exposition of this point is Berglöf (1995).

Implications for transition economies

How are these factors likely to influence the future development of financial systems in transition economies? From a historical point of view, finance in the transition economies is bank-based for good reasons. These include the inheritance of large state banks from the era of central planning and the particular difficulty of developing active securities markets when the contracting and information environments are highly imperfect. On the other hand, the view that technological progress will continue to diminish these information problems and shift the balance from bank-based to market-centred finance suggests that securities markets are likely to play a growing role over time in the transition economies, especially as initial conditions begin to weaken. Theories emphasising the interaction between bank-based and securities-based finance suggest that securities activities will have to grow in the region in order to play the efficiency-enhancing role required to complement the operation of commercial banks. These reasons explain why financial systems in the transition economies are heavily bank-based, and why they are likely to grow less so over time.

5.5 Policy implications and conclusion

The evidence and analysis of this chapter suggest that the choice for transition economies is not between bank- and securities-based finance but how to develop both. Central and eastern Europe, the Baltic states and the CIS are under-banked, but they are even more severely under-provisioned with securities markets. But both banking and securities activities have complementary roles to play in the allocation of resources. The problem for policy is thus to create an institutional and regulatory framework conducive to the development of both.

The experiences of the region also make clear that banks and securities markets develop together and respond to many of the same conditions. For example, both are held back by the same policy mistakes. Inflation hampers the development of the banking system without providing impetus to active security markets. High interest rates undermine both securities markets and provision of credit to the private sector by the banking system when attempts at stabilisation are not accompanied by budgetary reform. The experience of the transition economies thus suggests that stabilisation accompanied by sustained reductions in fiscal deficits is necessary if both banks and securities markets are to provide finance to customers other than just the government.[30]

Recent experience documents the importance of well-designed and vigorously enforced regulation for the operation of both banks and securities markets. Deep and liquid markets develop only when enterprises issuing publicly traded securities are subject to disclosure, auditing and accounting requirements that support the information environment for financial transactions. The rights of minority creditors must be secure for equity claims to be widely distributed. Providing credit particularly in that portion of the economy where information is less widely available, banks require deposit insurance and lender-of-last-resort services to protect them against the contagious losses of depositor confidence that can disrupt their operation when information is incomplete. To prevent them from taking on additional risk in response to the provision of this financial safety net, and because bank failures can have systemic implications, they must be subjected to prudential regulation. These arguments for strengthening financial supervision and regulation are familiar. The point here is that this need is equally pressing where policy makers aspire to build a banking system and where they seek to promote securities markets. Chapter 6 takes up these issues.

The fact that stock- and bond-market capitalisation and liquidity are even less adequate than bank finance suggests that policy makers will have to devote special efforts to promoting markets for stocks and bonds. Large-scale privatisation, with effective property rights and reliable and enforceable regulation is indispensable for the expansion of stock markets, and for these markets to play an active role in the allocation of resources. Development of non-bank financial institutions, such as insurance companies and pension funds, can provide a further impetus to the expansion of securities activities.[31]

Strengthening the performance of banks in transition economies, however, remains a vitally important task. Over the medium term, their financial systems are likely to remain primarily bank-based and the performance of their banks will be an important determinant of how rapidly their economies grow and how stable they will be. While Chapter 6 examines the extent to which the legal and regulatory frameworks in transition economies provide a foundation for sound finance, Chapter 7 analyses how competition and private ownership of banks influence their performance in terms of profitability and scale of activity. Chapter 8 concludes the report by examining ways in which the process of competition in banking can be strengthened and how more extensive and effective private ownership of banks can be promoted. Together with prudential regulation and supervision, use of these policy instruments is central to promoting the stable expansion of banking in transition economies.

[30] See Leijonhufvud and Rühl (1997).

[31] Chapter 7 of the *Transition Report* 1996 examines insurance companies and pension funds in transition economies.

References

F. Allen (1993), "Stock markets and resource allocation", in C. Mayer and X. Vives (eds.), *Capital Markets and Financial Intermediation* Cambridge University Press, Cambridge, pp. 81-107.

Bank Austria (1998), *Banking in Eastern Europe,* Bank Austria, Vienna.

E. Berglöf (1995), "Corporate governance in transition economies: The theory and its policy implications", M. Aoki and H.-K. Kim (eds.), *Corporate Governance in Transitional Economies,* World Bank, Washington, DC, pp. 59-98.

M. Boycko, A. Shleifer and R. Vishny (1995), *Privatizing Russia,* The MIT Press, Cambridge, MA.

J. Boyd and B. Smith (1996), "The coevolution of the real and financial sectors in the growth process", *World Bank Economic Review* Vol. 10, pp. 371-396.

G. Caprio Jr. and R. Levine (1994), "Reforming finance in transitional socialist economies", *World Bank Research Observer,* Vol. 9, pp. 1-24.

A. Demirgüç-Kunt and E. Detragiache (1997), "The determinants of banking crises: Evidence from developed and developing countries", International Monetary Fund, mimeo (May).

D. Diamond and P. Dybvig (1983), "Bank runs, deposit insurance, and liquidity", *Journal of Political Economy,* Vol. 91, pp. 401-19.

B. Eichengreen (1996), "Explaining Britain's economic performance: A critical note", *Economic Journal,* Vol. 106, pp. 213-18.

B. Eichengreen and A. Rose (1998), "Staying afloat when the wind shifts: External factors in emerging-market banking crises", NBER Discussion Paper, No. 6370 (January).

M. Gavin and R. Hausmann (1995), "The roots of banking crises: The macroeconomic context", in R. Hausmann and L. Rojas-Suarez (eds.), *Banking Crises in Latin America,* Johns Hopkins University Press, Baltimore, MD, pp. 27-61.

A. Gerschenkron (1964), *Economic Backwardness in Historical Perspective,* Harvard University Press, Cambridge, MA.

A. Greenspan (1998), "The globalization of financial markets", Board of Governors of the Federal Reserve System, unpublished manuscript (May).

D. Heymann and A. Leijonhufvud (1995), *High Inflation,* Oxford University Press, Oxford.

M. Jensen and W. Meckling, "Theory of the firm, managerial behaviour, agency costs and ownership structure", *Journal of Financial Economics,* Vol. 3, pp. 305-60.

G. Kaufman (1994), "Bank contagion: A review of the theory and evidence", *Journal of Financial Services Research,* Vol. 8, pp. 123-50.

A. Leijonhufvud and C. Rühl (1997), "Russian dilemmas", *American Economic Review,* Vol. 87, pp. 344-48.

R. Levine (1998), "Banks, markets, and structure: Implications and determinants", paper prepared for the Fourth Annual Conference on Development in Latin America and the Caribbean, San Salvador, 28-30 June.

M. Mendelson and J. Peake (1993), "Equity Markets in Economies in Transition", *Journal of Banking and Finance,* Vol. 17, pp. 913-29.

F. Modigliani, E. Perotti and P. van Oijen (1998), "Security versus bank finance", Tinbergen Institute Discussion Paper, No. 98-051/2.

S. Myers and N. Majluf, "Corporate financing and investment decisions when firms have information that investors do not have", *Journal of Financial Economics,* Vol. 13, pp. 187-221.

R. Pardy (1992), "Institutional reform in emerging securities markets", World Bank Policy Research Working Paper, No. 907.

C. Rühl (1998), "Transition economies in year eight: Growth prospects", N. Dimc (ed.), *The Competitiveness of Countries in Transition During Economic Depression and Recovery,* Open Society Institute, Ljubljana, pp. 10-47.

D. Soskice "German technology policy, innovation, and institutional frameworks", Wissenschaftscentrum Berlin Working Paper, 96-319.

J. Stiglitz and A. Weiss (1981), "Credit rationing in markets with imperfect information", *American Economic Review,* Vol. 71, pp. 393-410.

World Bank (1998), *Global Development Finance,* World Bank, Washington DC.

Legal foundations for sound finance

6

Law underpins sound finance in important ways. Its role is particularly important in transition economies, where market-based financial practices and reputations for prudent behaviour require time to become established. Law governs the practices of financial institutions and markets, helping to assure savers and investors that financial instruments and institutions are secure and that financial markets are transparent and fair. Legal rules, particularly with respect to contracts and property rights, enable financial commitments to be created and shape the form that they can take. But not only must these rules be in place, they must operate effectively to ensure that savers and investors have confidence in financial instruments, institutions and markets. Sound and stable financial systems thus require that financial laws be embedded in well-functioning legal and administrative systems.

In the absence of adequate foundations for sound finance, the confidence of savers and investors can easily be misplaced, particularly when they are inexperienced. There have been high-profile examples of misplaced confidence in transition economies – such as pyramid schemes that promise high returns that can only be met by attracting new investors. The MMM scheme in Russia promised annual returns of 2,000 per cent and attracted 5 million savers, while in Romania the Caritas scheme involved 20 per cent of the population by promising 800 per cent returns in 100 days.[1] But perhaps the most extreme examples of misplaced confidence were the Albanian schemes. They promised returns as high as 100 per cent in six months, sold claims to half the population, and attracted sums equivalent to total GDP. Their collapse contributed to civil unrest and a change of government.

While pyramid schemes are perhaps the most glaring consequence of weak financial laws, repeated episodes of financial instability reveal the extent of the challenge confronting governments to strengthen them. When markets drive the breadth and depth of financial activity, the challenge for the legal systems is to keep abreast of this activity. In market economies, banking crises have tended to occur when financial markets were recently liberalised but when supervision and regulation were not upgraded to cope with expanded activity.[2] In transition economies, the challenge has been to build the principles and practices of sound finance in step with the expansion of financial activity. Such synchronisation is undoubtedly difficult to achieve; and not surprisingly there have been many banking crises in transition economies. Not only did the severe economic upheavals early in the transition render many enterprises and banks insolvent, but banking crises have persisted even as the transition advances and the economies stabilise. Behind the Baltic banking crises (Latvia and Lithuania in 1995-96) was pervasive connected lending by new private banks that had rapidly expanded their activities. In the current Russian crisis, a number of banks have built up large open foreign exchange positions by writing forward contracts that are inadequately hedged. In each episode, there were serious gaps in the prudential regulation and supervision of banks that allowed imprudent exposures to go unchecked.

The challenge of enacting and enforcing sound financial law is further emphasised by the fact that the post-communist countries launched their transition to a market economy without adequate financial legal rules or supporting systems. There was simply no need for them under central planning. But what are the legal arrangements towards which the transition economies should be moving? Just as there is no archetype for a market economy, there is no unique set of laws and mechanisms for their enforcement that underpins sound finance. Indeed, there is wide variation in these institutional arrangements and practices in market economies. From this diversity, though, has come a range of experiences and many valuable lessons. Through several international forums government officials and regulators have begun to draw from these experiences to develop "core principles" for effective financial laws and regulations. These forums also serve as a mechanism for harmonisation of regulatory systems in increasingly integrated capital markets.

This chapter identifies core standards for effective financial laws in transition economies, helping to disseminate the recent work of several international financial forums and drawing on the lessons learned from the EBRD's experience as an investor in these economies. It then examines the extent to which the post-communist countries have enacted financial laws that embody these standards and have legal and administrative capability and political will to enforce them. The basis for this assessment is a survey of lawyers practising in the countries undertaken by the Office of the General Counsel at the EBRD. A key finding of the chapter is that transition economies have achieved greater progress in enacting than in implementing and enforcing sound financial laws. Moreover, their effectiveness is more advanced in banking than in securities activities, reflecting in part the dominance of banking in the financial systems of the region and the early priority placed on banking reform.

The remainder of the chapter is organised in four sections. The first sets out selected core principles for financial laws and regulations derived from international experience, emphasising those of particular importance in the context of transition economies. Section 6.2 reports on the results of a survey of lawyers practising in transition economies on the extent and effectiveness of their

[1] See Bhattacharya (1998) for a discussion of pyramid schemes in transition economies.

[2] See Chapter 5 for a discussion of this issue.

Box 6.1

A summary of the Basle Committee's "Core Principles" on banking regulation

Organisation of supervisory authority

An effective banking supervisory authority requires a clear framework of objectives set by legislation, operational independence to pursue them free of arbitrary political pressure, and accountability for achieving the objectives. The clear objective of a banking supervisor should be the enforcement of banking regulations that set out the minimum standards that banks must meet. To ensure compliance, the banking supervisor must have adequate resources, and must be able to gather and verify information and to apply sanctions when prudential requirements are not met. The gathering of information can be done through either reporting by banks or on-site inspections, although a combination of the two methods has proven to be more effective. An essential element of banking supervision is the ability to supervise on a fully consolidated basis so that any problems cannot simply be swept away by a bank into its affiliates. Also, supervisors must have a range of enforcement powers that can be applied to limit risk-taking and conserve the capital of a troubled bank, and to address management problems. In extreme circumstances, the banking supervisor must be able to revoke the banking licence.

Licensing

To define precisely the group of institutions to be supervised and to limit the potential for savers to be misled, there should be clearly established arrangements for defining and licensing a bank and for limiting the application of the name "bank" to licensed institutions. At a minimum, the activity of taking a deposit from the public should be reserved for institutions that are licensed and supervised as banks. Moreover, the licensing authority should determine that a new bank has suitable shareholders, adequate capital, feasible operating and financial plans, and management with sufficient expertise and integrity to operate the bank prudently. The licensing authority must have the right to set criteria and reject applications that do not meet the standards set. Clear and objective criteria can also reduce the potential for arbitrary political interference in the licensing process.

Prudential requirements

Sound banking requires that the inherent risks are recognised, monitored and managed, and prudential regulations and their enforcement play a critical role in ensuring that bank management performs these tasks effectively. These measures do not supplant management decisions but rather impose minimum prudential standards on banks and constraints on their risk-taking. The main instruments of prudential regulation should include: capital adequacy standards, loan classification and provisioning requirements, limits on large exposures, limits on connected lending, and requirements for liquidity and market risk management. In addition, supervisors should evaluate the credit and market risk management systems and internal controls of banks.

Accounting principles

Supervisors must be satisfied that banks maintain accurate accounts based on accounting principles that are appropriate for banks and that are generally acceptable internationally. Bank management must ensure that reports are verified and that external auditors determine that the reporting systems in place are adequate and provide reliable data. External auditors should express an opinion on the annual accounts and management report supplied to shareholders and the public. In assessing the adequacy of the auditors' work and the degree of reliance that can be placed on this work, supervisors must consider the extent to which the audit examined the quality of the loan portfolio, asset valuations, off-balance sheet positions and internal controls over financial reporting.

financial laws. This survey covers prudential supervision and regulation in banking, transparency and disclosures in securities activities, and regulation of collective investment schemes. The third section identifies priorities for improvements, while Section 6.4 briefly concludes the chapter.

6.1 Core principles of financial law

The widespread incidence and the high cost of financial instability have spurred a concerted international effort to learn from experience and to develop core principles for sound finance. An important part of this effort was an initiative by G-7 countries to bring together experts from advanced industrialised economies and from emerging market economies to develop a strategy for fostering financial stability in emerging markets.[3] This working group focused on three main aspects of financial stability: (1) the development of regulatory and supervisory arrangements that complement and support the operation of market discipline; (2) the creation of an institutional setting and financial infrastructure necessary for sound finance; and (3) the promotion of market discipline and effective corporate governance over financial institutions. This chapter focuses primarily on the first and second aspects of the framework for sound finance. Chapter 8 examines in depth how to strengthen market discipline and corporate governance in banking, the dominant type of financial activity in these economies.

Effective regulation and supervision

Approaches to effective regulation and supervision differ significantly between banking and securities activities, reflecting fundamental differences between the nature of these activities. Banking basically transforms the liquid deposits of many small and dispersed savers into illiquid loans to borrowers. These loans are extended on the basis of bank-client relationships and private information. This combination of liquid deposits and illiquid loans, however, is potentially unstable because of the risk that depositors will withdraw their money from a bank if its liquidity becomes doubtful and because of the limited information depositors have about banks. Prudential oversight in banking provides a measured alternative to the disruptive market discipline of bank runs and is often accompanied by government provision of deposit guarantees.

Securities activities, in contrast, are market-based and require transparency and public disclosure of information for the markets to function well. This information is necessary not only for the accurate valuation of equities and bonds in securities markets, but also for the holders of these securities to protect their rights and to perform a corporate governance role. Companies and their managers have a potential interest in voluntarily disclosing accurate financial information and refraining from insider dealing – to increase investor confidence and to lower the cost of finance. But they may also be tempted to engage in deception, particularly

[3] Together with the Czech National Bank and Bank for International Settlements, the EBRD sponsored a conference on "Building Stable, Market-Oriented Financial Systems in Central and Eastern Europe and the CIS" in Prague in March 1998 to help disseminate the work of the Emerging Markets Task Force. This conference brought together experts on financial sector fundamentals and reform and senior financial officials from the region.

Box 6.2

A summary of the IOSCO principles on regulation of securities activities

Responsibilities and resources of regulator

As in banking regulation, effective implementation of securities regulation requires that the regulatory authority has clearly defined responsibilities, operational independence to pursue these free from arbitrary political influence, and that it is held accountable for achieving the objectives. The responsibilities of the regulator should be set out clearly, preferably in law. Where there is a division of regulatory responsibilities across various types of financial services (banking, securities and insurance), the legislation should be designed to ensure that the division of responsibility avoids gaps or inequities in regulation. The regulator should have adequate powers, resources and capacity to perform its functions. In practical terms, this requires the powers of licensing, supervision, inspection, investigation and enforcement. It also requires that the regulatory agency receive adequate funding and be appropriately staffed.

Self regulation

The regulatory regime should make appropriate use of self-regulatory organisations (SROs), which can be a valuable complement to the regulator in achieving the objectives of securities regulation. There can be substantial benefits from self-regulation, including the observance of standards that go beyond governmental requirements and the ability to respond flexibly to changing market conditions. However, the effectiveness of an SRO may be compromised by conflicts of interest. The regulator should monitor and address the potential for such conflicts to arise.

Disclosure

The most important way of regulating issuers of securities and secondary markets is the requirement of full disclosure of information material to investors' decisions. To ensure effectiveness of disclosure requirements, accounting and auditing practices should be of a standard that is of an internationally acceptable level. Provided with relevant information, investors in both primary and secondary markets are better able to protect their own interests. Regulation of secondary markets should also promote transparency of trading by disclosing information about trades as they take place, including firm bids and offers for trades as well as prices and volumes of trades actually concluded. Regulation of trading in the secondary market should prohibit market manipulation, misleading conduct, insider trading and other fraudulent or deceptive conduct that may distort market pricing.

Licensing and prudential requirements

Supervision of market intermediaries (securities firms that manage individual portfolios, execute trading orders and deal in securities) should achieve investor protection by setting licensing and minimum operating standards for them. In particular, there should be initial and ongoing capital and other prudential requirements for market intermediaries. Capital adequacy standards should be designed to allow a market intermediary to absorb losses in the event of a large adverse market movement, and to provide the supervisory authority with the time to intervene if necessary to accomplish an orderly winding down of operations. Regulation should also ensure proper risk management in market intermediaries, including the periodic evaluation of their risk management processes.

when investors are inexperienced and when it is difficult to distinguish the financial facts from fiction. Public regulation of corporate disclosure, and of transparency and of fairness in securities markets, can be instrumental in building investor confidence in securities activities and in increasing their attractiveness as a source of finance for corporations.

Banking

The "Core Principles for Effective Banking Supervision and Regulation" of the Basle Committee on Banking Supervision provides an authoritative and comprehensive assessment of the components of an effective system for prudential supervision and regulation in banking.[4] The Committee consists of senior banking supervisors from G-10 countries and it consulted 16 other supervisory authorities in preparing the core principles. These principles cover issues ranging from the organisation, methods and powers of the supervisory authority to the licensing conditions, prudential regulations and information requirements applied to banks (see Box 6.1). The Basle Committee's Core Principles are intended to serve as a basic reference and to facilitate the review of existing arrangements and the design of programmes to strengthen them.

Securities regulation

The "Objectives and Principles of Securities Regulation" by the International Organisation of Securities Commissions (IOSCO) provides an authoritative and comprehensive assessment of the requirements for effective regulation of securities activities.[5] IOSCO is an international forum for securities regulators, with members from 81 countries. Its assessment sets out three main objectives of securities regulation: (1) the protection of investors; (2) ensuring that markets are fair, efficient and transparent; and (3) the reduction of systemic risk. In particular, investors should be protected from misleading, manipulative or fraudulent practices and misuse of client assets by intermediaries. Market structures should not favour some market users over others, and regulation should seek to prevent market manipulation and other unfair trading practices. When a financial institution fails, it should be able to wind down its business without loss to its customers and counterparties or systemic damage.

To provide guidance on achieving these objectives, IOSCO set out principles to be implemented as part of a legal and regulatory framework for securities and capital markets. These principles address the role of the regulator, enforcement of securities regulation and self-regulation, as well as disclosure requirements for issuers of securities and for secondary markets and prudential requirements for market intermediaries. Box 6.2 provides a brief summary of the principles.

Non-bank financial intermediaries: collective investment schemes[6]

Collective investment schemes include open-ended funds that redeem their shares at the market value of the underlying assets and closed-ended funds that have their shares traded in the secu-

4 Basle Committee on Banking Supervision (1997). See also Folkerts-Landau and Lindgrin (1998).

5 International Organisation of Securities Commissions (1998).

6 This section draws on International Organisation of Securities Commissions (1997,1998). Chapter 6 of the 1996 *Transition Report* examines the regulation of pension funds and insurance companies in transition economies. On insurance, see also International Association of Insurance Supervisors (1997a, 1997b).

Box 6.3

Secured transactions

Unlike the more developed countries with civil law roots, the transition economies could not rely on practices of banks and courts established over decades to create ways of effectively securing credit. Instead, these economies initially offered well-defined legal concepts such as the possessory pledge which were, however, ill adapted to the needs of a market economy. New, more effective and sophisticated economic legislation was needed. This legislation needed to be easy to understand and applicable for businesses, courts and enforcement authorities. This was the environment in which the EBRD found itself in 1992 when it was asked to assist in establishing modern laws for secured transactions in its countries of operations. Initially the EBRD produced a "model law" on secured transactions (see Rover and Simpson, (1994)). This was undertaken with the assistance of an advisory board of 20 lawyers from 15 jurisdictions. The principal purposes of producing the model were to:

- illustrate the principal components of a secured transactions law and the way in which they can be included in legislation;
- act as a reference point and checklist for the law reformer; and
- provide guidance as to expectations of international investors and lenders.

Since producing the model, the Legal Transition Team within the Office of the General Counsel of the EBRD has given assistance on reforming, or creating, secured transactions laws across the region. In doing so it has developed certain basic principles that are considered the heart of an effective law on secured transactions:

- To be of value, security should give a creditor a right to recover a claim out of an asset in case of failure of the borrower to meet his contractual obligation to repay the debt and interest in a timely manner.
- Security should give a creditor priority ahead of unsecured creditors, which continues in bankruptcy; without priority the risk of lending is not reduced.
- The existence of the security should be publicised to enable third parties to discover that security has been given and that consequently the debtor has limited power to offer the assets for further security or for sale.
- The owner of the secured asset should continue to be able to use the asset given as security. A system of merely possessory security has a heavy cost attached to it, the cost of depriving the pledgor of the right to use his asset.
- Enforcement rights, procedures and infrastructures should maximise the speed and amount of recovery but strike a balance with the need to protect the legitimate rights of debtors.
- Security legislation should apply to the broadest range of claims and assets. Any claim, any debt can be secured as long as it can be expressed in monetary terms. Any asset that is capable of being transferred should be capable also of being pledged, movables and immovables, tangibles and intangibles.
- A secured transactions law should enable the parties to adapt the security to their particular transaction. The law is there to facilitate credit transactions and within its basic framework secured transactions law should allow maximum flexibility as to how each transaction can be structured.
- Costs should be kept to a minimum, including the actual cost of creating, maintaining and enforcing the security.

These principles should be looked at in the context of the economic impact of security. Giving security should reduce the cost of borrowing. The size of the reduction will depend on an analysis of the security. In the past some banks' credit committees may just have asked about the value of the assets secured and checked that a legal opinion was being obtained. But increasingly we can expect sophisticated analysis to be made of the extent to which the security actually reduces the risk of non-payment.

In some markets the risk reduction can be estimated by looking at market statistics; for example, in many countries the recovery rate in the domestic house mortgage market is well established. But in new markets, such as those of the EBRD's countries of operations, and for less repetitive deals such as for large project financings, the effect of the security has to be quantified on a case-by-case basis. Although the quantification process may be less than perfect, it is useful because it gives the financier an estimate as to the value of the risk-reducing effect of the security. This value is the economic objective of sound, effective secured transactions laws.

It is this economic objective to increase the availability and decrease the cost of credit in its countries of operations that drives the EBRD's secured transactions project.

rities markets. These funds are particularly important in transition economies because of their role in mass privatisation programmes, such as those in the Czech Republic, Poland and Russia. Proper regulation of collective investment schemes is crucial if investor protection is to be achieved, since investors in these schemes rely upon the fund managers to act in their best interests.

The operation of collective investment schemes raises the potential for conflict of interests between the investors in the scheme and those that operate it (and their associates). To mitigate these conflicts, regulations would be required covering issues such as the best execution of trades, commissions and fees, related party transactions and underwriting arrangements. There should also be a licensing procedure for those who seek to operate a scheme, as well as clear disclosure of the investment policies and of all fees that may be levied under the scheme.

Legal and institutional infrastructure

Prudential supervision and regulation of financial institutions, and transparency and fairness of securities markets, are central to a sound and stable financial system. They only come into play, however, if savers and investors have the confidence and means to engage in financial activity. This requires the intensive use of legal and accounting services. The legal infrastructure serves to establish and enforce property rights and contracts, as well as creditor and shareholder rights. Accounting and auditing practices generate the reliable financial information required by savers and investors to ensure their rights are being respected and to perform an active corporate governance role. The availability and quality of these services are thus crucial factors in determining how well a financial system performs.

Legal infrastructure

An effectively functioning legal system based upon the rule-of-law underlies a sound financial system. The rule-of-law encompasses:[7]

[7] For a general discussion of the rule of law, see Carothers (1998).

- a system of government where institutions and officials are guided by and constrained by the law – that is, a government accountable to, not above, the law;
- a body of laws that is transparent, reasonably predictable, validly derived, and fairly and equitably applied;
- laws, principles and procedures that protect those civil, political and economic rights that have become enshrined as universal human rights; and
- a fair and effective legal system led by an independent and professionally competent judiciary that acts as the final arbiter of the law.

The rule-of-law provides an essential framework for investment and financial activity. Without a predictable, enforceable set of rules, uncertainty reins in an economy. Without transparent legal rules enforced by a competent judiciary, the costs of investment rise and economic growth prospects decline.[8] Entrepreneurs and firms require higher returns on their investments, raising capital becomes more expensive, and debtors may not repay debts knowing that laws and contracts are not consistently enforced. Lack of confidence in law enforcement and of fair, effective dispute resolution supervised by the courts also leads to the creation of alternative institutions, opens the door to criminal encroachment in the economy, and creates a fertile breeding ground for corruption and money laundering.

The rule-of-law as applied to financial activity requires the enforcement of financial contracts, the creation of efficient insolvency and secured-transactions laws, and the existence of clear standards for corporate governance. In transition economies, the creation of efficient insolvency and collateral laws and of standards for corporate governance pose particular challenges, because of their absence under central planning and the consequent lack of appropriate laws and practices in these areas. These issues are an ongoing concern of the EBRD and a priority for its legal transition activities. Boxes 6.3 and 6.4 provide detailed assessments of them and describe the EBRD's remedial activities.

Accounting and auditing practices

Effective financial regulation and supervision and the legal infrastructure supporting financial activity depend on the timely provision of financial information that is understandable and that can be relied upon by savers and investors. The best assurance that financial statements contain understandable information is if they are prepared and presented in accordance with accounting standards and principles that are generally acceptable internationally. The work of the International Accounting Standards Committee (IASC) in publishing International Accounting Standards has been instrumental both in influencing the content of national standards and in providing standards with which individual financial institutions and other enterprises may prepare their accounts.[9] The best assurance that such financial statements are reliable is if they have been audited to standards that are broadly acceptable internationally.

Rigorous accounting and auditing standards also help prevent money laundering and other financial crime, an important function given the serious, adverse impact such problems can have on both individual financial institutions and confidence in the financial system as a whole. In this area, the Financial Action Task Force on money laundering has made recommendations and established principles and guidelines that serve as the basis for the development of laws to combat money laundering.

EU financial services directives and accession

Given the composition of many of the international bodies concerned with promoting effective regulation and supervision of financial markets, it is not surprising that European Union requirements relating to financial services have influenced the content of worldwide principles. Nevertheless, EU standards are more immediately relevant for countries in the region with EU membership aspirations. The EC framework for financial services provides minimum standards for banks and other financial institutions, securities regulation, stock exchange regulation, company law and regulation of institutional investors, all based on the premise of universal banking and an open internal market.

Ten post-communist countries in central and eastern Europe and the Baltics (CEE) are signatories to Europe Agreements with the EU, which encourage them to move towards harmonisation of their legal and regulatory frameworks with the body of EU law: the *acquis communautaire*. An important aim of the accession process is the approximation of existing and future legislation in the financial services sector to that of the EU. Moreover, under the existing Europe Agreements, EU financial companies will have the right to operate on the territory of the respective accession candidate country by the end of a transition period at the latest. Accordingly, these countries will need to have in place a fully EU-compatible system of banking and financial services regulation by the date of accession.

As an aid to this process of approximation, in April 1995 the European Commission issued a White Paper identifying the key measures in each sector of the internal market.[10] The paper proposed a sequence under which the accession candidates should seek to approximate their domestic legislation to that of the EC. Specifically, it proposed that EC legislation in the financial services area should be adopted in two stages: the first involves the introduction of the basic principles for the establishment of financial institutions; the second (although some elements are important for the first stage) aims to strengthen prudential supervision of investment firms in order to bring them up to international standards. This second stage for the accession candidates focuses on the various EC provisions for free movement of capital and services in the financial sphere.

[8] Chapter 6 of the 1997 *Transition Report* examines the contribution that strengthening the rule-of-law can make to economic growth prospects in transition economies. For a more general discussion of the rule-of-law and economic growth, see Olson (1996) and Clague, Keefer, Knack and Olson (1996).

[9] See IASC (1998).

[10] See European Commission (1995).

Box 6.4

Corporate governance

Adequate company laws incorporating principles of good corporate governance are important for the development of market economies in the EBRD's countries of operations. If foreign and domestic equity capital is to flow significantly into companies, it is essential that the legislative framework applicable to such companies, as well as charter provisions and contractual agreements among shareholders, reflect principles of good corporate governance. Prospective investors, including the EBRD, need to be assured that the legislative and contractual frameworks within which corporate entities are structured and managed provide for adequate protection of their legitimate interests and expectations. As one of the largest investors in many countries of central and eastern Europe, the Baltics and the CIS, the EBRD seeks to assist in the development of such frameworks in these countries.

As a first step in this effort, the EBRD has created a set of guidelines, published in September 1997, to help companies understand some of the broader concerns that lenders and investors have when considering a potential loan or investment opportunity in the region (see EBRD (1997)). The Bank is also currently preparing a set of guidelines reflecting essential principles of good corporate governance. These guidelines will be used as a checklist for evaluating the status of applicable laws and regulations, and for reviewing and adapting the documents of the Bank's investee companies in its countries of operations. In addition, upon request by the relevant authorities and in appropriate circumstances, the Bank will also advise and assist the governments of its countries of operations in reforming their legal systems so as to give effect to the guidelines.

As an example of such assistance, and in response to the problems described above, the EBRD is currently assisting the Russian Federal Commission for Securities Market (FCSM) in improving the legal framework for good corporate governance. The Bank's assistance project, funded by the Japanese Government, aims to facilitate and promote a well-organised, modern, efficient capital market in the Russian Federation, as well as aiming to achieve higher standards in regulation of corporations and protection of rights of securities holders.

One of the primary tasks of the FCSM is to regulate the securities market. It does so through regulations on the issue and circulation of securities, supervision of stock exchanges, requirements to protect investors and rules guiding the formation and operation of mutual funds and other collective investments. An initial survey of Russian laws in the field of corporate governance shows that although there are reasonably good basic laws in place, there is still a need to improve the legal framework in certain areas.

The Russian Law on Joint Stock Companies (JSC) came into force on 1 January 1996. It has proven to be a fairly workable law, having created a solid legal framework for corporate activity. At the same time, its implementation has shown some obvious gaps and some JSC provisions require further adjustment or adaptation.

In 1997, Russia's FCSM launched investigations into four Russian oil companies (Sidanko, Yukos, Yuganskneftegaz and Samaraneftegaz) for possible violations of minority shareholder interests. The inquiry was initiated upon requests by Russian minority shareholders and foreign investors with holdings in subsidiaries of the oil companies claiming that the right of minority shareholders to participate in control of these companies was being violated by the owners of the parent companies. Disgruntled minority shareholders suspected that they were being cheated through suspect practices, such as parent companies compelling subsidiaries to sell oil to them at prices below market value and thus diminishing subsidiary profitability.

Another recent example of a corporate conflict involving minority shareholders occurred in the context of a convertible bond issue in December 1997 in Sidanko, a giant oil company with a few large shareholders and several funds holding a number of shares. The minority shareholders felt that the convertible bonds effectively diluted their shares. On 17 February 1998, the FCSM annulled Sidanko's convertible bond issue, holding that the convertible bond issue had indeed breached minority shareholder rights. However, the FCSM did give Sidanko approval to have a new bond issue as long as it arrived at an understanding with minority shareholders.

Examples such as those above suggest that there are still gaps in Russian corporate law that permit share dilutions. Additional priorities for reforming company law include procedures for the liability of directors and managers, external and internal audits, transactions with affiliated or connected persons, and general and special meetings.

As for Russian capital markets, at present the only federal law regulating activity on the securities market is the Law on the Securities Market, which became effective in April 1996; however, the provisions in this law are not comprehensive. Other applicable rules are contained either in a number of regulations issued by the FCSM in the form of sub-laws, or in various laws and presidential decrees. The rapid development of the Russian securities market requires further elaboration of more advanced rules which were not on the agenda two or three years ago. The gap between the needs of the market and the present legal framework inevitably results in unclear rules, and could cause mis-application of these rules. This lack of clarity creates instability and increases risks. It affects the relations between market participants and the perception of potential investors. This also prevents the FCSM from applying enforcement measures to bad faith market participants.

To boost the investors' confidence, the FCSM has initiated a State Programme for Protection of the Rights of Investors. The Programme, aiming to protect minority shareholders and improve corporate governance standards, encompasses 17 laws and regulations that the FCSM will develop. The Programme is expected to be presented to parliament at the end of 1998.

The experience of the European Union shows that regional integration can play a role in promoting the adoption of sound principles and practices in economies and in supporting their implementation. The fundamental principle of mutual recognition and a system of a single licence ensures that these directives provide a set of minimum norms, while at the same time avoiding the creation of obstacles to competition among financial institutions. The EU is thus well placed to help transition economies to respond to the challenges they face in strengthening the legal foundations for sound finance.

6.2 Progress in financial transition

Gauging the extent to which the financial laws of the region approximate international standards requires an assessment of both the normative laws and their effectiveness. To form this assessment, the EBRD's Office of the General Counsel conducted a survey of academic and practising lawyers and of other experts familiar with the financial laws and regulations of the region, covering at least three or four lawyers per country. These lawyers were selected on the basis of their known competence, demonstrated in connection with the EBRD's investment activities. The

Chart 6.1

Average ratings for extensiveness and effectiveness of legal rules in banking and securities activities

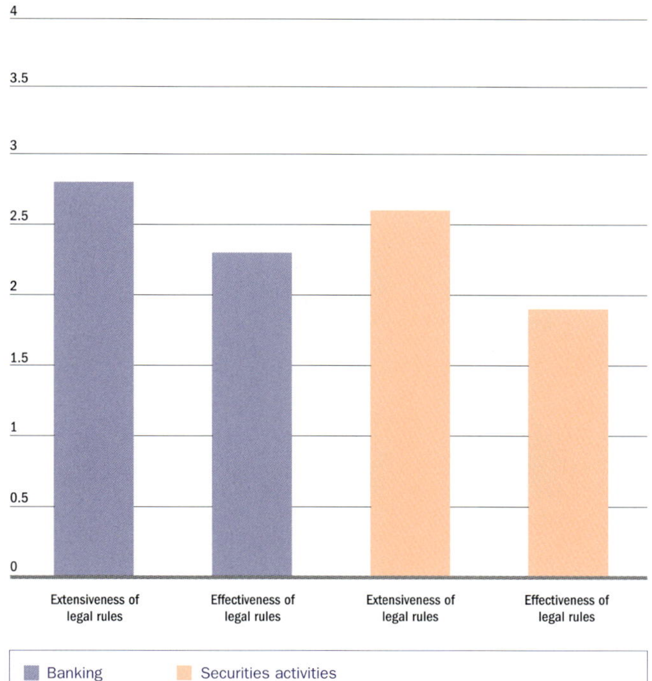

Source: EBRD.

survey questions were based in large part on core principles developed by the Basle Committee and IOSCO, outlined in the previous section. The survey also included a number of questions focused on the implementation and enforcement of core principles. For example, it contained questions about the effectiveness and frequency with which regulators take corrective action against failing banks, and against entities or individuals that violate securities laws. The survey thus attempted to measure how effectively countries in the region enforce financial laws and regulations so as to foster confidence in both banking and securities activities.

The survey questions were subdivided into separate sections dealing with banking and securities activities. The section on banking contained questions on: banking regulation and supervision, minimum financial requirements (for example, capital adequacy standards) and criteria for banking operations; the use of internationally acceptable accounting standards; and the ability of banking regulators to engage in enforcement and corrective action. The questions on securities activities focused on supervision and regulation, disclosure and transparency, enforcement, and the regulation of intermediaries.

To score the survey and to develop summary measures, a weighting system was used in which key questions related to principles that are most important to a well-functioning financial system were identified and given a heavy weight. For example, questions concerning the application of capital adequacy standards, public disclosure requirements, and use of internationally acceptable accounting standards were identified as having particular importance and weight. In this way, a numerical scoring system and criteria for ratings (scaled 1 to 4*) based on the survey results were developed. Numerical scores and rankings are for both the extensiveness and the effectiveness of laws and regulations applied to both banking and securities activities.

Table 6.1 summarises the survey results. The summary measures reported in this table reflect the subjective assessment of survey respondents, as well as of EBRD bankers and lawyers who have experience working on banking and capital market transactions in the field. For a few countries, the survey respondents provided significantly differing assessments. Where there were large discrepancies among a few respondents, recourse to the EBRD's in-house knowledge of that country's conditions was used to arbitrate among the differing views. Accordingly, while the purpose of the survey and resulting analysis is to give an impression of how the financial laws and regulations in the region approximate core international principles, some caution must be exercised in interpreting the results.[11]

Overview of results

The survey conducted for this chapter shows that, while many countries have well-developed laws with respect to both banking and securities activities, they continue to face serious problems with enforcement and implementation of these laws. Major impediments include a lack of trained regulatory personnel, a failure to conduct regular supervisory examinations of financial institutions, and an inability (due to a lack of capability or to political constraints) to take prompt and frequent corrective action with respect to problematic financial institutions. The survey revealed that the extensiveness of securities regulation has closed the gap with that of banking, but that the effectiveness of legal rules applied to securities activities continued to lag behind that of banking (see Chart 6.1). Additionally, the results of the commercial law survey (see Annex 2.1, Chapter 2) indicate that the lack of effective legislation in the areas of pledge and bankruptcy in many instances also creates a poor environment for financial transactions. Thus, there tends to be a correlation between the rankings of countries with respect to commercial law and financial law.

The survey results thus show a continuation of patterns identified in previous Transition Reports. In an analysis of financial institutions and markets in the 1995 *Transition Report* (Chapter 10), it was found that, despite initial setbacks, progress had been made in reforming and reshaping the banking systems in the region. As of 1995, many countries had enacted legal and regulatory frameworks for banks based on minimum international standards. It is interesting to note that, while prudential regulations in banking had developed towards minimum international standards, the capacity to enforce such regulations as assessed in 1995 was expanding at a slower pace. The laws applied to securities activities typically were also less developed than those in banking,

[11] The ranking of countries according to the survey results, nevertheless, corresponds closely with the assessments of EBRD economists on financial sector reform and development reported in Table 2.1 of Chapter 2. An important advantage of the survey is that it draws on legal practitioners' assessment of both the extensiveness and effectiveness of financial laws and regulations.

Table 6.1

Extent and effectiveness of financial laws and regulations

Country	Banking		Securities activities	
	Extensiveness	Effectiveness	Extensiveness	Effectiveness
Albania	2+	2	1+	1
Armenia	3	3–	2+	1
Azerbaijan	2	1	2	1
Belarus	2	2	1	1
Bosnia and Herzegovina	3	2	1	1
Bulgaria	4	4–	4	3
Croatia	3	3	4	3
Czech Republic	3	3–	4–	3
Estonia	3	3	4	2+
FYR Macedonia	3	3–	3	1
Georgia	2	2	1+	1
Hungary	4	4	4	4
Kazakhstan	2	2	2+	2
Kyrgyzstan	3–	2	1+	1
Latvia	3	3	4	2
Lithuania	3–	2+	3	2
Moldova	2+	2	3–	2
Poland	4	3	4	4
Romania	3	2+	3	3
Russian Federation	3–	2+	3	2
Slovak Republic	3	2	3	2
Slovenia	4	3	3+	2+
Tajikistan	2+	1	2–	1
Turkmenistan	2	1	1	1
Ukraine	2+	2	2	2–
Uzbekistan	2	1	2	1

Classification system for transition indicators:

The *extensiveness* of legal rules on banking and securities activities

1 Legal rules governing banking and securities are very limited in scope. For example, capital adequacy standards and restrictions on affiliated lending in banking do not exist. There may be no functioning stock exchange in this jurisdiction, or the capital markets' legal infrastructure may be in its earliest stage of development.

2 Legal rules governing banking and securities are somewhat limited in scope. Although regulations in banking have been amended to accord with core principles, at least one important area of regulation remains deficient – for example, capital adequacy, use of international accounting standards, use of consolidated comprehensive supervision. Oversight of securities markets is limited, and regulation of securities intermediaries and investment funds, for example, are either non-existent or rudimentary.

3 Legislation for banking and securities activities is reasonably comprehensive but would benefit from further refinement in some areas. Banking regulations generally conform to the Basle Committee's Core Principles, although regulations concerning bank insolvency and deposit protection may not have been adopted. Further refinement to regulation of securities intermediaries and/or investment funds and creation of shareholder depositories and registers is needed to achieve conformity with minimum international standards.

4 Comprehensive regulation exists with respect to banking and securities activities that conforms generally to minimum international standards. But refinement is still needed in at least one important aspect of either banking or securities regulation. For example, many countries in this category still need to enact rules concerning money laundering (including "know your customer" provisions), or bank insolvency. Legislation concerning shareholder depositories and registries is either non-existent or is in its early stages of implementation.

4* Banking and capital markets legislation and regulation is comprehensive and conforms to minimum international standards.

The *effectiveness* of legal rules on banking and securities activities

1 Legal rules governing financial institutions and markets are usually very unclear and often contradictory. The regulatory support of the laws is rudimentary. Supervisory mechanisms are either non-existent or poor. There are no meaningful procedures in place to make financial laws and regulations fully operational.

2 Legal rules are somewhat unclear and sometimes contradictory. Supervision of banking and securities activities exists on an ad hoc basis. But there are few, if any, meaningful procedures in place to enforce the law. There may be a lack of adequately trained staff in either banking or capital markets regulatory authorities.

3 Although legal rules governing banking and securities activities are reasonably clear, regulatory and supervisory support of the law may be inconsistent so as to create a degree of uncertainty. Although the regulator may have engaged in corrective actions against failing banks and securities markets practices, enforcement problems still exist.

4 Legal rules governing banking and securities activities are readily ascertainable. Banking and securities laws are generally well supported administratively and judicially, particularly regarding the efficient functioning of enforcement measures against failing institutions and illegal market practices. For example, the regulator has taken corrective action to liquidate failing banks. Enforcement actions against individuals and securities intermediaries are evident, but could still benefit from more systematic and rigorous enforcement. Courts have the authority to review enforcement decisions or other corrective actions for banks and/or securities firms.

4* Regulators possess comprehensive enforcement powers and exercise authority to take corrective action on a regular basis. Examination of securities intermediaries and licensing of intermediaries is frequent, as is the use of corrective action, such as prosecution for insider dealing, revocation of bank licences, liquidation of insolvent banks and consolidation of banks.

with the authorities in a number of countries in the region only just beginning to create the basic legal and regulatory framework for a securities market.

In the 1997 *Transition Report* (Chapters 2 and 5), it was found that the high-profile banking crises in several transition economies over the previous few years had provided further impetus to financial reform. After an initial period of rapid and virtually unregulated expansion, a widespread recognition emerged among countries at all stages of transition of the need to consolidate and strengthen the banking sector. It was also noted that some countries had taken significant strides in enhancing the supervisory capacities of central banks, tightening prudential regulations, and increasing capital requirements in an effort to prevent systemic problems from re-emerging in the financial sector. Despite this progress, improved supervision is, by its very nature, a long-term task in which the development of effective human skills is as important as enhanced regulatory structures.

Banking

Countries that receive low ratings (either a 1 or a 2 for extensiveness) have yet to implement standards with respect to capital adequacy, related party lending and transactions, and bank insolvency, do not promote the use of internationally acceptable accounting standards and do not require frequent on-site supervisory examinations (among other issues). These countries include Albania, Azerbaijan, Belarus, Georgia, Kazakhstan, Moldova, Tajikistan, Turkmenistan, Ukraine and Uzbekistan. CIS countries thus tend to lag behind in this dimension of reform (see Chart 6.2).

Countries that have received a 3 rating have reasonably comprehensive financial laws and regulations, but would benefit from further refinements in some areas so as to raise standards in line with core principles. For example, Russia has recently promoted the use of more generally acceptable accounting standards for banks, but has staggered its implementation of various prudential ratios in the banking sector. There are also serious gaps in the control of market risks, such as open foreign exchange positions assumed by Russian banks. Armenia is another country that has staggered its adoption of prudential regulations such as capital adequacy ratios.

Countries that receive a rating of 4 for extensiveness have comprehensive banking regulations, but some refinement is needed in at least one important area. The countries that receive this rating include several in central Europe invited to enter into accession negotiations with the European Union, in particular Hungary, Poland and Slovenia. Bulgaria also scores highly on the effectiveness of legal rules in banking, having significantly upgraded its regulations in the wake of its recent banking crisis.

Regarding specific aspects of banking regulation, minimum capital requirements and capital adequacy standards warrant specific consideration. The vast majority of countries have adopted minimum standards of prudential regulation, which in many respects accord with the Basle Committee's Core Principles. Most countries have introduced stricter licensing requirements and have increased the minimum capital needed for new financial institutions. In many countries the minimal requirement is the equivalent of US$ 5 million and in certain jurisdictions has reached the EU standard of ECU 5 million. As a result of stricter licensing and entry requirements, banks have been consolidated in many jurisdictions and some that fail to meet the requirements have been forced to merge or exit. However, the full impact of these measures has yet to be felt and there may be gaps in enforcement.

The Basle Committee's 8 per cent ratio of regulatory capital to total risk-adjusted assets is a minimum standard that is designed for countries with an established commercial banking sector and substantial international financial transactions. In emerging market economies, a higher percentage may be advisable given the more volatile economic environment and greater inherent risks in bank lending. Among transition economies, for example, Estonia, Latvia and Lithuania have a 10 per cent capital adequacy standard. In contrast, Armenia, Russia and Ukraine have yet to raise their standard to the 8 per cent level.

Chart 6.2

Average ratings for extensiveness and effectiveness of legal rules in banking by region

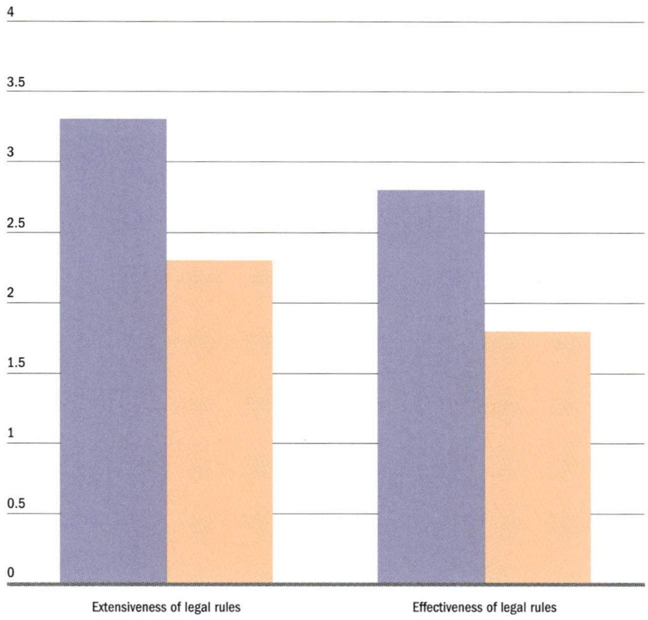

Source: EBRD.

The survey identified a number of problems associated with effective implementation of legal rules across many transition economies. Many bank supervisory staffs were significantly understaffed. Lack of financial resources as well as high staff turnover were two of the primary reasons for the problem. For example, while Poland receives high marks for its legal framework, it has had problems with on-site examinations due to a shortage of trained staff. But perhaps the most significant problem is the lack of use of internationally acceptable accounting standards. One troubling consequence of this is that the lack of requirements for consolidated accounts makes it difficult for supervisors to assess adequately the level of inter-affiliate lending and relationships between banks. In their assessments of banking in transition economies, the IMF and the Central European Working Group of the Institute for International Finance have also identified these issues as key problem areas.[12]

A particular challenge in the effective implementation of banking laws and regulations is the resolution of troubled banks. Here, the recent actions of the Hungarian regulator set a strong example. In August 1998, it issued an American-style "cease-and-desist order" against one of the largest commercial banks in Hungary, Postabank. This order restrained the management and suspended the board of directors. The Hungarian State Banking Supervision Office installed a commissioner to oversee the troubled bank's affairs. While several countries are to be commended for their use of prompt and corrective actions, the use of enforcement proceedings also points out some of the problems that exist with respect to prudential regulation. In particular, banking supervisors may lack autonomy with respect to corrective action. In Hungary, the State Banking Supervision Office must also seek prior consent

[12] See Institute for International Finance (1997) and International Monetary Fund (1998).

from a banking supervisory committee, comprised of members from the Ministry of Finance, the National Bank of Hungary and the Supervisor's office. The need for prior approval can constrain both the extent to and speed at which enforcement actions can take place.

Securities activities

While the extensiveness of securities laws is now broadly on a par with that of banking, their effectiveness remains less than that of banking. The problems affecting the development of viable securities markets are very similar throughout the region, though varying significantly in terms of magnitude. The lack of effective regulation and weaknesses in accounting and auditing continue to hold back the performance of equity markets. These markets are generally thin and illiquid with the exception of a small number of "blue-chip" shares (see Chapter 5). However, as certain markets have expanded, there has been some improvement in their regulatory structure and functioning, with Hungary and Poland being the most advanced in this respect.

While most transition economies now have functioning securities markets, those countries that received either a 1 or a 2 for extensiveness have either no stock exchange or alternatively an extremely rudimentary system of trading coupled with a minimal legislative framework. Azerbaijan and Georgia, for example, do not yet have a functioning stock exchange. More generally, most CIS countries receive a relatively low score for the extensiveness of legal rules for securities activities (see Chart 6.3).

Among those countries with functioning stock exchanges, most have adequate disclosure and transparency standards with respect to the provision of information to shareholders. However, the accounting information contained in financial statements is only infrequently prepared on the basis of internationally acceptable accounting standards. A number of countries have established an active securities commission or other regulatory body that enforces prudential regulations. For example, as discussed in Box 6.5, the Czech Securities Commission, which began operations in April 1998, is a government agency that possesses a range of enforcement powers.

Countries with still higher scores in the capital markets segment of the survey have greater safeguards with respect to investment funds. Poland, for example, enacted a new Law on Investment Funds (which came into force in February 1998). This law replaces a 1991 Law on Public Trading in Securities and Trust Funds, and requires that investment funds be established as joint-stock companies with capital of at least PLN 3 million. In October 1997, the Russian Federal Securities Commission also passed regulations on portfolio management and funds invested in securities. They require that only licensed broker-dealers may engage in portfolio management. Furthermore, a specific licence is required for broker-dealers who want to engage in portfolio management activities. Kazakhstan, by contrast, is only beginning to draft legislation with respect to fund management and the role of fund managers.

Chart 6.3

Average ratings for extensiveness and effectiveness of legal rules in securities activities by region

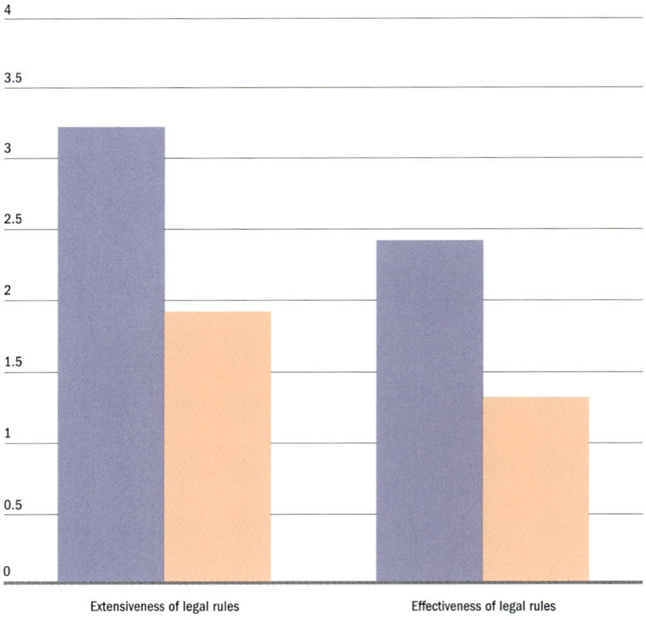

Source: EBRD.

6.3 Sound finance and transition: challenges for legal reform

The survey reveals that, while some countries in the region have significantly better financial laws than others, no country has a combination of legal rules and a supporting legal system that together meet minimum international financial standards. Bridging that gap requires legal reform, the nature of which must be responsive to the problems of the individual countries in adopting, and tailoring to their own circumstances, the minimum international standards discussed earlier and invigorating adopted laws with an enhanced respect for the rule-of-law.

A region-by-region perspective

For leading EU accession candidates in CEE (the Czech Republic, Estonia, Hungary, Poland and Slovenia), the adoption of EU standards and their effective implementation is a major priority. The immediate challenge for these countries is to raise the standards of financial disclosure imposed on market participants. In the other EU accession candidates (Bulgaria, Latvia, Lithuania, Romania and the Slovak Republic) the challenge is more basic and is to improve laws on the regulation of securities, introduce stricter capital adequacy requirements and improve financial disclosure.

Survey responses for Russia show that the primary transition challenge is to engender confidence in the financial markets, mainly by introducing more effective legal rules to make them more transparent, increasing financial stability overall and ensuring that financial obligations can be properly enforced. Effective regulation and supervision and the development of a better functioning

Box 6.5

Developing local capital markets

The experiences of East Asia and of central and eastern Europe, the Baltics and the CIS show that adequate and effective capital market regulation is essential for the development of stable domestic financial markets. Accordingly, the EBRD is increasingly focusing on the development of capital markets, not only to support its own investment goals, but also to further the development of sources of long-term finance for the private sector throughout the region.

A case study of the Czech Republic

The EBRD is currently undertaking a technical cooperation project to provide assistance to the Czech Republic in establishing a securities commission for the supervision and regulation of the Czech capital markets. This initiative followed from the period of financial instability in 1996 and 1997, when a number of events occurred in the Czech Republic that triggered a loss of confidence in the local capital markets. Contributing factors included significant problems in the banking sector, a rapidly mounting current account deficit, the slow pace of industrial restructuring, a progressive deterioration in the financial performance of some investment funds, and reports of illegal and fraudulent activity by market participants. An ensuing attack on the Czech koruna during the spring of 1997 led to a currency devaluation. These events contributed to a change of government in November 1997.

This situation led to strong demands for regulatory reforms and improved supervisory functions. As part of its reforms, the interim Czech government announced a number of measures intended to strengthen the regulation of the local capital markets, including the enactment of a law providing for the establishment of a securities commission.

The Law on the Securities Commission and on Amendments and Supplements to Other Laws (the Securities Commission Law) was approved by the Czech parliament on 13 January 1998. It transferred (effective 1 April 1998) the regulatory and supervisory functions with respect to the Czech capital markets from the Czech Ministry of Finance (MOF) to the Securities Commission. The Law provides for the establishment of the Commission and for its organisational structure and activity. Under the Securities Commission Law, the Commission possesses certain powers related to the regulation of the Czech capital markets and is required to act in a manner that will contribute to the "development and security" of these markets.

At the request of the Czech Minister of Finance, the EBRD is currently providing legal technical assistance to the Commission under a project funded by EU Phare. The primary objectives of the project are twofold:

First, the project aims to assist the Commission in: (i) reviewing and revising the Securities Commission Law, the Czech Securities Act of 1992 and related legislation; (ii) preparing regulations that will supplement the newly adopted Law; and (iii) facilitating integration with EU legislation (thereby accelerating the accession process).

Second, the project aims to provide assistance in establishing a regulatory authority which will enable the capital markets to function in an efficient, fair and transparent manner, thus increasing the level of confidence of the investor community. In particular, it aims at achieving: (i) the development of regulations and procedures for the proper functioning of the Commission; (ii) the development of regulations and procedures (e.g. licences and licensing procedures) for use by the Commission in order to ensure fairness, transparency, efficiency and consistency in the exercise of its powers; (iii) the development of an appropriate organisational and management structure as well as operating systems for the Commission; and (iv) training for commissioners and other Commission staff on matters related to the functioning of the Commission, to include workshops with experts from other countries.

It is intended that the project will have a significant impact on the transition through institution building in an area critical to private sector development. The project will also assist with the EU accession process by ensuring that the legislative and regulatory framework governing the Commission's activities and, more generally, the Czech capital markets, are consistent with EU directives and other norms.

Debt issues by the EBRD in local capital markets

In addition to its normal equity investments, the EBRD also contemplates issuing bonds denominated in local currency in certain of its countries of operations (one such issue has already been conducted in Hungary). Local currency issues by the Bank serve to enhance the credibility of the local debt capital market and encourage other domestic and foreign borrowers to participate in these markets, thus accelerating the transition process.

If such issues are to be brought to the market successfully, however, certain legal obstacles need to be overcome. In order to bring about the desired legislative and regulatory changes, including changes to the regulations and established practices of the relevant securities authorities and stock exchanges, a number of issues need to be addressed and the EBRD is currently identifying ways in which this can be done. These issues relate to, among other things: disclosure requirements, listing requirements, settlement and local clearing systems, tax treatment, accounting requirements and issues specific to foreign issuers, including monetary and exchange controls.

legal system are essential in order to rebuild confidence in the financial system to help the current crisis pass and to avoid it recurring. Moreover, only through strengthening the rule-of-law will Russia be able to encourage the development of a viable financial system and to reduce the pernicious effects of corruption.

Belarus, Bosnia and Herzegovina, Moldova and Ukraine, as well as the countries of the Balkan region (with exceptions in some respects for Croatia), share the need to improve their basic laws relating to both the enforcement of financial transactions and the privatisation of financial institutions. The challenges for the Central Asian countries are similar, with improved respect for the rule-of-law being a priority.

Responding to the challenges

The legal foundations of sound finance require not only that the right financial laws be created but that they be supported by a legal system that ensures they are effective. Legal reform programmes must thus extend beyond the mere enactment of normative laws to ensuring that they are actually implemented in a way that fosters confidence in their operation.[13] Box 6.5 provides an example of an EBRD legal reform project for the improvement of the Czech capital markets.

Efforts at legal reform will fail, however, if they do not attract sufficient political support. In particular, governments must give legal reform the needed legislative priority and budgetary support if the

[13] For a recent review of the financial legal reform process in general, see Norton (1998) and for the EBRD's approach to legal reform, see Taylor and April (1997).

right financial laws are to be enacted and their implementation funded. Constant sensitivity to, and expressed support for, the rule-of-law is also necessary if the public is to have confidence in the law-making process, the quality of the law produced by that process, and the independent role of a competent judiciary in interpreting the law.

6.4 Conclusion

This chapter helps disseminate recent work in international forums to develop core principles for financial laws and regulations, and assesses the extensiveness and effectiveness of these legal rules in the region relative to international standards. The analysis shows that many countries in central and eastern Europe, the Baltics and the CIS have made considerable, but not uniform, progress in establishing the basic legal and regulatory framework to support financial markets. However, the implementation and enforcement of laws have not kept pace with law-making activity, particularly in securities activities but also in banking. This lag both undermines the value of good normative laws and diminishes respect for the rule-of-law. This deficiency may exacerbate the region's vulnerability to financial crises. More generally, without respect for the rule-of-law, the transition process will not only prove slow, but existing achievements may well be reversed.

In advancing the transition, the countries of the region need to undertake the reforms necessary to increase their integration into the international financial system. This process entails necessary changes in the legal framework and financial practices in order to advance this goal. Further, EU accession countries face the challenge of harmonising their laws and institutions with the requirements of the *acquis communautaire.* As emphasised by the EC White Paper, integration into the international financial system must be based on the foundation of an effectively functioning domestic financial system.

While appropriate and effectively enforced financial laws are the foundation of sound finance, the building blocks of the financial sector are the financial institutions and markets themselves. The performance of these institutions and markets determines how well the financial sector as a whole functions and how effectively it contributes to economic growth and macroeconomic stability. Factors that shape the performance of a decentralised financial system are those that influence the performance of individual institutions and markets. Examples are the extent of private ownership of financial institutions and the effectiveness of their corporate governance practices, and the extent of competition in the market for financial services. Chapter 7 seeks to identify empirically those factors that shape the performance of banks in transition economies, the dominant type of financial institution in these economies. Chapter 8 considers the policies that can serve to promote the performance of banks, including ways to manage the process of competition among banks and to enhance their private ownership and corporate governance.

References

Basle Committee on Banking Supervision (1997), *Core Principles of Effective Banking Supervision,* BIS, Basle.

U. Bhattacgarya (1998), "On the possibility of Ponzi schemes in transition economies", Kelley School of Business, Indiana University, mimeo.

T. Carothers (1998), "The rule of law revival", *Foreign Affairs,* Vol. 77, pp. 95-106.

C. Clague, P. Keefer, S. Knack and M. Olson (1996), "Property and contract rights in autocracies and democracies", *Journal of Economic Growth,* Vol. 1, pp. 243-76.

EBRD (1997), *Sound Business Standards and Corporate Practices: A Set of Guidelines,* London.

European Commission (1995), *White Paper on the Preparation of the Associated Countries of Central and Eastern Europe for Integration into the Internal Market of the Union,* European Commission, Brussels.

D. Folkerts-Landau and C.-J. Lindgren (1998), *Toward a Framework for Financial Stability,* International Monetary Fund, Washington DC.

Group of Ten (1997), "A strategy for the formulation, adoption and implementation of sound principles and practices to strengthen financial systems", *Report of the Group of Ten (G-10) Working Party on Financial Stability in Emerging Markets.*

International Accounting Standards Committee (1998), *International Accounting Standards,* IASC, London.

International Association of Insurance Supervisors (1997a), *Insurance Supervisory Principle,* IAIS, Basle.

International Association of Insurance Supervisors (1997b), *Guidance on Insurance Regulation and Supervision for Emerging Market Economies,* IAIS, Basle.

International Organisation of Securities Commissions (1997), *Principles for the Supervision of Operators of Collective Investment Schemes,* IOSCO, Montreal.

International Organisation of Securities Commissions (1998), *Objectives and Principles of Securities Regulation,* IOSCO, Montreal.

Institute of International Finance, Central and Eastern European Working Group (1997), *Response to the Basle Core Principles,* IIF, Washington DC.

J. Norton (1998), "Reflections on the development of capital markets, stock exchanges and securities regulations in central and eastern Europe", in U. Drobnig, K. Hopt, K. Kötz and E-J Mestmäcker, *Systemtransformation in Mittel- und Osteuropa und ihre Folgen für Banken,* Börsen und Kreditsicherheiten, Hamburg.

M. Olson (1996), "Big bills left on the sidewalk: Why some nations are rich and others poor", *Journal of Economic Perspectives,* Vol.10, pp. 3-24.

J.-H. Rover and J. Simpson (1994), "Model law on secured transactions", EBRD, mimeo.

J. Taylor and F. April (1997), "Fostering investment law in transitional economies: A case for refocusing institutional reform", *Parker School Journal of East European Law,* Vol. 4, pp. 1-52.

Performance of financial institutions: lessons from transition banking

7

The extent to which banks in a post-communist country can mobilise and allocate capital efficiently and prudently is an important determinant of how well its real economy performs. Banks must mobilise domestic savings to fund the investment that is necessary to advance the transition and to sustain growth. They must allocate funds to the kind of investment that contributes strongly to structural change and enhanced productivity, particularly that by the private sector and small and medium-sized enterprises. Banks must also provide monetary payments without which markets can operate only at high cost. But how is it possible to judge whether the banks of a particular country are performing their role effectively? One approach is to focus on the overall economy. However, there are many factors in addition to the performance of banks that can influence economic growth and output fluctuations. Identifying the influence of each is not always possible, particularly when the time period is short, as it is for transition economies.

An alternative approach is to examine the performance of individual banks to form an assessment of how well they are performing as financial intermediaries. A basic measure of bank performance is profitability. The profits earned by a bank reflect the value to customers of its deposit taking and lending services. However, banking activities can generate profits in a variety of ways: by being more efficient and providing better services to customers; by using market dominance to set low deposit rates and high loan rates; or by trading in government debt and foreign exchange, particularly when the macroeconomy is unstable. Identifying the way in which profits are earned and interest margins are determined thus provides an indication of how well banks are serving the economy.

The scale of deposit taking and lending and the growth of this activity can also provide valuable indicators of banking performance. They provide measures of the extent to which banks have become integrated into the real economy and of whether this integration is increasing or decreasing. Given the widespread under-provision of financial services in transition economies, described in Chapter 5, increasing the depth and breadth of banking activity is of vital importance to the transition. But what factors are associated with the expansion of banking activity? Clearly, the overall economic environment can have a significant impact on the returns to real investment in the economy and thus on the opportunities to expand lending. It is also important to identify what types of banks in transition economies are responding to customer demands for more services in order to assess how the stable expansion of banking takes place and what policies can promote it.

This chapter assesses the performance of banks in transition economies. The selection of countries and banks for the analysis reflects the availability of data at the bank level and this availability is associated primarily with the quality of financial accounting and disclosure practices. It includes all countries of central and eastern Europe and the Baltic region, except Albania, Bosnia and Herzegovina, and four CIS countries: Belarus, Kazakhstan, Russia and Ukraine (16 in all). The banks covered by this chapter (452 in all) are the larger commercial and savings banks in each country and they account for the vast majority of the banking operations in their respective countries. This sample is selective within countries to the extent that it excludes smaller banks and those that do not publicly disclose their financial accounts (often banks that are chronically loss-making).

The analysis in this chapter finds that the profitability of banks has varied significantly depending on their market share and ownership structure, on the types of assets they hold and on the economic environment in which they operate. In particular, banks with a large share of their national retail deposit market have often been able to raise revenues above competitive levels. However, banks have tended to make losses on customer loans, even those with a large share of the loan market. In terms of bank assets, the holdings of government securities have been the main source of net revenue. Banks with less market power and with foreign participation have offered more competitive deposit and loan terms to their customers, suggesting that there is a competitive fringe of banks placing pressure on the dominant institutions. Private ownership of banks has also had a significant impact on performance. Newly formed and privatised banks have been more profitable than comparable state-owned banks, but undoubtedly the better state banks have been selected for privatisation.

The scale of banking activity has tended to increase in step with macroeconomic stabilisation and with progress in transition. In addition, banks with less market share and with foreign participation have expanded their customer loans (after allowing for inflation) more rapidly than other banks. There is evidence that a minority of financially weak banks is expanding its customer loans more rapidly than well-capitalised banks, although this is not a dominant feature of transition banking. These findings suggest that the process of competition, including foreign entry, is contributing to the needed expansion of banking activity, and that the application of prudential regulation is promoting sound banking in many but not all banks.

Taken together, these findings point to important roles for competition and private ownership – along with enforcement of prudential requirements, such as capital adequacy standards – in strengthening the performance of banks in transition economies. Chapter 8 examines in detail the key policy issues identified in this chapter, in particular those to enhance competition and to increase private ownership. The issues of prudential regulation in banking were considered in Chapter 6.

The remainder of the chapter consists of five sections. Section 7.1 reports on the overall scale and profitability of banks in transition economies and how they vary over time and across countries. It also provides a reliability check on the quality of the financial accounts (primarily loan quality) by examining the relationship between the real rates of growth in customer loans and the strength of banks' balance sheets. The second section examines the relationship between the profitability of banks, their market share and type of ownership and the overall economic environment in which they operate. Section 7.3 examines which banks in transition economies have a stronger customer orientation, focusing on the competitiveness of pricing and on the expansion of services (customer loans). The fourth section draws an overall assessment of bank performance in transition economies and compares these findings with evidence on bank performance in market economies. Section 7.5 concludes the chapter, identifying key policy issues and preparing the ground for Chapter 8.

7.1 Scale, financial performance and risk-taking in banking

This section reports on the scale, quality and financial performance of banks in the 16 transition economies covered by the chapter.[1] The measures of scale in banking are the levels of deposit taking and lending relative to the size of the overall economy in which they are provided. These activities embody the financial services that banks provide: mobilisation of savings, evaluation of investment projects, monitoring of loans and provision of payment services. As important as the scale of banking activity are its qualitative dimensions. And a particularly important dimension in transition economies is the maturity structure of lending. Measures of profitability (net income before taxes relative to total assets), net interest margins (interest revenues less interest expenses scaled by total assets) and capitalisation (equity relative to total assets) characterise a bank's financial performance. This characterisation is in terms of the flow of profits, the setting of interest rates on loans and deposits, and the adequacy of bank capital.

One of the (many) limitations of using accounting data to form judgements about bank performance is the ease with which banks can conceal problem loans, particularly in transition economies but even in industrialised market economies.[2] Therefore, the section also examines the relationship between the balance-sheet strength of banks and the quality of their lending. The growth rate of a bank's lending (adjusted for inflation) serves as a proxy for risk taking, based on the assumption that more rapid loan growth comes at the expense of greater risk. The other working assumption is that a bank's capitalisation determines in part its incentive for risk taking, with a less well-capitalised bank more likely to engage in risky activities because it has less of its own funds at risk.

Scale

A key finding in Chapter 5 is that the scale of banking in transition economies is significantly less than that in comparable market economies. This result holds regardless of whether the scale of banking is measured in terms of deposit taking (broad money) or lending (total domestic credit or credit to the private sector). The only measure of scale in which banks in transition economies lie above their benchmark from market economies is in lending to the public sector. This result suggests that transition economies suffer from an under-provision of bank intermediation, particularly in mobilising savings and in allocating credit to the private sector. The under-provision is particularly pronounced in countries of the former Soviet Union, in part because of the extreme macroeconomic instability that prevailed in these countries early in the transition.

Table 7.1 reports measures of banking scale for the 16 transition economies considered in detail in this chapter for the years 1993-97. While much of the variation across countries is due to "major events" (such as the near hyperinflation around the time of the break-up of the Soviet Union), more gradual changes over time and across countries point to additional factors that can influence the scale of banking activity. Among this group of countries, only six (Croatia, the Czech Republic, Estonia, Poland, the Slovak Republic and Slovenia) experienced growth in both deposit taking and lending to the private sector beyond that of nominal GDP over the period under consideration. Each of these countries has reached a more advanced stage of transition and has achieved a degree of macroeconomic stability and growth.[3] The more advanced transition economies that did not see a significant increase in banking activity in this period either experienced significant banking troubles (Latvia and Lithuania) or implemented a major banking consolidation programme (Hungary). The countries at less advanced stages of transition (Belarus, Kazakhstan, Russia and Ukraine) experienced continued decline in the scale of banking activity.

Quality

Bank lending in transition economies tends to be short term, reflecting the unsettled economic environment in which banks operate, the weak legal and accounting frameworks to support long-term, secured lending, and the need to develop credit skills and practices necessary for sound lending decisions. Progress in expanding the maturity structure of bank lending is thus an important indicator of how well banks in transition economies are able to perform as financial intermediaries.

Available evidence reveals that banks in transition economies have been able to achieve only modest progress in expanding the maturity of their lending. Chart 7.1 shows that the share of long-term loans in total customer loans increased to 48 per cent in 1995 from 33 per cent in 1993, before tapering off to 43 per cent in 1997.

1 See also Anderson, Berglöf and Mizsei (1996) and Anderson and Kegels (1998) for an overview of developments in transition banking.

2 On the origins of this problem in transition economies and on possible ways to overcome it, see Mitchell (1993, 1998) and Aghion, Bolton and Fries (1998).

3 The grouping of countries into those at more and less advanced stages of transition is based on the EBRD's transition indicators. See Chapter 2 of this and previous *Transition Reports* for a discussion of the transition indicators. Chapter 3 of this Report examines the macroeconomic performance and prospects of transition economies.

Table 7.1

Scale of deposit taking and lending in transition economies

Ratio of broad money to GDP (in per cent)

Country	1993	1994	1995	1996	1997	Country average
Belarus	–	39	15	15	18	22
Bulgaria	78	78	66	75	34	66
Croatia	26	20	25	34	42	29
Czech Republic	70	73	81	75	71	74
Estonia	28	26	25	27	30	27
FYR Macedonia	73	14	12	12	14	25
Hungary	50	46	43	42	42	45
Kazakhstan	–	13	12	9	10	11
Latvia	32	34	23	23	38	30
Lithuania	23	26	23	17	19	22
Poland	36	37	36	38	40	37
Romania	23	22	25	28	24	24
Russia	24	21	17	16	17	19
Slovak Republic	69	68	69	71	69	69
Slovenia	30	34	37	39	43	37
Ukraine	32	27	13	12	14	20
Annual average	*42*	*36*	*33*	*33*	*33*	*35*

Ratio of credit to the private sector to GDP (in per cent)

Country	1993	1994	1995	1996	1997	Country average
Belarus	–	18	6	7	9	10
Bulgaria	4	4	21	37	13	16
Croatia	47	29	31	29	38	35
Czech Republic	51	60	60	57	68	59
Estonia	11	14	15	18	26	17
FYR Macedonia	59	49	26	30	30	39
Hungary	28	26	23	22	24	25
Kazakhstan	45	25	7	6	5	18
Latvia	17	16	8	7	11	12
Lithuania	14	18	15	11	10	14
Poland	12	12	13	16	18	14
Romania	–	–	–	–	–	–
Russia	12	12	8	7	8	9
Slovak Republic	32	24	28	32	44	32
Slovenia	22	23	27	29	29	26
Ukraine	1	5	1	1	2	2
Annual average	*26*	*22*	*19*	*21*	*23*	*22*

Sources: IMF, *International Financial Statistics*, and EBRD.

However, data on the maturity structure of customer loans are available for only some banks in the region, in particular those in countries in central and eastern Europe that are at more advanced stages of transition and that have achieved a degree of macroeconomic stability. The share of long-term loans in total customer loans for other banks in the region is likely to be lower than that for banks that disclose the maturity structure of their loans.

Financial performance

Table 7.2 reports the profitability of banks in transition economies for the years 1993-97 measured as the ratio of net profits before taxes to total assets.[4] Across most countries and over all years, the average rate of return on bank assets was in the range of 1 to 3 per cent. In comparison, the profitability of banks in OECD countries for the years 1993-95 averaged 0.7 per cent of total assets. Across countries, Ukraine witnessed exceptionally high reported bank profitability, reflecting the generous profits that banks can earn in an unstable macroeconomic environment by investing in high-

[4] The source of the financial data on banks in transition economies is the BankScope database of Bureau van Dijk, which includes data on 10,227 banks worldwide and of which 452 are in transition economies. The data used in this chapter are from the May 1998 issue of BankScope.

Table 7.2

Average ratio of net income before taxes to total assets of banks in transition economies, 1993-97[1]

(in per cent)

Country	1993	1994	1995	1996	1997[2]	Country average
Belarus	5.7	4.6	3.1	0.1	na	3.4
Bulgaria	0.2	1.8	1.2	4.5	16	4.7
Croatia	3.5	-0.5	-2.5	-0.7	1.2	0.2
Czech Republic	0.5	1.0	0.8	-0.4	0.6	0.5
Estonia	4.1	0.8	2.5	2.9	3.0	2.7
FYR Macedonia	7.9	-0.6	2.0	2.2	1.7	2.6
Hungary	-5.2	1.3	1.6	1.7	0.6	0.0
Kazakhstan	0.0	2.8	3.6	5.1	2.8	2.9
Latvia	4.5	1.5	1.0	3.6	3.4	2.8
Lithuania	7.2	-2.6	-2.1	-1.1	0.3	0.3
Poland	2.9	1.4	3.3	3.5	1.7	2.6
Romania	5.9	4.2	5.0	-1.6	9.1	4.5
Russia	2.9	2.5	1.5	6.2	1.7	3.0
Slovak Republic	2.1	1.4	1.2	0.1	1.6	1.3
Slovenia	1.7	0.5	1.2	1.3	0.4	1.0
Ukraine	13.6	13.6	9.4	8.2	2.6	9.5
Annual average	*3.6*	*2.1*	*2.1*	*2.2*	*3.1*	*2.6*

Source: BankScope.

1 Averages for each country in any year are weighted by the total assets of each bank. Averages over years for a particular country and across countries for a particular year are unweighted.

2 Based on incomplete data.

yielding government debt and trading in foreign exchange.[5] Four countries (Croatia, the Czech Republic, Hungary and Lithuania) recorded average bank profitability below 1 per cent of total assets over the period. Over time there does not appear to be a significant trend in bank profitability in transition economies.

Chart 7.2 plots the distribution of profitability for all 452 banks and for each of the five years under consideration. The distribution for each year has a single peak (mode) and the spread (dispersion) of the distribution declines over time. This finding is consistent with the view that the convergence in overall economic conditions across countries has tended to equalise returns to banking activities across all banks in all countries. Similar findings are also obtained for all banks in five individual countries for which there are a large number of observations (Croatia, the Czech Republic, Hungary, Poland and Russia) (not shown), suggesting that competition among them is tending to equalise returns as well.[6] However, this sample of banks is biased in the way it has been constructed because it includes only those banks that publicly disclose their accounts. It may well be the case that only better-performing banks disclose their accounts, with some poorly performing banks being systematically excluded from the sample. It may also be the case that the disclosed financial accounts do not adequately measure the true financial performance of banks.

Chart 7.1

Long-term lending to customers

(in per cent)

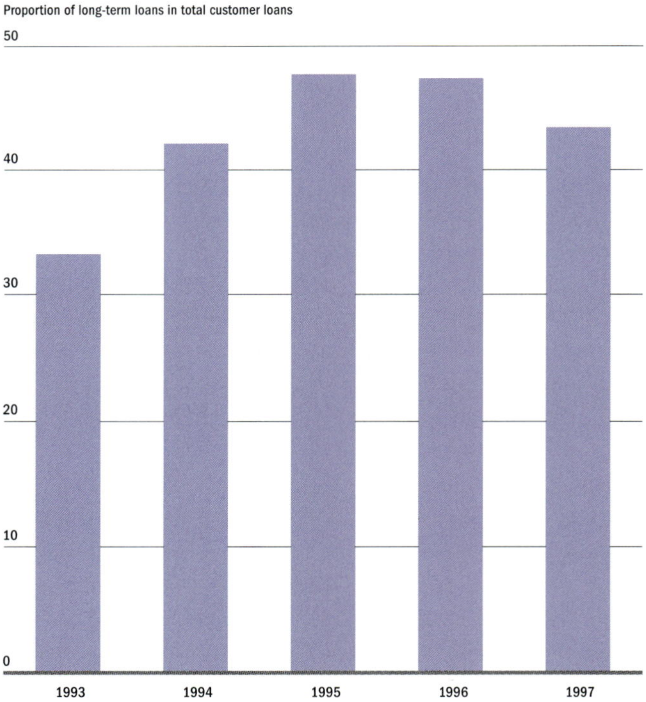

Source: BankScope.

5 It is important to recognise, however, that in periods of high inflation the real profitability of banks is significantly lower than their nominal profitability. Part of these nominal profits serves to maintain the real value of a bank's capital.

6 A separate analysis was performed for the countries where there are a sufficient number of observations to perform the statistical analysis. The composition of the sample of banks in transition economies is as follows: Belarus (9), Bulgaria (26), Croatia (34), Czech Republic (29), Estonia (14), FYR Macedonia (14), Hungary (34), Kazakhstan (13), Latvia (20) Lithuania (15), Poland (43), Romania (20), Russia (126), Slovak Republic (15), Slovenia (17) and Ukraine (23). The number of banks in each country is given in parentheses.

Table 7.3

Average ratio of net interest income to total assets of banks in transition economies, 1993-97[1]

(in per cent)

Country	1993	1994	1995	1996	1997[2]	Country average
Belarus	4.7	5.9	12.6	8.4	na	7.9
Bulgaria	-0.1	-3.1	1.7	5.7	2.4	1.3
Croatia	13.9	2.7	2.6	3.4	3.2	5.2
Czech Republic	4.6	3.9	3.1	2.6	3.3	3.5
Estonia	5.4	5.9	5.1	4.8	4.1	5.0
FYR Macedonia	16.0	16.0	10.3	8.9	6.2	11.5
Hungary	3.7	4.8	4.9	4.2	3.1	4.1
Kazakhstan	na	3.3	10.3	9.2	7.4	7.6
Latvia	6.8	8.0	7.5	6.3	0.4	5.8
Lithuania	10.5	8.9	6.8	5.3	3.9	7.1
Poland	3.8	4.7	5.1	4.9	2.3	4.2
Romania	9.5	6.4	7.3	5.1	10.7	7.8
Russia	3.3	3.0	6.7	11.3	4.0	5.7
Slovak Republic	4.8	4.6	4.0	2.8	2.8	3.8
Slovenia	5.9	1.9	3.4	4.1	4.3	3.9
Ukraine	16.3	21.8	15.0	15.5	9.2	15.5
Annual average	*7.3*	*6.2*	*6.6*	*6.4*	*4.5*	*6.2*

Source: BankScope.

[1] Averages for each country in any year are weighted by the total assets of each bank. Averages over years for a particular country and across countries for a particular year are unweighted.

[2] Based on incomplete data.

The net interest margin of banks – the difference between interest revenues and interest expenses scaled by their total assets – is a key determinant of bank profitability. The net interest margins generate the revenues of banks, from which operating expenses and loan loss provisions are paid. Table 7.3 reports the net interest margins of banks in transition economies over the years 1993-97. There is a significant decline in the average margins over time, falling to 5 per cent in 1997 (based on incomplete data) from 7 per cent in 1993. This effect could be due to greater macroeconomic stability and to progress in structural reform. In 1996, however, net interest margins still varied widely across countries, with the widest margins (above 8 per cent) in Belarus, FYR Macedonia, Kazakhstan, Russia and Ukraine. Those countries with higher margins tend to have made less progress in transition and in macroeconomic stabilisation. As a benchmark, the average net interest margin in OECD countries for the years 1993-95 was 2.3 per cent.

Table 7.4 reports the financial strength of banks' balance sheets in transition economies, specifically the ratio of equity to total assets. Over time and across countries, this ratio averages just above 9 per cent. There is an upward trend over time in the average ratio across the countries, rising from 8 per cent in 1994 to 12 per cent in 1997 (based on incomplete data). By 1996, most countries had achieved an average capital ratio of 8 per cent or more for those banks that publicly disclose their accounts. The exceptions were Belarus, Hungary, Kazakhstan, Lithuania, Romania and the Slovak Republic.

Taken together, the country-level evidence suggests that financial performance and scale of activity tend to move in opposite direc-

Chart 7.2

Frequency distribution of bank profitability, 1993-97

(in per cent)

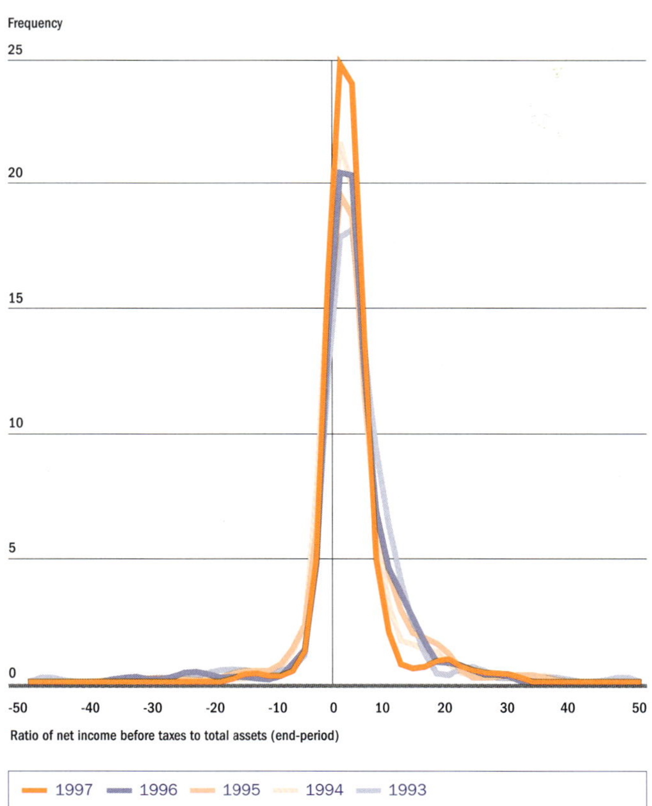

Source: BankScope.

Table 7.4

Average ratio of equity to total assets of banks in transition economies, 1993-97[1]

(in per cent)

Country	1993	1994	1995	1996	1997[2]	Country average
Belarus	1.2	1.9	8.4	5.2	na	4.2
Bulgaria	4.8	6.0	5.9	15.2	29.4	12.3
Croatia	15.1	16.8	14.4	14.8	11.0	14.4
Czech Republic	5.2	8.3	9.1	8.1	6.3	7.4
Estonia	8.0	6.5	9.5	9.5	9.0	8.5
FYR Macedonia	19	11.6	23.6	24.7	21.8	20.1
Hungary	4.6	6.6	8.0	7.5	8.4	7.0
Kazakhstan	6.1	4.9	10.6	-0.8	17.8	7.7
Latvia	11.9	13.9	12.9	13.5	10.9	12.6
Lithuania	6.4	6.1	1.2	5.7	7.5	5.4
Poland	4.6	6.1	7.1	9.1	7.7	6.9
Romania	8.9	9.7	9.3	3.5	13.2	8.9
Russia	11.2	10.9	8.9	13.8	12.8	11.5
Slovak Republic	6.2	6.9	6.8	6.0	7.1	6.6
Slovenia	16.3	9.9	10.4	10.2	11.6	11.7
Ukraine	4.7	4.6	8.6	13.2	8.2	7.9
Annual average	*8.4*	*8.2*	*9.7*	*10.0*	*12.2*	*9.6*

Source: BankScope.

1 Averages for each country in any year are weighted by the total assets of each bank. Averages over years for a particular country and across countries for a particular year are unweighted.

2 Based on incomplete data.

tions as the economic environment improves. In general, those countries at earlier stages of transition and with greater macroeconomic instability have had banking systems that are small in scale relative to the size of the economy in which they operate. They have had wide net interest margins and, in some cases, high rates of profitability. Progress in both transition and macroeconomic stabilisation has tended to be accompanied by an expansion of banking activity and by a narrowing of net interest margins. This narrowing of net interest margins, however, has not translated into a squeeze on profitability in most countries because banking costs have also tended to decline, including provisions against loan losses.

Risk taking

While accounting profits and equity provide a snapshot of banks' financial performance, it is important to recognise that financial accounts may not provide the complete picture, particularly with respect to risk taking and loan quality. Regardless of their initial risk, loans are scored in the accounts of banks at their face value. Only if a loan subsequently becomes non-performing would a valuation adjustment be made to the bank's financial accounts. Moreover, any problem loans in a bank's portfolios often appear in its financial accounts only well after the fact, reflecting the degree of discretion that can be involved in the accounting valuation of (non-tradable) loans. Since accounting measures of loan quality are a lagging indicator of true quality, an alternative measure is necessary.

One contemporaneous indicator of loan quality is the growth rate of lending (adjusted for inflation) of a bank and of a banking system as a whole, with higher growth coming at the expense of greater risk.[7] This trade-off can arise for two reasons. Within a bank, a high rate of loan growth can stretch thinly the (relatively fixed) capacity of a bank to evaluate lending opportunities and to monitor loans, contributing to deterioration in the quality of new loans. For a banking system as a whole, high loan growth can be associated with deterioration in new loan quality because of diminishing returns to investment. In addition, a bank is less likely to discount fully loans for their riskiness when the funding of the bank itself is based more on the strength of the government's guarantee of deposits than on shareholder equity. That is, banks are more likely to make risky loans when less of their equity is at risk. This propensity towards risk taking in weakly capitalised banks is a manifestation of the "moral hazard" in which a risk is more likely to be taken when the downside consequences are shouldered elsewhere.

Chart 7.3 plots the relationship between the growth of loans (adjusted for inflation) and the ratio of equity to total assets for all banks in the sample. For these banks, high rates of loan growth are not associated with low ratios of equity to total assets. This lack of association between loan growth and bank capitalisation suggests that loan growth is not based primarily on the strength of government guarantees.[8]

7 Several recent studies of banking crises find real loan growth to be a leading indicator of such crises. See, for example, Goldstein and Turner (1996), Honohan (1997) and Kaminsky and Reinhart (1998).

8 For five countries considered separately (Croatia, Czech Republic, Hungary, Poland and Russia), there is a similar positive but insignificant relationship between loan growth and bank capitalisation, except in the Czech Republic where the positive association is significant.

Chart 7.3

Real loan growth versus bank capitalisation

(in per cent)

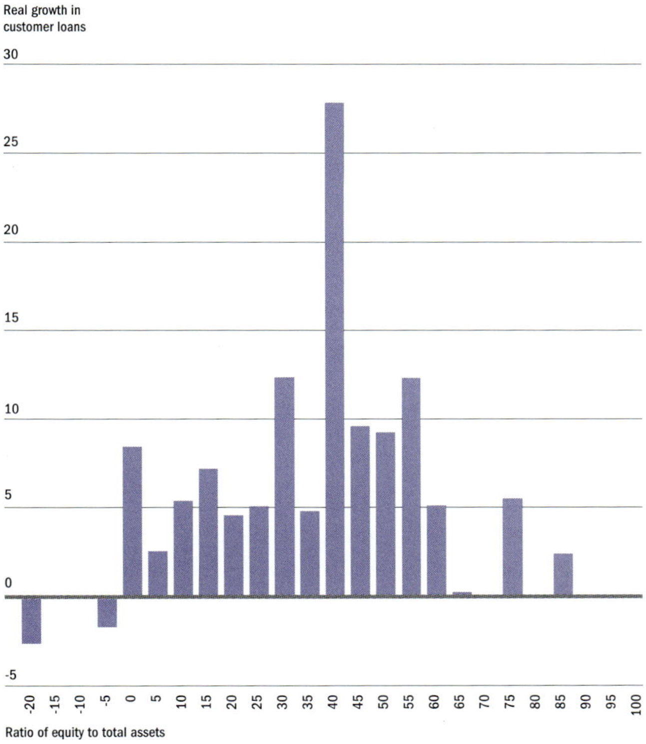

Source: BankScope.

Chart 7.4

Bank profitability versus deposit market share

(in per cent)

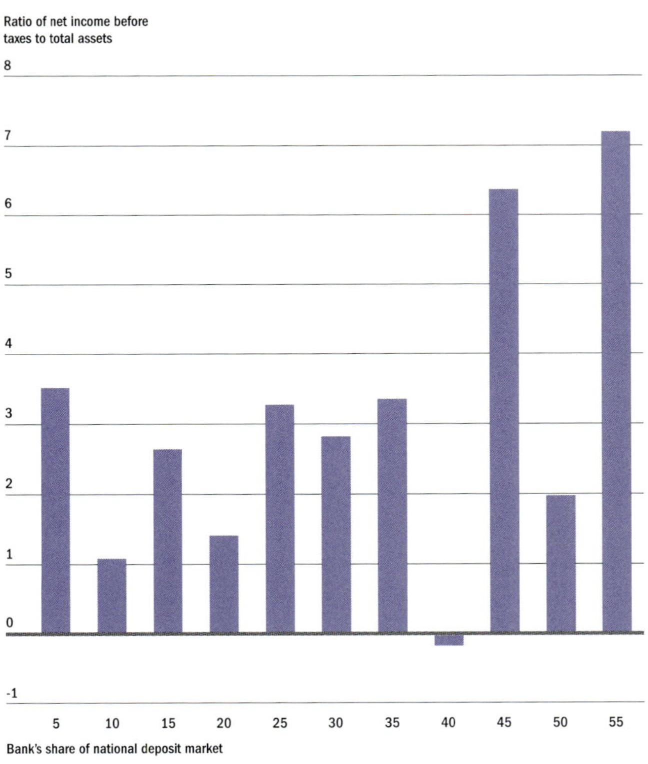

Source: BankScope.

There are several reasons, however, for interpreting this evidence with caution. First, as with the accounting valuation of loans, the ratio of equity to total assets is a lagging indicator of a bank's financial strength. The accounting measure of equity can overstate the true strength of a bank when non-performing loans have not been classified and provisioned against. Nevertheless, measured equity is somewhat less sensitive to mis-reporting than loan values are because it includes the equity contributions of shareholders as well as the cumulation of past reported profits and losses. Second, the results indicate the presence of a substantial minority of banks whose loan portfolios are growing on an inadequate foundation of shareholder equity. The behaviour of this minority of banks can give cause for concern even if it is not characteristic of the sample as a whole (as was the case of the US savings and loan crisis). Third, banks can engage in forms of risk taking other than rapid loan growth. A particular example is the large build-up of open foreign exchange positions by Russian banks, primarily by writing inadequately hedged forward contracts for foreign exchange.[9] In most transition economies, details on banks' off-balance-sheet exposures are not disclosed in their financial statements.

7.2 Bank profitability: country factors, market power and ownership

This section examines the factors that are associated with the variation in profitability of individual banks. Some of these factors can arise from outside the banks themselves and the banking systems in which they operate. A particular example is the high reported profits of Ukrainian banks, which are likely to be associated with the combination of macroeconomic instability, high interest rates and foreign exchange trading. This and other examples point to the potential significance of country factors in explaining variation in bank profitability. But factors at the level of a banking system and of individual banks might also be significant. Basic economic considerations suggest that both the degree of competition faced by a bank and its characteristics, such as its ownership and corporate governance, can have a significant influence on its performance.

As a preliminary analysis, Chart 7.4 plots profitability (measured as the rate of return on assets) and the bank's share of its national market for retail deposits. There is wide variability in profitability, but even so there is a statistically significant (though non-linear) relationship with market share. The profitability of banks with small market shares (up to 5 per cent) earn moderate rates of profit and this characterises a substantial part of the sample. As the market share increases, profitability tends to taper off. However, with market shares above 40 per cent, profitability rises substantially. It is important to note that, although there are very few banks with such large market shares, they account for a large proportion of total deposits.

Chart 7.5 shows the average profitability of banks grouped according to their ownership – new private, privatised, state-owned (by government and state-owned enterprises) and unknown ownership (either private or owned by a state-owned enterprise). The average profitability of banks with significant foreign partici-

[9] See Annex 1.1 to Chapter 1 on the Russian crisis.

Chart 7.5

Average bank profitability by ownership

(in per cent)

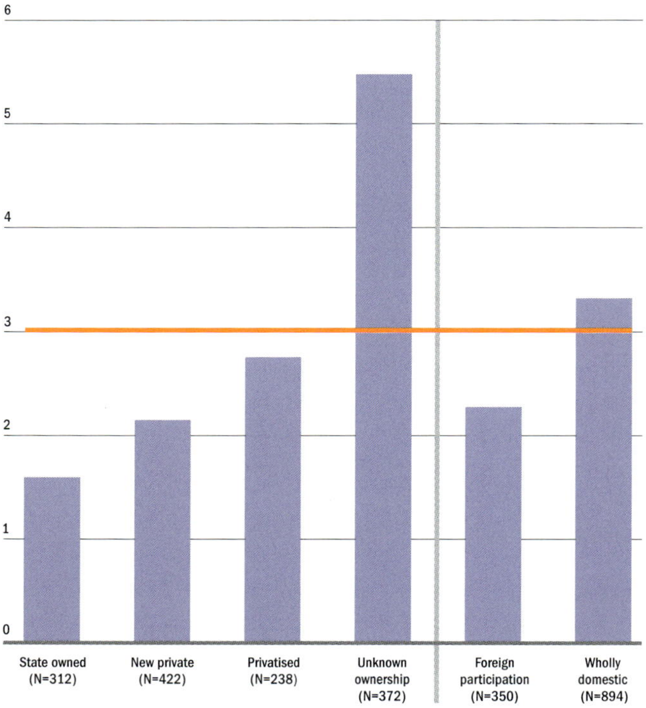

Profitability — Mean profitability

Source: BankScope.

pation is also shown. Privatised banks appear to achieve somewhat higher rates of profitability than new private banks and state-owned banks, but the difference is not dramatic. Given the findings about market share, it is unsurprising that the difference is not very large, since new private banks tend to have only a small share of their national markets for retail deposits. More surprisingly, banks in the group of unknown ownership are substantially the most profitable of all. These banks are concentrated in the earlier years of the sample and in Russia and Ukraine, where it is often not possible to distinguish between private ownership and ownership by state-owned enterprises based on available data. Since these banks are concentrated by time and by country, their profitability may reflect a blend of ownership and country effects.

As the above discussion illustrates, it is important to establish whether the relationships between bank profitability and both market share and ownership simply conceal the effect of other important factors. One way to identify the extent and significance of the many factors that might influence bank profitability is to use (multivariate) regression analysis based on a simple model of bank profitability.[10] This analysis can allow for the simultaneous influence of market shares and ownership characteristics of banks, as well as for country effects.

A key assumption in the analysis is that a bank sets its deposit and lending rate so as to maximise profits. This approach is appropriate in circumstances where banks have market power and where there are substantial differences among banks in the quality of their services.[11] Both circumstances can be expected in transition economies, where banking markets are often highly concentrated and quality differences among banks are large. This approach provides an estimate of the average contribution to profits associated with each type of banking activity, such as deposit taking from, and making loans to, customers.

There are several studies that follow this approach in analysing cross-country evidence from industrialised and developing market economies on the determinants of bank profitability and net interest margins. They yield several important results. First, the studies do not find a significant relationship between market structure and bank profitability, where market structure is measured by the share of the largest banks in total assets of the banking system.[12] In contrast, however, the analysis in this chapter relates profitability to more precise measures of market power. In particular, the analysis examines the impact on profitability of market shares of individual banks in deposit taking and lending rather than the overall concentration of a banking sector measured as the share of the largest banks in total assets. Second, the studies of bank profitability in market economies report that banking profits tend to increase with inflation and interest rates and to decrease with economic growth and structural reforms. These findings suggest that macroeconomic instability inflates banking profits (which are not adjusted for inflation) and that reforms to the legal and regulatory environment reduce the risks in banking activity.[13] Third, the studies find that foreign participation in banks is associated with significantly higher rates of profitability, particularly for banks in developing countries.[14]

The cross-country analysis of bank profitability in transition economies reported in this chapter is the only such study available for the post-communist countries.[15] Revenues net of interest expenses and loan losses (hereafter "net revenues") and operating costs receive separate consideration in the analysis to identify as clearly as possible the ways in which market share, ownership and country factors have an impact on profitability. This approach allows the identification of factors that enable a bank to enhance revenues or to reduce costs relative to other banks in the sample.

[10] See Freixas and Rochet (1998) for a detailed discussion of the microeconomic modelling of banks.

[11] See Berger and Mester (1997).

[12] See Barth, Nolle and Rice (1997) and Demirgüç-Kunt and Huzinga (1998).

[13] See Hanson and Rocha (1986) and Demirgüç-Kunt and Huzinga (1998).

[14] See Claessens, Demirgüç-Kunt and Huzinga (1997) and Demirgüç-Kunt and Huzinga (1998).

[15] Fries, Neven and Seabright (1998) provides a detailed presentation of the econometric evidence summarised in Sections 7.2 and 7.3 of this chapter.

Table 7.5

Contribution of deposit taking and lending to banking revenues

(in per cent)

Banking activity	Market share of deposits or loans 5%	25%	50%
Retail deposits	11	4	11
Customer loans	-8	-2	0
Memorandum item:			
Contribution of government securities holdings to banking revenues (independent of market share)	7	7	7

Source: Fries, Neven and Seabright (1998).

Table 7.6

Bank ownership and net revenues

(in per cent)

	Additional net revenue from deposit taking and lending relative to a state-owned bank
Privatised bank	1
New private bank	0
Bank with unknown ownership (either private or owned by a state-owned enterprise)	7

Source: Fries, Neven and Seabright (1998).

Net revenues

Market share

The contribution of deposit taking to net revenues is expressed as the difference between the inter-bank borrowing rate and the interest paid on deposits. This amount is the saving achieved by raising deposits from customers rather than by borrowing on the inter-bank market. The estimated average contribution of retail deposits to a bank's net revenues is positive, regardless of its market share in retail deposit taking. Moreover, as a bank's share of the retail deposit market increases, so too does the average contribution of deposits to net revenue, but the effect is non-linear. For a bank with a 5 per cent market share, the average contribution of an ECU 1 deposit to net revenues is ECU 0.11 (see Table 7.5). While for a bank with a 25 per cent market share, the average contribution of an ECU 1 retail deposit to net revenues is only ECU 0.04, the average for a bank with a 50 per cent market share is ECU 0.11. The extra ECU 0.07 earned from deposits by a bank with a 50 per cent versus 25 per cent market share provides an indication of the impact of market power in deposit taking on the net revenues. The fact that the retail deposits of small banks make a significant contribution to net revenues must arise from an effect other than market power, because small banks have no such power. For example, small banks on average may be able to better serve their customers by offering better quality services.[16]

The situation in the customer loan market is very different. The average contribution of customer loans to net revenues, which is expressed as the extent to which interest earned on loans (after loan losses) is above the inter-bank borrowing rate, is negative or nil regardless of their share of the customer loan market. For small banks with a 5 per cent share of the customer loan market the average contribution of an ECU 1 customer loan to net revenue is ECU -0.08. This average becomes less negative as a bank's share of the customer loan market increases, but even for a bank with a large market share (50 per cent) it just breaks even.[17]

On the asset side of banks' balance sheets, holdings of government securities appear to be the main source of net revenue. However, this result is restricted to a sample of only those banks that disclose their securities holdings (about two-thirds of the observations in the entire sample). Including government securities in the analysis of banks' net revenues (not reported) reveals that each ECU of securities held by a bank contributes on average about ECU 0.07 to net revenues and that this contribution is highly (statistically) significant.

Ownership

Various ownership variables have a significant association with net revenues. In particular, newly formed and privatised banks generate significantly higher net revenues than comparable state-owned banks. One channel through which ownership can influence net revenues is the quality of services provided by a bank, with some banks having a stronger customer-orientation and more differentiated services than others. For example, a newly formed bank seeking to attract customers and to expand its business may try to do so by offering a better quality service at wider margins than a similar state-owned bank (with the same market share and in the same country). However, new banks may also set wider interest margins because they make riskier loans. Over a short period of time, as for this analysis, high-risk loans may not have had sufficient time to turn into high loan losses.

Relative to the benchmark of state-owned banks, privatised banks have significantly higher net revenues, an association that increases with the scale of the privatised bank. Specifically, a privatised bank earns on average an extra ECU 0.01 per ECU of retail deposits and customer loans relative to a state-owned bank (see Table 7.6). Causality, of course, may run in either direction. Those state banks with the better financial performance have no doubt been the ones selected for privatisation, in some cases after their extensive recapitalisation by the government. Nevertheless, the EBRD's experience with bank privatisation is that the introduction of private ownership and, in some cases, new management can significantly strengthen the performance of former state banks (see Box 7.1).

[16] While the reported results are for the sample of all banks, it is also possible to analyse separately banks in Croatia, the Czech Republic, Hungary, Poland and Russia, where there are sufficient numbers of banks. Results similar to those for the entire sample of banks emerge from the samples of Czech, Hungarian, Polish and Russian banks, but not from the sample of Croatian banks (not reported). In the latter case, there is not a significant relationship between the market share of deposits and net revenues.

[17] The contribution of customer loans varies significantly between countries. The results for the Czech Republic are similar to the sample as a whole (a negative average contribution regardless of a bank's share of the customer loan market). However, in Croatia, Hungary, Poland and Russia, there is no significant relationship between customer loans and net revenues, suggesting that banks in these countries just break even on their customer loans on average.

Box 7.1

EBRD experience with bank privatisation

The EBRD has participated in nine privatisations of banks, either through the purchase of existing shares or new shares in capital increases, or through the conversion of subordinated debts or bonds into the equity of the local bank at the time of its privatisation. The experience from these investments varies according to the position of the privatised bank in the local market, the soundness of its financial position, the share of the government ownership in the bank, the strategic objectives and expectations of the authorities at privatisation, the experience of the local government in privatising banks, and the timetable of the privatisation.

In Hungary, the EBRD has played a major role in bank privatisation by participating in three successful transactions in which the largest Hungarian state banks were sold to a combination of strategic investors and the EBRD. The EBRD's stake in Magyar Külkereskedelmi Bank has been recently sold to an investor yielding a high return. In the case of Kereskedelmi es Hitelbank (K&H), the EBRD participated in the pre-privatisation phase of the bank by investing in a subordinated convertible bond, which at the time of privatisation was converted into equity. In this case, the EBRD knew about the privatisation schedule at the time of investment and provided convertible debt to both support the capital of K&H and increase the chance that the Hungarian government could speedily and profitably complete the privatisation of this institution. In Poland, the EBRD had a positive experience with the privatisation of Wielkopolski Bank Kredytowy (WBK), Bank Przemyslowo-Handlowy and of Powszechny Bank Kredytowy via its minority stake in Kredyt Bank, and in all three cases the value of the EBRD's investment has yielded a return higher than was originally expected. The investment in WBK has been sold to the strategic partner which invested with the EBRD at the time of WBK privatisation.

Common features of the success of these investments are the presence of a stable and strong shareholding structure emerging after privatisation, accompanied by a skilled management team with a vision for future developments in the local and regional markets and, in most of the above cases, a strong investor willing to dedicate management and financial resources to the success of its investment. Management, either existing or appointed after privatisation, remains the key success factor in all the above projects.

New banks for which the ownership is unknown (either private or owned by state-owned enterprises) have also tended to earn higher net revenues than comparable state-owned banks. This effect again increases with the scale of activity of the bank, with it earning an extra ECU 0.07 per ECU of retail deposits and customer loans relative to a comparable state-owned bank. The strength of this ownership effect, however, seems implausibly high and may be due to risky lending at high interest rates by banks with non-transparent ownership structures. The effect on net revenues associated with being a new private bank is insignificant.

Foreign participation in a bank's ownership (a 5 per cent or greater equity participation) is associated with significantly higher net revenues, but the association is greater with foreign participation in new private banks than in privatised banks. One explanation for this effect is that it is more difficult to restructure a privatised bank than it is to develop a strong customer-oriented bank from scratch.[18]

Country factors

In addition to market share and ownership, country factors have a significant influence on banks' net revenues. They tend to increase with the rate of inflation and the real rate of interest on bank loans and to decline with growth in output. Taken together, these results suggest that macroeconomic instability and high nominal interest rates have tended to inflate net revenues.[19] In periods of high inflation and nominal interest rates, banking margins often widen, in part to maintain the real value of a bank's capital. Regarding structural reform, the results show that advances in banking reform and overall progress in transition have a significant negative impact on net revenues in banking. This effect could be largely due to the association between progress in transition and macroeconomic stabilisation.[20] It could also be the case that progress in banking reform lowers costs (such as through better enforcement of loan contracts) and, in turn through competition, net revenues.

Operating costs

The primary determinant of a bank's operating costs is the scale of its combined deposit taking and lending activity. At the scale of banking activity in transition economies (which is very small relative to that in industrialised market economies), there appears to be significant economies of scale. In particular, operating costs on average increase by 0.8 per cent for a 1 per cent increase in scale (retail deposits plus customer loans). However, neither the market structure nor the ownership variables have any significant influence on costs.[21] Also, macroeconomic performance and progress in transition appear to have no significant influence on operating costs. The lack of influence of competitive pressure and ownership structures on operating costs, together with their significant influence on net revenues, suggests that much differentiation among banks in transition economies occurs in the deposit taking and lending activities, rather than in variation in operating costs and productive efficiency.

The analysis of operating costs, however, reveals that the average productivity of banks varies substantially across countries. The countries with less efficient banks, controlling for other factors, would appear to be Belarus, Kazakhstan and Ukraine, and those with the more efficient banks to be Croatia, the Czech Republic,

[18] However, in Russia, where foreign participation in banks is limited to a 12% share, this involvement is associated with reduced net revenues. This effect may reflect the weak position of foreign investors in Russian banks, particularly given the lack of protection on minority shareholder rights.

[19] The coefficient on the inflation rate and real rate of interest are equal in magnitude and statistical significance, implying that it is the nominal interest rate that influences net revenues.

[20] When both sets of variables (macroeconomic performance and structural reform) are included in the analysis, they tend to lose their statistical significance (not reported). See Fries, Neven and Seabright (1998) for details.

[21] There is weak evidence that advances in banking reform and progress in overall transition reduce operating costs in banking, but the effect is not statistically significant.

Poland, the Slovak Republic and Slovenia. This variation may reflect country differences in development of market-oriented banking skills, in adaptation of information-processing technology and in overall progress in transition.

Summary

Taken together, the above findings paint a fairly clear picture of the factors that shape the profitability of banking activity in transition economies.

- There is significant evidence that banks with a large share of the retail deposit market have been able to boost their earnings by paying captive depositors less than a competitive rate of interest.
- Customer loans have not been profitable investments for banks. In contrast to the deposit market, it appears that banks have been the captives of poorly performing or recalcitrant borrowers.
- The main source of profit on the asset side of banks' balance sheets has been the holding of government securities and the high returns they have yielded in some countries. However, high yields on government debt reflect the risks in premiums associated with macroeconomic stabilisation efforts, as in the current Russian crisis.
- State-owned banks have earned lower net revenues than have comparable banks that are privately owned (new private or privatised banks) or that have unknown ownership (either private or owned by a state-owned enterprise). The EBRD's experience with bank privatisation suggests that the better performance of privatised banks is not simply due to the fact that the better state banks have been the ones selected for privatisation.
- Macroeconomic factors have also had an important influence on the net revenues of banks. In particular, periods of high inflation and nominal interest have tended to boost bank profits, but in large part these profits only serve to preserve the real value of the bank's capital.

7.3 Serving the customer in transition banking

This section takes a close look at how the customer-orientation of banks in transition economies can be strengthened by considering which banks appear to be more responsive to their customers. It examines two key dimensions along which this orientation can be assessed – pricing (net interest margins) and service expansion (growth in customer lending and its maturity structure). As with the analysis of bank profitability, the particular focus here is on the relationship between dimensions of bank performance and the market power of banks, their ownership characteristics and country effects.

Net interest margins

The net interest margin – the difference between the interest revenues and interest expenses of a bank scaled by its total assets – provides a key measure of the pricing decisions of a bank and is an important determinant of its profitability. The margin represents the average difference between the amount a bank charges borrowers to extend loans and pays to savers to attract deposits. While it would be preferable for the purpose at hand to measure net the interest margin in terms of the average rate on customer loans less the average rate of return on retail deposits, the available data do not permit this calculation. Rather, the basis for the net interest margin calculation must be the entire activities of the bank. This measure includes activities where banks typically have less ability to set prices based on market power or quality of service, such as in purchasing government securities and in borrowing and lending in the inter-bank market.

What determines the differences in net interest margins from one bank to another? In particular, how much is due to differences between one country and another and how much is due to differences between one bank and another? A regression analysis of net interest margins was undertaken to provide some answers to these questions (not reported).[22]

Net interest margins tend to increase with the bank's share of its retail deposit market, a finding consistent with the previous analysis of net revenues. However, interest margins are not affected by the overall level of concentration in the deposit market (as measured by a five-bank concentration ratio), independently of the effect of the individual bank's own market share. This result suggests that, in a concentrated deposit market, the smaller banks on the competitive fringe of the market are not raising margins to match those of dominant banks. In other words, smaller banks appear to be placing downward pressure on net interest margins by setting higher deposit rates and lower loan rates. Banks with foreign participation also set significantly narrower net interest margins. A partial explanation for this result could be that banks with foreign participation tend to focus on financing needs of the local subsidiaries of multinational companies and the local "blue-chip" companies, essentially the lower risk borrowers. The relatively low credit risk of their loans may provide a partial explanation for their narrower margins.

Countries with high inflation and real interest rates and low rates of output growth have significantly higher margins than countries with a more stable macroeconomic environment. Once again, this result emphasises the importance of macroeconomic stability in strengthening the efficiency of intermediation in banking.

Expansion of customer loans

While it appears that the competitive fringe of smaller banks and those with foreign participation is placing downward pressure on net interest margins, it is also important to examine which banks are expanding and improving their services. The expansion of customer loans (adjusted for inflation) by banks with adequate capital is a priority in transition banking because of the significant under-provision of loans to the private sector, as demonstrated in Chapter 5. However, for a bank to actively seek to expand its loan portfolio, it must have both the opportunity and incentive to do so. The opportunity for a bank to expand customer lending is deter-

[22] Fries, Neven and Seabright (1998) provides details of this multivariate regression analysis.

mined largely by overall country factors, such as the degree of macroeconomic stability, rate of output growth and overall progress in transition. These factors shape the opportunity for profitable investments in the real economy, which in turn creates the demand for bank financing. For loans to be provided, though, banks must have an incentive to respond to this demand. This incentive can come from bank owners that are seeking to realise the most value from shareholdings and from competitive pressures. It is also important that any expansion of lending take place within a framework of effective prudential regulation, including capital adequacy standards. A regression analysis of the real growth of customer loans was undertaken to identify the influence of these basic factors that shape the supply of, and demand for, bank credit (not reported).[23]

The analysis yields several important results. Those banks with a smaller share of the deposit market tend to expand their customer loans (allowing for inflation) more rapidly than the dominant banks. Chart 7.6 illustrates the partial relationship between real growth in customer loans and a bank's share of the deposit market. This finding suggests that banks not benefiting from a dominant share of the profitable deposit market have been more likely to expand their customer loans in real terms. Foreign banks also tend to increase their customer loan more rapidly relative to the benchmark of state-owned banks. However, new private and privatised banks and those with unknown ownership on average expand their customer loans at the same rate as state-owned banks. Taken together, the results on market share and ownership suggest that banks competing to gain market share are more likely to expand their supply of customer loans in real terms, as are banks with foreign participation. However, this competition must be disciplined by the effective application of prudential regulations, including capital adequacy requirements.

Country factors appear to play a significant role in influencing the demand for bank credit. In particular, output growth is significantly associated with the real growth in customer loans. However, no significant effects from other country factors were identified.

7.4 An assessment of transition banking

The central question is: How have banks in transition economies performed their role as effective financial intermediaries in mobilising savings and in financing investment?

The analysis reveals how the difficult economic environment in which transition banks operate shapes their performance. Macroeconomic instability is associated with low levels of activity, high interest margins and, in some instances, high rates of profitability. Macroeconomic stabilisation and a recovery in growth bring with them some expansion in bank lending to customers. But the scale of banking in transition economies remains well below that in comparable market economies. One response of banks to their difficult operating environment is to accumulate holdings of government securities. While these instruments often yield high returns in transition economies, these returns reflect the

Chart 7.6

Real loan growth versus deposit market share

(in per cent)

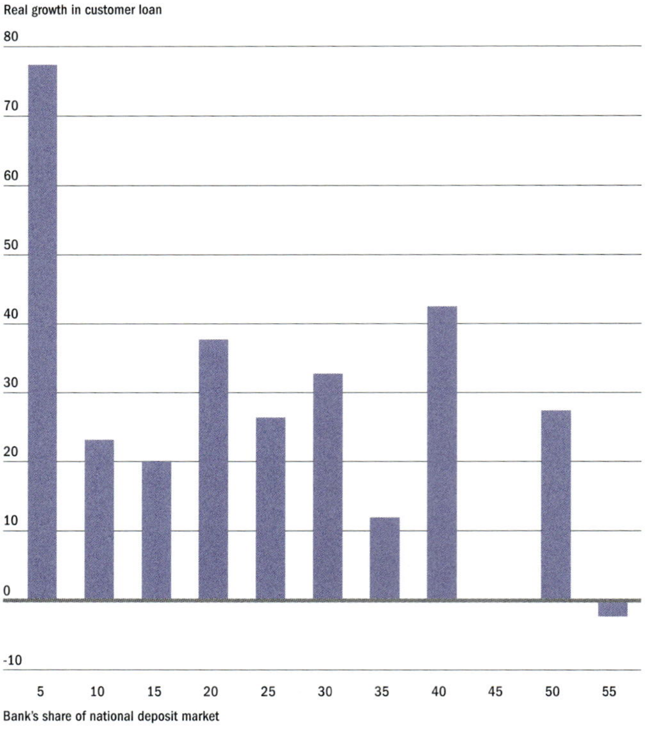

Source: BankScope.

underlying risk associated with macroeconomic stabilisation efforts. In particular, the returns include premiums for the risk of an outburst of inflation or an outright government default, as in the current Russian crisis.

The Russian crisis aside, the main loss-making assets for banks have been their customer loans. Because of large-scale changes in the structures of these economies and of bouts of macroeconomic instability, loans to the real sectors of the transition economies have been inherently risky. And on average, transition banks earn losses on these loans, even those banks with a large share of the loan market. In the more advanced transition economies of Croatia, Hungary and Poland, though, there is evidence that banks on average are able to break even on their customer loans. The profitable expansion of customer lending will thus require not only a stable macroeconomic environment but also a supportive legal and institutional framework. In addition, banks themselves must develop the skills and practices required for making sound loans.

Smaller banks in the region are expanding their customer loans more rapidly than the dominant banks, as they seek to develop new banking opportunities. The customers of smaller banks are naturally small and medium-sized enterprises (SMEs) and households. It is important to recognise the role of the banking sector in the expansion of the private activity, in particular development of SMEs. It will be the banks that will be the main source of external

[23] See Fries, Neven and Seabright (1998).

funds for SMEs. The banks will not provide a good service to SMEs without both a local presence and knowledge and competition to instil a strong focus on the customer. Hence, if a country attaches a priority to supporting SMEs, it should pay special attention to the effectiveness, and particularly the competitiveness, of its banking system.

Banks must also play an important role in mobilising savings if the transition is to advance successfully, but it appears that banks which dominate the retail deposit markets are able to boost their net revenues above the levels of banks with less share of the market. The ability of larger banks to attract deposits, while offering relatively low deposit rates, may arise from the perception that these institutions are "too-big-to-fail" compared with smaller institutions. But the relationship between market share and net revenues holds even for countries where there are credible explicit deposit insurance schemes and, thus, where size would not necessarily provide additional confidence to depositors. This result thus suggests that the concentrated banking markets of transition economies may impede the performance of banks in mobilising savings, pointing again to the importance of competition in banking.

Different types of bank ownership have been associated with variations in bank performance. Newly established and privatised banks achieve higher net revenues than comparable state-owned banks. While undoubtedly the better state-owned banks have been selected for privatisation, the EBRD's experience with bank privatisation supports the view that private ownership brings with it a stronger commercial orientation. Moreover, foreign participation in banks has been associated with their stronger revenue performance; however, this effect diminishes as the size of a bank increases. In larger banks, foreign participation typically involves investments in privatised banks. This result suggests that it may be more difficult for foreign participation to bring about a strong commercial orientation in a privatised bank than in a new private bank established with foreign involvement.

7.5 Conclusion

The analysis of this chapter identifies the impact that the overall economic environment as well as the market shares and ownership of banks have on their performance. Several priorities for strengthening the performance of banks in transition economies follow from this analysis. Progress in transition and stabilisation of the macroeconomy are necessary to increase the scale of key banking activities – mobilisation of deposits from savers and the allocation of credit to the private sector, in particular to SMEs. Macroeconomic stabilisation and growth have been accompanied by lower interest margins and by a real expansion in lending to customers. Moreover, the foundation for a stable expansion of banking activity requires a sound framework for the prudential supervision and regulation of banks, including capital requirements. There is no systematic evidence of weakly capitalised banks expanding their customer loans more rapidly than strongly capitalised banks, although the former characterises a significant minority of transition banks. A priority is thus the further strengthening of prudential oversight, as discussed in Chapter 6.

In addition to macroeconomic stability and effective prudential oversight, strengthening the performance of banks requires two additional measures. First, the reduction in market power, particularly in retail deposit taking, would serve to strengthen the banks' role in the mobilisation of savings and in strengthening their customer orientation. In particular, greater competition would put downward pressure on net interest margins, attract more savings into the banking sector and spur lending to customers. A key policy challenge in transition banking is thus to foster competition while maintaining stability of the overall banking system. Second, greater private participation in the banking sector would serve to strengthen the performance of banks. There is evidence that newly established and privatised banks are able to achieve higher net revenues than state-owned banks (other factors being equal). While the relatively high profitability of privatised banks is difficult to interpret because the better state-owned banks have been selected for privatisation, the EBRD's experience from investing in privatised banks points to the significant potential for enhancing operations. The wider private ownership of banks is thus another key priority in transition banking, but it is vital that private ownership brings with it effective corporate governance and prudent management. Chapter 8 examines in depth the policy challenges of strengthening competition and expanding private ownership in transition banking.

References

P. Aghion, P. Bolton and S. Fries (1998), "Optimal bank bailouts: The case of transition economies", EBRD Working Paper, No. 32.

R. Anderson, E. Berglöf and K. Mizsei (1996), *Banking Sector Development in Central and Eastern Europe: Forum Report of the Economic Policy Initiative,* Centre for Economic Policy Research, London.

R. Anderson and C. Kegels (1998), *Transition Banking: Financial Development in Central and Eastern Europe,* Oxford University Press, Oxford.

J. Barth, D. Nolle and T. Rice (1997), "Commercial banking structure, regulation and performance: an international comparison", US Comptroller of the Currency Economics Working Paper, No. 97-6.

A. Berger and L. Mester (1997), "Inside the black box: what explains differences in the efficiencies of financial institutions", *Journal of Banking and Finance,* Vol. 21, pp. 895-947.

S. Claessens, A. Demirgüç-Kunt and H. Huzinga (1997), "How does foreign entry affect the domestic banking market?", World Bank, mimeo.

A. Demirgüç-Kunt, and H. Huzinga (1998), "Determinants of commercial bank interest margins and profitability: Some international evidence", World Bank Policy Research Working Paper, No. 1900.

X. Freixas and J.-C. Rochet (1998), *Microeconomics of Banking,* The MIT Press, Cambridge, MA.

S. Fries, D. Neven and P. Seabright (1998), "Bank performance in transition economies", EBRD, mimeo.

M. Goldstein, and P. Turner (1996), "Banking Crises in Emerging Economies: Origins and Policy Options", BIS Economic Paper, No. 46.

J. Hanson and R. de Rezende Rocha (1986), "High interest rates, spreads and the cost of intermediation", World Bank Industry and Finance Series, No. 18.

P. Honohan (1997), "Banking system failures in developing and transition economies: Diagnosis and predictions", BIS Working Paper, No. 39.

G. Kaminsky and C. Reinhart (1998), "The twin crises: The causes of banking and balance of payments problems", IMF Staff Papers, Vol. 45, pp. 1-48.

J. Mitchell (1993), "Creditor passivity and bankruptcy: implications for economic reform", in C. Mayer and X. Vives (eds.), *Capital Markets and Financial Intermediation,* Cambridge University Press, Cambridge.

J. Mitchell (1998), "Strategic creditor passivity, regulation and bank bailouts", CEPR Discussion Paper, 1780.

Promoting the stable expansion of banking

8

A key challenge in the transition to a market economy is to expand the depth and breadth of financial activity. As Chapter 5 showed, the financial systems of transition economies provide less bank intermediation of savings and investment than those of comparable market economies. Even more severely under-developed are the securities markets of transition economies. While factors outside the financial sector can have a significant impact on its development, such as the degree of macroeconomic stability and progress in privatisation, it is important to consider those conditions within the financial sector that foster its stable expansion. Clearly, a sound prudential framework is fundamental to the stable expansion of financial activity and Chapter 6 examined progress of transition economies in building the required legal and regulatory institutions. Moreover, Chapter 7 identified the beneficial effects of competition and private ownership on banking performance, including both profitability and expansion of activity. This chapter complements the analysis of the preceding chapters by examining the policies that foster effective competition and private ownership in transition banking, including the resolution of failed banks, licensing requirements for new banks and bank privatisation. Within the financial sector, banking receives particular emphasis because of its vital role in the payments system and its dominant role in the intermediation of savings and investment in these economies.

The analysis of policies fostering competition in banking begins with the issue of exit and, in particular, the approaches to resolving failed banks. A credible threat of exit is clearly fundamental to the process of competition in any sector, including banking. However, this issue takes on particular importance in the banking sector, because the failure of one bank can sometimes spread through the banking system to weaken other institutions. Such contagion can arise from the web of inter-bank deposits that exist naturally in banking activity or from the perceptions of depositors and their general confidence. To protect retail depositors, governments engage in the prudential regulation of banks and, in sufficiently well developed systems, provide partial deposit guarantees. Governments also develop procedures for managing the resolution of failed banks, separate from the bankruptcy laws applied to non-financial firms. In principle, these special procedures aim to balance the objectives of minimising the systemic risks associated with the failure of an individual bank, of maximising the value of the assets of a failed bank, and of imposing accountability for performance and financial discipline. However, striking the right balance can be exceedingly difficult, particularly in periods of financial panic. Nevertheless, it is possible to design policies that strike a careful balance among these potentially conflicting objectives.

Once there is the prospect of orderly exits from banking, it becomes possible to open the system to competitive entry. Competition promotes the efficient allocation of capital by helping to ensure that deposit rates are attractive to savers and loan rates are affordable to borrowers. The process of competition also promotes the selection of banks on the basis of their ability to deliver the services their depositors and borrowers require at the lowest cost. Chapter 7 has shown that competition in transition banking must be strengthened, particularly in the market for retail deposits, but that the process of competition is already bringing benefits in terms of competitive interest rates and service expansion. Competition in banking, however, should not take the form of an unregulated free-for-all. The scope for fraud and other abuses is simply too great. Rather, effective competition in banking requires a balance between the number and the quality of banks. One clear constraint on the desirable number of banks is the capacity of the regulatory authority to supervise them effectively, a particularly important consideration in transition economies. Given the problems following episodes of liberal entry of new banks in these economies, the focus is now on ensuring that new entrants into banking are of high quality. This requires the fair and transparent application of licensing requirements that help to ensure that new banks are both prudent and capable.

Bank privatisation in transition economies is important because of the benefits it brings not only to the privatised bank but also to the process of competition. Privatisation can be expected to improve the capabilities and productivity of the bank, particularly by imparting a strong focus on the customer and by introducing effective corporate governance. Privatisation is also likely to lead to a hardening of the budget constraint on the bank by reducing the prospect of a generous government bailout if performance deteriorates. This financial discipline on banks serves to strengthen both the internal incentives within the bank and the process of competition in the banking system as a whole. However, there are many difficult trade-offs to address in the design of bank privatisation so as to achieve desirable post-privatisation ownership structures and effective corporate governance of privatised banks.

The remainder of the chapter is organised as follows. Section 8.1 looks at how to resolve bank failures. The section considers alternative frameworks for resolving bank failures in the context of transition economies, including schemes for mandatory corrective actions and conservatorship (direct control of bank management by the regulator) and for conditional bank recapitalisations. Section 8.2 turns to the issue of entry. Contrary to a simple belief that free entry must automatically strengthen competition and hence efficiency, it is important to recognise that the process of competition can be easily undermined by under-capitalisation of banks that engage in imprudent or fraudulent activities. The focus of this section is on licensing requirements for new banks to promote the entry of high-quality banks. Section 8.3 considers the allied problem of bank privatisation and corporate governance. The analysis emphasises that privatisation must be carried out in a way that minimises the risk of bank failure and bailouts while bringing in, to the extent possible, new management, skills and technology. There is a strong case for concentrated ownership of banks, in particular by strategic investors. There are also advantages in matching foreign strategic investors with domestic banking institutions to mesh superior banking skills and technology with local information about clients and loan opportunities.

8.1 Resolving bank failures

In the long run, healthy competition among banks should bring about the survival of only those institutions that are best able to serve their customers at the lowest cost. This selection process comes about not only through new entry and the expansion of the more capable and efficient banks, but also through the contraction and exit of weak institutions. However, important distortions arise in the banking sector at both ends of the competitive process. Deposit insurance tends to distort competition by, in effect, subsidising entry by less capable and efficient banks. Similarly, poorly performing banks may be allowed to survive, rather than exit, because they are perceived to be "too big to fail". One problem with exit is that closure of a weak bank can sometimes be more problematic than closure of a non-financial firm, because of the spill-over effects that liquidation can have on other banks. The threat of a generalised liquidity crisis can induce a government rescue of troubled banks even when they should be closed on the basis of their poor performance.

Such bank bailouts distort the competitive process. They also create a "moral hazard" problem in the way banks make loans and other investments, because the managers and shareholders of failed banks are shielded from the full consequences of their investment decisions. Although the rescue of larger banks may in certain circumstances be necessary to avoid a generalised liquidity crisis, such rescues must be designed carefully if distortions to competition and allied incentive problems are to be minimised. A key challenge facing transition economies is to impose more financial discipline and less generous bailouts for troubled banks.

Constraints on bank liquidations in transition economies

While the need for greater financial discipline in transition banking is clear, constraints on liquidation as a policy to resolve bank failures exist at several levels. As mentioned above, concern over the stability of the banking system as a whole is often invoked as a reason for generous bank bailouts. Moreover, banking regulators often do not have the independence or the incentive to act decisively as banking troubles become apparent. And in many cases, distressed banks actively conceal the extent of their problems from the regulatory authorities in a bid to avoid detection or to "gamble" their way out of trouble.

The extent to which the failure of an individual bank could spill over into a more generalised banking crisis depends on both the extent of the financial relationships among banks and the general perception of depositors. Banks often have large exposures among themselves that arise from the process of providing payment services to depositors and from the intermediation of savings into investment. The larger the bank, the larger these inter-bank exposures tend to be, although in principle the payment system can be designed to reduce them substantially. This aspect of banking is one source of the too-big-to-fail problem. Another source is the fact that a large bank has a large number of depositors and a run on a highly visible yet troubled bank can readily spill over into a wider banking panic and to strong political pressure for depositor protection.

While these considerations are important, there is often a tendency for regulators to follow the path of least resistance and to invoke generously the too-big-to-fail principle, particularly in transition economies where even the largest banks are very small relative to the economies in which they operate. Bank bailouts are often the path of least resistance because the bailout costs are spread widely over current and future taxpayers, while the benefits are concentrated on existing depositors. However, as stressed in Chapter 5, the experience with banking crises in transition economies suggests that they are less disruptive to the real economy in these countries than they are in other emerging market economies. While still significant, the impact is less dramatic even when large banks in a banking system have been liquidated, as in Estonia (1993) and Latvia (1995). Nevertheless, the response to more recent banking turmoil in transition economies has included wide application of the too-big-to-fail principle. For example, in Bulgaria the largest seven state banks that had become insolvent were recapitalised in 1996, while only small banks were liquidated. The failure of the fifth-largest bank in Croatia in April 1998 elicited a government bailout, despite evidence of possible fraud. Following the August 1998 financial crisis, the Russian authorities have proven reluctant to let the larger banks fail.

Related to the wide application of the too-big-to-fail principle is the issue of regulatory forbearance. There are two types of forbearance. One is simply procrastination or reluctance to face difficult decisions and a preference for shifting the problem to others in the future. This form of forbearance has no economic justification. The other form is a deliberate decision to let a distressed bank continue operations because the value of the bank as a going concern is greater than its liquidation value. To limit unjustified forbearance, it may be necessary both to reduce the discretion of regulators with respect to the timing of their intervention and to their ability to sustain a troubled bank.

It would be too simple to suggest, however, that the reluctance of regulators to resolve troubled banks in transition economies is largely due to lax incentives for the regulatory authorities. In fact, the broader economic, political and institutional environment in these economies often makes it difficult for regulators to act decisively. For example, there have been strong political pressures placed on banks to sustain large state-owned enterprises, particularly as governments have commonly been sensitive to changes in unemployment and associated fiscal costs. These pressures appear to have been greatest at the level of regional or provincial government. As a consequence, banks throughout the region have been reluctant to foreclose on state-owned enterprises when they have defaulted on their debt repayments and have generally been slow at shifting their lending away from these declining enterprises to the private sector. For the same reason, governments are often reluctant to see banking regulators act decisively to liquidate troubled banks and, in turn, to harden the budget constraints on loss-making enterprises.

The problem of bad loans not only continues to distort the allocation of capital and to restrict lending to the private sector, but also places pressure on banks' balance sheets. In some countries, such as the Baltic states, Croatia, Hungary, Poland and Slovenia, pervasive banking problems have brought about a comprehensive resolution of the bad debt problem. But despite these efforts at strengthening financial discipline, the bad-loan problem still looms large throughout the region (see Table 8.1).

The factors contributing to the bad-loan problem in transition economies, however, extend beyond the political pressure placed on banks and banking regulators. Banks themselves often have both the incentive and the ability simply to roll-over bad loans to conceal the extent of their problems, rather than to seek to recover non-performing assets. The managers of troubled banks, for example, may engage in this "creditor passivity" to preserve their positions in otherwise failing institutions.[1] Even if bank managers have an incentive to recover on bad loans, they often do not have the legal means to do so, since bankruptcy courts in most transition economies provide little prospect of recovering assets (see Annex 2.2 to Chapter 2 and Chapter 5 of the 1997 *Transition Report*). Moreover, weaknesses in accounting and auditing practices for banks and limited regulatory capacity often enable transition banks to engage without sanction in creditor passivity.

Table 8.1

Non-performing loans, 1994-97

(in per cent of total loans, end of period)

	1994	1995	1996	1997
Albania	–	35	40	49
Bulgaria	7	13	15	13
Croatia	12	13	11	10
Czech Republic	34	33	30	29
Hungary	18	10	7	4
Poland	29	21	13	10
Romania	19	38	48	57
Slovak Republic	30	41	32	33
Slovenia	22	13	14	12
Estonia	4	3	2	1
Latvia	10	19	20	10
Lithuania	27	17	32	28
Armenia	34	36	23	8
Azerbaijan	16	22	20	20
Belarus	8	12	14	13
Georgia	24	41	7	7
Kazakhstan	–	15	20	8
Kyrgyzstan	92	72	26	8
Moldova	16	9	17	10
Russian Federation	–	6	5	4
Turkmenistan	–	11	11	14
Ukraine	5	13	12	11
Uzbekistan	–	8	2	4

Sources: IMF and central banks.

These issues are not unique to transition economies. Experience with financial crises around the world suggests that the main incentive problems preventing the effective resolution of troubled banks are: (i) regulatory forbearance and a willingness to invoke generously the too-big-to-fail principle; (ii) political intervention to avoid bank liquidations and to provide unconditional bank bailouts; (iii) protection of bank shareholders in bailouts, which dulls banks' incentives to monitor management and increases their tendency to make risky investments; (iv) incentives for bank managers to under-report their non-performing assets and over-report capital; and, (v) deposit insurance – often implicit – that extends beyond protection of retail deposits and that undermines market discipline in banking.

Corrective actions, recapitalisation and liquidation

The obstacles to efficient bank liquidation outlined above make it all the more important to detect troubled banks early and to deal with them swiftly. But early and prompt intervention requires accurate financial reporting by banks and a system of "alarm bells" that can draw the regulator's attention to a bank in distress. If a distressed bank can be identified sufficiently early, it becomes possible to intervene before the situation becomes irrecoverable. A range of remedial actions are possible, from the formulation of a business plan to restore capital adequacy, to restrictions on permissible activities and payments and to rapid implementation of a recapitalisation plan. If a bank's balance sheet deteriorates to the point where its solvency is impaired and where no recapitalisation from shareholders is forthcoming, the banking regulator should place the bank into conservatorship for eventual recapitalisation or liquidation.

Each step, from the early identification of financial distress to the eventual recapitalisation or liquidation of a bank, involves crucial regulatory decisions and requires the participation of bank managers, shareholders, depositors, regulators and, inevitably, politicians. Yet providing all parties with the right incentives is not feasible. Instead compromises must be reached and some incentive problems must take priority over others. To address some of these problems, various regulations have either been implemented or proposed in several industrialised market economies. Some of these regulations can usefully be applied in transition economies, but new regulatory solutions specific to the situation faced by transition economies are also necessary.

Mandatory corrective actions and conservatorship: limiting forbearance and interference

In response to the problems of regulatory forbearance and potential political intervention, mandatory corrective action measures have recently been introduced in the United States, following the savings and loan crisis, and more recently in Japan. This frame-

[1] See Mitchell (1993), Berglof and Roland (1998), Aghion, Bolton and Fries (1998) and Mitchell (1998).

work for regulatory intervention relies on a series of alarm bells based on a bank's regulatory capital ratio, in particular the Basle Committee's risk-weighted capital adequacy standard.

The following illustration of the framework draws from the original US reform proposal.[2] When a bank's capital ratio drops somewhat below its required level – say to between 6 and 8 per cent – the traditional regulatory approach of working with an institution to nurse it back to financial health could still be appropriate. This approach could involve formulation of a business plan to restore capital adequacy, along with mandatory actions to limit risks such as reductions in concentrated loan exposures. If a troubled bank's capital ratio falls further – between 3 and 6 per cent – the regulator could impose a tough set of restrictions, such as suspension of dividend payments on equity, interest payments on subordinated debt and unauthorised payments to affiliated companies, and limits on deposit interest rates. The intervention could also require the formulation of a rapid recapitalisation plan that would be implemented if there is a further deterioration. If a bank's capital ratio falls below 3 per cent and the recapitalisation plan is not implemented, the regulators would be required to take the bank into conservatorship, for subsequent recapitalisation or liquidation.

While the set of prescribed actions provides a strategy for responding to banks that fall out of compliance with basic regulatory requirements, the principle of mandatory intervention aims to reduce regulatory forbearance and political interference. But the level of the thresholds, the nature of the intervention, as well as the strict limits on regulatory discretion in an intervention, need to be adjusted to the specific context of different transition economies. Given the limited capacity for regulatory enforcement in transition economies, corrective actions should be simple to administer, such as orders to cease payments and activities, and should aim at eliciting prompt shareholder support for a troubled bank. Such interventions could include suspension of dividend payments and interest payments on subordinated debt, prohibitions on unauthorised transfers to affiliated companies and limits on deposit interest rates. These measures would provide the shareholders of a troubled bank with a strong incentive to provide support so as to enhance the value of their claims and of the bank as a going concern. The failure of shareholders to recapitalise a troubled bank should result in its conservatorship.[3]

Conservatorship provides for control of a solvency-impaired bank by the regulator while preparations are made for its eventual resolution. This resolution can take the form either of a recapitalisation to satisfy minimum regulatory requirements followed by its sale to new shareholders or of an orderly liquidation. Following the sale or liquidation, any residual value should be returned to the subordinated debt holders and shareholders. The choice between recapitalisation and liquidation should be shaped by an assessment of the system-wide impact of liquidation (if any) and of the value of the bank as a going concern. If recapitalisation is warranted, there should be dilution of the initial shareholders and replacement of senior management, particularly if poor managerial performance was a main factor contributing to the failure. These measures are necessary to hold shareholders and managers accountable for bank performance.

Combating mis-reporting by banks

While mandatory corrective actions and conservatorship are, in principle, effective remedial actions for capital-impaired banks and devices to mitigate regulatory forbearance and interference, they can create incentives for bank managers to conceal asset quality problems and to overstate a bank's capital adequacy. If full disclosure triggers regulatory intervention and conservatorship, bank managers will inevitably attempt to under-report the size of their bad assets and over-state their capital, thus undermining the whole purpose of these rules. In most industrialised countries, where strict accounting standards are imposed on banks and where banks are subjected to close monitoring by markets and regulators, the scope for under-reporting is limited. Even so, judging by recent experience in Japan, it remains considerable. And in many transition countries the opportunities for banks to hide bad loans is much greater. In Russia, for example, it has sufficed to move bad loans to a subsidiary to remove them from the parent bank's accounts.[4] To limit a bank manager's ability to hide asset-quality problems, it is essential to introduce internationally recognised accounting and auditing standards for banks and, in particular, to insist on consolidation of the accounts of banks and their affiliates, as discussed in Chapter 6.

Where the ability of bank managers to mis-report remains largely unconstrained by reliable financial information about banks, as in many post-communist countries at earlier stages of transition, the mandatory corrective action and conservatorship framework is unlikely to function well. In this case, it would be desirable to move to a system for bank recapitalisation that gives troubled banks an incentive to reveal their asset quality problems (rather than to hide them) and to recover on bad loans and other non-performing assets. This incentive can be created by a recapitalisation scheme that takes the form of a "purchase" of non-performing assets at a premium to their market value or "subsidy" for each asset recovery.[5] Non-performing loans can either be acquired at a premium by a special government agency set up to recover on bad assets or they can remain on the books of the troubled bank for recovery, in which case it would receive recapitalisation in the form of a subsidy for asset recoveries. In either case, the subsidy element would aim to restore the bank's capital adequacy. This form of recapitalisation can create a direct incentive to recover on non-performing assets and to harden the budget constraints on enterprises and on other borrowers from banks, a priority in transition economies.

[2] See Benston, Brumbaugh, Guttentag, Herring, Kaufman, Litan and Scott (1989), as well as United States Department of the Treasury (1991).

[3] For a formal analysis of the incentive of bank shareholders to support a bank as its capital deteriorates and the failure of shareholder support to serve as a trigger for conservatorship, see Fries, Mella-Barral and Perraudin (1997).

[4] This loophole is due to the lack of consolidated supervision of banks.

[5] See Aghion, Bolton and Fries (1998). In contrast to this scheme, a conventional regulatory approach to recapitalisation involves the unconditional purchase of subordinated debt or preferred stock.

Whether bad assets should be transferred to a specialised workout agency or kept on the books of the troubled bank for recovery is a complex problem. The main arguments for keeping the responsibility for recoveries with the banks is that they tend to have better information about the loans, that the work-out of bad loans builds banking skills and that individual banks are less vulnerable to political interference than a government-owned agency. For instance, in Poland in 1993 bad loans were kept with the banks, but in order to receive recapitalisation, banks were forced to present a feasible workout strategy, which was supported by a special law on debt restructuring. By 1995, most of the bad loans targeted by the programme had been restructured.[6] The main arguments in favour of a specialised agency are that it allows for the concentration of expertise on asset recoveries, quickly eliminates the debt-overhang on banks' balance sheets and allows them to focus on new lending, thus helping to avoid a credit crunch. Experience with recent banking crises in the United States and the Nordic countries suggests that on the whole special debt-resolution agencies have played an important role in speeding up bank restructuring. However, a specialised agency in transition economies may be less effective in recovering on non-performing assets because of political pressure to maintain soft budget constraints on enterprises, as was the case in Slovenia.[7]

Another potential advantage of conditional recapitalisations is that – when carefully designed – they can limit the drain on fiscal resources by targeting recapitalisations at only truly insolvent banks. By conditioning recapitalisations on write-downs and restructuring of bad loans, it is possible to distinguish insolvent banks from solvent ones. This discrimination between solvent and insolvent banks can be fine-tuned by implementing a graded subsidy (or pricing) scheme for bad debts. This scheme would involve a greater unit subsidy (or price) per loan recovery when the proportion of written-down loans to total assets of the bank is higher. In this way, more insolvent banks – with a higher proportion of non-performing loans – receive a bigger unit recapitalisation than less insolvent banks with a lower fraction of bad loans.[8] In contrast, more standard recapitalisation methods based on purchases of subordinated debt or preferred stock cannot provide a mechanism for discriminating between truly solvent and insolvent banks. While the graded-subsidy scheme offers a potential way of overcoming the limited information for regulators about the financial condition of individual banks, its implementation would nevertheless require some general knowledge of how losses are distributed through the banking system.

Avoiding concentration and the "too-big-to-fail" problem

The distortions created by too-big-to-fail banks are largely the result of their market dominance. Policies to break-up the large state-owned banks or to curb increases in concentration through mergers of private banks are thus desirable. Such policies would not only have a direct impact on curbing monopolistic practices in banking as discussed in Chapter 7, but would also contribute to strengthening the credibility of bank closure rules and the threat of liquidation. Of course, breaking-up a large state bank in a transition economy is not an easy task and may be very costly. It requires new management teams and new capital, both of which are in scarce supply. Nevertheless, such break-ups are unlikely to be more difficult than forced spin-offs in large enterprises.

While the expansion of successful new private banks is fundamental to a successful transition in the banking sector, however, some mergers among private banks aim to achieve market dominance and a too-big-to-fail status. In particular, the flurry of merger proposals in the midst of the Russian crisis by key private banks, all of which were individually quite small, may have been driven in part by the aim of becoming quickly too-big-to-fail and to lobby the central bank for support.

Limiting deposit insurance to encourage market discipline

A system of full deposit insurance is extremely costly and is not justifiable on efficient risk-sharing or incentive grounds.[9] Indeed, most countries with an explicit deposit insurance scheme specify a ceiling on the compensation of each depositor and explicitly leave uncovered certain types of deposits, such as inter-bank deposits. However, whether countries have explicit deposit insurance with ceilings or indeed no formal scheme, all deposits often become *de facto* fully insured when a major bank fails. One recent attempt to avoid this outcome has been made in the United States. This approach aims to make it more difficult for depositors to be compensated over and above the prescribed limit by the discretion of the banking regulator in extending the coverage of deposit insurance beyond its prescribed limits. Any such extension would require approval of the legislature and the government, as well as the deposit insurance agency. Such credible commitments are desirable because they encourage large depositors, such as corporations and other banks, to take an interest in the bank's solvency, thereby introducing an element of market discipline.

Resolution rules for state-owned banks

The mandatory corrective action and conservatorship framework discussed above is designed to apply to privately owned banks with shareholders that have an incentive to preserve their ownership claims. These rules are not necessarily appropriate for state-owned banks. Recourse to shareholder support in this case often takes the form of unconditional government bailouts. However, the issue of how to resolve a failed state-owned bank is particularly important in transition economies. Many of these banks are (or have been) insolvent, owing to large loan exposures to declining state enterprises, and they often dominate the banking systems in which they operate. Ignoring the insolvency of state banks runs the risk of perpetuating soft budget constraints in both the enterprise and banking sectors and of distorting the process of competition.

[6] See Gary and Holle (1996) on the experience in Poland.

[7] On Slovenia, see van Wijnbergen (1998).

[8] See Aghion, Bolton and Fries (1998).

[9] For an extensive analysis of the design of deposit insurance schemes, see Garcia (1996).

Chart 8.1

Share of five largest banks in total bank assets, 1994-97

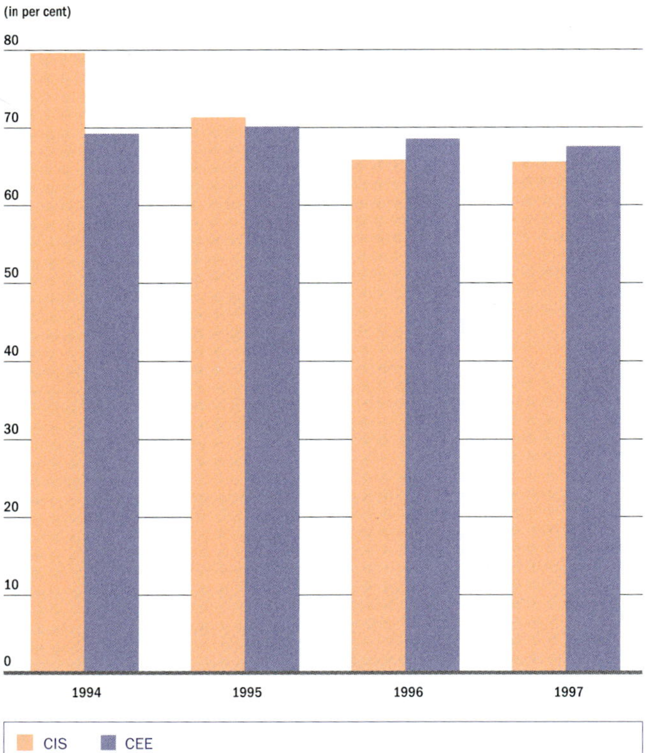

Source: National authorities – Unweighted averages for the regions.

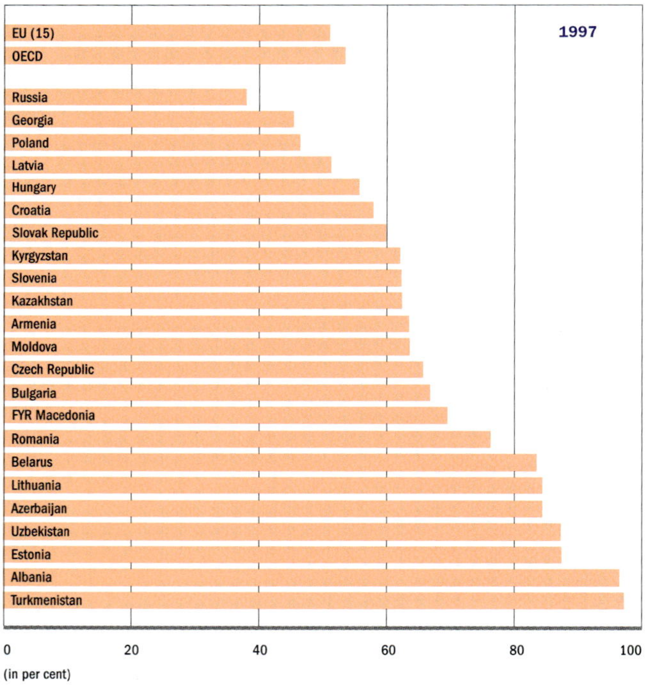

Source: National authorities.

How should government resolve the insolvency of state-owned banks? In transition economies, these banks often have significant value as a going concern, because of their size and extensive branch networks, and large inter-bank exposures. These considerations point to recapitalisation rather than liquidation of troubled state banks. Indeed, insolvent state banks have typically been recapitalised or targeted for restructuring. However, the challenge in recapitalising state banks is to ensure that this bailout does not become a source of a more generalised source of unconditional support, not only to state banks themselves, but also to enterprises. Again, the proposal of making recapitalisation conditional on the recovery of bad loans can help. This scheme would provide for the recapitalisation of state banks only on the condition that they recover on their non-performing assets. If the scheme is carefully designed – in the form of a graded subsidy for loan recoveries – it would also encourage state banks to reveal fully their non-performing assets, while keeping the fiscal costs of the recapitalisation to a minimum and preparing them for privatisation.

Responding to a system-wide crisis

The frameworks of mandatory corrective actions, conservatorship and conditional recapitalisation provide banks with an incentive to reveal bad assets and focus on the resolution of failed banks in an otherwise functioning banking system. However, if there is a general loss of confidence and widespread liquidity pressure on banks, more extensive, albeit temporary, support may be required.

First, the central bank may need to expand the provision of liquidity to banks through collateralised short-term lending to banks (discount facilities) or through open market operations. However, the provision of central bank loans must be restricted to solvent banks in need of short-term liquidity. Emergency loans to insolvent banks can easily be wasted by "end-game" strategies, whereby the managers and owners use the liquidity to strip an insolvent bank of assets and engage in capital flight. The crisis in Russia clearly demonstrates this limit to emergency liquidity support by the central bank. Second, the government may need to institute a more extensive guarantee of deposits, beyond that provided by any explicit deposit insurance scheme, in order to restore confidence. This extension should be temporary to limit the moral hazard problem. Moreover, the government should extend coverage only after other options have been exhausted and the costs have been fully taken into account. Nevertheless, the government may not be able to expand coverage quickly enough to contain the crisis. In Russia, the government's attempts to expand the coverage of deposit insurance have been seriously impeded by delays in the legislature, leaving the central bank to pursue a series of ad hoc measures. Failing these two measures, there is little alternative but to suspend the convertibility of bank deposits in currency.

Once confidence is restored, it is often necessary after a systemic crisis to recapitalise some affected banks. The new capital should come from private sources to the fullest extent possible, but some government funds may be required to cover the negative equity. As discussed above, conditions for the injection of government funds should include the dilution of initial shareholders and replacement of senior management.

8.2 Managing entry in banking

The deep financial turmoil in Russia in August 1998 not only raises forcefully the issue of resolving bank failures, but also illustrates a consequence of excessive entry of weak banks. A large number of small, under-capitalised banks can contribute to a generalised loss of confidence, especially when regulatory capacity is limited and enforcement is poor. But maintaining a monopolistic banking system is also undesirable, because in part it exacerbates the too-big-to-fail problem. Moreover, Chapter 7 provides evidence that transition banking should on the whole become more competitive, because banks that dominate the retail deposit market are able to boost their profits above competitive levels. But given the scarce regulatory capacity in transition economies, the process of entry must be disciplined to prevent-fraud and other abuses that can also distort interest rates.[10] The key issue to which these trade-offs point is how much the entry of new banks should be permitted and by what type of banks, provided there is an effective procedure for resolving bank failures.[11] It is important to recognise that effective competition in banking depends on both the number (market shares) and the quality of banks.

Chart 8.1 indicates that there has been some decline in the extent of concentration in banking since 1994 but that in both the CIS and central and east European countries the decline has been quite small. It also highlights the significant variation across countries. Further, when comparing concentration with that existing in industrialised market economies, the chart shows that the concentration of banking systems in most transition economies is generally higher than that for industrialised countries. It is notable that there is the least concentration in Russia. One implication of this comparison is that it may be desirable to strengthen the process of competition in most transition economies by encouraging new, high-quality entrants or through the break-up of dominant banks. In contrast, the relatively low bank concentration in Russia suggests that reducing the number of banks while raising their quality can enhance the process of competition.

There are several policies that can serve to ensure that entrants into banking are of high quality and that existing banks face effective competition. In particular, the allocation of licences to new banks should be based on clear and transparent prudential criteria, including minimum capital requirements and capital adequacy ratios. Entry policies should also ensure that connected lending is not a way for banks to meet these capital requirements. Foreign entry should be encouraged, particularly through the acquisition of stakes in existing banks. Existing dominant banks should be broken-up, but not into regional monopolies. There is a stronger case for break-ups on sectoral lines and as part of an overall programme for the restructuring and privatisation of state banks. Lastly, competition between existing and new banks should be fair. To this end, the bad debt problem of existing banks should be effectively resolved; state banks should be privatised; governments should maintain an arm's-length relationship with banks;[12] and deposit insurance should be made explicit and conditional upon meeting objective prudential criteria.

Benefits and costs of competition

Benefits

In principle, the benefits of competition in banking are the same as in other sectors of an economy. Competition promotes efficiency in the mobilisation of savings and the allocation of credit by ensuring that interest rates on deposits and loans are set at competitive levels. The lack of competition in retail deposit markets in transition economies appears to be one source of inefficiency in the setting of deposit rates (see Chapter 7). Competition also promotes the selection of banks on the basis of their ability to serve customers well at the lowest cost. For example, Chapter 7 provides evidence that those banks with only a small share of the deposit market and banks with foreign participation appear to be more responsive to customer demands. Although this evidence provides only a snapshot of the competitive process in transition banking, the smaller banks and those with foreign participation may be able to expand their operations and to place greater competitive pressure on the dominant banks, primarily the state-owned and privatised banks. Competition, by serving to curb the dominance of one or a few banks, also helps to reduce the too-big-to-fail problem, and thereby further reinforces the competitive process.

Costs

While an absence of competition in banking is undesirable, and even potentially dangerous, having too many banks and excessive competition can also be problematic. The limits on competition arise from several factors. First, the more banks there are, the harder it becomes to regulate each bank effectively, particularly in transition economies where regulatory capacity is scarce. A large number of weakly capitalised and poorly regulated banks can become a source both of instability and of distortions in interest rates. Second, competition in banking may induce banks to invest too early and too much in new market niches in order to pre-empt potential competitors. If such pre-emptive investment takes place before the investing bank has acquired the necessary information and expertise about the new sector or project and before it has acquired the necessary monitoring skills and capabilities to ensure profitability, then excessive competition in banking can lead to excessive risk-taking by banks. The plunge by Russian banks into writing forward contracts for foreign exchange illustrates this danger (see Annex 1.1 to Chapter 1). Third, excessive competition will reduce the banks' ability and incentives to undertake new innovative investments and to modernise their technologies and their internal organisation, while also ultimately discouraging the entry of new and sound banking institutions.[13]

Fostering competition in banking

While it is not possible to provide a simple formula for the appropriate number of banks and their qualities to ensure effective competition, the direction in which transition economies must

[10] For example, a bank engaged in pervasive connected lending can distort the deposit market by setting high deposit rates to attract deposits that it had no intention of honouring.

[11] In the absence of effective procedures for responding to bank failures, the process of competition becomes seriously distorted and (second-best) restrictions on entry may be warranted.

[12] The controversial loans-for-shares scheme in Russia, whereby favoured banks received large shareholdings in state-owned enterprises in return for financing the government's budget deficit, clearly violated the arm's-length principle.

[13] This is the well-known Schumpetarian trade-off between the allocative efficiency from competition and the incentive for innovation and entry created by monopoly profits.

move is clear. Reducing the dominance of state-owned and privatised banks is a priority in most transition economies. The notable exception is Russia, where the priority is to increase the quality of banks operating while reducing their number. This section examines ways of fostering more effective competition in banking, in particular the break-up of dominant banks and the entry of new domestic and foreign banks. Raising the quality of banks in Russia centres largely on the resolution of failed banks, which is considered in the previous section of this chapter.

Breaking-up dominant banks

Breaking-up dominant state banks as part of their restructuring and privatisation may be desirable in principle, but the dimension along which a dominant bank is broken up can have significant consequences for competition. For example, in Poland the former Monobank was divided in 1989 into a central bank and nine state commercial banks operating on a regional basis. Each of these banks was awarded a large branch network within its own region of operation, in effect creating regional monopolies. While being clearly ineffective in stimulating competition in banking, these regional break-ups have the additional disadvantage of being unable to mitigate the too-big-to-fail problem because of the concentration of losses in the event of failure. Should bank break-ups be avoided altogether? The answer is not necessarily. The dominant state banks that have been broken up do inherit the retail networks and information about borrowers, unlike new entrants. This consideration suggests that where the break-up of dominant state banks is pursued, it should be organised more on sectoral rather than geographic terms and implemented alongside privatisation.

It is important to emphasise that, while privatisation may help to ensure that banks operate under competitive conditions, there is a conflict between policies, such as bank break-ups, which are aimed at reducing market power, and privatisation that may lead governments to maintain market power. Often governments have a strong financial interest in boosting receipts from bank privatisation by selling banks with significant market power. These considerations, and more generally the difficulty in implementing efficient bank break-ups, should also encourage governments to rely on a disciplined entry policy as a key, complementary instrument for promoting sound competition in the banking sector.

Domestic entry

The main instrument for regulating entry in banking – in terms of both the number of entrants and their quality – is the granting of banking licences. In early stages of transition, emphasis in some countries was placed on liberal licensing to encourage a large number of new banks to form, based on the view that through a process of competition among them, some strong banks would emerge to form a core of the banking system. In other words, greater emphasis was placed on the number of banks, rather than their quality, in shaping the process of competition. The Czech Republic, Poland and Russia are clear cases in point. But the emergence of a large number of small, weakly capitalised, poorly regulated and often fraudulent banks quickly led to the reversal of the policy and the temporary suspension of the granting of new licences. As the suspensions were lifted, the focus shifted to licensing requirements that serve to ensure high-quality entrants.

There are several ways that bank licensing can help to ensure that new banks are both prudent and capable.[14] Foremost among them is the setting of minimum initial capital requirements. This requirement acts as an "entry fee" to discipline the inflow of new banks, preventing the proliferation of undercapitalised banks and serving to ensure that real capital is at risk in new banks. The amount of minimum capital should be set at a level sufficient to finance the initial business of the bank and to provide it with liquidity in the early stages of development. It is also important that shareholders finance the initial capital out of their own net worth and not on the basis of borrowed funds, including loans from the new bank itself or from other banks. Should a bank's capital fall below the required minimum level, it would no longer be in compliance with licensing requirements and would risk losing its licence. In practice, it is important that banks start with more capital than the required minimum, so as to be able to sustain losses and yet remain in regulatory compliance. While minimum capital requirements vary across countries, EU directives set the level at ECU 5 million.

To ensure that new banks are capable, licensing procedures often apply a "fit-and-proper" test to the shareholders and managers of a new bank and evaluate its proposed governance structure and internal controls. This criterion requires that the shareholders and managers have integrity and be technically qualified and experienced in banking. Their track record of performance in banking and compliance with the law should therefore be carefully considered. It is also important that the proposed ownership structure and corporate governance arrangements are transparent and in accordance with sound business practices. While this assessment of the capabilities of a new bank inevitably introduces a subjective element into the licensing process, the procedures themselves should be transparent and fair, with the licensing authority vested in an independent yet accountable agency.

A key issue in transition economies, however, is the ability to enforce effective regulation. Chapter 6 has shown that even in the relatively advanced transition economies, the capacity to enforce prudential regulations and licensing requirements remains limited. This outcome in part is attributable to weaknesses in the legal infrastructure. But it is also due to a lack of regulatory resources. For example, in terms of the ratio of banking supervisory staff, weighted by the number of banks, most transition countries, particularly those further east, have ratios currently well below Western standards.

Foreign entry

Chart 8.2 shows that foreign entry has become more important over time in transition economies, but with considerable variation across countries. The evidence reported in Chapter 7 suggests that foreign entry has generally contributed to improved performance of the banking sector. These findings are not surprising: foreign

[14] See Folkerts-Landau and Lindgrin (1998) for a discussion of bank licensing procedures that can promote high-quality entry into banking.

Chart 8.2

Share of majority foreign-owned banks in total bank assets, 1994-97

(in per cent)

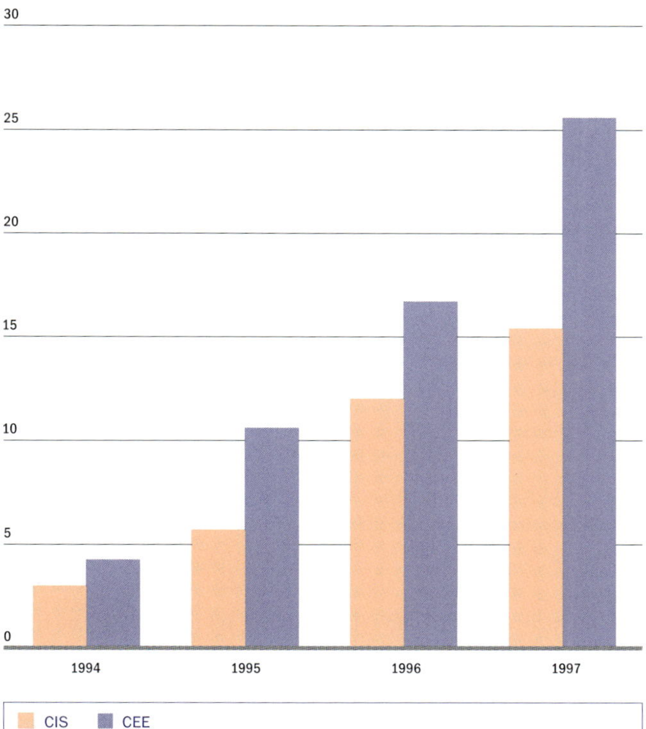

Source: National authorities – Unweighted averages for the regions.

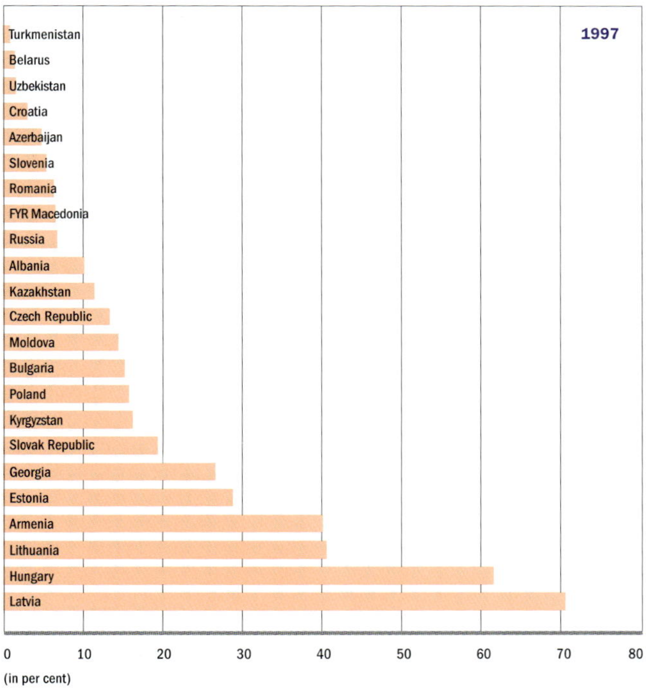

Source: National authorities.

institutions can more easily satisfy relatively high capital adequacy ratios, since they have access to relatively inexpensive sources of finance from their home country. In addition, foreign banks have reputations based on their established track records and transparent financial accounts, which contribute further to improving their access to capital. Moreover, foreign banks typically bring with them advanced technologies and banking skills, thereby allowing them to screen loans and to monitor them more effectively than local banks, ultimately raising the overall level of investment. Lastly, foreign entry is likely to reduce the scope for connected lending, since foreign shareholders of local banks are unlikely to borrow from the banks in which they invest.

While the positive effects of increasing foreign entry on competition and efficiency appear to be uncontroversial, the question remains as to the particular ways in which foreign investors should be allowed to take controlling positions in domestic banking sectors. Two broad approaches have been taken in the region. The first is to allow foreign investors to establish new banks in the country. This approach has been pursued in Hungary. The second is to allow foreign participation in the domestic banking system through shareholding in existing banks. For example, both Poland and Russia have required foreign institutions to take stakes in former state-owned banks or troubled private banks as a precondition for licensing.

There are benefits and limits to each approach. While it is easier to introduce modern banking practices and monitoring technologies in new banks, they may have difficulties in establishing their own retail network in the country and thus in competing with existing domestic banks. This limitation should encourage governments to accept greater foreign equity participation in existing domestic banks. Obstacles to such participation are the potential dilution of domestic shareholders' claims and the need for a robust regulatory regime to encourage financial disclosure by domestic banks. Another obstacle is the persistence of a large fraction of non-performing banks in domestic banks' portfolios. This points to a close relationship between entry policies and the resolution of failed banks. With both the entry of foreign banks and foreign participation in existing banks, there is the additional advantage that their effective regulation in their home countries will tend to improve the enforcement of regulation in the transition economy. Given that foreign participation can bring significant benefits to both existing domestic banks and to new ones, banking regulation should aim to open the banking systems to non-discriminatory access by foreign banks. Indeed, this is a requirement of the EU Association Agreements signed by 10 countries in central and eastern Europe.

8.3 Bank privatisation and corporate governance

Privatisation to date has mostly been concentrated on enterprises (see Chapter 2). Bank privatisation has been held back by a combination of factors, including the scale of bad debts in the portfolios of state banks, opposition by vested interests – including incumbent personnel and favoured debtors – as well as a lack of clarity in legal rules and oversight. Yet, privatisation of state banks can make a substantial contribution to enhancing their performance. Allowing the participation of outside investors – domestic and foreign – will lead to the adoption of new banking technologies as well as the reduction in scope for political factors to drive lending decisions. At the same time, bank privatisation can harden the budget constraints of both banks and firms and ultimately ensure greater stability in the sector. Given the particular problems that exit and entry can pose in banking and that have

Chart 8.3

Share of majority state-owned banks in total bank assets, 1994-97

(in per cent)

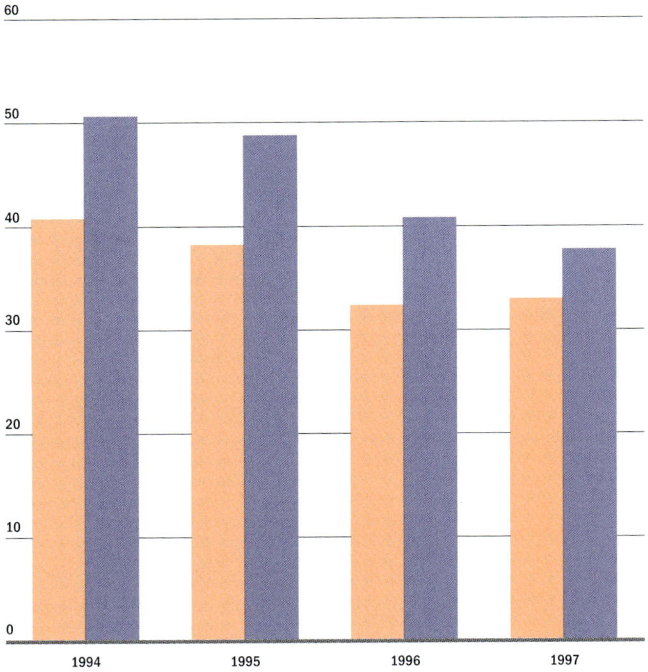

Source: National authorities – Unweighted averages for the regions.

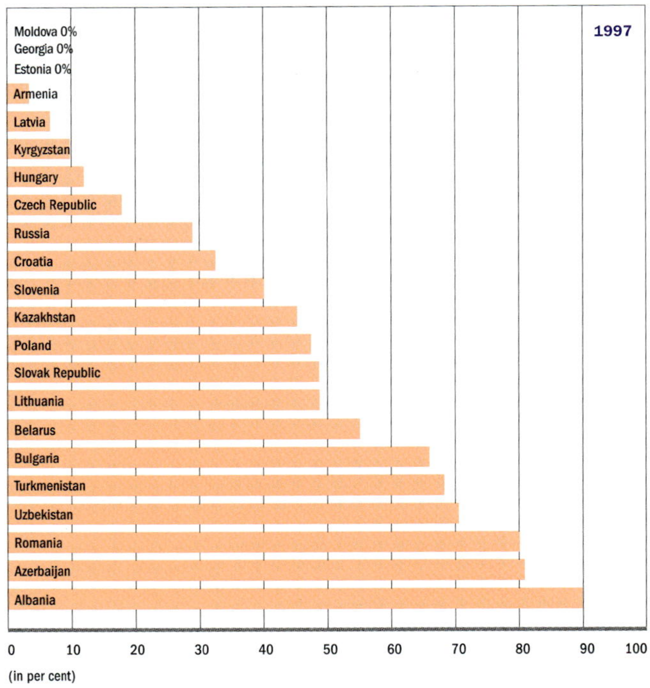

Source: National authorities.

been highlighted in sections 8.1 and 8.2, the manner of privatisation will itself affect the way in which the process of competition is managed in banking.

Why privatise?

There is now significant empirical evidence across developing and industrialised countries and those in transition that the benefits of privatising firms generally outweigh the costs.[15] These benefits will be sensitive to the sector in which the privatised firm operates and to whether privatisation has been associated with more or less competition. However, it is important to recognise that differences between banks and firms will affect the scale and way in which such benefits are manifested.

First, as indicated in Section 8.1, bank failures are not the same as firm failures. Systemic risks tend to force governments to rescue some banks. Thus, it must be a central consideration to implement ownership changes in ways that help reduce expectations that a bank will be bailed out in the future, and hence provide the appropriate incentives for bank managers not to indulge in overly risky behaviour.

Second, privatisation limits the scope for intervention by government in the allocation of credit, while also breaking the nexus of state control over both bank regulation and managerial decisions in banking. This will provide a framework for better investment decisions by banks and make regulatory oversight more credible.

Third, privatisation can also be expected to improve productivity at the level of the individual bank, particularly through the introduction of better monitoring. This would not only improve the bank's own performance but should help banks function more effectively as active creditors to firms. Although such changes could in principle be divorced from ownership through transfer of expertise – as through twinning arrangements with foreign banks – experience suggests that these arrangements are not as successful as changes in ownership structure in improving lending practices.[16]

There are cases, however, where delaying privatisation may make sense. For example, when adequate supervisory or regulatory authority is not in place, the argument for rapid privatisation is weaker. This also applies to the large savings banks – such as Sberbank in Russia – which continue to mobilise the bulk of household deposits. The very scale of their depositor base and the underlying assumption regarding deposit insurance suggests that some caution be exercised in privatisation. In particular, the objective must be to avoid disturbing confidence among depositors – particularly important given the recent history of large inflation taxes on deposits and, in some cases, outright confiscation of savings – and creating private monopolies.

Experience with bank privatisation

While bank privatisation has recently accelerated in central Europe and Russia, much remains to be done. Furthermore, even

[15] See, Chapter 4 of the 1997 *Transition Report* and Galal, Jones, Tandon and Vogelsang (1994).

[16] See Meyendorff and Snyder (1997).

when privatisation has gone ahead, governments have often retained strategic stakes in privatised banks. This has, for example, been the case in the Czech Republic. Chart 8.3 shows that banks with state ownership exceeding 50 per cent are still important in terms of their share of total assets. Moreover, where privatisation has taken place, the approach taken has varied widely across countries.

In central European countries, privatisation has largely proceeded in an orderly manner. In the Czech Republic, for example, banks were included in the first wave of voucher privatisation. The government retained its position as a major shareholder and, while initially ownership was dispersed among voucher holders, subsequent resale to investment funds has led to greater concentration.[17] Recently, the Czech government has begun to sell its residual shareholdings in banks, largely to foreign banks. In Poland, by contrast, a mixed approach to privatisation has been adopted, combining preferential distribution of rights to incumbent managers and staff, some public offerings and, in a minority of cases, placement of shares with foreign strategic investors, as in the case of Bank Slaski. Drawing in foreign strategic investment has been a major feature in the Hungarian bank privatisations.

Further east, the privatisations that have occurred have generally been led by incumbent bank managers who have successfully exploited the inability of the government to organise an orderly transfer of ownership rights. A distinctive feature has been to secure the participation not only of insiders – the managers and employees of banks – but also the participation of borrowers that historically benefited from loans granted in a regime of soft budget constraints. Evidence from Russia, for example, shows that the power of managers has been key in driving privatisation.[18] In Russia, bank managers were initially given control rights to decide whether to create single-branch banks or to join larger banks to be privatised. They were also commonly accorded veto power over the amount of shares to be purchased by a single shareholder. Faced with the need to raise capital, they turned to their existing clients as the new shareholders. When these firms were subsequently privatised, banks took ownership stakes in their clients. This behaviour led to the creation of cross-holding patterns between the newly privatised banks and their main debtor enterprises. In addition, post-privatisation managers have commonly issued new equity to dilute holdings and to ensure dispersed ownership structures.[19]

The key point to be emphasised is that when privatisation has occurred by giving incumbent managers the ownership claims that go with their *de facto* control of enterprises, there is the danger that prior lending patterns and links will be maintained. This risk is particularly great if there is a continued expectation of recourse to public resources to compensate for bad decisions. Since insider-led privatisations will not usually facilitate access to external finance – since there cannot generally be a credible commitment to pay back investors – such banks will be more prone to rely on government rescue, including re-nationalisation.

The speed of bank privatisation has also been conditioned by the presence of bad loans. While again responses have varied substantially, the evidence suggests that rapid privatisation – preferably with the participation of foreign investors – following recapitalisation is likely to be the best way of stemming any future demand for additional public support to cover bad loans. The worst possible approach has been to recapitalise without addressing the ownership structure and associated lending patterns that have given rise to the problem in the first place. This is the key lesson from recent events in Bulgaria.

How privatisation occurs also has major implications for market power and the associated problem of too-big-to-fail banks. One approach (see section 8.2 above) is to break up or restructure prior to privatisation. The strategy is consistent with the overall objective of achieving a banking structure where a manageable number of high-quality banks, adequately capitalised and accessible for regulation, would dominate. Aside from reducing the scope for exercising market power, this approach has merit when addressing the bailout problem.

Lastly, it is important to place individual privatisations in context. Bank privatisations have occurred in the framework of emerging universal banking systems, similar to the German banking model (see Chapter 5). In principal, universal banking ought to be able to help banks encourage restructuring in firms by behaving as active investors. Indeed, it could be argued that by taking on equity – through swaps, for example – banks will be provided with the incentives to reduce the bad loans problem and enforce better governance. Yet several factors caution against any simple conclusions. In the first place, privatised banks may suffer from the same lack of managerial expertise and capacity to monitor loans as state banks, at least initially. Second, the problem of connected lending has remained a key concern, particularly in contexts where bank privatisation has been insider-led. Universal banking may actually exacerbate this problem if robust regulatory authority is not in place.[20]

Privatisation and corporate governance

While bank privatisation in transition economies has taken a variety of forms, what is desirable and what is not desirable in these various approaches? In particular, what are the desirable attributes of ownership structure that are likely to be associated with better corporate governance, and ultimately efficiency, following privatisation? There are three general dimensions along which the ownership of banks can vary: concentrated versus dispersed ownership; insider versus outside owners; and foreign versus domestic owners.

[17] For example, only 7% of the initial 49% of vouchers awarded to citizens were still owned by individuals by 1993.

[18] Meyendorff and Snyder (1997).

[19] See the case study of Zhilotsbank in Abarbanell and Meyendorff (1997).

[20] In central Europe exposure to individual borrowers is generally restricted to around 25% of a bank's own funds. However, it is not clear whether enforcement is effective.

Concentrated versus dispersed ownership

Both theory and empirical work indicate that, in the case of firms, dispersed ownership is generally best avoided.[21] Does this result apply to banks? In general, the answer is clearly affirmative. Capital markets in the transition economies are characterised by their small size and illiquidity (see Chapter 5). One consequence is that take-over threats will generally not be credible.[22] Hence markets will not be able to exert corporate control and discipline bank managers so that they pursue profit-maximising objectives. Therefore, for banks, as well as firms, a core of large investors will generally be the best guarantor of effective monitoring of managers. But while concentrated ownership is an important element in good corporate governance, it is important to recognise that concentration – particularly in the setting of the transition economies – raises important problems in its own right.

There are a number of contexts in which the role of big shareholders in disciplining managers may be ineffectual. The first is the case of connected lending where bank shareholders are at the same time borrowers from the bank. This phenomenon, as we have already seen, is quite widespread in the transition economies. It gives rise to a major conflict of interest and resulting lending practices may primarily respond to the private interests of the dominant shareholders, rather than to the interests of the bank or minority shareholders. Intimately related to this problem is the case of financial-industrial groups. When banks and their main shareholders form part of the same group, experience suggests that shareholders tend to be ineffectual in restraining risky investments undertaken by managers.[23] Recent Russian experience with financial-industrial groups, loosely modelled on East Asian ownership forms, suggests that ownership of banks by individual groups should be avoided and, to the extent that such structures exist, they will require very close monitoring and regulation (see Box 8.1).[24]

Concentrated ownership of banks can also raise the scope for collusion. This appears to be particularly the case where government has retained a significant ownership stake in newly privatised banks, as in Hungary. While the way in which such influence will be used will depend on the specific objectives of the parties, there is an obvious danger that this will translate into inefficient lending practices. In addition, there is the danger that minority shareholders will be expropriated or their interests ignored. This risk is exacerbated in most transition economies by a lack of rules to protect minority shareholders, as well as by the low level of transparency in the absence of international accounting standards in consolidated accounts.

While concentrated ownership brings clear governance benefits, alongside some potential risks, dealing with the latter is far from clear cut. Rules on lending exposures and other constraints will be important ancillary instruments, as will imposing the requirement of independent audits by accounting firms on a regular basis. All of these depend for their effectiveness, however, on adequate regulatory authority – a large assumption in many of the transition economies. This suggests that, wherever possible, attempts should be made to limit explicitly the formation of financial-industrial groups, and to try to ensure at privatisation an adequate separation of investors and borrowers.

Types of owners

If in the transition context there is a compelling case for concentrated, rather than dispersed, ownership as a mechanism for ensuring effective corporate governance, the obvious and allied question is what types of owners for banks will generally be preferable? In particular, are there reasons for favouring insider or outsider ownership or foreign as against domestic owners?

Throughout the region, incumbent managers or insiders have played a major role in the privatisations that have occurred to date.[25] Certainly, insider privatisation can proceed rapidly, since there is no need to search for strategic investors, and insiders will not only be willing to hold formal authority through privatisation but may also try to block outsiders acquiring stakes. But while possibly convenient, insider privatisation faces a clear conflict of interest between the private objectives of managers and employees and the implementation of sound lending practices required to maximise the value of the bank. Unable to bring new capital to the table, hence unable to make new investments in technology, and more likely to be implicated in connected lending practices, insiders will be hard pressed to address the fundamental inefficiencies present in banks.

There is a strong case for involving outside interests in privatisation and, in particular, ensuring the participation of strategic investors. This argument turns not only on the incentive problems that arise when insiders dominate, but also on the pressing need for banks in the transition economies to improve the technology of banking and the selection and monitoring of investment projects in particular. Importing managerial skills and providing better oversight are at the core of the privatisation problem.

To achieve these objectives, the acquisition of controlling positions in privatised banks by strategic foreign investors offers substantial benefits. Aside from helping the transfer of new technology to privatised banks, such investors can infuse capital at a lower cost, since foreign institutions generally enjoy access to international markets. Foreign investors should be able to comply with capital requirements more efficiently, while the risk of collu-

[21] See, for example, Chapter 5 of the 1995 *Transition Report* and Shleifer and Vishny (1997).

[22] Identifying a take-over target will be difficult if information about the current operations of banks is not reflected in the market price of their shares. Investors willing to take controlling positions in the bank may also not find sufficient large blocks of shares available for sale from existing shareholders.

[23] For example, evidence from Japan shows that when the bank and its main shareholders belong to the same group or *keiretsu*, concentration of shareholding by members of the group has commonly led to the pursuit of riskier investment projects, such as the increase in real estate lending in the 1980s. Not only have large shareholders shown an unwillingness to discipline managers but they have also prevented other shareholders from disciplining the managers. See Dinc (1998).

[24] An associated – but different – issue is that of cross-holdings by banks. These can easily exacerbate systemic risk due to interconnection through inter-bank operations.

[25] See Chapter 5 of the 1997 *Transition Report*.

Box 8.1

Financial-industrial groups in Russia

Financial-industrial groups (FIGs) have become major players in the Russian economy. FIGs are defined as business groups constituted by a parent company. The parent company holds residual control rights over the assets of the group and may be constituted either as a new joint-stock company or as a group member after the acquisition of shares from the other firms in the group. The decision to form a FIG can be taken either by the government (as when a state-owned firm is involved) or voluntarily by private initiative. The formation of FIGs has been actively encouraged by the government. There is significant heterogeneity among these groups but broadly there are two main types: (1) industry-led groups formed either by large industrial firms that set up their own agent or 'pocket' bank for operational needs, as well as established regional holding groups and, (2) bank-led groups formed either by direct acquisition of industrial firms by banks or as a result of debt-equity swaps after privatisation. We focus especially on bank-led groups where banks hold important positions on the board of directors of industrial firms.

FIGs: Benefits versus costs

In principle, FIGs offer several advantages. First, concentrated ownership tends to improve corporate governance. Second, the interests of shareholders and creditors are aligned, as these roles are played by the same institution. With control rights over the group's assets being held by the parent company, this might favour an efficient allocation of funds within the group, and help overcome any liquidity problems in financing profitable projects. For instance, Perotti and Gelfer (1998) find that investment undertaken by firms belonging to FIGs tends to be less sensitive to internal liquidity than the investment undertaken by independent firms. This may be particularly advantageous in contexts where information asymmetries between banks and firms exist and where an inability to enforce bankruptcy undermines creditors and leads to reductions in long-term finance. Lastly, FIGs may permit greater horizontal and vertical integration consistent with gaining economies of scale and scope.

These potential benefits need to be set against the probable costs associated with FIGs. A primary concern must be the risk that FIGs will permit misallocations of credit and investment. This can arise because the composition of FIGs may be primarily designed to serve government interests and hence will create conflicts of interest in the allocation of credit. Among other effects, this may lead banks to succumb to pressure from government to support certain industries that may be declining. Further, the risk of collusion between FIGs and the government can be conducive to rent-seeking behaviour that will undermine market efficiency. The privileges granted to FIGs with respect to wealth transfers within the group – together with the lack of transparency of these operations – can facilitate the expropriation of minority shareholders, through a variety of devices, including transfer pricing and share dilution.

There is also a flip side to the argument for banks having equity stakes in firms; it can lead to an undesirable composition of the banks' portfolios. This risk is reinforced whenever banks hold positions in the same companies as owners and creditors. Increased risk is not compensated by higher capital ratios. Indeed in Russia, capital adequacy requirements imposed by government are actually lower for banks integrated in FIGs than for the rest of the banking sector. As a result, the likelihood of bank failure increases.

FIGs may also be a source of market power. To encourage their formation, the Russian government granted major privileges with respect to taxation, investment guarantees and access to financial credit on favourable terms. These privileges tend to place barriers to entry, pre-empting potential rivals from entering the industry. In addition, the cross-shareholding pattern that characterises FIGs may lead to mutual forbearance decreasing the extent of competition. Anti-competitive behaviour has been facilitated by ineffectual regulation. Lastly, FIGs tend to be large and because of that raise the problem of being potentially 'too-big-to-fail'. All these factors suggest that the costs of encouraging the formation of FIGs have outweighed the benefits.

sion with the domestic authorities will tend to be reduced when new bank owners include foreign investors. Experience from other countries strongly supports the view that foreign entry can raise competition and efficiency, assuming that adequate regulatory controls are put in place.[26]

There are several constraints on foreign participation. The first is political and involves opposition by citizens and government to foreign ownership. The second is that foreign owners may lack sufficient information regarding the quality of domestic borrowers, although this is likely to be offset by superior monitoring technology. An interesting approach that has attempted to address these constraints has been the privatisation of Bank Handlowy in Poland. In this case, one of the government's objectives was to generate adequate revenues from the privatisation for financing the pension system. They also had to satisfy a perceived desire for a significant ownership stake to remain in Polish hands. To achieve this, Polish citizens, bank employees and some institutional investors were allocated nearly two-thirds of the equity but these holdings were dispersed. Although the state notionally held on to a further 30 per cent, it retained only 8 per cent of the voting rights. A core group of foreign investors with only 26 per cent equity share actually received a controlling stake. That control was made contingent on signing explicit cooperation agreements that guaranteed transfer of expertise and know-how while providing some protection against take-over by initially restricting the possibility for share disposal.[27]

The importance of strategic investors raises the associated question of whether investment funds can be suitable owners of banks. For example, recent Czech experience suggests that after voucher privatisation investment funds have achieved greater concentration by acquiring vouchers directly from the government or from individual investors. However, the evidence also suggests that funds in the Czech Republic and elsewhere have as yet exerted little beneficial influence on governance. Part of the reason may be that dispersing the ownership of the investment funds will give rise to an incentive problem involving the behaviour of managers of both the fund and the bank. The extent of this problem depends in part on the design of the investment fund. With an open-end fund, investors can redeem their shares at current market value, and the resources of the fund expand or

[26] For instance, in New Zealand the largely foreign-owned banking system is subject to very transparent supervision, both in the country and in the bank's country of origin. The gains from foreign participation depend strongly on having appropriate incentives for banks to disclose information and a robust regulatory regime.

[27] See Kawalec (et al. 1997).

shrink depending on its performance. By contrast, if the fund is closed-end, so that shares cannot be redeemed, investors are locked in and fund managers may not have enough incentive to ensure banks in their portfolios perform well. In fact, evidence from the Czech Republic shows that concentrated ownership by investment funds (mostly closed-end) of firms or banks is not positively correlated with their performance.

8.4 Conclusion

This chapter has examined the key policy challenges in promoting the expansion of banking activities in transition economies, which are central to their nascent financial sectors. The starting point of this analysis has been the recognition that effective competition and private ownership of banks can serve to enhance their performance, but that banks are different from firms in several key respects. Governments fear bank failures because of the risk of contagion to other institutions in the system; they also commonly provide prudential regulation of banks and partial guarantees of deposits. These actions are taken with the objectives of securing stability and protecting retail depositors. The legacies from central planning in the banking sector include not only weak regulatory institutions that are inexperienced in managing the process of competition in banking but also banks that are inexperienced in market-based finance. At the same time, the structure of control in banks has facilitated the perpetuation of connected lending and, in some cases, soft budgets for both banks and firms.

These features of transition banking point to the importance of clarifying the way in which failed banks are to be resolved. The introduction of a framework of mandatory corrective actions and conservatorship can provide both a strategy for responding to banks that fall out of compliance with basic regulatory requirements and for mitigating the problems of regulatory forbearance and political interference. However, for this framework to function well, the regulatory authorities must have access to reliable financial information about banks. While this regulatory capacity does not yet exist, an alternative framework may be required until the capacity is put in place. One approach would be to move to a system of bank recapitalisation that gives troubled banks an incentive to reveal their asset quality problems and to recover on bad loans and other non-performing assets. This incentive can be created by a scheme that takes the form of a purchase of non-performing assets at a premium to their market value or a subsidy for each asset recovery. Non-performing loans could be either acquired at a premium by a special government agency set up to recover on bad assets or they could remain on the books of the troubled bank for recovery. In the latter case, the bank would receive a recapitalisation in the form of a subsidy for asset recoveries.

The steps to achieve a consistent framework for bank oversight, corrective actions and closure have to be considered in tandem with a strategy on entry. While there are likely to be clear welfare gains if entry is associated with increased competition, it is important to recognise that effective competition depends on both the number of banks and their quality. In the context of the transition economies, the chapter has argued that there is a strong case for giving greater weight to the quality of banks than might normally be the case. Indeed, experience shows that where permissive bank licensing has led to extensive entry, inadequate oversight has resulted in fragile, under-capitalised banking systems. Russia is the clearest case in point. An alternative approach is to be more restrictive in terms of entry, where a principal objective is to achieve high quality in the system through the presence of a smaller number of well-capitalised banks. Prudential licensing requirements, effectively and fairly applied, and non-discriminatory access to domestic and foreign entry can help to raise the quality of banks.

Lastly, a more efficient banking system in the transition economies requires a strong emphasis on privatisation. Privatisation reduces the scope for political factors to dominate in lending decisions and radically improves the incentives of both bank and firm managers. To realise those gains requires, however, sufficient concentration in the structure of ownership so as to provide appropriate corporate governance, as well as types of owners that are less likely to perpetuate connected lending and other practices so characteristic of the previous system. In these respects, the insider-led privatisation that has been widespread cannot be recommended. Rather, greater emphasis should be placed on attracting strategic investors, both foreign and domestic.

References

J. Abarbanell and J. Bonin, (1997), "Bank privatisation in Poland: The case of Bank Slaski", *Journal of Comparative Economics,* Vol. 25, No.1, pp. 31-61.

J. Abarbanell and A. Meyendorff (1997), "Bank privatisation in post-communist Russia: The case of Zhilsotsbank", *Journal of Comparative Economics,* Vol. 25, No.1, pp. 62-96.

P. Aghion, P. Bolton and S. Fries (1998), "Optimal Design of Bank Bailouts: The Case of Transition Economies", EBRD Working Paper, No. 31.

R. Anderson and C. Kegels (1998), *Transition Banking: Financial Development of Central and Eastern Europe,* Oxford University Press, Oxford.

G.Benston, R. D. Brumbaugh Jr., J. Guttentag, R. Herring, G. Kaufman, R. Litan and K. Scott (1989), *Blueprint for Restructuring America's Financial Institutions: Report of a Task Force,* The Brookings Institution, Washington DC.

E. Berglof and G. Roland (1998), "Soft Budget Constraints and Banking in Transition Economies", *Journal of Comparative Economics,* Vol. 26, pp. 18-40.

I. S. Dinc (1998), "The Shareholding Structure of Japanese Banks and Their Real State Lending in the 1980s", Tokyo University, mimeo.

EBRD (1995), *Transition Report* 1995, EBRD, London.

EBRD (1997), *Transition Report* 1997, EBRD, London.

A. Faure-Grimaud and J.-C. Rochet (1998), "Bank privatisation in transition economies", IDEI, mimeo.

D. Folkerts-Landau and C.-J. Lindgrin (1998), *Toward a Framework for Financial Stability,* International Monetary Fund, Washington DC.

S. Fries, P. Mella-Barral and W. Perraudin (1997), "Optimal bank reorganisation and the fair pricing of deposit insurance", *Journal of Banking and Finance,* Vol. 21, pp. 441-468.

A. Galal, L. Jones, P. Tandon and I. Vogelsang (1994), *The Welfare Consequences of Selling Public Enterprises: An Empirical Analysis,* Oxford University Press, Oxford.

G. Garcia (1996), "Deposit insurance: Obtaining the benefits and avoiding the pitfalls", IMF Working Paper, No. WP/96/83.

C. Gray and A. Holle (1996), "Bank-led restructuring in Poland: the Bank conciliation process in action", *Economics of Transition,* Vol. 4, No. 2, pp. 349-370.

E. E. Karlova (1997), "Financial-Industrial Groups, Industrial Policy, and Competition in the Russian Federation", World Bank, mimeo.

S. Kawalec (1997), "Bank privatisation: The case of Bank Handlowy w Warszawie SA", Bank Handlowy, mimeo.

A. Meyendorff and E. Snyder (1997), "Transactional Structures of Bank Privatisations in Central Europe and Russia", *Journal of Comparative Economics,* Vol.25, No.1, pp. 5-30.

J. Mitchell (1993), "Creditor passivity and bankruptcy: implications for economic reform", in C. Mayer and X. Vives (eds.), *Capital Markets and Financial Intermediation,* Cambridge University Press, Cambridge.

J. Mitchell (1998), "The Problem of Bad Debts: Cleaning Banks' Balance Sheets in Economies of Transition", ECARE, mimeo.

E. Perotti and S. Gelfer (1998), "Investment Financing in Russian Financial-Industrial Groups", University of Amsterdam, mimeo.

P. Rey and J.-C. Rochet (1998), "Banking competition, stability and innovation in transition economies", GREMAQ-IDEI, mimeo.

J.-C. Rochet and J. Tirole (1996), "Interbank Lending and Systemic Risk", *Journal of Money, Credit and Banking,* 28, (4), pp. 733-762.

A. Shleifer and R. Vishny (1997), 'A Survey of Corporate Governance' *Journal of Finance,* 52 (2), pp. 737-783.

E. Snyder and R. Kormendi (1997), "Privatisation and Performance of the Czech Republic's Komercni Banka", *Journal of Comparative Economics,* Vol.25, No.1, pp. 97-128.

United States Department of the Treasury (1991), *Modernising the Financial System: Recommendations for Safer, More Competitive Banks,* Government Printing Office, Washington DC.

Transition assessments for each country

Since 1994, the EBRD has presented annual assessments of the transition for each country in its *Transition Reports.* These assessments have highlighted key developments and issues central to the process of transition in a wide range of areas, including: enterprises, markets and trade, financial institutions, fiscal and social safety net reform, and legal transition.

This year, the format and contents of these transition assessments have been changed to provide greater comparability across countries and a stronger focus on the key transition challenges facing each country. The text discusses the main aspects of reform at the current stage of the transition process. The analysis is more topical and selective than in the past, in order to focus the attention on the most important developments and issues. The text is grouped into six broad dimensions of reform: liberalisation, privatisation, enterprises, infrastructure, financial sector, and fiscal and social sector. The key reform challenges facing the country are summarised at the beginning of the text. The assessment is complemented by a timeline of important historical events in the transition process.

In order to provide a quantitative foundation for analysing progress in transition and to promote cross-country comparability, each transition assessment includes a data table. The table is grouped into the same six categories as the text. On the left-hand side of the table, "snapshots" provide an overview of selected institutional and legal arrangements as of October 1998. On the right-hand side, the time series data provide indicators of progress in transition within each category.

The data presented in these assessments are by no means comprehensive and cannot give a complete account or precise measurement of progress in transition. Some entries, such as the exchange rate regime and the privatisation methods, are useful only for information and carry no normative content. Other variables may have normative content, but their evaluation may vary depending on different practical and theoretical interpretations.

The data should be interpreted with caution as their quality varies across countries and categories. The data are based on a wide variety of sources, including national authorities, EBRD staff estimates, and other international organisations. To strengthen the degree of cross-country comparability, much of the data were collected through standardised EBRD surveys of national authorities. The technical notes at the end of this section provide definitions of the variables, along with country-specific qualifications.

Albania

1991

Mar Small-scale privatisation begins

1992

Apr Two-tiered banking system established

July Full current account convertibility introduced

July Exchange rate unified

July All quantitative controls on foreign trade removed

Aug Most prices liberalised

1993

Apr Restitution law for non-agricultural land adopted

May Privatisation of housing begins

June Privatisation agency established

July First foreign-owned bank opened

July Enterprise restructuring agency established

1994

Jan Modernisation of tax administration begins

Aug T-bills market initiated

1995

Apr Voucher privatisation begins

July Competition law enacted

July Land titles introduced

Oct Bankruptcy law enacted

1996

Feb Central bank independence law adopted

Mar Securities and exchange commission established

May Stock exchange established

July VAT introduced

July First enterprise liquidated

Dec First pyramid scheme collapsed

1997

Mar Widespread rioting and looting

July Law on transparency adopted

Oct VAT increased

Nov Emergency IMF assistance approved

Nov Pyramids placed under international administration

Key reform challenges

- **The failed pyramid schemes and the resulting civil unrest in early 1997 have seriously undermined the economy. The situation has improved, but law and order has not yet been fully restored.**
- **Pressing ahead with market-oriented reforms and strengthening public institutions will be crucial to attract much-needed investment finance. The new IMF programme is a signal that these challenges can be credibly addressed.**
- **Further progress in liquidating or restructuring the three state banks is an important prerequisite for the emergence of a functioning banking system. In light of the pyramid crisis, tighter financial markets regulation will be necessary to restore public confidence.**

Liberalisation

Efforts have been made to improve customs procedures and further liberalise the trade regime.
During the civil unrest in early 1997, most custom and tax offices were destroyed and smuggling became the norm. In the second half of 1997, customs collection was temporarily carried out by the Italian and Greek customs offices, which helped to reverse the free-fall in government revenues. Since then, most customs offices have been reopened and the EU is assisting in improving collection and modernising customs accounts. At the end of 1997, import duty exemptions on wheat and on investment goods expired. An export ban on certain metals was removed in early 1998. Further liberalisation and harmonisation of trade rules, such as the removal of discriminatory excise taxes on imports, will be required to achieve WTO entry.

Significant reforms have created the conditions for a functioning land market.
Comprehensive land privatisation occurred early in the transition process, with 92% of agricultural land privatised by the end of 1993. However, land could not be traded effectively, partly due to lack of registration; only 3% of land had been registered by mid-1997. This has constrained consolidation of agricultural land, where most farmers cultivate small tracts and often produce for their own consumption only. A new land law, passed by parliament in May 1998, has considerably simplified procedures for the sale of agricultural land. Land registries covering all districts are now open. Whereas under the previous law, land could not be sold until all plots in a district were registered, the new law allows for the sale of land on an individual basis. Registration is, however, sometimes problematic due to unresolved restitution issues.

Privatisation

A regulatory framework to privatise remaining state-owned SMEs is now in place.
Albania made very rapid early progress in privatising agriculture, bringing the private sector share in GDP to over 50% by the end of 1994. However, few industrial enterprises were privatised and the 1995 mass voucher programme was interrupted by the 1997 crisis. In March 1998, parliament approved a new regulatory framework for the privatisation of the remaining 470 SMEs with full or partial state ownership. Unviable companies are to be transferred to local authorities. The other enterprises are to be transformed into joint-stock companies and auctioned off.

There are plans to privatise the large natural resource and infrastructure monopolies.
The government intends to transform the state monopolies in transport, telecommunications, energy, mining and water into joint-stock companies. Their privatisation is envisaged on a case-by-case basis, primarily through international tenders. The mining sector will be particularly attractive as Albania boasts substantial deposits of copper and chrome. In December 1997, copper exploration rights for the Munelle site were sold to a Canadian investor. Production by the state-owned copper monopoly Albaker resumed in March 1998, after a one year stoppage resulting from the civil unrest. The state oil company, Albpetrol, is engaged in some joint ventures, but is plagued by financial difficulties.

Enterprises

Enterprises are recovering gradually from the 1997 crisis.
In the wake of the crisis, output collapsed in many sectors, while agricultural production remained at close to its 1996 level. The economy has shown signs of recovery in 1998, especially in construction and services. Agriculture continues to account for over half of GDP, although its contribution to exports is much smaller. Enterprises remain hampered by the poor quality of infrastructure, significant security problems in some regions and by corruption. Survey results indicate that the cost of corruption to firms could be as high as 8% of their turnover. The government has launched an anti-corruption programme supported by the World Bank.

Some large enterprises have been restructured, but market discipline remains weak.
The Enterprise Restructuring Agency set up in 1993 to deal with 32 problem firms has been relatively successful in restructuring these firms, reducing employment from 50,000 at their peak to 7,000 at the end of 1995. However, only 10 have been privatised and only one smaller enterprise liquidated. Financial discipline is weak,

Liberalisation			1994	1995	1996	1997
Exchange rate regime	managed float	Share of administered prices in CPI	na	na	na	na
Current account convertibility	full	Administered prices in "EBRD-15" basket	na	na	na	na
Interest rate liberalisation	limited *de jure*	Share of trade in GDP	18.8	18.3	21.4	18.8
Wage regulation	no	Tariff revenue (% of imports)	10.9	9.9	8.0	8.7
Privatisation						
Primary privatisation method	MEBOs	Private sector share in GDP	50	60	75	75
Secondary privatisation method	vouchers	Privatisation revenues (% of GDP)	1.17	0.14	0.19	0.27
Tradability of land rights	limited *de facto*	Number of small firms privatised	2,775	2,821	na	na
Enterprises						
Protection of shareholder rights	ineffective	Budgetary subsidies (% of GDP)	1.2	0.6	0.4	0.5
Bankruptcy proceedings	ineffective	Credit to enterprises (% of GDP)	4.9	5.0	5.1	4.6
Competition office	no	Labour productivity in industry (% change)	na	na	na	na
Infrastructure						
Independent telecoms regulator	yes	Main telephone lines per 100 inhabitants	1.4	1.3	1.9	2.3
Separation of railway accounts	no	Railway labour productivity (1989=100)	33.6	33.3	37.6	21.4
Independent electricity regulator	yes	Electricity tariff, US¢/kWh (collection ratio in %)	na	na	3.0 (50)	3.0 (50)
Financial institutions						
Deposit insurance	no	Number of banks (of which foreign-owned)	6 (3)	6 (3)	8 (3)	9 (3)
Secured transactions law	restricted	Asset share of state-owned banks	97.8	94.5	93.7	89.9
Insider dealing prohibited	yes	Bad loans (% of total loans)	na	34.9	40.1	91.3
Securities commission	yes	Stock market capitalisation (% of GDP)	na	na	na	na
Fiscal and social sector						
Private pension funds	no	Tax revenues (% of GDP)	19.1	17.7	15.3	13.7
Share of population in poverty	na	Earnings inequality (Gini coefficient)	na	na	na	na

including among the large state enterprises, which have high arrears to the utilities and to the budget.

Infrastructure

Poor infrastructure is constraining economic growth prospects.
Even before the crisis, Albania's infrastructure was quite underdeveloped relative to other east European countries. The widespread destruction and looting have made matters even worse. Most roads and bridges are in very poor condition. There are almost daily power cuts. Water runs only a few hours a day in most apartments. International financial institutions are assisting in financing the large investment agenda.

Poor revenue collection is inhibiting the restructuring of the electricity sector.
The national electricity utility is virtually insolvent despite the fact that prices are close to cost recovery. This is partly the result of the 1997 crisis, which led to a drop in electricity production of over 50%. Another problem is poor revenue collection. Many people are stealing electricity and the large loss-making state enterprises in oil and mining have accumulated large payment arrears. As a first step towards restructuring, the government plans to award a management contract to a private operator, while rehabilitating the hydropower plants and the networks.

Telecommunications companies are to be sold to foreign strategic investors.
The government intends to privatise parts of the state-owned mobile phone company, AMC, and the state-owned fixed-line monopoly, Telekomi Shqiptar, through international tender in 1999. It has drafted a law for liberalising the market which would abolish Telekomi's monopoly on fixed-line services.

Financial institutions

The pyramid schemes are being liquidated and the central bank's supervisory capabilities strengthened.
Following the collapse of the pyramid schemes in 1997, they have all been closed down and the lengthy process of liquidation and asset recovery is under way. Recovered assets will be sold and proceeds distributed to depositors, most likely in 1999. It is estimated that US$ 25-50 million could be recovered, far below the US$ 1 billion deposited in these schemes. A new bank law has been drafted to strengthen prudential regulations, improve the supervisory powers of the central bank and prevent any recurrence of the pyramid schemes.

Plans to privatise the defunct banking sector are in preparation.
The financial sector is small and in very poor condition. Most financing activities take place outside the banking system and the stock market. The banking system has been dominated by three state banks – National Commercial Bank (NCB), Rural Commercial Bank (RCB) and the Savings Bank (SB) – which together account for more than 90% of all banking assets. They suffer from an extremely high proportion of doubtful and non-performing loans, reaching over 90% of total loans in 1997 (up from 40% in 1996). The stock of total credit to enterprises is very low and new lending to the private sector is minimal. There are plans to sell NCB to foreign strategic investors. A governance contract between SB and the government is in place and all new loans have to be approved by selected foreign advisers. The RCB was put into liquidation in January 1998. Most of its assets were transferred to SB, and its bad debts have been transferred to the Credit Restructuring Agency. The stock market remains insignificant and trading is limited to treasury bills and privatisation vouchers.

Fiscal and social sector

The fiscal revenue crisis has led to cuts in public sector employment.
The fiscal deficit, resulting from a large informal economy, worsened significantly following the pyramid crisis. Tax revenues for 1997 dipped to about 10% of GDP and would have fallen even further had VAT not been raised from 12.5% to 20% in October. The general budget deficit amounted to over 12% of GDP. Further efforts were made to contain the deficit, including expenditure cuts in the public sector wage bill. In the first four months of 1998, employment in state budgetary institutions was cut by 11,000, and further cuts are planned for the rest of the year. A public sector wage freeze was, however, terminated in February 1998.

There are plans to increase social assistance in order to cushion the hardships resulting from the pyramid collapse.
Social assistance is a cornerstone of the new IMF and World Bank programmes signed in early 1998. An increase in real terms will be required to provide a safety net for the significant share of the population that lost almost all its assets, including apartments, after the collapse of the pyramid schemes. No direct compensation for pyramid depositors will be paid other than the proceeds from selling assets recovered from the pyramid schemes.

Armenia

CIS member · WTO observer

1991

- Jan — Land reform begins
- May — Small-scale privatisation begins
- Sept — Independence from Soviet Union

1992

- Jan — VAT introduced
- Jan — Foreign trade registration abolished
- Aug — Privatisation law adopted
- Dec — Central bank law adopted

1993

- May — Stock exchange established
- Nov — New currency (dram) introduced

1994

- Jan — First privatisation programme adopted
- Feb — Tradability of land permitted
- May — Cease-fire in Nagorno-Karabakh
- Oct — Voucher privatisation begins

1995

- Apr — Large-scale privatisation begins
- Apr — Export surrender requirement eliminated
- May — Bankruptcy law adopted
- June — Foreign bank ownership allowed
- July — Most prices liberalised
- Sept — Banking crisis peaked
- Sept — T-bills market initiated

1996

- Mar — First foreign-owned bank opened
- June — Banking law amended
- July — IAS audit of banking system

1997

- Jan — Bankruptcy law enacted
- May — Full current account convertibility introduced
- June — Electricity law adopted

Key reform challenges

- **The renewed momentum of privatisation should be combined with improvements in corporate governance and in financial discipline on firms.**
- **Foreign investment will remain constrained without stronger efforts to alleviate infrastructure bottlenecks, to enhance legal and regulatory reforms, and to introduce greater transparency and predictability.**
- **The financial sector is not yet effectively mobilising and channelling domestic savings into new and productive investments. A sound legal and regulatory framework is still not in place for the capital market and for non-bank financial institutions.**

Liberalisation

Negotiations for WTO membership have accelerated.
Armenia has a liberal foreign trade regime with a simple two-band import tariff (at 0% and 10%), no taxes on exports and no substantial quantitative trade restrictions. The remaining inconsistencies with WTO provisions – relating primarily to customs fees and the valuation of goods at customs – are likely to be brought into compliance with WTO regulations by the time of accession, which is expected soon. In September 1997, an Interim Agreement with the EU came into force, which liberalised trade with the EU in goods (except for steel, textiles and coal) and granted Armenia "most favoured nation" status.

Price controls on flour have been eliminated.
The privatisation of state-owned bakeries and flourmills during 1997 and early 1998 has eliminated state controls on profit margins for flourmills, thus eliminating the implicit price controls on bread.

Privatisation

Privatisation has recovered momentum ...
Though the privatisation process had slowed considerably in 1996 and early 1997, the pace began to accelerate after a new Privatisation Minister was appointed in November 1997. A new Law on Privatisation and the government's new privatisation programme were adopted in December 1997, placing greater emphasis on cash auctions and giving foreign investors the same rights as domestic investors. The minimum purchase price for enterprises sold in voucher auctions was lowered from 50% to 25% of the appraised value. These measures sparked a surge of new sales. From October 1997 to mid-1998, over 1,200 SMEs were privatised. In addition, international tenders were announced for 18 of the largest enterprises. Six have been sold and seven are in the process of being privatised. By mid-1998, 70% of medium-sized and large enterprises and over 80% of small enterprises had been privatised.

... with increased foreign participation in cash auctions.
The international tenders for large-scale enterprises have spurred increased foreign participation in privatisation. The government installed in March 1998 has encouraged the involvement of the Armenian Diaspora in the process. Recent sales through international tender have included the telephone operator Armentel, the Yerevan Cognac Factory, and the Armenia and Ani hotels. FDI increased from US$ 22 million in 1996 to US$ 51 million in 1997, equivalent to 3% of GDP. The cumulative inflow of FDI of US$ 91 million since 1989 remains one of the lowest in the region, but FDI had already reached nearly US$ 100 million in the first half of 1998.

Enterprises

Corporate governance is dominated by insider ownership.
Voucher privatisation has resulted in corporate governance structures characterised by insider ownership, as public participation in the programme was low and no alternative investment vehicles were set up to counterbalance managers. The relatively underdeveloped securities market has done little to redistribute ownership.

The pace of enterprise restructuring remains slow.
Industrial output, which started to show positive growth in 1994, grew by less than 1% in 1997. Industrial productivity, which grew strongly in the period 1994-96 (largely driven by labour shedding), declined by 2% in 1997. Some structural change is evident from export flows, with exports to non-CIS countries representing nearly 60% of total exports in 1997, up from 30% in 1994. Nearly 75% of these exports are precious and non-precious metals. Investment in privatised enterprises has been low and many privatised enterprises remain overstaffed. According to one official survey, about one in four employees were on compulsory leave.

Financial discipline remains weak.
Tax arrears increased to 2.6% of GDP at the end of 1997, compared with nearly 2% of GDP at the end of 1996. State-owned firms were responsible for about 70% of these arrears. Bankruptcies are rare and have tended to focus on small enterprises. By mid-1998, only eight of the nearly 2,000 medium-sized and large enterprises originally targeted for privatisation had been liquidated. Enterprises targeted for privatisation cannot be declared bankrupt and liquidation procedures can be initiated only after three privatisation attempts have failed. The government has announced financial rehabilitation plans for some large state-owned enterprises on the verge of bankruptcy, such as the large chemicals company Nairit.

Liberalisation			1994	1995	1996	1997
Exchange rate regime	managed float	Share of administered prices in CPI	na	6.2	7.7	7.0
Current account convertibility	full	Administered prices in "EBRD-15" basket	2	2	1	1
Interest rate liberalisation	full	Share of trade in GDP	43.3	34.8	32.9	31.5
Wage regulation	no	Tariff revenue (% of imports)	0.8	1.1	1.9	2.6
Privatisation						
Primary privatisation method	vouchers	Private sector share in GDP	40	45	50	55
Secondary privatisation method	MEBOs	Share of small firms privatised	7.7	28.1	55.8	77.8
Tradability of land rights	full except foreigners	Share of medium/large firms privatised	na	18.3	51.3	72.3
Enterprises						
Protection of shareholder rights	partly effective	Budgetary subsidies (% of GDP)	12.8	0.9	0.1	0.4
Bankruptcy proceedings	partly effective	Credit to enterprises (% of GDP)	10.7	6.5	4.9	5.0
Competition office	no	Labour productivity in industry (% change)	8.8	20.3	20.2	-2.1
Infrastructure						
Independent telecoms regulator	no	Main telephone lines per 100 inhabitants	15.6	15.5	15.4	17.0
Separation of railway accounts	no	Railway labour productivity (1989=100)	26.3	20.3	16.9	19.9
Independent electricity regulator	yes	Electricity tariff, US¢/kWh (collection ratio in %)	0.4 (na)	1.5 (na)	2.2 (76)	3.3 (80)
Financial institutions						
Deposit insurance	no	Number of banks (of which foreign-owned)	41 (1)	35 (1)	33 (1)	30 (1)
Secured transactions law	yes	Asset share of state-owned banks	1.9	2.4	3.2	3.4
Insider dealing prohibited	na	Bad loans (% of total loans)	34.0	36.1	22.6	7.9
Securities commission	yes	Stock market capitalisation (% of GDP)	na	na	0.2	1.0
Fiscal and social sector						
Private pension funds	no	Tax revenues (% of GDP)	na	12.7	12.9	14.9
Share of population in poverty	44%	Earnings inequality (Gini coefficient)	0.321	0.381	na	na

Infrastructure

A wide-ranging reform programme has been announced for the energy sector.
In December 1997, the government approved a programme for the financial rehabilitation and privatisation of the energy sector. The programme provides for periodic revisions of electricity, water and gas tariff increases towards full cost recovery, measures to improve tariff collection ratios and reductions in subsidies to major energy consumers. Electricity tariffs were raised by 20% in September 1997, but further increases scheduled for April 1998 have been delayed. Privatisation of energy enterprises is under way, with eight small hydropower plants privatised by July 1998.

Armentel, the telecommunications operator, was privatised at the end of 1997.
In December 1997, the Greek telecommunications company OTE bought 90% of Armentel. The remaining 10% was retained by the government. Cash proceeds from the sale amounted to US$ 142 million, part of which went to a US company that held 49% of Armentel before the sale. The new owner assumed Armentel's US$ 47 million of external debt and agreed to invest US$ 300 million over 10 years. Under the agreement, OTE has obtained 15-year exclusivity on fixed systems and 5-year exclusivity on mobile systems. Telephone rates will remain unchanged up to 1999, when further tariff increases will be capped to the rate of inflation. The government plans to establish an independent telecoms regulator.

Financial institutions

A bank rehabilitation programme has shown some signs of success.
A bank rehabilitation programme was launched in early 1996, when most of Armenia's 35 commercial banks were insolvent according to international accounting standards (IAS). From January 1998, minimum capital requirements have been raised to US$ 600,000, with gradual increases up to US$ 1 million by the year 2000. New IAS requirements have also been implemented. Three of the largest problem banks, successors of the Soviet-era specialised banks, have been restructured and were in compliance with new prudential regulations at the end of 1997. The state has gradually reduced its ownership in banks and currently owns only the State Savings Bank. The government is negotiating to sell down its remaining 28% stake in Ardshibank, which accounted for 70% of total banking assets before the rehabilitation programme and now accounts for only 11%. These measures have paved the way for a recovery of the banking sector. The share of classified loans in total loans has declined from 23% in December 1996 to under 10% as of mid-1998. The capital of the banking system increased by nearly 50% in 1997. Only seven of the remaining 29 commercial banks reported a net loss at the end of 1997.

Volume on the capital markets has modestly increased, but the regulatory framework is highly underdeveloped.
There are four stock exchanges in Armenia. The number of firms listed on the largest one, the Yerevan Stock Exchange, has increased from nine in 1996 to 65 in mid-1998. Trading volumes are still very low and are concentrated in Treasury bills. Much of the legal and regulatory framework for capital markets is still under preparation.

Fiscal and social sector

A comprehensive tax reform is showing some early positive results.
In May 1997, a new tax law was adopted to improve tax administration, broaden the tax base and reduce the tax burden. New laws were also adopted on VAT, excise tax, profit tax, property tax and income tax. These laws expand the VAT tax base, while introducing new progressive scales for profit and income tax. Tax exemptions have been reduced, including those for firms with foreign participation, and collection procedures have been improved. Tax revenues increased from 12.9% to 14.9% of GDP from 1996 to 1997 and more than doubled in nominal terms in the first quarter of 1998. However, tax arrears still stood around 15% of total tax revenues in 1997, a 30% rise in nominal terms from 1996, despite a scheme introduced in early 1997 to allow firms to clear tax arrears without penalties.

Necessary reforms in the social sector have been delayed.
A fundamental reform of the pension system, approved as early as 1995, has still not been implemented. Some efforts were made in 1997 and early 1998 to improve pension targeting, reduce the payroll taxes for pensions, and increase pension allowances. In December 1997, the government adopted a new law on compulsory social security payments, according to which workers must contribute 3% of their salaries while payments made by employers are regressively tied to the minimum wage. Poverty and inequality remain severe problems, despite increasing social safety net expenditures from 10% of total budgetary expenditures in 1996 to 15% in 1997. The government has announced plans to replace universal social benefits with better-targeted family allowances, but these reforms have been postponed until January 1999.

Azerbaijan

CIS member · WTO observer

1991

June Law on private ownership adopted

Oct Independence from Soviet Union

1992

Jan Most prices liberalised

Jan VAT introduced

Aug New currency (manat) introduced

Aug Central bank law enacted

1993

Jan Small-scale privatisation law adopted

Aug Interbank currency exchange begins trading

1994

Jan Manat becomes sole legal tender

Apr Privatisation programme announced

May Cease-fire in Nagorno-Karabakh

July Bankruptcy law adopted

July Bank consolidation begins

Sept First international oil PSA

1995

Mar Exchange rate unified

Apr First IMF programme approved

Aug Railway law adopted

1996

Mar Small-scale privatisation begins

June Export surrender requirement abolished

Aug Land reform law adopted

Sept T-bills market initiated

Sept Bank restructuring begins

1997

Mar Voucher privatisation begins

June BIS capital adequacy enacted

June Amended bankruptcy law enacted

June New customs code adopted

July Telecoms law adopted

Dec Northern pipeline to Novorossiisk opened

Key reform challenges

- **Several key large-scale state enterprises are scheduled for privatisation in 1998. Ensuring effective post-privatisation corporate governance will remain a major challenge.**
- **Improvements in the legal business environment, including the functioning of the courts, the reduction of overlapping jurisdictions within government, and the accountability of the state bureaucracy, are necessary to sustain the privatisation process and promote private sector development.**
- **Despite Azerbaijan's substantial oil-related revenues, the commercialisation of infrastructure remains an important challenge to ensure efficient service delivery and to improve the mix of public and private investment.**

Liberalisation

Market competition remains severely impaired, despite price liberalisation.
With the liberalisation of producer prices in agriculture in 1997, price controls are now limited to public utilities and rents. However, high costs arising from bottlenecks in infrastructure and regional instability, combined with concentrated industrial structures, still limit the extent of competition. In agriculture, rural services and the marketing of rural produce are still predominantly provided by a single state-owned concern. A new competition law is under preparation with EU assistance.

Trade liberalisation is progressing towards the requirements of WTO accession.
In 1997, average tariffs were unified at rates of 15%, 5% and 0% for consumer goods, intermediates and most capital goods respectively. De facto state trading monopolies still persist in some sectors such as cotton. With World Bank and IMF assistance, the government is to introduce a new foreign trade charter in line with WTO requirements by December 1998. Azerbaijan already complies with the IMF's Article VIII on current account transactions; formal acceptance is envisaged by early 1999.

Privatisation

Small-scale privatisation is almost complete; medium- and large-scale privatisation began in 1997.
At the end of 1996, there were 3,200 state-owned medium-sized and large enterprises in Azerbaijan, representing an official book value of US$ 12 billion (excluding the state oil company). By mid-year 2000, the authorities plan to privatise over 70% of these assets, encompassing all sectors but natural resources and some infrastructure (e.g. roads and railways). The majority of enterprises are to be privatised through a mass privatisation scheme, which combines several privatisation methods. Following corporatisation under the management of the State Property Committee (SPC), a minimum of 50% of the shares of each enterprise will be sold through voucher auctions, up to 15% will be transferred to employees, and the remainder will be sold via cash auctions. The first auction was held in August 1997. By June 1998, 711 enterprises had been privatised. A limited number of strategic enterprises, mainly in extractive and petrochemical industries, banking and infrastructure – selected on a case-by-case basis by the President – are to be sold through investment tenders.

Despite the accelerated pace of implementation, mass privatisation lacks transparency.
Two main factors have impeded the transparency of mass privatisation. First, the process by which the SPC allocates voucher bids and determines the auction price lacks accountability. Allegations of auction-fixing have been made. Second, the total portfolio of enterprises to be offered for voucher auctions has not yet been determined, as a result of conflicts between the SPC and the state holding companies that control non-privatised assets. The resulting uncertainty has led to low redemption values of privatisation vouchers (less than 10% of the total 32 million vouchers) and wide fluctuations in secondary market prices.

Despite new production sharing agreements, state control of the oil sector remains pervasive.
Since 1994, 13 production sharing agreements in the oil sector have been signed with international companies. Under these agreements, the oil sector will benefit from substantial private investment, although the Azeri partner to all of these deals, the State Oil Corporation of the Azerbaijan Republic (SOCAR), remains a quasi-governmental institution.

Enterprises

Implementation of bankruptcy procedures remains weak.
The implementation of the new bankruptcy law adopted in June 1997 has been hampered by the fact that procedures cannot be initiated against enterprises in the privatisation process. Moreover, the transfer of ownership often implicitly entails a write-down of liabilities that might prevent potential bankruptcies. Many industrial concerns are kept in operation through implicit subsidies from the public utilities. Although utility prices cover operational costs, payment arrears continue to rise; for electricity, gas and water, arrears stood at 3.9% of GDP by end-1997 (up from 3% a year earlier).

The establishment of effective post-privatisation corporate governance is a major reform challenge.
Privatisation so far has largely transferred ownership to enterprise insiders, with little

Liberalisation			1994	1995	1996	1997
Exchange rate regime	managed float	Share of administered prices in CPI	na	na	na	na
Current account convertibility	limited	Administered prices in "EBRD-15" basket	4	3	3	3
Interest rate liberalisation	full	Share of trade in GDP	58.4	33.8	33.5	28.3
Wage regulation	no	Tariff revenue (% of imports)	1.1	1.6	1.9	4.3
Privatisation						
Primary privatisation method	vouchers	Private sector share in GDP	20	25	25	40
Secondary privatisation method	direct sales	Share of small firms privatised	na	na	33.0	71.0
Tradability of land rights	full except foreigners					
Enterprises						
Protection of shareholder rights	ineffective	Budgetary subsidies (% of GDP)	5.4	2.2	2.1	0.7
Bankruptcy proceedings	ineffective	Credit to enterprises (% of GDP)	34.4	14.4	15.7	15.5
Competition office	no	Labour productivity in industry (% change)	-21.9	-16.1	16.1	9.9
Infrastructure						
Independent telecoms regulator	no	Main telephone lines per 100 inhabitants	8.5	8.3	8.5	na
Separation of railway accounts	no	Railway labour productivity (1989=100)	19.2	8.5	9.2	11.7
Independent electricity regulator	no	Electricity tariff, US¢/kWh (collection ratio in %)	0.7 (na)	2.0 (39)	2.5 (41)	2.7 (56)
Financial institutions						
Deposit insurance	no	Number of banks (of which foreign-owned)	210 (1)	180 (2)	136 (3)	99 (3)
Secured transactions law	restricted	Asset share of state-owned banks	77.6	80.5	77.6	80.9
Insider dealing prohibited	yes	Bad loans (% of total loans)	15.7	22.3	20.2	19.9
Securities commission	no	Stock market capitalisation (% of GDP)	na	na	na	na
Fiscal and social sector						
Private pension funds	no	Tax revenues (% of GDP)	12.0	7.4	10.8	10.6
Share of population in poverty	na	Earnings inequality (Gini coefficient)	na	na	na	na

control exercised by outside shareholders. The development of effective post-privatisation corporate governance is hampered by the lack of a securities market, which prevents the tradability of shares in privatised firms and limits the financial discipline that would derive from a functioning capital market. Residual state interference remains a problem in large enterprises.

FDI has increased significantly – and not only in the oil sector.
Total FDI in 1997 was over US$ 1 billion, of which almost half was invested in non-oil-related sectors. Foreigners have participated in privatisation and through greenfield investments. Sectors of particular interest have been textiles (several cotton ginneries were privatised and sold to Turkish investors), food processing (the Ganja beer factory was sold to a French investor) as well as energy generation. The economic impact of these investments has yet to be felt. According to official data, production in the non-oil branches of industry stagnated in 1997.

Infrastructure

Electricity tariffs have been increased and privatisation of energy distribution is planned.
Increases in household tariffs and the elimination of privileged access to free gas and electricity during 1997 have reduced the cross-subsidies from industry to households. However, collection rates remain low for both types of consumers. Three regional grids drawn from the national grid are to be privatised as part of a pilot scheme starting in late 1998. The government's medium-term Public Investment Programme also calls for large external investments in rehabilitating power plants.

The regulatory environment for commercial infrastructure remains inadequate.
Regulatory and operational responsibilities in the telecommunications and transport sectors have not yet been separated. Telecommunications are among those strategic enterprises currently being considered for privatisation by special presidential decree, most likely through an international investment tender. Commercialisation of the operational functions of the road authority is planned, but is not likely before 1999.

Financial institutions

A bank restructuring programme is being implemented, including plans for privatisation of the largest state bank.
An action plan for each of the four remaining state-owned banks (which account for 80% of total bank assets) has been developed for 1997-98 with support from international financial institutions. The plan entails reorganisation, restructuring and recapitalisation of the banks, with a view to privatise those banks where long-term viability can be ensured. International Bank, the strongest of the four, is scheduled for privatisation after a US$ 44 million government recapitalisation. Following an increase to US$ 1.25 million in July, minimum capital requirements are set to reach US$ 5 million by 2001, which is likely to lead to further consolidation of the 84 commercial banks currently operating. Foreign banks face significant restrictions in obtaining licences and must seek approval for increases in statutory capital.

Securities market legislation has been passed but remains to be implemented.
Currently, only Treasury bills are being issued and secondary trading remains thin. A Securities Law and a Collateral Law were recently passed establishing the legislative framework for the issuance and secondary market trading of corporate securities. The Securities Law makes provisions for a Securities Commission to regulate the market, though this has yet to be established. A National Registry and Depository Agency is to be set up by October 1998. Foreigners cannot receive a licence for investment banking.

Fiscal and social sector

Fiscal policy undergoes further reforms.
The government has implemented a series of fiscal reforms in line with IMF recommendations, including the integration of all spending agencies into a unified treasury account. In order to prevent excessive real appreciation of the exchange rate, the government is committed to keeping oil-related fiscal revenues in a special account at the central bank. Such funds are usually not available for general government expenditure. In 1997, tax administration was strengthened but tax collection rates remain as low as 50% for some taxes and total revenues amounted to only 18% of GDP. Significant budgetary arrears persist to public utilities.

War-related social problems remain a significant challenge.
Approximately 800,000 internally displaced persons are currently living in Azerbaijan, partly contributing to the 19% unemployment rate. In 1995, around 60% of the population were estimated to live below the official poverty line, although the actual number may be lower due to unreported earnings. The World Bank is financing the rehabilitation of areas affected by the war.

Belarus

CIS member · WTO observer

1990

Oct Small-scale privatisation begins

1991

May Bankruptcy law adopted

July Independence from Soviet Union

1992

Jan VAT introduced

May New currency (Belarussian rouble) introduced

Dec Competition law adopted

1993

Jan Privatisation law adopted

Mar Stock exchange established

1994

Feb T-bills market initiated

Apr Voucher privatisation begins

Aug Belarussian rouble becomes sole legal tender

1995

Jan Customs Union with Russia and Kazakhstan

Apr Investment funds' licences suspended

June Most prices liberalised

1996

Jan Currency corridor established

Apr Interbank currency exchange nationalised

May State share in commercial banks increased

Aug Price controls re-introduced

1997

Feb Currency corridor abandoned

Apr Belarussian-Russian Union Treaty

Key reform challenges

- **High growth rates have been fuelled by subsidised credits to industry and agriculture as well as exports to and financial support from Russia; these sources of growth are unsustainable.**
- **The currency crisis of March 1998 and ensuing inflation have led the government to tighten and extend price and convertibility controls and to increase state intervention in the economy.**
- **The lack of structural reforms and increased macroeconomic instability have created a highly uncertain and difficult investment climate which is undermining the process of market-oriented transition.**

Liberalisation

Loose monetary policy sparked a currency crisis that has been further exacerbated by the financial turmoil in Russia.
In March 1998, the Belarussian rouble plunged by 30% following a 107% increase in net domestic credit by the central bank (NBB) during 1997. The currency continued to plummet during the year, especially following the Russian crisis in August. The spread between the official and the parallel interbank market rate widened to 200% by mid-September. Lacking adequate foreign reserves, the NBB has been unable to stabilise the rouble. This led the government to pursue a range of administrative interventions in the market to prevent price increases and further devaluation. These measures have not succeeded in reining in inflation or stemming the rouble's decline.

The government has reversed earlier progress on foreign trade and exchange rate liberalisation.
In December 1997, the NBB introduced some flexibility for commercial banks in setting cash exchange rates, though the non-cash rate remained administratively determined. However, the NBB reintroduced convertibility restrictions following the currency crisis. The president issued a decree requiring cash exchange rates to be restored to pre-crisis levels. Exporters are now required to surrender 40% of their foreign exchange earnings to the state at a highly over-valued exchange rate. Since mid-August 1998, exporters are not allowed to accept payments in Belarussian roubles from foreign customers. The crisis also prompted new restrictions on external trade: the government introduced a list of imported goods and services, including basic food and consumer products, for which hard currency payment became mandatory.

The government reintroduced price controls to keep inflation within official targets.
Previously, the government maintained direct price controls on basic food products and utility tariffs, as well as de facto limits on monthly price increases of 2%. Following an acceleration of inflation in the aftermath of the currency decline, the government ordered both private and public enterprises to return prices to their pre-crisis levels and banned any further price increases above 2% per month. This restriction was lifted for imported products in the beginning of September 1998. This has led to shortages of consumer goods, especially food products, leading the government to introduce limited food rationing in certain cities and a ban on exports of selected food products.

Privatisation

The privatisation of large state enterprises has stalled.
Privatisation was launched in 1993 with the objective of privatising two-thirds of all enterprises by the year 2000. Approximately 33% of the targeted firms had been transformed into joint-stock companies and partially privatised by mid-1998. However, the number of enterprises with a state share of less than 51% was estimated at 26% of the total number originally targeted for privatisation. In the second half of 1997 through April 1998, 160 communal (mostly small) enterprises were privatised. In contrast, none of the five large enterprises targeted for privatisation in November 1997 have been privatised. A presidential decree in June 1998 ordered the nationalisation of one of the largest department stores in Minsk, which had been privatised a year earlier, and banned the privatisation of two other major department stores.

Some existing administrative obstacles to privatisation have been removed.
A presidential decree on privatisation in March 1998 eliminated the requirement for parliamentary approval of annual lists of firms to be privatised, eased the terms for buy-outs of leased state property and unprofitable enterprises, and gave local authorities full rights to privatise local facilities and restructure companies. This decree might accelerate the privatisation of small enterprises.

Enterprises

Official statistics show an acceleration of industrial production ...
According to official figures, industrial output grew by 18% in 1997 and by 13% during the first half of 1998. This was driven by a 50% increase in exports to Russia in 1997, as well as a 16% increase in gross investment. Industrial sector wages rose by more than 30% in real terms during 1997, outpacing the 19% increase in labour productivity during the same year. Official figures report a decline in the share of loss-making enterprises in the industrial sector from 18% in 1996 to 13% in 1997. For the economy

Liberalisation			1994	1995	1996	1997
Exchange rate regime	managed float	Share of administered prices in CPI	60	45	30	27
Current account convertibility	limited	"Administered prices in ""EBRD-15"" basket"	5	5	5	5
Interest rate liberalisation	limited *de facto*	Share of trade in GDP	61.7	47.0	45.9	60.1
Wage regulation	yes	Tariff revenue (% of imports)	4.9	3.4	3.7	1.0
Privatisation						
Primary privatisation method	MEBOs	Private sector share in GDP	15	15	15	20
Secondary privatisation method	vouchers	Share of firms privatised	11.7	14.3	19.7	25.5
Tradability of land rights	limited *de jure*	Privatisation revenues (% of GDP)	0.30	0.26	0.00	0.15
Enterprises						
Protection of shareholder rights	ineffective	Budgetary subsidies (% of GDP)	6.3	3.4	2.9	1.3
Bankruptcy proceedings	ineffective	Credit to enterprises (% of GDP)	16.5	5.5	10.9	11.7
Competition office	no	Labour productivity in industry (% change)	-12.6	-1.5	11.1	20.0
Infrastructure						
Independent telecoms regulator	no	Main telephone lines per 100 inhabitants	18.6	19.0	20.8	22.6
Separation of railway accounts	no	Railway labour productivity (1989=100)	33.6	29.9	na	na
Independent electricity regulator	no	Electricity tariff, US¢/kWh (collection ratio in %)	na	na	1.5 (80)	1.1 (87)
Financial institutions						
Deposit insurance	yes	Number of banks (of which foreign owned)	48 (na)	42 (1)	38 (1)	38 (2)
Secured transactions law	restricted	Asset share of state-owned banks	69.2	62.3	54.1	55.2
Insider dealing prohibited	na	Bad loans (% of total loans)	8.4	11.8	14.2	12.7
Securities commission	no	Stock market capitalisation (% of GDP)	na	na	na	na
Fiscal and social sector						
Private pension funds	no	Tax revenues (% of GDP)	41.6	34.4	32.0	34.7
Share of population in poverty	23%	Earnings inequality (Gini coefficient)	na	na	na	na

as a whole, the share of loss-making firms is estimated to lie between 20% and 25%. However, inter-enterprise arrears amounted to over 40% of GDP by the end of 1997. Not one enterprise has been declared bankrupt under the 1991 Bankruptcy Law.

... though this growth is based on state subsidies to unprofitable state enterprises and agriculture.

The government continues to support state-owned enterprises by means of directed credits and budgetary funds to write off arrears. However, enterprise arrears to the budget increased during 1997, with profit tax arrears more than doubling in nominal terms. In December 1997, the government borrowed BRB 500 billion from the NBB to write off energy arrears accumulated by state-owned enterprises. In March 1998, a presidential decree deferred repayment of debts by agricultural enterprises to the budget and non-budgetary funds until 2000. The government also ordered commercial banks to open a BRB 2 trillion subsidised credit line to agricultural enterprises, on top of the BRB 0.5 trillion of soft credits allocated in February 1998. The weak financial position of agricultural enterprises is reflected in their substantial wage arrears. In December 1997, unpaid wages in collective farms were nearly 55% of the total payroll, compared with wage arrears of 10.5% for the whole economy.

The state continues to increase its control over decision-making at the enterprise level.

A presidential decree granting the state a "golden share" in the management of enterprises became effective in January 1998. The decree gives the state the right to veto enterprise decisions on reorganisation, liquidation, alterations of the statutory fund, and managerial changes. Another presidential decree added further uncertainty to the investment climate by cancelling existing tax and customs privileges to foreign investors and giving the president direct responsibility for granting such privileges. Net foreign investment was nearly US$ 190 million (1.4% of GDP) in 1997. The increasing isolation from the international community and the growing macroeconomic instability are likely to constrain further inflows of FDI.

Infrastructure

Utility prices still do not reflect cost-recovery levels.

Despite the government's intention to raise utility tariffs to achieve full cost recovery in 1998, fears of accelerating inflation have slowed the implementation of tariff reform. By mid-April 1998, the government had increased water and sewerage tariffs by 30% and, in May 1998, heating tariffs by nearly 20%; but inflation has outpaced most of these tariff increases. According to official sources these changes imply cost recovery ratios of 29% for water and 37% for sewerage.

Financial institutions

Key prudential regulations have been delayed to avoid bank closures ...

At the beginning of 1998, 27 commercial banks were operating in Belarus following the ongoing liquidation of nine banks and the suspension of the licences of two banks. Three majority state-owned banks account for nearly 75% of the total loans of the banking system. By January 1998, only 12 of the 27 banks had met the NBB's statutory requirements established two years earlier, including a minimum statutory capital requirement of ECU 2 million. The NBB has successively postponed the implementation of such requirements to avoid bank closures. A new deadline has been set for January 1999.

... while the government has extended its control over the financial system.

The state re-imposed control over the NBB in early 1998 following the currency crisis. The government dismissed the central bank's board and put the NBB under direct supervision of the government. According to a presidential decree of July 1998, the currency and stock exchanges are to be unified, implying the nationalisation of the Belarus Stock Exchange, 60% of which is currently in private hands. The merger would also shift supervision of the currency exchange market from the NBB to the Ministry of Finance and the Securities Committee.

Fiscal and social security reform

Budgetary performance remains under control but lacks transparency.

Tax revenues accounted for nearly 32% of GDP in the first half of 1998, one of the highest ratios in the CIS, reflecting high tax ratios and close monitoring of compliance with tax regulations. The general budget deficit reported by the authorities was 2.7% of GDP in 1997. The general budget includes all the extrabudgetary funds except the Presidential Fund, whose size and accounts are not disclosed, and the Social Protection Fund, which spends the equivalent of 13% of GDP. It also excludes quasi-fiscal operations arising from subsidised directed credits, which were estimated at 3% of GDP in 1997.

Bosnia and Herzegovina[†]

Key reform challenges

- **Constitutional structure and political antagonism have frustrated hopes for rapid reform. Important reform legislation has been passed under international pressure; the challenge now is implementation.**
- **The creation of a common central bank and currency and steps towards a common customs area may gradually deepen the internal economic integration.**
- **With legislation for enterprise and bank privatisation largely in place, tangible results are now required. However, laws need to be changed to improve the tax and regulatory environment for private business.**
- **With reconstruction advancing, the lack of commercialisation and inter-Entity cooperation remain key obstacles in the reform of infrastructure.**

Liberalisation

A unified customs tariff has been adopted.
A simple import tariff (unified across Entities) was adopted in November 1997 and is to be applied from 1999. It consists of four tariff categories (between 0% and 15%) with an unweighted average rate of about 7%. The law eliminates most tariff exemptions and quantitative restrictions (in practice only restrictions on certain agricultural exports have been maintained by the RS). While intra-FBH cooperation between authorities is gradually improving, trade between the Entities continues to be restricted by the absence of integrated payment systems and, more importantly, curbs aimed at preventing arbitrage between the Entities' differing tax systems.

Full exchange-rate convertibility has been established under the currency board.
A new currency, the konvertibilna marka (KM), has been introduced in stages since the establishment of the central bank of Bosnia and Herzegovina (CBBH) in August 1997. The KM was introduced under strict currency board rules at a rate of one KM per DM. The law permits no restrictions on the convertibility of the KM. Since mid-1998 all receipts and payments to the State budget are settled in KM and the Entities have committed to promoting use of the KM on their territories. KM banknotes have been tendered since June against the now-defunct Bosnian dinar or hard currency but other currencies can be freely utilised in transactions. The Yugoslav dinar and Croatian kuna continue to be used in the RS and Croat-majority areas of the FBH, respectively, while the Deutschmark is widely employed throughout Bosnia and Herzegovina.

Privatisation

Privatisation legislation has been passed.
The legislative and institutional framework for the privatisation of enterprises, banks and apartments had been essentially completed by March 1998. A State umbrella law on privatisation aimed at ensuring fair treatment of refugees and non-discrimination was passed in July 1998. Legislation on privatisation-investment funds is under consideration. Natural restitution claims will introduce some uncertainty into the privatisation process. A restitution law has been held up, pending a decision on a cut-off date (1945 or 1919, the latter vastly increasing the scope of restitution) and is not expected before 1999, well after the start of privatisation. The RS embarked on mass privatisation in 1996 under a scheme that was criticised by international observers and subsequently cancelled by a new government in early 1998. In June, a new privatisation law was passed that is broadly comparable with the FBH law, though some adjustments will need to be made to achieve consistency with the State umbrella law.

Privatisation in FBH set to begin.
All non-private shares in the estimated 1,250 enterprises with State, social or mixed ownership are in principle subject to privatisation against a mix of cash and certificates. Certificates are being issued for claims against the State including frozen foreign currency accounts, back wages for the army, restitution claims and general claims based on duration of employment. Documented interest by strategic foreign and local investors takes precedence over certificate privatisation. So-called "strategic enterprises" (approximately 40% of the book value of privatisable assets) are to be subject to a different procedure calling for individual parliamentary approval. First auctions under the small-scale privatisation programme (minimum 35% cash bid with the rest payable in certificates) were scheduled for September 1998, but have been delayed. Several large enterprises might be offered before end-1998, with up to 100% of shares exchanged for certificates.

Obstacles remain regarding implementation.
The privatisation process in FBH faces a number of uncertainties, including information problems and a highly decentralised implementation process. The authority of the Federation Privatisation Agency is limited to enterprises with assets in more than one Canton. The 10 Cantonal Privatisation Agencies (CPAs) are at varying stages of development and few of them are ready for implementation according to schedule. There are further problems regarding the ownership status of enterprises, given unclear documentation of minority "internal" shares issued to employees under a pre-war privatisation scheme and pre-war shareholdings across Entities. There were also cases of asset stripping and illegal privatisation, which may have to be reversed. Taking also into account possible restitution claims, legal and political action could conceivably delay the privatisation process and the revitalisation of privatised enterprises.

Enterprises

No active restructuring has been undertaken so far.
The pre-war economy of Bosnia and Herzegovina was dominated by around 10 large conglomerates responsible for more than half of GDP. Despite advice from donors to begin breaking up the conglomerates, there has been little active pressure to restructure. Together, today's state-owned enterprises accounted for 80% of pre-war output. Production of the conglomerates collapsed during the war and it appears that they have not fully participated in the economy's revival since 1995. More than 90% of registered firms are private, in both FBH and RS. Although these firms tend to be very small, they are active in sectors (such as construction, trade and services) that have benefited disproportionately from the inflow of reconstruction funds.

Financial discipline is weak.
In the absence of privatisation, the structure of enterprise control and financing remains essentially the same as in the former Yugoslavia. Shares in "socially-owned" enterprises were nationalised during the war and are now owned by the FBH and RS, respectively. However, effective control was retained by management. Public enterprises own the largest banks in both FBH and RS and are their largest depositors and borrowers. While bank liquidity is constrained under currency board rules, the closeness between banks and enterprises weakens financial discipline and some banks continue to run up substantial bad loans. Past bankruptcy legislation was geared more to protecting workers than creditors. A new law was enacted in June 1998.

The business climate is poor.
The legacy of the war includes a damaged infrastructure, severed supply links within Bosnia and Herzegovina, and political uncertainty. In addition, private businesses generally face a difficult or even hostile tax and administrative environment that has shed little of its socialist legacy. Inconsistent tax treatment tends to distort competition and tops the list of concerns of businessmen in surveys. Social payroll taxes in the FBH, though reduced from 100-200% only two years ago, remain very high at 65%. Business legislation in both Entities remains a patchwork of sometimes inconsistent laws and regulations, dating back mostly to the SFRY and wartime administrations. If followed to the letter, business registration in the FBH can take a year, which – together with the tax regime – invites informal activity. Legislative initiatives to mend these

problems have been taken with donor assistance, but have been subject to delay.

Infrastructure

Reconstruction is progressing.
Bosnia and Herzegovina's infrastructure was severely damaged during the war. About US$ 2 billion in reconstruction assistance over 3-4 years was envisaged for this sector under the priority reconstruction programme, with more than half of this amount now in various stages of financing and implementation. While international assistance has generally focused on capital expenditure, operating costs (except in telecoms) continue to be heavily subsidised by Entity and local budgets. Improved commercial practices and inter-Entity cooperation are the key near-term challenges in infrastructure. The idea of privatising infrastructure services has been floated but would seem to be a longer-term proposition, except in the telecoms sector where it is targeted for 1999.

Lack of inter-Entity cooperation is a serious obstacle.
All infrastructure systems are split along ethnic lines. Lack of cooperation between the Entities invites and perpetuates inefficient solutions. In the power sector, joint dispatching could substantially increase the efficiency of the system and reduce capital costs, given very different technical characteristics (hydropower dominates in the Croat-controlled area, thermal power in the Bosniak and Serb areas). Separate water supply systems duplicate facilities across ethnic boundaries. The railway infrastructure has not been interconnected, thus limiting its commercial use, although there has been recent agreement to improve matters. In telecoms, the dividing lines left by the war bear little relation to the original design of the network. All three operators have made efforts to reconfigure their networks to fit the new realities. The first inter-Entity telecoms link was put into operation in September 1997 – though with very low capacity – and two more are under construction.

Tariff structures are highly distorted.
Tariffs, metering, billing and collection procedures as well as organisational and accounting practices remain highly inadequate in most infrastructure services. Average tariffs differ substantially between utilities in the three ethnic areas, with those in power and telecoms based on cost-recovery in the Croat-majority areas, but considerably lower in the Bosniak-majority area and, in particular, in the RS. Heavy cross-subsidisation of households by industrial users is a shared feature in the power sector, while telecoms subsidise postal services, except in the RS. The most serious challenge, however, is the low payments discipline, especially among public sector clients, and outright theft. Social considerations and the effort to sustain economic recovery have argued against the cut-off of supplies. Together with technical losses, theft amounted to 30-35% of power sector revenues in 1997, and payments arrears in this sector represented between 56% of annual sales (RS) and 160-200% (Croat-majority area). Cash revenues of the Sarajevo-based gas-distribution company represented just 5% of operating costs in 1997, while in district heating the corresponding figure was 24%. Few customers are paying for water and sewage services. Telecoms utilities have fared somewhat better, with average collection ratios ranging from 72% (Telekom Srpske) to 91% (Sarajevo-based PTT BiH). Comprehensive new telecoms legislation, a key step towards improved performance, has been drafted with EBRD assistance, but its approval has been delayed repeatedly.

Financial institutions

Financial intermediation remains limited.
The banking sector in both Entities continues to consist of large and insolvent state banks on the one hand (25 in total), and growing but still very small private banks on the other (39). While the assets of the banking system represented around 60% of GDP at end-1997, the vast majority of these assets (more than 80%) are irrecoverable. Adjusted for bad assets, the balance sheet of state banks is likely to be similar in size to that of the private banks. Banks have not yet overcome depositor scepticism (after hyperinflation, confiscation of deposits and post-war bank failures) nor have banks moved significantly from fee-based to core banking functions. Credit to the private sector represented only 1.7% of GDP, and household deposits 3.3%. Term lending is funded almost exclusively from donor credit lines.

Legislation on the privatisation and liquidation of state banks is now in place.
Federation legislation enabling the financial restructuring, privatisation and liquidation of state banks came into force in April 1998. A similar set of laws is under preparation in the RS. Bank Privatisation Agencies were set up during the summer of 1998 in both RS and FBH. Privatisation is based on the principles that no fiscal resources are to be used, that strategic investors are to be preferred, that solvent banks are to be privatised within 28 months from the effectiveness of the law, and that insolvent banks are to be liquidated within 24 months. Liquidation would also automatically follow a failure to privatise.

State banks are to be restructured.
The law transfers ownership in state banks from public enterprises to the Ministry of Finance. Upon preparation of opening balance sheets, solvency is established after shortening balance sheets by transferring assets and liabilities related to pre-war foreign debt and frozen foreign exchange deposits to the Ministry and writing off assets impaired by war. For the seven largest state banks in the FBH, accounting for 80% of banking sector assets, this procedure is expected to lead to a reduction of consolidated assets from DM 5.6 billion to DM 0.4 billion. All but two banks are estimated to be solvent and would be offered for sale through competitive bidding and, failing that, direct negotiation, with the rest slated for liquidation. In the RS, the bad asset problem appears to be of a similar dimension. Citizens will receive certificates for use in enterprise privatisation against their frozen foreign exchange deposits with the banks. The foreign-funded loans taken off the banks' balance sheets will be written off – although enterprises will only see their corresponding liability cancelled upon privatisation.

Confidence is gradually being built.
Independent banking agencies were established in the Federation in 1996 (FBA) and in RS in the first half of 1998. Both agencies now have the power to intervene and liquidate problem banks. The recent failure of three private banks in FBH, however, revealed serious understaffing at the FBA, which has been focusing its scarce supervisory capacity on the larger state banks. New commercial banking laws introducing international standards for licensing, loan classification and prudential rules are under consideration by legislatures in both Entities, and passage of a deposit insurance scheme is expected in late 1998.

Fiscal and social sector

Fiscal and social policy is affected by the decentralised nature of the State.
Despite recent progress, budget planning and control remain somewhat chaotic. The Dayton Constitution calls for a proliferation of State, Entity and lower-level political and administrative bodies, each with a claim on authority over economic management. The State of Bosnia and Herzegovina has no revenue authority of its own, but relies on transfers from the Entities. After disruptions in the servicing of the external debt in 1997, the transfer mechanism was strengthened by reducing the scope for discretion by the Entities. Budgets within the Federation are highly decentralised. Revenue sources accounting for approximately three-quarters of the total are assigned to the Cantons, along with most social and infrastructure expenditure. Since Cantons differ enormously in their revenue-raising capacity, and inter-cantonal transfers are politically difficult, this may cause widely differing provision of basic public services. There are also very large differences in budget volumes between the Entities. Whereas consolidated Federation budget revenue was equivalent to 28% of Bosnia and Herzegovina's GDP in 1997, revenues in RS (with one-third of the country's population) apparently amounted to only 2.7% of total GDP.

† The territorial constitutional entities distinguished in this assessment include the State of Bosnia and Herzegovina, the Federation of Bosnia-Herzegovina ("Federation" or FBH), the Republika Srpska (RS) and the Cantons of the Federation. FBH and RS are referred to as the "Entities".

Bulgaria

EU Association Agreement · WTO member · EFTA member · CEFTA member

1991

Feb Most prices liberalised
Feb Import controls removed
Feb Exchange rate unified
May Competition law enacted
May Competition agency established
July T-bills market initiated

1992

Feb Restitution law enacted
Apr Privatisation law adopted
May Stock exchange begins trading

1993

Jan Small-scale privatisation law adopted
Feb Large-scale privatisation begins
July EFTA membership

1994

Mar Currency crisis
June Privatisation law amended
July Bankruptcy law adopted

1995

Jan EU Association Agreement
Feb Railway law adopted
July Securities law adopted
July Securities and exchange commission established
Dec Social insurance law adopted

1996

May Bankruptcy law amended
May Special restructuring programme enacted
June Bank restructuring initiated
Oct Mass privatisation programme begins
Dec WTO membership

1997

Feb Financial crisis peaks
July Currency board introduced
July First bank privatised
Oct New stock exchange begins trading

Key reform challenges

- **In the wake of the economic crisis of 1996, the government implemented a radical stabilisation and structural reform programme in mid-1997. Rapid privatisation of enterprises is key to a sustainable economic recovery.**
- **The banking system has been strengthened by the exit of insolvent banks and improved prudential regulations. Pressing ahead with bank privatisation will be crucial for strengthening market-oriented financial intermediation.**
- **Recent tax reforms have strengthened the fiscal position. The planned overhaul of the pension system is important in order to keep expenditures under control in the long run.**

Liberalisation

Bulgaria joins CEFTA.
Bulgaria signed an accession agreement with the Central European Free Trade Association in July 1998 and will become a full member in January 1999. Bulgaria has also applied to join the European Union, but is currently not among the "first-wave" candidates.

A currency board has been effective in restoring confidence.
A currency board was introduced in July 1997 as a centrepiece of the reform programme. It has been effective in restoring macroeconomic stability by imposing tight constraints on fiscal and monetary policy.

Privatisation

Privatisation is accelerating after years of delay.
Between 1992 and 1997, roughly 20% of total enterprise assets were privatised via both cash sales and voucher-based mass privatisation. In 1997 alone, around 4% of total enterprise assets were privatised through cash sales, including some of the largest state-owned enterprises in the chemicals and metals sectors, as well as the world trade centre.

A greater variety of privatisation methods is being used.
Amendments to the Privatisation Law were adopted in March 1998, supporting a broader range of privatisation methods. Since late 1997, foreign consultants have acted as intermediaries in "pool" privatisations which combine groups of assets of varying quality by industry. A list of enterprises suitable for this type of privatisation comprises 92 state-owned enterprises and 22 hydropower stations. By mid-1998, only one privatisation contract had been concluded under this framework. The government also plans to privatise more companies through public offerings on the stock exchange. In May 1998, the electric equipment producer Elkabel became the first enterprise to be privatised in this fashion.

Privatisation via cash sales is complemented by a second "wave" of mass privatisation.
The first wave of mass privatisation ended in mid-1997. A second wave, under which around 5% of the original state-owned assets are to be privatised, began in July 1998. Newly issued investment coupons can be purchased by the population and used in a variety of transactions, including auctions, tenders, management and employee buy-outs, and for buying shares in pension funds. The second wave gives preferential treatment to workers and management by offering them deferred payment options.

Enterprises

The increasing number of insider privatisations raises some concern.
Enterprise reform has shifted away from state-administered liquidation and restructuring towards greater reliance on privatisation. Enterprise restructuring has accelerated, but continues to be hampered by vested interests and the inexperience of the courts in bankruptcy cases. Complex legal rules, for example on licensing, create some scope for corruption, although the government has made efforts to limit the discretion of civil servants. In addition, most companies privatised to insiders lack access to finance for post-privatisation restructuring. Recent legislation has removed preferential treatment of managers and employers in privatisation, after an increasing number of MEBOs threatened to raise corporate governance problems.

The enterprise isolation and liquidation programmes have produced some positive results.
Economy-wide losses of state-owned enterprises fell from US$ 1.3 billion in 1996 to US$ 0.3 billion in 1997. This is due in part to the "liquidation programme" which was completed in 1997. Under this programme, 59 large and 86 small firms, accounting for 28% of the total losses of state-owned enterprises in 1995, were closed. The programme of enterprise "isolation", which combines restructuring with limits on further borrowing, covers 71 enterprises. Their share in total enterprise losses decreased from 50% in 1995 to 10% in 1997. Losses of the 30 utilities in the programme fell particularly strongly, as a result of tariff increases, efficiency improvements and better bill collection. The performance of the other 41 industrial enterprises remains mixed and further liquidations are expected. Progress with their privatisation or liquidation has been slow and the duration of the programme has been extended until mid-1999. So far an estimated 5% of state-owned enterprise assets have been privatised through liquidation.

Liberalisation			**1994**	**1995**	**1996**	**1997**
Exchange rate regime	currency board	Share of administered prices in CPI	42	46	48	14
Current account convertibility	full	Administered prices in "EBRD-15" basket	6	6	6	2
Interest rate liberalisation	full	Share of trade in GDP	40.6	40.4	48.8	45.4
Wage regulation	yes	Tariff revenue (% of imports)	7.0	7.6	4.6	na
Privatisation						
Primary privatisation method	direct sales	Private sector share in GDP	40	45	45	50
Secondary privatisation method	vouchers	Share of small firms privatised	2.6	7.2	15.2	21.1
Tradability of land rights	full except foreigners	Share of assets privatised	2.1	3.1	7.2	25.6
Enterprises						
Protection of shareholder rights	partly effective	Budgetary subsidies (% of GDP)	1.3	1.2	0.8	0.8
Bankruptcy proceedings	partly effective	Credit to enterprises (% of GDP)	50.7	40.8	63.4	10.6
Competition office	yes	Labour productivity in industry (% change)	12.6	7.3	2.1	-3.8
Infrastructure						
Independent telecoms regulator	no	Main telephone lines per 100 inhabitants	33.5	30.6	31.3	32.4
Separation of railway accounts	yes	Railway labour productivity (1989=100)	73.1	77.4	73.8	83.2
Independent electricity regulator	no	Electricity tariff, US¢/kWh (collection ratio in %)	1.4 (82)	2.2 (85)	3.5 (85)	3.5 (85)
Financial institutions						
Deposit insurance	yes	Number of banks (of which foreign-owned)	40 (1)	41 (3)	42 (3)	28 (7)
Secured transactions law	yes	Asset share of state-owned banks	na	na	82.2	66.0
Insider dealing prohibited	yes	Bad loans (% of total loans)	6.8	12.6	14.6	12.9
Securities commission	yes	Stock market capitalisation (% of GDP)	na	na	na	0.0
Fiscal and social sector						
Private pension funds	no	Tax revenues (% of GDP)	na	na	26.5	26.6
Share of population in poverty	33%	Earnings inequality (Gini coefficient)	na	na	0.291	na

Financial discipline of state-owned enterprises remains weak.
At the end of 1997, the share of overdue credits in total credits to state-owned firms reached 19%, up from 17% the previous year. Roughly a quarter of tax revenues were not collected. Tax arrears, many of which date back to 1991, are concentrated among a few large state-owned industrial enterprises. Regulation has been introduced to reimburse wage arrears with investment coupons.

Infrastructure

Price rises in energy and district heating are paving the way for further reform.
Tariff increases have improved the financial health of most utilities over the past year, but further tariff increases are scheduled in order to finance much-needed investment. There are plans to restructure the state electricity monopoly and all 22 hydropower plants are scheduled to be privatised in 1999. In district heating, a particularly inefficient sector, tariffs were raised significantly in 1997 and 1998.

The privatisation of state telecommunications is under preparation.
The government is preparing an international tender for 51% of the Bulgarian Telecommunication Company (BTC). An additional stake (5%-15%) is to be sold to its employees, and further shares are to be floated on the stock exchange. However, the government plans to keep a "golden share". It is envisaged that a mobile licence will be awarded to the buyer in an effort to increase the attractiveness of the tender.

Financial institutions

The health of the banking sector has improved with macro-stabilisation ...
The financial position of the banking sector has improved substantially since the economic crisis in 1996. Fifteen of the weakest banks have exited the market, although liquidation of closed banks is proceeding slowly. The share of classified loans in total loans has decreased. The required capital adequacy ratio is gradually being raised from 8% at the end of 1997 to 10% by the end of 1998 and 12% by the end of 1999. Average capital adequacy of the banking system rose from 11% in 1996 to 29% in 1997, and by August 1998 all banks were complying with the 8% capital adequacy standard. As of mid-1997, all banks have also met the DM 10 million minimum capital requirement. Since mid-1997, banks have been more reluctant to extend new enterprise credit, partly as a result of their limited rights in bankruptcy procedures.

... but the pace of bank privatisation has been slower than anticipated.
The banking sector is dominated by five large state-owned banks, accounting for around two-thirds of total bank assets. Privatisation, a core element of the general reform programme, has advanced slowly. In mid-1997, the United Bulgarian Bank was bought by foreign investors, including the EBRD. After repeated delays, 78% of Postbank was sold to a consortium of international investors in August 1998. Three other banks are to be privatised by 1999, leaving only two banks in state ownership. Biochim Bank is to be run under a foreign management contract for up to two years before being privatised. The State Savings Bank will be transformed into a state-owned commercial bank lending to small businesses and households, according to a law passed in April 1998.

The stock exchange is still in its infancy.
Trading on the Bulgarian Stock Exchange, created by merging two exchanges, began in October 1997. There are few securities on the market and the legal framework remains underdeveloped. An amendment to the securities law in early 1998 should improve minority shareholder protection and information disclosure. It has also paved the way for privatisations through the stock exchange.

Fiscal and social sector

Tax reforms were initiated in 1997, though continued reforms are necessary.
The reforms include streamlining tax rules, abolishing exemptions and strengthening tax administration. "Large taxpayer units" were opened to improve tax compliance of the 1,200 largest corporations, which together provide 65% of total tax revenues. Although still very low, tax revenues as a share of GDP have increased in the first half of 1998 in comparison with the same period of 1997. Much of the increase is due to higher VAT receipts.

Pension reform has become a priority.
The current state pay-as-you-go pension system is in dire need of reform. There are an estimated 76 pensioners for every 100 contributors. Draft legislation has been prepared for the introduction of a "multi-pillar" pension system based on the Polish model. A reformed state scheme and a mandatory private scheme are to be introduced in 2000. Legislation for additional voluntary private contributions is expected to be approved by early 1999.

Croatia

WTO observer

1991

Apr Privatisation law adopted

June Independence from Yugoslavia

1992

July Large-scale privatisation begins

1993

Jan IAS adopted

Oct Macroeconomic stabilisation programme

Oct Banking law adopted

1994

Mar Stock exchange begins trading

May New currency (kuna) introduced

June Railways established as joint stock company

1995

Jan Electricity law adopted

May Full current account convertibility introduced

June Competition law adopted

Oct BIS capital adequacy enacted

Nov Bank rehabilitation begins

1996

Jan Securities and investment fund law enacted

Mar Pliva lists shares in London

July T-bills market initiated

July Most non-tariff import barriers removed

Oct Securities and exchange commission established

1997

Jan Restitution law enacted

Jan Bankruptcy law enacted

Feb First sovereign Eurobond

May Competition agency established

Key reform challenges

- **A successful conclusion of the voucher privatisation programme and further sales of residual state shareholdings could help improve corporate governance, if complemented by accelerated efforts to develop the capital markets.**
- **The restructuring of large state-owned enterprises, including in the oil, telecoms, rail and shipyard sectors, should be complemented by greater private sector involvement and the development of regulatory institutions in infrastructure.**
- **Priority in banking reform should now shift to the privatisation of rehabilitated banks and the strengthening of supervision and the enforcement of prudential regulations.**
- **Overhauling the pay-as-you-go pension system is essential for the future stability of public finances.**

Liberalisation

Progress has been made towards joining the WTO.
After removing most non-tariff barriers in 1996, Croatia boasts a transparent trade regime with an unweighted average import tariff of 10%. The average tariff on agricultural products is 35%. The government has made further progress in negotiating WTO accession and adjusting legislation to this end. In January 1998, existing discriminatory excise taxes were removed on all imports except of alcohol and tobacco. In March 1998, a new law on public procurement became effective. Accession is expected in 1999 and CEFTA entry thereafter.

Short-term capital controls have been tightened, while the financial sector is being prepared for further liberalisation.
In response to a domestic credit boom partly financed by foreign borrowing, the central bank introduced new reserve requirements on short-term foreign borrowing and deposits in April 1998. Croatia continues, however, to open its financial sector to foreign competition, in line with WTO requirements. In May 1998, the government put forward an amendment to the banking law that eliminates some remaining restrictions on the market access of foreign banks.

Privatisation

The state has retained significant ownership stakes in the enterprise sector ...
While there are few exclusively state-owned companies, the state retains significant ownership stakes in many large companies. Only about half of Croatian employees in the enterprise sector work in fully private enterprises, roughly a quarter each in new private and fully privatised firms. A further 20% work in firms with minority stakes by the state. The other 30% of the workforce is in state-owned enterprises, half of which is accounted for by 10 fully state-owned infrastructure companies.

... but the long-delayed voucher privatisation programme has been implemented.
More than two years after a new privatisation law was passed to accelerate the sluggish privatisation process, one of its integral parts – a mass voucher privatisation programme – is finally under way. Some 225,000 voucher holders are to acquire shares in 471 firms, either directly or through one of seven competing privatisation funds. By mid-1998, the funds had collected about 90% of all vouchers. During three bidding rounds in mid-1998, about 80% of the assets (with a book value of US$ 2 billion) were sold. The voucher funds are to be listed on the Zagreb Stock Exchange.

Enterprises

Labour productivity is growing, although corporate governance remains poor.
Productivity in industry has been growing at over 10% per annum in 1997 and early 1998. This has been driven both by output growth and by continued labour shedding, especially in manufacturing where employment has contracted by about 40% since 1989. Enterprise restructuring is, however, inhibited by poor corporate governance that typically results from the absence of a strong majority shareholder and from large residual state holdings. As a result of a privatisation process largely by management and employee buy-outs, small shareholders (mostly employees) own the great majority of shares in privatised companies. The state Privatisation Fund and the state Pension Fund – the largest shareholders in many majority privatised companies – have not taken an active role in management and enterprise restructuring. Restructuring also remains far from complete in most state-owned companies, including the oil company INA.

Some access has been maintained to international capital, despite the turmoil in other emerging markets.
While the turmoil in emerging markets has negatively affected capital flows to Croatia throughout 1998, many large companies continued to have access to international finance. Most syndicated loans have gone to state-owned infrastructure companies, but a few large private companies have also been able to tap international capital markets. In May 1998, the Croatian Privatisation Fund and the EBRD sold 17% of the pharmaceutical company Pliva in a secondary public offering on the London Stock Exchange. Access of enterprises to domestic bank credit is better than in many other transition economies, but most loans are indexed to the Deutschmark, exposing enterprises to exchange rate risk.

Liberalisation			1994	1995	1996	1997
Exchange rate regime	managed float	Share of administered prices in CPI	na	na	na	na
Current account convertibility	full	Administered prices in "EBRD-15" basket	4	3	3	3
Interest rate liberalisation	full	Share of trade in GDP	33.7	33.2	32.3	35.3
Wage regulation	yes	Tariff revenue (% of imports)	10.4	9.6	8.9	8.0
Privatisation						
Primary privatisation method	MEBOs	Private sector share in GDP	40	45	50	55
Secondary privatisation method	vouchers	Share of medium/large firms privatised	na	60.6	na	67.5
Tradability of land rights	full	Privatisation revenues (% of GDP)	0.37	0.50	0.52	0.12
Enterprises						
Protection of shareholder rights	partly effective	Budgetary subsidies (% of GDP)	2.0	1.8	1.9	1.9
Bankruptcy proceedings	partly effective	Credit to enterprises (% of GDP)	27.2	28.1	25.0	29.6
Competition office	yes	Labour productivity in industry (% change)	1.6	5.8	11.4	12.0
Infrastructure						
Independent telecoms regulator	no	Main telephone lines per 100 inhabitants	25.2	27.2	30.9	33.5
Separation of railway accounts	yes	Railway labour productivity (1989=100)	35.3	40.1	40.9	42.5
Independent electricity regulator	no	Electricity tariff, US¢/kWh (collection ratio in %)	7.3 (na)	8.2 (na)	7.9 (na)	7.0 (na)
Financial institutions						
Deposit insurance	yes	Number of banks (of which foreign-owned)	50 (na)	54 (1)	57 (4)	61 (7)
Secured transactions law	yes	Asset share of state-owned banks	55.5	51.9	36.2	32.6
Insider dealing prohibited	yes	Bad loans (% of total loans)	12.2	12.9	10.7	9.8
Securities commission	yes	Stock market capitalisation (% of GDP)	1.6	2.4	15.4	22.5
Fiscal and social sector						
Private pension funds	no	Tax revenues (% of GDP)	43.2	44.4	44.7	43.7
Share of population in poverty	na	Earnings inequality (Gini coefficient)	na	na	na	na

Shipyards recover after progress in restructuring.

Croatia has revived its position as one of Europe's major ship producers. After five years of rapid decline, shipyard production picked up sharply in 1996 and stabilised in 1997. Orderbooks point to further growth. Restructuring of the industry has led to a reduction of employment from over 21,000 in 1991 to about 11,000 at the end of 1997. Some of this reflects the spin-off of non-core units from the vertically integrated yards, while some was achieved through state-sponsored redundancy and early retirement packages. Restructuring is far from complete, however. The state continues to provide substantial subsidies to the sector; privatisation of the top five yards is not imminent.

Infrastructure

Railways reform is under preparation.

Cost recovery in railways operations is about 45%. The financial shortfall is financed mostly by state subsidies, which have amounted to around 1% of GDP in recent years. Much of the loss is generated in the passenger segment, where cost recovery is only 30%. A reform programme is being developed with World Bank and EBRD assistance. It includes further staff reductions with severance payments, closure of the least profitable lines and privatisation of ancillary activities. A new railway law, which sets the legal framework for commercially oriented reforms, will become effective in January 1999.

Financial institutions

The collapse of the fifth-largest bank highlights weaknesses in the banking sector.

After a run on its deposits, Croatia's fifth-largest bank, Dubrovačka Banka, became insolvent in April 1998. It was swiftly bailed out by the central bank and put under rehabilitation. The crisis has highlighted structural problems in the banking sector. With over 60 banks, Croatia appears over-banked and consolidation pressures are growing. Asset quality is thought to be overstated and many banks are under-provisioned. Bank supervision is still imperfect and prudential regulation not sufficiently enforced. High single-debtor exposure and related-party lending are common problems, as demonstrated in Dubrovačka Banka prior to its collapse. The central bank has ordered a re-audit of 12 banks, while the IMF continues to provide technical support in the reform process. A new bank law, strengthening central bank supervisory powers and raising minimum capital requirements, went through a first reading in parliament in mid-1998.

Privatisation of successfully rehabilitated banks commences.

A milestone in Croatia's bank rehabilitation programme was the successful rehabilitation of Privredna Banka, formerly Croatia's largest bank and the last of the four banks originally identified for rehabilitation. The bank returned to profitability in 1997 after the state took on a large share of its bad debts and injected fresh capital. Privatisation of the four rehabilitated banks is now a key challenge. In a first step, the state shares in Slavonska Banka were sold to the EBRD and an Austrian bank in mid-1998.

The fledgling stock market is evolving despite share price decline.

The capital market is still in its infancy with only five companies (three banks, one pharmaceutical firm and one shipyard) listed on the top tier of the stock exchange. However, listings on the second tier have continued to increase and the listing of investment funds participating in the voucher privatisation process is expected in 1999. Initial public offerings remain very rare, however, and have been made less attractive by falling share prices in the first half of 1998. There are plans to establish a central depository agency.

Fiscal and social sector

The introduction of VAT has streamlined the tax system.

VAT was introduced at a single rate of 22% in January 1998, replacing the sales tax. The measure has eliminated tax differentials across goods, in particular between food and non-food items. The change has also increased tax revenues. Tax revenues of the central budget are expected to reach 28% of GDP in 1998, while payroll taxes for pensions, health care and other social funds will generate an additional 16% of GDP.

Medium-term fiscal pressures necessitate pension reform.

Croatia's pay-as-you-go pension system is expected to exert considerable strain on the country's finances in the future. There are about 1.3 million people in registered employment and 0.9 million pension beneficiaries. The high number of pensioners is a result of unfavourable demographics, a low retirement age (60 for men and 55 for women) and liberal early retirement policies. Expenditures by the state Pension Fund have grown from 9% of GDP in 1994 to 13% in 1997. Pensions are funded primarily through a 21.5% payroll tax, but a growing funding gap has led to increased transfers from the budget. Reform plans include a "multi-pillar" pension system with both private and public provision of pensions.

Czech Republic

EU Association Agreement · OECD member · WTO member · EFTA member · CEFTA member

1990

Jan Two-tiered banking system established

July First Eurobond

1991

Jan Exchange rate unified

Jan Most prices liberalised

Jan Most foreign trade controls lifted

Jan Small-scale privatisation begins

Feb Restitution law adopted

Mar Competition law adopted

1992

Feb T-bills market initiated

May Voucher privatisation begins

May First bank privatised

July EFTA membership

1993

Jan Czechoslovakia splits into Czech and Slovak Republics

Jan VAT introduced

Feb New currency (koruna) introduced

Mar First Czech Eurobond

Mar CEFTA membership

Apr Stock exchange begins trading

Apr Bankruptcy law enacted

1994

Mar Second wave of voucher privatisation begins

Nov First corporate Eurobond

1995

Jan WTO membership

Oct Full current account convertibility introduced

Dec OECD membership

1996

Jan BIS capital adequacy enacted

Oct Forced administration of largest private bank

Nov Competition agency established

1997

Apr Austerity package announced

May Currency crisis

May Second austerity package announced

Oct First large power company sold to foreigners

Key reform challenges

- **Further progress in bank privatisation and effective implementation of recent financial sector reforms will strengthen investor confidence and prepare for EU accession.**
- **Unclear ownership structures resulting from privatisation have slowed the process of industrial restructuring which will become increasingly urgent in the run-up to EU accession.**
- **Although the retirement age is being increased over time, a fundamental pension reform would help address the fiscal burdens that will be placed on the state pension system by an ageing population.**

Liberalisation

Wage restraints in the public sector and state-controlled enterprises have remained.

Fiscal policy was tightened at the time of the currency crisis in May 1997, when the currency fell by about 10% against the former currency basket and the fixed exchange rate regime was replaced by a managed float against the DM. Restrictions on wage growth in the public sector and state-controlled enterprises were included in fiscal austerity packages of April and May 1997. The first package declared a freeze in the government sector real-wage bill; the second package included a freeze in the nominal wage bill of the state sector in 1998. These wage ceilings dampened overall annual real wage growth to around 3% in 1997 and -2% in the first quarter of 1998.

Rent deregulation has continued.

The government increased rents by 27% in July 1998, moving them closer towards market prices. The slow pace of rent deregulation has inhibited the establishment of an efficient housing market, especially in Prague where rents on the non-regulated market are several times higher than regulated rents. This has opened arbitrage possibilities for incumbent tenants.

Privatisation

Some steps have been taken to dispose of the state's residual ownership stakes.

Mass voucher privatisation, undertaken in two waves, was the dominant method of privatisation. It is estimated that 58% of large companies were privatised via vouchers, compared with 14% privatised via direct sales. The state retains significant stakes in a number of companies, among them utilities, mines, steel-mills and three of the four large banks. Earlier plans by the interim government to privatise a range of large enterprises have been put on hold following the election of a new government.

Enterprises

Corporate governance continues to lack transparency ...

The two waves of mass voucher privatisation have resulted in corporate ownership structures initially dominated by closed-end Investment and Privatisation Funds (IPFs). Although the role of IPFs is gradually declining, corporate governance problems remain as a result of a general lack of transparency. Some controlling shareholders have been criticised for transferring funds out of the enterprises they own. These issues, as well as concerns over the lack of minority shareholder rights, have depressed the market value of companies (most firms trade below par value on the stock market) and contributed to the lack of investor confidence.

... but regulation of investment funds has been tightened ...

Partly in response to the corporate governance problems, parliament approved an amendment to the Investment Companies Law in mid-1998 which requires closed-end investment funds to be open by 2002, with earlier deadlines if they trade at certain discounts. This requirement and new regulations on fund management will force investment funds to become more transparent and thus more attractive for investors. Furthermore, a fund's holding in any one company will be limited to 11%, the previous limit being 20%.

... and enterprise restructuring has intensified.

Since 1995, IPFs and other investors have consolidated their ownership in a "third wave" of privatisation; most privatised companies now have a majority or dominant owner. This has contributed to an accelerated pace of enterprise restructuring, marked by three consecutive years of productivity growth of around 10% in manufacturing. While productivity growth was mainly driven by production in 1995, reductions in employment was an important contributing factor in 1996 and 1997. Firm profitability remains low, however, often as a result of high indebtedness. The financial problems of the enterprise sector are reflected in growing inter-enterprise and tax arrears. In order to speed up bankruptcy procedures, the Bankruptcy Law was amended in January 1998, requiring insolvent companies to file for bankruptcy without delay and finalise liquidation within 18 months of an order.

Infrastructure

Improvements in transport infrastructure have been delayed by fiscal constraints.

The European Commission has emphasised the need to increase investment in infrastructure, especially in the transport system, in preparation for EU accession. The amounts of investment are substantial: the trans-European transport networks alone are estimated to require 1.2–1.5% of GDP annually in new investment. International rail

Liberalisation			1994	1995	1996	1997
Exchange rate regime	managed float	Share of administered prices in CPI	18.1	17.4	17.4	13.3
Current account convertibility	full	Administered prices in "EBRD-15" basket	4	4	4	2
Interest rate liberalisation	full	Share of trade in GDP	36.4	46.3	43.6	47.6
Wage regulation	no	Tariff revenue (% of imports)	4.1	2.6	2.6	1.7
Privatisation						
Primary privatisation method	voucher	Private sector share in GDP	65	70	75	75
Secondary privatisation method	direct sales	Share of medium/large firms privatised	57.9	66.7	71.6	74.2
Tradability of land rights	full except foreigners	Privatisation revenues (% of GDP)	1.61	1.12	0.20	0.43
Enterprises						
Protection of shareholder rights	partly effective	Budgetary subsidies (% of GDP)	3.1	2.7	2.2	2.4
Bankruptcy proceedings	partly effective	Credit to enterprises (% of GDP)	67.9	61.7	58.4	56.0
Competition office	yes	Labour productivity in industry (% change)	4.9	11.1	9.6	11.1
Infrastructure						
Independent telecoms regulator	no	Main telephone lines per 100 inhabitants	20.9	23.2	27.3	31.8
Separation of railway accounts	no	Railway labour productivity (1989=100)	80.0	84.0	83.2	80.2
Independent electricity regulator	no	Electricity tariff, US¢/kWh (collection ratio in %)	3.2 (95)	3.7 (95)	3.9 (95)	3.7 (95)
Financial institutions						
Deposit insurance	yes	Number of banks (of which foreign-owned)	47 (13)	45 (13)	44 (14)	41 (15)
Secured transactions law	restricted	Asset share of state-owned banks	19.2	18.9	17.6	17.9
Insider dealing prohibited	yes	Bad loans (% of total loans)	34.0	33.3	30.0	28.8
Securities commission	yes	Stock market capitalisation (% of GDP)	30.9	40.3	32.3	30.0
Fiscal and social sector						
Private pension funds	yes	Tax revenues (% of GDP)	40.5	40.0	38.8	37.8
Share of population in poverty	1%	Earnings inequality (Gini coefficient)	0.260	0.271	na	na

routes crossing the Czech Republic are being gradually improved. Motorway construction slowed down significantly, however, when fiscal policy was tightened in 1997.

Increases in gas and energy prices have improved cost recovery.
The government increased household electricity prices by 24% and gas tariffs by 27% in July 1998, reducing the cross-subsidy from industry to households. The Ministry of Finance has indicated that energy prices will need to be raised further to achieve cost recovery.

Financial institutions

New legislation will increase transparency in the financial sector.
Amendments to the Banking Law, which became effective in 1998, will strengthen the powers of the central bank (CNB) and disentangle the often non-transparent relationships between banks, investment funds and industrial enterprises. Banks will be required to separate their commercial and investment banking operations, representatives from the banks are prohibited from sitting on the supervisory boards of industrial companies, and limits have been placed on banks' holdings in any one industrial company. The CNB will have greater powers in limiting participation of any investor in the banking sector.

Privatisation of state-controlled banks is progressing.
The banking sector remains dominated by four large banks, three of them state-controlled, with state stakes ranging from 45% in Ceska Sporitelna and 48.7% in Komercni Banka to 65.7% in CSOB. The fourth, IPB, had its minority state share sold to a Japanese bank in March 1998. Two months later, the viable part of Agrobanka (formerly the largest private bank, under central bank administration since 1996) was sold to a US investment company. Overall, the process of bank privatisation has been cumbersome, partly due to the bad loan problem; the share of bad loans in total loans of 29% in mid-1998 is high, even in the central European context, and many of these loans are concentrated among the four largest banks. At the end of 1997, the Klaus government finally approved plans for the full privatisation of the other three large banks. The new government has indicated its intention to privatise them by the year 2000.

A semi-independent Securities and Exchange Commission has been established.
During the last few years, the Czech stock market consistently under-performed the stock markets in the neighbouring countries, mainly because of the lack of transparency and violations of minority shareholder rights. In an effort to restore investor confidence, a Securities and Exchange Commission (SEC) was established in April 1998. It has powers to impose fines up to CZK 100m (US$ 3 million), revoke licences, block suspicious trades and capital transfers, and approve or reject share issues. However, the SEC is not fully independent and its staff are appointed and funded by the government. Efforts to improve the transparency and liquidity of the stock exchange have continued. They included the removal of share issues with low turnover from the free market in October 1997 and measures to facilitate trading on the stock exchange in May 1998.

Fiscal and social sector

The deficits of state-owned financial institutions were disclosed.
Public finances have been made more transparent by the disclosure of the deficits of the three state-owned financial institutions which were set up to restructure the bad loans of Czech banks. The size of these deficits effectively doubles the size of domestic debt to about 20% of GDP and implies that the consolidated fiscal deficits were in the range of 2-3% of GDP in recent years.

Further pension reforms are under consideration.
Expenditures on pensions accounted for about 10% of GDP. Although the retirement age is being gradually increased – from 60 to 62 years for men and from 53-57 to 57-61 years for women – the actual number of pensioners has grown due to new early retirement options. Further pressure is expected as a result of an ageing population, but little progress has been made in preparing a fundamental pension reform. Proposals include the transition from a pay-as-you-go to a mixed system, including mandatory participation in private pension funds. At present individuals already have an option to contribute to private pension schemes, with incentives provided by the state.

Estonia

EU Association Agreement† · WTO observer · EFTA member

1990

Jan	Central bank established
Dec	State trading monopoly abolished

1991

Aug	Independence from Soviet Union
Oct	Tradability of land rights enacted
Dec	Small-scale privatisation begins

1992

June	Exchange rate unified
June	New currency (kroon) and currency board introduced
Aug	Large-scale privatisation begins
Sept	Bankruptcy law enacted
Dec	Most prices liberalised
Dec	Banking crisis

1993

June	Securities law enacted
June	Securities and exchange commission established
July	Privatisation law adopted
July	Privatisation agency established
Nov	Import tariffs abolished

1994

Jan	VAT introduced
Jan	Non-tariff trade restrictions removed
Jan	Flat-rate income tax introduced
Aug	Full current account convertibility introduced
Sept	BIS capital adequacy enacted

1995

Jan	IAS introduced
Feb	First bank privatised

1996

June	Stock exchange begins trading
June	EFTA membership

1997

Jan	Last bank privatised
May	Electricity law adopted

Key reform challenges

- **The effort to bring legislation in line with EU requirements will imply substantial commitments in a wide range of areas and reform of public administration.**
- **The success of new privatisation efforts in infrastructure will depend upon substantial restructuring and the continued development of an effective regulatory framework.**
- **In spite of a tightening of prudential regulations in the financial sector, recent troubles at a number of private Estonian banks have highlighted the need to strengthen the effectiveness of central bank supervision.**

Liberalisation

EU accession will require further progress in price liberalisation and competition policy.
A new competition law, closely modelled on EU directives, is effective from October 1998 and addresses shortcomings in state aid, anti-trust legislation and merger rules. Further harmonisation with EU guidelines will also require the elimination of exclusive rights in telecommunications and air, railway and maritime transport, as well as the abolition of state monopolies in oil shale and electricity supply. Further price liberalisation is needed as administratively controlled prices still account for 24% of the CPI.

The currency board remains the anchor of a liberal trade and exchange rate regime.
The government has recently reaffirmed its commitment to the currency board, which has pegged the Estonian kroon against the Deutschmark at a rate of 8:1 since June 1992. The peg will be transferred to the Euro in January 1999 at the current DM-Euro conversion rate. Estonia abolished all tariff and non-tariff barriers to foreign trade early in the transition, although the harmonisation of trade policy with the EU's Common External Tariff will require the reintroduction of tariff protection for some commodities. After some delays, WTO accession is now likely in early 1999.

Privatisation

The privatisation of industrial and service companies is almost complete.
According to the Estonian Privatisation Agency, 471 enterprises were sold through tender for a total of EEK 4.4 billion between 1993 and 1997. This included contractual agreements for additional investments worth EEK 4.3 billion and employment guarantees for over 56,000 workers. In addition, 1,338 enterprises were sold in auctions for a total of EEK 0.6 billion between 1991 and 1997. In April 1998, the government adopted a privatisation programme which entails the privatisation of 20 commercial enterprises (including the sale of Liviko alcohol producer and Moe Spirit distillery) and major infrastructure companies.

Land privatisation is accelerating.
A weak institutional structure and legal uncertainties have hampered the development of a land market. Only around 17% of total land had been privatised by the end of 1997. Amendments to the Law on Land Reform in late 1997 and the recent completion of 95% of existing restitution claims are expected to accelerate land privatisation. The government plans to privatise at least 27% of total land by the end of 1998. In addition, the government intends to remove the current restrictions on land purchases by foreigners by the end of 1998, in line with EU requirements.

Enterprises

Improved corporate governance has been the result of sales to strategic investors and high levels of FDI.
Competition from imports, privatisation and high levels of FDI have provided the major impetus for enterprise restructuring. The thrust of the privatisation effort (modelled on the German Treuhand) has been to find effective owners for enterprises and to promote corporate governance rather than to maximise privatisation revenues. In 1995-97, investment and employment guarantees in many privatised enterprises have been fulfilled and at times been exceeded by a wide margin. The 1992 Bankruptcy law has also been applied actively.

High growth in labour productivity has been a result of successful enterprise restructuring.
After substantial industrial downsizing, Estonia's economic structure resembles that of advanced market economies, with a share of manufacturing in GDP around 15-17%. Labour productivity in manufacturing grew by 18% in 1997, driven mainly by higher output growth rather than by falling employment. Some labour shedding in the manufacturing sector continues, though at a much slower pace compared with the early transition period.

Infrastructure

Telecoms privatisation has been postponed.
Government plans to sell 49% of Eesti Telekom, through an issue of global depository receipts and a public offering on the local stock exchange, have been postponed following the turmoil in emerging markets. A new Telecommunications Law came into force in January 1998 and a new regulatory Telecommunications Board is to be established by the end of 1998 in accordance with EU requirements.

Privatisation in the energy sector makes progress ...
In September 1998, the government sold its remaining stake of 10% in Eesti Gas, the main gas distributor, to Finland's Neste.

Liberalisation			1994	1995	1996	1997
Exchange rate regime	currency board	Share of administered prices in CPI	21.1	18.0	24.0	24.0
Current account convertibility	full	Administered prices in "EBRD-15" basket	3	3	3	3
Interest rate liberalisation	full	Share of trade in GDP	66.1	62.0	53.2	61.1
Wage regulation	no	Tariff revenue (% of imports)	0.0	0.0	0.0	0.0
Privatisation						
Primary privatisation method	direct sales	Private sector share in GDP	55	65	70	70
Secondary privatisation method	vouchers	Share of small firms privatised	78.9	88.1	94.7	99.6
Tradability of land rights	full except foreigners	Share of medium/large firms privatised	57.1	86.5	95.4	99.0
Enterprises						
Protection of shareholder rights	partly effective	Budgetary subsidies (% of GDP)	0.9	0.5	0.4	0.3
Bankruptcy proceedings	effective	Credit to enterprises (% of GDP)	14.1	14.9	18.1	25.6
Competition office	no	Labour productivity in industry (% change)	6.7	0.4	3.7	17.8
Infrastructure						
Independent telecoms regulator	no	Main telephone lines per 100 inhabitants	24.5	27.7	29.9	32.1
Separation of railway accounts	yes	Railway labour productivity (1989=100)	47.7	50.8	55.0	74.2
Independent electricity regulator	yes	Electricity tariff, US¢/kWh (collection ratio in %)	1.6 (99)	3.0 (100)	3.2 (98)	3.4 (97)
Financial institutions						
Deposit insurance	yes	Number of banks (of which foreign-owned)	22 (1)	18 (4)	15 (3)	12 (3)
Secured transactions law	restricted	Asset share of state-owned banks	28.1	9.7	6.6	0.0
Insider dealing prohibited	yes	Bad loans (% of total loans)	3.5	2.4	2.0	2.1
Securities commission	yes	Stock market capitalisation (% of GDP)	na	na	17.2	25.2
Fiscal and social sector						
Private pension funds	no	Tax revenues (% of GDP)	39.5	38.4	37.0	37.1
Share of population in poverty	40%	Earnings inequality (Gini coefficient)	na	na	na	na

There are plans to privatise two power stations (although the state will maintain a 51% stake in one of them), the distribution companies and power transmission in 1998 and 1999. The oil shale company Eesti Polevkivi has been transformed into a joint-stock company with 16 subsidiaries in preparation for future privatisation. The energy law of January 1998 sets up a new Energy Market Inspectorate in charge of setting tariffs and provides for real tariff increases over the next two years.

... while privatisation plans have been made for railways.

The blueprint privatisation plan for the railways company, Eesti Raudtee, envisages the sale of shares in all of its subsidiaries before the end of 1998. After selling the first 40 km of track to private operators at the end of 1997, the state will retain ownership of most of the remaining rail infrastructure for now. The new Railway Law, conforming to EU guidelines, came into force in January 1998. A supervisory body for railway administration is to be set up by the end of 1998.

Financial institutions

Weaknesses in corporate governance of banks have been exposed.

High-profile cases of serious mismanagement at two Estonian banks have raised questions regarding the quality of corporate governance and supervision of Estonia's banking sector. At Houipank, the central bank discovered that equity had been pledged by senior managers to back a loan to finance purchases of the bank's shares by the very same managers. At Eesti Maapank, mismanagement of the bank's equity portfolio during the autumn of 1997, including possibly fraudulent behaviour, brought about losses that have resulted in the bank's bankruptcy. However, Maapank is relatively small (with 3.5% of the country's banking assets) and its failure did not significantly affect public confidence in the banking system.

Financial regulations have been improved.

Since mid-1997, the coverage of reserve requirements has been extended and prudential regulations tightened to rein in the rapid expansion of banking sector credit to the economy and improve supervision. The measures focus on consolidating financial accounts, limiting open foreign exchange exposure and increasing capital adequacy (from 8% to 10%). The Estonian banking system is expected to meet all the prudential guidelines set out in the 25 principles of the Basle Committee before the end of 1998. The authorities are also taking measures to strengthen the banking supervision department of the central bank. In addition, a number of new laws have been drafted in line with EU legislation, including amendments to the Credit Institutions Law and a draft Securities Law. A new deposit guarantee fund came into effect in October 1998, which limits compensation to 90% of deposits up to a maximum amount of EEK 20,000.

Bank consolidation is under way.

Capital adequacy requirements and stock market falls have taken their toll on bank profits and are leading to bank consolidation. With the central bank pressing banks to expand their capital base and restrain their lending, banks are looking for merger opportunities to increase their assets. In 1998, merger agreements were signed between Tallina Pank and Uhispank, as well as Hansapank and Hoiupank. The turmoil in financial markets has forced the central bank to withdraw the licences of ERA Pank and Evea Pank and to take temporary controlling stakes in Forekspank and Estonian Investment Bank, which are intending to merge.

Fiscal and social sector

External imbalances have forced the government to tighten fiscal policies.

The tax structure has remained unchanged since 1994 when a flat-rate income tax of 26% was introduced. However, since the middle of 1997 the authorities have tightened other fiscal policies. These include the implementation of greater budgetary control on local governments through a new local authority financing law (May 1997), the establishment of the Stabilisation Reserve Fund into which fiscal surpluses are transferred (October 1997), and the introduction of excise taxes on tobacco and petrol (beginning of 1998).

Medium-term fiscal pressures have initiated pension reform.

Despite the gradual increase in the retirement age, the ratio of pension beneficiaries to contributors is estimated to increase from the current 0.6 to 0.85 by 2045. In response to the build-up of contingent pension liabilities, the Estonian authorities are in the process of moving from the pay-as-you-go pension system to a three-tier partially funded scheme. The first tier (to become operational in January 1999) will provide a minimum pension financed by a 33% social tax. The second tier (to be introduced in 2001) will offer additional pension coverage financed by mandatory individual contributions. The third tier (introduced in July 1998) consists of voluntary contributions administered by private pension funds and insurance companies.

† Signed on 12 June 1995, currently in the process of ratification.

FYR Macedonia

WTO observer

1991

Sept Independence from Yugoslavia

1992

Apr New currency (denar) introduced

Apr Two-tiered banking system established

June Securities and exchange commission established

1993

May BIS capital adequacy enacted

June Privatisation law adopted

Nov First credit auction by Central Bank

1994

Jan Sales taxes streamlined

Jan Bank credit ceilings introduced

Feb Greek embargo imposed

1995

Mar Banking rehabilitation law adopted

Sept Greek embargo lifted

1996

Mar Stock exchange begins trading

Apr Banking law adopted

June Telecoms law adopted

July Trade reforms enacted

Aug Import restrictions eliminated

1997

Mar TAT Savings House collapsed

July Securities law enacted

July New land law enacted

July Devaluation of denar

Nov Electricity law adopted

Key reform challenges

- **Continued efforts to move away from insider privatisation and to attract foreign investment will improve corporate governance and support further progress in enterprise restructuring.**
- **Effective implementation of the new bankruptcy law and new prudential regulations for banks would help improve financial discipline and market efficiency.**
- **The financial sector remains relatively underdeveloped with a thin loan market and a large burden of bad loans. The stock market is at an early stage of development.**

Liberalisation

A comprehensive wage freeze has expired.
A six-month wage freeze, introduced to contain inflationary pressures after the 14% devaluation in July 1997, lapsed at the end of the year. The freeze extended to all budgetary entities and all enterprises that were not fully privately owned, encompassing about 80% of all employees. Partly as a result of this measure, real wages fell by 4% during the second half of 1997.

Tax incentives have been introduced to tackle long-term unemployment.
The unemployment rate stood at 36%, according to a 1997 labour force survey, though the true rate is most likely lower due to activities in the informal economy. About three-quarters of the unemployed were without a job for over 18 months and almost half for over 4 years. In January 1998, the government implemented a programme to stimulate employment. It provides a two-year waiver of social security contributions for newly hired employees who have been unemployed for over a year or whose previous firm has gone bankrupt. However, the exemption only applies to firms that have increased their workforce since December 1997. The exemption was subsequently extended to cover new entrants to the labour market.

Privatisation

Privatisation is continuing, with the focus shifting towards public utilities.
By mid-1998, roughly four-fifths of all formerly "socially-owned" enterprises identified for privatisation had been privatised, mostly through management and employee buy-outs. However, most of these are SMEs. There are a number of large loss-making industrial enterprises with majority state ownership which are being restructured and are to be sold to strategic investors or otherwise liquidated. The government is also preparing international tenders for stakes in telecoms, energy and the oil refinery.

The pace of privatisation in the agricultural sector has increased.
Agriculture accounts for about 11% of GDP and nearly 20% of employment. Privatisation in this sector has lagged behind the rest of the economy, but the pace increased in 1998. By May, 70% of all agricultural enterprises had been privatised (representing about 40% of employment in the sector); the rest are scheduled for privatisation by the end of the year. After some initial delays, substantial progress is being made on the restructuring and privatisation of the large agro-kombinats, with the assistance of the World Bank.

Enterprises

Enterprise restructuring is progressing gradually.
Although the economic environment has been relatively stable for several years, improvements in corporate governance have been slow. This is due in part to the prevalence of management and employee buy-outs in the privatisation process, which can act as a hindrance to enterprise restructuring. As of March 1998, enterprises sold to outsiders accounted for less than 15% of employees in privatised enterprises. Nevertheless, industrial productivity has been improving slowly, reflecting both increasing output and a continued decline in employment. The government has taken further measures to support the restructuring process by relaxing restrictions on hiring and firing workers and by discouraging insider privatisations. All companies will be required to produce accounts in line with international accounting standards from January 1999.

A new bankruptcy law has strengthened creditors' rights.
Financial discipline has been weakened by continued lending of banks to loss-making enterprises with a poor debt service record and by an ineffective bankruptcy law inherited from the former Yugoslavia. Under this law, a debtor was often allowed a period of several months within which it could clear its debts. The cumbersome judicial process led to a large backlog of cases in the courts. While the number of bankruptcy cases filed has been very large, few have led to liquidation. Instead, bankruptcy was often a way for firms to restructure and emerge from the proceedings with a reduced debt burden and workforce. A new bankruptcy law became effective in May 1998, giving creditors more rights, reducing the number of bankruptcy cases where assets are small relative to the judicial costs, and enhancing the likelihood that filed cases result in liquidation. The government also plans to initiate bankruptcy proceedings against enterprises that are in arrears to the public utilities or the budget.

FDI is finally rising as investors respond to an improved investment climate.
Cumulative inflows of FDI from 1993 to 1997 amounted to only US$ 65 million, which compares unfavourably with other transition economies – both in per capita and GDP terms. Foreign investors have been

Liberalisation			1994	1995	1996	1997
Exchange rate regime	fixed	Share of administered prices in CPI	na	15.0	19.6	19.6
Current account convertibility	full	Administered prices in "EBRD-15" basket	2	2	2	2
Interest rate liberalisation	limited *de facto*	Share of trade in GDP	37.4	32.8	33.1	41.9
Wage regulation	no	Tariff revenue (% of imports)	10.5	12.5	11.4	7.0
Privatisation						
Primary privatisation method	MEBOs	Private sector share in GDP	35	40	50	50
Secondary privatisation method	direct sales	Number of medium/large firms privatised	na	na	148	92
Tradability of land rights	limited *de jure*	Share of firms privatised	na	37.8	57.1	70.8
Enterprises						
Protection of shareholder rights	partly effective	Budgetary subsidies (% of GDP)	3.1	2.7	2.0	0.3
Bankruptcy proceedings	partly effective	Credit to enterprises (% of GDP)	na	10.6	14.4	14.2
Competition office	no	Labour productivity in industry (% change)	-1.4	6.6	-9.0	14.6
Infrastructure						
Independent telecoms regulator	no	Main telephone lines per 100 inhabitants	16.1	16.5	17.0	17.4
Separation of railway accounts	na	Railway labour productivity (1989=100)	23.7	27.0	47.2	na
Independent electricity regulator	no	Electricity tariff, US¢/kWh (collection ratio in %)	2.7 (90)	2.8 (90)	3.1 (90)	3.5 (90)
Financial institutions						
Deposit insurance	yes	Number of banks (of which foreign-owned)	6 (3)	6 (3)	8 (3)	9 (3)
Secured transactions law	yes	Asset share of state-owned banks	na	na	0.0	0.0
Insider dealing prohibited	na	Bad loans (% of total loans)	na	na	42.8	35.6
Securities commission	yes	Stock market capitalisation (% of GDP)	na	na	na	0.3
Fiscal and social sector						
Private pension funds	no	Tax revenues (% of GDP)	na	na	37.9	36.1
Share of population in poverty	na	Earnings inequality (Gini coefficient)	0.253	0.270	0.250	na

deterred by high political risk in the region. Their participation in the privatisation process amounted to less than 2% of equity privatised. The situation has improved sharply in 1998, facilitated by an improved economic climate and greater emphasis on sales to outsiders in privatisation. Several large foreign investments have been concluded or are at an advanced stage of preparation, including the sale of state shares in FYR Macedonia's steel company to a foreign strategic investor for about US$ 20 million. Planned privatisations in utilities and the banking sector are also attracting foreign interest. A new agency to promote foreign investment was established in January 1998 and efforts are being made to remove bureaucratic obstacles faced by investors.

Infrastructure

Utility prices remain below cost recovery.
Many utility prices, including electricity and phone tariffs, remain below the regional average. Movement towards cost recovery is expected, however, especially as these sectors are being prepared for privatisation. To this end, the government plans to put in place independent regulatory bodies, which will be responsible for setting tariffs for heat, electricity and gas.

Telecommunications is being prepared for privatisation.
The government plans to privatise infrastructure on a case-by-case basis. A pre-privatisation programme for Macedonian Telecommunications is being implemented, including the preparation of a regulatory framework. The government intends to sell at least one-third of the shares to an international strategic investor.

Financial institutions

Prudential regulation and banking supervision have been tightened in order to tackle the bad loan problem.
The banking sector's health has improved since 1995, when a large amount of bad loans were transferred from the balance sheets of banks to the newly created Bank Rehabilitation Agency. Bank profitability increased markedly in 1997 and most banks are now well capitalised and provisioned. The share of bad loans has decreased from 70% in 1992 to around 36% at the end of 1997. However, many banks continue to lend to enterprises with a poor debt service record and maintain high exposure to single parties, partly because banks have acquired enterprise shares in debt-for-equity swaps. A new Bank Act, effective since April 1998, foresees stricter limits on connected lending and single-debtor exposure. It also requires banks to sell down assets acquired in debt-for-equity swaps. The supervisory powers of the central bank have been strengthened. During 1997, it closed a number of savings houses, including the largest one (TAT) which was running a pyramid scheme. It has also performed full on-site inspections at the three largest banks.

The largest commercial bank is to be fully privatised.
Stopanska Banka (SB) remains the dominant bank in FYR Macedonia, with about 35% of the sector's assets. The state is SB's single largest shareholder, with a 23% share. A programme to rehabilitate and fully privatise SB is well advanced and should be finalised by the end of 1998. The deal involves the EBRD, the IFC and Erste Bank from Austria. The privatisation of SB will be a significant step forward in making the sector more competitive and will also help to eliminate soft lending practices.

Stock market activity is increasing, but market capitalisation remains very low.
The stock market started trading in early 1996 and remains relatively undeveloped, despite higher trading volumes in 1998. Total market capitalisation was only around US$ 10 million at the end of 1997. Almost all activity takes place on the "Third Market", where the only requirement for participation is the submission of the latest financial statement of the issuer.

Fiscal and social sector

VAT is to replace the sales tax.
In mid-1998, parliament was discussing the introduction of VAT in 1999. It would replace the sales tax, which is currently levied at rates varying from 5% to 25%. A pilot programme for VAT has been implemented.

Pension reform is envisaged.
Despite a fairly young population, pension expenditures amounted to over 10% of GDP in 1997. The state pension fund is financed primarily through a 20% payroll tax, but additional funds have to be transferred from the central budget. Under the current IMF programme, the government is committed to reforming the pension system by raising the retirement age and introducing private pension plans.

Georgia

CIS member · WTO observer

1991

Apr Independence from Soviet Union

Aug Exchange rate unified

1992

Jan Tax reform

Feb Most prices liberalised

Mar Controls on foreign trade lifted

Mar VAT introduced

1993

Mar Small-scale privatisation begins

1994

Jan First foreign-owned bank opened

Dec Export tax to non-CIS countries abolished

1995

Jan Trade regulations streamlined

June Central bank law enacted

June State order system abolished

June Privatisation of State Bread Corporation

June Voucher privatisation begins

Oct New currency (lari) introduced

1996

Feb Banking law enacted

Mar Tradability of land enacted

June Competition law enacted

June First bank privatised

June Voucher privatisation ends

Sept BIS capital adequacy enacted

Sept Competition agency established

Dec Full current account convertibility introduced

Dec Last bank privatised

1997

Jan Bankruptcy law enacted

May New privatisation law adopted

June Electricity law adopted

Aug T-bills market initiated

Key reform challenges

- **The increased momentum in the privatisation of medium-sized and large enterprises should be matched by similar efforts in the agricultural sector to privatise land and promote the effective functioning of land markets.**
- **The ongoing reforms in the energy and transport sectors, including private sector involvement and the commercialisation of state enterprises, will help to rebuild infrastructure.**
- **Further strengthening of prudential regulations and the formal establishment of a capital market will support the growth of private enterprises.**
- **Increasing fiscal revenues and reducing corruption and tax avoidance would provide the additional resources needed to improve the social safety net.**

Liberalisation

Further trade liberalisation is being pursued in preparation for WTO accession.

Georgia has a very liberal trade regime with a maximum import tariff of 12%. The first round of multilateral talks with the WTO took place in March 1998. Accession is conditional upon the introduction of new legislation, in particular a new Law on Foreign Trade which would introduce WTO standards in the areas of customs fee, customs valuation, rules of origin, anti-dumping and sanitary measures. The new Law on Customs Tariffs adopted in March 1998 abolished the system of minimum import prices which applied to 16 food items. The government has also prepared a draft law to abolish export restrictions on scrap metal and timber.

Privatisation

Privatisation has accelerated with the introduction of "zero price" cash auctions.

In May 1997, a new law was introduced to speed up the privatisation process. At that time, about half of the 1,115 medium-sized and large enterprises earmarked for privatisation had been sold, mostly through management and employee buy-outs and voucher auctions. However, the privatised firms accounted for only about 10% of the total book value of these companies. Cash auctions were introduced at the end of 1996, but failed to attract bidders due to high minimum prices. The new law allows for auctions without floor prices ("zero price auctions"). Two such auctions in July 1997 and March 1998 sold over 300 of the remaining 550 enterprises.

The government has started to privatise "strategic" enterprises.

In August 1997, the president abolished a decree suspending the privatisation of so-called "strategic" enterprises – a group of around 50 enterprises mostly in heavy industry. They are being privatised on a case-by-case basis due to their significant restructuring and investment requirements. Some were sold at the zero price auction in early 1998 and others were sold through tenders and specialised auctions. Tenders for 10-year management contracts with a buy-out option for management at the end of the term have also been used. These contracts include quantitative targets for investment, output and employment. Under this framework, a consortium of Georgian and foreign investors won the tender for a 51% stake in Rustavi Metallurgical, the country's largest iron and steel plant, in January 1998. Three months later, a Russian firm won the tender for 75% of Chiatura Manganese, a large refining plant. These two companies account for almost half of the book value of the strategic enterprises.

Land privatisation is hampered by the lack of a system for land registration.

Agriculture accounts for almost a third of GDP, for half of the labour force and for 80% of self-employment. Economic efficiency in agriculture is limited by the slow pace of land privatisation and the lack of a functioning land market. In mid-1998 the share of privatised land was 26%, though the share is about 60% if the breakaway regions of Abkhazia and South Ossetia are excluded. The establishment of an active land market is impaired by the lack of a system for land registration; the World Bank is supporting a pilot scheme for registers in two districts. Draft laws on the privatisation of non-farming land were discussed by parliament in June 1998.

Enterprises

Output is growing rapidly, but enterprise restructuring has been slow.

The economic recovery is well under way after the collapse of GDP caused by the break-up of the Soviet Union and the civil war from 1991 to 1993. However, capacity utilisation in industry was only around 30% at the end of 1997. Exports are growing rapidly, but their 10% share in GDP is low for a small open economy. The structural change away from industry and towards services and informal activities has been very pronounced. Industry now accounts for only about 10% of GDP, down from 30% prior to the transition. The restructuring process of larger industrial enterprises has been slow, mainly due to remaining state ownership and concerns about employment. Tacis and the World Bank are currently supporting the restructuring of eight privatised enterprises. The 1997 Bankruptcy Law has not yet resulted in a liquidation.

Liberalisation			1994	1995	1996	1997
Exchange rate regime	managed float	Share of administered prices in CPI	na	9.0	7.5	7.5
Current account convertibility	full	Administered prices in "EBRD-15" basket	5	5	4	3
Interest rate liberalisation	limited *de facto*	Share of trade in GDP	45.1	18.6	13.0	13.5
Wage regulation	no	Tariff revenue (% of imports)	0.3	0.5	2.1	5.0
Privatisation						
Primary privatisation method	voucher	Private sector share in GDP	20	30	50	55
Secondary privatisation method	direct sales	Share of small firms privatised	22.7	62.5	81.5	93.8
Tradability of land rights	limited *de facto*	Share of medium/large firms privatised	12.3	36.2	60.7	73.1
Enterprises						
Protection of shareholder rights	ineffective	Budgetary subsidies (% of GDP)	13.8	1.1	1.0	1.5
Bankruptcy proceedings	partly effective	Credit to enterprises (% of GDP)	7.8	4.0	2.2	2.5
Competition office	yes	Labour productivity in industry (% change)	na	na	na	na
Infrastructure						
Independent telecoms regulator	no	Main telephone lines per 100 inhabitants	9.6	10.3	10.5	na
Separation of railway accounts	no	Railway labour productivity (1989=100)	na	na	na	na
Independent electricity regulator	yes	Electricity tariff, US¢/kWh(collection ratio in %)	1.6 (20)	3.5 (35)	2.8 (55)	3.1 (68)
Financial institutions						
Deposit insurance	no	Number of banks (of which foreign-owned)	226 (1)	101 (3)	61 (6)	53 (8)
Secured transactions law	restricted	Asset share of state-owned banks	67.9	45.8	0.0	0.0
Insider dealing prohibited	no	Bad loans (% of total loans)	23.9	40.5	6.6	6.6
Securities commission	no	Stock market capitalisation (% of GDP)	na	na	na	na
Fiscal and social sector						
Private pension funds	no	Tax revenues (% of GDP)	3.0	3.6	5.3	7.1
Share of population in poverty	na	Earnings inequality (Gini coefficient)	na	na	na	na

The government has launched an anti-corruption initiative.

The President has identified corruption as one of the main obstacles to reform, particularly to tax collection. An anti-corruption commission was formed in 1998 which drafted a law creating a special service to fight corruption.

Infrastructure

Wide-ranging reforms of the energy sector are to be implemented.

Georgia's hydropower plants have suffered from a lack of maintenance, leading to frequent power cuts throughout the country. To raise the funds for their renovation, a wide-ranging reform programme is under preparation. Electricity tariffs have moved towards cost recovery. Household tariffs have been raised to the level of industrial tariffs (about US$ 0.035 per kWh) and discounts for both types of consumers have been eliminated. The increase in the collection ratio from 55% in 1996 to 68% in 1997 has reduced the hidden subsidisation through arrears and increased financial discipline. The 1997 Electricity Law separates regulation from ownership and has established an independent regulatory body. The government plans to reorganise and privatise local distribution. The tendering process for a 75% stake in Tbilisi's major distribution company, Telasi, is already under way. At a later stage, other distribution and generation companies are to be privatised while the transmission company will remain in state hands.

International bodies are supporting reforms and investments in the transport sector.

Georgia's geographical position makes it an important transport link between the Black and Caspian Seas and between Russia and Turkey. The EU, the World Bank and the EBRD are supporting projects to rebuild the transport infrastructure, which has suffered from war damage and a lack of maintenance. The projects are linked to institutional reforms. The new railways law, presently under draft, will establish the Georgian Railways as a state-owned joint stock company, separate regulation from operation and reduce cross-subsidies between passenger and freight services. In connection with the regeneration of the Black Sea port of Poti, the government is considering various proposals for private sector involvement.

Financial institutions

After rapid consolidation, the banking sector is healthier, but still fragile and very small.

The banking sector has consolidated since early 1995 when there were more than 200 banks, most of them undercapitalised with a high proportion of bad loans. Since then, the central bank has reviewed bank licences, raised minimum capital requirements and introduced prudential regulations. By mid-1998, the number of certified banks had fallen to 48 and the average bad loan portfolio to about 7%. Agrobank, one of the three large formerly state-owned banks, has been partly sold to a Russian bank. The sector remains fragile, however, and further consolidation could result from the planned stepwise increase of capital requirements. Financial intermediation is still under-developed, with total banking assets representing only 5% of GDP and banking activity concentrated on short-term loans.

Comprehensive legislation is being prepared to establish a formal capital market.

Securities are currently traded on an informal market. In 1997, the Ministry of Finance issued the first Treasury bills, with 1 and 3 month maturities. A new Law on Securities is being considered by parliament. It covers the brokerage and registration of shares and bonds, investments of insurance companies and private pension funds, and the establishment of a stock exchange and an independent Securities and Exchange Commission. The stock exchange is expected to open in early 1999.

Fiscal and social sector

Fiscal pressures have prompted a new tax code and measures to tackle tax evasion.

The share of tax revenues in GDP is the lowest in the CIS and tax arrears amounted to 30% of tax revenues in 1997. Wage and pension arrears owed by the state have accumulated in early 1998. A tax code approved in late 1997 has broadened the tax base, mainly by abolishing exemptions on VAT and excise taxes. Further measures were introduced in 1998, including an increased excise tax on cigarettes, an environmental tax on petrol and diesel, and an income tax on small business. The adjustment of VAT on agricultural goods to the standard 20% rate is under discussion. Tax and customs administration continue to be strengthened.

Social safety net reforms have been limited by low public resources.

The flat-rate pension was raised to compensate for electricity price increases, but remains below US$ 10 per month. Other social transfers are similarly small and partly determined by local authorities. Given the financial pressures on the state, greater private involvement in the pension system is envisaged. A law submitted to parliament in early 1998 foresees the introduction of private pension plans.

Hungary

EU Association Agreement · OECD member · WTO member · EFTA member · CEFTA member

1990

Mar Large-scale privatisation begins

Mar State property agency established

June Stock exchange established

1991

Jan Most prices liberalised

Jan Competition law enacted

Jan Small-scale privatisation begins

1992

Jan Bankruptcy law enacted

Jan BIS capital adequacy enacted

Mar EU Association Agreement

Aug State asset management agency established

1993

Mar CEFTA membership

Sept Bankruptcy law amended

Oct EFTA membership

1994

July First bank privatised

1995

Jan WTO membership

May Privatisation law adopted

May State property and asset management agencies merge

Dec Telecoms becomes majority foreign-owned

Dec Restitution law enacted

Dec Securities and exchange commission established

1996

Jan Full current account convertibility introduced

Jan State finance reform

Mar IMF programme

Apr Customs law enacted

May OECD membership

Oct New customs law enacted

Dec Financial sector supervision law adopted

Dec IAS introduced

1997

Jan Currency basket changed

Jan New competition law enacted

July Pension reform adopted

Key reform challenges

- **The state retains control in some privatised enterprises through golden shares or minority stakes, which could affect post-privatisation governance.**
- **The development of a strong SME sector remains constrained by a lack of access to credit, though improvements could come from growing competition in the banking sector.**
- **The start of a new pension system and the reassertion of central government control over the deficit-ridden state pension and health funds are important first steps in the much-needed reform of the welfare system.**

Liberalisation

EU accession leads to further progress on trade liberalisation.
Hungary was a founding member of the WTO. Its trade regime is liberal with an average tariff of 5% in 1997. The EU Association Agreement removed most tariff and quantitative trade restrictions by the end of 1997, with the exception of agricultural products, textiles and steel. The new government has announced plans to phase out existing export subsidies for agricultural producers in line with EU standards.

International capital flows have been further liberalised.
A new package of measures was introduced in January 1998 to liberalise international capital flows. The measures allow OECD-based enterprises to issue foreign-currency denominated securities with maturities above one year in Hungary. Reporting requirements for foreign credits of over US$ 50 million were scrapped for loans with a maturity of over one year, as was the central bank's ability to postpone such loans. The new package also gives Hungarians the right to purchase real estate abroad.

Privatisation

The state retains "golden" shares and long-term ownership stakes in some privatised companies.
An amendment to the Privatisation Law in July 1997 identifies privatised enterprises in which the state is to maintain a significant ownership stake. In 27 enterprises, ranging from energy and telecoms to agribusiness, the state will retain a golden share, which entitles it to a wide range of powers, such as the right to veto changes in product lines and to approve mergers, share conversions and divestments. In 116 enterprises, the state will retain a long-term ownership stake. However, the amendment also includes plans for a further divestiture of state shares in blue-chip companies through public offerings.

The privatisation process is nearly completed.
The Hungarian Privatisation and State Holding Company (APV Rt.) has made significant progress in completing the privatisation process. In 1997, shares in 158 companies were sold yielding higher than expected revenues of US$ 1.8 billion. Among the most important privatisations in 1997-98 were the international public offerings of minority stakes in the telecoms company Matáv (the largest IPO in Hungary to date), OTP bank, and the oil and gas company MOL (reducing the government's share from 59% to 42%). The privatisation process is scheduled to be completed by the end of 1998, with revenues for this year expected at around US$ 500 million. Subsequently, APV Rt. will focus its activities primarily on portfolio management of the state's remaining ownership stakes, including minority stakes in privatised enterprises.

Enterprises

Foreign direct investment has enhanced the competitiveness of Hungarian enterprises ...
Enterprises with majority foreign ownership (excluding banks) accounted for around 16% of total gross value added in 1996. This figure has most likely increased further, given the progress in privatisation and above-average output growth of foreign companies. In 1997, output grew by 56% and productivity by 43% in a range of FDI-intensive sectors, such as machinery, computers, telecoms equipment, electrical and electronic goods, and automobiles. Exports of FDI-intensive sectors were up by similar amounts. The manufacturing sector as a whole recorded 15% growth in output and productivity and 10% in exports. These trends have broadly continued in early 1998. Major multinational companies are beginning to relocate their research activities to Hungary.

... while SMEs have been recovering more slowly.
Hungary's strong output recovery has not yet fully reached its SME sector, which is the backbone of the domestically owned private sector. Despite evidence that some multi-nationals are increasingly relying on domestic inputs, the number of SMEs is declining (as distinguished from micro-enterprises), suggesting that the sector is still facing serious difficulties. One problem is the lack of access to bank credit, with collateral requirements reportedly up to three times the value of a loan, although growing competition in the banking sector may soften this constraint over time.

Infrastructure

The telecommunications sector may be liberalised further.
Hungary's telecoms company, Matáv, was corporatised in 1991, and privatised in 1993 and 1995, with 67% sold to a German-

Liberalisation			1994	1995	1996	1997
Exchange rate regime	crawling peg, with band	Share of administered prices in CPI	11.8	12.9	12.8	15.9
Current account convertibility	full	Administered prices in "EBRD-15" basket	2	2	2	2
Interest rate liberalisation	full	Share of trade in GDP	22.6	31.5	34.3	45.3
Wage regulation	no	Tariff revenue (% of imports)	12.7	13.1	9.9	5.3
Privatisation						
Primary privatisation method	direct sales	Private sector share in GDP	55	60	70	75
Secondary privatisation method	MEBOs	Share of small firms privatised	57.8	66.0	77.2	87.7
Tradability of land rights	full except foreigners	Privatisation revenues (% of GDP)	0.71	2.70	3.28	0.60
Enterprises						
Protection of shareholder rights	partly effective	Budgetary subsidies (% of GDP)	4.5	3.8	3.9	3.3
Bankruptcy proceedings	effective	Credit to enterprises (% of GDP)	17.9	16.5	17.4	20.1
Competition office	yes	Labour productivity in industry (% change)	7.3	11.2	9.1	14.5
Infrastructure						
Independent telecoms regulator	yes	Main telephone lines per 100 inhabitants	16.9	18.5	26.1	30.5
Separation of railway accounts	yes	Railway labour productivity (1989=100)	84.8	87.7	88.5	95.6
Independent electricity regulator	yes	Electricity tariff, US¢/kWh (collection ratio in %)	4.0 (90)	5.9 (90)	6.0 (90)	6.8 (90)
Financial institutions						
Deposit insurance	yes	Number of banks (of which foreign owned)	43 (17)	42 (21)	41 (25)	41 (30)
Secured transactions law	yes	Asset share of state-owned banks	62.8	52.0	16.3	12.0
Insider dealing prohibited	yes	Bad loans (% of total loans)	17.6	10.3	7.2	3.6
Securities commission	yes	Stock market capitalisation (% of GDP)	4.2	5.8	34.7	36.2
Fiscal and social sector						
Private pension funds	yes	Tax revenues (% of GDP)	39.9	37.2	35.9	34.8
Share of population in poverty	2%	Earnings inequality (Gini coefficient)	0.337	na	na	na

American consortium of strategic investors for a total of US$ 1.7 billion. In November 1997, a further 19% was sold by the state through a simultaneous flotation on the Budapest and New York stock exchanges. Matáv's exclusivity rights on fixed-line services expire at the end of 2002. It is likely that competition in fixed-line services would be allowed by the time Hungary becomes an EU member.

After privatisations in energy generation and distribution, progress in the reform of the energy sector has recently slowed down.
Between 1995 and 1997, six electricity generating companies and six regional gas distribution companies were sold to foreign investors, raising revenues of almost US$ 4 billion. However, the new private owners have criticised the government's tariff policy, which has repeatedly postponed some of the scheduled price increases, most recently in October 1998. The introduction of legislation necessary to carry out the privatisation of the national grid operator, MVM, has been delayed. The technological upgrading of the country's four state-owned Soviet-built nuclear power plants is proceeding slowly. The EU Energy Charter Treaty, which came into effect in July 1998, guarantees foreign energy suppliers free entry into the Hungarian market.

Financial institutions

Divestiture of remaining state assets in the banking sector has continued.
Direct state ownership of share capital in the banking sector has continued to decline, falling to 20% by mid-1998 as a result of several privatisations. Following a recapitalisation of Postabank (the second-largest bank) in May 1998, the state's shareholding in this bank increased to 50%, though recent management changes have set the stage for potential re-privatisation. Plans to sell the remaining 29% stake in K&H (Commercial Bank) have been delayed by unfavourable market conditions and the priorities of the new government.

There has been a strong expansion of bank credits to enterprises.
Progress in bank recapitalisation and privatisation has led to increased competition for corporate clients. Interest margins have fallen to below 4% and real credit growth to the enterprise sector was 20% in 1997. While access to credit for medium-sized enterprises remains tight, increasing competition among Hungary's 38 commercial banks is forcing the most dynamic players into the small business and retail markets. Given low margins and high costs, a process of consolidation in the banking sector is expected.

There was continued progress in the development of the securities market, but share prices have fallen substantially following the Russian crisis.
The successful initial public offering of shares in the main telecoms company, Matáv, which raised US$ 1.3 billion in the midst of the Asian crisis, demonstrated the high investor confidence in the Budapest Stock Exchange (BSE), eastern Europe's most developed capital market. Market capitalisation in US dollar terms tripled during 1997, fuelled by buoyant share prices and 10 new listings on the BSE. However, in the wake of the Russian crisis, the stock index has declined substantially, with share prices losing almost half their value within a month and falling to their pre-1997 levels.

Fiscal and social sector

The new multi-pillar pension system was implemented in January 1998.
Hungary became the first country in eastern Europe to adopt a "multi-pillar" pension system. Since July 1998, all new labour force entrants (and optionally existing workers) make mandatory contributions to both the existing pay-as-you-go system (the first pillar) and to a fully-funded second pillar, based on a system of personal savings accounts held in privately managed pension funds. A voluntary third pillar is also available for top-up contributions. The pension reform also includes an increase in the retirement age, a change in the indexation formula for state pensions to net wage growth, and tighter eligibility criteria. These measures should limit the budgetary costs of lower contributions to finance existing pension liabilities. The World Bank is supporting this reform with a US$ 150 million loan. Disability pension reform is planned for 1999.

The new government has plans to reform health care.
The health system is run by the State Health Fund, an extrabudgetary entity with substantial operational autonomy and no effective accountability. The efficiency of service delivery remains poor. The health care system is financed by payroll taxes of 15% and 4% for employers and employees respectively. However, a large funding gap in the Fund, partly resulting from growing arrears of insurance contributions, has made transfers from the budget necessary. In August 1998, the government re-established its direct control over the Health Fund (together with the State Pension Fund) as a first step in streamlining its operations and increasing its accountability for costs.

Kazakhstan

CIS member · WTO observer

1991

June	Securities and stock exchange law adopted
Dec	Independence from Soviet Union

1992

1993

Apr	Securities and stock exchange law amended
Nov	New currency (tenge) introduced

1994

Apr	First voucher auction
Apr	T-bill issues introduced
June	Competition agency established
Nov	Most prices liberalised

1995

Jan	Customs union with Russia and Belarus
Feb	Most foreign trade licences abolished
Apr	Central bank law enacted
Apr	Rehabilitation Bank and Enterprise Restructuring Agency set up
Apr	Anti-monopoly legislation introduced
June	State orders in agriculture abolished
July	New tax code introduced
July	Prohibition of barter trade
Aug	Abolition of foreign exchange surrender
Dec	Privatisation law enacted
Dec	Telecoms law adopted

1996

June	IMF programme
June	Last voucher auction
June	Third stage privatisation programme begins
July	Full current account convertibility introduced
Nov	New accounting standards adopted
Dec	First sovereign Eurobond

1997

Jan	New bankruptcy law enacted
June	Pension reform law adopted
July	First ADR issue
Oct	Stock exchange begins trading

Key reform challenges

- **Budgetary pressures related to low oil prices and high borrowing costs raise the urgency of proceeding with the "blue-chip" privatisation programme.**
- **Impressive efforts in pension reform still face important implementation obstacles to achieving the envisaged benefits in domestic savings and capital market development.**
- **Resolution of the legal status of the Caspian Sea has opened up the development of new pipeline routes that could boost Kazakhstan's natural resource sector. This development will depend on continued inflows of FDI.**

Liberalisation

Price liberalisation is largely complete, but cross-subsidies persist in utilities.
Consumer price liberalisation was largely completed by 1995, with the exception of regulated prices for utilities (gas, electricity, water), rents, transport and telephony. Utility prices have been gradually adjusted towards cost recovery levels but higher rates for business and government customers subsidise lower rates for households.

Membership negotiations for the WTO are in progress.
Kazakhstan, which has a liberal trade regime, is in the advanced stages of negotiations for WTO membership. However, membership in the Customs Union with Belarus, Kyrgyzstan, Russia and Tajikistan may delay further tariff reductions because of the need to maintain a unified tariff structure within the union. The group has decided to coordinate application to the WTO among its members.

Privatisation

Rapid progress has been made in the privatisation of medium-sized and large enterprises ...
Small-scale privatisation was officially completed in 1997, with more than 13,000 enterprises sold through cash auctions and vouchers. There remains some state ownership in the health, education and social service sectors. Following an early focus on voucher auctions, large-scale privatisation has progressed rapidly through cash auctions encompassing 1,600 enterprises by mid-1998. There are still 400 state enterprises to be sold through this method. Case-by-case sales of strategic enterprises have attracted considerable foreign participation, especially in the power and utility sectors. In 1997, two oil companies, a copper plant, a manganese plant, and a 40% stake in Kazakhtelecom were sold to strategic foreign investors. Plans to hold initial public offerings for seven of the 13 blue-chip companies previously excluded from the privatisation programme have been delayed, due partly to the unfavourable international economic environment.

... though the state retains significant residual holdings.
Though official estimates report that over 70% of all enterprise assets have been privatised, only 30% of large enterprises are in majority private ownership and the state continues to retain large stakes in privatised enterprises. In addition, 330 very large enterprises, accounting for an estimated 35% of GDP, remain fully state-owned.

Enterprises

There have been renewed efforts to promote the restructuring of loss-making enterprises ...
Kazakhstan has experimented with several means to facilitate the restructuring of loss-making enterprises. An initial reliance on management contracts was effectively abandoned in favour of state-led restructuring under the management of the State Property Committee and the Rehabilitation Bank (RB), the latter concerned primarily with financial work-outs in insolvent enterprises. In 1997, 46 enterprises were transferred to the RB and, as of mid-1998, 26 enterprises had been either liquidated or offered for sale with the rest remaining in RB's portfolio. The new bankruptcy law was also amended in early 1998 to apply to agriculture.

... but financial discipline has remained weak.
The build-up of arrears remains an important source of soft budget constraints. Loss-making enterprises continue to run significant arrears to suppliers, workers and the state budget, despite the government's effort to eliminate "mutual settlements" whereby tax obligations are offset against budgetary arrears.

The natural resource sector has attracted large inflows of foreign direct investment.
FDI inflows to Kazakhstan have been among the highest in the CIS. In cumulative per capita terms, FDI has exceeded US$ 300 over 1989-98, second only to Azerbaijan. About 80% of this investment went to the non-renewable resource sector, in particular oil and gas. A Foreign Investment Advisory Council was established in 1998.

Infrastructure

Progress on the legal status of the Caspian Sea will facilitate pipeline development.
The signing of the Caspian Pipeline Consortium and a memorandum with China mark important milestones in the development of a transport infrastructure, creating the potential for the construction of a pipeline from Kazakhstan to the West of China. In the summer of 1998, a bilateral agreement with Russia was signed, accepting the legal definition of the Caspian as a sea – a definition crucial to Kazakhstan's

Liberalisation			1994	1995	1996	1997
Exchange rate regime	managed float	Share of administered prices in CPI	na	na	na	na
Current account convertibility	full	Administered prices in "EBRD-15" basket	3	3	3	0
Interest rate liberalisation	full	Share of trade in GDP	31.8	31.7	31.1	30.9
Wage regulation	no	Tariff revenue (% of imports)	4.2	3.9	2.0	1.5
Privatisation						
Primary privatisation method	vouchers	Private sector share in GDP	20	25	40	55
Secondary privatisation method	direct sales	Share of small firms privatised	41.7	60.0	79.5	100.0
Tradability of land rights	full except foreigners	Privatisation revenues (% of GDP)	na	0.71	2.20	3.20
Enterprises						
Protection of shareholder rights	ineffective	Budgetary subsidies (% of GDP)	na	na	na	na
Bankruptcy proceedings	ineffective	Credit to enterprises (% of GDP)	26.8	7.1	4.5	4.5
Competition office	yes	Labour productivity in industry (% change)	-12.1	0.1	12.3	17.4
Infrastructure						
Independent telecoms regulator	no	Main telephone lines per 100 inhabitants	11.7	11.8	11.6	13.3
Separation of railway accounts	no	Railway labour productivity (1989=100)	31.5	29.3	28.2	26.5
Independent electricity regulator	yes	Electricity tariff, US¢/kWh (collection ratio in %)	3.0 (73)	2.6 (75)	1.8 (70)	4.0 (50)
Financial institutions						
Deposit insurance	no	Number of banks (of which foreign-owned)	184 (6)	130 (6)	101 (9)	82 (22)
Secured transactions law	yes	Asset share of state-owned banks	na	24.3	28.4	45.4
Insider dealing prohibited	no	Bad loans (% of total loans)	na	14.9	19.9	7.7
Securities commission	yes	Stock market capitalisation (% of GDP)	na	na	na	5.9
Fiscal and social sector						
Private pension funds	yes	Tax revenues (% of GDP)	12.3	13.0	11.3	12.0
Share of population in poverty	50%	Earnings inequality (Gini coefficient)	na	na	na	na

claims for independent access to offshore oil and gas resources.

Privatisation of utilities raises regulatory challenges.
Kazakhstan has made considerable progress in privatising its utilities with the privatisation of more than 80% of the generation capacity in the power sector, the sale of a large minority stake in the national telecoms operator, and the awarding of a 15-year concession to a private operator for parts of its gas distribution network. However, attempts to attract investors into the remaining parts of the energy distribution system have been complicated by tension between foreign operators and public agencies over the operators' attempts to improve collection rates by cutting off customers. The Anti-Monopoly Committee, responsible for price regulation, became independent again in July 1998, after attempts to subordinate it to the Ministry of Industry.

Financial institutions

The banking sector has been strengthened through privatisation and foreign entry ...
Improvements in compliance with rules on capital adequacy, single-debtor exposure and connected lending have contributed to a decline in the number of banks and branches. Mandatory IAS accounting will be applied by 2000. The majority of the banking sector's assets are privately owned. A majority stake in the country's second-largest bank, comprising about a quarter of the banking system's total assets, is scheduled to be sold to private investors by the end of 1998. The state-owned Turan-Alem Bank was reprivatised in April 1998. Twenty banks with foreign ownership comprise about 22% of the banking sector's capital. Following the abolition of a 25% restriction on the share of foreign capital in the banking sector, foreign participation is likely to increase further. The largest private domestic bank, Kazkommertsbank, issued a GDR in 1997 and a Eurobond in 1998.

... but the sector is still highly concentrated with a legacy of non-performing loans.
The two largest banks in Kazakhstan (one private, the other state-owned) control more than 50% of deposits and 40% of outstanding loans. While improvements in credit assessment and loan work-outs have reduced the share of sub-standard loans, new lending to the private sector remains small.

The stock exchange is still at an early stage of development.
In September 1997, the Kazakhstan Stock Exchange was formally launched. Though the exchange has an infrastructure, regulatory framework and listing requirements that conform to international standards, trading is still minor, due primarily to delays in the privatisation of blue-chip companies. The over-the-counter market is more active, but lacks transparency. With the launch of the stock market and pension reform and in anticipation of blue-chip privatisation, a growing number of new non-bank financial institutions (including brokerages and private pension funds) have recently been licensed, in addition to insurance and leasing companies.

Fiscal and social sector

Pension reform is launched ...
In January 1998, Kazakhstan launched the first comprehensive pension reform in the CIS, to transform the existing pay-as-you-go system into a fully funded system. Employees make mandatory payments of 10% of their wages into a personal retirement account, in addition to contributions for existing pension liabilities financed through a 15% payroll tax – to be reduced to 5% over the next 10 years. Mandatory contributions can be made to public or private pension funds and may be topped up through voluntary savings. The minimum capitalisation requirements for private funds is US$ 1 million; at least 50% of their funds must be invested in domestic government securities, 10% in domestic equity and 10% in securities of international financial institutions. Twelve pension funds, three asset management companies and five custodial banks have been licensed as of mid-1998. In preparation for the reform, all pension arrears, which stood at 1.7% of GDP, were cleared at the end of 1997.

... but implementation has been difficult.
Low collection rates for mandatory contributions in the first half of 1998 reflect bottlenecks in administrative capacity and delays in the establishment of a contractual regime governing relations between pension funds, asset management companies and custodial banks. Even more problematic has been the lack of attractive private investment opportunities. The replacement ratio of 60% under the public pension system sets very high benchmarks for returns on investments in private pension accounts, potentially raising excessive expectations. Lastly, rules regarding the possibility for withdrawal of contributions and the purchase of annuities still need to be drafted.

Kyrgyzstan

CIS member · WTO observer

1991

June Banking laws adopted

Aug Independence from Soviet Union

Dec Small-scale privatisation begins

1992

Jan Most prices liberalised

1993

May Exchange rate unified

May New currency (som) introduced

May T-bills market initiated

1994

Apr Competition law introduced

May Enterprise restructuring agency established

May Most export taxes eliminated

1995

Mar Full current account convertibility introduced

May Stock exchange begins trading

June BIS capital adequacy enacted

Oct Liquidation phase of restructuring programme begins

1996

Jan VAT introduced

July New tax code introduced

Sept Securities and exchange commission established

1997

Jan Electricity law adopted

May Suspension of utilities privatisation

July IAS introduced

July Customs union with Russia, Kazakhstan and Belarus

Oct New bankruptcy law enacted

Key reform challenges

- **After its suspension in 1997, the acceleration of the medium- and large-scale privatisation programme – as well as further progress in agricultural reform – will provide a stronger foundation to support the substantial reforms in other areas.**
- **Further development of the financial sector would increase the availability of medium- and long-term capital for enterprises.**
- **Despite high growth in recent years, GDP per capita remains very low and about half the population are living at a subsistence level. Social reforms and increased tax collection will be necessary to ensure progress in alleviating poverty.**

Liberalisation

Kyrgyzstan is the first CIS country to join the WTO.
Final negotiations for WTO entry have been concluded successfully and Kyrgyzstan signed a membership agreement with the WTO in October 1998. Formal membership is expected by the end of the year. As a result, trade restrictions will continue to be reduced over the next few years.

The central bank has discontinued foreign exchange auctions.
The central bank discontinued its weekly auction of foreign currency to commercial banks in July 1998. In line with IMF recommendations, the central bank will now intervene directly in the inter-bank market for foreign exchange.

Privatisation

Large-scale privatisation resumes.
Small-scale privatisation was initiated in 1991 and proceeded relatively quickly, mostly via cash auctions. The mass privatisation programme for medium-sized and large enterprises started in 1994 and involved a combination of voucher and cash auctions. In early 1997, minority stakes in some large public monopolies were included in the voucher programme and controlling stakes were to be offered to foreign strategic investors. However, the privatisation process was suspended in May 1997 pending investigations into price rigging and corruption. The government has resumed the programme and formulated a new plan for the privatisation of about 300 medium-sized and large enterprises until the year 2000, including public monopolies in telecoms, energy, mining, railways and the national airline.

Land reform is being accelerated.
Agriculture accounts for about half of GDP and over a third of the labour force. Kyrgyzstan has made significant progress in developing a private market in agriculture. More than half of all land has been distributed to the public with land rights of up to 99 years. In 1997, more than 80% of agricultural output was produced by private farms. Full private land ownership had been prohibited by the constitution; however, a referendum in October 1998 approved a constitutional amendment introducing private land ownership. To facilitate the transfer of land rights and the use of land as collateral, new laws on land registration and mortgages are being considered by parliament.

Enterprises

Productivity growth is driven by agriculture and gold mining.
Kyrgyzstan's rapid GDP growth in recent years has been fuelled largely by significant increases in productivity in agriculture, especially in the private sector, and by the start of production at the Kumtor gold mine in January 1997. Productivity growth in the agricultural sector, however, is unlikely to continue to grow in 1998. The manufacturing sector is dominated by the Kumtor gold mine, which in 1997 contributed nearly 30% of exports and about 11% of GDP. Enterprise restructuring in other sectors has generally been uneven. The liquidation of large, loss-making state enterprises under the Enterprise Reform and Resolution Agency is nearing completion; three of the five remaining enterprises are due to be sold.

Efforts have been made to improve corporate governance and the investment climate.
The privatisation process has led to ownership structures dominated by managers and employees of privatised companies. Improvements in corporate governance have been slow, however, partly due to a lack of market discipline. The government is attempting to remedy this situation by gradually eliminating subsidies and directed credits and by instituting liquidation procedures for enterprises failing to pay outstanding arrears within a certain time. The 1997 Bankruptcy Law is now being put slowly into practice. In order to attract more foreign direct investment, an Agency for Foreign Investment was established in November 1997. Yet foreign interest remains limited, mainly because of the remote land-locked location of the country and the small regional market. A notable joint venture is the Kumtor gold mine, which is one-third owned by a Canadian company and two-thirds owned by the state.

Infrastructure

Electricity prices are to be raised significantly.
In April 1998, the government announced that electricity prices will be raised by an average of 70% over two years. This will help to raise prices towards cost-recovery levels and will counterbalance losses from declining exports of electricity to Kazakhstan and Uzbekistan. However, theft and non-payment are widespread and the effect of the price increase on low-income households means that these problems are likely to increase. Overcoming such obstacles is

Liberalisation			1994	1995	1996	1997
Exchange rate regime	managed float	Share of administered prices in CPI	na	na	na	na
Current account convertibility	full	Administered prices in "EBRD-15" basket	na	na	na	na
Interest rate liberalisation	limited *de facto*	Share of trade in GDP	36.2	33.3	36.2	37.9
Wage regulation	no	Tariff revenue (% of imports)	0.9	2.1	2.0	2.2
Privatisation						
Primary privatisation method	vouchers	Private sector share in GDP	30	40	50	60
Secondary privatisation method	MEBOs	Share of firms privatised	51.7	59.0	62.0	63.8
Tradability of land rights	limited *de facto*	Privatisation revenues (% of GDP)	na	0.00	0.50	0.08
Enterprises						
Protection of shareholder rights	partly effective	Budgetary subsidies (% of GDP)	na	6.9	4.7	3.7
Bankruptcy proceedings	partly effective	Credit to enterprises (% of GDP)	3.0	2.1	1.2	1.4
Competition office	no	Labour productivity in industry (% change)	-19.4	-3.3	22.2	56.4
Infrastructure						
Independent telecoms regulator	yes	Main telephone lines per 100 inhabitants	7.3	7.7	7.5	7.6
Separation of railway accounts	no	Railway labour productivity (1993=100)	na	42.8	49.6	48.7
Independent electricity regulator	yes	Electricity tariff, US¢/kWh (collection ratio in %)	0.7 (65)	1.0 (70)	2.3 (75)	2.0 (80)
Financial institutions						
Deposit insurance	no	Number of banks (of which foreign-owned)	18 (3)	18 (3)	18 (3)	20 (3)
Secured transactions law	yes	Asset share of state-owned banks	77.3	69.7	5.0	9.8
Insider dealing prohibited	yes	Bad loans (% of total loans)	92.2	72.0	26.1	7.5
Securities commission	yes	Stock market capitalisation (% of GDP)	na	0.3	0.3	2.8
Fiscal and social sector						
Private pension funds	yes	Tax revenues (% of GDP)	na	15.0	12.7	13.1
Share of population in poverty	76%	Earnings inequality (Gini coefficient)	0.443	0.395	0.428	na

important for the planned liberalisation of the sector. The government intends to replace indirect subsidies to low-income households in the form of low utility prices with direct transfers. A privatisation strategy for the state energy company, Kyrgyzenergo, is due to be submitted to parliament in September 1998. At present, Kyrgyzenergo is about 90% state-owned but it is envisaged that this share would fall to less than 50% after privatisation.

Financial institutions

The banking sector is generally healthy, but lending to enterprises remains minimal.

The central bank has continued to strengthen bank supervision and prudential regulation, including the introduction of Basle capital adequacy standards in mid-1995 and a stepwise increase in minimum capital requirements to about US$ 1 million by January 1999. The sector's health has improved significantly over time, especially given the continuous exit of the least profitable banks. By mid-1998, the 20 banks in the sector were in general conformity with prudential requirements, with relatively high solvency ratios and strict limits on connected lending and foreign currency exposure. The share of non-performing loans in total loans has fallen dramatically since 1996.

The financial sector is still under-developed, but the first private pension fund is now operating.

Despite the increasing health of the banking sector, the loan market remains very thin, with loans to enterprises accounting for less than 5% of GDP. Banks are more active in Treasury bills. Credit lines from the World Bank and the EBRD continue to be a vital source of medium- and long-term capital for SMEs. The non-banking financial sector is also still in its infancy. Trading on the Kyrgyz Stock Exchange in the first four months of 1998 was only US$ 1.5 million. Stock market capitalisation, by contrast, rose to almost a third of GDP. However, more than 90% of market capitalisation is accounted for by the full book value of the state energy monopoly, Kyrgyzenergo, which was "pre-listed" at the end of 1997 for subsequent privatisation, though trading has not begun. The first non-governmental pension fund was registered in April 1998. It has paid-in capital of US$ 100,000 and has so far registered around 1,500 contributors.

Fiscal and social sector

Tax revenues remain low but measures to improve collection are being implemented.

Tax revenues accounted for about 13% of GDP in 1997, a slight improvement from a year earlier, but down from the 15% in 1995. The low tax revenues are partly due to difficulties with tax collection from state enterprises. During 1998, both income tax and VAT collection have improved. The government plans to raise revenues further through a number of measures, including the removal of a wide range of discretionary tax exemptions, simplification and extension of VAT, and increased compliance through closer monitoring of tax returns and payments.

There are severe constraints on public spending.

As a result of the problems in revenue generation and a budget deficit of almost 10% of GDP, public spending has been severely constrained. This is particularly problematic in the social sphere, where a growing funding gap in the Social Fund (the umbrella for pensions, health, employment and other social assistance by the state) has necessitated rising transfers from the budget. In 1997, this budget subsidy amounted to about 1.5% of GDP. In response to these pressures, some pension reforms have been introduced in 1998 including an increase in the pension age.

Poverty remains widespread despite strong economic growth.

GDP has grown rapidly since 1994, but a recent World Bank survey has revealed that the proportion of people living on less than US$ 40 a month has risen from two-fifths in 1993 to three-fifths in 1996. The minimum wage increase to 100 soms (US$ 6) per week in January 1998 is unlikely to have a significant impact on poverty alleviation. The government is preparing a strategy to reduce poverty and enhance the social safety net, and it intends to maintain or increase spending on health and education in real terms.

Latvia

EU Association Agreement† · WTO member · EFTA member

1990

Nov Exchange rate unified

1991

Sept Independence from Soviet Union

Nov Small-scale privatisation begins

1992

Jan Most prices liberalised

Jan First foreign-owned bank opened

Jan VAT introduced

May Central bank law enacted

Oct IAS introduced

1993

Feb Tradability of land enacted

June New currency (lat) introduced

Nov Railways established as joint stock company

Dec T-bills market initiated

1994

Jan BIS capital adequacy enacted

Feb Privatisation law adopted

Feb Privatisation agency established

June Full current account convertibility introduced

1995

Jan First bank privatised

Aug Stock exchange begins trading

1996

June EFTA membership

Sept Bankruptcy law enacted

1997

Apr Latvian Gas privatised

June Competition law enacted

Dec First GDR issue

Key reform challenges

- **Pressing on with the restructuring and privatisation of larger firms and infrastructure would solidify recent progress in enterprise restructuring, which has been evidenced by rapidly growing productivity.**
- **Ongoing efforts to improve prudential regulation of banks and non-bank financial institutions should be continued, especially in light of the negative spill-over effects from the Russian crisis.**
- **The timely introduction of key reform elements in the pension system should be complemented by the establishment of strong institutions to regulate the system.**

Liberalisation

The process of liberalisation is moving forward, spurred by accession efforts to the WTO and the EU.
Latvia is scheduled to accede formally to the WTO by the end of 1998. Upon accession, Latvia has agreed to cap agricultural tariffs at 50%. In support of Latvia's application to the EU, a Competition Council and a Competition Board were established at the beginning of 1998 to strengthen the enforcement of competition legislation.

Privatisation

The privatisation of medium-sized and large enterprises is progressing.
Comprehensive privatisation of medium-sized and large companies began in February 1994, later than in the other two Baltic countries. By June 1998, around 50% of the assets in formerly state-owned enterprises had been sold, including stakes in Ventipils Nafta oil terminal (56%) and Latvian Gas (58%). The Latvian Privatisation Agency adopted a case-by-case approach regarding the privatisation method. In most larger enterprises, several methods were combined, including international tenders, direct sales, public auctions and public offerings on the stock exchange. The focus has recently shifted to preparing the privatisation of infrastructure and to privatising the Latvian Shipping Company (Lasco). Lasco is to be sold to a foreign strategic investor through a capital increase, while minority stakes are to be sold through a local and an international public offering. Around 50 entities including ports, the postal service, the railway company, agricultural research institutions and road maintenance units are excluded from the privatisation list.

The development of land and real estate markets is in progress.
Since 1997 land plots have been offered in conjunction with enterprise privatisation and the process of land registration has notably accelerated. There are plans to privatise half of the local government-owned housing by the end of 1998. Legislation on mortgages was approved in September.

Enterprises

Progress in enterprise restructuring is reflected in rapid growth.
Productivity growth in industry turned positive in 1996 and continued to grow in 1997, reflecting both a further decline of employment and a sharp upturn of output. There are growing capital investments for upgrading facilities and products. Restructuring as measured by productivity growth is most advanced in major export industries such as wood and furniture. Inflows of FDI between 1993 and 1997 amounted to US$ 1 billion. The majority of these investments were made in transport and communications (45%), with industry receiving only 24% of the total flow. Financial discipline of enterprises has improved over recent years. Tax arrears declined from 40% of annual tax revenues in 1996 to 30% in 1997. Subsidies amounted to only 0.4% of GDP in 1997, virtually all directed to agriculture.

The privatisation process has led to concentrated ownership of large firms.
Of the 33 non-financial companies listed on the stock exchange where ownership data is available, more than 60% are majority-owned by other legal entities, often by holding companies. In this sample, firms with significant foreign stakeholdings had the highest net profit to equity ratio in 1997, followed by firms controlled by financial institutions. Firms controlled by managers or the state were less profitable.

Efforts are under way to improve the investment climate.
Organic growth of new enterprises has often been hindered by red tape coupled with inefficient and sometimes corrupt bureaucracy. Latvian authorities are making efforts to overcome these obstacles. New regulations for licensing requirements were introduced in October 1997, halving the number of business activities subject to licensing and improving administration. An anti-corruption programme has been prepared with World Bank assistance.

Infrastructure

Further liberalisation of telecommunications is planned.
While mobile telephony has been liberalised, exclusive rights for the provision of fixed-line services were awarded to Lattelekom, which was established in 1994 as a joint venture between the state (51%) and a consortium of European operators (49%). In return for the fixed-line monopoly, Lattelekom was expected to ensure full digitalisation of the network within eight years. This target no longer appears feasible, partly due to delays in tariff reform. The authorities intend to speed up liberalisation in conjunction with the EU application process. A new telecoms

			1994	1995	1996	1997
Liberalisation						
Exchange rate regime	fixed	Share of administered prices in CPI	na	16.6	17.8	19.6
Current account convertibility	full	Administered prices in "EBRD-15" basket	2	2	2	2
Interest rate liberalisation	full	Share of trade in GDP	32.1	37.3	36.8	40.9
Wage regulation	no	Tariff revenue (% of imports)	3.1	1.8	1.5	1.4
Privatisation						
Primary privatisation method	vouchers	Private sector share in GDP	55	60	60	60
Secondary privatisation method	direct sales	Share of assets privatised	0.1	8.2	19.3	38.2
Tradability of land rights	full except foreigners	Privatisation revenues (% of GDP)	0.34	0.38	0.18	0.97
Enterprises						
Protection of shareholder rights	partly effective	Budgetary subsidies (% of GDP)	0.2	0.4	0.3	0.4
Bankruptcy proceedings	partly effective	Credit to enterprises (% of GDP)	16.4	7.8	7.2	10.7
Competition office	yes	Labour productivity in industry (% change)	9.5	-1.0	8.6	28.0
Infrastructure						
Independent telecoms regulator	yes	Main telephone lines per 100 inhabitants	25.8	28.0	29.8	30.2
Separation of railway accounts	yes	Railway labour productivity (1989=100)	48.8	50.2	65.5	75.4
Independent electricity regulator	no	Electricity tariff, US¢/kWh (collection ratio in %)	3.2 (85)	3.6 (85)	5.6 (94)	6.1 (98)
Financial institutions						
Deposit insurance	yes	Number of banks (of which foreign-owned)	56 (na)	42 (11)	35 (14)	32 (15)
Secured transactions law	restricted	Asset share of state-owned banks	7.2	9.9	6.9	6.8
Insider dealing prohibited	yes	Bad loans (% of total loans)	11.0	19.0	20.0	10.0
Securities commission	yes	Stock market capitalisation (% of GDP)	na	na	3.0	6.2
Fiscal and social sector						
Private pension funds	no	Tax revenues (% of GDP)	30.9	32.4	33.1	34.0
Share of population in poverty	23%	Earnings inequality (Gini coefficient)	0.325	0.346	0.349	na

law is being drafted which would strengthen regulation and introduce competition in fixed-line services. There are also plans to sell down the state's minority stake in Lattelekom.

The energy sector has moved towards full cost recovery, but privatisation remains unresolved.
In 1994, Latvian authorities adopted a package of measures to reduce customer arrears and to bring energy tariffs to full cost-recovery levels. The payments discipline has improved, with collection ratios increasing from 80% in 1993 to 98% in 1997. The pre-privatisation strategy of Latvenergo remains controversial. The proposal of the Latvian Privatisation Agency is based on the separation of power generation and distribution before privatisation. Others prefer privatising Latvenergo as a vertically integrated monopoly. In March 1998, the privatisation of the utility was suspended, pending further consideration of both proposals.

A new railways law sets the legal framework for wide-ranging reforms.
A new railway law conforming with EU legislation is to become effective in November 1998. Its key provisions include the establishment of a quasi-independent regulator, third-party access to the railway infrastructure, establishment of a Railway Fund to finance infrastructure development and the introduction of public service contracts for non-profitable passenger services. These contracts between Latvian Railways and the state and local governments will reimburse the net cost of providing passenger services and thus eliminate the cross-subsidy currently paid by freight revenues. At present, passenger services account for about one fifth of total revenues and cost recovery for these services is less than 50%.

Financial institutions

Regulation and supervision continue to be strengthened.
Following the 1995-96 banking sector crisis, prudential regulation and supervision of banks has been tightened. The expansion of leasing companies and other non-bank financial institutions, mostly affiliated with existing commercial banks, has prompted an amendment to the Credit Institutions Act in March 1998, to supervise banking groups on a consolidated basis from January 1999. The government also set up a working group to develop coordinated monitoring of all financial instruments offered by the growing number of "universal" banks. A deposit insurance scheme became effective in October 1998, bringing legislation in line with EU requirements. The high Russian exposure of some Latvian banks has led to sharp losses in the aftermath of the Russian crisis and to the bankruptcy of the ninth-largest bank. In response to these problems, the central bank plans to tighten regulation regarding regional exposure.

The stock market has become more active.
Trading volumes and market capitalisation on the Riga Stock Exchange expanded rapidly in 1996 and 1997. In mid-1998, market capitalisation amounted to 11% of GDP, up from 3% at the end of 1996. Over the same period the number of listed shares increased from 34 to 65. After rapid growth of share prices until October 1997, equities started to follow the downturn in Asian and Russian stock markets.

Fiscal and social sector

Further progress is made on pension reform, though with difficulties in implementation.
In 1996, pension expenditure reached 11% of GDP and the ratio of pensioners to contributors was 80%. Latvia is gradually moving away from the "pay-as-you-go" scheme towards a mixed system. Legislation for the operation of private pension funds that would collect voluntary private contributions became effective in July 1998. Transition to the new system has been hampered by the lack of a public information campaign and a fully equipped agency to handle regulation and administration. The underdevelopment of local capital markets is inhibiting the effectiveness of the new system.

First steps have been taken to streamline the public sector.
Salaries in the public sector are low and staff turnover is high, which adversely affects the state's administrative capacity. To tackle these problems, the government has completed the first civil service census and prepared a programme for the reorganisation of the public sector. The programme aims to eliminate duplication between various agencies, cut staff and contract out some services. A restructuring scheme for state ministries has already been implemented on a pilot basis.

† Signed on 12 June 1995, currently in the process of ratification.

Lithuania

EU Association Agreement† · WTO observer · EFTA member

1990

- Feb Central Bank established
- Mar Independence from Soviet Union

1991

- Feb Voucher privatisation begins
- July Restitution law adopted

1992

- Apr Export surrender requirement abolished
- Sept Two-tiered banking system re-established
- Sept Bankruptcy law enacted
- Sept Stock exchange established
- Oct Most prices liberalised
- Nov Competition law enacted
- Nov Competition agency established

1993

- July Litas becomes sole legal tender
- July New trade regime adopted
- Sept Stock exchange begins trading
- Nov Free trade agreement with Russia

1994

- Apr Currency board introduced
- May VAT introduced
- May Full current account convertibility introduced
- July T-bills market initiated
- July Land law enacted
- Oct Export duties abolished

1995

- Jan EFTA membership
- June First phase of privatisation completed
- July Cash privatisation begins
- Dec Financial sector turmoil
- Dec First sovereign Eurobond

1996

- Mar BIS capital adequacy enacted
- July First GDR issue

1997

- Feb First corporate Eurobond
- Oct New bankruptcy law enacted

Key reform challenges

- **As the focus of privatisation shifts to infrastructure, strengthening the enforcement capacity of regulatory institutions will be a crucial factor determining its success.**
- **Despite the recent success of privatisation tenders, the introduction of direct sales has raised concerns about the transparency and consistency of the government's role in the process.**
- **Following the banking crisis of 1996, the planned privatisations of Agricultural Bank and State Savings Bank would contribute to further strengthening of the banking system.**

Liberalisation

Lithuania has maintained a stable exchange rate and an open trade regime.
The Litas Stability Law of 1994 requires full reserve cover of base money, as in other countries with a currency board, though it does provide some flexibility. The fixed exchange rate remains a key component of the trade and exchange rate regime. Lithuania's application for WTO membership is at an advanced stage, although concerns about relatively high customs duties on grain, oil products and sugar have pushed back the expected entry date to mid-1999.

Harmonisation of competition policy with EU standards is in progress.
Lithuania is responding to two key elements of the EU's directives on competition policy: the monitoring of state aid and anti-trust legislation. Following the requirements under the EU Association Agreement, the role of monitoring of state aid policies has been delegated to the Competition Office. A new Law on Competition is expected to be adopted in late 1998, harmonising the legislative framework with EU standards. In 1997, the Competition Office investigated 44 cases and imposed 36 fines totalling almost 800,000 litas (US$ 200,000).

Privatisation

Successful tenders of strategic enterprises have increased revenues.
After privatising 30% of all state enterprise assets by means of voucher privatisation through mid-1995, the strategy in the second phase of privatisation has shifted to cash sales. Revenues were initially small due to the unattractiveness of the assets offered and the conditions attached to sales. In 1997 and the first half of 1998, however, privatisation revenues have grown substantially following the inclusion of 14 strategic enterprises, mainly in infrastructure, which were offered in international investment tenders. The sale of Lithuanian Telecommunications in July 1997 alone raised US$ 510 million, increasing total revenues from cash privatisation to US$ 564 million. Further sales agreements have recently been concluded and could raise cumulative privatisation revenues to over US$ 700 million by the end of 1998.

The reliance on direct negotiations for further privatisations raises concerns over political interference.
In November 1997, an existing legal requirement that all privatisations go through tenders was abandoned. Since then, the government has entered into direct negotiations with an American investor in the planned sale of significant minority stakes in the main oil pipeline, an oil refinery and the oil terminal at Butinge (currently under construction). While direct negotiations may accelerate cash privatisation, they also provide an opportunity for the authorities to intervene in the outcomes of privatisation in a way that could affect the attractiveness of future privatisations.

Enterprises

Structures of corporate governance are controlled largely by insiders.
Voucher privatisation led to the transfer of up to 50% of enterprise shares to employees and management at preferential prices. Insider ownership was further consolidated through the post-privatisation dilution of residual state shares via the formation of manager-controlled investment companies that participated in the tenders of remaining state shares of large enterprises. In some cases, managers have transformed privatised companies into closed corporations to fend off take-over bids. Foreign investment has been limited largely to retail trade and light industry, though recently it has begun to extend to other sectors. However, while enterprises with majority state ownership have tended to perform below the average for all enterprises, there is no strong evidence that insider ownership has negatively affected enterprise performance.

Enterprise restructuring has varied across sectors.
In 1997, the source of productivity growth in industry shifted from labour shedding to output growth. However, this general trend masks significant sectoral differences in the economy. Output growth is the main source of productivity improvements in labour-intensive sectors, while employment reduction has been the driving force behind productivity growth in the manufacturing and transport sectors. Investment levels and profit margins also differ across sectors, with food processing, apparel and chemicals recording the best performance. Lithuania's largest industrial company, an oil refinery, remains subject to demand constraints and is operating substantially below capacity. The superior performance of labour-intensive sectors reflects the reorientation of exports in line with the country's comparative advantage.

Liberalisation			1994	1995	1996	1997
Exchange rate regime	currency board	Share of administered prices in CPI	na	na	na	na
Current account convertibility	full	Administered prices in "EBRD-15" basket	6	2	2	2
Interest rate liberalisation	full	Share of trade in GDP	50.4	50.7	48.9	49.9
Wage regulation	no	Tariff revenue (% of imports)	3.2	1.4	1.2	1.3
Privatisation						
Primary privatisation method	vouchers	Private sector share in GDP	50	55	65	70
Secondary privatisation method	direct sales	Number of medium/large firms privatised	537	440	11	46
Tradability of land rights	full except foreigners	Privatisation revenues (% of GDP)	0.40	0.16	0.10	0.27
Enterprises						
Protection of shareholder rights	partly effective	Budgetary subsidies (% of GDP)	1.7	1.1	1.3	0.9
Bankruptcy proceedings	partly effective	Credit to enterprises (% of GDP)	17.8	15.9	11.7	10.9
Competition office	yes	Labour productivity in industry (% change)	-12.1	12.0	8.5	4.6
Infrastructure						
Independent telecoms regulator	yes	Main telephone lines per 100 inhabitants	24.1	25.4	26.8	28.3
Separation of railway accounts	yes	Railway labour productivity (1989=100)	35.4	32.3	35.6	37.9
Independent electricity regulator	yes	Electricity tariff, US¢/kWh (collection ratio in %)	na	3.6 (85)	3.8 (85)	4.0 (85)
Financial institutions						
Deposit insurance	yes	Number of banks (of which foreign-owned)	22 (0)	12 (0)	12 (3)	11 (4)
Secured transactions law	yes	Asset share of state-owned banks	48.0	62.5	54.9	48.8
Insider dealing prohibited	yes	Bad loans (% of total loans)	27.0	16.7	32.2	28.3
Securities commission	yes	Stock market capitalisation (% of GDP)	2.5	6.3	15.9	22.8
Fiscal and social sector						
Private pension funds	no	Tax revenues (% of GDP)	31.4	31.6	28.8	32.1
Share of population in poverty	46%	Earnings inequality (Gini coefficient)	0.349	0.341	0.350	na

Financial discipline has strengthened, but bankruptcy procedures still face administrative bottlenecks.
With the reduction of direct subsidies, new off-budget support to enterprises emerged in the form of tax exemptions and arrears. The stock of tax arrears was 3% of GDP by the end of 1997. However, tax exemptions for "special enterprises" expired at the end of 1996, reducing the implicit government subsidies. The Bankruptcy Law, which became effective in October 1997, streamlines court procedures and better prioritises creditor claims. However, the number of concluded bankruptcy cases remains small due to the lack of qualified administrators.

Infrastructure

Lithuanian Telecommunications was sold to a strategic investor in mid-1998.
The telecoms sector in Lithuania has been liberalised since 1995, except for the operation of fixed-line networks and the provision of national fixed-line telephone services. A new Law on Telecommunications was adopted in June 1998, ensuring equal access to interconnection networks, in line with EU requirements. The law also establishes an independent regulator, although the setting of maximum tariffs remains the responsibility of the government. A controversial aspect of the law is the granting of exclusivity rights for the provision of fixed-line services to Lithuanian Telecommunications (LT) until December 2002. The exclusivity clause contributed to the successful sale of a 60% stake in LT to a Swedish-Finnish consortium in June, the largest privatisation to date.

The unbundling of the heat and electricity sectors is proceeding, albeit slowly.
Tariff reform and tariff increases to cost-recovery levels in electricity and district heating have been the first steps in restructuring the energy sector. A government commission, established in November 1996 to advise on tariff policy, has devised a pricing formula based on operating cost plus a profit margin. Some of the assets of the state-owned energy monopoly have been decentralised and transferred to the municipalities, which are now responsible for the provision of district heating services. The city of Kaunas is considering the introduction of a private concessionaire to operate its system. Plans also exist to separate and privatise the power distribution networks from Lithuanian Energy. However, privatisation in the energy sector will require further improvements in the regulatory framework.

Financial institutions

The liquidation and privatisation of remaining state-owned banks is leading to a consolidation of the banking sector.
As of mid-1998, 10 commercial banks (two state-owned, four domestic private, and four foreign-controlled) were operating, one less than at the end of 1997. Concentration is high, with the four largest institutions holding 85% of all banking sector assets. The country's third-largest bank, the state-owned State Commercial Bank (SCB) was liquidated in March 1998, after a privatisation attempt failed to attract bidders. Taking into account the transfer of SCB's performing assets to the state-owned Savings Bank, the share of assets controlled by the two remaining state banks has declined to 45% by mid-1998. Plans to sell the remaining state shares in Agricultural Bank (87%) have been postponed in the aftermath of the Russian crisis. The government also plans to privatise the Savings Bank in 1999.

A legislative amendment gives more regulatory powers to the Securities Commission.
The regulatory framework for Lithuania's securities market has improved as a result of amendments to the Securities Law. The amendments require more comprehensive disclosure requirements for listed companies, provide sanctions against insider trading, streamline trading lists, and enhance the supervisory and sanctioning powers of the Securities Commission. In August 1998, there were seven listed companies with substantial trading volumes (on the "official list") and 56 other listed companies with smaller trading volumes (on the "current list"). After a strong expansion in 1997, with trading volume up 480% and a sharp increase in the number of listed companies, the Lithuanian stock index has fallen substantially in 1998, following the crises in Russia and other emerging markets.

Fiscal and social sector

Revenue shortfalls in the Social Security Fund highlight the need for comprehensive pension reform.
The Social Security Fund, SoDra, has been facing a financing gap since 1996, which has been covered by short-term borrowing from commercial banks, a costly and potentially unsustainable solution. A reform of the current pay-as-you-go pension system – including the tightening of eligibility criteria, changes in the indexation formula, and increases in the retirement age – will be required to restore SoDra's balance. The government has drafted legislation to establish private open-ended pension funds to serve as depositories for voluntary retirement savings.

† Signed on 12 June 1995, currently in the process of ratification.

Moldova

EU Partnership and Cooperation Agreement · CIS member · WTO observer

1991

Aug Independence from Soviet Union

1992

Jan Most prices liberalised

Jan State trading monopoly abolished

Feb Competition law adopted

June New tax system introduced

Sept Exchange rate unified

1993

Mar Cash privatisation begins

Mar Privatisation with patrimonial bonds begins

Apr Most quantity controls on exports removed

Nov New currency (leu) introduced

1994

July Securities and exchange commission established

1995

Jan VAT introduced

Mar T-bills market initiated

June Full current account convertibility introduced

June Stock exchange established

June Trade in listed shares begins

June Enterprise restructuring agency established

1996

Jan New central bank law becomes effective

Jan New financial institutions law becomes effective

1997

June First sovereign Eurobond

July New VAT law enacted

July New land law adopted

Sept New privatisation law adopted

Key reform challenges

- **The reform process would gain new momentum through an acceleration of privatisation, including international tenders of energy and large companies.**
- **Further progress is also required in the restructuring of loss-making firms, combined with effective implementation of the new bankruptcy rules.**
- **Fiscal and social reform, including increased revenue collection from the corporate sector and further cuts in subsidies to agriculture, would help reduce the large budget deficit.**
- **The establishment of a market-oriented agricultural sector would be strengthened by further progress in the restructuring and privatisation of large state farms and by the implementation of an effectively functioning land market.**

Liberalisation

Some adjustments to the foreign trade regime have been made, but WTO accession is not imminent.
Moldova has a fairly liberal trade regime with an unweighted average import tariff of 9%. Negotiations for accession to the World Trade Organisation (WTO) commenced in mid-1997. Progress has been made in adapting the trade regime to WTO requirements. Discriminatory application of excise duties has been ended; rules of origin and customs valuation consistent with the WTO have been enacted; a law on government procurement through competitive selection has been introduced; and a number of intellectual property agreements have been undertaken. Further progress is required, including the abolition of VAT exemption for domestically produced agricultural goods and the introduction of a new customs classification. Moldova's application for developing country status has been rejected.

Privatisation

Progress in privatisation has recently been slow, with little foreign interest.
By the beginning of 1997, 60% of industry, 70% of trade and services, 44% of construction and transport, 40% of agricultural products and 85% of public housing had been privatised. There was little further progress during 1997 and the first half of 1998, when only a fraction of the small enterprises offered in cash auctions were actually sold, and not one large enterprise privatised. Foreign interest has been low, following the cancelled tender for the state tobacco company in 1996. Minimum prices in auctions have often been prohibitively high, publicity has been poor and there have been problems with the legal framework. Three important candidates for immediate privatisation through international tender are the wine, cement and tobacco industries.

Land reform has moved forward.
Individual private farms accounted for about 10% of total farmland at the beginning of 1998, while most land is owned by collective farms, joint-stock companies with state ownership and cooperatives. Land was made tradable in 1997 through the new Law on the Normative Price of Land and the establishment of a national land cadastre for registering and titling land. Furthermore, land can now be used as collateral following changes in the Collateral Law in 1997. These improvements should lead to the evolution of an agricultural land market. Purchases of land under non-farm enterprises from the state have been slow, however, partly due to the high prices demanded by the state and partly because companies with partial state ownership are not allowed to purchase land.

Enterprises

Enterprise restructuring is continuing, partly through the state-run ARIA programme.
Employment in manufacturing fell by 10% in 1997, due to enterprise closure and restructuring, and the decline in output slowed. These factors led to positive productivity growth. However, dispersed share ownership gives a high degree of insider control, which stands in the way of enterprise restructuring. About a third of enterprises remain loss-making. Since the Bankruptcy Law was amended in mid-1997, proceedings have started against only three companies and these were initiated by the state rather than creditors. Some restructuring is taking place through the state Agency for Enterprise Restructuring (ARIA) which works with large firms heavily indebted to the state. Restructuring under the ARIA programme involves debt restructuring (including temporary freezing of tax liabilities), spin-offs of non-core assets, staff reductions, the establishment of marketing and trade departments, and the introduction of quality controls. Of the 60 companies that had registered with ARIA, 28 had completed the programme by mid-1998.

Restructuring of large farms is being expanded.
The share of agriculture in GDP was 30% in 1997; 50% with the inclusion of agro-processing. As of October 1997, agriculture and agro-processing had arrears of about US$ 800 million to the budget, social fund, commercial banks, workers and suppliers. The profitability of large farms rose from an average of -10% in 1996 to 4% in 1997, though this includes direct and indirect subsidies. As of early 1998, 70 out of 1,000 large farms had been broken up and privatised under a pilot project undertaken with the assistance of USAID. This programme has now been extended and the intention is to break up and then privatise 650 farms by 1999.

Liberalisation			1994	1995	1996	1997
Exchange rate regime	managed float	Share of administered prices in CPI	na	na	na	na
Current account convertibility	full	Administered prices in "EBRD-15" basket	0	0	0	0
Interest rate liberalisation	full	Share of trade in GDP	45.8	47.2	48.4	45.2
Wage regulation	yes	Tariff revenue (% of imports)	1.1	1.4	2.0	2.4
Privatisation						
Primary privatisation method	vouchers	Private sector share in GDP	20	30	40	45
Secondary privatisation method	direct sales	Number of small firms privatised	na	na	na	90
Tradability of land rights	full	Privatisation revenues (% of GDP)	na	0.32	0.43	0.81
Enterprises						
Protection of shareholder rights	partly effective	Budgetary subsidies (% of GDP)	na	na	na	na
Bankruptcy proceedings	partly effective	Credit to enterprises (% of GDP)	10.6	13.7	15.1	15.1
Competition office	no	Labour productivity in industry (% change)	-23.6	12.0	15.6	na
Infrastructure						
Independent telecoms regulator	no	Main telephone lines per 100 inhabitants	12.3	13.0	14.0	14.6
Separation of railway accounts	no	Railway labour productivity (1989=100)	32.1	28.3	26.5	27.6
Independent electricity regulator	yes	Electricity tariff, US¢/kWh (collection ratio in %)	4.3 (64)	3.2 (92)	3.1 (87)	4.7 (92)
Financial institutions						
Deposit insurance	no	Number of banks (of which foreign-owned)	21 (1)	22 (1)	21 (2)	22 (4)
Secured transactions law	yes	Asset share of state-owned banks	0.0	0.0	0.0	0.0
Insider dealing prohibited	yes	Bad loans (% of total loans)	16.3	9.2	17.3	10.2
Securities commission	yes	Stock market capitalisation (% of GDP)	na	0.00	0.02	0.03
Fiscal and social sector						
Private pension funds	no	Tax revenues (% of GDP)	25.1	28.8	27.4	29.3
Share of population in poverty	65%	Earnings inequality (Gini coefficient)	0.379	0.390	na	na

Infrastructure

Efforts to privatise the state telecommunications company continue.
A 40% stake in MoldTelecom, the state monopoly for fixed line telephone services, was offered for international tender in 1997. One of the two bidders, a French-Danish consortium, withdrew from the tender late in 1997 and the price offered by the other bidder, the Greek telecom company OTE, was considered too low by parliament. Following the breakdown of negotiations with OTE in mid-1998, the government now intends to offer 51% of MoldTelecom in 1999. An international tender to set up a GSM mobile telephone network was won by a joint venture between a French, a Romanian and two Moldovan companies, which started operations in February 1998.

The gas industry is to be consolidated and privatised.
In March 1998, parliament approved a plan to consolidate the gas industry into one company, Moldova Gas, comprising the Moldovan and Trans-Dniestrian distribution networks and a pipeline joint venture with Gazprom. The new company would be owned 50% by Gazprom (in a debt-for-equity swap), 36% by the government and 14% by the secessionist Trans-Dniestria region. The Gazprom stake only partially settles Moldova's US$ 650 million arrears with the company and in June 1998 – as a result of a continuing payments dispute – Gazprom cut Moldova's gas supplies in half.

Electricity prices have been increased.
Electricity prices were increased twice in 1997 and price differentials between customer categories were diminished, reducing the cross-subsidy from industry to households. A third price rise to the level of full cost recovery is planned, though no date has been specified. There are proposals to privatise five electricity distribution companies and three combined heat and power generating plants, the latter satisfying around 25% of Moldova's power demand in winter. The first tenders are expected in late 1998. An independent energy regulating body, set up in August 1997, has yet to assume any price-setting powers.

Financial institutions

Prudential regulations and accounting standards have been improved.
Moldova's banking sector is relatively healthy compared with other countries in the CIS. Minimum capital requirements were doubled to lei 8 million (US$ 1.7 million) in January 1998. Capital adequacy standards were raised to 8% of risk-weighted assets. As of end-1997, all 22 banks were in compliance with these new standards and average capital adequacy was 24%. In October 1997, accounting procedures in line with International Accounting Standards were introduced. Around 10% of total loans are non-performing. A number of banks which could not fulfil central bank standards were closed in 1997 and two new banks were opened. There are no state-owned commercial banks in Moldova.

New regulation on investment funds has been enacted.
The number of shares traded on the Moldovan stock exchange rose from US$ 2.5 million in 1996 to about US$ 40 million in 1997. Around 70% of transactions involved share swapping between Privatisation Investment Funds which followed a new law limiting the holding of a fund in a firm to a maximum of 25%. Other non-bank institutions remain underdeveloped. The insurance sector collected premiums of less than 1% of GDP in 1997 and there are very few private pensions.

Fiscal and social sector

Some efforts have been made to reduce wage and pension arrears and to streamline the tax system.
The general public deficit rose to 7.5% of GDP in 1997, despite unbudgeted receipts of US$ 40 million from the sale of 21 MIG fighters to the USA. In response to the persistent fiscal imbalance, the government froze public sector wages and pensions for 1997 at 1996 levels. Slow progress in energy, health and education reform has hampered further expenditure rationalisation. The state has made efforts to reduce its payables, leading to 50% reductions in wage and pension arrears in 1997. As of April 1998, the state owed US$ 50 million in overdue wages and US$ 90 million in overdue pensions. Corporate tax revenues fell significantly in 1997, partly due to tax amnesties and to weak implementation. Revenues from indirect taxes rose after petrol and diesel excise taxes were doubled in 1997 and the excise taxes on wine and cigarettes were raised. New corporate and personal income tax codes were introduced in January 1998, reducing the number of tax brackets from four to two (20% and 32%) and broadening the tax base.

Poland

EU Association Agreement · OECD member · WTO member · EFTA member · CEFTA member

1990
- Jan Most prices liberalised
- Jan Most foreign trade controls removed
- Jan Small-scale privatisation begins
- Jan Competition law adopted
- Jan Competition agency established
- Apr Privatisation law adopted

1991
- Apr Stock exchange begins trading
- May T-bills market initiated

1992
- Jan Tax reform
- Mar EU Association Agreement
- Dec Banking law amended

1993
- Feb Financial restructuring law adopted
- Mar CEFTA membership
- Apr Mass privatisation programme begins
- Apr First bank privatised
- May BIS capital adequacy enacted
- July VAT introduced
- Nov EFTA membership

1994
- Sept IAS introduced
- Dec National Investment Funds (NIFs) established

1995
- Jan Wage restrictions redefined
- May Agricultural import restrictions changed
- June First sovereign Eurobond
- June Full current account convertibility introduced
- July WTO membership
- July State enterprises allocated to NIFs
- July Railway law adopted

1996
- Apr First corporate Eurobond
- Aug New privatisation law adopted
- Nov OECD membership

1997
- May Energy law adopted
- June Securities law amended
- Aug Pension reform begins
- Dec Electricity law adopted

Key reform challenges

- **A new government and the beginning of EU accession negotiations have given a new impetus to structural reforms, though major investments will be required to comply with EU directives, especially in infrastructure.**
- **The new government has ambitious plans for privatisation of large enterprises, but implementation so far has been slow. Restructuring of difficult sectors – coal, steel and agriculture – is a priority but proposed measures have met with resistance.**
- **The completion of bank restructuring and privatisation would enhance competition and alleviate some of the remaining inefficiencies in the banking sector.**

Liberalisation

EU accession negotiations began in March 1998.
Among the key challenges for accession are: the restructuring of the agricultural, coal and steel sectors; the strengthening of environmental standards; and the reform of regional and local government. The World Bank has estimated the direct costs of EU directives at US$ 6.6 billion over the period 1998-2000 (approximately 1.5% of GDP on an annual basis).

New legislation paves the way for full capital account liberalisation.
In September 1998, a new foreign exchange bill came into effect, radically liberalising the foreign exchange regime and setting the groundwork for full capital account liberalisation by 2000. This includes full liberalisation of all current and long-term capital transactions as well as safeguard mechanisms to prevent destabilisation of the zloty.

Privatisation

Privatisation guidelines call for the sale of most remaining state-owned enterprises by 2001.
The government unveiled in May 1998 its draft privatisation guidelines through 2001, which call for the sale of most remaining state assets, placing particular emphasis on large enterprises in infrastructure, heavy industry, mining and finance. There remain about 2,863 state-owned enterprises, with an estimated book value equivalent to 30-35% of GDP. About three-quarters of the top Polish companies by turnover are still state-owned. Particularly large privatisation revenues (PLN 13-14 billion) are expected for 1999, with the scheduled sales of parts of the energy, coal and chemical sectors as well as the state insurance company (PZU). Privatisation receipts increased to 1.5% of GDP in 1997.

Enterprises

Plans are being prepared for restructuring "difficult" sectors.
Many of the remaining large state-owned companies are in problem sectors – including defence, hard-coal mining, steel, chemicals and shipbuilding – which have been a continued drain on public resources. These sectors will also be a focus of EU accession negotiations. The government has made the restructuring and privatisation of these difficult sectors a major priority. Plans for restructuring the steel and coal sectors were approved in mid-1998. Nearly a third of all coal mines – roughly 70 mines – are to be closed. Employment in the steel sector will be halved through a market-driven consolidation, while keeping output constant. Two of the largest steel plants are being prepared for privatisation.

Tax arrears rose in 1997.
At the end of 1997, the total stock of arrears on taxes and social contributions amounted to almost 6% of general government revenue. The share of arrears on social contributions has been increasing over time, amounting to almost half of total arrears by the end of 1997. Nineteen large state-owned firms, mostly in heavy industry, accounted for over a third of economy-wide arrears on social contributions.

Progress on corporate governance remains slow.
The financial performance of the private sector continues to lag behind the public sector, reflecting institutional weaknesses associated with the methods of privatisation and the functioning of corporate governance. Corporate governance is regulated primarily by the 1934 Commercial Code, based largely on German law. Supervisory boards have responsibility for approving companies' by-laws and statutes, approving annual financial statements, and endorsing profit distributions, but have little direct influence over strategic management decisions. Companies are not required to send shareholder proxies prior to meetings. There have been few examples of activism by outside shareholders.

Infrastructure

The 1997 Energy Law has paved the way for accelerated reform in the sector.
The law provides for the unbundling of electric power generation, transmission and distribution and opens parts of the sector to competition and private sector participation. It gives the government two years to abandon subsidies to district heating, natural gas and electricity, and also establishes an independent Energy Regulatory Agency. The first foreign investor in the Polish power industry was Electricité de France, which bought 55% of the Elektrocieplownia Krakow heat-and-power generator at the end of 1997.

			1994	1995	1996	1997
Liberalisation						
Exchange rate regime	crawling peg, with band	Share of administered prices in CPI	12.0	12.0	11.6	10.6
Current account convertibility	full	Administered prices in "EBRD-15" basket	na	na	na	na
Interest rate liberalisation	full	Share of trade in GDP	18.8	20.0	21.2	24.2
Wage regulation	yes	Tariff revenue (% of imports)	18.5	15.2	10.7	na
Privatisation						
Primary privatisation method	direct sales	Private sector share in GDP	55	60	60	65
Secondary privatisation method	MEBOs	Share of medium/large firms privatised	21.8	27.0	34.1	35.7
Tradability of land rights	full except foreigners	Privatisation revenues (% of GDP)	0.76	0.92	1.03	1.47
Enterprises						
Protection of shareholder rights	partly effective	Budgetary subsidies (% of GDP)	3.3	2.9	2.5	na
Bankruptcy proceedings	effective	Credit to enterprises (% of GDP)	18.2	17.5	18.8	19.8
Competition office	yes	Labour productivity in industry (% change)	13.9	7.0	9.9	13.9
Infrastructure						
Independent telecoms regulator	no	Main telephone lines per 100 inhabitants	13.1	14.8	16.9	19.4
Separation of railway accounts	yes	Railway labour productivity (1989=100)	78.4	83.0	84.4	87.4
Independent electricity regulator	yes	Electricity tariff, US¢/kWh (collection ratio in %)	4.9 (90)	6.2 (95)	6.7 (97)	6.2 (97)
Financial institutions						
Deposit insurance	yes	Number of banks (of which foreign-owned)	82 (11)	81 (18)	81 (25)	83 (29)
Secured transactions law	yes	Asset share of state-owned banks	72.3	67.8	62.9	47.5
Insider dealing prohibited	yes	Bad loans (% of total loans)	28.7	20.9	13.2	10.4
Securities commission	yes	Stock market capitalisation (% of GDP)	3.8	3.8	7.0	9.8
Fiscal and social sector						
Private pension funds	no	Tax revenues (% of GDP)	39.6	38.7	38.3	na
Share of population in poverty	13%	Earnings inequality (Gini coefficient)	0.281	0.290	na	na

Restructuring of the railway sector has begun.
The Transport Ministry awarded the first licences for nationwide railway services to independent operators in June 1998. This involves a gradual move away from the State Railway's monopoly and a harmonisation with EU legislation.

Financial institutions

Despite some progress, competition in the banking sector is still limited.
While the portfolios of most major banks have been cleaned up, further development has been hampered by the slow pace of privatisation and by restrictions on foreign entry and competition. Foreign banks have been required, in most cases, to take over existing troubled Polish banks in order to obtain licences. However, remaining restrictions on the entry of foreign banks will be lifted in 1999. Polish banks will also face new competition from pension funds over domestic investment opportunities. Inefficiencies remain, as is illustrated by the slow adjustment of bank lending rates to changes in central bank rates.

The pace of bank privatisation is slowly picking up.
In one of the largest privatisations to date, the state floated 85% of the shares of Bank Handlowy in 1997. In October 1997, a public offering was held for 70% of the shares of another sizeable bank, PBK-Warsaw, albeit after the first tender was cancelled by the previous government. The state continues to own or retain significant stakes in several large banks - Bank Przemyslowo Handlowy (BPH), PKO-BP (the savings bank) and BGZ (the agricultural bank). The strategic approach of the authorities has been to rehabilitate and recapitalise banks prior to privatisation. Preparations are being made to sell off the state's stake of around 40% in BPH. There are no immediate plans for the rehabilitation and privatisation of the savings bank and the agricultural bank, both of which are in need of extensive restructuring.

The insurance market is still dominated by a loss-making state-owned firm.
The state-owned non-life insurer, PZU, and its life insurance subsidiary continue to dominate the insurance market. Under the 1995 Insurance Law and the EU Association Agreement, branches and agencies of foreign insurance companies will be granted access to the Polish market in 1999. To prepare for the increase in competition, the government is planning to restructure and privatise the loss-making PZU.

The securities market has been growing, but remains small.
Poland's regulations in this sector are now close to international standards and comply mostly with EU directives. A revised law on public trading in securities came into effect in early 1998 creating a legal framework for collective investment vehicles, including open-end funds, closed-end funds and mixed funds. A legal framework for derivative trading has been introduced and it has become easier for listed companies to issue stocks. Despite sustained growth, however, the market remains small, with a stock market capitalisation equivalent to nearly 10% of GDP. Initial public offerings in 1997 raised about 1% of GDP. There are no publicly traded corporate bonds and only a few municipal bonds.

Fiscal and social sector

The government has proposed new legislation to streamline local government.
The reform effectively represents a return to the set-up prevailing until the mid-1970s. This will involve a significant decentralisation of public finances, shifting revenues equivalent to 10% of GDP to local and regional authorities and creating a new tier of government. This new layer of government will play a key role in the decentralisation of the management of health care and education.

Tax reform is aimed at reducing the high tax burden and moving towards EU standards.
The government's medium-term programme involves gradual cuts in the three rates of personal income tax, from 20%, 32% and 44% in 1997 to 19%, 30% and 40% in 1998. The corporate profits tax rate will be cut by 2% a year, falling to 32% in 2000. Further reform plans include a reduction of tax breaks. An increasing share of revenue will be provided by indirect taxes. VAT rates have been increased for a number of items with lower rates than the standard 22%. Reforms are under way to harmonise tax laws and accounting regulations with EU standards. Major adjustments in excise taxes are still required.

A multi-pillar pension system will begin operation in 1999.
The new system is to comprise three pillars: a reformed pay-as-you-go social insurance fund, mandatory pension funds and additional voluntary insurance. The pensionable age will be set at 62 for both men and women. Three of the key bills underlying the reform were passed in 1997, and three more bills, building the oversight and regulatory capabilities, were under examination by parliament in mid-1998.

Romania

EU Association Agreement · WTO member · EFTA member · CEFTA member

1990

Dec Two-tiered banking system established

1991

Mar Railway law adopted

Apr Banking legislation adopted

Aug Privatisation law enacted

Sept Mass voucher privatisation begins

1992

Jan Small-scale privatisation begins

May State trading monopoly abolished

1993

May EFTA member

July VAT introduced

1994

Jan BIS capital adequacy enacted

Mar T-bills market initiated

Dec Securities and exchange commission established

1995

Jan WTO membership

Mar New privatisation law adopted

June Bankruptcy law enacted

June New restitution law adopted

July Most prices liberalised

Aug Second voucher privatisation begins

Nov Stock exchange begins trading

1996

Oct OTC market established

1997

Jan Competition law enacted

Feb First corporate Eurobond

Feb Enterprise liquidation programme begins

Mar Exchange rate unified

June First sovereign Eurobond

July CEFTA membership

Key reform challenges

- **The pace of enterprise restructuring and privatisation will have to accelerate in order to strengthen market-based incentives, eliminate tax arrears and restart economic growth.**
- **The state-dominated banking sector, troubled by a large bad loan portfolio, remains limited in its ability to provide efficient financial intermediation. The rehabilitation and restructuring of the main state-owned banks is a vital element of the reform agenda.**
- **Future macroeconomic stabilisation efforts to control the fiscal deficit and the current account deficit will not be sustainable unless enterprise and financial sector reforms are accelerated.**

Liberalisation

After substantial tariff reductions, new protective measures are planned.
Before joining CEFTA in mid-1997, Romania had introduced a package of import tariff reductions, including drastic reductions on some food products. The unweighted average tariff for agricultural and food products fell to 32%, down from 122% in 1996. In mid-1998, a slight increase of selected agricultural import tariffs was agreed with CEFTA members to cushion some of the adverse effects on farmers and food processors resulting from the earlier liberalisation. The government also plans to introduce a 6% import surcharge.

Full current account convertibility has been established.
After unifying the exchange rate in early 1997, Romania introduced full current account convertibility in March 1998. The foreign exchange and Treasury bill markets were liberalised, but some restrictions on capital account transactions remain.

Privatisation

Large-scale privatisation has continued to lag behind schedule.
Progress in privatisation has been slower in Romania than in most other transition economies in central and eastern Europe. At the end of 1996, more than three-quarters of the total book value of companies allocated to the State Ownership Fund (SOF) was still state owned. The reform programme of early 1997 gave more decision-making power to the SOF, shifting focus to direct sales. More recently, increasing emphasis has been placed on IPOs and sales to foreign strategic investors. In November 1997, a Ministry of Privatisation was established. Despite these measures, the pace of privatisation has remained very slow. The SOF still maintains a portfolio of 5,500 enterprises to be privatised. Five "Regies Autonomes", Romania's large state enterprises, have been transformed into fully state-owned joint-stock companies in preparation for their privatisation.

Enterprises

The restructuring and liquidation of loss-making state enterprises has been slow.
Industrial output has continued to fall. By mid-1998, inter-enterprise and tax arrears had reached 13% and 8% of GDP respectively. Little progress has been made in the restructuring of loss-making state-owned enterprises, including the Regies Autonomes. Plans for closing some of the biggest loss-makers – agreed with the IMF and the World Bank in 1997 – have not been realised. However, a rationalisation programme was implemented successfully in the mining sector. In addition, the government pressured the Regies Autonomes to develop reorganisation plans. One such plan, for the national oil company Petrom, was submitted in May 1998. It includes the liquidation of unprofitable units, the divestiture of the distribution network and substantial reduction of employment in preparation for its privatisation.

Agricultural reform is proceeding slowly.
Agriculture accounts for about 20% of GDP and 30% of employment. Until 1997, the sector was characterised by strong state intervention and a non-functioning land market. Since April 1998, a new law has facilitated the transfer of agricultural land by accelerating restitution and clarifying ownership rights. Access to working capital and investment credit has been tight since the restructuring of the state agricultural bank, Banca Agricola. Directed credits were abolished in 1997, but farmers continue to benefit from interest rate subsidies.

Infrastructure

The government has recently approved plans for the restructuring of the energy sector.
The energy sector suffers from over-staffing and poor payment discipline by state-owned clients. In preparation for its restructuring, the national electricity company, Renel, was transformed into a fully state-owned joint-stock company, renamed Conel, in the summer of 1998. The government also approved a plan to split the industry into separate companies for nuclear, hydro and thermal generation, as well as for transmission and distribution. Under new draft legislation, the nuclear power company would be spun off, while the remaining four companies would be subsidiaries of Conel. The proposed legislation would also allow for the further subdivision and privatisation of the generation and distribution companies. A regulatory agency for the energy sector is being created within the Ministry of Trade and Industry. In the medium term, it is envisaged that the regulator would become independent and assume full responsibility for the setting of network access charges

			1994	1995	1996	1997
Liberalisation						
Exchange rate regime	managed float	Share of administered prices in CPI	na	18	18	7
Current account convertibility	full	Administered prices in "EBRD-15" basket	5	5	5	2
Interest rate liberalisation	full	Share of trade in GDP	21.0	24.3	26.2	27.0
Wage regulation	no	Tariff revenue (% of imports)	5.0	5.2	4.3	4.0
Privatisation						
Primary privatisation method	MEBOs	Private sector share in GDP	35	40	60	60
Secondary privatisation method	direct sales	Share of small firms privatised	23.1	33.5	65.0	95.5
Tradability of land rights	full except foreigners	Share of medium/large firms privatised	4.8	13.9	22.0	28.4
Enterprises						
Protection of shareholder rights	partly effective	Budgetary subsidies (% of GDP)	3.8	4.1	4.3	2.6
Bankruptcy proceedings	partly effective	Credit to enterprises (% of GDP)	14.5	15.3	14.6	5.8
Competition office	yes	Labour productivity in industry (% change)	10.1	20.0	12.1	1.0
Infrastructure						
Independent telecoms regulator	no	Main telephone lines per 100 inhabitants	12.3	13.1	14.0	16.0
Separation of railway accounts	yes	Railway labour productivity (1989=100)	46.5	56.4	79.9	58.5
Independent electricity regulator	no	Electricity tariff, US¢/kWh (collection ratio in %)	4.3 (88)	4.2 (94)	4.2 (96)	6.0 (96)
Financial institutions						
Deposit insurance	yes	Number of banks (of which foreign-owned)	20 (3)	24 (6)	31 (8)	33 (11)
Secured transactions law	restricted	Asset share of state-owned banks	80.4	84.3	80.9	80.2
Insider dealing prohibited	yes	Bad loans (% of total loans)	18.5	37.9	48.0	57.0
Securities commission	yes	Stock market capitalisation (% of GDP)	na	0.4	1.3	6.8
Fiscal and social sector						
Private pension funds	no	Tax revenues (% of GDP)	28.2	28.7	26.7	26.0
Share of population in poverty	22%	Earnings inequality (Gini coefficient)	0.276	0.278	0.303	na

and retail tariffs. It is also planned that there will be competition between generators for large customers (distribution companies and large industrial companies) in line with the "negotiated access" model of the EU Energy Directive. There are also plans to restructure the national gas company, Romgaz.

The planned privatisation of the national telecoms operator, Romtelecom, has been delayed.
The State Ownership Fund has recently announced the intention to privatise the dominant operator, Romtelecom, through the sale of a 51% controlling stake to a strategic investor, rather than the previously proposed 35% stake. Romtelecom was corporatised in September 1997 and still holds exclusivity rights on basic voice telephony until 2003. Competition is allowed in all telecoms services other than basic telephony, including data transmission and cable TV. In the mobile sector, two GSM operators have been active since 1997. In addition, there are plans to issue two DCS-1800 licences, one already purchased by Romtelecom. A telecommunications law was passed in June 1996, with plans to create an independent regulator.

Financial institutions

The banking sector is underdeveloped with a large bad loan portfolio.
The banking sector remains dominated by five large state-owned banks, which account for about three-quarters of total banking sector assets. These banks have extended credit to loss-making state enterprises and thus accumulated large amounts of bad loans. For the banking sector as a whole, the share of doubtful and loss-making credits in total credits grew from 19% at the end of 1994 to 57% at the end of 1997. Total provisions cover only half of all non-performing loans. New lending has fallen sharply, with total outstanding loans to enterprises declining from 15% of GDP in 1996 to 6% in 1997. This was mainly the result of high inflation during 1996 and 1997 and did not necessarily reflect more prudent lending practices. Banks remain subject to political interference, the lack of structural adjustment in the real sector of the economy and the current recession.

First steps have been taken in the difficult process of bank privatisation.
In June 1998, the government announced that two state-owned banks, Banc Post and the Romanian Development Bank, are to be sold to foreign strategic investors. These two medium-sized and relatively healthy banks would be the first to be privatised. Together, they account for around 10% of the total assets of the banking system. Two of the large remaining state-owned banks, Banca Agricola and Bancorex, are currently undergoing a restructuring programme, the former with support of international financial institutions.

Bank supervision is inadequate.
The regulatory framework has been improved recently with the adoption of three new laws on banking strengthening the supervisory authority of the central bank (NBR). Effective bank supervision remains, however, constrained by political interference. A decision by the NBR to revoke two bank licences was overruled by the courts in December 1997. A month earlier, the NBR took on its books five-year bonds worth about US$ 1 billion, issued by the Ministry of Finance to cover bad debts of the two largest state-owned banks, indicating weaknesses in central bank independence and the continued use of inflationary bail-out operations.

Stock market listings are increasing, but secondary trading is still low.
In August 1998, the Bucharest Stock Exchange registered 110 companies, of which 18 were listed on the first tier. RASDAQ, the over-the-counter market, has about 5,500 listed companies. Both markets have continued to grow and can be expected to play a larger role in the future, as their importance in the privatisation process is gradually increasing. The market for government securities, on the other hand, is still underdeveloped. Although foreign banks are active in the primary market for Treasury bills and bonds, there is no functioning secondary market.

Fiscal and social sector

Poor tax revenue collection has impeded efforts to reduce the fiscal deficit.
Some efforts have been made to reduce the fiscal deficit (3.6% of GDP in 1997), partly by cutting subsidies and streamlining the tax system. However, with GDP expected to decline by about 4% in 1998 and with increasingly lax tax discipline, fiscal revenues could decline further. Arrears to the state budget were around US$ 3 billion, or 8% of GDP, in mid-1998, much of it owed by the state-owned utilities. Large state-owned companies are often unwilling or unable to pay their taxes in full and the authorities are not yet able to efficiently tax newly emerging private enterprises. Tax changes in 1998 reduced profit and wage taxes, but increased VAT and excise taxes. The net effect has been a loss in revenue.

Russian Federation

EU Partnership and Cooperation Agreement · CIS member · WTO observer

1990

June	Sovereignty proclaimed

1991

Oct	Reform programme announced
Nov	State organs of the USSR abolished
Dec	Dissolution of Soviet Union and creation of the CIS
Dec	VAT introduced

1992

Jan	Most prices liberalised
Jan	Small-scale privatisation begins
Jan	State trading monopoly abolished
June	Mass privatisation programme adopted
July	Exchange rate unified
Oct	Voucher privatisation begins

1993

Mar	Bankruptcy law enacted
May	T-bills market initiated
July	New currency (Russian rouble) introduced
Nov	Rouble zone collapsed

1994

July	Voucher privatisation completed
July	Cash-based privatisation begins
Oct	Currency crisis
Dec	Chechen war begins

1995

Jan	Customs union formed with Belarus and Kazakhstan
July	Currency corridor introduced
Aug	Interbank market crisis
Nov	First shares-for-loans auctions conducted

1996

Mar	3-year IMF programme agreed
Apr	Foreign trade liberalisation completed
June	Full current account convertibility introduced
Aug	Chechen war ends
Nov	First sovereign Eurobond

1997

May	First regional Eurobond
July	Privatisation law adopted
July	First corporate Eurobond
Sept	Admission to Paris Club
Dec	London Club deal completed

Key reform challenges

- **Resolving the economic crisis will require re-establishing macroeconomic stability, reviving the payments system and restructuring the banking sector.**
- **Decisive action on reforming an inefficient fiscal system is now more important than ever, given the collapse of foreign financing.**
- **Improving financial discipline, corporate governance, minority shareholder rights and bankruptcy will be the key to economic recovery and long-term growth.**
- **The crisis provides an opportunity to address the most difficult issues of corruption and vested interests that have undermined stabilisation and reform.**

Liberalisation

The rouble was devalued and capital controls have been re-imposed.
Despite a US$ 22.6 billion IMF-led rescue package in July 1998, investor confidence continued to erode and pressure on the rouble intensified. On 17 August, the government widened the exchange-rate corridor from a +/–15% band around 6.2 roubles to the US dollar to a band of 6.0 to 9.5 roubles to the US dollar, and imposed a 90-day moratorium on foreign debt service by domestic banks and enterprises. Shortly afterwards, additional pressure on the rouble forced the central bank (CBR) to let the currency float beyond the new corridor. Currency trading has been suspended repeatedly and the market has fragmented.

Many regions imposed price and trade controls.
With surging prices and declining imports, many regional governments, including the City of Moscow, have introduced price controls, ranging from ceilings on profit margins to administered price-setting. To prevent food shortages, some regional governments have also placed restrictions on the movement of selected locally produced goods out of the region.

Privatisation

Privatisation plans were put on hold.
The privatisation programme for 1998 envisaged full or partial privatisation of over 70 medium-sized and large companies, with a revenue target of about US$ 3 billion. The collapse of the equity market, continued devaluation fears and the deteriorating investment climate have undermined these plans. Three attempts in 1998 to privatise Rosneft, the last state-owned integrated oil company, failed. Other high-profile plans to privatise shares of "blue-chip" companies in the oil (Lukoil) and gas (Gazprom), telecoms (Svyazinvest) and aviation sectors have been postponed repeatedly.

Uneven progress has been made in land reform.
Two new laws on land registration and on mortgages were enacted in 1998, representing a significant step in the development of the property market. However, the continued delay in the adoption of a market-oriented Land Code remains a major obstacle to both the urban and rural property markets. The parliament has consistently rejected the free sale of land. A few regions, including Samara, Saratov and Tatarstan, have taken matters into their own hands by adopting legislation allowing for the free trade of land in their regions.

Enterprises

Lack of a credible bankruptcy threat has been a key problem.
A new bankruptcy law was enacted in March 1998. Though much improved, it is biased against private creditors, overemphasises restructuring at the expense of liquidation and provides extensive rights to local authorities in the bankruptcy of large enterprises. In May, an accelerated bankruptcy procedure was introduced, allowing bankrupt enterprises to be sold as going concerns. The progress in improving the legal and regulatory framework has not been matched by effective implementation, thus weakening the bankruptcy threat. By backtracking in a number of high-profile bankruptcy cases, the government has shown a lack of political will to allow the market to select enterprises for survival.

Financial discipline has been undermined by widespread arrears and barter.
In the absence of a credible bankruptcy threat, enterprises have increasingly resorted to financing themselves by accumulating arrears towards tax authorities, banks, suppliers and workers, as well as through non-monetary forms of payments, such as barter, monetary surrogates, offsets and payments-in-kind. Total overdue arrears of the enterprise sector amounted to 43% of GDP in August 1998. Non-monetary forms of payments accounted for about 60% or more of the average industrial firm's sales. This trend has greatly reduced financial transparency and accountability at the firm level, distorted market signals and weakened incentives for enterprise restructuring. Arrears and barter represent a major indirect subsidy to many firms. The problem has largely contributed to the state's continued fiscal weakness.

The protection of minority shareholder rights has been particularly weak.
Around 60% of Russia's medium-sized and large companies are majority-owned by insiders. The dominance of managers also extends to many companies with substantial outside ownership. Minority shareholders have frequently been subjected to a range of abuses including restricted access to shareholder meetings, share dilutions, and discriminatory transfer pricing and share-

Liberalisation			1994	1995	1996	1997
Exchange rate regime	managed float	Share of administered prices in CPI	na	na	na	na
Current account convertibility	full	Administered prices in "EBRD-15" basket	3	2	2	2
Interest rate liberalisation	full	Share of trade in GDP	20.3	20.5	19.1	17.9
Wage regulation	no	Tariff revenue (% of imports)	18.7	8.7	6.0	6.7
Privatisation						
Primary privatisation method	vouchers	Private sector share in GDP	50	55	60	70
Secondary privatisation method	direct sales	Privatisation revenues (% of GDP)	0.11	0.38	0.12	0.90
Tradability of land rights	limited *de jure*	Number of firms privatised	23,000	8,414	3,675	1,546
Enterprises						
Protection of shareholder rights	partly effective	Budgetary subsidies (% of GDP)	na	na	6.2	6.4
Bankruptcy proceedings	ineffective	Credit to enterprises (% of GDP)	12.1	8.5	7.2	8.7
Competition office	yes	Labour productivity in industry (% change)	-14.3	5.5	3.2	3.0
Infrastructure						
Independent telecoms regulator	no	Main telephone lines per 100 inhabitants	16.2	17.0	17.5	18.2
Separation of railway accounts	no	Railway labour productivity (1989=100)	57.4	80.9	73.6	77.9
Independent electricity regulator	yes	Electricity tariff, US¢/kWh (collection ratio in %)	2.2 (50)	2.3 (50)	3.0 (50)	3.2 (50)
Financial institutions						
Deposit insurance	no	Number of banks (of which foreign-owned)	na	2,295 (19)	2,029 (23)	1,697 (26)
Secured transactions law	yes	Asset share of state-owned banks	na	na	na	29.0
Insider dealing prohibited	yes	Bad loans (% of total loans)	na	5.9	5.1	3.5
Securities commission	yes	Stock market capitalisation (% of GDP)	0.1	4.6	9.4	29.4
Fiscal and social sector						
Private pension funds	yes	Tax revenues (% of GDP)	34.8	35.9	32.7	32.2
Share of population in poverty	38%	Earnings inequality (Gini coefficient)	0.446	0.471	0.483	na

swaps within holding companies, especially in the oil and gas sector. The Federal Securities Commission took some measures against high-profile violations of minority shareholder rights. In July 1998, the government issued a programme to improve the framework for minority shareholder rights and strengthen disclosure and accounting requirements.

Infrastructure

Resistance to the reform of natural monopolies remains substantial.
Reform of the natural monopolies is critical both to improving the government's fiscal position and hardening enterprise budget constraints. Though political opposition to major structural reforms in this area remains substantial, some measures have been adopted, largely driven by fiscal concerns. The regulatory framework has been strengthened with a focus on phasing out cross-subsidies, improving transparency, reducing non-payments and encouraging private sector participation. Some high-level management changes have also been made, especially in the main electricity provider, UES. However, the implementation of reforms has been uneven.

Financial institutions

The banking system is in crisis.
Due to a weak regulatory structure, commercial banks were allowed to develop large foreign-currency exposure. The sharp devaluation of the rouble in August 1998, combined with the forced restructuring of domestic government securities (which accounted for a large part of banking assets) plunged much of the banking system into insolvency. To prevent explicit defaults of banks on their foreign debt and derivatives contracts, the government declared a 90-day moratorium on principal repayments of private debts to non-residents. The crisis led to bank runs, a breakdown in the payments system, disruptions in tax collection, and the collapse of financial intermediation in the economy. The central bank's initial response exacerbated the problems through indiscriminate liquidity injections and inconsistent efforts to provide guarantees for household deposits.

Securities trading has come to a halt.
Following the stock market boom in 1996 and 1997, declining investor confidence sparked a collapse in equity prices in 1998 and a surge in yields on state securities to unsustainable levels, well above 100% in real terms. With investors unwilling to roll over short-term government debt and the government unable to finance its deficit at such interest rates, the government finally imposed an involuntary restructuring of Treasury bills and bonds in August. As of early October, the terms of the restructuring were still subject to further negotiations. Primary issues and secondary trading of state securities have been halted, though new, very short-term bills have been issued since September. By the end of September, the stock market had fallen by more than 90% from its level one year earlier. Trading volumes have been minimal.

Fiscal and social sector

The tax regime is a serious obstacle to a sound investment climate.
An onerous and arbitrarily applied tax regime has been a key deficiency of Russia's business climate, causing massive tax evasion and avoidance, while weakening the state's fiscal position. After repeated failures, the first part of the new Tax Code was finally adopted in July 1998 clarifying and streamlining the tax system. An earlier ban on tax off-sets in the federal budget has not been fully implemented. However, a major effort to reform individual taxes, as part of an IMF-sponsored stabilisation programme in June, largely failed, as the parliament passed the tax-reducing measures but rejected the key revenue-raising measures.

Some progress has been made in controlling budgetary expenditures.
From late 1997, the government began to make sharp spending cuts by overhauling budgetary organisations and introducing conditionality on regional transfers. The result was a primary surplus of the federal budget in the first half of 1998, though the continued accumulation of expenditure arrears raised sustainability concerns.
A new Budget Code was adopted in August, strengthening control over budget implementation and clarifying the interrelationships among federal and regional budgets and off-budgetary funds. The implementation of these measures will take considerable time.

The lack of an efficient social safety net has inhibited the overall reform process.
The current social safety net, largely inherited from the Soviet period, is characterised by a large number of untargeted social benefits and price subsidies for housing and public utilities. Enterprises still provide many social services, while tight fiscal positions have prevented federal and local authorities from shouldering a larger share of the costs. Low unemployment benefits (accounting for roughly 10% of the average wage) together with the lack of a well-functioning housing market sharply constrain labour mobility. Inadequate progress in reforming the social safety net has become a major bottleneck in reforms at the grass-roots level.

Slovak Republic

EU Association Agreement · WTO member · EFTA member · CEFTA member

1990

Jan	Two-tiered banking system established

1991

Jan	Exchange rate unified
Jan	Most foreign trade controls lifted
Jan	Most prices liberalised
Jan	Small-scale privatisation begins
Feb	Restitution law adopted

1992

Feb	T-bills market initiated
May	Voucher privatisation begins
July	EFTA membership

1993

Jan	Czechoslovakia splits into Czech and Slovak Republics
Feb	New currency (koruna) introduced
Mar	CEFTA membership
Apr	Stock exchange begins trading
June	New bankruptcy law enacted

1994

Jan	First corporate Eurobond
July	First sovereign Eurobond
Aug	New competition law enacted

1995

Jan	WTO membership
Sept	Second wave of voucher privatisation cancelled
Sept	Strategic enterprises excluded from privatisation
Oct	Full current account convertibility introduced
Dec	First municipal Eurobond

1996

Dec	BIS capital adequacy enacted

1997

Aug	Enterprise revitalisation law enacted
Sept	New wage regulation enacted
Dec	Third-largest bank collapsed

Key reform challenges

- **The continued survival of unprofitable firms and the large volume of inter-enterprise arrears and bad loans are clear signs of weak market discipline. Making bankruptcy proceedings more effective is crucial to improve market efficiency.**
- **Improving transparency in privatisation and regulation would encourage foreign investment.**
- **Progress in restructuring and privatising the three dominant banks would significantly improve financial intermediation.**
- **Reforms in the healthcare system and in public transport would help alleviate pressures on public spending and enhance market efficiency.**

Liberalisation

The koruna has been allowed to float.
On 1 October 1998, the central bank abolished the exchange rate peg against the DEM/USD basket with its +/–7% fluctuation band. A week later, the koruna traded at about 15% below the old parity, implying a devaluation of 9%. A large current account deficit had encouraged speculative attacks against the currency ever since the Czech currency crisis in May 1997.

International trade and capital flows have been liberalised.
In an effort to comply with OECD standards, further steps have been taken to liberalise international capital flows. In December 1997, the short-term Treasury bill market was opened to foreign investors. In April 1998, limits on foreign exchange purchases by Slovak subjects were lifted and short-term capital flows liberalised. In compliance with a WTO decision, the 7% import surcharge introduced in mid-1997 was gradually phased out and reduced to zero in October 1998. The surcharge was part of a larger package of import restrictions introduced to stem the widening current account deficit.

New wage regulations apply to most enterprises.
At the end of 1997, the government introduced a comprehensive wage regulation scheme, for both public and private enterprises, in an effort to contain rapid real wage growth. The scheme limits wage growth in firms to between 6% and 12%, depending on the firm's performance. In the first half of 1998, average real wage growth in industry slowed down and – in contrast to 1997 – was below labour productivity growth.

Privatisation

Privatisation via direct sales has continued at a fast pace.
The National Property Fund has continued to sell off its residual shareholdings. From 1996 to 1997, the book value of privatisable shares held by the Fund fell from about US$ 2 billion to US$ 0.7 billion, although this probably overstates the market value of residual state shares. After further sales in 1998, the large-scale privatisation programme is nearing completion, with total assets privatised amounting to a book value of almost US$ 10 billion. However, the National Property Fund and other ministries still manage companies excluded from the privatisation process. These account for about 30% of the book value of all productive state assets and include utilities, the postal service, telecoms, railways, some agricultural enterprises, as well as the savings bank and the main insurance company (SP).

The style of privatisation has been controversial.
The privatisation process has been criticised for a lack of transparency in the timing of sales, the choice of buyers, and the special terms and conditions offered to select buyers. In February 1998, around 8% of Slovnaft, the large petrochemical company, whose shares are actively traded on the stock exchange, was sold for half the market price to a previously unknown company. In another surprise move, the National Property Fund sold 74% of the large aluminium producer ZSNP in July 1998 to a newly founded holding company whose ownership was uncertain. The average price for all direct sales completed in 1997 was only 18% of the average book value. New owners have also been able to reduce their subsequent instalments by undertaking investments in the privatised company. This practice has led to high, but not necessarily efficient, capital expenditures of enterprises.

Enterprises

Enterprise restructuring progresses, but profitability remains generally low.
Labour productivity in industry has grown steadily since 1992, driven primarily by output growth since 1994. Though industrial employment fell sharply early in the transition, it has since stabilised. The private sector has consistently recorded faster output and employment growth than the public sector. Despite these signs of progress, firm profitability remains generally low and has deteriorated in many cases. While profits of SMEs rose in 1997, the profitability of larger enterprises declined sharply. Among medium-sized and large enterprises, there are as many profitable as loss-making firms.

The absence of effective bankruptcy proceedings has undermined market discipline.
The virtual absence of bankruptcy continues to inhibit the exit of unprofitable firms and to weaken financial discipline. Inter-enterprise arrears amounted to 18% of GDP in 1997, roughly unchanged from 1996. An amend-

			1994	1995	1996	1997
Liberalisation						
Exchange rate regime	managed float	Share of administered prices in CPI	na	na	na	na
Current account convertibility	full	Administered prices in "EBRD-15" basket	na	na	na	na
Interest rate liberalisation	full	Share of trade in GDP	48.4	50.0	53.1	49.0
Wage regulation	yes	Tariff revenue (% of imports)	3.4	3.3	2.9	3.5
Privatisation						
Primary privatisation method	direct sales	Private sector share in GDP	55	60	70	75
Secondary privatisation method	vouchers	Share of medium/large firms privatised	59.6	66.9	71.3	79.4
Tradability of land rights	full except foreigners	Share of assets privatised	32.3	43.3	52.0	62.0
Enterprises						
Protection of shareholder rights	ineffective	Budgetary subsidies (% of GDP)	3.2	2.8	2.4	na
Bankruptcy proceedings	ineffective	Credit to enterprises (% of GDP)	53.5	52.0	54.5	48.0
Competition office	yes	Labour productivity in industry (% change)	6.8	4.0	2.5	4.8
Infrastructure						
Independent telecoms regulator	no	Main telephone lines per 100 inhabitants	18.7	20.8	23.2	25.9
Separation of railway accounts	no	Railway labour productivity (1989=100)	74.1	83.9	75.1	77.1
Independent electricity regulator	no	Electricity tariff, US¢/kWh (collection ratio in %)	2.9 (95)	3.1 (95)	3.2 (95)	2.9 (95)
Financial institutions						
Deposit insurance	yes	Number of banks (of which foreign-owned)	19 (4)	25 (9)	24 (9)	25 (9)
Secured transactions law	restricted	Asset share of state-owned banks	66.9	61.2	54.2	48.7
Insider dealing prohibited	yes	Bad loans (% of total loans)	30.3	41.3	31.8	33.4
Securities commission	no	Stock market capitalisation (% of GDP)	7.8	7.1	12.1	9.7
Fiscal and social sector						
Private pension funds	no	Tax revenues (% of GDP)	38.8	39.7	39.6	na
Share of population in poverty	1%	Earnings inequality (Gini coefficient)	na	na	na	na

ment to the bankruptcy law became effective in February 1998 to facilitate proceedings. However, "strategic" enterprises and enterprises under the new "revitalisation" programme remain excluded. The 1997 Law on Revitalisation of Enterprises induced over 1,000 companies to apply for tax and debt relief, further weakening market discipline. Recently, the size of the programme has been scaled back significantly.

FDI remains low, but efforts have been made to attract foreign investors.
After abandoning the second wave of mass voucher privatisation in 1995, privatisation has continued via direct sales – usually to former management or domestic holding companies. As foreigners have been virtually excluded from the privatisation process, they have played little role in the development of corporate governance. Inflows of FDI accounted for only 0.9% of GDP in 1997. Some notable ventures include a Volkswagen plant and a joint venture between US Steel and the large Slovak steelmaker VSZ, signed in early 1998. The government has recently made efforts to attract foreign investors. In July 1998, it introduced corporate income tax relief of 75% for the first five years of foreign direct investments exceeding US$ 30 million, subject to conditions on investment and output growth.

Infrastructure

Little progress has been made to reform the loss-making railways sector.
The state railways are expected to generate a loss of about US$ 100 million in 1998, only slightly down from the 1997 level. Losses are driven primarily by low tariff revenues in passenger services, where cost recovery is estimated at less than 30%. Freight traffic, by contrast, usually generates a small surplus. Beyond the need to increase productivity, reforms such as corporatising freight and passenger traffic and reducing the cross-subsidy between them would substantially enhance efficiency.

The state has further reduced subsidies in key infrastructure sectors.
Partly in response to fiscal pressures, the government raised VAT on postal and telecoms services from 6% to the standard 23% in January 1998. The subsidy for heating was cut drastically in 1998.

Financial institutions

The banking sector has been weakened by high interest rates and non-performing loans.
The banking sector has suffered since May 1997 when the central bank sharply reduced liquidity to defend the currency against speculative attacks. High and sometimes volatile interest rates drove up real lending rates and stifled enterprise credit. The sector remains burdened by a large portfolio of bad loans. The volume of doubtful and loss-making loans increased slightly during 1997, accounting for around a third of all outstanding loans.

The collapse of the third-largest bank has highlighted the problems of the major state banks.
The banking system remains dominated by three state-controlled banks, which account for about half of all assets in the banking sector and for the lion's share of bad loans. Capital adequacy is below the required 8% in these banks. In December 1997, the third-largest bank – IRB – collapsed with estimated losses of almost US$ 100 million. It was put under forced administration of the central bank and received a significant liquidity injection. In June 1998, the state-owned Slovak Insurance Company (SP) acquired a 66% stake in IRB through a capital increase. SP commands about 60% of the US$ 0.5 billion insurance market; its dominant shareholders, the National Property Fund and steel producer VSZ, were also the largest shareholders of IRB prior to its collapse. Little progress has been made in the restructuring and privatisation of the other two large state banks, VUB and the state Savings Bank.

Capital markets have been hampered by a sharp decline in share prices.
The Slovak stock index (SAX) fell by 41% during the first half of 1998. Foreign interest in shares remained muted, partly as a result of negative trends in other emerging markets. This has slowed down the development of capital markets. There has been only one new share listing on the top tier of the stock market since October 1995. Low liquidity was cited as the main reason for postponing the introduction of derivatives trading on the stock exchange planned for mid-1998.

Fiscal and social sector

A large funding gap is emerging in the healthcare sector.
Healthcare spending accounted for more than 6% of GDP in 1997. The system is financed through six public health insurance companies, which collect contributions paid through payroll taxes. As spending on healthcare grew much more quickly than contributions, arrears by the insurance companies to healthcare providers have been accumulating rapidly during the first half of 1998.

Slovenia

EU Association Agreement† · WTO member · EFTA member · CEFTA member

1991

June Independence from Yugoslavia
June Central bank established
Oct New currency (tolar) introduced
Oct Bank rehabilitation agency established
Dec Restitution law adopted

1992

Sept Enterprise rehabilitation begins
Nov Privatisation law adopted
Dec First large enterprise liquidated

1993

Jan Rehabilitation of largest bank begins
Mar Foreign trade law adopted
Apr Competition law enacted

1994

Jan Bankruptcy law enacted
Jan Investment companies law adopted
Mar New securities law adopted
June Most prices liberalised
Aug BIS capital adequacy enacted
Nov New privatisation law adopted

1995

Feb Capital account controls introduced
June EU Association Agreement
July EFTA membership
July WTO membership
Sept Full current account convertibility introduced
Sept Competition agency established

1996

Jan CEFTA membership
July First Eurobond
July Capital account restrictions relaxed
July Liquidation of Komercialna Banka Triglav initiated

1997

Feb First GDR issue
June Restrictions on foreign portfolio investments relaxed
June Telecoms law adopted
July Restriction on real estate ownership

Key reform challenges

- **A large number of legislative initiatives will be required for EU entry in the first wave, including the introduction of VAT, further price liberalisation and opening of the financial sector to international competition.**
- **Removing existing capital account restrictions and encouraging greater inflows of FDI would promote Slovenia's integration into the world economy and improve corporate governance standards.**
- **Privatisation has entered a more difficult phase, shifting to the financial sector, larger state-owned companies and private sector involvement in infrastructure.**

Liberalisation

Price liberalisation has accelerated in preparation for EU accession.
Administered prices still accounted for about 28% of the retail price index and 20% of the consumer price index in 1997. Price liberalisation has intensified (since mid-1997). Price controls for bread, milk and pork have been removed, while flour, sugar and oil products are still controlled. Prices for petrol and diesel oil have been raised significantly, bringing them closer to EU levels.

The new Wage Act is likely to contain public sector wage growth.
During 1997, wages in the public sector grew more quickly than in the private sector, despite being subject to wage regulation. The new Wage Act adopted in mid-1997 has changed the rules for public sector and minimum wage indexation. Full indexation to retail prices on a quarterly basis was replaced by an annual partial indexation to consumer prices. This is expected to contain public sector wage growth during price liberalisation as the share of controlled prices in the RPI is greater than the CPI.

Significant progress in capital account liberalisation is required before EU accession.
International financial flows to Slovenia remain fairly restricted by capital controls that are not compatible with EU membership. Deposit requirements apply to most foreign loans and deposits, 40% of which must be placed in a non-interest-bearing account with the central bank. A reduced deposit requirement of 10% applies to loans or deposits with a maturity of more than 7 years; no deposit is required if the loan is used for the import of capital goods. Most portfolio flows are restricted by a requirement that investors set up (often very costly) custodial accounts with local banks. In October 1998, further restrictions were introduced on portfolio flows forcing foreign investors to hold Slovene shares for at least 7 years.

Privatisation

With privatisation of "socially managed" enterprises nearly complete, progress has been slow in privatising large firms.
By July 1997, the privatisation agency had approved 1,420 privatisation programmes for the approximately 1,600 remaining "socially managed" enterprises. By July 1998, 90% of these privatisation programmes had reached the final stage. The remaining 180 enterprises have either been liquidated or transferred to the State Development Fund for restructuring. However, some large loss-making enterprises in the metal and oil sectors were not included in the original privatisation law and are still fully or majority state-owned.

Enterprises

After years of productivity growth driven mainly by falling employment, there are signs of accelerating output growth.
The manufacturing sector has recorded positive productivity growth since 1994, driven almost exclusively by declining employment in the range of 5% a year, while output and value added have grown very slowly. Falling employment has been more the result of bankruptcies than of enterprise restructuring. Since early 1998, however, productivity growth has been driven by higher production as employment levels have stabilised. Exports, two-thirds of which go to the EU, are also growing more rapidly. Aggregate net profits of commercial companies are still negative, with most losses concentrated among state-owned enterprises. Inter-enterprise arrears are common among state-owned companies and utilities and are often settled through multilateral debt offsets.

Corporate governance remains poor, dominated by insiders with low levels of FDI.
Privatisation through management and employee buy-outs has effectively perpetuated the Yugoslav system of "social management" of enterprises. This entails high labour representation on supervisory boards and disproportionate control by managers and employees *vis-à-vis* outside shareholders. Most enterprises have undergone little restructuring. The existing ownership structures are likely to prevail for some time as shares in privatised enterprises cannot be sold on the secondary market for at least two years after privatisation. Also, share purchases of more than 25% of a company are subject to approval by the Securities Market Agency. Another factor inhibiting improvements in corporate governance is the lack of foreign capital in Slovenia. FDI has been discouraged by excluding foreigners from the privatisation process and by the gradual introduction of capital account restrictions since 1995. FDI inflows increased from 1.0% of GDP in 1996 to 1.8% in 1997, but early figures for 1998 indicate a reversal of this upward trend.

Liberalisation			1994	1995	1996	1997
Exchange rate regime	managed float	Share of administered prices in CPI	18.4	22.5	22.4	20.4
Current account convertibility	full	Administered prices in "EBRD-15" basket	5	5	5	4
Interest rate liberalisation	limited *de facto*	Share of trade in GDP	48.6	47.1	46.7	48.3
Wage regulation	yes	Tariff revenue (% of imports)	7.0	7.1	na	na
Privatisation						
Primary privatisation method	MEBOs	Private sector share in GDP	30	45	45	50
Secondary privatisation method	vouchers	Share of firms privatised	7.0	26.0	62.0	72.0
Tradability of land rights	full except foreigners	Privatisation revenues (% of GDP)	0.00	0.39	0.41	0.54
Enterprises						
Protection of shareholder rights	partly effective	Budgetary subsidies (% of GDP)	1.6	1.6	1.2	1.3
Bankruptcy proceedings	partly effective	Credit to enterprises (% of GDP)	17.6	19.5	20.0	19.6
Competition office	yes	Labour productivity in industry (% change)	11.4	7.2	6.6	5.2
Infrastructure						
Independent telecoms regulator	no	Main telephone lines per 100 inhabitants	28.7	30.9	33.3	36.4
Separation of railway accounts	yes	Railway labour productivity (1989=100)	78.4	99.2	86.1	na
Independent electricity regulator	no	Electricity tariff, US¢/kWh (collection ratio in %)	6.8 (92)	7.4 (95)	7.4 (95)	9.4 (97)
Financial institutions						
Deposit insurance	yes	Number of banks (of which foreign-owned)	44 (6)	41 (6)	36 (4)	34 (4)
Secured transactions law	restricted	Asset share of state-owned banks	39.8	41.7	40.7	40.1
Insider dealing prohibited	yes	Bad loans (% of total loans)	22.0	13.2	14.3	12.3
Securities commission	yes	Stock market capitalisation (% of GDP)	1.5	1.8	4.9	10.9
Fiscal and social sector						
Private pension funds	no	Tax revenues (% of GDP)	23.9	23.9	24.7	24.9
Share of population in poverty	1%	Earnings inequality (Gini coefficient)	0.275	0.358	0.298	na

New powers have been granted to the State Development Fund.
The State Development Fund – set up to restructure, liquidate or privatise enterprises that were too unprofitable to be privatised – was transformed into the Development Corporation of Slovenia (SRD) in 1997. The scope of its activities has been widened to include financing and restructuring enterprises that have not yet been privatised and privatised enterprises in financial distress.

Infrastructure

Reform of telecommunications is planned in preparation for EU accession.
The Telecommunications Act and the Postal Service Act of May 1997 created two legally separate public companies, Pošta Slovenije and Telekom Slovenije. The latter will remain the sole provider of telephone services until the year 2000, when the market is to be opened up for international competition in line with EU requirements. A partial privatisation, with 8% of its shares going to employees, is to take place soon. Further stakes may be offered later, but the government plans to keep at least 51%. In mobile services, a second GSM licence (after the first went to a subsidiary of Telekom Slovenije) was awarded in June 1998, following an international tender.

A new Energy Act is being drafted in preparation for EU accession.
The energy sector is almost fully state-owned, except for the oil and gas sectors where the state is a minority shareholder. Most energy companies are unprofitable and face large stocks of receivables. Household electricity prices are gradually being adjusted upwards. The drafting of the new Energy Act will provide a legal framework for the electricity, district heating and gas sectors, harmonising legislation with EU directives on energy markets and the competition law.

Financial institutions

The banking sector is generally healthy, but remains protected and uncompetitive.
The successful conclusion of a bank rehabilitation programme in mid-1997 has strengthened the banking sector. Profits are rising, the share of non-performing loans in total loans declined to 12% at end-1997 and all banks satisfy the 8% capital adequacy ratio. However, competition is inadequate as evidenced by the fact that the top three banks (two of which are majority state-owned) account for half of the sector's assets. An inter-bank agreement on fixing deposit rates was renewed for the third time in early 1998. There is no law on bank privatisation and majority state-owned banks still account for about 40% of assets. Foreign banks are not allowed to open branches and no new foreign-owned banks have been licensed since 1994. A new banking law to bring legislation in line with EU directives has not yet been introduced.

A new tax on banks is intended to encourage lending to enterprises.
Lending to enterprises accounts for only 40% of bank assets and 20% of GDP. To encourage lending to non-financial enterprises, a 2% tax on inter-bank loans, fixed investments and assets of banks, and deposits with the central bank was introduced in December 1997.

The stock market has expanded rapidly, but remains relatively small.
Stock market capitalisation has grown to 13.2% of GDP in mid-1998, from 4.9% in 1996. This expansion mainly reflects new listings of previously privatised companies, but has also been supported by a 33% rise in share prices from mid-1997 to mid-1998, largely unaffected by the Asian crisis. Stock market growth is, however, limited by the capital account restrictions introduced in early 1997. These restrictions contributed to a reduction of foreign portfolio inflows from US$ 637 million in 1996 to US$ 236 million in 1997.

Fiscal and social sector

The introduction of VAT has been postponed.
The 1991 tax reform created a tax system similar to that of EU countries. The replacement of the 20% sales tax by VAT, scheduled for January 1998, has been postponed to July 1999. The introduction of VAT and excise taxes are requirements for EU accession.

The government has defined its long-run strategy for pension and healthcare reform.
Expenditures of the pension and health funds accounted for 13.3% and 6.8% of GDP in 1997. With a moderately ageing population, the "pay-as-you-go" pension system financed through payroll taxes is unsustainable, especially as there are already 450,000 pensioners and only 743,000 employed. There are plans for a gradual increase of the retirement age from the current 58 for men and 53 for women. It is also intended to introduce a "multi-pillar" pension system comprising compulsory state-funded, compulsory privately funded and voluntary private elements. In healthcare, a mix of private and public insurance and service provision is envisaged.

† Signed on 10 June 1996, currently in the process of ratification.

Tajikistan

CIS member

1991

Sept Independence from Soviet Union

Dec Central bank law adopted

Dec Joint-stock companies law adopted

1992

Jan Most prices liberalised

Jan VAT introduced

Mar Bankruptcy law enacted

1993

Dec Wage indexation law enacted

Dec Competition law adopted

1994

Sept Interim cease-fire arranged

1995

May New currency (Tajik rouble) introduced

May State trading monopoly abolished

May Exchange rate unified

Aug Licences for agricultural trade eliminated

Aug Banking regulations adopted

1996

May New privatisation programme begins

May IMF programme

Dec Guidelines on land trade adopted

Dec Central bank law adopted

1997

June Peace agreement concluded

Key reform challenges

- **With the conclusion of a peace agreement in June 1997, the government has adopted an ambitious reform plan under a recently approved three-year IMF programme.**
- **While progress on small-scale privatisation has been swift, large-scale privatisation has only just begun. Further progress in the implementation of land reform will also be required to consolidate private ownership in the agricultural sector.**
- **The domestic banking system needs to be restructured to encourage domestic savings and expand financial intermediation from its current low levels.**

Liberalisation

Price liberalisation is largely completed.
With the removal of the last remaining price controls on agricultural goods (grain and bread) in 1996, most prices have been liberalised with the exception of water, rents, communal services and transportation. In 1997, some water usage charges were increased. However, electricity tariffs still fall below cost recovery levels.

Following the conclusion of a new peace agreement, a liberal exchange and trade regime has been re-established.
Tajikistan has a liberal foreign trade and exchange regime, with a uniform import tariff of 5% as of 1998 (albeit with some exemptions), and de facto full current account convertibility. Regular foreign exchange auctions have been reintroduced in early 1998 after their cancellation in late 1996. Acceptance of the IMF's Article VIII is planned for late 1998. Temporary protectionist measures introduced in late 1996, including controls on cotton exports, new export taxes, high import duties and special excise taxes, have been fully eliminated. Tajikistan is preparing its application for WTO membership and has recently joined the customs union with Russia, Kyrgyzstan, Kazakhstan and Belarus.

Privatisation

Small-scale privatisation accelerated in 1997; completion is planned for 1999.
Following a revision of the privatisation law in May 1997, small-scale privatisation accelerated during 1997 and 50% of units in this category had been privatised by the end of the year. The government's commitments under the new IMF programme include the completion of small-scale privatisation by March 1999.

A timetable for corporatisation and privatisation of large enterprises has been drawn up.
Medium-sized and large enterprises remain predominantly state-owned, with only 13 firms out of a total of over 400 privatised in 1997. However, in 1998, 120 of these enterprises were transformed into joint-stock companies in preparation for privatisation and about 30 firms were privatised by auctions. The government plans to issue international tender documents for all cotton ginneries by December 1998 and to complete the corporatisation of all privatisable assets by March 1999.

Land ownership is gradually shifting to private hands.
The revised land code of December 1996 allows farmers to be granted lifetime leases to farmland with transfer and inheritance rights. Under this type of privatisation method, the share of agricultural land in private hands has continued to increase. Government commitments under the new IMF programme include the full marketability of land and the sale of 60 (out of 1,200) state-owned farms by early 1999, which would bring the share of privatised agricultural land to around 25%, up from 16% in 1996.

Enterprises

The revival of the cotton sector underlines the benefits of private sector involvement, while little restructuring has taken place in large state-owned enterprises.
Tajikistan's internationally competitive products include cotton, hydroelectric power and aluminium. The abolition of the state order system for cotton and the entry of private marketing companies contributed to an increase in output by 15% in 1997. However, the state-owned electricity company (Barki Tajik) and aluminium producer (TADAZ) are examples of the slow process of restructuring in industry, which is plagued by inter-enterprise and wage arrears and large debts. TADAZ was operating at 40% capacity and paid for only 9% of its electricity bill in 1996. The separation of non-core activities from TADAZ is planned for the end of 1998 as part of its general restructuring programme.

Steps have been taken to harden budget constraints and to improve the legal environment for private businesses.
Directed credits from the central bank (NBT) to priority sectors, which constituted half of the stock of bank credit in mid-1997, have been reduced sharply, following a presidential decree in July 1997 to strengthen the NBT's autonomy. State enterprises have been instructed to insist on payment before delivery and utilities to cut off non-paying customers. Recent steps to improve the investment climate include a revision of the previously ineffective bankruptcy law and the law on joint-stock companies, while laws on property and foreign investment are planned for 1998-99.

Liberalisation			1994	1995	1996	1997
Exchange rate regime	managed float	Share of administered prices in CPI	na	na	na	na
Current account convertibility	limited	Administered prices in "EBRD-15" basket	2	1	0	0
Interest rate liberalisation	limited *de facto*	Share of trade in GDP	78.1	178.9	76.1	69.4
Wage regulation	no	Tariff revenue (% of imports)	3.5	27.1	0.7	1.1
Privatisation						
Primary privatisation method	MEBOs	Private sector share in GDP	15	15	20	20
Secondary privatisation method	voucher	Share of small firms privatised	22.0	28.0	36.0	50.0
Tradability of land rights	limited *de jure*	Share of medium/large firms privatised	8.2	8.2	8.5	11.3
Enterprises						
Protection of shareholder rights	ineffective	Budgetary subsidies (% of GDP)	12.3	6.9	0.7	0.6
Bankruptcy proceedings	ineffective	Credit to enterprises (% of GDP)	na	8.5	4.0	5.8
Competition office	no	Labour productivity in industry (% change)	na	na	na	na
Infrastructure						
Independent telecoms regulator	no	Main telephone lines per 100 inhabitants	4.5	4.5	4.2	3.8
Separation of railway accounts	no	Railway labour productivity (1989=100)	na	na	na	na
Independent electricity regulator	no	Electricity tariff, US¢/kWh (collection ratio in %)	na	na	na	na
Financial institutions						
Deposit insurance	no	Number of banks (of which foreign-owned)	na	17 (0)	21 (0)	24 (0)
Secured transactions law	yes	Asset share of state-owned banks	na	na	na	na
Insider dealing prohibited	yes	Bad loans (% of total loans)	na	na	na	na
Securities commission	no	Stock market capitalisation (% of GDP)	na	na	na	na
Fiscal and social sector						
Private pension funds	no	Tax revenues (% of GDP)	na	16.7	11.7	13.3
Share of population in poverty	na	Earnings inequality (Gini coefficient)	na	na	na	na

Infrastructure

Economic integration and market expansion are hampered by inadequate transport infrastructure.
Tajikistan's mountainous geography creates substantial transportation problems. The long civil war led to the decay of existing transport infrastructure. A key bottleneck is the lack of a railway linking the northern to the southern part of the country.

The potential for hydroelectric power generation remains unused due to lack of investment and inadequate incentives.
Tajikistan's hydroelectric potential is estimated at kWh 120 billion, but the country produced only kWh 15 billion in 1996, down by over 15% since 1991. The power generation and transmission equipment is outdated and power cuts are frequent. The tariff structure creates few incentives for improvements in operational efficiency. Households currently pay 0.1 US cents per kWh, while industrial customers pay 1.5 US cents (with preferential rates for large customers). Marginal costs of power generation and transmission are estimated at 3 US cents per kWh. The government has committed itself to a tariff review to move towards cost recovery by 2001.

Financial institutions

Financial intermediation is very low.
The five largest banks account for about 90% of the total stock of commercial bank credit. These banks still function to some extent as specialised banks of the Soviet era and have served as intermediaries for on-lending directed credits. They are burdened with substantial non-performing loans (estimated at 30% in the case of one of the country's strongest banks, Orienbank) and are severely underprovisioned. With the banking system as whole undercapitalised and unrestructured, financial intermediation is extremely weak.

Prudential regulations have been tightened, but enforcement remains weak.
Since 1996, the NBT has begun to put in place minimum reserve requirements and standard prudential regulations, which were revised in 1998. Nevertheless, only one of the major existing banks meets these requirements. The enforcement of banking supervision is weak, and the NBT lacks the adequate staff to exercise effective monitoring.

A financial sector restructuring programme has recently been agreed with IMF and World Bank.
The new bank restructuring programme envisages external audits of the major state-owned banks, a clear timetable for fulfilment of all prudential requirements and the withdrawal of licences in the case of non-compliance. Prudential ratios have been tightened and minimum capital requirements are to be increased to US$ 500,000 in January 1999 and to US$ 1 million by 2000. Financial sector reforms also include the introduction of a government treasury bill market, the adoption of a new laws on banking and collateral (effective since June 1998), and the move towards credit auctions as the primary vehicle for channelling liquidity to the banking sector.

Fiscal and social safety net reform

Despite a significant decrease in the fiscal deficit, poor tax collection and administration continue to weaken government revenues.
The recent sharp decline in the budget deficit was due primarily to a reduction in government expenditures associated with the peace dividend following the ceasefire. The main fiscal challenge now lies in increasing revenues, which declined from almost 17% of GDP in 1995 to just over 13% in 1997. This reflects in part problems in tax collection and administration, which have resulted in a stock of tax and custom duties arrears of TR 18 billion (3% of GDP) by end-1997. To improve tax enforcement, branches of the State Treasury have been established in local districts during 1997.

Poverty remains a major problem.
Wage arrears and high inflation have increased poverty. Annual per capita income is less than US$ 200 – by far the lowest of all transition economies. Payroll taxes of 38% of the wage bill are levied on employers to finance the state pension and social security funds. In addition, the government grants compensation payments to poor households to replace previous price subsidies, although effective disbursements have been low. With around 70% of the population living in rural areas, a revival of the agricultural sector is perhaps the most important ingredient in alleviation of poverty. The World Bank has recently granted a US$ 50 million loan to be used primarily for investments in social infrastructure, such as health and education.

Turkmenistan

CIS member

1991

Oct	Independence from Soviet Union

1992

June	Bankruptcy law adopted

1993

July	Foreign exchange reserves controlled by president
Oct	Company legislation enacted
Oct	Gas exports to Europe interrupted
Oct	VAT introduced
Oct	Central bank law adopted
Nov	New currency (manat) introduced
Nov	Foreign exchange law adopted

1994

May	Small-scale privatisation begins
Aug	State trading monopoly reinforced
Sept	National privatisation programme adopted

1995

Jan	State treasury system introduced
July	Flat rate income tax introduced
Dec	Inter-bank market established

1996

Jan	Most prices liberalised
Feb	First foreign currency auction
Apr	BIS capital adequacy enacted
May	Barter trade in cotton, oil, wool banned
Aug	First T-bills issued
Dec	Land reform decreed

1997

Mar	Hydrocarbon resources law enacted
Mar	Gas deliveries halted to non-paying CIS customers
Apr	Large-scale privatisation law adopted
Dec	First gas through non-CIS pipeline delivered to Iran

Key reform challenges

- **With much of industry and banking still under state control, privatisation continues to lag. The new private sector remains stifled by government interventions, cumbersome registration procedures, and little access to credit and foreign exchange.**
- **The establishment of a social safety net to alleviate poverty and an unemployment insurance system to cope with redundancies from enterprise restructuring could be partially financed by a reduction of direct and indirect state subsidies.**
- **Conclusion of an IMF agreement could provide a significant stimulus to structural reforms, and help attract additional FDI into the oil and gas sectors, while supporting the very fragile balance of payments position.**

Liberalisation

Some progress has been made in price liberalisation.
After further price liberalisation in 1997 (including on butter, meat, milk, oil, sugar and tea), price controls now apply only to flour and bread, utilities, communal services, rents, petrol, transportation and building materials. Some utility prices have recently been raised, but most remain far below cost recovery levels. Electricity, gas and water, as well as rents, remain free of charge for households. State procurement prices for cotton and wheat have been kept at their January 1997 levels, a decline of 30% in real terms by mid-1998. A doubling of petrol prices to US$ 0.15 per litre in January 1998 was reversed soon after implementation.

The exchange rate has been unified, but access to foreign exchange remains controlled.
The commercial and official exchange rates were unified in April 1998, implying a depreciation of the official rate by 25%. However, the government continues to screen access to the central bank's non-cash foreign exchange auctions, thereby implicitly regulating imports by enterprises. Moreover, surrender requirements on hard currency export earnings remain in place. Control over surrendered foreign exchange has partially shifted to the central bank. Subject to sufficient reserves, the new system provides individuals with better access to foreign exchange.

Privatisation

Little progress has been made in privatisation.
Turkmenistan is lagging in both small- and large-scale privatisation. Line ministries continue to exert effective control over the corporate sector. In April 1997, a presidential decree earmarked 345 medium-sized and large enterprises for privatisation by 2000 and established equal rights for participating foreigners. Another decree in August 1997 highlighted a sub-set of 83 enterprises for corporatisation and privatisation through auctions by the end of the year. A central share registry was established at the State Agency for Foreign Investment (SAFI). However, only four medium-sized and large enterprises were sold during 1997. Small-scale privatisation has also slowed down, primarily because of excessive price expectations in the cash auctions which became the primary privatisation method in December 1996. In January 1998, a new Privatisation Centre was created at SAFI with the immediate aim to privatise 18 large state enterprises through international investment tenders. A modest acceleration of privatisation occurred in the first half of 1998 when 30 medium-sized companies were sold.

Land reform shows some results, but state interference remains pervasive.
Following a decree on land reform in December 1996, most land has been allocated to individual farmers for a two-year lease and eventual private ownership. However, registration of land titles has been slow due to a lack of administrative capacity. The first positive results were evident in the much improved 1997 and 1998 harvests. Yet ownership rights remain contingent on fulfilment of government-determined output targets for cotton and wheat. State control is also exercised through the allocation of collectively owned assets, input supplies and subsidised rural credit. Most individual plots are small and ownership rights do not extend to the sale of land.

Enterprises

Gas exports have been severely disrupted, while other sectors have recorded some improvements.
Turkmenistan's economy has been dominated by the gas sector, which in 1996 accounted for close to half of GDP and three-quarters of industrial production and export revenues. In 1997, gas supplies to CIS customers were disrupted, following disputes about rapidly accumulating payments arrears; their resumption has been stalled by disagreements with Gazprom over transit fees through Russia. This led to a 49% decline in gas production, dragging down industrial production by 30%. Other sectors of the economy recorded significant output growth in 1997; the oil sector, which recently attracted sizeable FDI, saw production rise by 11%. Construction output was up by over 40%, supported by substantial amounts of foreign project finance. Other output stimuli came from foreign greenfield investments, for instance in the textiles sector. By contrast, the state-owned cotton fibre industry has sharply contracted, following the poor cotton harvest in 1996.

Liberalisation			1994	1995	1996	1997
Exchange rate regime	fixed	Share of administered prices in CPI	na	na	na	na
Current account convertibility	limited	Administered prices in "EBRD-15" basket	na	7	7	4
Interest rate liberalisation	limited *de facto*	Share of trade in GDP	86.4	74.1	83.1	48.0
Wage regulation	yes	Tariff revenue (% of imports)	0.4	1.4	0.7	1.8
Privatisation						
Primary privatisation method	MEBOs	Private sector share in GDP	15	15	20	25
Secondary privatisation method	direct sales	Number of small firms privatised	1,064	404	214	97
Tradability of land rights	limited *de jure*	Number of medium/large firms privatised	4	2	5	4
Enterprises						
Protection of shareholder rights	ineffective	Budgetary subsidies (% of GDP)	1.0	1.1	0.8	0.7
Bankruptcy proceedings	ineffective	Credit to enterprises (% of GDP)	6.7	8.5	5.8	8.9
Competition office	no	Labour productivity in industry (% change)	-22.9	-5.9	9.6	-29.8
Infrastructure						
Independent telecoms regulator	no	Main telephone lines per 100 inhabitants	7.6	7.1	7.4	na
Separation of railway accounts	no	Railway labour productivity (1991=100)	42.2	26.3	28.7	27.9
Independent electricity regulator	no	Electricity tariff, US¢/kWh (collection ratio in %)	0 (0)	0 (0)	0 (0)	0 (0)
Financial institutions						
Deposit insurance	no	Number of banks (of which foreign-owned)	na	14 (3)	15 (3)	15 (3)
Secured transactions law	restricted	Asset share of state-owned banks	na	26.1	64.1	68.3
Insider dealing prohibited	no	Bad loans (% of total loans)	na	11.2	11.4	13.9
Securities commission	no	Stock market capitalisation (% of GDP)	na	na	na	na
Fiscal and social sector						
Private pension funds	no	Tax revenues (% of GDP)	8.0	10.6	13.9	21.1
Share of population in poverty	48%	Earnings inequality (Gini coefficient)	na	na	na	na

Inter-enterprise arrears have risen rapidly.
The revenue crisis in the gas sector has spread throughout the economy, with overdue payments to suppliers increasing to 42% of GDP by March 1998. A netting out operation among enterprises reduced arrears to 23% of GDP by August. However, arrears are likely to remain a substantial problem as they partially reflect continued weak financial discipline. Market discipline is also weakened by the failure to apply effectively the 1992 Bankruptcy Law.

The new private sector has expanded, but the business environment remains difficult.
Improved access to foreign exchange and the resulting increase in shuttle trade have relaxed input constraints and supported a moderate growth in the number of private enterprises. However, enterprise registration remains generally cumbersome and entrepreneurial activity is hampered by continued government interference and lack of access to credit. A waiver of the 30% corporate profit tax for small enterprises with total profits below approximately US$ 550 was abolished in April 1998.

Infrastructure

Road and port rehabilitation projects foster institutional reforms.
EBRD projects are contributing to the rehabilitation of the Ashgabad-Mary road and the port at Turkmenbashi. Both projects include open tendering for public works and the commercialisation of the government departments managing these public assets. Open tendering and financial accountability of government represent a significant departure from the existing practice of closed bilateral negotiations for foreign construction work, supported by public foreign borrowing.

Lack of progress on energy tariffs limits the scope for commercialisation.
Given the wealth of gas and oil resources, Turkmenistan possesses significant potential for power generation. However, commercially-oriented financing of investments in energy generation and distribution is unlikely as long as rations of free electricity and gas are provided to households. The reversal of the price increase for petrol shows that progress in reducing indirect social transfers via controlled prices on goods and utilities is likely to be slow.

Financial institutions

State control over the banking sector is pervasive.
The three largest banks, one state-owned and two owned by state enterprises, control 80% of all banking sector assets. Three-quarters of domestic currency credit goes to state-owned enterprises. Access to credit in foreign currency is screened by the State Agency for Foreign Investment and usually tied to import requirements. Manat credit auctions which began in early 1997 were abolished soon afterwards. Directed credits to agriculture have continued and contributed significantly to the growth of manat-denominated credit in 1997. Interest rates on these credits are usually close to zero. Interest rates for all other loans have been liberalised in principle, but in practice this freedom is often limited by government discretion. As a result of state interference and weak credit appraisal skills, banks are burdened with non-performing loans, which increased by over 40% during the first four months of 1998.

A securities market remains to be developed.
Treasury bills have been issued since mid-1996 at irregular intervals and have been placed directly with commercial banks. They are not tradable and accounted for less than 1% of GDP at the end of 1997. Currently, the central bank controls the money supply primarily through foreign exchange auctions.

Fiscal and social sector

The role of state in resource mobilisation and allocation remains substantial.
The presentation of the budget now includes the Oil and Gas Fund, the Foreign Exchange Reserve Fund and the Transport Fund. With these funds, total fiscal revenues equalled 47% of GDP in 1997, much above other countries in the former Soviet Union. The expenditures of the funds remain outside the control of the Ministry of Finance, although during 1997 some expenditures from the Oil and Gas Fund were sequestered for financing budget subsidies, of bread and flour in particular.

The underlying fiscal position has weakened considerably.
The public sector continues to be overstaffed and relatively inefficient. Government expenditures rose sharply in 1997, as a result of substantial public sector wage increases. Real wages in the public sector were increased by two-thirds in April 1998. In light of falling gas revenues and profit taxes, the government has sharply reduced public investment (by as much as 1.5% of GDP in the revised 1998 budget) and slashed price subsidies on several controlled goods. The combination of reduced public investment and social transfers is causing hardship for the population at large.

Ukraine

EU Partnership and Cooperation Agreement · CIS member · WTO observer

1991

Mar	Land code enacted
Aug	Independence from Soviet Union
Oct	Central bank law adopted
Dec	Securities and stock exchange law adopted

1992

Feb	Competition agency established
Mar	Small- and large-scale privatisation begins
May	Bankruptcy law enacted
June	Stock exchange begins trading
Nov	Interim currency (karbovanets) introduced
Dec	VAT introduced

1993

Jan	Income tax law adopted
Aug	Multiple exchange rates reintroduced

1994

Oct	Most prices liberalised
Oct	Most export quotas and licences abolished
Oct	Exchange rate unified
Nov	Voucher privatisation begins

1995

Jan	New corporate profits tax introduced
Mar	T-bills market initiated
June	Securities and exchange commission established
Dec	Indicative export prices removed

1996

Jan	Licensing requirement for grain exports abolished
Mar	Grado bank placed under forced administration
Sept	New currency (hryvnia) introduced

1997

Mar	Land code amended
Apr	Full current account convertibility introduced
June	Export surrender requirement revoked
July	New corporate tax rate introduced
Aug	First sovereign Eurobond
Oct	VAT rate changed

Key reform challenges

- **The sharp fall in the currency in September 1998 will necessitate tight budgetary policies and an acceleration of structural reforms. Successful implementation of the new IMF programme will be crucial.**
- **Further progress in the sale of large enterprises to strategic investors will promote improvements in corporate governance if the privatisation procedures are transparent and the residual state shares in enterprises are managed effectively.**
- **Weak financial discipline – in the form of tax, wage and inter-enterprise arrears as well as barter – is a key constraint on the development of the enterprise sector. Progress in enterprise restructuring will depend on measures to tighten these soft budget constraints, but also on attracting more FDI and strengthening domestic financial institutions.**

Liberalisation

New foreign exchange controls have been imposed.
The collapse of the Russian rouble in August 1998 led to strong pressures on the hryvnia. As part of the authorities' anti-crisis measures, the currency band was widened to 2.5 to 3.5 hryvnia to the US dollar at the beginning of September, leading to a depreciation of over 50% within a month. In order to keep the currency within the new band, the central bank also introduced a number of restrictions on the foreign exchange market, including a 50% export surrender requirement.

New trade barriers affect progress towards WTO accession.
Negotiations on Ukraine's accession to the WTO have continued, with some progress in bilateral discussions. Many trading partners have, however, expressed their concern at the increase in import tariffs and trade barriers, especially to agricultural trade. The recent US$ 150 million joint venture between Daewoo of South Korea and Avtozaz to increase auto production in Ukraine has provoked criticism regarding certain tax exemptions and constraints on imports of used cars, which appear to contravene the most-favoured nation rules of the WTO.

Liberalisation of the grain market could generate higher returns to farmers.
In December 1997, the state purchase of grain was abolished allowing farmers to sell most of their grain through commodity exchanges, which could increase the returns to farmers. In practice, the state remains a major influence in the market as it claims a large proportion of marketed grain as payment for inputs and past debts, and to boost grain reserves.

Privatisation

Further progress is made in large-scale privatisation ...
Privatisation legislation adopted in 1998 envisages the virtual completion of the Mass Privatisation Programme (MPP) by the end of the year. By July 1998, over 7,800 of the original 9,500 medium-sized and large enterprises included in the MPP had been privatised (defined as more than 70% of shares sold). To accelerate the programme, cash sales were introduced and the floor price for all forms of share sales was eliminated. The government's need to raise funds for the budget has given added stimulus to the sale of the 200 largest enterprises via open tender for cash or via investment tender to strategic investors. However, by mid-year only 40 of these enterprises had been privatised. Continuing disagreements between the President and parliament have held back the pace of privatisation. Following a Constitutional Court ruling, the President decreed that the State Property Fund was subordinate to the Council of Ministers.

... though the pace of agricultural privatisation lags behind.
Privatisation in the agricultural sector has been thwarted by constraints on the sale of land. The focus of privatisation in the agro-industrial sector will be on the 440 grain elevators owned by the main grain marketing company. The small-scale privatisation programme was largely completed at the end of 1997, with over 45,400 enterprises privatised.

Enterprises

Weak financial discipline continues to hamper enterprise restructuring.
The dominant role of insiders in newly privatised firms coupled with persistent weaknesses in financial discipline and in the enforcement of bankruptcy law have contributed to the slow pace of industrial restructuring. There are several indicators of continued soft budget constraints on enterprises: by mid-1998, inter-enterprise arrears amounted to over 80% of GDP, wage arrears were 5% of GDP (excluding budgetary wage arrears), and barter trade constituted some 42% of industrial sales. Though the number of reviewed bankruptcy cases has risen steadily, from about 2,000 for the whole of 1995 to over 1,700 during the first quarter of 1998, the complexity of procedures and the lack of trained staff have limited the implementation of the 1992 law. In addition, an estimated 50% of all enterprises reported losses in the first few months of this year. Estimates of the size of the informal economy vary, but range between 40% and 50% of recorded GDP.

Foreign direct investment remains relatively weak.
Net FDI flows were US$ 581 million in 1997 and increased to US$ 518 million during the first half of 1998, taking the cumulative

Liberalisation			1994	1995	1996	1997
Exchange rate regime	fixed, with band	Share of administered prices in CPI	na	na	na	na
Current account convertibility	full	Administered prices in "EBRD-15" basket	6	2	2	2
Interest rate liberalisation	yes	Share of trade in GDP	40.4	41.9	39.6	35.2
Wage regulation	no	Tariff revenue (% of imports)	1.6	1.7	1.2	1.9
Privatisation						
Primary privatisation method	vouchers	Private sector share in GDP	30	34	40	50
Secondary privatisation method	MEBOs	Share of medium/large firms privatised	12.2	12.7	53.3	72.4
Tradability of land rights	limited *de jure*	Privatisation revenues (% of GDP)	0.21	0.13	0.25	0.13
Enterprises						
Protection of shareholder rights	ineffective	Budgetary subsidies (% of GDP)	na	na	na	na
Bankruptcy proceedings	ineffective	Credit to enterprises (% of GDP)	11.9	6.7	6.1	6.0
Competition office	yes	Labour productivity in industry (% change)	-21.4	-4.0	2.4	6.1
Infrastructure						
Independent telecoms regulator	no	Main telephone lines per 100 inhabitants	15.7	16.1	18.1	18.6
Separation of railway accounts	no	Railway labour productivity (1989=100)	46.9	46.1	40.7	42.4
Independent electricity regulator	yes	Electricity tariff, US¢/kWh (collection ratio in %)	1.0 (60)	3.5 (65)	3.7 (70)	3.3 (80)
Financial institutions						
Deposit insurance	no	Number of banks (of which foreign-owned)	228 (1)	230 (1)	229 (6)	227 (12)
Secured transactions law	restricted	Asset share of state-owned banks	na	na	na	na
Insider dealing prohibited	na	Bad loans (% of total loans)	na	na	na	na
Securities commission	yes	Stock market capitalisation (% of GDP)	na	na	na	6.1
Fiscal and social sector						
Private pension funds	no	Tax revenues (% of GDP)	37.3	32.6	34.2	34.3
Share of population in poverty	41%	Earnings inequality (Gini coefficient)	na	na	0.413	na

stock of FDI to just under US$ 2.5 billion. Foreign investors can own up to 100% of a Ukrainian company; however, there has been a lack of clarity and stability regarding the regulatory environment and there are unresolved questions regarding land ownership.

Infrastructure

Utility prices for residential consumers have been increased.
Electricity prices for residential consumers, which remain well below those for industrial consumers, were raised by an average of 23% in May 1998. Higher tariffs are one element of the government's financial recovery plan for the power sector, following the postponement of a similar tariff increase last year. Gas prices were raised by 18% in July 1998 for residential consumers – an increase necessitated by the fall in the value of the hryvnia and the high dependence on imported gas.

Infrastructure privatisation is under way.
Tenders for the sale of power distribution companies commenced at the end of 1997. Packages of shares of up to 40% were offered to strategic investors either for cash or future investment, with the state retaining at least 25% in each company. Initial interest of potential strategic investors was limited, partly because of concerns over price and the transparency of procedures. By July 1998, however, cash tenders for large share packages had been completed for 10 distribution companies; the State Property Fund also announced plans to sell stakes in the main power generating companies in 1999.

Financial institutions

The rescheduling of domestic government debt threatens to weaken liquidity in the banking sector.
The banking sector remains small and undercapitalised. The five sectoral banks created from the initial break-up of the former monobank account for over 70% of total assets in the banking sector. Two of these banks are state-owned (the savings bank and the foreign trade bank); the remaining three have been privatised, although ownership is widely dispersed. In early 1998, total bank assets were estimated at almost US$ 12 billion on the basis of local accounting standards, with a large share in treasury bills. The voluntary rescheduling of some of this government debt in September 1998 will weaken liquidity in the sector. The central bank (NBU) has introduced international accounting standards for all banks, which is likely to result in an increase in the level of loan loss provisions. As of early 1998, the share of non-performing loans in total loans was 20-25% according to unofficial estimates. In April 1998, the NBU abolished the 15% limit on the extent of foreign bank ownership in an attempt to strengthen both capital and competition. By mid-1998 there were 25 banks in Ukraine with foreign capital; their share of total capital is estimated at 12%.

The legal framework of the securities market continues to be strengthened.
The Ukraine Stock Exchange is the largest of four stock exchanges. Since mid-1996, there has also been an over-the-counter electronic share trading system, PFTS. The first share market indices were introduced in 1997. Total turnover on the PFTS increased to an average of US$ 4-6 million per week in early 1998, as both the membership and the number of listed stocks increased. Although there were expectations of further growth resulting from the large-scale privatisation programme, the markets have weakened in the aftermath of the Asian crisis and the financial turmoil in Russia. The Securities and Stock Market State Commission, established in 1995, is currently preparing regulations to implement the law on the National Depository System which took effect in January 1998.

Fiscal and social sector

The government has proposed reductions in the budget deficit.
Lowering the budget deficit is a key element in Ukraine's macroeconomic stabilisation efforts. The 1998 budget, approved at the end of last year, projected a deficit of 3.3% of GDP. However, the deficit exceeded this level in the first half of the year, while public wage and pension arrears amounted to a further 2% of GDP by mid-1998. The Asian and Russian crises have accentuated the funding problems as many non-resident investors left the Treasury bill market, while higher interest rates on both domestic and international markets led to higher debt servicing costs. In September 1998, after consultations with both domestic banks and the non-resident holders of T-bills, the government announced (separate) rescheduling terms of its debt. At the same time, and as one of the main conditions of the new 3-year IMF programme agreed in early September, the government proposed a combination of expenditure cuts and tax changes to reduce the deficit to 2.8% of GDP this year and to lower it further in 1999.

The government is considering proposals to reform the pension system.
The level of the state pension is very low, less than a third of average wages. The government is considering draft legislative proposals to reform the pension system, which include the phasing out of preferential pensions and the establishment of voluntary private pension funds.

Uzbekistan

CIS member · WTO observer

1991

Feb Company law adopted

Sept Independence from Soviet Union

1992

Dec Pledge law adopted

1993

1994

Jan New currency (som) introduced

Apr Stock exchange established

May Bankruptcy law adopted

May Foreign investment law adopted

1995

May Foreign investment law amended

Aug Telecoms law adopted

Dec IMF programme

1996

Mar First T-bills issued

Apr Banking law adopted

Apr Land law amended

June Privatisation programme adopted

Aug Bankruptcy law amended

Oct IMF programme suspended

Dec Competition law adopted

1997

Mar Bank accounting standards adopted

Nov Custom duties and export licensing abolished

Key reform challenges

- **Liberalising the trade and exchange rate regimes and reducing state control of the financial sector are crucial to enhance efficiency and encourage investment.**
- **Accelerating privatisation and reducing the state's role in partially privatised enterprises will promote the emergence of a market-oriented enterprise sector.**
- **To finance expenditures on poverty and infrastructure, fundamental reform of the fiscal and social systems is required; this should encompass replacing indirect subsidies through low utility tariffs with direct transfers to low-income households.**

Liberalisation

The multiple exchange rate regime has taken firm roots.
An IMF stand-by credit facility expired at the end of 1996, pending commitments by the government to unify the exchange rate and to move towards current account convertibility. The multiple exchange rate regime was institutionalised at the beginning of 1997 and supports activities and investments in the government's priority sectors. The highly overvalued "auction rate" and "commercial bank rate" are used for converting export revenues under the obligatory surrender requirement. The rates also apply to selected importers, giving them privileged access to foreign exchange. The widely used (though illegal) black market exchange rates were almost twice as high as the formal rates in mid-1998.

Non-tariff trade restrictions give the state wide-ranging control over international trade.
Negotiations on WTO membership and on a Partnership and Co-operation Agreement with the EU are inhibited by the lack of progress on foreign exchange and trade liberalisation. The state has a trading monopoly in the export of cotton and gold, which generate most of the foreign exchange earnings. Since late 1996, import contracts have to be registered, giving authorities effective control over imports. Since February 1998, imports have to be prepaid in hard currency and these payments can only be processed by authorised banks.

Privatisation

The mass privatisation programme is proceeding at a slow pace.
The mass privatisation programme started in 1996 and minority stakes in about 150 enterprises were sold to Privatisation Investment Funds (PIFs) in 16 auctions. Individuals can participate in the process by purchasing stakes in the PIFs. The second phase of the programme has been delayed. The secondary market for shares has almost completely dried up since the government prohibited managers from buying shares in their own companies in early 1998.

Some large companies are to be sold to foreign investors.
The government is planning to privatise six large enterprises through international tenders. The government has announced that it intends to offer 25% of the state-owned aircraft manufacturer and 47% of the Almalyk Metallurgical Factory by the end of 1998. The World Bank has offered technical assistance in these privatisations.

Enterprises

The state continues to exert control on the management of many enterprises.
Although the management of corporatised and partially privatised companies is independent de jure, there is wide scope for direct administrative control by the state. In many cases, a large part of the 49% shareholding available for privatisation has been transferred to other state entities. The State Property Committee, which is in charge of the privatisation process, maintains some influence on the management of partially privatised companies. The state exercises further control by channelling direct and indirect subsidies to priority sectors. Indirect subsidies include privileged access to foreign exchange at the official exchange rates, credits at negative real interest rates and subsidised inputs.

Legislation has been adopted to encourage foreign direct investment.
Foreign direct investment has been relatively low, although there are some major joint ventures in tobacco, gold mining and the automotive sector. In May 1998, laws on foreign investment became effective to stimulate further investment. Foreign investors receive tax holidays and can import duty-free capital goods, unlike Uzbek companies. Nevertheless foreign investors still face bureaucratic hurdles such as import contract registration, business registration, and licensing and customs delays.

Promoting SMEs is among the government's declared priorities.
A presidential decree of April 1998 halves to US$ 150,000 the minimum capital threshold required for new enterprises. In May 1998, the Cabinet of Ministers proposed a strategy to reduce bureaucratic procedures that complicate the creation, registration and activity of SMEs. Credit to new businesses is provided in part by the state "Business Fund". Despite these efforts, the emergence of a strong SME sector has been hampered by the absence of currency convertibility, by the lack of access to bank credit and by an underdeveloped legal system with often contradictory laws that leave much discretion to civil servants.

Reforms in the agricultural sector continue at a slow pace.
The agricultural sector is largely unreformed. The state has almost full control over the vital cotton industry. The state sets

			1994	1995	1996	1997
Liberalisation						
Exchange rate regime	managed float	Share of administered prices in CPI	na	na	na	na
Current account convertibility	limited	Administered prices in "EBRD-15" basket	na	na	na	na
Interest rate liberalisation	limited *de jure*	Share of trade in GDP	49.8	33.5	28.5	26.3
Wage regulation	yes	Tariff revenue (% of imports)	2.5	2.9	1.8	2.2
Privatisation						
Primary privatisation method	MEBOs	Private sector share in GDP	20	30	40	45
Secondary privatisation method	direct sales	Privatisation revenues (% of GDP)	0.74	0.81	0.81	0.52
Tradability of land rights	limited *de jure*	Number of firms privatised	9,744	5,645	1,644	1,231
Enterprises						
Protection of shareholder rights	ineffective	Budgetary subsidies (% of GDP)	1.9	3.4	4.0	3.2
Bankruptcy proceedings	ineffective	Credit to enterprises (% of GDP)	46.5	18.5	19.2	20.8
Competition office	yes	Labour productivity in industry (% change)	10.5	-1.6	4.1	6.3
Infrastructure						
Independent telecoms regulator	no	Main telephone lines per 100 inhabitants	6.9	7.6	6.7	7.2
Separation of railway accounts	no	Railway labour productivity (1989=100)	na	na	na	na
Independent electricity regulator	no	Electricity tariff, US¢/kWh (collection ratio in %)	na	na	na	na
Financial institutions						
Deposit insurance	no	Number of banks (of which foreign-owned)	31 (1)	29 (1)	30 (3)	30 (3)
Secured transactions law	restricted	Asset share of state-owned banks	46.7	38.4	75.5	70.6
Insider dealing prohibited	yes	Bad loans (% of total loans)	8.0	na	2.0	4.0
Securities commission	yes	Stock market capitalisation (% of GDP)	na	na	1.3	3.9
Fiscal and social sector						
Private pension funds	no	Tax revenues (% of GDP)	22.5	27.7	32.2	28.1
Share of population in poverty	29%	Earnings inequality (Gini coefficient)	na	na	na	na

production targets and prices, supplies all inputs and procures the bulk of the crop. Individual farms have to fulfil a state order quota, before being allowed to market the remaining cotton. All exports have been effectively centralised in four state foreign trade agencies. Land continues to be owned mostly by the state. A Land Code came into force in July 1998, declaring land state property that cannot be traded or mortgaged, except in cases where there are specific provisions in other pieces of (yet unspecified) legislation.

Infrastructure

Greater private sector involvement in telecommunications is envisaged.

The telecommunications infrastructure is very poor. Uzbekistan has one of the lowest penetration rates among transition economies (seven main telephone lines per 100 people), though some progress has been made in upgrading existing fixed line networks. The government plans to sell stakes in local telephone and postal companies to foreign investors. It has opened the mobile telephone market to competition by offering five new licences. In November 1997, an international consortium formed a joint venture with the state telecoms company to upgrade long-distance and international phone networks.

Energy sector reform is focused on increasing capacity.

There are currently no plans to introduce more cost-reflective prices for fuel and electricity. Household electricity tariffs are very low. It is estimated that about 30% of energy is lost as a result of inefficiencies in production and distribution. The government plans to increase the country's energy-generating capacity through a number of investments. Unlike its neighbours, Kazakhstan and Azerbaijan, which have attracted much foreign direct investment, most funding comes in the form of sovereign-guaranteed loans. In June 1998, an international tender for the exploration and development of six oil and gas fields was announced.

Financial institutions

The banking sector remains dominated by the state.

The banking system remains dominated by the state-owned National Bank of Uzbekistan, which accounts for about 60% of all banking assets. Many banks are used for directing subsidised credit to state-owned enterprises and farms. Most commercial banks effectively act as government agencies, enforcing tax, trade and wage regulations. All companies not part of a foreign joint venture are required to keep one single bank account for tax tracking purposes.

Financial reforms are needed to restore confidence in the banking system.

From late 1996, with the assistance of the World Bank, commercial banks started to set aside reserves against non-performing loans. All banks are required to follow a new chart of accounts introduced in early 1997, but implementation has been difficult. The persistence of the Soviet-era distinction between cash and non-cash money reduces confidence in the banking system and incurs resource misallocation costs. Most business transactions must be performed by bank transfer. Cash transactions – with the exception of salary payments and some business travel expenses – are illegal.

Securities markets are developing slowly, but secondary trading is negligible.

Lack of convertibility of the currency and occasional violations of shareholder rights have discouraged foreign investors. A large proportion of the shares on both the stock exchange and the over-the-counter market were bought by state-owned or state-controlled entities. Secondary trading has been low and limited to a few companies.

Fiscal and social sector

A new tax code became effective in January 1998.

The standard corporate profit tax has been reduced from 37% to 35%, although some enterprises pay a lower rate. Numerous exemptions and differential treatment of sectors continue to create distortions and make the tax regime less transparent. According to the new tax code, VAT is levied on imports that were previously exempt. The standard VAT rate has been raised from 18% to 20%, whereas the lower 10% VAT rate on basic food products has been kept unchanged. Discriminatory excise taxes of 50% and 75% have been imposed on tobacco and alcohol imports, respectively. Moreover, there is a 1% "environmental" tax levied on the assets of non-agricultural enterprises.

The social security system has been reorganised.

The social safety net consists partly of family allowances, but also relies heavily on indirect benefits such as subsidised central heating, urban transport and housing. A presidential decree of June 1998 increased the minimum wage by almost 50% to around 1,100 soms per month (US$ 6 at the black market rate), monthly wages in the state sector by 50% and pensions by an average of 60%.

Notes on definitions and options:

Liberalisation

Exchange rate regime
Options: *currency board, fixed, fixed with band, crawling peg, crawling peg with band, managed float, floating.*

Current account convertibility
Options: *full* (full compliance with Article VIII of IMF Agreement), *limited* (restrictions on payments or transfers for current account transactions).

Interest rate liberalisation
Options: *full* (banks are free to set deposit and lending rates), *limited de facto* (there are no legal restrictions on banks to set deposit and lending rates, but limitations arise from substantial market distortions, such as directed credits or very poorly functioning or high illiquid money or credit markets), *limited de jure* (restrictions on the setting of interest rates by banks through law, decree or central bank regulation).

Wage regulation
Restrictions or substantial taxes on the ability of some enterprises to adjust the average wage or wage bill upward; options: *yes, no.*

Share of administered prices in CPI
Administered prices are defined as those prices subject to regulation by the state.

Administered prices in "EBRD-15" basket
"EBRD-15" basket consists of flour/bread, meat, milk, petrol, cotton textiles, shoes, paper, cars, television sets, cement, steel, coal, wood, rents, inter-city bus service.

Share of trade in GDP
The average of exports and imports as a share of GDP.

Privatisation

Primary privatisation method
Options: *vouchers* (distribution of investment coupons at a symbolic price), *direct sales* (sales to outsiders), *MEBOs* (management/ employee buy-outs), *liquidations.*

Secondary privatisation method
Options and definitions as above.

Tradability of land rights
Options: *full* (no substantial restrictions on the tradability of land rights beyond administrative requirements; no discrimination between domestic and foreign subjects), *full except foreigners* (as "full", but with some differential treatment of foreigners), *limited de facto* (substantial de facto limitations on the tradability of land, for example due to the lack of enforceability of land rights, a non-existent land market, or significant obstruction by government officials), *limited de jure* (legal restrictions on the tradability of land rights), *no* (land trade prohibited).

Private sector share in GDP
The "private sector shares" of GDP represent rough EBRD estimates, based on available statistics from both official (government) and unofficial sources. The underlying concept of private sector value added includes income generated by the activity of private registered companies as well as by private entities engaged in informal activity in those cases where reliable information on informal activity is available.

Share of medium/large firms privatised
Defined as the ratio between the cumulative number of medium-sized or large firms privatised to year-end and the total number of medium-sized or large firms initially identified for privatisation; a firm is considered privatised if more than 50% of its equity has been transferred to the private sector.

Share of small firms privatised
Defined as the ratio between the cumulative number of small firms privatised by year-end and the total number of small firms initially identified for privatisation.

Share of firms privatised
Defined as the ratio between the cumulative number of firms privatised by year-end and the total number of firms initially identified for privatisation; a firm is considered privatised if more than 50% of its equity has been transferred to the private sector.

Share of assets privatised
Cumulative share of the book value of assets of all formerly state-owned enterprises transferred to the private sector as a percentage of the book value of all assets of formerly all state-owned enterprises initially identified for privatisation.

Number of medium/large firms privatised
Number of medium-sized or large firms privatised during the year; a firm is considered privatised if more than 50% of its equity has been transferred to the private sector.

Number of small firms privatised
Number of small firms privatised during that year; a firm is considered privatised if more than 50% of its equity has been transferred to the private sector.

Enterprises

Protection of shareholder rights
The effectiveness of legal protections of shareholder rights as determined by a country-by-country survey of domestic and foreign lawyers and legal experts; options: *effective, partly effective, ineffective.*

Bankruptcy proceedings
The effectiveness of court proceedings in encouraging creditors to use judicial settlement and liquidation proceedings as determined by a country-by-country survey of domestic and foreign lawyers and legal experts; options: *effective, partly effective, ineffective.*

Competition office
Competition or anti-monopoly office exists separately from any ministry, though it may not be fully independent; options: *yes, no.*

Credit to enterprises (% of GDP)
Stock of domestic bank credit to enterprises, end-of-year, as a percentage of GDP

Labour productivity in industry (% change)
Labour productivity is calculated as the ratio of industrial production and industrial employment; changes refer to annual averages.

Infrastructure

Independent telecoms regulator
Independent body, but the scope of power may differ across countries; options: *yes, no.*

Separation of railway accounts
Accounts for freight and passenger operations are separated; options: *yes, no.*

Independent electricity regulator
Independent body, but the scope of power may differ across countries; options: *yes, no.*

Railway labour productivity (1989=100)
Productivity measured as the ratio of the number of traffic units (passenger – Kms plus freight tonne – Kms) and the total number of railway employees.

Electricity tariff, US- cents/kWh (collection ratio in %)
Refers to the average retail tariff; the collection ratio is defined as the ratio of total electricity payments received (in cash and non-cash) and total electricity charges.

Financial institutions

Deposit insurance
Deposits in all banks are covered by a formal deposit insurance scheme; options: *yes, no.*

Secured transactions law
Non-possessory security over movables permitted; options: *yes, restricted.*

Insider dealing prohibited
Insider dealing is prohibited by law, decree or central bank regulation; options: *yes, no.*

Securities commission
Securities and exchange commission exists separately from any ministry, though it may not be fully independent; options: *yes, no.*

Number of banks (of which foreign-owned)
Number of commercial and savings banks, excluding savings cooperatives; foreign-owned banks are defined as banks with foreign ownership exceeding 50%, end-of-year.

Asset share of state-owned banks
Share of total assets of majority state-owned banks in total bank sector assets, the state is defined to include the federal, regional and municipal levels, as well as the state property fund and the state pension fund, state-owned banks are defined as banks with state ownership exceeding 50%, end-of-year.

Bad loans (% of total loans)
Refers to non-performing loans, excluding loans transferred to state rehabilitation agency/consolidation bank, end-of-year.

Stock market capitalisation (% of GDP)
Market value of all shares listed on the stock market as a percentage of GDP, end-of-year.

Fiscal and social sector

Private pension funds
Options: *yes, no.*

Share of population in poverty
Percentage of population living on less than US$ 4 (in 1990 US$ at PPP) a day per person.

Tax revenues (% of GDP)
Tax revenues include direct and indirect taxes and payroll taxes.

Earnings inequality (Gini coefficient)
The Gini coefficient measures the distribution of employees' earnings. A higher coefficient implies a higher degree of earnings inequality. The Gini coefficient is derived from the cumulative distribution of earnings across the workforce ranked in order of ascendance. It is defined as one half of the mean difference between any two observations in the earnings distribution divided by average earnings. Its possible values range between 0 and 1. The Gini coefficients presented in the table are calculated using monthly earnings data as reported by employers. Small employers are often excluded, and some data refer to the public sector only. All data in this category are from UNICEF, International Child Development Centre, Regional Monitoring Report, 1998.

Sources: National authorities (including EBRD surveys), IMF, World Bank, IFC, WTO, OECD, UNICEF, UNDP and EBRD staff estimates.

Country footnotes:

Albania

Number and assets of banks exclude branches of foreign banks. Independent electricity and telecoms regulators are in place, but most regulatory functions are still carried out by the government. Bad loans includes loans of banks under forced administration.

Azerbaijan

Bad loans refers to overdue credits.

Belarus

The exchange rate regime is characterised by multiple exchange rates (official non-cash rate, market cash rate, black market rate and parallel interbank market); the official rate is administratively set and the market cash rate is subject to a maximum ceiling. The EBRD-15 basket does not include prices for coal, wood, rents and inter-city bus service. Tariff revenues refer to taxes on international trade. Bad loans include prolonged and doubtful debts.

Bulgaria

The exchange rate is fixed at a rate of 1,000 leva to the DM. Domestic credit includes all claims on the non-government sector, including claims on non-financial state-owned enterprises, private enterprises, the public and non-bank financial institutions; it includes credit in local as well as in foreign currencies. Share of assets privatised refers to total cumulative share of assets of all formerly state-owned enterprises transferred to the private sector, including voucher privatisation in 1997.

Croatia

Wage regulation exists as incomes policy for the public sector. Tariff revenues refers to all taxes on international trade. Land is tradable, but the right to trade land applies to foreigners only on a reciprocity basis and foreigners cannot acquire certain types of land (including agricultural) from the state. Privatisation revenues excludes swaps with frozen foreign currency deposits. Securities and exchange commission is not fully operational as of mid-1998. There are no private pension funds, but private insurance companies offer life insurance and pension schemes.

Czech Republic

Share of administered prices in CPI excludes health insurance, motor insurance, customers' fees for radio and TV and fees by local authorities; these items represent about 5% of the CPI. Labour productivity in industry refers to manufacturing. The new telecoms law is expected to establish independence of the Czech Telecommunications Office from the Ministry of Transport and Communications. Asset share of state-owned banks excludes Ceska Sporitelna and Kommercni Banka, which have a state share of 45% and 48.7% respectively. Bad loans excludes loans on the books of Kosolidacni banka, banks in receivership and the loan of CSOB to Slovenská inkasní jednotka.

Estonia

The exchange rate is fixed at a rate of 8 kroon to the DM. Tariff revenues does not include differential excise taxes on imports. Domestic credit to enterprises refers to domestic credit to private sector including households. The new competition law, effective from October 1998, foresees greater independence for the existing Competition Board.Labour productivity in industry refers to manufacturing. According to the recently approved telecommunications law, a new regulatory body is to be established by the end of 1998. Number of banks includes Merita-Nordbanken branch and investment banks. Bad loans refers to provisions for non-collectible loans.

FYR Macedonia

While the exchange rate is officially a managed float, since July 1997 there has been a *de facto* peg to the DM at a rate of 30.9 denar. Number and assets of banks exclude branches of foreign banks. Bad loans also includes loans of banks under forced administration.

Hungary

The exchange rate is a pre-announced crawling peg to a currency basket of 70% DM and 30% US$, with band of +/– 2.25%. Labour productivity in industry refers to manufacturing.

Kazakhstan

Tariff revenues refers to taxes on international trade. Credit to enterprises includes credit to households. The state share of banking sector assets increased in 1997 following the merger of private owned Alem bank and state-owned Turan bank into a new state-owned institution.

Kyrgyzstan

Share of firms privatised refers to cumulative share of privatised companies of total number of state-owned enterprises as of 1991; an enterprise is considered privatised if there is a decision to reorganise it as a joint-stock company. Budgetary subsidies refer to transfers and subsidies. The increase in industrial labour productivity in 1997 is due primarily to the rise in production at the Kumtor gold mine. The figure for 1997 stock market capitalisation excludes the state energy company, Kyrgyzenergo, which was pre-listed on the Stock Exchange in December 1997.

Latvia

The exchange rate has been informally fixed to the Special Drawing Rights (SDR) since February 1994 and has maintained a constant exchange rate of LVL 0.7997 per SDR. Foreign entities are allowed to own land under joint venture with Latvian entities whereby Latvian entities have a majority stake. Share of assets privatised refers only to assets transferred to the Latvian Privatisation Agency (established in 1994) and does not include all formerly state-owned assets. Labour productivity in industry refers to manufacturing. The Telecommunications Tariff Council (TTC) is in charge of regulating tariffs while other regulatory activities are performed by the Ministry of Transport and Communications, The securities commission is part of the Ministry of Finance, but the members of the commission are independently appointed by and reports to parliament.

Lithuania

The exchange rate is fixed at a rate of 4 litai to the US$. Tariff revenues refer to all taxes on foreign trade. Tradability of land rights is full for non-agricultural land; ownership of agricultural land is constitutionally prohibited for foreigners and partially restricted for Lithuanian legal persons. The first phase of privatisation was conducted from 1991-95 where medium-sized and large enterprises were privatised by methods of public subscription of shares and public tender, accepting vouchers as the main payment method; the second phase, from 1996, is conducted against cash. Labour productivity in industry refers to manufacturing. The State Energy Inspectorate issues licences while the State Commission for Energy Pricing regulates tariffs. A new law, expected to be ready for parliamentary approval by October 1998, will establish a new independent regulatory body.

Moldova

Tariff revenues refers to all taxes on foreign trade. The 1997 figure for small enterprises privatised refers to cash privatisation only; privatisation through vouchers peaked in 1994-95, with 1,350 small firms (and 1,150 medium-sized and large firms) privatised. The National Energy Regulatory Commission does not yet have price setting authority. The asset share of state-owned banks is zero for all four years, after four state-owned banks were majority privatised in 1994 (and fully privatised by the end of 1995). Bad loans refers to doubtful and loss credits.

Poland

The exchange rate is a pre-announced crawling peg to a currency basket of 45% US$, 35% DM, 10% £, 5% FF and 5% SWF, with a fluctuation band of +/– 10%. Labour productivity in industry refers to manufacturing. The telecoms law submitted to parliament in October 1997 would establish an independent telecommunications regulator. There exists an energy regulatory agency, but tariffs for final users are still set by the Ministry of Finance. There were no private pension funds as of October 1998 although the regulator had received 14 applications for licences for pension funds, which will be established in 1999.

Romania

Credit to enterprises excludes credits in foreign currencies. Labour productivity in industry refers to manufacturing. The new energy law submitted to parliament in June 1998 foresees the creation of an independent electricity regulator. Bad loans includes overdue loans and interest classified as doubtful and loss-making; data for bad loans for Credit Bank CEC between 1994 and 1996 and Dacia Felix Bank in 1997 are not included. Stock market capitalisation (% of GDP) includes listings on the Bucharest Stock Exchange and RASDAQ over-the-counter market.

Russia

The exchange rate was allowed to fluctuate within a band of +/– 15% around 6.2 roubles to the US$ until August, when the band was at first widened and then abolished; since then, the exchange rate has been determined by a managed float, although with a fragmented foreign exchange market. Tariff revenues refer to all taxes on international trade. While the Russian authorities introduced tight measures on capital controls, current account convertibility has officially remained in place (as of early October 1998); however, trading on the currency market has repeatedly been suspended and recently two foreign exchange markets have been introduced. Electricity tariff figures are averages of the Siberian, Northern, Southern, Volga, Far East and Ural regions and the Federation; collection ratios are estimated. Although there is no general deposit insurance, depositors of Sberbank, the state-owned savings bank, are covered by a formal deposit insurance scheme. Insider dealing is prohibited, but no penalties are specified and no market surveillance system exists.

Slovak Republic

The exchange rate was fixed to a basket of DM (60%) and the US$ (40%), with a +/– 7% fluctuation band; on 1 October 1998 the band was abolished and the currency has been determined by a managed float. Tariff revenues refers to import tariffs, customs duties and import surcharge. Three methods have been almost equally important in the privatisation process: vouchers, direct sales to outsiders and MEBOs. Stock market capitalisation data are taken from the IFC *Emerging Stock Markets Factbook* 1998; they refer only to listed and registered shares, but exclude shares on the free market.

Slovenia

Labour productivity in industry refers to manufacturing.

Turkmenistan

The official exchange rate has been fixed at 5,200 manat to the US$ since April 1998; the commercial bank rate (applying to all cash transactions) has fluctuated around the level of 5,350 manat to the US$; there is an additional parallel market on which the manat depreciated 7,000 to the US$ following the Russian crisis. Tariff revenues refer to differential excise taxes on imports; Turkmenistan does not levy import tariffs. Industrial production excludes oil and gas extraction. Households are entitled to a free electricity allowance of 45 kWh per family member per month; excess usage is charged at just under 1 US cent per kWh.

Ukraine

The currency band was widened in early September from the original hryvnia 1.80-2.25 to the US$, to 2.25-3.50; by early October, the official rate for the hryvnia had fallen almost to the bottom of the new band. Tariff revenues refers to taxes on international trade and transactions. Although there is no general deposit insurance, depositors of the Savings Bank are covered by a formal deposit insurance scheme.

Uzbekistan

The exchange rate is determined by a managed float, but there are multiple exchange rates, most of which are not determined by market forces. Tariff revenues refer to custom duties and export taxes. Number of firms privatised includes enterprises that are corporatised and only partially privatised.

Selected economic indicators for each country

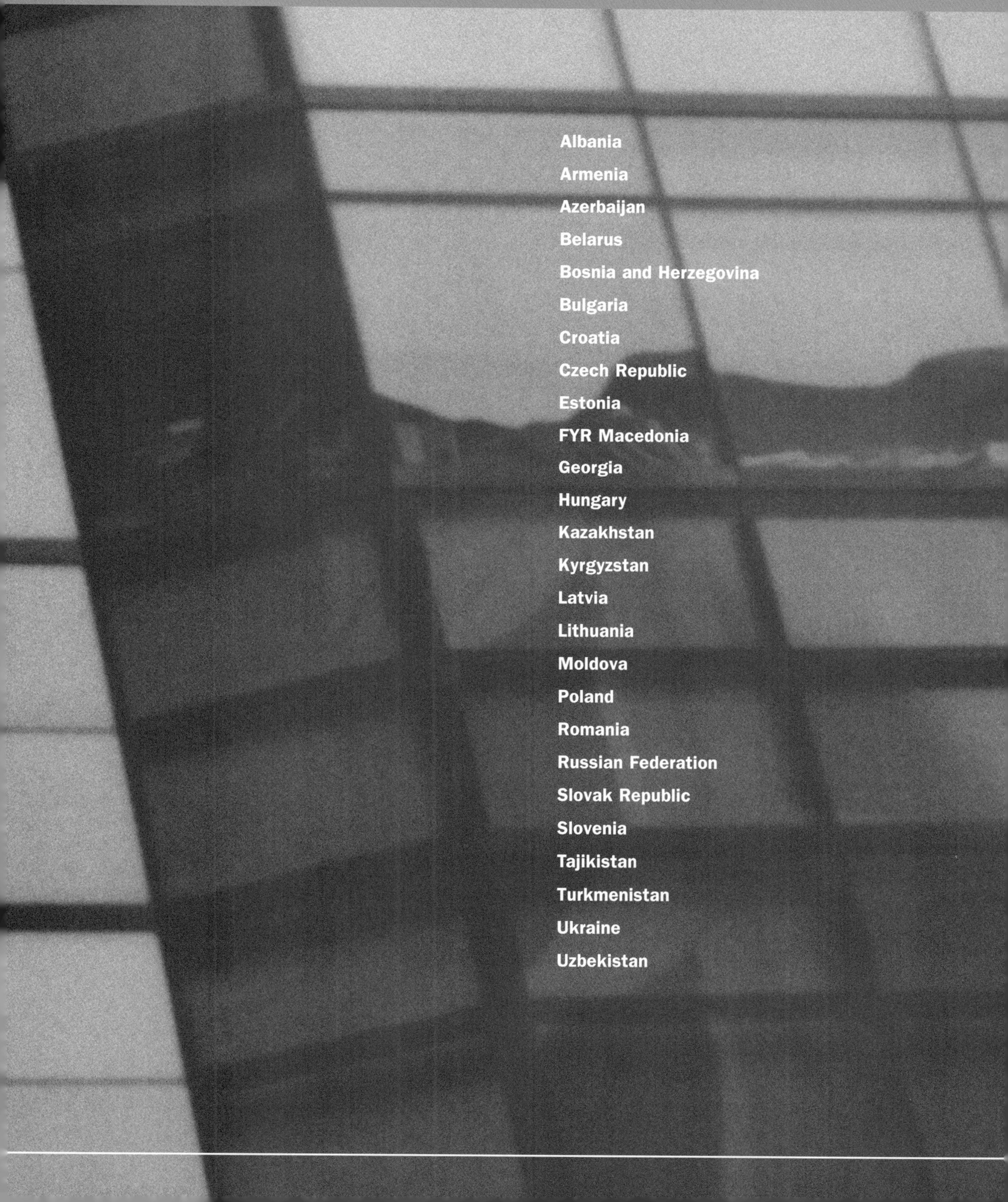

Albania
Armenia
Azerbaijan
Belarus
Bosnia and Herzegovina
Bulgaria
Croatia
Czech Republic
Estonia
FYR Macedonia
Georgia
Hungary
Kazakhstan
Kyrgyzstan
Latvia
Lithuania
Moldova
Poland
Romania
Russian Federation
Slovak Republic
Slovenia
Tajikistan
Turkmenistan
Ukraine
Uzbekistan

Albania

	1991	1992	1993	1994	1995	1996	1997 *Estimate*	1998 *Projection*
Output				*(Percentage change)*				
GDP at constant prices	-27.7	-7.2	9.6	9.4	8.9	9.1	-7.0	9.0
Industrial gross output	-42.0	-51.2	-10.0	-2.0	1.0	15.8	-5.6	na
Agricultural gross output	-17.4	18.5	10.4	10.3	10.6	0.5	1.0	na
Employment				*(Percentage change)*				
Labour force (annual average)	6.2	-4.2	0.4	1.3	1.8	1.8	na	na
Employment (annual average)	0.0	-28.9	-3.2	9.7	5.7	-2.5	na	na
				(In per cent of labour force)				
Unemployment (end-year) [1]	8.3	27.9	29.0	19.6	16.9	12.4	na	na
Prices and wages				*(Percentage change)*				
Consumer prices (annual average) [2]	35.5	226.0	85.0	22.6	7.8	12.7	32.1	21.9
Consumer prices (end-year) [2]	104.1	236.6	30.9	15.8	6.0	17.4	42.1	10.0
Wages in budgetary institutions (end of period)	na	na	64.5	46.9	25.6	20.0	0.0	na
Government sector				*(In per cent of GDP)*				
General government balance [3]	-31.0	-20.3	-14.4	-12.4	-10.3	-12.1	-12.7	-13.9
General government expenditure	61.9	44.0	34.9	31.2	30.8	29.0	27.6	na
Monetary sector				*(Percentage change)*				
Broad money (end-year)	104.4	152.7	75.0	40.6	51.8	43.8	28.4	na
Domestic credit (end-year)	100.1	68.0	27.7	35.3	23.6	26.4	8.6	na
				(In per cent of GDP)				
Broad money	69.1	54.1	40.2	37.7	47.8	55.0	64.4	61.9
Interest and exchange rates				*(In per cent per annum, end-year)*				
Refinancing rate	na	40.0	34.0	25.0	20.5	24.0	34.0	na
Treasury bill rate (three-month maturity)	na	na	na	10.0	14.7	21.1	35.3	na
Deposit rate (one year) [4]	5.0	32.0	23.0	16.5	13.7	19.1	27.8	na
Lending rate (one year) [5]	8.0	39.0	30.0	20.0	21.0	28.8	43.0	na
				(Lek per US dollar)				
Exchange rate (end-year)	25.0	98.7	100.9	95.0	94.5	103.7	149.8	na
Exchange rate (annual average)	14.6	81.3	105.6	95.4	93.0	104.8	149.6	na
External sector				*(In millions of US dollars)*				
Current account	-249	-434	-365	-279	-176	-245	-276	-399
Trade balance [6]	-208	-454	-490	-460	-474	-692	-519	-675
Exports [6]	73	70	112	141	205	229	167	226
Imports [6]	281	524	602	601	679	921	685	901
Foreign direct investment, net	8	32	45	65	89	97	42	95
Gross reserves (end-year), excluding gold [7]	1	72	147	204	240	280	306	na
External debt stock	628	811	936	1,012	683	732	760	na
				(In months of current account expenditures, excluding transfers)				
Gross reserves (end-year), excluding gold [7]	0.04	1.4	2.3	3.2	3.5	3.1	4.5	na
				(In per cent of current account revenues, excluding transfers)				
Debt service	33.0	37.2	16.8	19.6	2.4	6.0	6.2	na
Memorandum items				*(Denominations as indicated)*				
Population (in millions, end-year)	3.3	3.2	3.2	3.2	3.2	3.2	3.2	na
GDP (in billions of lek)	16.5	53.2	125.3	187.9	224.7	281.0	338.9	450.0
GDP per capita (in US dollars)	346	222	388	620	745	799	708	na
Share of industry in output (at current prices)	32.1	16.9	13.9	12.4	11.5	12.2	na	na
Share of agriculture in output (at current prices)	42.5	54.2	54.6	55.1	55.9	55.4	na	na
Current account/GDP (in per cent)	-22.1	-66.3	-30.8	-14.2	-7.3	-9.1	-12.2	-13.7
External Debt minus Reserves (in US$ millions)	627	739	789	808	443	452	454	na
External Debt/GDP (in per cent)	55.7	123.9	78.9	51.4	28.3	27.3	33.5	na
External Debt/Exports (in per cent)	860.3	1158.6	835.7	717.7	333.2	319.7	455.1	na

Note:

Data for 1991-96 represent official estimates of outturns as reflected in publications from the national authorities, the International Monetary Fund, the World Bank, the OECD, PlanEcon and the Institute of International Finance. Data for 1997-98 reflect EBRD evaluations, partly based on information from these sources.

Methodological notes can be found on pp. 232-234.

Armenia

	1991	1992	1993	1994	1995	1996	1997 Estimate	1998 Projection
Output				*(Percentage change)*				
GDP at constant prices	-17.1	-52.6	-14.8	5.4	6.9	5.8	3.1	6.0
Industrial gross output	na	na	-28.0	5.6	2.6	1.2	0.9	na
Agricultural gross output	na	na	-18.5	3.1	4.0	1.7	-5.9	na
Employment				*(Percentage change)*				
Labour force (end-year)	na	na	1.4	-2.2	-0.8	0.1	1.6	na
Employment (end-year)	2.6	-5.6	-2.2	-3.6	-0.8	-2.7	-2.6	na
				(In per cent of labour force)				
Unemployment [1]	na	1.8	5.3	6.7	6.7	9.2	10.7	na
Prices and wages				*(Percentage change)*				
Consumer prices (annual average)	na	na	3,500	5,273	176.7	18.7	14.0	11.0
Consumer prices (end-year)	na	na	10,896	1,885	31.9	5.8	21.8	3.0
Gross average monthly wages (annual average)	na	na	na	2,760	240.0	71.0	30.0	na
Government sector				*(In per cent of GDP)*				
General government balance [2]	-1.9	-13.9	-54.7	-10.5	-11.0	-9.3	-6.3	-5.8
General government expenditure	28.0	46.7	82.9	42.9	26.6	23.7	24.5	na
Monetary sector				*(Percentage change)*				
Broad money (end-year)	na	na	1,077.2	729.5	62.5	32.8	29.6	na
Domestic credit (end-year)	na	na	864.8	1,437.2	66.4	27.6	8.2	na
				(In per cent of GDP)				
Broad money	na	na	71.5	13.5	7.9	8.3	8.9	na
Interest and exchange rates				*(In per cent per annum, end-year)*				
Interbank interest rate (weighted average)	na	na	na	na	na	48.6	36.4	na
Treasury bill rate (three-month maturity)	na	na	na	na	37.8	41	56	na
Deposit rate [3]	na	na	na	na	63	32	26	na
Lending rate [3]	na	na	na	na	12	66	54	na
				(Dram per US dollar)				
Exchange rate (end-year)	na	2.1	75	406	402	435	495	na
Exchange rate (annual average)	na	na	9	289	406	414	491	na
External sector				*(In millions of US dollars)*				
Current account (excl. official transfers)	na	-195	-315	-231	-483	-428	-472	-535
Trade balance [4]	na	-102	-78	-128	-354	-470	-560	-500
Exports [4]	na	83	156	216	271	290	233	300
Imports [4]	na	185	234	344	625	760	793	800
Foreign direct investment, net	na	0	0	3	19	22	51	170
Gross reserves (end-year), excluding gold [5]	0	0	0	32	107	168	238	na
External debt stock	na	na	na	200	371	611	786	na
				(In months of imports of goods and services)				
Gross reserves (end-year), excluding gold [5]	na	na	na	0.7	1.6	2.3	3.1	na
				(In per cent of exports of goods and services)				
Debt service	na	na	na	3.0	20.6	20.3	16.4	na
Memorandum items				*(Denominations as indicated)*				
Population (in millions, end-year)	3.6	3.7	3.7	3.7	3.7	3.7	3.7	na
GDP (in millions of dram)	na	na	4,265	187,049	522,285	660,311	798,555	939,580
GDP per capita (in US dollars)	na	na	125	173	344	426	435	na
Share of industry in GDP (in per cent)	na	na	25.8	29.1	24.3	23.8	25.2	na
Share of agriculture in GDP (in per cent)	na	na	49.1	43.5	38.7	33.0	30.1	na
Current account/GDP (in per cent) [6]	na	na	-67.3	-35.7	-37.5	-26.8	-29.0	-28.7
External Debt minus Reserves (in US$ millions)	na	na	na	168	264	443	548	na
External Debt/GDP (in per cent)	na	na	na	30.9	28.8	38.3	48.3	na
External Debt/Exports (in per cent)	na	na	na	92.8	136.9	210.7	337.3	na

Note:

Data for 1991-96 represent official estimates of outturns as reflected in publications from the national authorities, the International Monetary Fund, the World Bank, the OECD, PlanEcon and the Institute of International Finance. Data for 1997-98 reflect EBRD evaluations, partly based on information from these sources.

Methodological notes can be found on pp. 232-234.

Azerbaijan

	1991	1992	1993	1994	1995	1996	1997 Estimate	1998 Projection
Output				(Percentage change)				
GDP at constant prices	-0.7	-22.6	-23.1	-19.7	-11.8	1.3	5.8	6.7
Industrial gross output	-8.9	-30.4	-19.7	-24.8	-21.4	-6.7	0.2	na
Agricultural gross output	-2.6	-25.0	-15.4	-13.0	-6.8	3.1	-6.9	na
Employment [1]				(Percentage change)				
Labour force (end-year)	na	na	0.5	-3.1	1.6	5.1	0.2	na
Employment (end-year)	na	-1.7	-0.2	-2.3	-0.5	2.0	0.2	na
				(In per cent of labour force)				
Unemployment	na	15.4	16.0	15.2	17.0	19.4	19.3	na
Prices and wages				(Percentage change)				
Consumer prices (annual average)	107	912	1,129	1,664	411.7	19.7	3.5	0.9
Consumer prices (end-year)	126	1,395	1,294	1,788	84.5	6.5	0.4	3.9
Gross monthly average wages in industry (annual average)	83	871	701	576	355	53	33	na
Government sector				(In per cent of GDP)				
General government balance [2]	na	na	-15.3	-12.1	-4.9	-2.8	-1.7	-3.6
General government expenditure	na	na	55.9	45.9	22.4	20.4	21.4	na
Monetary sector				(Percentage change)				
Broad money (end-year)	na	na	821	1,114	24.0	18.9	33.6	na
Domestic credit (end-year)	na	na	480	841	61.0	33.2	11.1	na
				(In per cent of GDP)				
Broad money	na	39.0	54.9	55.9	12.2	11.3	13.4	na
Interest and exchange rates				(In per cent per annum, end-year)				
Interbank interest rate [3]	na	13	144	406	144	36	22.9	na
Treasury bill rate (three-month maturity)	na	na	na	na	na	34	14.3	na
Deposit rate [4]	na	10	34	406	90	13	11.5	na
Lending rate [5]	na	60	257	406	107	33	21.5	na
				(Manat per US dollar)				
Exchange rate (end-year)	na	45	238	4,330	4,440	4,098	3,888	na
Exchange rate (annual average)	na	na	120	1,432	4,417	4,301	3,983	na
External sector				(In millions of US dollars)				
Current account	153	488	2	-121	-318	-811	-915	-1,480
Trade balance [6]	60	489	-5	-163	-275	-549	-567	-850
Exports [6]	295	1,275	716	682	680	789	808	750
Imports [6]	336	786	721	845	955	1,338	1,375	1,600
Foreign direct investment, net [7]	na	na	20	22	282	661	1,093	1,155
Gross reserves (end-year), excluding gold [8]	na	0	0	2	119	214	467	na
External debt stock	na	na	na	230	420	560	590	na
				(In months of imports of goods and services)				
Gross reserves (end-year), excluding gold [8]	na	0	0	0	1.2	2.0	4.0	na
				(In per cent of exports of goods and services)				
Debt service	na	na	na	na	7.9	9.7	7.4	na
Memorandum items				(Denominations as indicated)				
Population (in millions, end-year)	7.24	7.30	7.36	7.42	7.47	7.51	7.57	na
GDP (in billions of manat) [9]	2.7	24.1	157	1,873	10,669	13,663	15,352	17,500
GDP per capita (in US dollars) [10]	na	364	223	173	323	423	509	na
Share of industry in GDP	23.6	29.4	25.0	20.4	27.3	25.8	24.8	na
Share of agriculture in GDP	30.4	25.9	26.9	32.2	25.1	24.7	20.0	na
Current account/GDP (in per cent)	na	na	na	-9.2	-13.2	-25.5	-23.7	-32.7
External Debt minus Reserves (in US$ millions)	na	na	na	228	301	346	123	na
External Debt/GDP (in per cent)	na	na	na	17.6	17.4	17.6	15.3	na
External Debt/Exports (in per cent)	na	na	na	33.7	61.8	71.0	73.0	na

Note:
Data for 1991-96 represent official estimates of outturns as reflected in publications from the national authorities, the International Monetary Fund, the World Bank, the OECD, PlanEcon and the Institute of International Finance. Data for 1997-98 reflect EBRD evaluations, partly based on information from these sources.

Methodological notes can be found on pp. 232-234.

Belarus

	1991	1992	1993	1994	1995	1996	1997 Estimate	1998 Projection
Output				*(Percentage change)*				
GDP at constant prices	-1.2	-9.6	-7.6	-12.6	-10.4	2.8	10.4	5.0
Industrial gross output	1.0	-9.4	-10.0	-17.1	-11.7	3.5	17.6	na
Agricultural gross output	na	-9.0	3.7	-14.3	-4.7	2.4	-5.5	na
Employment				*(Percentage change)*				
Labour force (end-year)	-2.2	-2.9	-0.6	-2.4	-5.7	0.1	-2.5	na
Employment (end-year)	-2.5	-2.6	-1.3	-2.5	-6.2	-1.0	-2.0	na
				(in per cent of labour force)				
Unemployment [1]	0.1	0.5	1.4	2.1	2.7	3.9	2.8	na
Prices and wages				*(Percentage change)*				
Consumer prices (annual average)	na	969	1,188	2,200	709	53	64	50
Consumer prices (end-year)	na	1,559	1,996	1,960	244	39	63	60
Producer prices (annual average)	150	2,330	1,536	2,171	462	34	89	na
Producer prices (end-year)	na	3,275	2,316	1,867	122	31	90	na
Gross average monthly wages (annual average)	na	838	1,107	1,504	669	61	87	na
Government sector				*(In per cent of GDP)*				
General government balance [2]	na	0.0	-1.9	-2.5	-1.9	-1.6	-2.1	-3.0
General government expenditure	na	46.0	56.2	50.0	44.6	42.6	46.8	na
Monetary sector				*(Percentage change)*				
Broad money (end-year)	na	na	na	1,111	158.4	52.4	111.4	na
Domestic credit (end-year)	na	na	na	na	157.4	58.5	115.5	na
				(In per cent of GDP)				
Broad money	na	na	58.1	39.0	15.0	14.8	17.9	na
Interest and exchange rates				*(In per cent per annum, end-year)*				
Refinancing rate	na	30	210	300	66	35	40	na
Treasury bill rate (three-month maturity)	na	na	na	320	70	37	38	na
Deposit rate (one year)	na	na	65	90	101	32	15	na
Lending rate (one year)	na	na	72	149	175	64	33	na
				(Belarussian roubles per US dollar)				
Exchange rate (end-year) [3]	na	15	698	10,600	11,500	15,500	31,230	na
Exchange rate (annual average) [3]	na	17	269	3,666	11,533	13,292	26,191	na
External sector				*(In millions of US dollars)*				
Current account	na	na	-1,113	-641	-254	-503	-799	-950
Trade balance [4]	na	377	-1,051	-710	-528	-1,149	-1,335	-1,350
Exports [4]	na	3,580	2,812	2,641	4,621	5,790	7,383	7,000
Imports [4]	na	3,203	3,863	3,351	5,149	6,939	8,718	8,350
Foreign direct investment, net	na	na	18	11	7	70	190	50
Gross reserves (end-year), excluding gold [5]	na	na	37	101	377	369	394	na
External debt stock	na	570	969	1,321	1,623	1,785	1,869	na
				(In months of imports of goods and services)				
Gross reserves (end-year), excluding gold [5]	na	na	0.1	0.4	0.8	0.6	0.5	na
				(In per cent of exports of goods and services)				
Debt service	na	0.0	0.5	4.5	3.9	3.2	na	na
Memorandum items				*(Denominations as indicated)*				
Population (in millions, end-year)	10.2	10.2	10.2	10.3	10.3	10.3	10.2	na
GDP (in billions of Belarussian roubles)	86	92	986	17,815	119,813	184,174	351,043	553,000
GDP per capita (in US dollars)	na	524	358	472	1,007	1,346	1,314	na
Share of industry in GDP	na	40.4	30.9	30.8	31.4	35.3	37.4	na
Share of agriculture in GDP	na	23.8	18.3	15.0	17.7	15.9	15.0	na
Current account/GDP (in per cent)	na	na	-30.4	-13.2	-2.4	-3.6	-6.0	-7.7
External Debt minus Reserves (in US$ millions)	na	na	932	1,220	1,246	1,416	1,475	na
External Debt/GDP (in per cent)	na	na	26.4	27.2	15.6	12.9	13.9	na
External Debt/Exports (in per cent)	na	na	34.5	50.0	35.1	30.8	25.3	na

Note:
Data for 1991-96 represent official estimates of outturns as reflected in publications from the national authorities, the International Monetary Fund and the World Bank.
Data for 1997-98 reflect EBRD evaluations, partly based on information from these sources.

Methodological notes can be found on pp. 232-234.

Bosnia and Herzegovina

	1991	1992	1993	1994	1995	1996	1997 Estimate	1998 Projection
Output				(Percentage change)				
Real GDP [1]	-20	na	na	na	32	46	39	30
Federation	na	na	na	na	na	55	37	na
Republika Srpska	na	na	na	na	na	25	42	na
Industrial output								
Federation	na	na	na	na	341	122	30	na
Republika Srpska	na	na	na	na	-13	20	34	na
Employment				(Percentage change)				
Employment [2]	na	na	na	na	53.1	10.9	3.3	na
Prices and wages				(Percentage change)				
Retail prices (annual average)								
Federation	114	73,109	44,069	780	-4.4	-24.5	13.4	5
Republika Srpska (YUD-based) [3]	114	7,461	$2.2*10^{15}$	1,061	117.6	65.9	2.7	10
Republika Srpska (DM-based) [4]	na	na	na	na	12.9	17.2	-6.7	na
Gross average monthly wages								
Federation	na	na	na	na	na	290	58	na
Republika Srpska	na	na	na	na	-31	43	64	na
Government sector				(In per cent of GDP)				
Consolidated government balance [7]	na	na	na	-10.6	-0.3	-3.7	-1.2	-1.9
Federation	na	na	na	na	na	-2.5	-0.4	na
Republika Srpska	na	na	na	na	na	-0.1	0.0	na
Consolidated government expenditure	na	na	na	28.1	34.0	43.4	32.6	na
Federation	na	na	na	na	na	12.9	15.0	na
Republika Srpska	na	na	na	na	na	13.1	6.1	na
Monetary sector				(Percentage change)				
Broad money [5]	na	na	na	na	9	96	25	71
Domestic credit [5]	na	na	na	na	-13	14	17	na
				(In per cent of GDP)				
Broad money [5]	na	na	na	11.4	12.8	15.6	12.5	na
Exchange rates				(Dinar/KM per DM)				
Exchange rate (end-year) [6]	na	na	na	na	100	100	1	na
Exchange rate (annual average) [6]	na	na	na	na	100	100	1	na
External sector				(In millions of US dollars)				
Current account	na	na	na	-177	-193	-748	-1,046	-1,815
excluding official transfers	na	na	na	-492	-570	-1,306	-1,468	-2,005
Trade balance	na	na	na	-803	-930	-1,546	-1,629	na
Exports [8]	2,120	495	7	91	152	336	570	na
Imports [8]	1,673	429	60	894	1,082	1,882	2,199	na
of which humanitarian aid in-kind	na	na	na	561	459	246	360	na
Foreign Investment	na	na	na	0	0	0	0	na
Gross official international reserves	na	na	na	92	213	459	684	na
External debt stock	na	na	na	na	3,361	3,620	4,076	na
				(In months of merchandise imports)				
Gross official reserves	na	na	na	1.2	2.4	2.9	3.7	na
				(In per cent of exports of goods and non-factor services)				
Debt service	na	na	na	na	118	63	31	na
Memorandum items:				(Denominations as indicated)				
Population (in millions) [9]	4.38	4.24	4.11	4.14	4.12	4.0	4.1	na
GDP (US$ millions)	8,670	na	na	1,964	2,157	3,327	4,455	5,956
Federation	na	na	na	1,008	1,392	2,032	2,464	na
Republika Srpska	na	na	na	956	765	1,295	1,991	na
GDP per capita (US dollars)	1,979	na	na	474	524	832	1,087	na
Current account (excluding official transfers)/GDP (in per cent)	na	na	na	-25.1	-26.4	-39.3	-33.0	-33.7
External Debt minus Reserves (in US$ miilions)	na	na	na	na	3,148	3,161	3,392	na
External Debt/GDP (in per cent)	na	na	na	na	156	109	91	na
External Debt/Exports (in per cent)	na	na	na	na	2,211	1,077	715	na

Note:
Data for 1991-96 represent official estimates of outturns as reflected in publications from the national authorities and the International Monetary Fund. Data for 1997-98 reflect EBRD evaluations, partly based on information from these sources. Data refer to the entire territory of Bosnia and Herzegovina, unless otherwise indicated.

Methodological notes can be found on pp. 232-234.

Bulgaria

	1991	1992	1993	1994	1995	1996	1997 Estimate	1998 Projection
Output and expenditure				(Percentage change)				
GDP at constant prices [1]	-11.7	-7.3	-1.5	1.8	2.1	-10.9	-6.9	4.0
Private consumption	-15.7	1.0	-0.7	-2.6	-1.8	-7.5	-15.7	na
Public consumption	-10.3	-14.6	-12.6	-11.5	-7.4	-31.8	-14.2	na
Gross fixed investment	-19.9	-7.3	-17.5	1.1	8.8	-13.5	-22.1	na
Industrial gross output	-21.0	-6.4	-6.2	6.0	-5.4	-8.3	-7.0	na
Agricultural gross output	4.3	-14.8	-30.2	9.5	14.5	-18.1	6.0	na
Employment				(Percentage change)				
Labour force (end-year)	-4.3	-3.3	-0.1	-3.1	-0.6	1.4	-0.4	na
Employment (end-year)	-13.0	-8.1	-1.6	0.6	1.3	0.1	-2.7	na
				(In per cent of labour force)				
Unemployment	11.1	15.3	16.4	12.8	11.1	12.5	13.7	na
Prices and wages				(Percentage change)				
Consumer prices (annual average)	333.5	82.0	73.0	96.3	62.0	123.0	1,082	25.0
Consumer prices (end-year)	338.9	79.4	63.8	121.9	32.9	310.8	578.5	10.0
Gross average monthly earnings in industry, public sector (annual average)	na	132.8	55.1	53.9	57.7	95.0	na	na
Government sector				(In per cent of GDP)				
General government balance [2]	na	-5.2	-10.9	-5.8	-5.6	-10.4	-2.1	-2.0
General government expenditure	45.6	43.6	48.1	45.7	41.3	42.3	33.4	na
Monetary sector				(Percentage change)				
Broad money (end-year)	110.0	53.6	47.6	78.6	39.6	124.3	359.5	na
Domestic credit (end-year)	148.0	51.8	56.0	37.1	15.7	220.2	255.4	na
				(In per cent of GDP)				
Broad money	76.0	79.0	78.3	79.5	59.6	45.7	28.1	na
Interest and exchange rates				(In per cent per annum, end-year)				
Interbank interest rate (up to 30-day maturity)	na	na	68.3	108.0	44.2	448.8	2.0	na
Treasury bill rate (less than one-year maturity)	na	na	58.4	92.0	42.7	477.2	7.9	na
Deposit rate (one month)	57.7	45.3	53.6	72.3	25.3	211.8	3.0	na
Lending rate (less than one year)	83.9	64.6	83.7	117.8	51.4	480.8	6.7	na
				(Leva per US dollar)				
Exchange rate (end-year)	21.9	24.5	32.7	66.0	70.7	487.4	1,777	na
Exchange rate (annual average)	18.1	23.3	27.6	54.1	67.2	177.9	1,641	na
External sector				(In millions of US dollars)				
Current account	-406	-801	-1,386	-203	-59	117	433	-100
Trade balance [3]	404	-212	-885	-17	120	209	381	-200
Exports [3]	2,734	3,956	3,727	3,935	5,345	4,890	4,925	4,400
Imports [3]	2,330	4,169	4,612	3,952	5,224	4,703	4,544	4,600
Foreign direct investment, net	56	42	40	105	82	100	497	300
Gross reserves (end-year), excluding gold [4]	331	935	655	1,002	1,236	483	2,159	na
External debt stock	11,802	12,548	13,890	11,411	10,229	9,660	10,095	na
				(In months of current account expenditures, excluding transfers)				
Gross international reserves (end-year), excluding gold [4]	0.8	1.9	1.2	2.1	2.2	0.9	4.2	na
				(In per cent of exports of goods and nonfactor services)				
Debt service	na	38.1	33.7	19.3	15.4	19.3	15.5	na
Memorandum items				(Denominations as indicated)				
Population (in millions, end-year)	8.6	8.5	8.5	8.4	8.4	8.4	8.3	na
GDP at market prices (in billions of leva) [1]	136	201	299	526	880	1,749	17,103	22,500
GDP per capita (in US dollars)	872	1,012	1,276	1,157	1,538	1,189	1,227	na
Share of industry in GDP [1]	37.4	40.5	35.0	32.1	32.7	30.2	29.4	na
Share of agriculture in GDP [1]	14.3	11.7	10.3	12.0	13.1	14.6	25.9	na
Current account/GDP (in per cent)	-5.4	-9.3	-12.8	-2.1	-0.5	1.2	4.2	-0.8
External Debt minus Reserves (in US$ millions)	11,471	11,613	13,235	10,409	8,993	9,177	7,936	na
External Debt/GDP (in per cent)	157.4	145.6	128.3	117.5	78.1	98.3	96.9	na
External Debt/Exports (in per cent)	431.7	317.2	372.7	290.0	191.4	197.5	205.0	na

Note:

Data for 1991-96 represent official estimates of outturns as reflected in publications from the national authorities, the International Monetary Fund, the World Bank, the OECD, PlanEcon and the Institute of International Finance. Data for 1997-98 reflect EBRD evaluations, partly based on information from these sources. 1998 data are from the macroeconomic framework for the budget (passed late 1997).

Methodological notes can be found on pp. 232-234.

Croatia

	1991	1992	1993	1994	1995	1996	1997 Estimate	1998 Projection
Output				(Percentage change)				
GDP at constant prices	-21.1	-11.7	-8.0	5.9	6.8	6.0	6.5	4.2
Industrial gross output	-28.7	-14.6	-6.0	-2.6	0.3	3.1	6.8	na
Agricultural gross output	-7.2	-13.5	4.5	-2.9	0.7	1.5	na	na
Tourism [1]	-85.2	11.7	29.2	59.4	-45.3	94.3	49.3	na
Employment				(Percentage change)				
Labour force (annual average)	na	na	na	-1.0	-1.3	-4.1	-0.1	na
Employment (annual average) [2]	-13.7	-12.7	-2.6	-4.2	-3.3	-1.4	-1.7	na
				(In per cent of labour force)				
Unemployment	13.2	13.2	14.8	14.5	14.5	16.4	17.5	na
Prices and wages				(Percentage change)				
Retail prices (annual average)	123	666	1,518	97.6	2.0	3.5	3.6	5.8
Retail prices (end-year)	250	938	1,149	-3.0	3.8	3.4	3.8	6.0
Producer prices (annual average)	146	825	1,512	77.6	0.7	1.4	2.3	na
Producer prices (end-year)	412	1,079	1,076	-5.5	1.6	1.5	1.6	na
Average monthly earnings (annual average) [3]	69	309	1,477	137.1	34.0	12.3	13.1	na
Government sector [4]				(In per cent of GDP)				
Government balance	na	-3.9	-0.8	1.6	-0.9	-0.4	-1.3	-0.5
Government expenditure	na	36.1	35.0	40.6	44.9	45.6	46.1	na
Monetary sector				(Percentage change)				
Money (M1, end-year)	na	na	na	111.9	24.6	37.9	20.9	na
Domestic credit (end-year)	na	na	na	9.1	10.9	1.0	15.5	na
				(In per cent of GDP)				
Broadest Money (M4, end-year)	na	na	25.8	20.0	24.9	34.1	42.3	na
Interest and exchange rates				(In per cent per annum, end-year)				
Interbank interest rate (overnight)	na	2,182	34.5	8.5	27.3	9.7	8.5	na
Refinancing rate (three-months)	na	na	97.4	14.0	27.0	9.5	9.0	na
Deposit rate [5]	na	434	27.4	5.0	6.1	4.2	4.4	na
Lending rate [5]	na	2,333	59.0	15.4	22.3	18.5	14.1	na
				(kuna per US dollar)				
Exchange rate (end-year)	na	0.80	6.56	5.63	5.32	5.54	6.30	na
Exchange rate (annual average)	0.02	0.26	3.58	6.00	5.23	5.43	6.16	na
External sector				(In millions of US dollars)				
Current account	-589	823	600	786	-1,283	-881	-2,435	-1,737
Trade balance [6]	-536	-303	-960	-1,323	-3,238	-3,651	-5,224	-4,778
Exports [6]	3,292	3,127	3,904	4,260	4,633	4,546	4,206	4,416
Imports [6]	3,828	3,430	4,864	5,583	7,870	8,197	9,430	9,195
Foreign direct investment, net	na	13	77	95	83	509	196	450
Gross reserves (end-year), excluding gold [7]	0	167	616	1,405	1,895	2,314	2,539	na
External debt stock (end-year)	2,978	2,736	2,490	2,820	3,340	4,810	6,660	na
				(In months of imports of goods and services)				
Gross reserves (end-year), excluding gold [7]	0.0	0.4	1.2	2.5	2.5	2.8	2.7	na
				(In per cent of exports of goods and services)				
Debt service	12.3	8.9	9.5	7.6	9.9	8.5	11.5	na
Memorandum items				(Denominations as indicated)				
Population (in millions, end-year)	4.51	4.47	4.64	4.65	4.67	4.49	4.53	na
GDP (in billions of kuna)	0.4	2.7	39.0	87.4	98.4	107.3	119.1	131.2
GDP per capita (in US dollars)	4,028	2,291	2,342	3,139	4,029	4,392	4,267	na
Share of industry in GDP	29.5	29.0	30.8	27.9	23.6	na	na	na
Share of agriculture and fishing in GDP	9.7	13.5	12.8	10.4	10.0	na	na	na
Current account/GDP (in per cent)	-3.2	8.0	5.5	5.4	-6.8	-4.5	-12.6	-8.5
External Debt minus Reserves (in US$ millions)	2,978	2,569	1,874	1,415	1,445	2,496	4,121	na
External Debt/GDP (in per cent)	16.4	26.7	22.8	19.3	17.8	24.4	34.4	na
External Debt/Exports (in per cent)	90.5	87.5	63.8	66.2	72.1	105.8	158.3	na

Note:

Data for 1991-96 represent official estimates of outturns as reflected in publications from the national authorities, the International Monetary Fund, the World Bank, the OECD, PlanEcon and the Institute of International Finance. Data for 1997-98 reflect EBRD evaluations, partly based on information from these sources.

Methodological notes can be found on pp. 232-234.

Czech Republic

	1991	1992	1993	1994	1995	1996	1997 Estimate	1998 Projection
Output and expenditure				*(Percentage change)*				
GDP at constant prices [1]	-11.5	-3.3	0.6	3.2	6.4	3.9	1.0	-1.0
Private consumption	-28.5	15.5	2.9	5.3	6.9	7.0	1.6	na
Public consumption	-8.7	-3.2	0.0	-2.3	-1.6	4.3	-1.8	na
Gross fixed investment	-17.5	8.8	-8.1	17.3	21.0	8.7	-4.9	na
Exports of goods and services	na	6.7	7.5	0.4	16.1	5.4	10.2	na
Imports of goods and services	na	22.0	10.2	7.8	22.0	12.9	6.7	na
Industrial gross output	-22.3	-7.9	-5.3	2.1	8.7	1.8	4.5	na
Agricultural gross output	-8.9	-12.1	-2.3	-6.0	5.0	-1.4	-5.9	na
Employment				*(Percentage change)*				
Labour force (end-year)	na	na	2.1	-1.7	0.4	1.4	-2.3	na
Employment (annual average)	na	-2.6	-1.6	0.8	2.6	0.8	-1.3	na
				(In per cent of labour force)				
Unemployment (end-year)	4.1	2.6	3.5	3.2	2.9	3.5	5.2	na
Prices and wages				*(Percentage change)*				
Consumer prices (annual average)	56.6	11.1	20.8	10.0	9.1	8.8	8.5	11.0
Consumer prices (end-year)	52.0	12.7	18.2	9.7	7.9	8.6	10.0	9.0
Producer prices (annual average)	70.3	10.0	9.2	5.4	7.6	4.8	4.9	na
Producer prices (end-year)	na	9.3	11.4	5.6	7.2	4.4	5.7	na
Gross average monthly earnings in industry (annual average)	16.7	19.6	23.8	15.8	18.1	17.7	13.5	na
Government sector				*(In per cent of GDP)*				
General government balance [2]	-1.9	-3.1	0.5	-1.2	-1.8	-1.2	-2.1	-2.4
General government expenditure	na	na	41.9	43.3	42.8	41.8	41.6	na
Monetary sector				*(Percentage change)*				
Broad money (end-year)	**26.8**	20.7	19.8	19.9	19.8	9.2	10.1	na
Domestic credit (end-year)	na	14.6	18.1	14.0	5.9	9.1	4.6	na
				(In per cent of GDP)				
Broad money	na	69.4	70.3	73.9	75.6	72.2	73.8	na
Interest and exchange rates				*(In per cent per annum, end-year)*				
Interbank interest rate (up to 30-day maturity)	na	12.7	6.7	12.6	11.0	12.6	17.5	na
Discount rate	na	9.5	8.0	8.5	9.5	10.5	13.0	na
Deposit rate [3]	na	6.3	7.0	6.9	6.9	6.7	8.1	na
Lending rate [3]	na	13.3	14.1	12.8	12.7	12.5	13.9	na
				(Koruna per US dollar)				
Exchange rate (end-year)	**27.8**	**28.9**	29.8	28.2	26.7	27.3	34.7	na
Exchange rate (annual average)	**29.5**	**28.3**	29.2	28.8	26.6	27.1	31.7	na
External sector				*(In billions of US dollars)*				
Current account	**0.3**	**-0.3**	0.1	0.0	-1.4	-4.3	-3.2	-1.7
Trade balance [4]	**-0.5**	**-1.9**	-0.3	-0.9	-3.7	-5.9	-4.6	-3.0
Exports [4]	**8.3**	**8.4**	13.0	14.0	21.5	21.7	22.5	27.0
Imports [4]	**8.8**	**10.4**	13.3	14.9	25.1	27.6	27.1	30.0
Foreign direct investment, net	**na**	**1.0**	0.6	0.7	2.5	1.4	1.3	1.0
Gross reserves (end-year), excluding gold [5]	0.7	0.8	3.9	6.2	14.0	12.4	9.8	na
External debt stock (convertible currency)	6.7	7.1	8.5	10.7	16.5	20.8	21.4	na
				(In months of imports of goods and services)				
Gross reserves (end-year), excluding gold [5]	**0.8**	**0.8**	2.7	3.9	5.6	4.2	3.4	na
				(In per cent of exports of goods and services)				
Debt service	na	12.4	6.5	13.1	9.3	10.4	15.1	na
Memorandum items				*(Denominations as indicated)*				
Population (in millions, end-year)	10.3	10.3	10.3	10.3	10.3	10.3	10.3	na
GDP (in billions of koruna)	750	847	1,002	1,143	1,339	1,533	1,650	1,812
GDP per capita (in US dollars)	2,467	2,906	3,337	3,856	4,896	5,483	5,050	na
Share of industry in GDP	na	40.2	34.9	33.6	34.1	33.8	35.0	na
Share of agriculture in GDP	6.0	6.1	6.5	3.8	5.3	5.1	4.8	na
Current account/GDP (in per cent)	1.2	-1.0	0.3	-0.1	-2.7	-7.6	-6.1	-3.1
External Debt minus Reserves (in US$ billions)	6.0	6.2	4.6	4.5	2.5	8.4	11.6	na
External Debt/GDP (in per cent)	26.4	23.7	24.7	26.9	32.8	36.9	41.0	na
External Debt/Exports (in per cent)	80.8	83.8	65.4	76.3	77.1	96.1	94.8	na

Note:

Data in bold type refer to former Czechoslovakia. Data for 1991-96 represent official estimates of outturns as reflected in publications from the national authorities, the International Monetary Fund, the OECD, PlanEcon and the Institute of International Finance. Data for 1997-98 reflect EBRD evaluations, partly based on information from these sources.

Methodological notes can be found on pp. 232-234.

Estonia

	1991	1992	1993	1994	1995	1996	1997 Estimate	1998 Projection
Output and expenditure				*(Percentage change)*				
GDP at constant prices	-13.6	-14.2	-9.0	-2.0	4.3	4.0	11.4	5.0
Private consumption	na	na	na	1.0	4.0	2.5	na	na
Public consumption	na	na	na	1.1	6.7	4.3	na	na
Industrial sales	na	na	-19	-3.0	2.0	3.4	13.4	na
Agricultural gross output	na	na	na	na	0.2	-6.3	-1.5	na
Employment				*(Percentage change)*				
Labour force (end-year) [1]	na	na	na	-0.4	-3.5	-0.7	-1.4	na
Employment (annual average) [1]	na	na	na	-2.2	-5.3	-1.6	-1.7	na
				(In per cent of labour force)				
Unemployment [1]	na	na	6.5	7.6	9.7	10.0	10.5	na
Prices and wages				*(Percentage change)*				
Consumer prices (annual average)	211	1,076	90	48	29	23	11	11
Consumer prices (end-year)	304	954	36	42	29	15	12	8
Producer prices (annual average)	na	na	75	36	26	15	9	na
Producer prices (end-year)	na	na	na	33	22	10	8	na
Gross monthly earnings in manufacturing (annual average)	na	na	93	72	36	24	20	na
Government sector				*(In per cent of GDP)*				
General government balance [2]	5.2	-0.3	-0.7	1.3	-1.3	-1.5	2.2	2.5
General government expenditure	n.a.	34.9	40.3	39.2	41.4	40.5	37.4	na
Monetary sector				*(Percentage change)*				
Broad money (end-year)	na	59	93	40	34	35	41	na
Domestic credit (end-year)	na	30	53	42	66	101	87	na
				(In per cent of GDP)				
Broad money	na	28	33	34	33	35	39	na
Interest and exchange rates				*(In per cent per annum, end-year)*				
Interbank interest rate (up to 30-day maturity)	na	na	na	na	6.0	5.8	14.7	na
Deposit rate (over one year) [3]	na	na	na	8.8	8.7	10.5	10.8	na
Lending rate (over one year) [4]	na	na	na	17.5	15.8	13.9	11.2	na
				(kroon per US dollar)				
Exchange rate (end-year)	na	12.9	13.9	12.4	11.5	12.4	14.3	na
Exchange rate (annual average)	na	na	13.2	13.0	11.5	12.0	13.9	na
External sector				*(In millions of US dollars)*				
Current account [5]	na	36	22	-166	-166	-399	-564	-576
Trade balance [5]	na	-90	-145	-356	-674	-1,021	-1,129	-1,250
Exports (merchandise) [5]	na	461	812	1,329	1,857	1,814	2,298	2,800
Imports (merchandise) [5]	na	551	957	1,684	2,531	2,835	3,427	4,050
Foreign direct investment, net	na	na	157	215	199	111	128	200
Gross reserves (end-year), excluding gold [6]	na	170	386	443	580	637	764	na
External debt stock [7]	na	na	161	187	287	1,499	2,651	na
				(In months of current account expenditures, excluding transfers)				
Gross reserves (end-year), excluding gold [6]	na	2.8	3.7	2.5	2.3	2.2	2.1	na
				(In per cent of exports of goods and non-factor services)				
Debt service	na	na	1.4	0.4	0.6	2.2	3.6	na
Memorandum items				*(Denominations as indicated)*				
Population (in millions, end-year)	1.56	1.53	1.51	1.49	1.48	1.46	1.45	na
GDP (in millions of kroons)	na	13,054	21,610	29,645	40,705	52,446	65,080	76,400
GDP per capita (US dollars)	na	663	1,085	1,530	2,405	2,981	3,230	na
Share of industry in GDP	na	27.5	22.0	21.1	20.7	19.8	19.4	na
Share of agriculture in GDP	na	12.6	9.8	9.0	7.1	6.8	6.3	na
Current account/GDP (in per cent)	na	na	1.3	-7.3	-4.7	-9.2	-12.0	-10.5
External Debt minus Reserves (in US$ millions)	na	na	-225.1	-256.4	-292.9	862.5	1,886.8	na
External Debt/GDP (in per cent)	na	na	9.9	8.2	8.1	34.4	56.5	na
External Debt/Exports (in per cent)	na	na	19.8	14.1	15.5	82.6	115.3	na

Note:

Data for 1991-96 represent official estimates of outturns as reflected in publications from the national authorities, the International Monetary Fund, the World Bank, the OECD, PlanEcon, Stockholm Institute of East European Economics and the Institute of International Finance. Data for 1997-98 reflects EBRD evaluations, partly based on information from these sources.

Methodological notes can be found on pp. 232-234.

FYR Macedonia

	1991	1992	1993	1994	1995	1996	1997 Estimate	1998 Projection
Output				(Percentage change)				
GDP at constant prices	-12.1	-21.1	-9.1	-1.8	-1.2	0.8	1.5	5.0
Industrial gross output	-17.2	-13.0	-9.0	-7.0	-6.0	2.0	3.4	0.0
Agricultural gross output	17.1	0.5	-23.5	7.1	4.0	1.2	5.5	na
Employment				(Percentage change)				
Labour force (annual average) [1]	1.3	1.3	-3.6	-2.4	-1.5	na	1.4	na
Employment (annual average)	-6.5	-5.2	-5.6	-6.0	-9.9	na	-4.7	na
				(In per cent of labour force)				
Unemployment (annual average) [2]	19.2	27.8	28.3	31.4	37.7	31.9	36.0	na
Prices and wages				(Percentage change)				
Retail prices (annual average)	114.9	1,690.7	338.4	126.5	16.4	2.5	1.3	1.3
Retail prices (end-year)	230	1,925	230	55	9.0	-0.6	2.7	1.4
Producer prices in industry (annual average)	112.0	2,198.2	258.3	84.6	3.9	-0.2	4.5	na
Producer prices in industry (end-year)	281.5	2,148.6	177.8	28.5	2.2	-0.6	8.6	na
Net average monthly wages in industry (annual average)	79.2	1,084.1	454.0	105.8	11.1	3.6	2.3	na
Government sector				(In per cent of GDP)				
General government balance [3]	na	-9.6	-13.8	-2.9	-1.2	-0.5	-0.4	-0.8
General government expenditure	na	48.2	55.3	50.5	43.1	41.5	39.4	na
Monetary sector				(Percentage change)				
Broad money (end-year)	na	na	na	na	-2.7	-0.1	24.5	na
Domestic credit (end-year)	na	na	na	na	-22.3	-11.5	6.8	na
				(In per cent of GDP)				
Broad money	na	na	25.6	14.2	12.3	11.9	14.1	na
Interest and exchange rates				(In per cent per annum, end-year)				
Refinancing rate	na	719	848	66	30	18.4	14.2	na
Discount rate	na	250	295	33	15	9.2	8.9	na
Deposit rate [4]	na	435	322	32	9	9	9	na
Lending rate [5]	na	1,100	367	87	25	20	20	na
				(Denar per US dollar)				
Exchange rate (end-year)	na	na	44.5	40.6	38.0	41.4	54.9	na
Exchange rate (annual average)	na	na	23.6	43.2	38.0	39.9	49.9	na
External sector				(In millions of US dollars)				
Current account	-262	-19	15	-180	-230	-288	-275	-238
Trade balance [6]	-225	-7	43	-186	-235	-317	-388	-349
Exports [6]	1,150	1,199	1,056	1,086	1,204	1,147	1,201	1,325
Imports [6]	1,375	1,206	1,013	1,272	1,439	1,464	1,589	1,674
Foreign direct investment, net	na	0	0	24	13	12	30	45
Gross reserves (end-year), excluding gold [7]	na	na	105	149	257	249	254	na
External debt stock	744	758	818	844	1,060	1,121	1,141	na
				(In months of current account expenditures, excluding transfers)				
Gross reserves (end-year), excluding gold [7]	na	na	1.2	1.3	1.9	2.0	1.9	na
				(In per cent of current account revenues, excluding transfers)				
Debt service	na	na	13.1	15.8	10.1	10.8	9.2	na
Memorandum items				(Denominations as indicated)				
Population (in millions, end-year)	2.2	2.2	2.2	2.1	2.1	2.0	2.0	2.0
GDP (in millions of denar)	920	11,791	59,161	136,033	153,132	157,302	165,989	176,550
GDP per capita (in US dollars)	na	na	1,141	1,500	1,887	1,950	1,663	na
Share of industry (including mining) in GSP [8]	na	29.4	25.1	19.3	19.2	19.5	19.0	na
Share of agriculture in GSP [8]	na	14.4	9.8	10.4	10.7	11.0	10.8	na
Current account/GDP (in per cent)	na	na	0.6	-5.7	-5.7	-7.3	-8.3	-7.5
External Debt minus Reserves (in US$ millions)	na	na	713	695	803	872	887	na
External Debt/GDP (in per cent)	na	na	32.6	26.8	26.3	28.4	34.3	na
External Debt/Exports (in per cent)	64.7	63.2	77.5	77.7	88.0	97.7	95.0	na

Note:

Data for 1991-96 represent official estimates of outturns as reflected in publications from the national authorities, the International Monetary Fund, the World Bank, the OECD, PlanEcon and the Institute of International Finance. Data for 1997-98 reflect EBRD evaluations, partly based on information from these sources.

Methodological notes can be found on pp. 232-234.

Georgia

	1991	1992	1993	1994	1995	1996	1997 Estimate	1998 Projection
Output				*(Percentage change)*				
GDP at constant prices	-20.6	-44.8	-25.4	-11.4	2.4	10.5	11.0	9.0
Industrial gross output	-24.4	-43.3	-21.0	-39.1	-9.9	6.8	8.1	na
Agricultural gross output	-10.1	-34.2	-42.0	11.6	19.9	5.1	7.1	na
Employment [1]				*(Percentage change)*				
Labour force (end-year)	na	-19.5	-5.5	-5.5	9.3	5.1	18.6	na
Employment (end-year)	na	-21.2	-9.7	-2.4	10.5	5.4	15.7	na
				(In per cent of labour force)				
Unemployment	0.2	2.3	6.6	3.6	2.6	11.6	5.2	na
Prices and wages				*(Percentage change)*				
Consumer prices (annual average)	79	887	3,125	15,607	163	39.4	7.3	4.0
Consumer prices (end-year)	na	1,177	7,488	6,474	57	14.3	7.1	5.0
Gross average monthly wages in manufacturing (annual average)	na	na	1,950	23,315	103	159	49	na
Government sector				*(In per cent of GDP)*				
General government balance [2]	-3.0	-25.4	-26.2	-7.4	-4.5	-4.4	-3.8	-2.5
General government expenditure	33.0	35.7	35.9	23.5	11.6	14.1	14.4	na
Monetary sector				*(Percentage change)*				
Broad money (end-year)	na	464	4,319	2,229	135.2	41.9	45.5	na
Domestic credit (end-year)	na	724	2,048	3,448	84.6	59.6	54.5	na
				(In per cent of GDP)				
Broad money	na	40.3	20.1	5.6	4.9	4.5	5.5	na
Interest and exchange rate				*(In per cent per annum, end year)*				
Interbank interest rate (three-month)	na	na	na	na	na	47.6	32.1	na
Treasury bill rate (three-month maturity) [3]	na	na	na	na	na	na	44.0	na
Deposit rate (three-month)	na	na	na	na	17.9	16.1	12.6	na
Lending rate (three-month)	na	na	na	na	69.8	53.2	45.0	na
				(Lari per US dollar)				
Exchange rate (end-year)	na	na	0.10	1.28	1.23	1.27	1.30	na
Exchange rate (annual average)	na	na	na	1.10	1.29	1.26	1.30	na
External sector				*(In millions of US dollars)*				
Current account	na	-248	-354	-278	-218	-278	-347	-500
Current account (excluding transfers)	na	-319	-485	-448	-407	-418	-535	-670
Trade balance [4]	na	-378	-448	-365	-338	-351	-484	-600
Exports [4]	na	267	457	381	363	417	463	500
Imports [4]	na	645	905	746	700	768	947	1,100
Foreign direct investment, net	na	na	na	8	6	54	189	255
Gross reserves (end-year), excluding gold [5]	na	0.7	1.0	41	157	158	173	na
External debt stock	na	95	544	999	1,225	1,371	1,539	na
				(In months of current account expenditures, excluding transfers)				
Gross reserves (end-year), excluding gold [5]	na	0.01	0.01	0.7	2.7	2.7	2.2	na
				(In per cent of current account revenues, excluding transfers)				
Debt service [6]	na	na	na	na	7.3	9.7	8.6	na
Memorandum items				*(Denominations as indicated)*				
Population (in millions, end-year)	5.4	5.4	5.4	5.4	5.4	5.4	5.4	na
GDP (in millions of lari)	na	0.19	16.4	1,373	3,694	5,724	6,797	7,800
GDP per capita (US dollars)	na	213.6	194.9	228.2	537.6	846.5	968.3	na
Share of industry in GDP	na	12.6	6.3	21.3	14.5	10.3	9.6	na
Share of agriculture in GDP	na	54.5	67.7	28.7	38.0	31.0	28.2	na
Current account/GDP (in per cent)	na	na	na	-22.6	-7.6	-6.1	-6.6	-8.4
External Debt minus Reserves (in US$ millions)	na	94	543	957	1,069	1,213	1,366	na
External Debt/GDP (in per cent)	na	na	na	81.4	42.5	30.0	29.4	na
External Debt/Exports (in per cent)	na	35.6	118.9	262.3	337.6	328.8	332.6	na

Note:

Data for 1991-96 represent official estimates of outturns as reflected in publications from the national authorities, the International Monetary Fund, the World Bank, the OECD, and the Institute of International Finance. Data for 1997-98 reflect EBRD evaluations, partly based on information from these sources.

Methodological notes can be found on pp. 232-234.

Hungary

	1991	1992	1993	1994	1995	1996	1997 Estimate	1998 Projection
Output and expenditure				*(Percentage change)*				
GDP at constant prices	-11.9	-3.1	-0.6	2.9	1.5	1.3	4.4	4.6
Private consumption	-5.6	0.0	1.9	-0.2	-7.1	-3.4	0.9	na
Public consumption [1]	-2.7	4.9	27.5	-12.7	-4.1	-5.4	2.0	na
Gross fixed investment	-10.4	-2.6	2.0	12.5	-4.3	6.3	8.8	na
Exports of goods and services	-13.9	2.1	-9.1	13.7	13.4	7.4	26.4	na
Imports of goods and services	-6.1	0.2	20.2	8.8	-0.7	5.7	25.5	na
Industrial gross output	-18.3	-9.7	4.0	9.6	4.6	3.3	11.0	na
Agricultural gross output	-6.2	-20.0	-9.7	3.2	2.6	4.0	-1.9	na
Employment				*(Percentage change)*				
Labour force (end-year) [2]	-3.7	-3.6	-4.2	-2.6	-1.1	-0.5	-1.8	na
Employment (end-year) [2]	-9.6	-9.3	-5.4	-1.4	-0.7	0.3	0.3	na
				(In per cent of labour force)				
Unemployment [3]	7.4	12.3	12.1	10.4	10.4	10.5	10.4	na
Prices and wages				*(Percentage change)*				
Consumer prices (annual average)	35.0	23.0	22.5	18.8	28.2	23.6	18.3	15.0
Consumer prices (end-year)	32.2	21.6	21.1	21.2	28.3	19.8	18.4	13.5
Producer prices (annual average)	32.6	12.3	10.8	11.3	28.9	21.8	20.4	na
Producer prices (end-year)	23.5	18.8	10.3	19.9	30.2	20.1	19.5	na
Gross average monthly earnings in manufacturing (annual average)	25.6	25.9	24.7	23.5	21.3	21.6	22.1	na
Government sector				*(In per cent of GDP)*				
General government balance [4]	-2.9	-6.8	-5.5	-8.4	-6.7	-3.1	-4.9	-4.9
General government expenditure	55.4	59.4	60.6	60.9	53.9	48.3	52.9	na
Monetary sector				*(Percentage change)*				
Broad money (end-year)	35.7	27.6	15.7	13.0	20.1	22.5	19.4	na
Domestic credit (end-year) [5]	17.7	0.6	20.9	18.0	12.8	6.5	11.7	na
				(In per cent of GDP)				
Broad money	54.8	59.4	56.8	52.2	48.7	48.6	47.4	na
Interest and exchange rates				*(In per cent per annum, end-year)*				
Interbank interest rate (up to 30-day maturity)	na	na	21.8	31.3	27.8	23.2	19.7	na
Treasury bill rate (three-month maturity)	na	na	24.3	31.6	30.1	21.7	19.2	na
Deposit rate (one year)	33.0	14.7	17.2	23.6	26.1	20.1	17.6	na
Lending rate (one year)	35.5	28.8	25.6	29.7	32.2	24.0	20.8	na
				(Forints per US dollar)				
Exchange rate (end-year)	75.6	84.0	100.7	110.7	139.5	164.9	203.5	na
Exchange rate (annual average)	74.8	79.0	92.0	105.1	125.7	152.6	186.8	na
External sector				*(In billions of US dollars)*				
Current account	0.3	0.3	-3.5	-3.9	-2.5	-1.7	-1.0	-1.6
Trade balance [6]	0.2	0.0	-3.2	-3.6	-2.4	-2.6	-1.7	-2.4
Exports [6]	9.3	10.0	8.1	7.6	12.8	14.2	19.6	22.0
Imports [6]	9.1	10.1	11.3	11.2	15.3	16.8	21.4	24.4
Foreign direct investment, net	1.5	1.5	2.3	1.1	4.5	2.0	2.1	1.5
Gross reserves (end-year), excluding gold [7]	3.9	4.3	6.7	6.7	12.0	9.7	8.4	na
External debt stock	22.7	21.4	24.6	28.5	31.7	27.6	23.7	na
				(In months of current account expenditures, excluding transfers)				
Gross reserves (end-year), excluding gold [7]	3.7	3.6	5.1	5.0	6.7	5.1	3.6	na
				(In per cent of current account revenues, excluding transfers)				
Debt service [8]	33.3	34.2	43.1	54.5	47.1	47.8	43.6	na
Memorandum items				*(Denominations as indicated)*				
Population (in millions, end-year)	10.34	10.31	10.28	10.25	10.21	10.17	10.14	na
GDP (in billions of forints)	2,498	2,943	3,548	4,365	5,614	6,894	8,446	10,185
GDP per capita (in US dollars)	3,230	3,613	3,752	4,052	4,374	4,441	4,462	na
Share of industry in GDP	25.1	23.4	22.5	22.1	23.5	na	na	na
Share of agriculture in GDP	8.5	7.2	6.6	6.7	7.2	na	na	na
Current account/GDP (in per cent)	0.8	0.9	-9.0	-9.4	-5.6	-3.7	-2.2	-3.4
External Debt minus Reserves (in US$ billions)	18.7	17.1	17.9	21.8	19.7	17.8	15.3	na
External Debt/GDP (in per cent)	67.8	57.6	63.7	68.7	70.9	61.0	52.5	na
External Debt/Exports (in per cent)	244.7	213.8	303.4	374.6	247.1	194.3	120.9	na

Note:

Data for 1991-96 represent official estimates of outturns as reflected in publications from the national authorities, the International Monetary Fund, the World Bank, the OECD, PlanEcon and the Institute of International Finance. Data for 1997-98 reflect EBRD evaluations, partly based on information from these sources.

Methodological notes can be found on pp. 232-234.

Kazakhstan

	1991	1992	1993	1994	1995	1996	1997 Estimate	1998 Projection
Output				(Percentage change)				
GDP at constant prices	-13.0	-2.9	-9.2	-12.6	-8.2	0.5	2.0	1.0
Industrial value added	-1.0	-14.0	-14.0	-27.5	-8.6	0.3	4.0	na
Agricultural value added	-9.0	1.0	-6.9	-21.0	-24.4	-5.0	1.9	na
Employment				(Percentage change)				
Labour force (end-year)	na	na	na	-3.0	-3.0	-2.0	-2.2	na
Employment (end-year) [1]	-1.0	-1.9	-5.8	-3.9	-7.8	-12.3	-16.5	na
				(In per cent of labour force)				
Unemployment [2]	0.0	0.5	0.6	0.8	1.7	3.6	4.1	na
Prices and wages				(Percentage change)				
Consumer prices (annual average)	79	1,381	1,662	1,892	176	39.1	17.4	10.0
Consumer prices (end-year)	137	2,984	2,169	1,160	60.4	28.6	11.3	9.0
Gross average monthly wages in industry (annual average)	na	na	na	1,538	178.0	30.8	30.0	na
Government sector				(In per cent of GDP)				
General government balance [3]	-7.9	-7.3	-1.4	-7.2	-2.5	-3.1	-3.7	-5.5
General government expenditure	32.9	31.8	25.2	25.9	19.9	18.6	20.3	na
Monetary sector				(Percentage change)				
Broad money (end-year)	211	391	692	576	106	13.8	32.3	na
Domestic credit (end-year)	289	1,343	653	745	-23.6	-12.4	33.5	na
				(In per cent of GDP)				
Broad money (end-year)	na	45.0	20.9	13.4	11.6	9.5	10.4	na
Interest and exchange rates				(In per cent per annum, end-year)				
Refinancing rate	na	na	240	230	52.5	35.0	18.5	na
Treasury bill rate (three-month maturity)	na	na	na	354	58.8	32.6	16.1	na
Deposit rate [4]	na	na	na	na	44.4	30.0	12.6	na
Lending rate [4]	na	na	na	na	58.3	45.0	22.9	na
				(Tenge per US dollar)				
Exchange rate (end-year)	na	0.8	6.1	54.3	64.0	73.8	75.9	na
Exchange rate (annual average)	na	0.4	1.9	36.0	61.0	68.2	75.6	na
External sector				(In millions of US dollars)				
Current account	-1,300	-1,900	-400	-905	-516	-752	-953	-1,800
Trade balance [5]	-3,200	-1,100	-400	-920	-222	-326	-385	-1,100
Exports [5]	10,200	3,600	4,800	3,285	5,164	6,292	6,769	6,300
Imports [5]	13,400	4,700	5,200	4,205	5,387	6,618	7,154	7,400
Foreign direct investment, net	na	na	473	635	964	1,137	1,320	1,200
Gross reserves (end-year), excluding gold [6]	na	na	640	1,220	1,660	1,980	2,252	na
External debt stock	na	1,478	1,848	2,717	3,428	3,889	4,587	na
				(In months of imports of goods and services)				
Gross reserves (end-year), excluding gold [7]	na	na	1.5	3.5	3.2	3.1	3.2	na
				(In per cent of exports of goods and services)				
Debt service	na	4.3	1.4	3.3	2.7	4.6	5.8	na
Memorandum items				(Denominations as indicated)				
Population (in millions, end-year)	16.7	16.9	16.9	16.7	16.5	16.3	15.7	na
GDP (in billions of tenge)	na	2	29	424	1,014	1,416	1,702	1,900
GDP per capita (in US dollars)	na	296	916	704	1,008	1,274	1,434	na
Share of industry in GDP	38.0	34.7	28.7	29.1	23.5	21.2	20.4	na
Share of agriculture in GDP	29.0	30.4	16.4	14.9	12.3	12.0	10.8	na
Current account/GDP (in per cent)	na	-38.0	-2.6	-7.7	-3.1	-3.6	-4.2	-7.5
External Debt minus Reserves (in US$ millions)	na	na	1,208	1,497	1,768	1,909	2,335	na
External Debt/GDP (in per cent)	na	29.6	11.9	23.1	20.6	18.7	20.4	na
External Debt/Exports (in per cent)	na	41.1	38.5	82.7	66.4	61.8	67.8	na

Note:

Data for 1991-96 represent official estimates of outturns as reflected in publications from the national authorities, the World Bank, the International Monetary Fund, the OECD, PlanEcon and the Institute of International Finance. Data for 1997-98 reflect EBRD evaluations, partly based on information from these sources.

Methodological notes can be found on pp. 232-234.

Kyrgyzstan

	1991	1992	1993	1994	1995	1996	1997 Estimate	1998 Projection
Output				(Percentage change)				
GDP at constant prices	-5.0	-19.0	-16.0	-20.0	-5.4	7.1	6.5	4.0
Industrial gross output	-0.3	-26.4	-25.3	-27.9	-12.5	3.9	20.0	na
Agricultural gross output	-10	-5	-10	-15	4	13	na	na
Employment				(Percentage change)				
Labour force (annual average)	na	0.4	-3.1	-1.5	2.0	0.6	na	na
Employment (annual average) [1]	0.4	4.7	-8.5	-2.1	-0.3	0.0	na	na
				(In per cent of labour force)				
Unemployment rate [2]	0.0	0.1	0.2	0.7	3.0	4.5	3.2	na
Prices and wages				(Percentage change)				
Consumer prices (annual average)	85	855	772	228.7	52.5	30.4	25.5	12.0
Consumer prices (end-year)	170	1,259	1,363	95.7	31.9	35.0	14.7	12.0
Producer prices (annual average)	na	na	650	211.6	36.8	32.4	na	na
Producer prices (end-year)	na	na	225	96.7	27.0	39.4	14.8	na
Gross average monthly wages (annual average) [3]	na	na	na	191.3	66.7	26.5	27.3	na
Government sector				(In per cent of GDP)				
General government balance [4]	na	na	na	na	-17.0	-9.0	-9.4	-8.1
General government expenditure	na	na	na	na	33.7	24.9	26.3	na
Monetary sector				(Percentage change)				
Broad money (end-year)	84	428	180	125.0	76.7	22.9	24.7	na
Net domestic assets	na	761	307	83.5	96.8	17.7	8.2	na
				(In per cent of GDP)				
Broad money	na	na	13.2	12.9	17.1	14.3	14.3	na
Interest and exchange rates				(In per cent per annum, end-year)				
Refinancing rate [5]	na	na	276.8	89.5	45.8	45.9	na	na
Treasury bill rate (three-month maturity)	na	na	na	73.0	44.0	57.0	23.1	na
Deposit rate [6]	na	na	na	na	na	24.8	32.0	na
Lending rate [6]	na	na	na	na	na	58.3	50.1	na
				(Som per US dollar)				
Exchange rate (end-year) [7]	1.7	414.5	8.0	10.7	11.0	16.7	17.4	na
Exchange rate (annual average) [7]	1.8	222.0	6.1	10.9	10.8	12.9	17.4	na
External sector				(In millions of US dollars)				
Current account balance	na	-61	-162	-124	-242	-425	-139	-165
Trade balance [8]	-41	-74	-166	-119	-179	-252	-15	-40
Exports [8]	3,845	258	335	340	409	531	631	630
Imports [8]	3,886	332	501	459	588	783	646	670
Foreign direct investment, net	na	na	10	45	96	46	83	29
Gross reserves (end-year), including gold [9]	na	na	46	96	123	129	200	na
External debt stock	na	na	290	414	585	753	935	na
				(In months of imports of goods and services)				
Gross reserves (end-year), including gold [10]	na	na	1.1	2.5	2.5	1.8	3.0	na
				(In per cent of merchandise exports)				
Debt service	na	na	0.6	5.0	19.5	12.9	8.0	na
Memorandum items				(Denominations as indicated)				
Population (in millions, beginning of year)	4.4	4.5	4.5	4.5	4.5	4.6	4.6	na
GDP (in millions of som)	92.6	741.3	5,355	12,019	16,145	23,399	29,300	34,000
GDP per capita (in US dollars)	na	na	195.1	245.0	331.3	379.2	366.0	na
Share of industry in GDP	27.5	32.1	25.1	20.5	12.0	11.9	15.5	na
Share of agriculture in GDP	35.3	37.3	39.0	38.3	40.6	46.6	43.4	na
Current account/GDP (in per cent)	na	-1,827	-18.5	-11.3	-16.2	-23.4	-8.3	-7.5
External Debt minus Reserves (in US$ millions)	na	na	243.8	318.1	462.2	624.1	734.4	na
External Debt/GDP (in per cent)	na	na	33.0	37.5	39.1	41.5	55.5	na
External Debt/Exports (in per cent)	na	na	86.5	121.7	143.0	141.7	148.2	na

Note:

Data for 1991-96 represent official estimates of outturns as reflected in publications from the national authorities, the International Monetary Fund, the World Bank, the OECD, PlanEcon and the Institute of International Finance. Data for 1997-98 reflect EBRD evaluations, partly based on information from these sources.

Methodological notes can be found on pp. 232-234.

Latvia

	1991	1992	1993	1994	1995	1996	1997 Estimate	1998 Projection
Output and expenditure				(Percentage change)				
GDP at constant prices	-10.4	-34.9	-14.9	0.6	-0.8	3.3	6.5	4.0
Industrial gross output	na	-46.2	-38.1	-9.5	-6.3	1.4	6.1	na
Agricultural gross output [1]	-1.7	-28.6	-18.2	-15.0	3.1	-5.3	4.9	na
Employment				(Percentage change)				
Labour force (annual average)	-1.0	2.9	-8.8	-1.6	-1.9	-1.8	0.8	na
Employment (annual average)	-0.9	-3.7	-7.4	-3.2	-1.3	-2.7	1.9	na
				(In per cent of labour force)				
Unemployment	na	2.3	5.8	6.5	6.6	7.2	7.0	na
Prices and wages				(Percentage change)				
Consumer prices (annual average)	172	951	108	36	25.0	17.6	8.4	5.3
Consumer prices (end-year)	262	959	35	26	23.1	13.1	7.0	4.6
Gross average monthly earnings in industry (annual average)	na	na	na	60	24.1	14.9	21.6	na
Government sector				(In per cent of GDP)				
General government balance [2]	na	-0.8	0.6	-4.1	-3.5	-1.4	1.4	1.0
General government expenditure	na	28.2	35.2	38.2	38.2	38.0	38.2	na
Monetary sector				(Percentage change)				
Broad money (end-year)	153	170	84	47.7	-23.1	19.9	38.7	na
Domestic credit (end-year)	91	304	146	65.7	-25.4	6.0	36.1	na
				(In per cent of GDP)				
Broad money	na	na	32	34	22	22	26	na
Interest and exchange rates				(In per cent per annum, end-year)				
Interbank interest rate	na	na	na	37.8	21.1	9.7	3.7	na
Treasury bill rate (three-month maturity)	na	na	na	21.5	33.4	10.1	3.6	na
Deposit rate (less than one year)	na	na	28.4	18.8	15.0	10.0	5.3	na
Lending rate (less than one year)	na	na	70.8	36.7	31.1	20.3	12.1	na
				(lats per US dollar)				
Exchange rate (end-year)	na	0.835	0.595	0.548	0.537	0.556	0.590	na
Exchange rate (annual average)	na	0.669	0.674	0.560	0.528	0.551	0.581	na
External sector				(In millions of US dollars)				
Current account	na	25	314	-9	-159	-217	-345	-514
Trade balance [3]	na	-40	3	-300	-579	-798	-848	-1,000
Exports [3]	na	800	1,054	1,022	1,368	1,488	1,838	1,900
Imports [3]	na	840	1,051	1,322	1,947	2,286	2,686	2,900
Foreign direct investment, net	na	43	51	155	244	376	515	344
Gross reserves (end-year), excluding gold [4]	na	na	432	545	506	654	704	na
External debt stock [5]	na	na	na	na	1,440	2,044	2,775	na
				(In months of imports of goods and services)				
Gross reserves (end-year), excluding gold [6]	na	na	4.9	4.9	3.1	2.5	2.4	na
				(In per cent of exports of goods and services)				
Debt service [6]	na	0.0	1.0	4.8	4.5	3.3	5.5	na
Memorandum items				(Denominations as indicated)				
Population (in millions, end-year)	2.7	2.6	2.6	2.5	2.5	2.5	2.5	na
GDP (in millions of lats)	143	1,005	1,467	2,043	2,349	2,829	3,211	3,518
GDP per capita (US dollars)	na	578	837	1,459	1,780	2,054	2,211	na
Share of industry in GDP [7]	35.9	28.4	23.2	20.2	22.6	21.1	21.3	na
Share of agriculture in GDP [7]	21.9	17.2	11.7	9.4	10.4	8.7	7.2	na
Current account/GDP (in per cent)	na	1.7	14.4	-0.2	-3.6	-4.2	-6.2	-8.6
External Debt minus Reserves (in US$ millions)	na	na	na	na	934	1,390	2,071	na
External Debt/GDP (in per cent)	na	na	na	na	32.4	39.8	50.2	na
External Debt/Exports (in per cent)	na	na	na	na	105.3	137.4	151.0	na

Note:

Data for 1991-96 represent official estimates of outturns as reflected in publications from the national authorities, the International Monetary Fund, the World Bank, the OECD, PlanEcon and the Institute of International Finance. Data for 1997-98 reflects EBRD evaluations, partly based on information from these sources.

Methodological notes can be found on pp. 232-234.

Lithuania

	1991	1992	1993	1994	1995	1996	1997 Estimate	1998 Projection
Output				(Percentage change)				
GDP at constant prices	-5.7	-21.3	-16.2	-9.8	3.3	4.7	5.7	3.0
Industrial gross output	na	na	-34.4	-26.5	5.2	1.3	0.7	na
Agricultural gross output [1]	-5	-24	-8	-18	10	10	6	na
Employment				(Percentage change)				
Labour force (annual average)	2.7	-1.2	-1.1	-6.4	0.7	1.8	-1.2	na
Employment (annual average)	2.4	-2.2	-4.2	-5.8	-1.9	0.9	0.3	na
				(In per cent of labour force)				
Unemployment	0.3	1.3	4.4	3.8	6.2	7.1	5.9	na
Prices and wages				(Percentage change)				
Consumer prices (annual average)	225	1,021	410	72.1	39.5	24.7	8.9	5.5
Consumer prices (end-year)	345	1,161	189	45.0	35.5	13.1	8.5	4.2
Producer prices (annual average)	148	1,517	398	44.7	28.3	17.2	6.4	na
Producer prices (end-year)	na	2,407	132	33.8	20.6	12.8	0.8	na
Gross average monthly earnings in industry (annual average) [2]	na	na	na	68.4	42.8	34.8	30.7	na
Government sector [3]				(In per cent of GDP)				
General government balance	2.7	0.5	-3.3	-5.5	-4.5	-4.5	-1.8	-3.6
General government expenditure	38.7	31.5	35.1	38.5	36.8	34.1	34.7	na
Monetary sector				(Percentage change)				
Broad money (M2, end-year)	143.0	245.3	100.2	63.0	28.9	-3.5	34.1	na
Domestic credit (end-year)	na	na	109.4	78.1	10.7	1.8	37.6	na
				(In per cent of GDP)				
Broad money	na	39.2	23.1	25.8	23.3	17.2	19.0	na
Interest and exchange rates				(In per cent per annum, end-year)				
Interbank interest rate	na	na	98.3	24.9	22.4	10.7	7.6	na
Treasury bill rate (three-month maturity)	na	na	na	na	22.4	10.8	9.4	na
Deposit rate [4]	na	na	39.3	8.9	8.0	na	na	na
Lending rate [4]	na	na	88.3	29.8	23.9	16.0	11.5	na
				(Litai per US dollar)				
Exchange rate (end-year) [5]	110	379	3.9	4.0	4.0	4.0	4.0	na
Exchange rate (annual average) [5]	38	177	4.3	4.0	4.0	4.0	4.0	na
External sector				(in millions of US dollars)				
Current account	na	203	-86	-94	-614	-723	-981	-1,563
Trade balance [6]	na	101	-155	-205	-698	-896	-1,147	-1,651
Exports [6]	na	1,142	2,026	2,029	2,706	3,413	4,192	4,123
Imports [6]	na	1,041	2,180	2,234	3,404	4,309	5,340	5,774
Foreign direct investment, net [7]	na	na	30	31	72	152	328	800
Gross reserves (end-year), excluding gold [8]	na	44	350	525	757	772	1,010	na
External debt stock [9]	na	59	325	529	845	2,340	3,194	na
				(In months of merchandise imports)				
Gross reserves (end-year), excluding gold [8]	na	0.5	1.9	2.8	2.7	2.2	2.3	na
				(In per cent of merchandise exports)				
Debt service	na	na	0.4	2.7	4.5	8.7	18.1	na
Memorandum items				(Denominations as indicated)				
Population (in millions, mid-year)	3.74	3.74	3.73	3.72	3.71	3.71	3.70	3.70
GDP (in millions of litai/litai equivalent)	415	3,406	11,590	16,904	24,103	31,569	38,201	41,530
GDP per capita (in US dollars)	289	514	715	1,142	1,624	2,127	2,581	na
Share of industry in GDP	45.3	38.8	36.0	28.1	26.7	26.3	24.4	na
Share of agriculture and forestry in GDP	16.7	14.3	14.9	11.0	11.9	12.4	12.8	na
Current account/GDP (in per cent)	na	10.6	-3.2	-2.2	-10.2	-9.2	-10.3	-15.1
External Debt minus Reserves (in US$ millions)	na	15.4	-25.6	3.6	87.6	1,568	2,184	na
External Debt/GDP (in per cent)	na	3.1	12.2	12.5	14.0	29.6	33.4	na
External Debt/Exports (in per cent)	na	5.2	16.0	26.1	31.2	68.6	76.2	na

Note:

Data for 1991-96 represent official estimates of outturns as reflected in publications from the national authorities, the International Monetary Fund, the World Bank, the OECD, PlanEcon and the Institute of International Finance. Data for 1997-98 reflect EBRD evaluations, partly based on preliminary estimates for 1996 from these sources.

Methodological notes can be found on pp. 232-234.

Moldova

	1991	1992	1993	1994	1995	1996	1997 Estimate	1998 Projection
Output				(Percentage change)				
GDP at constant prices	-17.5	-29.1	-1.2	-31.2	-3.0	-8.0	1.3	-2.0
Industrial gross output	na	na	0.3	-27.7	-3.9	-6.5	-4.0	na
Agricultural gross output	na	na	9.9	-24.3	3.7	-11.9	10.7	na
Employment				(Percentage change)				
Labour Force (end-year)	na	na	-17.6	0.0	-0.2	-27.3	na	na
Employment (end-year)	na	-1.0	-17.7	-0.4	-0.5	-27.6	na	na
				(In per cent of labour force)				
Unemployment	na	0.1	0.7	1.1	1.4	1.8	1.6	na
Prices and wages				(Percentage change)				
Consumer prices (annual average)	98	1,276	789	330	30.2	23.5	11.8	13.0
Consumer prices (end-year)	151	2,198	837	116	23.8	15.1	11.2	30.0
Producer prices (annual average)	na	na	na	205	255.3	31.2	15.3	na
Producer prices (end-year)	na	na	6947	215	46.6	20.4	13.4	na
Gross average monthly wages in manufacturing (annual average)	na	na	na	na	40.7	38.3	25.4	na
Government sector				(In per cent of GDP)				
General government balance [1]	0.0	-26.2	-7.4	-8.7	-5.7	-6.7	-7.5	-8.0
General government expenditure	24.7	56.6	29.4	40.6	39.7	38.7	41.8	na
Monetary sector				(Percentage change)				
Broad money (end-year)	na	361.7	320.2	115.7	65.2	15.3	34.0	na
Domestic credit (end-year)	na	550.0	333.8	116.6	55.8	18.5	27.8	na
				(In per cent of GDP)				
Broad money	69.5	43.3	15.8	13.0	16.5	16.2	19.2	na
Interest and exchange rates				(In per cent per annum, end-year)				
Interbank interest rate (up to 30 days maturity)	na	na	na	na	na	31.2	24.5	na
Treasury bills rate (three-month maturity)	na	na	na	na	52.9	39.0	25.5	na
Deposit rate (one year)	na	na	na	na	32.5	22.0	20.4	na
Lending rate (one year)	na	na	na	na	41.9	35.3	29.9	na
				(Leu per US dollar)				
Exchange rate (end-year) [2]	na	0.4	3.6	4.3	4.5	4.7	4.7	na
Exchange rate (annual average) [2]	na	0.2	1.5	4.1	4.6	4.6	4.6	na
External sector				(In millions of US dollars)				
Current account	na	-39	-182	-82	-149	-256	-292	-293
Trade balance [3]	na	-37	-180	-54	-70	-254	-319	-330
Exports [3]	na	868	451	618	739	802	823	790
Imports [3]	na	905	631	672	809	1,056	1,142	1,120
Foreign direct investment, net	na	17	14	18	73	56	64	100
Gross reserves (end-year), excluding gold [4]	na	na	89	179	257	315	366	na
External debt stock	na	16	255	503	670	795	1,205	na
				(In months of current account expenditures, excluding transfers)				
Gross reserves (end-year), excluding gold [4]	na	na	1.7	2.9	3.0	3.0	3.3	na
				(In per cent of current account revenues, excluding transfers)				
Debt service	na	na	na	2.3	8.2	5.7	17.4	na
Memorandum items				(Denominations as indicated)				
Population (in millions, end-year)	4.4	4.4	4.3	4.4	4.3	4.3	4.3	na
GDP (in millions of leu)	26	192	2,210	5,780	7,545	8,828	9,998	11,100
GDP per capita (US dollars)	na	231.7	310.0	327.2	386.4	444.5	504.0	na
Share of industry in GDP	na	na	39	33	28	28	29	na
Share of agriculture in GDP	na	na	32	29	33	31	30	na
Current Account/GDP (in per cent)	na	-3.0	-11.9	-5.8	-9.0	-13.4	-13.5	-15.6
External Debt minus Reserves (in US$ millions)	na	na	165.5	323.6	413.4	479.9	839.0	na
Exterenal Debt/GDP (in per cent)	na	1.3	16.7	35.3	40.5	41.4	55.6	na
External Debt/Exports (in per cent)	na	1.9	56.4	81.3	90.7	99.2	146.4	na

Note:

Data for 1991-96 represent official estimates of outturns as reflected in publications from the national authorities, the International Monetary Fund, the World Bank, the OECD, PlanEcon and the Institute of International Finance. Data for 1997-98 reflect EBRD evaluations, partly based on information from these sources.

Methodological notes can be found on pp. 232-234.

Poland

	1991	1992	1993	1994	1995	1996	1997 Estimate	1998 Projection
Output and expenditure				*(Percentage change)*				
GDP at constant prices	-7.0	2.6	3.8	5.2	7.0	6.1	6.9	5.2
Private consumption	6.3	2.3	5.2	4.3	3.6	8.7	7.0	na
Public consumption	10.2	6.4	3.8	2.8	2.9	3.4	3.4	na
Gross fixed investment	-4.4	2.3	2.9	9.2	16.9	20.6	21.9	na
Exports of goods and services	-1.7	10.8	3.2	13.1	23.6	12.5	9.9	na
Imports of goods and services	29.6	1.7	13.2	11.3	24.3	28.0	16.7	na
Industrial gross output	-8.0	2.8	6.4	12.1	9.7	8.7	10.8	na
Agricultural gross output	-1.6	-12.7	6.8	-9.3	10.7	0.7	1.0	na
Employment				*(Percentage change)*				
Labour force (end-year)	1.9	-0.4	0.7	0.6	-1.0	0.4	na	na
Employment (end-year)	-4.3	-2.8	-1.7	1.1	2.9	3.5	na	na
				(In per cent of labour force)				
Unemployment (end-year)	11.8	13.6	16.4	16.0	14.9	13.2	10.5	na
Prices and wages				*(Percentage change)*				
Consumer prices (annual average)	70.3	43.0	35.3	32.2	27.8	19.9	14.9	11.0
Consumer prices (end-year)	60.4	44.3	37.6	29.4	21.6	18.5	13.2	10.0
Producer prices (annual average)	40.9	34.5	31.9	25.3	25.4	12.4	12.2	na
Producer prices (end-year)	35.7	31.5	37.0	27.9	18.9	11.2	11.5	na
Gross average monthly earnings in manufacturing (annual average) [1]	63.1	38.7	35.4	36.7	32.7	26.9	21.5	na
Government sector				*(In per cent of GDP)*				
General government balance [2]	-6.7	-6.7	-3.1	-3.1	-2.8	-3.3	-3.1	-3.1
General government expenditure [2]	49.0	49.5	50.5	48.9	47.9	47.5	48.1	na
Monetary sector [3]				*(Percentage change)*				
Broad money (end-year)	37.0	57.5	36.0	38.2	34.9	29.4	29.1	na
Domestic credit (end-year)	158.7	55.6	44.2	30.1	20.1	29.7	26.4	na
				(In per cent of GDP)				
Broad money	31.6	35.8	35.9	36.7	36.5	37.5	39.6	na
Interest and exchange rates				*(In per cent per annum, end-year)*				
Interbank interest rate (up to 30-day maturity)	36.7	30.8	25.2	21.1	24.7	21.2	24.8	na
Treasury bill rate (three-month maturity)	na	41.4	33.7	27.0	24.2	18.8	23.5	na
Deposit rate [4]	36.0	32.0	25.0	26.0	22.0	18.3	19.5	na
Lending rate [5]	40.0	39.0	35.0	31.0	24.0	23.3	25.8	na
				(Zloty per US dollar)				
Exchange rate (end-year)	1.10	1.58	2.13	2.44	2.47	2.88	3.52	na
Exchange rate (annual average)	1.06	1.36	1.81	2.27	2.43	2.70	3.28	na
External sector				*(In billions of US dollars)*				
Current account	-2.0	0.9	-0.6	2.3	5.5	-1.3	-4.3	-6.5
Trade balance [6]	0.1	0.5	-2.3	-0.8	-1.8	-8.2	-11.3	-14.0
Exports [6]	12.8	14.0	13.6	17.0	22.9	24.4	27.2	31.0
Imports [6]	12.7	13.5	15.9	17.8	24.7	32.6	38.5	45.0
Net unclassified transactions [7]	1.3	1.8	2.2	3.2	7.8	7.2	6.1	na
Foreign direct investment, net [8]	0.1	0.3	0.6	0.5	1.1	2.8	3.0	4.0
Gross reserves (end-year), excluding gold [9]	3.6	4.1	4.1	5.8	14.8	17.8	20.4	na
External debt stock	48.0	47.6	47.2	42.2	43.9	40.4	38.1	na
				(In months of current account expenditures, excluding transfers)				
Gross reserves (end-year), excluding gold [9]	2.5	2.9	2.6	3.2	6.1	5.8	5.9	na
				(In per cent of current account revenues, excluding transfers)				
Debt service	68.9	19.3	20.1	14.3	6.7	7.6	5.9	na
Memorandum items				*(Denominations as indicated)*				
Population (in millions, end-year)	38.3	38.4	38.5	38.6	38.6	38.6	38.7	na
GDP (in billions of zloty)	82.5	114.9	155.8	210.4	288.7	362.8	445.1	520.0
GDP per capita (in US dollars)	2,037	2,197	2,234	2,399	3,084	3,486	3,512	na
Share of industry in GDP [10]	40.2	34.0	32.9	32.2	29.2	27.1	na	na
Share of agriculture in GDP	6.8	6.7	6.6	6.2	6.4	6.0	na	na
Current account/GDP (in per cent)	-2.6	1.1	-0.7	2.5	4.6	-1.0	-3.1	-4.5
External Debt minus Reserves (in US$ billions)	44.4	43.5	43.1	36.4	29.1	22.6	17.7	na
External Debt/GDP (in per cent)	61.5	56.4	54.9	45.6	36.9	30.0	28.1	na
External Debt/Exports (in per cent)	375.0	340.0	347.1	248.2	191.7	165.6	139.9	na

Note: Data for 1991-96 represent official estimates of outturns as reflected in publications from the national authorities, the International Monetary Fund, the World Bank, the OECD, PlanEcon and the Institute of International Finance. Data for 1997-98 reflect EBRD evaluations, partly based on information from these sources.

Methodological notes can be found on pp. 232-234.

Romania

	1991	1992	1993	1994	1995	1996	1997 Estimate	1998 Projection
Output and expenditure				(Percentage change)				
GDP at constant prices	-12.9	-8.8	1.5	3.9	7.1	3.9	-6.6	-5.0
Private consumption	na	-7.5	0.9	2.4	12.9	11.1	-5.7	na
Public consumption	na	2.2	2.7	11.7	0.7	7.0	-2.3	na
Gross fixed investment	na	11.0	8.3	20.7	6.9	3.7	-15.9	na
Exports of goods and services	na	12.9	11.1	19.0	17.0	0.2	2.1	na
Imports of goods and services	na	7.5	4.4	28.0	16.3	5.2	-4.7	na
Industrial gross output	-22.8	-21.9	1.2	3.3	9.4	9.9	-5.9	na
Agricultural gross output	-8.6	-12.2	13.4	3.2	4.5	1.8	3.1	na
Employment				(Percentage change)				
Labour force (end-year)	1.8	-1.8	-3.0	0.0	-7.1	-4.9	-0.7	na
Employment (end-year)	-0.5	-3.0	-3.8	-0.5	-5.2	-1.2	-3.1	na
				(In per cent of labour force)				
Unemployment [1]	3.0	8.2	10.4	10.9	9.5	6.6	8.8	na
Prices and wages				(Percentage change)				
Consumer prices (annual average)	161.1	210.4	256.1	136.7	32.3	38.8	154.8	60.0
Consumer prices (end-year)	222.8	199.2	295.5	61.7	27.8	56.9	151.4	45.0
Producer prices (annual average)	11.5	6.1	9.6	4.8	2.3	4.1	8.1	na
Producer prices (end-year)	250.5	104.0	195.4	73.4	32.0	60.4	154.3	na
Net monthly average earnings (annual average)	120.6	170.0	196.5	137.7	48.9	-51.9	98.3	na
Government sector				(In per cent of GDP)				
General government balance [2]	3.3	-4.6	-0.4	-1.9	-2.6	-4.0	-3.6	-5.5
General government expenditure	38.7	42.0	34.2	33.9	34.5	34.1	34.3	na
Monetary sector				(Percentage change)				
Broad money (end-year)	101.2	79.6	141.0	138.1	71.6	66.0	75.9	na
Domestic credit (end-year)	116.5	34.6	139.7	115.4	89.5	80.8	50.8	na
				(In per cent of GDP)				
Broad money	46.9	30.8	22.3	21.4	25.2	27.7	24.9	na
Interest and exchange rates				(In per cent per annum, end year)				
Interbank interest rate (up to 30-day maturity)	19.5	43.6	61.4	64.3	45.2	55.3	90.3	na
Treasury bills rate (three-month maturity)	na	na	na	na	45.0	55.0	98.0	na
Deposit rate (one year)	na	28.3	42.5	49.5	32.4	38.9	34.1	na
Lending rate (one year)	na	49.5	86.4	61.8	47.5	53.6	55.6	na
				(Lei per US dollar)				
Exchange rate (end-year)	189	460	1,276	1,767	2,578	4,035	8,023	na
Exchange rate (annual average)	76	308	760	1,655	2,033	3,083	7,168	na
External sector				(In millions of US dollars)				
Current account	-1,290	-1,518	-1,239	-516	-1,732	-2,611	-2,338	-3,400
Trade balance [3]	-1,345	-1,373	-1,130	-483	-1,605	-2,494	-1,971	-2,600
Exports [3]	3,538	4,286	4,882	6,067	7,882	8,061	8,427	8,400
Imports [3]	4,883	5,659	6,012	6,550	9,487	10,555	10,398	11,000
Foreign direct investment, net	37	73	97	341	417	263	1,224	900
Gross reserves (end-year), excluding gold[4]	695	826	995	592	334	551	2,194	na
Total external debt stock	2,131	3,240	4,249	5,563	6,645	8,332	9,315	na
				(In months of current account expenditures, excluding transfers)				
Gross reserves (end-year), excluding gold [4]	1.5	1.5	1.7	0.9	0.4	0.5	2.2	na
				(In per cent of current account revenues, excluding transfers)				
Debt service	2.3	8.9	6.2	8.7	11.5	14.8	20.2	na
Memorandum items				(Denominations as indicated)				
Population (in millions, end-year)	23.2	22.8	22.7	22.6	22.6	22.6	22.5	na
GDP (in billions of lei)	2,204	6,029	20,036	49,768	72,560	109,515	249,750	383,616
GDP per capita (in US dollars)	1,245	859	1,161	1,331	1,579	1,572	1,549	na
Share of industry in GDP	37.9	38.3	33.8	35.6	34.6	36.0	35.6	na
Share of agriculture in GDP	18.9	19.0	21.0	19.8	19.9	19.1	18.8	na
Current account/GDP (in per cent)	-4.1	-8.0	-4.5	-1.4	-5.0	-7.2	-7.1	-7
External Debt minus Reserves (in US$ millions)	1,436	2,414	3,254	4,971	6,311	7,781	7,036	na
External Debt/GDP (in per cent)	7.4	16.6	16.1	18.5	18.6	23.5	26.5	na
External Debt/Exports (in per cent)	65.8	64.9	74.7	77.3	70.7	86.4	93.8	na

Note:

Data for 1991-96 represent official estimates of outturns as reflected in publications from the national authorities, the International Monetary Fund, the World Bank, the OECD, PlanEcon and the Institute of International Finance. Data for 1997-98 reflect EBRD evaluations, partly based on information from these sources.

Methodological notes can be found on pp. 232-234.

Russian Federation

	1991	1992	1993	1994	1995	1996	1997 *Estimate*	1998 *Projection*
Output and expenditure				*(Percentage change)*				
GDP at constant prices	-5.0	-14.5	-8.7	-12.7	-4.1	-3.5	0.8	-5.0
Private consumption	na	na	-5.5	-9.2	-5.5	-5.6	2.0	na
Public consumption	na	na	-7.2	-2.7	1.2	-1.5	-2.0	na
Gross fixed investment	na	na	-25.8	-26.0	-7.5	-18.5	-5.0	na
Exports of goods and services	na	na	-2.1	4.9	7.3	-6.0	4.0	na
Imports of goods and services	na	na	-9.6	9.2	8.4	-14.7	7.0	na
Industrial gross output	-8.0	-18.0	-14.1	-20.9	-3.3	-4.0	1.9	na
Agricultural gross output	-3.7	-9.0	-4.4	-12.0	-7.6	-5.1	0.1	na
Employment				*(Percentage change)*				
Labour force (annual average)	na	na	-1.1	-1.6	-1.8	0.4	0.0	na
Employment (annual average)	-2.0	-2.3	-1.7	-6.2	-0.2	-0.6	-1.8	na
				(In per cent of labour force)				
Unemployment (annual average)	0.0	4.8	5.3	7.1	8.3	9.2	10.9	na
Prices and wages				*(Percentage change)*				
Consumer prices (annual average)	92.7	1,526.0	875.0	311.4	197.7	47.8	14.7	40.0
Consumer prices (end-year)	161.0	2,506.1	840.0	204.4	128.6	21.8	10.9	150.0
Producer prices (annual average)	na	1,767.9	941.9	337.4	236.5	50.8	19.7	na
Producer prices (end-year)	345.0	3,279.1	895.0	233.0	175.0	25.6	7.4	na
Gross average wages (large & medium-sized companies)	80.1	994.0	878.5	272.7	123.6	70.8	19.7	na
Government sector				*(In per cent of GDP)*				
General consolidated government balance [1]	na	-4.1	-7.4	-9.0	-5.7	-8.3	-7.4	-8.0
General consolidated government expenditure [1]	na	37.2	40.7	45.9	37.0	40.1	40.7	na
Monetary sector				*(Percentage change)*				
Broad money (end-year)	125.9	642.6	416.1	166.4	125.8	30.6	28.4	na
Net domestic assets (end-year)	na	na	770.0	359.8	70.7	80.6	14.8	na
				(In per cent of GDP)				
Broad money	68.4	37.4	21.4	16.0	13.9	13.1	14.2	na
Interest and exchange rates				*(In per cent per annum, end-year)*				
Treasury bill rate (all maturities)	na	na	103.2	136.8	100.8	38.7	36.6	na
Central bank refinance rate (uncompounded)	na	na	210.0	180.0	160.0	48.0	28.0	na
Lending rate	na	na	na	na	224.9	66.9	35.3	na
Deposit rate	na	na	na	na	69.6	34.5	7.4	na
				(Roubles per US dollar)				
Exchange rate (end-year) [2]	0.169	0.415	1.247	3.550	4.640	5.570	5.974	na
Exchange rate (annual average) [2]	0.067	0.222	0.992	2.097	4.459	5.126	5.785	na
External sector				*(In billions of US dollars)*				
Current account [3]	na	na	na	9.3	7.9	12.1	3.3	4.0
Trade balance [3]	na	na	na	17.8	20.8	23.1	17.3	17.0
Exports [3]	na	na	na	69.6	81.5	90.2	88.8	80.0
Imports [3]	na	na	na	48.5	64.0	73.9	72.2	63.0
Foreign direct investment, net	na	na	na	0.5	1.7	1.7	3.8	1.5
Gross reserves (end-year), including gold	na	4.5	8.9	6.5	17.2	15.3	17.8	na
External debt stock [4]	67.0	107.7	112.7	119.9	120.4	125.0	123.5	na
				(In months of current account expenditures, excluding transfers)				
Gross reserves (end-year), including gold	na	na	na	1.1	2.3	1.9	2.1	na
				(In per cent of current account revenues, excluding transfers)				
Public debt service due [5]	na	na	na	25.4	20.8	17.4	12.8	na
Public debt service paid [5]	na	na	na	7.0	7.3	7.2	7.1	na
Memorandum items				*(Denominations as indicated)*				
Population (in millions, end-year) [6]	148.7	148.7	148.4	148.3	148.0	147.5	147.2	na
GDP (in billions of roubles)	1.4	19.0	171.5	610.7	1,585	2,200	2,602	3,461
GDP per capita (in US dollars)	140.5	575.6	1,165	1,964	2,402	2,910	3,056	na
Share of industry in GDP	na	46.0	43.9	43.6	41.5	41.8	42.5	na
Share of agriculture in GDP	na	13.4	8.5	6.8	9.6	9.8	9.7	na
Current account/GDP (in per cent)	na	na	na	3.2	2.2	2.8	0.7	1.4
External Debt minus Reserves (in US$ billions)	na	103.2	103.8	113.4	103.2	109.7	105.7	na
External Debt/GDP (in per cent)	320.6	125.8	65.2	41.2	33.9	29.1	27.5	na
External Debt/Exports (in per cent)	na	na	na	172.3	147.7	138.6	139.1	na

Note: Data for 1991-97 represent official estimates of outturns as reflected in publications from the national authorities, Russian Economic Trends and Economist Intelligence Unit. Data for 1998 reflect EBRD evaluations, partly based on information from these sources.

Methodological notes can be found on pp. 232-234.

Slovak Republic

	1991	1992	1993	1994	1995	1996	1997 Estimate	1998 Projection
Output and expenditure				*(Percentage change)*				
GDP at constant prices	-14.6	-6.5	-3.7	4.9	6.9	6.6	6.5	5.0
Private consumption	-28.4	-6.4	-1.5	0.0	3.4	6.9	6.3	na
Public consumption	-17.8	9.9	-2.2	-11.2	3.0	20.3	0.1	na
Gross fixed investment	-25.2	-4.5	-5.4	-4.6	5.3	39.8	14.5	na
Exports of goods and services	na	na	-0.5	14.2	3.1	-0.3	6.1	na
Imports of goods and services	na	na	-0.8	-3.6	9.6	20.3	-2.3	na
Industrial gross output	-19.4	-9.2	-3.8	4.9	8.3	2.5	2.7	na
Agricultural gross output	-7.4	-13.9	-8.1	4.8	2.4	2.7	na	na
Employment				*(Percentage change)*				
Labour force (annual average) [1]	na	na	na	-2.6	1.4	1.0	-0.6	na
Employment (annual average)	-14.4	0.3	-0.1	-1.8	2.2	0.8	-0.4	na
				(In per cent of labour force)				
Unemployment [1]	na	na	12.2	13.7	13.1	11.1	11.6	na
Prices and wages				*(Percentage change)*				
Consumer prices (annual average)	61.2	10.1	23.2	13.4	9.9	5.8	6.1	7.5
Consumer prices (end-year)	58.3	9.1	25.1	11.7	7.2	5.4	6.4	9.0
Producer prices (annual average)	68.8	5.3	17.2	10.0	9.0	4.1	4.5	na
Producer prices (end-year)	50.6	6.1	18.8	9.4	7.1	4.7	4.4	na
Gross average monthly earnings in manufacturing (annual average) [2]	16.3	16.4	22.4	18.3	15.9	14.7	11.9	na
Government sector [3]				*(In per cent of GDP)*				
General government balance	na	na	-7.0	-1.3	0.2	-1.9	-3.8	-4.0
General government expenditure	na	na	51	48	47	49	51	na
Monetary sector				*(Percentage change)*				
Broad money (M2, end-year)	na	na	16.8	20.1	19.2	16.5	9.1	na
Domestic credit (end-year)	na	na	na	9.2	7.8	14.4	3.2	na
				(In per cent of GDP)				
Broad money (M2, end-year)	na	64	67	68	69	72	69	na
Interest and exchange rates				*(In per cent per annum, end-year)*				
Interbank interest rate (30-day maturity)	na	na	16.2	5.9	9.7	16.1	26.6	na
Discount rate	9.5	9.5	12.0	12.0	9.8	8.8	8.8	na
Lending rate [4]	na	na	14.1	14.4	14.8	13.2	16.2	na
Deposit rate [4]	na	na	8.7	9.2	8.2	6.2	8.7	na
				(Koruna per US dollar)				
Exchange rate (end-year)	27.84	28.90	33.20	31.28	29.57	31.90	34.81	na
Exchange rate (annual average)	29.49	28.29	30.77	32.04	29.74	30.65	33.62	na
External sector				*(In billions of US dollars)*				
Current account	na	na	-0.60	0.66	0.39	-2.10	-1.34	-1.95
Trade balance [5]	na	na	-0.93	0.06	-0.23	-2.29	-1.47	-2.12
Exports [5]	na	na	5.45	6.69	8.58	8.83	8.79	9.58
Imports [5]	na	na	6.38	6.63	8.81	11.12	10.26	11.70
Foreign direct investment, net	0.08	0.10	0.11	0.24	0.19	0.20	0.05	0.22
Gross reserves (end-year), excluding gold [6]	na	na	0.45	1.75	3.42	3.47	3.28	na
External debt stock	na	na	3.38	4.66	5.68	7.67	9.90	na
				(In months of imports of goods and services)				
Gross reserves (end-year), excluding gold [6]	na	na	0.7	2.5	3.9	3.2	3.2	na
				(In per cent of exports of goods and services)				
Debt service	na	na	8.6	8.8	9.3	10.8	17.3	na
Memorandum items				*(Denominations as indicated)*				
Population (in millions, end-year)	5.3	5.3	5.3	5.3	5.4	5.4	5.4	na
GDP (in billions of koruna)	320	332	370	441	517	576	654	730
GDP per capita (in US dollars)	2,052	2,213	2,258	2,571	3,240	3,495	3,624	na
Share of industry in GDP	na	37.9	35.4	30.6	32.2	30.0	28.2	na
Share of agriculture in GDP	na	6.2	6.6	7.4	5.6	5.2	4.8	na
Current account/GDP (in per cent)	na	na	-5.0	4.8	2.3	-11.2	-6.9	-9.6
External Debt minus Reserves (in US$ billions)	na	na	2.9	2.9	2.3	4.2	6.6	na
External Debt/GDP (in per cent)	na	na	28.1	33.9	32.7	40.8	50.9	na
External Debt/Exports (in per cent)	na	na	62.0	69.6	66.2	86.9	112.5	na

Note:

Data for 1991-96 represent official estimates of outturns as reflected in publications from the national authorities, the International Monetary Fund, the World Bank, the OECD, PlanEcon and the Institute of International Finance. Data for 1997-98 reflect EBRD evaluations, partly based on information from these sources.

Methodological notes can be found on pp. 232-234.

Slovenia

	1991	1992	1993	1994	1995	1996	1997 Estimate	1998 Projection
Output and expenditure				(Percentage change)				
GDP at constant prices	-8.9	-5.5	2.8	5.3	4.1	3.1	3.8	4.0
Private consumption	-11.0	-3.6	13.9	3.8	9.2	2.6	2.8	na
Public consumption	0.3	-1.7	5.3	2.1	2.5	2.2	5.8	na
Gross fixed investment	-11.5	-12.9	10.7	12.5	17.1	6.9	8.7	na
Exports of goods and services	-20.1	-23.5	0.6	10.5	1.0	2.5	9.9	na
Imports of goods and services	-22.4	-22.9	17.6	10.7	11.6	1.3	9.6	na
Industrial gross output	-11.6	-12.6	-2.5	6.6	2.3	1.2	4.7	na
Agricultural gross output	-2.5	-6.7	-4.2	4.2	1.6	1.7	0.7	na
Employment				(Percentage change)				
Labour force (end-year)	na	na	0.3	-1.7	-0.9	-0.8	0.5	na
Employment (annual average)	-5.1	-4.1	-3.6	-1.3	-0.1	-0.4	0.2	na
				(In per cent of labour force)				
Unemployment [1]	8.2	11.5	14.4	14.4	13.9	13.9	14.4	na
Prices and wages				(Percentage change)				
Consumer prices (annual average) [2]	117.7	207.3	32.9	21.0	13.5	9.9	8.4	8.5
Consumer prices (end-year) [2]	247.1	92.9	22.8	19.5	9.0	9.0	8.8	7.0
Producer prices (annual average)	124.1	215.7	21.6	17.7	12.8	6.8	6.1	na
Producer prices (end-year)	311.8	76.2	18.6	18.2	7.9	5.8	6.8	na
Net average monthly wages (annual average) [3]	82.5	198.5	52.0	28.3	19.4	14.8	11.5	na
Government sector				(In per cent of GDP)				
General government balance [4]	2.6	0.2	0.3	-0.2	0.0	0.3	-1.1	-1.0
General government expenditure	41.1	45.6	46.7	46.1	45.7	44.9	45.7	na
Monetary sector				(Percentage change)				
Broad money (end-year)	na	131.6	64.2	50.8	32.2	19.4	23.8	na
Domestic credit (end-year)	na	90.1	101.4	27.2	35.1	13.2	13.5	na
				(In per cent of GDP)				
Broad money	na	28.1	32.8	38.3	42.2	43.8	47.7	na
Interest and exchange rates				(In per cent per annum, end-year)				
Interbank interest rate (average)	na	60.5	34.7	24.7	15.9	10.2	9.8	na
Treasury bill rate (on tolar part of twin bills)	na	50.9	30.2	26.3	19.4	10.3	14.5	na
Deposit rate (one year and over)	na	53.8	33.9	32.2	24.4	13.6	16.6	na
Lending rate (short-term working capital)	na	72.2	42.6	38.5	28.0	18.3	20.3	na
				(Tolar per US dollar)				
Exchange rate (end-year) [5]	56.7	98.7	131.8	126.5	126.0	141.5	169.2	na
Exchange rate (annual average) [5]	27.6	81.3	113.2	128.8	118.5	135.4	159.7	na
External sector [6]				(In millions of US dollars)				
Current account	131	926	192	600	-23	39	37	-80
Trade balance [7]	-262	791	-154	-338	-954	-882	-772	-785
Exports [7]	3,869	6,683	6,083	6,829	8,350	8,370	8,407	8,853
Imports [7]	4,131	5,892	6,237	7,168	9,305	9,252	9,179	9,638
Foreign direct investment, net [7]	41	113	111	128	176	186	321	200
Gross reserves (end-year), excluding gold [8]	112	716	770	1,480	1,802	2,279	3,297	na
External debt stock	1,866	1,741	1,873	2,258	2,970	4,010	4,176	na
				(In months of current account expenditures, excluding transfers)				
Gross reserves (end-year), excluding gold [8]	0.4	1.2	1.2	2.1	2.0	2.5	3.6	na
				(In per cent of current account revenues, excluding transfers)				
Debt service	7.0	5.2	5.5	5.4	6.9	8.6	8.5	na
Memorandum items				(Denominations as indicated)				
Population (in millions, annual average)	2.0	2.0	2.0	2.0	2.0	2.0	2.0	na
GDP (in billions of tolars)	349	1,018	1,435	1,853	2,221	2,553	2,907	3,265
GDP per capita (in US dollars)	6,333	6,280	6,370	7,231	9,418	9,429	9,101	na
Share of industry in GDP (current prices, in per cent)	36.0	32.1	29.3	30.4	28.6	27.9	28.7	na
Share of agriculture in GDP (current prices, in per cent)	5.2	5.2	4.5	4.0	3.9	3.9	3.9	na
Current account/GDP (in per cent)	1.0	7.4	1.5	4.2	-0.1	0.2	0.2	-0.4
External Debt minus Reserves (in US$ millions)	1,754	1,026	1,103	778	1,168	1,731	879	na
External Debt/GDP (in per cent)	14.7	13.9	14.8	15.7	15.8	21.3	23.2	na
External Debt/Exports (in per cent)	48.2	26.1	30.8	33.1	35.6	47.9	49.7	na

Note:

Data for 1991-96 represent official estimates of outturns as reflected in publications from the national authorities, the International Monetary Fund, the World Bank, the OECD, PlanEcon and the Institute of International Finance. Data for 1997-98 reflect EBRD evaluations, partly based on information from these sources.

Methodological notes can be found on pp. 232-234.

Tajikistan

	1991	1992	1993	1994	1995	1996	1997 Estimate	1998 Projection
Output				*(Percentage change)*				
GDP at constant prices	-7.1	-29.0	-11.0	-18.9	-12.5	-4.4	1.7	3.0
Industrial gross output	-5.6	-26.8	-12.0	-31.2	-13.6	-23.9	-2.8	na
Agricultural gross output	-4.4	-26.7	-4.4	0.1	-21.5	-17.8	1.8	na
Employment				*(Percentage change)*				
Employment (end-year)	1.7	-3.1	-3.3	-0.1	0.8	-6.8	na	na
				(In per cent of labour force)				
Unemployment [1]	na	0.3	1.2	1.7	2.0	2.7	2.9	na
Prices and wages				*(Percentage change)*				
Consumer prices (annual average)	112	1,157	2,195	350	609	418	87.8	46.3
Consumer prices (end-year)	204	1,364	7,344	1.1	2,133	40.5	163.6	10.1
Producer prices (annual average)	163	1,320	1,080	328	1,080	449	113	na
Producer prices (end-year)	184	5,926	5,996	302	628	78	159	na
Gross average monthly wages (annual average)	64	461	746	116	109	283	187	na
Government sector				*(In per cent of GDP)*				
Central government balance [2]	-16.4	-28.4	-23.6	-10.2	-11.2	-5.8	-3.3	-3.3
Central government expenditure	49.6	55.0	50.7	54.8	26.5	17.9	17.0	na
Monetary sector				*(Percentage change)*				
Broad money (end-year)	68	579	1,429	159	413	143	117	na
Domestic credit (end-year)	na	na	na	125	393	146	176	na
				(In per cent of GDP)				
Broad money	na	na	9.1	8.6	24.5	10.7	8.5	na
Interest and exchange rates				*(In per cent per annum, end-year)*				
Interbank interest rate (up to 30-day maturity)	na	na	na	na	153	72	72	na
Deposit rate (up to three-month maturity) [3]	30	30	30	30	100	85	118	na
Lending rate (up to three-month maturity) [3]	30	30	30	30	500	124	136	na
				(Tajik rouble per US dollar)				
Exchange rate (end-year) [4]	2	415	1,247	3,550	285	328	747	na
Exchange rate (annual average) [4]	2	222	930	2,204	135	298	564	na
External sector				*(In millions of US dollars)*				
Current account	na	53	-208	-170	-54	-76	-60	-69
Trade balance [5]	na	-55	-204	-148	-41	-38	-64	-70
Exports [5]	na	na	456	559	839	770	746	740
Imports [5]	na	na	660	707	880	806	810	810
Foreign direct investment, net	na	na	9	12	17	20	11	18
Gross reserves (end-year), excluding gold [6]	na	na	2	1	4	14	30	na
External debt stock	na	0	509	760	817	868	1,039	na
				(In weeks of merchandise imports)				
Gross reserves (end-year), excluding gold [6]	na	na	0.2	0.1	0.3	1.0	2.1	na
				(In per cent of exports of goods)				
Debt service (due) [7]	na	na	5.7	9.7	25.5	32.6	12.5	na
Memorandum items				*(Denominations as indicated)*				
Population (in millions, end-year)	5.6	5.6	5.7	5.8	5.9	6.0	6.1	na
GDP (in millions of roubles until 1994, millions of Tajik roubles thereafter)	10,540	64,760	707,060	1,786,490	64,843	308,474	632,000	952,000
GDP per capita (in US dollars)	1,116	52	133	141	82	174	179	na
Share of industry in GDP [8]	31.6	36.4	32.8	22.1	35.3	20.5	19.5	na
Share of agriculture in GDP [8]	26.1	27.1	21.0	19.0	15.3	27.7	27.6	na
Current account/GDP (in per cent)	na	18.1	-27.4	-21.0	-11.2	-7.3	-5.4	-5.5
External Debt minus Reserves (in US$ millions)	na	na	507	759	813	854	1,009	na
External Debt/GDP (in per cent)	na	0.0	66.9	93.8	170.1	83.9	92.7	na
External Debt/Exports (in per cent)	na	na	111.6	136.0	97.4	112.7	139.3	na

Note:

Data for 1991-96 represent official estimates of outturns as reflected in publications from the national authorities, the International Monetary Fund, the World Bank, the OECD, PlanEcon and the Institute of International Finance. Data for 1997-98 reflect EBRD evaluations, partly based on information from these sources.

Methodological notes can be found on pp. 232-234.

Turkmenistan

	1991	1992	1993	1994	1995	1996	1997 Estimate	1998 Projection
Output				*(Percentage change)*				
GDP at constant prices	-4.7	-5.3	-10.0	-18.8	-8.2	-8.0	-26.0	5.0
Industrial gross output [1]	5	-15	5	-25	-6	19	-20	na
Agricultural gross output	na	-9	8	-11	-7	-49	14	na
Employment				*(Percentage change)*				
Labour force (end-year)	2.6	2.7	2.9	2.5	10.9	4.0	na	na
Employment (end-year)	1.9	0.1	4.4	1.4	0.5	0.4	-0.2	na
				(In per cent of labour force)				
Unemployment [2]	2.0	na	na	na	3.0	na	na	na
Prices and wages				*(Percentage change)*				
Consumer prices (annual average)	103	493	3,102	1,748	1,005	992	84	19
Consumer prices (end-year)	155	644	9,750	1,328	1,262	446	22	28
Gross average monthly wages in industry (annual average)	na	na	na	na	686	969	135	na
Government sector				*(In per cent of GDP)*				
General government balance [3]	2.5	13.2	-0.5	-1.4	-1.6	-0.2	0.01	-4.0
General government expenditure	38.2	42.2	19.2	10.4	12.5	16.9	29.2	na
Monetary sector				*(Percentage change)*				
Broad money M3 (end-year)	na	na	na	984	454	413	82	na
Domestic credit (end-year)	na	na	na	915	405	1,391	88	na
				(In per cent of GDP)				
Broad money M3	na	na	22.0	15.6	11.3	8.2	11.8	na
Interest and exchange rates				*(In per cent per annum, end-year)*				
Interbank interest rate (up to one-month maturity)	na	na	na	na	55	121	39	na
Treasury bill rate (one-month maturity)	na	na	na	150	60	120	40	na
Deposit rate (up to one year) [4]	na	na	50	206	80	130	47	na
Lending rate (up to one year) [4]	na	na	108	300	70	200	48	na
				(Manat per US dollar)				
Official exchange rate (end-year)	na	na	2	75	200	4,070	4,165	na
Official exchange rate (annual average)	na	na	2	19	111	3,232	4,143	na
Commercial exchange rate (end-year) [5]	na	na	30	75	2,400	5,055	5,090	na
Commercial exchange rate (annual average) [5]	na	na	na	63	426	3,924	5,256	na
External sector				*(In millions of US dollars)*				
Current account	na	na	776	85	23	44	-596	-696
Trade balance [6]	590	1,140	1,100	485	441	159	-245	-431
Exports [6]	1,238	2,149	2,693	2,176	2,084	1,691	759	689
Imports [6]	648	1,009	1,593	1,691	1,644	1,532	1,004	1,120
Foreign direct investment, net	na	na	79	103	233	129	108	110
Gross reserves (end-year), excluding gold [7]	na	na	818	927	1,165	1,172	1,287	na
External debt stock	na	na	168	418	550	667	1,360	na
				(In months of current account expenditures, excluding transfers)				
Gross reserves (end-year), excluding gold [7]	na	na	6.2	5.1	6.3	7.9	10.5	na
				(In per cent of current account revenues, excluding transfers)				
Debt service	na	na	na	1.8	12.6	16.6	34.6	na
Memorandum items				*(Denominations as indicated)*				
Population (in millions, end-year)	3.8	3.8	3.95	4.05	4.48	4.66	4.70	na
GDP (in billions of manat)	na	na	9	141	1,072	7,608	9,646	11,670
GDP per capita (in US dollars)	na	na	1,191	552	562	417	390	na
Share of industry in GDP (in per cent)	20	59	55.1	73.2	52.2	50.0	44.3	na
Share of agriculture in GDP (in per cent)	46	19	11.5	9.0	30.3	17.5	19.8	na
Current account/GDP (in per cent)	na	na	16.5	3.8	0.9	2.3	-32.5	-32.8
External Debt minus Reserves (in US$ millions)	na	na	-650	-509	-615	-505	73	na
External Debt/GDP (in per cent)	na	na	3.6	18.7	21.9	34.4	74.1	na
External Debt/Exports (in per cent)	na	na	6.2	19.2	26.4	39.4	179.2	na

Note:

Data for 1991-96 represent official estimates of outturns as reflected in publications from the national authorities, the International Monetary Fund, the World Bank, the OECD, PlanEcon and the Institute of International Finance. Data for 1997-98 reflect EBRD evaluations, partly based on information from these sources.

Methodological notes can be found on pp. 232-234.

Ukraine

	1991	1992	1993	1994	1995	1996	1997 *Estimate*	1998 *Projection*
Output				*(Percentage change)*				
GDP at constant prices	-11.6	-13.7	-14.2	-23.0	-12.2	-10.0	-3.2	0.0
Industrial gross output	-4.8	-6.4	-8.0	-27.3	-12.0	-5.7	-1.8	na
Agricultural gross output	-13.0	-8.3	1.5	-16.5	-3.6	-9.5	-0.8	na
Employment				*(Percentage change)*				
Labour force (end-year)	na	na	-1.7	-0.3	1.0	-5.0	na	na
Employment in industry (end-year)	na	na	-5.5	-11.5	-6.5	-8.6	na	na
				(In per cent of labour force)				
Unemployment	0.0	0.3	0.4	0.4	0.5	1.1	2.3	na
Prices and wages				*(Percentage change)*				
Consumer prices (annual average)	91	1,210	4,735	891	376	80	16	11
Consumer prices (end-year)	161	2,730	10,155	401	182	40	10	22
Producer prices (annual average)	125	2,384	4,619	1,144	488	52	8	na
Producer prices (end-year)	163	3,828	9,668	774	172	17	5	na
Gross average monthly wages in industry (annual average)	na	na	2,475	727	421	71	14	na
Government sector				*(In per cent of GDP)*				
General government balance [1]	na	-25.4	-16.2	-9.1	-7.1	-3.2	-5.6	-3.0
General government expenditure [1]	na	58.4	54.5	45.8	37.4	31.6	34.8	na
Monetary sector				*(Percentage change)*				
Broad money (end-year)	na	na	758	540	116	35	34	na
Domestic credit (end-year)	na	na	981	480	191	43	33	na
				(In per cent of GDP)				
Broad money	na	na	31.8	26.6	12.7	11.6	13.1	na
Interest and exchange rates				*(In per cent per annum, end-year)*				
Refinancing rate	na	80	240	252	110	40	35	na
Treasury bill rate (three-month maturity) [2]	na	na	na	na	164	62	41	na
Deposit rate [3]	na	82	149	209	70	34	18	na
Lending rate [3]	na	77	184	250	123	80	49	na
				(Hryvnia per US dollar)				
Exchange rate (annual average, auction rate) [4]	1.74	242	10,668	31,700	147,307	1.83	1.86	na
Exchange rate (annual average, official rate)	na	na	0.05	0.32	1.47	1.83	1.86	na
Exchange rate (end-year, official rate)	na	0.01	0.13	1.04	1.79	1.89	1.90	na
External sector				*(In billions of US dollars)*				
Current account	-2.9	-0.6	-0.8	-1.2	-1.2	-1.2	-1.3	-1.2
Trade balance [5]	-3.4	-0.6	-2.5	-2.6	-2.7	-4.3	-4.2	-3.0
of which with non-FSU countries	-2.7	0.5	0.5	1.0	0.6	-0.2	0.8	na
Exports [5]	50.0	11.3	12.8	13.9	14.2	15.5	15.4	14.5
of which to non-FSU countries	7.3	6.0	5.2	6.0	6.5	6.7	8.6	na
Imports [5]	53.4	11.9	15.3	16.5	16.9	19.8	19.6	17.5
of which from non-FSU countries	10.0	5.5	4.7	5.0	5.9	6.9	7.8	na
Foreign direct investment, net	na	0.2	0.2	0.1	0.4	0.5	0.6	0.7
Gross reserves (end-year), excluding gold [6]	na	0.5	0.2	0.6	1.1	2.0	2.4	na
External debt stock	na	0.5	3.7	7.7	8.1	9.2	11.8	na
				(In weeks of imports of goods and services)				
Gross reserves (end-year), excluding gold [6]	na	0.5	0.1	2.3	3.7	5.2	5.5	na
				(In per cent of exports of goods and services)				
Debt service	na	na	1.3	11.4	6.5	6.0	9.4	na
Memorandum items				*(Denominations as indicated)*				
Population (in millions, end-year)	51.9	52.0	52.1	51.9	51.7	51.3	50.9	na
GDP (in millions of hryvnia)	3	51	1,483	12,038	54,516	81,520	92,484	102,700
GDP per capita (in US dollars)	na	404	629	725	718	858	976	na
Share of industry in GDP	45.8	43.5	29.9	39.0	34.6	31.0	34.0	na
Share of agriculture in GDP	24.4	20.3	21.6	16.0	14.9	6.7	6.0	na
Current account/GDP (in per cent)	na	na	-2.4	-3.2	-3.2	-2.7	-2.6	-2.9
External Debt minus Reserves (in US$ billions)	na	0.0	3.5	7.1	7.0	7.2	9.4	na
External Debt/GDP (in per cent)	na	na	11.2	20.5	21.8	20.7	23.7	na
External Debt/Exports (in per cent)	na	4.4	28.9	55.4	57.0	59.4	76.6	na

Note:

Data for 1991-96 represent official estimates of outturns as reflected in publications from the national authorities, the International Monetary Fund, the World Bank and Ukraine Economic Trends (TACIS). Data for 1997-98 reflect EBRD evaluations, partly based on information from these sources.

Methodological notes can be found on pp. 232-234.

Uzbekistan

	1991	1992	1993	1994	1995	1996	1997 Estimate	1998 Projection
Output and expenditure				(Percentage change)				
GDP at constant prices	-0.5	-11.1	-2.3	-4.2	-0.9	1.6	2.4	2.0
Industrial value added	-3.8	-23.9	1.5	-3.4	2.0	-7.0	2.2	na
Agricultural value added	-0.4	-9.7	-4.2	-6.6	-5.6	1.7	4.9	na
Employment				(Percentage change)				
Labour force (end-year) [1]	na	na	na	na	1.2	1.3	1.4	na
Employment (end-year)	4.0	0.2	-0.1	-1.3	3.7	1.3	1.4	na
				(In per cent of labour force)				
Unemployment [2]	0.0	0.1	0.3	0.4	0.4	0.4	0.4	0.6
Prices and wages				(Percentage change)				
Consumer prices (annual average)	82	645	534	1,568	305	54	72	40
Consumer prices (end-year)	169	910	885	1,281	117	64	50	33
Producer prices (annual average)	147	3,275	2,545	1,428	499	107	52	na
Producer prices (end-year)	311	1,300	1,919	1,422	215	72	40	na
Gross average monthly wages (annual average)	51	612	1,148	963	252	102	71	na
Government sector				(In per cent of GDP)				
Consolidated central government balance [3]	-3.6	-18.4	-10.4	-6.1	-4.1	-7.3	-2.3	-3.0
Consolidated central government expenditure	52.7	43.4	46.4	35.3	38.7	41.6	32.8	na
Monetary sector				(Percentage change)				
Broad money (end-year)	na	468	784	680	144	113	36	na
Domestic credit (end-year)	na	na	na	na	55.2	268.5	70.0	na
				(In per cent of GDP)				
Broad money	na	69.4	53.5	32.8	18.1	19.6	16.4	na
Interest and exchange rates				(In per cent per annum, end-year)				
Treasury bill rate (three-month maturity)	na	na	na	na	na	36	26	na
Deposit rate (one year)	7	10	30	60	90	40	39	na
Lending rate (one year)	na	na	na	100	105	60	59	na
				(Som per US dollar)				
Exchange rate (end-year) [4]	2.0	415	1,247	25.0	36.0	55.0	80.2	na
Exchange rate (annual average) [4]	0.6	222	1.0	11.4	30.2	41.1	66.7	na
External sector				(In millions of US dollars)				
Current account	7,225	-236	-429	119	-21	-980	-584	-492
Trade balance [5]	688	-234	-378	214	237	-706	-72	-242
Exports [5]	11,829	1,424	2,877	2,940	3,475	3,534	3,695	3,845
Imports [5]	11,141	1,659	3,255	2,727	3,238	4,240	3,767	4,125
Foreign direct investment, net	na	9	48	73	-24	90	167	60
Gross reserves (end-year), including gold [6]	na	79	1,022	1,330	1,867	1,901	1,167	na
External debt stock	0	65	948	1,101	1,782	2,331	2,594	na
				(In months of imports of goods and services)				
Gross reserves (end-year), including gold [7]	na	0.6	3.8	5.9	6.9	5.4	3.7	na
				(In per cent of exports of goods and services)				
Debt service	na	0.4	0.7	10.5	15.8	9.0	9.8	na
Memorandum items				(Denominations as indicated)				
Population (in millions, end-year)	20.9	21.3	21.9	22.3	22.7	23.1	23.6	na
GDP (in millions of som)	61.5	447.0	5,095	64,878	302,787	560,147	962,200	1,305,000
GDP per capita (in US dollars)	na	na	232	251	442	590	611	na
Share if industry in GDP	26	27	25	19	20	20	19	na
Share of agriculture in GDP	37	35	28	38	32	26	29	na
Current account/GDP (in per cent)	na	na	-8.4	2.1	-0.2	-7.2	-4.1	-3.8
External Debt minus Reserves (in US$ millions)	na	-14	-74	-229	-8.5	430	1427	na
External Debt/GDP (in per cent)	na	na	18.6	19.3	17.8	17.1	18.0	na
External Debt/Exports (in per cent)	0.0	4.6	33.0	37.4	51.3	66.0	70.2	na

Note:

Data for 1991-96 represent official estimates of outturns as reflected in publications from the national authorities, the International Monetary Fund, the World Bank, the OECD, PlanEcon and the Institute of International Finance. Data for 1997-98 reflect EBRD evaluations, partly based on information from these sources.

Methodological notes can be found on pp. 232-234.

Methodological notes

Albania

1 Unemployment as a percentage of domestic labour force is much higher (17% in 1995). Emigrant workers abroad accounted for 18% of the total labour force in 1995.

2 Figures for 1997 are based on the information from parts of Albania where data collection was possible.

3 General government includes the state, municipalities and extrabudgetary funds. Budget balance on a commitment basis.

4 Until 1995 the figures show the floor of the band set by the Bank of Albania (central bank). Thereafter data refer to weighted average interest rates on new 12-month deposits in commercial banks.

5 Until 1995 data refer to the guideline rate announced by the Bank of Albania (central bank). Thereafter data refer to weighted average interest rates for 1-year loans by commercial banks.

6 Data from the balance of payments.

7 Foreign exchange reserves of monetary authorities.

Armenia

1 Registered unemployement. Unofficial estimates place the true rate of unemployment at 25% in 1997.

2 Consolidated accounts of the Republican government and the local authorities.

3 Weighted average rate for maturities of 15 days to less than one year.

4 Data from the balance of payments.

5 Foreign exchange reserves of monetary authorities.

6 Excluding official transfers.

Azerbaijan

1 Employment and labour force data (from IMF) differ from official statistics. Labour force data is corrected for the working age population outside the labour force. Unemployment is based on survey data. Less than 5% of all unemployed are registered.

2 General government includes the state, municipalities and extrabudgetary funds.

3 Central bank's compounded refinancing rate 1992-95. Interbank offer rate thereafter.

4 1993-95: Minimum rate for household time deposits, weighted average thereafter, compounded.

5 1993-95: Minimum lending rate for private enterprises, weighted average thereafter, compounded.

6 Data from the balance of payments.

7 Foreign direct investment including portfolio investment and oil bonus payments to the government.

8 Foreign exchange reserves of monetary authorities. Data on ratio to imports of goods and services are from the IMF and exclude oil sector operations.

9 GDP figure in roubles for 1991 was converted at the rate of 10 roubles per manat.

10 GDP per capita figures for 1992-93 are estimates from the IMF. The manat became official legal tender only in January 1994. Figures thereafter are based on Manat GDP.

Belarus

1 Officially registered unemployment.

2 General government includes the state, municipalities and extrabudgetary funds but excludes the Presidential Fund.

3 Official non-cash exchange rate. The premium on the parallel market was 30% in 1997, but reached 300% in August 1998. Belarus US-dollar GDP would decline from a projected 12.2 bn in 1998, at the official non cash rate, to 8.7 bn at the parallel market rate.

4 Data from the balance of payments.

5 Foreign exchange reserves of monetary authorities.

Bosnia and Herzegovina

1 Data are taken from the World Bank. However the IMF tends to report lower rates of growth, especially for Republika Srpska.

2 Bosniak-majority area prior to September 1996, Federation thereafter. Before September 1996 data includes personnel that are not actually working but for whom contributions (pension, health) are paid.

3 Index based on prices denominated in FR Yugoslavia dinars.

4 YUD based index, converted into DM using parallel market exchange rate.

5 Country-wide monetary aggregates.

6 Refer to Bosnian dinar. Since August 1997, Bosnia and Herzegovina has a common Central Bank. The new currency, the convertible Mark (KM) is pegged to the Deutschmark at 1:1 under currency board rules.

7 Excludes municipal government operations for RS. Data for 1996 and subsequent years exclude military expenditures financed by external grants. No net financing of the budget deficit, other than arrears, in 1996-98.

8 Data for 1992-93 are based on limited customs data for the Bosniak-majority area. 1994-97 data are rough estimates for the whole territory of Bosnia and Herzegovina.

9 Data include refugees abroad.

Bulgaria

1 There are several breaks in the national accounts data. Until 1993, figures include holding gains. In 1995, the industrial classification changed shifting the relative weights of industry and agriculture in GDP. Using the old classification, industry as a share of GDP is 32.4% in 1996 and the share of agriculture in GDP is 12.8%.

2 General government includes the state, municipalities and extrabudgetary funds.

3 Data from the balance of payments.

4 Foreign exchange reserves of monetary authorities.

Croatia

1 Nights spent by foreign tourists.

2 Excluding small enterprises, self-employed people, farmers, employees of the Ministry of Defence.

3 Earnings per employee. Until 1994 net wages, gross wages thereafter.

4 Consolidated central government.

5 Weighted average over all maturities.

6 Data from the balance of payments. Data for 1991-92 exclude trade with republics of former Yugoslavia.

7 Foreign exchange reserves of monetary authorities.

Czech Republic

1 GDP and GDP component data in 1984 constant prices up to and including 1993; 1994 prices thereafter.

2 General government includes the state, municipalities and extrabudgetary funds, but excludes privatisation revenues.

3 Weighted average over all maturities.

4 Data from the balance of payments. Data for 1991-92 represent the Czech Republic's share of the total for Czechoslovakia. Break in series in 1995 due to a change in the reporting system.

5 Foreign exchange reserves of monetary authorities.

Estonia

1 New series based on the ILO methodology. Figures for 1997 are based on the data for the second quarter.

2 General government includes the state, municipalities and extrabudgetary funds.

3 Weighted average annual interest rate of time deposits.

4 Weighted average annual interest on kroon loans.

5 Data from balance of payments.

6 Foreign exchange reserves of monetary authorities.

7 There is a break in the debt series between 1995 and 1996. The data for 1996 and 1997 is from the Central Bank of Estonia. The Central Bank calculation of gross debt includes loans from foreign companies to their subsidiaries, other loans, trade finance credit, currency deposits, and other liabilities.

FYR Macedonia

[1] Figures on employment and labour force up to 1995 are based on census data and are not comparable with later years, which are based on the ILO methodology.

[2] The figure provided in this table up to 1995 refers to officially registered unemployment. From 1996, they are based on a labour force survey.

[3] General government includes the state, municipalities and extrabudgetary funds.

[4] Household deposit rate (3-6 months). Minimum rate offered.

[5] Lending rate to small businesses. Minimum rate offered.

[6] Data from the balance of payments.

[7] Foreign exchange reserves of monetary authorities.

[8] GSP is the value added concept of former Yugoslavia, which excludes the value added by the government, financial and some personal services.

Georgia

[1] Up to 1996 refers to registered employment. Figures from 1997 are from the SDS Household Survey.

[2] General government includes the state, municipalities and extrabudgetary funds.

[3] Treasury bills were introduced in August 1997.

[4] Data from the balance of payments.

[5] Foreign exchange reserves of monetary authorities.

[6] Following debt restructuring.

Hungary

[1] Data for public expenditure and imports in 1993-94 include payments for Russian military equipment. Government consumption excludes social transfers, which are included in household final consumption.

[2] Data on labour force and employment from 1993 onwards are from the labour force survey. This includes employment in enterprises with less than 10 employees, which has been growing rapidly over the past years. Officially registered employment declined by 5.6% in 1996 and 1.7% in 1997.

[3] Registered unemployed. Data from the labour force survey indicates a lower rate of 8.7% in 1997.

[4] General government includes the state, municipalities and extrabudgetary funds.

[5] Change in domestic credit includes the forint debt arising from valuation changes on external government debt; government bonds of Ft 48.3 billion issued against outstanding rouble claims taken over by the government; and consolidation bonds with a total value of Ft 560 billion (around 12% of 1994 GDP) issued over the course of 1993-96.

[6] Data from balance of payments. Balance of payments data include trade from and to free export zones. These data have in the past deviated from mirror data of trade partners. Customs-based trade data, which exclude trade from free export zones prior to 1997, show considerably higher trade growth in 1994 but lower growth in 1995-96.

[7] Foreign exchange reserves of monetary authorities.

[8] Debt service in 1996-97 includes substantial prepayments to international financial institutions and commercial creditors.

Kazakhstan

[1] Full-time employees.

[2] Unemployed registered with the Public Employment Service.

[3] General government includes the state, municipalities and extrabudgetary funds. Balance includes privatisation revenues.

[4] Deposit rate for time deposits of individuals. Lending rate for short-term credits. Following a change in definition, data for 1997 are not comparable with previous years.

[5] Data from the balance of payments.

[6] Foreign exchange reserves of monetary authorities.

[7] Foreign exchange reserves of monetary authorities in months of merchandise imports until 1995.

Kyrgyzstan

[1] An industrial sector enterprise survey conducted by the ILO in 1995 found that employment fell by about one-third between 1991 and 1994.

[2] Registered unemployed.

[3] Wages in the whole economy including December bonuses.

[4] General government includes the state, municipalities and extrabudgetary funds. They also include expenditure under the foreign financed PIP. General government expenditure includes net lending.

[5] Simple average of National Bank's credit auction rates, until 1996. Credit auctions were discontinued at the end of January 1997 and the three-month treasury bill rate has become the official reference rate. The re-financing rate is set as a fixed multiple of the T-bill rate.

[6] Weighted average over all maturities.

[7] Roubles per dollar until 1992; som per dollar thereafter.

[8] Data from the balance of payments.

[9] Foreign reserves of monetary authorities.

[10] Excluding Kumtor gold imports.

Latvia

[1] Agricultural value added.

[2] General government includes the state, municipalities and extrabudgetary funds.

[3] Data from the balance of payments.

[4] Foreign exchange reserves of monetary authorities.

[5] Includes non-resident currency and deposits and loans to foreign subsidiaries.

[6] In months of imports and per cent of exports of goods until 1995 and goods, services and income thereafter.

[7] In per cent of gross value added at current prices.

Lithuania

[1] Including forestry.

[2] Gross average monthly earnings in manufacturing.

[3] The general government sector includes the state, municipalities and extrabudgetary funds. Government expenditure includes net lending.

[4] Weighted average rate of commercial banks.

[5] Roubles per US dollar for 1991; talonai per US dollar for 1992; and litai per US dollar for 1993-95.

[6] Data from the balance of payments.

[7] Covers only investment in equity capital for 1993 and 1994; equity capital and reinvested earnings for 1995 and 1996.

[8] Foreign exchange reserves of monetary authorities.

[9] Includes non-resident currency and deposits and loans to foreign subsidiaries.

Moldova

[1] General government includes the state, municipalities and extrabudgetary funds.

[2] Up to July 1993 the Russian rouble was the legal tender in Moldova. On 9 August 1993 the Moldovan rouble was introduced. On 29 November 1993 the Moldovan leu, equal to 1,000 Moldovan roubles, was introduced.

[3] Data from balance of payments.

[4] Foreign exchange reserves of monetary authorities.

Poland

[1] Gross wages are those before deducting income taxes. Prior to 1993, the change in wages is net of income taxes.

[2] General government includes the state, municipalities and extrabudgetary funds. General government balance excludes privatisation receipts. Data are on a cash basis. Government expenditure includes net lending.

[3] Beginning in 1992, data are based on a new system of accounts and an improved reporting system.

[4] Beginning in 1995, weighted average of rate offered by commercial banks on household deposits. Prior to 1995, lowest rate offered on six-month time deposits.

[5] Beginning in 1995, weighted average rate charged by commercial banks on lowest risk loans. Prior to 1995, lowest rate charged by commercial banks to prime borrowers.

[6] Balance of payments data based on banking statistics and presented on a settlements basis. On the basis of customs questionnaires, exports are virtually the same as on a settlements basis, while imports are higher (about 20% in 1994-96).

7 Sales of foreign exchange from kantors (small foreign-exchange bureaux) to commercial banks. A survey by the National Bank of Poland in 1995 indicated that about 85-90% of such transactions were associated with border trade (including services).

8 Balance of payments data based on banking statistics and presented on a settlement basis. Estimates of foreign direct investment on the basis of voluntary reports to the State Foreign Investment Agency (PIAZ), as reported in the IMF Balance of Payments Statistics Yearbook, show much larger inflows, with the cumulative stock of FDI from 1989 reaching US$ 19.2 billion at end-1997. Inflows for 1997 alone were reported as US$ 6.6 billion. The difference between the two series arises in part from investments-in-kind and reinvested earnings.

9 Foreign exchange reserves of monetary authorities.

10 Beginning in 1993, industry is classified according to the Polish version of the NACE-EKD classification system. The 1993 index includes VAT and excise taxes; from 1994 onwards it excludes VAT; and from 1996 it excludes excise taxes.

Romania

1 Registered unemployment.

2 General government includes the state, municipalities and extrabudgetary funds.

3 Data from the balance of payments.

4 Foreign exchange reserves of monetary authorities (from 1994: National Bank only).

Russian Federation

1 General consolidated government includes the federal, regional and local budgets and extrabudgetary funds, and excludes transfers.

2 Data in new (denominated) roubles per US dollar. One new rouble = 1,000 old roubles.

3 Data from the consolidated balance of payments, which covers transactions with both CIS and non-CIS countries.

4 Data includes public debt only. From 1992 debt to former Comecon countries is included.

5 Difference between due and paid arises from incomplete debt rescheduling with part of the creditors.

6 Data as of 1 January of the following year.

Slovak Republic

1 Based on labour force surveys.

2 Refers to industrial wages from 1990-93.

3 General government includes the state, municipalities and extrabudgetary funds.

4 Lending and deposit rates are weighted averages over all maturities. Lending rate excludes loans at zero interest rate since 1995.

5 Data from the balance of payments.

6 Foreign exchange reserves of monetary authorities.

Slovenia

1 Registered unemployment based on labour force surveys (consistent with ILO methodology). Unemployment was estimated at (in per cent): 7.3 in 1991, 8.3 in 1992, 9.1 in 1993, 9 in 1994, 7.4 in 1995, 7.3 in 1996 and 7.1 in 1997.

2 On 1 January 1998 the consumer price index became the new official measure of inflation, replacing the previously used retail price index. Data for 1991 refers to the retail price index.

3 Data for 1991 covers only the social (public) sector. Data for subsequent years take into account private enterprises employing three or more persons.

4 General government includes the state, municipalities and extrabudgetary funds.

5 For the period prior to 8 October 1991 (the date of the introduction of the tolar) measured as the multiple of 10,000 dinars that would buy one US dollar. The tolar was introduced at an exchange rate of 10,000 dinar per tolar.

6 Data for 1991 exclude transactions with former Yugoslav republics.

7 Data from the balance of payments.

8 Foreign exchange reserves of the Bank of Slovenia (central bank).

Tajikistan

1 Officially registered unemployed. The World Bank estimates the true unemployment rate at about 30% of the labour force.

2 Excludes transfers from the State budget to the Pension Fund and Employment Funds.

3 Interest rates were set by the parliament until June 1995.

4 Roubles per US dollar until 1994; Tajik roubles per US dollar thereafter.

5 Data from the balance of payments.

6 Foreign exchange reserves of monetary authorities.

7 In per cent of merchandise exports only. Exports are adjusted to count only net exports of alumina and electricity.

8 Figures are based on current prices. Variations in the shares thus reflect, inter alia, changes in relative prices. The share for 1997 is based upon January to September 1997 GDP figures.

Turkmenistan

1 Official data, which does not include gas and electric power, cotton ginnery and cooking oil industries. EBRD estimates suggest that industrial output decline in 1997 would be closer to 30% if these items were included.

2 Every Turkmen citizen is guaranteed employment, thus official unemployment does not exist. These figures are household survey estimates, but do not include substantial public sector overemployment.

3 General government includes the state, municipalities and some extrabudgetary funds. However, until 1997, most quasi-budgetary expenditures of sectoral ministries fell outside the budget and several off-budget funds were in operation.

4 Deposit and lending rates are quoted for legal entities at joint-stock banks accounting for the bulk of financial transactions in the banking sector. 1993-96 rates are the highest of the total range. Variations by type of counterparties and maturities are substantial. All interest rates are annual uncompounded.

5 The commercial exchange rate refers to the rate at which citizens can purchase foreign exchange. Official quotations are available since the end of 1995. The average figures for 1994 and 1995 are IMF estimates of the market exchange rate. Since April 1998, the official and commercial exchange rates have been unified at 5,200 manats to the US dollar.

6 Data from balance of payments. From 1996 exports of gas are recorded fob and transit costs are added to imports. The current account on a cash basis (excluding the flow accumulation of gas payment arrears) was in (small) deficit over 1993-96.

7 Foreign exchange reserves of the central bank plus the foreign exchange reserve fund. The ratio is to imports only in 1993.

Ukraine

1 General government includes the state, municipalities and extrabudgetary funds, excluding pension fund from 1994.

2 Treasury bills were introduced in March 1995.

3 Weighted average over all maturities.

4 Roubles per US dollar until 1991; karbovanets per US dollar until 1995; and hryvnia per US dollar from 1996.

5 Data from the balance of payments.

6 Foreign exchange reserves of monetary authorities.

Uzbekistan

1 Labour force data from Uzbek Economic Trends. Data prior to 1994 not available.

2 Officially registered unemployment. No labour force survey based estimates available.

3 Includes extrabudgetary funds but excludes local government.

4 Roubles per US dollar untill 1993; official rate of som per US dollar thereafter. The black market rate in 1997 was on average 100% higher.

5 Data from the balance of payments.

6 Reserves in millions of som were converted to millions of US dollars using the average official exchange rate reported above.

7 As a share of merchandise exports only.

Order form

The *Transition Report* and the *Transition Report Update* can be ordered from the UK in the following ways:

By mail order:
Please photocopy and complete the form below and return it to
The Stationery Office Publications Centre, PO Box 276,
London SW8 5DT, UK
or fax to +44 171 873 8200

By telephone:
Please ring +44 171 873 9090

Please send me

copy/copies of the *Transition Report* 1998, price £30. ISBN 1 898802 10 6

copy/copies of the *Transition Report Update* 1999, price £15. ISBN 1 898802 11 4

Please register a standing order for me to receive future editions of the *Transition Report* and *Transition Report Update* on publication

Please debit my Access/Visa/Amex/Connect Account No.

Expiry date

Signature

I enclose a cheque for £ **made payable to The Stationery Office Ltd.**

Please charge to my Stationery Office Account No.

Name

Address

Postcode

The *Transition Report* and *Transition Report Update* are also available through the following companies:

Canada
Renouf Publishing Company Ltd, 5369 Canotek Road, Unit 1,
Ottawa, Ontario K1J 9J3
Tel: (613) 745 2665 Fax: (613) 745 7660

France
World Data, 10 rue Nicolas Flamel, 75004 Paris
Tel: (1) 4278 0578 Fax: (1) 4278 1472

La Documentation Française, 29 Quai Voltaire, 75344 Paris Cedex 7
Tel: (1) 4015 7000 Fax: (1) 4015 7230

Germany
UNO-Verlag, Poppelsdorfer Allee 55, 53115 Bonn
Tel: 0228 212940 Fax: 0228 217492

Russia
Dinternal, Khlebny Pereulok 2/3, 121069 Moscow
Tel: 095 203 0763/202 4066 Fax: 095 203 0673

USA
Bernan Associates, 4611-F Assembly Drive, Lanham, MD20706-4391
Tel: 1 800 274 4888 (toll free) Fax: (301) 459 0056

In case of difficulty, please fax The Stationery Office Export Department, Fax: +44 171 873 8203, for details of your nearest stockist, or contact the EBRD Publications Desk
Tel: +44 171 338 7553; Fax: +44 171 338 6102;
E-mail: pubsdesk@ebrd.com